PLUNKETT'S TELECOMMUNICATIONS INDUSTRY ALMANAC 2022

The Only Comprehensive Guide to the Telecommunications Industry

Jack W. Plunkett

Published by:
Plunkett Research®, Ltd., Houston, Texas
www.plunkettresearch.com

PLUNKETT'S TELECOMMUNICATIONS INDUSTRY ALMANAC 2022

Editor and Publisher:
Jack W. Plunkett

Executive Editor and Database Manager:
Martha Burgher Plunkett

Senior Editor and Researchers:
Isaac Snider
Michael Cappelli

Editors, Researchers and Assistants:
Keith Carnes
Blake Lee
Ekaterina Lyubomirova
Annie Paynter
Gina Sprenkel

Information Technology Manager:
Rebeca Tijiboy

Special Thanks to:
Cellular Telecommunications & Internet Association (CTIA)
Cisco Visual Networking Index (VNI)
eMarketer
Federal Communications Commission (FCC)
Gartner, Inc.
International Telecommunication Union (ITU)
Telecommunications Industry Association
U.S. Bureau of the Census
U.S. Bureau of Economic Analysis
U.S. Bureau of Labor Statistics
U.S. Department of Commerce

Plunkett Research®, Ltd.
P. O. Drawer 541737, Houston, Texas 77254 USA
Phone: 713.932.0000   Fax: 713.932.7080
www.plunkettresearch.com

Plunkett Research®, Ltd.
P. O. Drawer 541737
Houston, Texas 77254-1737
Phone: 713.932.0000, Fax: 713.932.7080 www.plunkettresearch.com

<u>ISBN13 #</u> 978-1-62831-606-3 (eBook Edition # 978-1-62831-952-1)

Limited Warranty and Terms of Use:

Users' publications in static electronic format containing any portion of the content of this book (and/or the content of any related Plunkett Research, Ltd. online service to which you are granted access, hereinafter collectively referred to as the "Data") or Derived Data (that is, a set of data that is a derivation made by a User from the Data, resulting from the applications of formulas, analytics or any other method) may be resold by the User only for the purpose of providing third-party analysis within an established research platform under the following conditions: (However, Users may not extract or integrate any portion of the Data or Derived Data for any other purpose.)

a) Users may utilize the Data only as described herein. b) User may not export more than an insubstantial portion of the Data or Derived Data, c) Any Data exported by the User may only be distributed if the following conditions are met:

  i) Data must be incorporated in added-value reports or presentations, either of which are part of the regular services offered by the User and not as stand-alone products.
  ii) Data may not be used as part of a general mailing or included in external websites or other mass communication vehicles or formats, including, but not limited to, advertisements.
  iii) Except as provided herein, Data may not be resold by User.

"Insubstantial Portions" shall mean an amount of the Data that (1) has no independent commercial value, (2) could not be used by User, its clients, Authorized Users and/or its agents as a substitute for the Data or any part of it, (3) is not separately marketed by the User, an affiliate of the User or any third-party source (either alone or with other data), and (4) is not retrieved by User, its clients, Authorized Users and/or its Agents via regularly scheduled, systematic batch jobs.

<u>LIMITED WARRANTY; DISCLAIMER OF LIABILITY</u>: While Plunkett Research, Ltd. ("PRL") has made an effort to obtain the Data from sources deemed reliable, PRL makes no warranties, expressed or implied, regarding the Data contained herein. This book and its Data are provided to the End-User "AS IS" without warranty of any kind. No oral or written information or advice given by PRL, its employees, distributors or representatives will create a warranty or in any way increase the scope of this Limited Warranty, and the Customer or End-User may not rely on any such information or advice. <u>Customer Remedies</u>: PRL's entire liability and your exclusive remedy shall be, at PRL's sole discretion, either (a) return of the price paid, if any, or (b) repair or replacement of a book that does not meet PRL's Limited Warranty and that is returned to PRL with sufficient evidence of or receipt for your original purchase.

<u>NO OTHER WARRANTIES</u>: TO THE MAXIMUM EXTENT PERMITTED BY APPLICABLE LAW, PRL AND ITS DISTRIBUTORS DISCLAIM ALL OTHER WARRANTIES AND CONDITIONS, EITHER EXPRESSED OR IMPLIED, INCLUDING, BUT NOT LIMITED TO, IMPLIED WARRANTIES OR CONDITIONS OF MERCHANTABILITY, FITNESS FOR A PARTICULAR PURPOSE, TITLE AND NON-INFRINGEMENT WITH REGARD TO THE BOOK AND ITS DATA, AND THE PROVISION OF OR FAILURE TO PROVIDE SUPPORT SERVICES. <u>LIMITATION OF LIABILITY</u>: TO THE MAXIMUM EXTENT PERMITTED BY APPLICABLE LAW, IN NO EVENT SHALL PRL BE LIABLE FOR ANY SPECIAL, INCIDENTAL OR CONSEQUENTIAL DAMAGES WHATSOEVER (INCLUDING, WITHOUT LIMITATION, DAMAGES FOR LOSS OF BUSINESS PROFITS, BUSINESS INTERRUPTION, ABILITY TO OBTAIN OR RETAIN EMPLOYMENT OR REMUNERATION, ABILITY TO PROFITABLY MAKE AN INVESTMENT, OR ANY OTHER PECUNIARY LOSS) ARISING OUT OF THE USE OF, OR RELIANCE UPON, THE BOOK OR DATA, OR THE INABILITY TO USE THIS DATA OR THE FAILURE OF PRL TO PROVIDE SUPPORT SERVICES, EVEN IF PRL HAS BEEN ADVISED OF THE POSSIBILITY OF SUCH DAMAGES. IN ANY CASE, PRL'S ENTIRE LIABILITY SHALL BE LIMITED TO THE AMOUNT ACTUALLY PAID BY YOU FOR THE BOOK.

PLUNKETT'S TELECOMMUNICATIONS INDUSTRY ALMANAC 2022

CONTENTS

Continued on next page

Continued from previous page

INTRODUCTION

PLUNKETT'S TELECOMMUNICATIONS INDUSTRY ALMANAC is designed as a general source for researchers of all types.

The data and areas of interest covered are intentionally broad, ranging from the trends relating to landline and wireless telephone service, to emerging technology, to an in-depth look at the major for-profit firms (which we call "THE TELECOMMUNICATIONS 350") within the many industry sectors that make up the telecom sector.

This reference book is designed to be a general source for researchers. It is especially intended to assist with market research, strategic planning, employment searches, contact or prospect list creation and financial research, and as a data resource for executives and students of all types.

PLUNKETT'S TELECOMMUNICATIONS INDUSTRY ALMANAC takes a rounded approach for the general reader and presents a complete overview of the telecommunications field (see "How To Use This Book"). For example, you will find trends in unified communications, 5G wireless markets, satellites and VOIP, along with easy-to-use charts and tables on all facets of telecommunications in general: from the sales and profits of the leading telecom companies to statistics relating to revenues, cellular communications and internet access.

THE TELECOMMUNICATIONS 350 is our unique grouping of the biggest, most successful corporations in all segments of the telecommunications industry. Tens of thousands of pieces of information, gathered from a wide variety of sources, have been researched and are presented in a unique form that can be easily understood. This section includes thorough indexes to THE TELECOMMUNICATIONS 350, by geography, industry, sales, brand names, subsidiary names and many other topics. (See Chapter 4.)

Especially helpful is the way in which PLUNKETT'S TELECOMMUNICATIONS INDUSTRY ALMANAC enables readers who have no business background to readily compare the financial records and growth plans of telecommunications companies and major industry groups. You'll see the mid-term financial record of each firm, along with the impact of earnings, sales and strategic plans on each company's potential to fuel growth, to serve new markets and to provide investment and employment opportunities.

No other source provides this book's easy-to-understand comparisons of growth, expenditures, technologies, corporations and many other items of great importance to people of all types who may be studying this, one of the largest industries in the world today.

By scanning the data groups and the unique indexes, you can find the best information to fit your personal research needs. The major companies in telecommunications are profiled and then ranked using several different groups of specific criteria. Which firms are the biggest employers? Which companies earn the most profits? These things and much more are easy to find.

In addition to individual company profiles, a thorough analysis of trends in telecommunications sectors is provided. This book's job is to help you sort through easy-to-understand summaries of today's trends and technologies in a quick and effective manner.

Whatever your purpose for researching the telecommunications field, you'll find this book to be a valuable guide. Nonetheless, as is true with all resources, this volume has limitations that the reader should be aware of:

- Financial data and other corporate information can change quickly. A book of this type can be no more current than the data that was available as of the time of editing. Consequently, the financial picture, management and ownership of the firm(s) you are studying may have changed since the date of this book. For example, this almanac includes the most up-to-date sales figures and profits available to the editors as of mid-2021. That means that we have typically used corporate financial data as of late-2020.

- Corporate mergers, acquisitions and downsizing are occurring at a very rapid rate. Such events may have created significant change, subsequent to the publishing of this book, within a company you are studying.

- Some of the companies in THE TELECOMMUNICATIONS 350 are so large in scope and in variety of business endeavors conducted within a parent organization, that we have been unable to completely list all subsidiaries, affiliations, divisions and activities within a firm's corporate structure.

- This volume is intended to be a general guide to a vast industry. That means that researchers should look to this book for an overview and, when conducting in-depth research, should contact the specific corporations or industry associations in question for the very latest changes and data. Where possible, we have listed contact names, toll-free telephone numbers and internet site addresses for the companies, government agencies and industry associations involved so that the reader may get further details without unnecessary delay.

- Tables of industry data and statistics used in this book include the latest numbers available at the time of printing, generally through late-2020. In a few cases, the only complete data available was for earlier years.

- We have used exhaustive efforts to locate and fairly present accurate and complete data. However, when using this book or any other source for business and industry information, the reader should use caution and diligence by conducting further research where it seems appropriate. We wish you success in your endeavors, and we trust that your experience with this book will be both satisfactory and productive.

Jack W. Plunkett
Houston, Texas
August 2021

HOW TO USE THIS BOOK

The two primary sections of this book are devoted first to the telecommunications industry as a whole and then to the "Individual Data Listings" for THE TELECOMMUNICATIONS 350. If time permits, you should begin your research in the front chapters of this book. Also, you will find lengthy indexes in Chapter 4 and in the back of the book.

> **📹 Video Tip**
> For our brief video introduction to the Telecommunications industry, see www.plunkettresearch.com/video/telecommunications.

THE TELECOMMUNICATIONS INDUSTRY

Chapter 1: Major Trends Affecting the Telecommunications Industry. This chapter presents an encapsulated view of the major trends that are creating rapid changes in the telecommunications industry today.

Chapter 2: Telecommunications Industry Statistics. This chapter presents in-depth statistics including an industry overview.

Chapter 3: Important Telecommunications Industry Contacts – Addresses, Telephone Numbers and Internet Sites. This chapter covers contacts for important government agencies, industry organizations and trade groups. Included are numerous important Internet sites.

THE TELECOMMUNICATIONS 350

Chapter 4: THE TELECOMMUNICATIONS 350: Who They Are and How They Were Chosen. The companies compared in this book were carefully selected from the telecommunications industry, on a global basis. Many of the firms are based outside the U.S. For a complete description, see THE TELECOMMUNICATIONS 350 indexes in this chapter.

Individual Data Listings:
Look at one of the companies in THE TELECOMMUNICATIONS 350's Individual Data Listings. You'll find the following information fields:

Company Name:
The company profiles are in alphabetical order by company name. If you don't find the company you are seeking, it may be a subsidiary or division of one of the firms covered in this book. Try looking it up in

the Index by Subsidiaries, Brand Names and Selected Affiliations in the back of the book.

Industry Code:

Industry Group Code: An NAIC code used to group companies within like segments.

Types of Business:

A listing of the primary types of business specialties conducted by the firm.

Brands/Divisions/Affiliations:

Major brand names, operating divisions or subsidiaries of the firm, as well as major corporate affiliations—such as another firm that owns a significant portion of the company's stock. A complete Index by Subsidiaries, Brand Names and Selected Affiliations is in the back of the book.

Contacts:

The names and titles up to 27 top officers of the company are listed, including human resources contacts.

Growth Plans/ Special Features:

Listed here are observations regarding the firm's strategy, hiring plans, plans for growth and product development, along with general information regarding a company's business and prospects.

Financial Data:

Revenue (2020 or the latest fiscal year available to the editors, plus up to five previous years): This figure represents consolidated worldwide sales from all operations. These numbers may be estimates.

R&D Expense (2020 or the latest fiscal year available to the editors, plus up to five previous years): This figure represents expenses associated with the research and development of a company's goods or services. These numbers may be estimates.

Operating Income (2020 or the latest fiscal year available to the editors, plus up to five previous years): This figure represents the amount of profit realized from annual operations after deducting operating expenses including costs of goods sold, wages and depreciation. These numbers may be estimates.

Operating Margin % (2020 or the latest fiscal year available to the editors, plus up to five previous years): This figure is a ratio derived by dividing operating income by net revenues. It is a measurement of a firm's pricing strategy and operating efficiency. These numbers may be estimates.

SGA Expense (2020 or the latest fiscal year available to the editors, plus up to five previous years): This figure represents the sum of selling, general and administrative expenses of a company,

including costs such as warranty, advertising, interest, personnel, utilities, office space rent, etc. These numbers may be estimates.

Net Income (2020 or the latest fiscal year available to the editors, plus up to five previous years): This figure represents consolidated, after-tax net profit from all operations. These numbers may be estimates.

Operating Cash Flow (2020 or the latest fiscal year available to the editors, plus up to five previous years): This figure is a measure of the amount of cash generated by a firm's normal business operations. It is calculated as net income before depreciation and after income taxes, adjusted for working capital. It is a prime indicator of a company's ability to generate enough cash to pay its bills. These numbers may be estimates.

Capital Expenditure (2020 or the latest fiscal year available to the editors, plus up to five previous years): This figure represents funds used for investment in or improvement of physical assets such as offices, equipment or factories and the purchase or creation of new facilities and/or equipment. These numbers may be estimates.

EBITDA (2020 or the latest fiscal year available to the editors, plus up to five previous years): This figure is an acronym for earnings before interest, taxes, depreciation and amortization. It represents a company's financial performance calculated as revenue minus expenses (excluding taxes, depreciation and interest), and is a prime indicator of profitability. These numbers may be estimates.

Return on Assets % (2020 or the latest fiscal year available to the editors, plus up to five previous years): This figure is an indicator of the profitability of a company relative to its total assets. It is calculated by dividing annual net earnings by total assets. These numbers may be estimates.

Return on Equity % (2020 or the latest fiscal year available to the editors, plus up to five previous years): This figure is a measurement of net income as a percentage of shareholders' equity. It is also called the rate of return on the ownership interest. It is a vital indicator of the quality of a company's operations. These numbers may be estimates.

Debt to Equity (2020 or the latest fiscal year available to the editors, plus up to five previous years): A ratio of the company's long-term debt to its shareholders' equity. This is an indicator of the overall financial leverage of the firm. These numbers may be estimates.

Address:

The firm's full headquarters address, the headquarters telephone, plus toll-free and fax numbers where available. Also provided is the internet address.

Stock Ticker, Exchange: When available, the unique stock market symbol used to identify this firm's common stock for trading and tracking purposes is indicated. Where appropriate, this field may contain "private" or "subsidiary" rather than a ticker symbol. If the firm is a publicly-held company headquartered outside of the U.S., its international ticker and exchange are given.

Total Number of Employees: The approximate total number of employees, worldwide, as of the end of 2020 (or the latest data available to the editors).

Parent Company: If the firm is a subsidiary, its parent company is listed.

Salaries/Bonuses:

(The following descriptions generally apply to U.S. employers only.)

Highest Executive Salary: The highest executive salary paid, typically a 2020 amount (or the latest year available to the editors) and typically paid to the Chief Executive Officer.

Highest Executive Bonus: The apparent bonus, if any, paid to the above person.

Second Highest Executive Salary: The next-highest executive salary paid, typically a 2020 amount (or the latest year available to the editors) and typically paid to the President or Chief Operating Officer.

Second Highest Executive Bonus: The apparent bonus, if any, paid to the above person.

Other Thoughts:

Estimated Female Officers or Directors: It is difficult to obtain this information on an exact basis, and employers generally do not disclose the data in a public way. However, we have indicated what our best efforts reveal to be the apparent number of women who either are in the posts of corporate officers or sit on the board of directors. There is a wide variance from company to company.

Hot Spot for Advancement for Women/Minorities: A "Y" in appropriate fields indicates "Yes." These are firms that appear either to have posted a substantial number of women and/or minorities to high posts or that appear to have a good record of going out of their way to recruit, train, promote and retain women or minorities. (See the Index of Hot Spots For Women and Minorities in the back of the book.) This information may change frequently and can be difficult to obtain and verify. Consequently, the reader should use caution and conduct further investigation where appropriate.

Glossary: A short list of telecommunications industry terms.

Chapter 1

MAJOR TRENDS AFFECTING THE TELECOMMUNICATIONS INDUSTRY

Major Trends Affecting the Telecommunications Industry

1) Introduction to the Telecommunications Industry
2) The Coronavirus' Effect on the Telecommunications Industry
3) Landline Subscribers Cancel Service/ Bundled Services Pick Up Market Share
4) 5G Wireless Networks to Rollout Worldwide, Enabling the Internet of Things (IoT)/Massive Investments Required
5) Wi-Fi Enables Wireless Traffic Growth, Including the Internet of Things (IoT)
6) Chinese, Indian and African Cellphone Markets Skyrocket
7) Wireless Service Subscriptions Worldwide Reach 9.0 Billion
8) Handset Makers Adopt Android, Push Advanced 4G and 5G Smartphones
9) VOIP (Telephony over the Internet) Continues To Revolutionize the Telecommunications Industry
10) Telecom Equipment Makers Face Intense Competition from Manufacturers in China/Huawei Faces Controversy
11) Telecom Companies, Including AT&T and Verizon, Compete Fiercely Against Cable in the TV, Internet and Telephone Market
12) Fiber-to-the-Home (FTTH) Gains Traction
13) Global Internet Market Tops 4.9 Billion Users/Ultrafast Broadband Expands, both Fixed and Wireless
14) Telecommunications Systems Move Online Including Unified Communications, Telepresence
15) Carriers Reinstate Unlimited Access Plans for Smartphones/Face Intense Subscription Price Competition
16) Smaller Satellites (SmallSats and CubeSats) and Low Earth Orbit Revolutionize Telecommunications
17) The Internet of Things (IoT) and M2M to Boom, Enhanced by Artificial Intelligence (AI)

1) Introduction to the Telecommunications Industry

📹 Video Tip

For our brief video introduction to the Telecommunications industry, see www.plunkettresearch.com/video/telecommunications.

No other industry touches as many technology-related business sectors as telecommunications, which, by definition, encompasses not only the traditional areas of local and long-distance telephone service, but also advanced technology-based services including wireless communications, the internet, fiber-optics and satellites, as well as the software and hardware that enable these fields. Telecom is also deeply intertwined with entertainment of all types.

Cable TV systems, such as Comcast, are aggressively offering local telephone service and high-speed internet access. The relationship between the telecom and cable sectors has become even more complex as traditional telecommunications firms such as AT&T are selling television via the internet, and competing directly against cable for consumers' entertainment dollars.

Consequently, the various organizations that monitor the global telecommunications industry have their own ways of estimating total revenues, and their own thoughts on including, or not including, specific business sectors. Does "telecom" include equipment manufacturing and certain types of consulting? Or, should it be considered as services only, such as subscriber lines and data networks?

Information and Communication Technologies (ICT) is a term that is used to help describe the relationship between the myriad types of hardware, software, services and networks that make up the global information and telecommunications system. Sectors considered to be ICT include landlines, private networks, the internet, wireless communications, (including subscriber fees) and satellites. ICT is also generally considered to include cloud computing, computers and software. Globally, in the broadest possible sense, ICT was expected by Plunkett Research to grow to $1.9 trillion by 2021.

Telecommunications remains one of the major providers of employment in the world, with 680,000 employees in the U.S. alone as of mid-2021, and that number reflects only jobs in pure telecommunications service sectors.

There were approximately 9.1 billion wireless service subscriptions worldwide as of 2021, This is immense growth from about 4 billion at the end of 2008 and only 1.41 billion back in 2003. However, the actual number of individuals holding those subscriptions is somewhat less, as many people have more than one wireless device.

Experts at Cisco, with their Cisco Visual Networking Index, estimated that by 2022, the global number of internet-connected mobile devices would reach 3.6 per capita (nearly 28.5 billion devices).

Wireless service providers have set service prices low enough to be affordable for vast numbers of people, even in very low-income nations. Inexpensive cellphones are now indispensable to consumers from Haiti to Africa to New Guinea. Simple handsets can be bought for as little as $20 in such markets, and they can be topped-off with a segment of prepaid minutes for as little as 50 cents. Smartphones are more expensive, but good smartphones that are internet-capable are on the market at modest prices.

The International Telecommunication Union (ITU) estimates global landlines at 915 million as of 2019, down from 1.21 billion in 2009. This is only 11.9 landlines per 100 global population. Clearly, the worldwide boom in telecommunications is in wireless subscriptions and internet access—not in old-fashioned landlines.

Several major factors are creating deep changes in the telecommunications sector today, including: a) a shift in business and commercial telephones to VOIP (Voice Over Internet Protocol) services, that is, telephone via the internet; b) a shift in residential and personal telephone use from landline services to wireless; c) intense competition between cable, satellite and wired services providers; d) soaring growth in the amount of data and video accessed via the internet and over wireless devices for information and entertainment, especially video; the e) introduction of advanced, much more cost-effective satellites, f) rapid growth in machine-to-machine communications (the Internet of Things) and g) the continuing evolution of advanced wireless technologies, including more powerful smartphones and ultra-high-speed 5G services. Simply put, a vast number of telecommunications service users prefer to make their phone calls, download data, view entertainment and otherwise access the internet via smartphones, not fixed telephones or PCs plugged into the wall.

Ingenuity, innovation, cost control, mergers between large companies and a reasonable approach to spending and investment will help to move the telecom industry ahead while it goes through these evolutionary changes. New technologies promise continuous advancement. The cost of a cellphone call has become a bargain worldwide. Meanwhile, competition among handset makers is more intense than ever. On the higher end, manufacturers are adding advanced new features to smartphones on a regular basis. These phones now contain significant computing power and memory, to the extent that today's smartphones easily have more computer processing power than a PC of 15 years ago, at a fraction of the size and weight of a PC. Improved cellphone service has prompted tens of millions of consumers to cancel their landlines altogether, eating into traditional revenue streams at AT&T and Verizon, among others.

As more consumers recognize the promise, and good value, of phone service using VOIP, millions of households and businesses worldwide have signed up for this less-expensive service as an alternative to landlines, often through their cable providers as part of a bundle of services. A handful of firms, such as Comcast, lead the VOIP market, along with relatively young companies like Skype (a Microsoft subsidiary) and Vonage. Savvy consumers realize that some VOIP services are essentially free, such as certain international calls on Skype or Viber.

At the same time, local phone companies, led by Verizon and AT&T, as well as some cable companies, are laying fiber-optic cable directly to the neighborhood, and even directly into the home and office, in order to retain customers with promises of ultra-high-speed internet connections and enhanced entertainment offerings online. If mobile phone owners are dropping their landlines, while VOIP over cable takes even more landline customers away, then the best weapon that traditional telcos can use in their battle for market share is very high-speed internet. AT&T and its peers are focusing on bundled service packages (combining wireless accounts, very high-speed internet access and TV, in addition to VOIP or landlines).

AT&T took a significant strategic step in mid-2015 by completing its acquisition of satellite TV firm DIRECTV for $48.5 billion. However, in 2021, AT&T made an agreement to spin-off its TV subscription businesses (DIRECTV, AT&T TV and U-Verse) into a joint-venture with private equity firm TPG Capital.

In June 2018, AT&T completed a massive acquisition of Time Warner, Inc., adding such entertainment content as HBO, Warner Bros. and Turner to AT&T's businesses.

Telephone giant Verizon completed a strategic acquisition of AOL in 2015, largely to acquire AOL's superb online advertising technologies. In mid-2017, Verizon acquired Yahoo!'s online businesses, also to boost Verizon's advertising capabilities.

Meanwhile, government regulations are evolving quickly, which will bring even bigger changes to business strategies. In Europe and the U.S., regulators want much greater control over the practices of internet carriers and the ways in which they provide reliable access to consumers. Overall, the telecommunications industry is in a state of continuous technological and economic flux driven by intense competition and new technologies.

2) The Coronavirus' Effect on the Telecommunications Industry

The outbreak of the Coronavirus pandemic was a boon to the entire telecommunications industry. Hundreds of millions of workers around the world began working at home, along with students of all ages studying at home, all of whom rely on telecom to communicate with clients, coworkers and teachers more than ever before. The telepresence app Zoom especially benefitted, reporting about 265,400 customers that employ more than 10 workers in the February through April 2020 quarter, up 354% over the previous quarter.

In addition, Zoom reported usage of up to 300 million meeting participants per day, compared to 10 million per day in December 2019. The firm's phenomenal success has been shared to a lesser extent by competitors including Microsoft Teams, Google Classroom and Google Hangouts, Cisco Webex Meetings, Blackboard Collaborate and BlueJeans Meetings among others.

The Coronavirus pandemic's effects on the telecommunications industry include:
- Increased use of mobile phones and devices as more people work/study remotely
- Increased use of/demand for high-speed internet for everything from ecommerce shopping to streaming entertainment and video conferencing
- Increased demand for cloud-based services of all types

There are some negative effects on the industry as well. Mobile phones and internet access are among the last expenses that consumers cut during economic downturns. Nonetheless, there are millions of consumers in less-developed nations who have seen dramatic drops in income due to the virus. No doubt, some of them are no longer able to support their telecommunications expenses. Likewise, large numbers of businesses, particularly small businesses, have been forced to close as a result of the virus-related economic downturn, which means that millions of business telecommunications accounts have been closed worldwide.

3) Landline Subscribers Cancel Service/ Bundled Services Pick Up Market Share

Massive numbers of American cellphone users have given up their landline telephones. Cutting off the landline saves consumers a significant amount of money each month. According to the National Health Interview Survey (NHIS), 61.8% of U.S. households had wireless-only phone service as of December 2020, up from only 10.5% back in December 2006. (The NHIS makes this survey each year in order to keep track of what types of telephones that households might use to contact EMS and medical offices.)

There is more at work here than simply saving money. Consumers, particularly younger people, prefer their smartphones to any other communications medium. They use them for phone calls, text messages, email and internet access. It would not be convenient for them to switch back and forth from a cellphone to a landline, and a landline doesn't offer the advanced features and rich experience of a cellphone (particularly a smartphone, which is now carried by more than 80% of U.S. cellphone subscribers.) This same pattern is true throughout the world.

AT&T is successfully evolving from a landline-only company to a leading provider of cellphones, satellite TV, internet access and TV/film entertainment via the internet. Wireless, internet and entertainment are now the dominant strategies for major telecom firms.

At the same time, large numbers of homes have adopted internet-based VOIP phones, often from their cable providers. With new developments in technologies such as VOIP and enhanced, more reliable 4G cellular service (and even faster 5G in many cities), the demand for wired phone service will continue to fall.

AT&T is pushing its U-verse high speed internet and TV package, while Verizon is boosting its own FiOS high speed internet service. Both services offer TV via the internet that is similar in nature to the program choices offered by leading cable companies. They have implemented massive investments that are bringing fiber-optic cable directly to the home and office, or at least directly into the neighborhood. Fiber to the Premises (FTTP) enables these firms to add fast access to enhanced entertainment, such as video on demand, as an important part of their bundled services. At the same time, they are able to offer internet access at extremely high speeds. In mid-2018, AT&T closed its landmark acquisition of

Time Warner, adding large amounts of entertainment content to its business assets such as HBO and CNN.

Verizon offers its FiOS bundles to residential customers in a number of major U.S. cities. Consumers can receive a local landline, unlimited long-distance in the U.S. and Canada, along with several enhanced phone features, plus FiOS internet access and FiOS Digital TV.

4) 5G Wireless Networks to Rollout Worldwide, Enabling the Internet of Things (IoT)/Massive Investments Required

Fast wireless systems make it possible for subscribers to receive high-quality music, video and other features, and to connect interactively with the internet at high speeds. Fast wireless, combined with high-resolution color screens and cameras on smartphones, means that subscribers are using their handsets to play games, access Facebook, get detailed news or financial data, watch mobile TV and shop online. Smartphone owners are filming videos with their phones and then posting them to social media. They are also viewing internet sites featuring store and restaurant listings, as well as advertising, based on the location of the user. Film and video sites Netflix, Hulu and YouTube are immense drivers of traffic.

The next big thing in wireless internet service is 5G technology. The concept enables blinding download speeds from one gigabyte per second (Gbps), to perhaps as high as 10 Gbps. Part of the appeal is 5G's low latency (response time) of as little as one millisecond, compared to 4G's 50 milliseconds.

Ultrafast 5G wireless service will be the critical backbone that will enable IoT on a vast scale. Far beyond simply improving smartphone services, 5G will connect sensors and devices to networks, gathering data and enabling machine-to-machine communications at near instantaneous speeds. For example, it will be of vital, real-time use in robotics and self-driving cars and trucks.

In theory, 5G wireless can be more than 50 times faster than 4G. A test in New York City found that 5G enabled the download of a 2.1 GB movie file in two minutes, 57 seconds, compared to about one hour for a 4G download of the same film. However, actual 5G downloads achieved vary from city-to-city and carrier-to-carrier, and the movie download cited above may take a much longer tie to complete in some places. Actual users of 5G in 2020 often found lower than expected speed increases, as 5G networks and equipment are still in early stages of roll-out.

In the U.S., Sprint and T-Mobile completed a merger in April 2020. The combined businesses, operating under the T-Mobile name, intend to invest approximately $40 billion in infrastructure by 2022, developing what they expect to be one of the first nationwide 5G networks. Sprint and T-Mobile hope that the combined companies, with 90 million total customers, can operate more efficiently while aggressively establishing advanced 5G wireless services.

South Korea's largest mobile carriers (SK Telecom Co. and KT Corp.), manufacturers including Samsung Electronics Co. and LG Electronics, Inc. and the South Korean government have been true 5G pioneers. In April 2019, both SK Telecom and KT Corp. launched their first 5G commercial services. Initially subscribers who wanted to access 5G were limited to a certain Samsung Galaxy handset, but the variety of enabled handsets will grow quickly.

The EU and South Korea agreed to cooperate to develop systems, establish standards and acquire radio frequencies necessary to implement 5G networks. The partnership will be led by Europe's 5G PPP (backed by Telefonica SA and Nokia Oyj) and South Korea's 5G Forum.

The United Nations' International Telecommunication Union (ITU) agreed on a set of requirements for 5G technology in 2018. Download speeds should be at least 20 gigabits per second, response times should be less than 1 millisecond, and at least 1 million devices should be able to connect within a high-traffic area equal to one square kilometer. In practical terms, a full-length, high-resolution movie should transmit in two seconds. Carriers, equipment manufacturers and tech companies must agree to work together to establish seamless connections around the world, along with methods of managing these connections.

U.S. cellphone service providers have invested billions of dollars in enhancing their networks over recent years. By 2020, 78% of U.S. cellphone users were on smartphones, according to Plunkett Research estimates, compared to only 61% in early 2013.

Subscribers wanting 5G were initially limited to a small number of devices capable of using the service. However, by 2021 5G had been rolled out, at least to some extent, in most major metro markets and was in use on a variety of devices.

However, all major wireless device makers are investing heavily in the design of 5G-capable handsets. As services roll out to more and more cities worldwide, consumers' demand for new handsets will accelerate and will generate tremendous new revenues for handset makers. Apple is expected to launch a 5G iPhone (the iPhone 12) in late 2020, but may delay it due to supply chain problems brought on by the Coronavirus pandemic. The earliest models of true 5G handsets were expensive, and, due to high energy consumption, lacked the long battery endurance enjoyed by typical smartphones. (5G smartphones are designed to work with lower speed 4G networks when necessary. For example, if the handsets reach high temperatures, they will switch to 4G to conserve power.) However, 5G will improve rapidly, and consumers will eventually adopt them in massive quantities, as long as monthly subscription fees are reasonable and handset prices fall to reasonable levels. All-in-all, this is terrific news for handset manufacturers, as it has become more and more daunting to create improvements to today's smartphones that are compelling enough to get consumers to upgrade.

Despite these positives, 5G infrastructure faces a long and expensive rollout. In a recent report, Deloitte Consulting estimated that U.S. conversion to 5G would require carriers to invest a combined $130 billion to $150 billion. Other analysts believe that deployment of 5G (outside of urban areas with the highest population densities) will take more than 10 years due to the expense and the necessity of cooperation among carriers and local municipalities. According to CTIA, in 2020, the U.S. had 154,000 cellular service towers. However, an additional 769,000 transmission must be created by 2026 to achieve full 5G coverage, due to the fact that 5G has shorter range and requires more antennas. Analysts at Evercore estimated in 2021 that it could be two years before two-thirds of Americans can have 5G service that is notably better than 4G.

While 4G mobile phone service can travel fairly long distances and transmissions come and go from tall towers, the fastest-service (known as high-band) 5G antennae must be spaced fairly close together. Carriers will be competing to offer the fastest possible speeds within dense cities. Consequently, carriers will be placing small 5G antennae on street lights, the sides of buildings and other unique spots. Seeing this boom of new antenna locations as a potential source of tax revenue, some U.S. cities have been attempting to charge high permit fees to the carriers for each new antenna deployed. Unfortunately, the super-fast high-band systems may not be able to penetrate walls, creating the need for even more antennae. Slower low- and mid-band systems are likely to be used in areas that are not as densely populated.

5G may also increase cybersecurity threats since it will eventually connect to vast numbers of devices, pieces of equipment and remote sensors as the Internet of Things grows. Its potential use in autonomous vehicles, factories, transportation systems, utilities and smart-city infrastructure raises security concerns.

Chinese mobile equipment manufacturer Huawei Technologies Co., which was previously a dominant player in the global 5G market, faced cybersecurity doubts among certain foreign governments in recent years, resulting in U.S. and Australian government bans of Huawei 5G equipment. The bans, in addition to other Huawei restrictions in the U.K. and a number of EU countries, have opened doors for other cellular equipment makers to gain market share and play larger roles in establishing global standards. In the U.S., a number of smaller companies such as Airspan Networks (www.airspan.com), Altiostar (www.altiostar.com), Mavenir (www.mavenir.com), JMA Wireless (jmawireless.com) and Parallel Wireless (www.parallelwireless.com) ae pushing ahead using open-standard 5G software.

Satellite provider Dish is spending an estimated $10 billion to launch a 5G wireless service. The service will be focused on creating wide-area networks for major enterprises, capable of powering the Internet of Things (IoT). Dish will be working with Dell Technologies' RAN (Radio Access Network) architecture and a strategy known as "edge" computing which enables faster IoT data processing. Dish is hoping that its service will cost much less to operate than those of traditional competitors.

Meanwhile, some carriers have been advertising a "lite" version of 5G, optimistically referred to as 5GE—the E stands for "evolution." Such service is technically based on an enhanced 4G system. Another technology is 5G NR ("new radio"), which upgrades existing 4G networks with regard to home internet access. For example, Verizon offers the 5G NR Enhanced Gateway modem made by D-Link.

High speed mobile access is a global phenomenon. China ranks number one in the world in the total number of high-speed internet subscribers. India's high-speed wireless count is soaring, thanks to massive investments in infrastructure, along with intense competition that keeps prices low. China's Huawei Technologies is investing heavily in 5G technology development and plans to compete head-on with the world's other

technology giants in hopes to own very significant market share in 5G equipment.

Faster speed may also be achieved through new routers which support Wi-Fi 6 (also known as 802.11ax). They enable more devices in crowded areas to exchange data, such as texts and tweets, more quickly. Peak download speeds max out at 9.6 gigabits per second. In addition, Bluetooth 5 is a new standard with improved wireless range and reliability. Growing numbers of devices are compatible with Bluetooth 5.

SPOTLIGHT: pCell

Artemis Networks, www.artemis.com, may solve wireless network traffic jams with a technology called the pCell mobile wireless data transmission system. Compared to conventional cell towers, which share spectrum capacity and suffer slow performance when many users are on the network simultaneously, pCell uses interference caused by closely placed antennas to create a unique and clear wireless signal for each user on the network. The firm claims that all pCell service is full speed, no matter how many users are involved.

---

5) Wi-Fi Enables Wireless Traffic Growth, Including the Internet of Things (IoT)

While cellular phone companies are investing billions of dollars in technologies to give their subscribers enhanced services such and 4G mobile internet, Wi-Fi is more vital than ever for wireless access. As the number of cellular device subscriptions for smartphones, tablets, laptops and aircards has soared, so has the demand placed upon cellular networks. Wi-Fi acts as a vital relief valve. Wireless device owners increasingly want to access immense files, such as Netflix movies on demand. If the world's rapidly increasing wireless data traffic relied solely on cellular networks, the system would be under severe stress. However, since wireless device owners frequently have access to Wi-Fi as an alternative for a large portion of the day, they can switch to Wi-Fi from cellular as needed, reducing their total cellular subscription costs and dramatically reducing the load placed on cellular networks. The role played by Wi-Fi will remain vitally important, even as ultrafast 5G cellular networks are rolled out. At the same time, Wi-Fi will become even more important to the world's technology users as connected devices proliferate in the rapidly growing Internet of Things (IoT).

Experts at Cisco, with their Cisco Visual Networking Index, estimated that by 2022, the global number of internet-connected mobile devices will reach 3.6 per capita (nearly 28.5 billion devices). Smartphones will represent about 44% of these devices and connections. More than 50% of mobile traffic is offloaded to Wi-Fi rather than remaining on cellular networks.

Wi-Fi routers have very high theoretical data transfer speeds, but actual speeds rely on local internet connections. On the fixed end, each Wi-Fi network is tied into an internet router. This means that the actual download speed enjoyed by the Wi-Fi user is limited to the speed of the internet service connected to the router. If a user has a local internet connection with a 50 meg download speed via a cable modem, then the local Wi-Fi system will also be limited to 50 meg.

Wi-Fi is now advancing through enhanced technologies. Recent enhancements include MU-MIMO (multi-user, multiple-input, multiple-output), which allows a Wi-Fi device to handle data requests from multiple sources at once. Another recent technology known as OFDMA (orthogonal frequency-division multiple access) can split a Wi-Fi channel into many data pipes simultaneously. Kumu Networks, Inc., a startup based in Santa Clara, California (kumunetworks.com), has developed "full duplex" technology that enables Wi-Fi to transmit and receive simultaneously, effectively doubling the speed and capability of the network.

In early 2019, Amazon acquired Eero, a Wi-Fi startup that makes small wireless routers for home use, promising no Wi-Fi dead zones within the home. The acquisition enables Amazon to compete with Google's OnHub Wi-Fi routers.

Amazon and Apple are using devices such as iPhones, smartwatches, "smart" speakers and personal digital assistants such as Alexa to provide connectivity and power wireless networks. The companies use their wireless networks, such as Amazon's Sidewalk, as well as Apple's AirTag and Find My Network, to allow the devices to transmit tiny bits of data from any available wireless connection, thereby supplementing Wi-Fi networks and reducing wireless communication problems. Data is encrypted for security.

6)   Chinese, Indian and African Cellphone Markets Skyrocket

China is the world's largest cellular market, with more than 1.6 billion subscriptions as of late 2020 (out of a population of about 1.449 billion). China

Mobile Ltd. is China's largest carrier with 941.7 million subscriptions as of April 2021. 4G connections were dominant in China by 2017, and 5G posted rapid growth beginning in 2020.

India had 1.18 billion wireless subscribers in early 2021 (out of a population of about 1.39 billion). India has seen phenomenal growth in subscriptions in recent years due to aggressive competition among telecom firms and the issue of licenses by the Indian government. Relatively new to the mobile phone market in India is Jio, a 4G carrier launched by the giant industrial conglomerate Reliance Industries, which has invested more than $20 billion in infrastructure to deliver high-speed connectivity throughout India. It led the market by December 2020 with 411.53 million subscribers. Bharti Airtel had 343.27 million wireless customers as of December 2020, followed by Vodafone Idea with 284.78 million (Vodafone merged with Idea Cellular, Ltd. In 2018) and BSNL with 125.88 million.

Between April and June 2020, Jio Platforms raised $15.2 billion in new investment capital in 11 deals. Facebook acquired a 10% stake for $5.7 billion, followed by agreements with American private equity firms KKR, Vista, General Atlantic, TPG, L Catterton and Silver Lake, as well as United Arab Emirates' Mubadala and the Abu Dhabi Investment Authority. Google recently announced a $4.5 billion deal in which it will collaborate with Reliance Industries on a new low-cost (less than $100) smartphones for the Jio network, to compete directly with units sold by Chinese vendors including Xiaomi and BBK Electronics.

The cellphone market in the continent of Africa is also growing quickly. In a continent where land-based telephone lines are concentrated in only a few areas, cellular service is the first modern infrastructure many Africans enjoy. There were an estimated 1 billion wireless subscriptions in Africa as of 2018. GSMA Intelligence expected this to grow to 1.3 billion by 2020, Phones marketed to these areas tend to be simple. Costs are kept extremely low to make the phones affordable. Nokia and Vodafone are targeting the very low-cost market, as are specialty manufacturers such as ZTE Corp., a Chinese handset maker with phones starting under $20. The African market for more sophisticated smartphones is on the rise.

Charging the batteries in cellphones is a major challenge in the emerging world, where electric supply is often not reliable or of limited availability. ZTE introduced a solar-powered handset, the Coral-200, which can retail in the $40 range.

Substantial growth in cellphone use in Africa is being fueled by two factors: First, both handsets and services are extremely inexpensive there, which is vital in this low-income market. Next, and equally important for most users throughout the continent, cellphones provide the only reliable, affordable, easy-to-obtain access to modern communications.

7) Wireless Service Subscriptions Worldwide Reach 9.0 Billion

Around the world, the wireless market continues to grow. As of 2021, there were 483.8 million mobile devices of all types in use in the U.S. (according to Plunkett Research estimates). This amount was up from only 233 million in 2006. On a global basis, Plunkett Research estimates there were 9.0 billion subscriptions as of mid-2020.

However, the actual number of individuals who subscribe to wireless connections is considerably lower than the total number of subscriptions. There are several reasons for this. In emerging nations, many people have multiple service subscriptions. Subscribers own and swap multiple SIM, or network subscription cards, on a frequent basis within their handsets, depending on the level of service quality available in a given location, or the balance left in a prepaid subscription account. In developed nations, subscribers may own multiple devices that require subscriptions, such as aircards, smartphones and tablets.

Cellphone manufacturers are continuously adding new features, cellphone service providers are offering more minutes per dollar spent and a growing number of consumers are discontinuing their landline phones. In 2020, 61.8% of U.S. households were wireless-only, according to the National Health Interview Survey, up from 31.6% in 2011.

Cellular companies are facing increased competition that is resulting in lower prices. The companies are also competing to purchase increased wireless spectrum in order to serve ever-growing downloads of data and video via wireless devices.

8) Handset Makers Adopt Android, Push Advanced 4G and 5G Smartphones

For 2020, analysts at Gartner reported that 1.38 billion mobile phone units were sold worldwide. The company also forecast 1.54 billion unit sales for 2021. Advanced smartphone features on modestly-priced handsets are helping to fuel sales.

Upstart competitors have been growing in the mobile handset business. However, this is a very challenging, highly competitive business. Profit margins can be very thin (outside of Apple's enormously profitable iPhone business).

A firm in China called Xiaomi Corp. rapidly grew to be a major competitor in the handset manufacturer race. Xiaomi's phones are full-featured but sold at near cost. The company is shipping its phones worldwide, with English versions bearing the brand "Mi." The firm's strategy is to build long-term revenues by selling services, such as music, video and games. Mi also quickly became one of India's leading brands in terms of market share. Meanwhile, India's Micromax, the largest smartphone vendor in India, is also making its phones available to Western consumers, at modest prices.

Phones are also featuring larger screens, especially in China. Large screens had been slow to catch on in the U.S. until the launch of the very popular Apple iPhone "Plus" models, which feature large screens.

Google forced transparency and open software on the cellular market in one bold act during 2007, with the launch of its Android wireless device operating system. Android is readily usable, at no fee, by any or all of the world's manufacturers. At the same time, it is open to the world's software and mobile app developers, free of charge. Google's highly successful strategy was to offer an open platform for mobile devices that is flexible and free, thus setting itself up to be the leader in mobile search and related services. The result is that Google is the envy of all other mobile search providers and all other mobile operating system creators. Google's Android is the most popular smartphone operating system worldwide.

Google's Android and Apple's iOS put additional competitive pressure on Microsoft in the mobile arena. Microsoft offers its Windows mobile operating system, which combines potential access to its Office suite of applications, Xbox LIVE gaming and a wide array of apps. However, Microsoft is running far behind Apple and Android in the mobile market.

The biggest news in the handset industry is the massive investments that manufacturers are making in order to launch state-of-the-art handsets capable of accessing ultra-fast 5G cellular networks. Such networks can offer ultrafast service, including internet downloads, at speeds of more than 50 times those of 4G networks. 5G service is steadily rolling out in major cities worldwide, and consumers are excited about the prospect of near-instantaneous download of full-length movies, higher resolution for images and fast access to all online services.

Pioneers in 5G handsets include Samsung, OnePlus, Motorola, Huawei, Xiaomi and LG. Apple's 5G iPhone was first released in October 2020.

9)   VOIP (Telephony over the Internet) Continues to Revolutionize the Telecommunications Industry

Local exchange telephone companies continue to face a dismal market for landlines. The popularity of smartphones is one reason, but another big threat to traditional phone lines is phone calls made over the internet. The rapid proliferation of high-speed access to the internet in homes and offices makes internet-based telephony a logical next step for a wide variety of businesses and consumers. Most newly installed telephone systems in mid-size to large business offices are based on Voice over Internet Protocol (VOIP), with virtually all telephone equipment manufacturers now offering VOIP equipment. Likewise, massive numbers of consumers around the globe are adopting VOIP for their long-distance services, particularly via the extremely popular Skype service, which is owned by Microsoft.

The fact that phone service can be provided online enables cable companies to compete head-on with telephone companies, since cable offers internet service as well as entertainment programming. Consequently, many households are subscribing to cable bundles that include VOIP, internet and entertainment/TV (and dropping their traditional landlines).

This makes cable companies major, direct competitors to traditional telephone companies. The competitive landscape has become even more complicated now that software companies are also getting into VOIP-type services. For example, WhatsApp, a global text messaging service owned by Facebook, offers VOIP features, putting it in direct competition with Skype. Viber, part of Japan's Rakuten, Inc., is another popular service used worldwide.

VOIP transforms phone calls into digital format, which is transmitted across the internet almost effortlessly and, more tellingly, cheaply. Rapid growth is occurring outside the U.S., particularly in nations where very high-speed broadband is commonplace in homes and offices. In emerging nations, VOIP growth has been fueled by its low cost.

Some VOIP services are essentially free of cost, or extremely inexpensive, but they offer limited services that often make or receive calls only with other members of the same service. This is how Skype got started. The strategy of Skype and similar firms has been to first offer free services, and then sell value-added subscriptions.

What a full-featured VOIP subscription offers is really a local telephone number bundled with long-distance service, at rates far cheaper than plans sold by other carriers, especially for international calls. In addition, many VOIP providers do not charge extra fees for services such as voice mail, call-waiting, caller ID and do-not-disturb, which temporarily blocks calls from certain parties and directs them to voice mail. Additional features are three-way calling as well as message retrieval and system settings via phone, web site or e-mail from any location worldwide.

A particularly interesting feature of VOIP service gives subscribers the ability to choose almost any area code as the prefix to their phone numbers. This means that a business or home can be located in Portland, Oregon, for example, but have an area code for Miami, Florida. This can be convenient for businesses that want to create local phone numbers for virtual locations in several cities or countries. Both businesses and consumers have the ability to set up toll-free numbers via VOIP as well.

Google offers its Voice app, but until recently users could only receive incoming calls. However, the company expanded Voice capability to VOIP calling, with all calls within the U.S. free of charge and international calls at low cost without roaming fees. The service works using Wi-Fi networks.

Not surprisingly, there are a large number of players in the VOIP service market. A leader in this technology is the aforementioned Vonage, a New Jersey-based firm. In addition to relatively new firms like Vonage and Net2Phone, however, are the traditional telephone companies, such as Verizon and AT&T, as well as cable companies like Cablevision Systems, Comcast and Bright House. These companies followed Vonage's lead into VOIP, and all offer some type of VOIP service.

One of the more interesting players in VOIP is Skype. Skype works on peer-to-peer technology; that is, users must download the free Skype software to their computers or smartphones. They can then make unlimited, free-of-charge VOIP calls to other computers that contain Skype software. Several users may participate in a conference call at once. Microsoft has integrated Skype's features into many of its products, such as its extremely popular Xbox game machines. Skype's challenge was to move beyond the distribution of free software, in order to generate significant subscription-based fees.

VOIP service is already a highly competitive market. Consequently, consumers can look forward to more new features and better service while prices drop. It can be vastly cheaper to operate an internet-based phone company than a traditional landline provider, because VOIP service providers don't have to invest in billions of dollars' worth of telephone equipment—instead, they rely on the internet as the backbone of their services. (Of course, this means that your VOIP telephone service is only as reliable as your internet connection.)

10) Telecom Equipment Makers Face Intense Competition from Manufacturers in China/Huawei Faces Controversy

Telephone service providers around the world have been facing up to vast changes in telecom technology. They have invested hundreds of billions of dollars in advanced switching equipment capable of providing ultra-fast internet service, wireless service and VOIP. Such investments involve massive purchases of state-of-the-art equipment. In the not too distant past, American companies were the world's leading makers of telecom equipment. Today however, there is intense global competition.

China-based telecom equipment manufacturers are booming. For example, Huawei Technologies Co., Ltd. has become a global leader. Chinese firms such as Datang Telecom Technology and ZTE Corp. are winning major contracts with telecom service providers around the world, including large sales of VOIP equipment, wireless infrastructure and network equipment. China has gained respect as a base for the manufacture of technology gear of very high quality. ZTE historically had sold to customers in China, elsewhere in Asia, and Africa. However, the firm is now aggressively marketing to telecom companies on a worldwide basis. ZTE has opened offices in U.S. cities and in Canada, as well as dozens of offices throughout Europe, Latin America, Africa and Asia/Pacific.

Nonetheless, some corporations and governments are uncomfortable installing and relying upon vital telecom equipment that has been designed and manufactured by Chinese firms. Particularly in today's environment of concerns about Chinese hackers gaining access to proprietary and highly sensitive corporate and government via the internet, some observers are worried that security breaches may be built into equipment made by companies like Huawei and its competitor ZTE, with or without the knowledge of corporate management. Unfounded or not, the debate about national security and foreign equipment has not been particularly detrimental to either Huawei or ZTE, as both have rapidly grown into global leaders in the telecommunications equipment industry.

In addition to a growing dependence upon wireless devices and ever-faster internet access, major corporations are committing to VOIP for their future telecommunications needs. VOIP not only saves on their voice communication costs, it also saves on costs for data and video. This is due to the fact that voice, video and data are able to run on the same network under VOIP.

Chinese competition was particularly hard on equipment maker Alcatel-Lucent. The France-based firm was the result of the merger of a leading European firm, Alcatel, and a leading U.S. telecom gear manufacturer, Lucent. The company faced eroding revenues and sometimes large losses for several years until its acquisition by Nokia in 2016.

While Chinese telecom equipment makers have gained market share, many U.S. firms continue to do well in particular sectors. An industry giant is Cisco Systems, Inc., one of the world's leading makers of IP-based networking and communications technology. Additional leading firms include F5 Networks (internet traffic management tools), Ciena Corp. (network infrastructure equipment) and Viavi Solutions (formerly part of JDS Uniphase, which has split into two firms including Viavi).

The next phase of global telecom equipment purchases will focus on upgrading services to ultra-fast 5G networks.

11) Telecom Companies, Including AT&T and Verizon, Compete Fiercely Against Cable in the TV, Internet and Telephone Market

Telecommunications companies like AT&T and Verizon are competing fiercely to take television viewers away from their cable and satellite competitors. Telecom companies are competing directly against cable companies by offering television programming in addition to telephone service and high-speed internet access.

Broadcast, cable and satellite TV providers are competing by positioning themselves with value-added content and services, such as enhanced interactive TV, video on demand and expensive programming such as made-for-TV movies and exclusive major league sports coverage.

AT&T took a significant strategic step in mid-2015 by completing its acquisition of satellite TV firm DirecTV for $48.5 billion. This made AT&T into America's largest TV distributor, with a combined subscribership of nearly 25 million at the end of 2017 when counting DirecTV's satellite customers, AT&T's U-verse TV via internet customers and AT&T TV customers. However, as of early 2021, the company was losing subscribers in droves. AT&T lost 7 million U.S. pay TV subscribers between 2019 and the end of 2020. In February 2021, the company agreed to sell 30% of its pay TV services (including Dish, U-Verse and AT&T TV) to TPG Capital, a private equity firm, for $1.8 billion. Operations of the three services will be run jointly under a new company called DirecTV.

Comcast Corp. suffered the loss of 404,000 residential pay-TV subscribers in the first quarter of 2021. The firm also reported losing 87,000 business video customers for the quarter.

In April 2016, the U.S. Federal Communications Commission and the Justice Departments approved Charter Communications' $65.5 billion acquisition of Time Warner Cable and Bright House Networks, which was completed in May of that year. However, a number of restrictions were set to protect streaming video providers and ensure the availability of relatively inexpensive broadband services to low income consumers (broadband is considered a utility in the U.S.). The new combined Charter entity became the second-largest broadband provider in the U.S.

Verizon is also investing heavily in the delivery of TV over its internet connections. The firm offers a full menu of hundreds of TV channels (including HD channels) plus an on-demand library of thousands of movies. The service, called FiOS, also provides premium channel packages for additional fees, as well as single or multi-room DVR. It provides subscribers with a very high-speed internet access service for speedy downloads.

The prospect of selling television subscriptions is a boon to telephone companies, since it gives them a highly coveted entertainment service to add to their phone service offerings. They have the ability to bundle services that might include any or all of the following: internet access, landline telephone, long-distance, VOIP telephony, cellular telephone and television—all on one discounted bill. The major telephone service providers have been in a tough spot in the past few years, with revenues from landline customers declining as more consumers switch to cellular phones and VOIP as their standard methods of communication. Delivering entertainment via the internet lines gives them a way to develop significant new revenues.

12) Fiber-to-the-Home (FTTH) Gains Traction

The major telephone firms are looking for ways to increase revenues through enhanced services while retaining their customer bases. One such way is through the delivery of ultra-high-speed internet access, combined with enhanced entertainment and telephone options, often by installing true fiber-to-the-home (FTTH) networks.

Under traditional telephone and internet service, homes are served by copper wires, which are limited to relatively slow service. However, old-fashioned copper networks are not up to the demands of today's always-on internet consumers. Fiber-optic cable might be used in trunk lines to connect regions and cities to each other at the switch and network level, but speed drops significantly once the service hits local copper lines.

Things are much more advanced in major markets today. In an AT&T project, fiber is being brought into special hubs in existing neighborhoods. From those hubs, fast services are delivered into the home with advanced technologies on short, final runs of copper wire.

FTTH, in contrast, delivers fiber-optic cable all the way from the network to the local switch directly into the living room—with this system, internet delivery speeds and the types of entertainment and data delivered can be astounding. Google's "Google Fiber" service offers extremely fast download speeds of 1,000 Mbps (one gigabit), roughly 50 to 100 times faster than typical DSL or cable service. Recently, Google offered the service in cities including Atlanta, Georgia; Austin, Texas; Charlotte, North Carolina; Kansas City, Missouri; Kansas City, Kansas; Nashville, Tennessee; and Provo Utah, among others. This puts tremendous competitive pressure on other internet access companies. It also makes consumers wonder why they have been paying high monthly rates for slow service for many years. In response, AT&T has begun providing 1,000 Mbps service in several major cities. The long-term result is going to be much better, faster internet access in major U.S. cities, at a reasonable cost.

Verizon has completed a multi-year FTTH program that makes it the U.S. leader in FTTH. Verizon's FTTH (called FiOS) offers exceptional speeds up to 1 gigabit.

The Fiber-to-the-Home Council (www.ftthcouncil.org) tracks FTTH trends. In many cases, FTTH has been provided by local government or by subdivision developers who are determined to provide leading-edge connectivity as a value-added feature to new homes.

FTTH technologies, though expensive, may save the Bells from being trampled by the cable companies. Fiber-optic networks can give consumers extremely fast internet connections. Such ultra-high-speeds will also allow consumers to download movies in seconds and make videoconferencing a meaningful reality for businesses. (Additional fiber terms used in the industry include FTTP for Fiber-to-the-premises and FTTO for fiber-to-the-office.)

FTTH has been widely adopted in South Korea, Hong Kong, Japan, the United Arab Emirates and Taiwan, according to the FTTH Councils of Asia-Pacific, Europe and North America.

13) Global Internet Market Tops 4.9 Billion Users/Ultrafast Broadband Expands, both Fixed and Wireless

The majority of American cellphones are now smartphones. Big improvements in the devices, such as the latest iPhones and Android-based units, along with enhanced high-speed access via 4G networks, are fueling this growth. In addition, most major e-commerce, news and entertainment sites have carefully designed their web pages to perform reasonably well on the "third screen," that is, cellphones (with TV being the first screen and desktop or laptop computers being the second screen). Globally, the number of internet users was more than 4.9 billion as of late 2020, (including wireless).

Internet access speeds continue to increase dramatically. Google launched its "Google Fiber" ultra-high-speed internet service in Kansas City, Kansas in 2012, and soon expanded into Austin, Texas; Provo, Utah; and Atlanta, Georgia. This system allows homes and businesses to have 1 gigabit per second access, roughly 100 to 200 times the speed of typical DSL or mobile broadband. More than 1,000 U.S. towns and cities applied for the service when it was first announced, but Google is gauging the results of this initial effort before making any decisions about rolling it out.

AT&T initially launched a similar 1 gigabit service in competition with Google in the Austin area called AT&T FIBER. The firm offers this fast service in dozens of cities across the U.S.

What will widespread use of fast internet access mean to consumers? The opportunities for new or enhanced products and services are endless, and the amount of entertainment, news, commerce and personal services designed to take advantage of broadband will continue to grow rapidly. For example, education support and classes via broadband is rapidly growing into a major industry.

Broadband in the home is essential for everyday activities ranging from children's homework to shopping to managing financial accounts. Online entertainment and information options, already vast, will grow daily. Some online services are becoming indispensable, and always-on is the new accepted standard. The quality of streaming video and audio is becoming clear and reliable, making music and movie downloads extremely fast, and allowing internet telephone users to see their parties on the other end as if they were in the same room. Compression and caching techniques are evolving, and distribution and storage costs are expected to plummet. A very significant portion of today's radio, television and movie entertainment is migrating to the web.

14) Telecommunications Systems Move Online Including Unified Communications, Telepresence

VOIP (internet-based telephony or Voice Over Internet Protocol) is only the first step in the telecommunications revolution taking place online. The next generation is known as "unified communications," a technology pursued by Microsoft, Cisco and many others. Special software operating on a local office server, or in the cloud, enables each office worker to have access, via the desktop PC (and via mobile devices with remote access), to communications tools that include VOIP phone service, e-mail, voice mail, fax, instant messaging (IM), collaborative calendars and schedules, contact information such as address books, audio conferencing and video conferencing.

For example, to make a phone call with unified communications you open your communications screen, click on a name in your address book, and the call is placed via VOIP. To send a fax, you click on a contact's fax number in your address book, click on the item you want to fax in your documents folder, and the fax is gone. When you have an incoming phone call, your screen will tell you what number is calling and match that number to a name in your address book. You might take the call, or you might send it to voice mail with one click. In the same way that you currently save and archive e-mails, you can digitally record, save, review and archive phone calls.

Mobility, security and advanced collaboration with coworkers are among the features emphasized.

Network equipment giant Cisco is pushing a next-generation video-conferencing technology it refers to as "TelePresence." Cisco provides hardware and software needed to fully equip a state-of-the-art video conferencing room. Such a room may include as many as three 65-inch plasma monitors, advanced high-speed cameras, projectors, microphones, speakers that are set up so that the sound seems to come directly from the participant who is talking, along with appropriate software. There are virtually no delays in the conversation, and images are crisp and life-like. Indeed, the image of a participant, from the chest up, is life-size. High bandwidth and extremely reliable, fast internet connections are prerequisites. Cisco offers a smaller system for use in individual offices and a large telepresence room designed for group training and team meetings. (The company also offers much simpler Unified IP Phone sets with video touchscreens for person-to-person meetings that turns any flat panel display into a telepresence system for small meeting rooms,)

However, the quality of a telepresence meeting relies very heavily on the quality of the equipment involved. For many major corporate users, near life-like quality is required, such as that delivered by Cisco's TelePresence equipment.

The advantages to telepresence systems such as Cisco's are based on making remote meetings more effective and life-like, while enhancing collaboration and communications, as well as greatly reducing the need for expensive, time-consuming business travel. The goal is to have results from teleconference meetings that near the results of F2F (face-to-face) meetings. High-end equipment makers are feeling strong competition from startups and lower-priced products.

Another player in videoconferencing is LifeSize Communications based in Austin, Texas. LifeSize uses high-definition (HD) cameras to send video streams over ordinary internet hardware, and was previously owned by Logitech before spinning off as a standalone company. Another noteworthy entrant to the telepresence market is Vidyo, Inc., a New Jersey firm which offers a mid-priced, three- to 20-screen videoconferencing room. In May 2019, Vidyo was acquired by Enghouse Systems Limited for approximately $40 million.

SPOTLIGHT: Zoom Video Communications, Inc.

Zoom Video Communications, Inc. designs and develops cloud-based video and web conferencing software. Zoom's software unifies cloud video conferencing, online meetings, group messaging and conference room solutions into one simple-to-use platform. The company's products work across multiple room systems. Zoom's software conferencing application program interface (API) runs within a business' conference room or workspace. Cloud video conferencing features include HD video and voice, full-screen with gallery views, dual stream/dual screen, feature-rich mobile apps and various ways to join the conferences (Zoom Room, view-only, voice only and more). The firm also offers a hybrid cloud service with 24/7 online monitoring and instant global service backup. Partner integrations provide content sharing, scheduling/starting meetings, unified log-in, marketing/process automation and room collaboration. Pricing plans range from free to $100 per month, among other options. Zoom is headquartered in San Jose, California, with additional U.S. offices in California, Colorado and Kansas, as well as international offices in Sydney, London, Paris and Amsterdam. The Coronavirus pandemic spurred phenomenal growth in Zoom meetings. The firm reported usage of up to 300 million meeting participants per day in the first quarter of 2020, compared to only 10 million per day in December 2019. For all of 2020, the firm reported over 3.3 trillion meeting minutes facilitated.

Meanwhile, for simpler needs and smaller budgets, startups such as Fuze, formerly FuzeBox, and Blue Jeans Network offer inexpensive subscription software that uses smartphones, tablets and PCs to provide videoconferencing. Both companies have signed big name corporate customers, including Facebook for Blue Jeans Network and Groupon for Fuze. Cisco offers its own subscription-based software. Over the mid-term, watch for more Cloud-based subscription options that offer videoconferencing and telepresence at a fraction of full-blown conference room system prices.

15) Carriers Reinstate Unlimited Access Plans for Smartphones/Face Intense Subscription Price Competition

Starting in 2016, competition among the U.S.'s major cellphone carriers grew to very intense levels as price wars drove subscription rates to new lows.

After years of charging users for the amount of data they consumed, carriers one-by-one reinstated unlimited access plans in order to stay competitive.

Carriers must look to the future needs of their subscribers and realizing that massive amounts of capital investment will be needed on a continuous basis in order to provide the fast internet service that customers want. The wireless industry has very clearly evolved from a voice-based business to a data- and video-based business, and pricing plans must support this change while providing the cash that carriers need for capital expenditures. Hundreds of billions of dollars will be invested in a gradual, global rollout of ultra-fast 5G wireless networks over the mid-term. A recent IHS Markit study estimated that 5G will create $3.5 trillion in global economic output and 22 million global jobs by 2035.

The continued growth of mobile video, mobile music, web sites tailored to the mobile screen, as well as social media tools such as Facebook will lead to ever-higher download levels. The Cisco Visual Networking Index (VNI) forecasts mobile (cellular) speeds will more than triple by 2023, reaching 43.9 Mbps. Cisco further estimates that 82% of all Internet traffic will be video by 2022. In fact, landline internet service companies, both cable and DSL, face the same challenges and opportunities from growing bandwidth use due to online videos, the download of full-length feature films from firms like Netflix, and other popular web trends.

Meanwhile, billions of text messages are sent every day around the world. New mobile messaging tools from firms like WhatsApp, GroupME and textPlus enable mobile users to send and receive text messages via internet sites, rather than via the cellular carriers' services. For example, WhatsApp (www.whatsapp.com) offers an app that enables users to send each other text messages via a smartphone's internet connection. Facebook acquired WhatsApp for $19 billion in 2014.

Cellular service providers are seeking unique ways to increase their revenues in an environment where subscription rates will remain fiercely competitive between providers. One way to increase total revenue is to increase mobile advertising. This explains Verizon's recent acquisitions of advertising technologies and sites, including its 2016 agreement to purchase the online assets of Yahoo! In 2021, both AT&T and Verizon were offering discounts or incentives generous enough to pay for high-end smartphones such as Apple's iPhone 12.

Cable companies, including Comcast Corp. and Charter Communications, Inc., are now offering mobile phone service, often bundled with cable service. Subscribers enjoy low prices and the ability to adjust their phone plans quickly and easily. As of late 2020, traditional wireless companies remained dominant with almost 50 times as many mobile-phone subscribers as the cable companies. However, the cable companies are aggressively seeking mobile business as a way to make up for growing losses of pay TV subscribers.

16) Smaller Satellites (SmallSats and CubeSats) and Low Earth Orbit Revolutionize Telecommunications

Until recently, satellites orbiting the Earth were large, heavy craft. In recent years, however, a growing fleet of smaller satellites has been launched, ranging from the size of kitchen refrigerators down to golf balls. These relatively tiny SmallSats have an exponentially growing number of uses and, thanks to their miniaturization coupled with rocket technology innovation, are far cheaper to launch and maintain than ever before. A class of the smallest SmallSats are called CubeSats, which, according to NASA, refers to a class of nanosatellites that use a standard size and form factor. The standard CubeSat size uses one standard module or unit ("1U") measuring 10x10x10 centimeters, and is extendable to larger sizes; 1.5, 2, 3, 6 and even 12U. They are particularly easy to launch because they have electronic and physical interfaces that allow 1U modules to stack together in a dispenser that increases payload in a rocket, sometimes called a "secondary payload." CubeSats were originally developed in 1999 by California Polytechnic State University at San Luis Obispo (Cal Poly) and Stanford University to provide a platform for education and space exploration.

Satellites of all sizes are being streamlined to rely more on 3-D printing which saves manufacturing costs and increases orbit efficiency. For example, Boeing Co. is incorporating 3-D printing in the development of its 502 Phoenix satellites.

Internet Research Tip: CubeSats

For more on CubeSats, see NASA's web site which includes comprehensive images, videos and media resources:
www.nasa.gov/mission_pages/cubesats/index.html

Some of the uses for these new baby satellites include gathering weather data to aid farmers, transportation and logistics firms, and disaster relief workers. Environmental impact data can be used by government agencies to monitor deforestation, polar icecap and ocean changes over time. Satellites are also bringing internet service to all parts of the globe, including rural areas that other providers cannot reach, at speeds of up to 25 megabits per second (enough to stream video). Internet providers such as Hughes Network Systems (owned by EchoStar Corp.) plan to beam even faster service from satellites in the near future through mid-term.

SmallSats promise vast increases in cost-efficiency, utility and flexibility. Today's state-of-the-art satellites feature computer circuitry that can be reprogrammed from the ground, on an as-needed basis. This is vast improvement over traditional satellites. SmallSats are easier and faster to manufacture as well.

Thanks to advanced technologies and miniaturization, today's tiny satellites are much lighter in weight than former generations. This means that a launch rocket can carry a much higher number of satellites in one payload. This is important, because launch costs are one of the major investments required in completing the tasks required to get satellites into service. Entrepreneur Elon Musk, founder of electric car company Tesla, is revolutionizing satellite launches. His SpaceX firm has shown that rocket bodies can be recovered and reused in a highly efficient manner. His methods are slashing the cost of putting satellites into orbit.

A firm called OneWeb is launching a revolutionary system that may eventually encompass from 650 to 2,500 low-Earth orbit (LOE) satellites. This will drive down costs and improve performance in telecommunications and internet applications. Unfortunately, after raising $1.7 billion and launching only 75 satellites, OneWeb took bankruptcy in the spring of 2020 during the Coronavirus pandemic. It was quickly acquired, in July 2020, by the UK Department for Business, Energy and Industrial Strategy.

Space launch firm SpaceX is laying plans for its own system, called Starlink, of as many as 12,000 LOE satellites. The first 60 units were launched in May 2019. This firm, associated with Tesla founder Elon Musk, will have significant advantages, since it operates an extremely cost-effective rocket launch service. Starlink's satellites will be deployed at three different altitudes. Its satellites weight only about 200 kilograms each. A grouping of 60 of these units can provide up to 1 terabit per second of bandwidth.

LEO satellites are typically in orbit at altitudes of 400 to 1,000 miles, and are used for telecommunications and internet access. Because of their low altitude, the time required to send and receive Earth signals is shorter. This can be extremely advantageous in many circumstances. For example, passengers on cruise ships are dependent upon satellite systems for internet access, which traditionally has been much slower than land-based access. LEO satellites are speeding up ship-board internet to the extent that movies, gaming and intense business applications are much more practical.

Cruise ships are perfect customers for fast internet access via low-orbit satellites. RCL (Royal Caribbean Lines), one of the world's largest cruise lines, is working with the O3b satellite constellation to offer its passengers the ultimate in floating connectivity. (Users report that speed is definitely higher than on other cruise ships, but still subject to the fluctuations that satellite service is known for.) RCL claims that it offers more bandwidth than every other cruise ship in the world combined. Guests are encouraged to Tweet, Skype, Stream movies (using accounts with DIRECTV, Netflix or Hulu), connect with friends or play Xbox Live with gamers worldwide. Its newest ships even offer live, global gaming rooms.

Facebook developed a technology called Terragraph which uses unlicensed airwaves to transmit signals. These signals are sent via small radio nodes mounted on homes, buildings or streetlights. This system makes it possible to create high speed wireless coverage without extending physical fiber to every house. The technology utilizes ultra-high-frequency airwaves that afford high speeds over short distances.

Amazon is investing $10 billion to launch more than 3,200 low-Earth-orbit satellites between 2020 and 2029. The network, called Project Kuiper, received FCC approval in July 2020 and promises to provide reliable, affordable broadband service to underserved communities around the globe.

17) The Internet of Things (IoT) and M2M to Boom, Enhanced by Artificial Intelligence (AI)

The phrase "Internet of Things" or "IoT" will become increasingly commonplace. It refers to wireless communications known as M2M or machine-to-machine. M2M can be as simple as a refrigerator that lets a smartphone app know when you are running low on milk (via Wi-Fi) to a vast, exceedingly complex network of wireless devices connecting all of the devices in a massive factory. Analysts at network device giant Cisco expect M2M connections to grow dramatically and rapidly, to 14.7

billion by 2023, while they expect the consumer segment to have almost 75% of total devices and connections.

A Wireless Sensor Network (WSN) consists of a grouping of remote sensors that transmit data wirelessly to a receiver that is collecting information into a database. Special controls may alert the network's manager to changes in the environment, traffic or hazardous conditions within the vicinity of the sensors. Long-term collection of data from remote sensors can be used to establish patterns and make predictions, as well as to manage surveillance in real time. Another term that is coming into wide use is M2M2P or machine-to-machine-to-people. The "to-people" part refers to the fact that consumers, workers and professionals will increasingly be actively involved in the gathering of data, its analysis and its usage. For example, M2M2P systems that automatically collect data from patients' bedsides; analyze, chart and store that data; and make the data available to doctors or nurses so that they may take any necessary actions are becoming increasingly powerful. Such systems, part of the growing trend of electronic health records (EHR), can also include bedside comments spoken into tablet computers by physicians that are transcribed automatically by voice recognition software and then stored into EHR.

The long-term trend of miniaturization is playing a vital role in M2M. Intel and other firms are working on convergence of MEMS (microelectromechanical systems—tiny devices or switches that can measure changes such as acceleration or vibration), RFID (wireless radio frequency identification devices) and sometimes tiny computer processors (microprocessors embedded with software). In a small but powerful package, such remote sensors can monitor and transmit the stress level or metal fatigue in a highway bridge or an aircraft wing, or monitor manufacturing processes and product quality in a factory. In our age of growing focus on environmental quality, they can be designed to analyze surrounding air for chemicals, pollutants or particles, using lab on a chip technology that already largely exists. Some observers have referred to these wireless sensors as "smart dust," expecting vast quantities of them to be scattered about the Earth as the sensors become smaller and less expensive over the near future. Energy efficiency is going to benefit greatly, particularly in newly-built offices and factories. An important use of advanced sensors will be to monitor and control energy efficiency on a room-by-room, or even square meter-by-square meter, basis in large buildings.

In an almost infinite variety of possible, efficiency-enhancing applications, artificial intelligence (AI) software can use data gathered from smart dust to forecast needed changes, and robotics or microswitches can then act upon that data, making adjustments in processes automatically. For example, such a system of sensors and controls could make adjustments to the amount of an ingredient being added to the assembly line in a paint factory or food processing plant; increase fresh air flow to a factory room; or adjust air conditioning output in one room while leaving a nearby hallway as is. The ability to monitor conditions such as these 24/7, and provide instant analysis and reporting to engineers, means that potential problems can be deterred, manufacturing defects can be avoided and energy efficiency can be enhanced dramatically. Virtually all industry sectors and processes will benefit.

Look for data sensors in homes to proliferate over the near- to mid-term. In the insurance business, live data emanating from sensors in homes could lead to more intelligent policies. Monitoring data via smartphone could be a significant opportunity for companies in the senior care, child care and pet care sectors.

Internet Research Tip: The Internet of Things Connections Counter and Infographic:

Network equipment maker Cisco has posted a "Connections Counter" online, which provides a running count of people and things connected to the internet, newsroom.cisco.com/ioe . This page also provides many useful links to Internet of Things resources.

In addition, Cisco posts a highly informative Internet of Things page at www.cisco.com/web/solutions/trends/iot/overview.html which includes a one-minute IoT video.

Meanwhile, French technology firm SigFox offers a simple, inexpensive wireless network, designed specifically for M2M needs. The network transmits data at a rate of 100 bits per second, which is slower by a factor of 1,000 than most smartphone networks, but does so cheaply while it fills simple transmission needs such as those from many wireless sensors (such as Whistle, a clip-on collar sensor that tracks dog activity levels). Base stations use a wireless chip that costs only $1 to $2, and customers pay modest service charges per year per device. As of early-2020, SigFox had deployed its technology in about 63 countries.

Intel and other firms have developed methods that enable such remote sensors to bypass the need for internal batteries. Instead, they can run on "power harvesting circuits" that are able to reap power from nearby television signals, FM radio signals, Wi-Fi networks or RFID readers.

Memory chips used in sensors are much smaller than those in smartphones and laptops, opening a major opportunity for manufacturers such as Adesto Technologies. The firm makes chips that store between 32 kilobits and one megabit of data, making them a good fit for small monitors such as fitness data tracking wristbands. Future applications might include location-based beacons in retail stores that alert nearby customers to selected items by cellphone. Smoke detectors with small memory chips could sense battery life, while blood transfusion bags could track their locations, ages and content viabilities.

Internet Research Tip: Internet of Things (IoT) Networks:

For more information on wireless network systems and remote sensors, see:

Analog Devices, Inc. (which acquired Linear Technology Corp.), www.analog.com/en/applications/technology/smartmesh-pavilion-home.html%20#

Moog, Inc., www.moog.com

C3ai, c3iot.com/industries

Chapter 2

TELECOMMUNICATIONS INDUSTRY STATISTICS

CONTENTS:

Telecommunications Industry Statistics and Market Size Overview

	Number	Unit	Year	Source
U.S. Telecommunications Spending (ICT)[1], 2021**	1.9	Tril. US$	2021	PRE
U.S. Telecommunications Spending (ICT)[1], 2020**	1.8	Tril. US$	2020	TIA
Worldwide Telecommunications Spending (ICT)**	7.1	Tril. US$	2020	PRE
Landline				
Total Wireline Retail Local Telephone Service Connections, U.S.	107.0	Mil. Units	Jun-19	FCC
Global Landline Subscriptions	915.0	Mil. Units	2019	ITU
Global Landlines per 100 inhabitants	11.9	Per 100 inhabitants	2019	ITU
Wireless				
Total Wireless Service Revenues, U.S.	197.5	Bil. US$	2021	PRE
Households with Wireless-only Service, U.S.	61.8	%	Dec-20	NHIS
Portion of Mobile Consumers with a Smartphone, U.S.	85.0	%	2020	Pew
Mobile Advertising Spending, U.S.	113.2	Bil. US$	2020	eMarketer
Mobile Cellular Subscriptions, Worldwide*	105.0	Per 100 inhabitants	Jun-20	ITU
Mobile Broadband Subscriptions, Worldwide	75.0	Per 100 inhabitants	Jun-20	ITU
Total Mobile Phone Shipment	1.8	Mil. Units	2021	Gartner
Mobile Application Downloads, Worldwide	218	Bil. Units	2020	App Annie
Mobile App Store Revenue, Worldwide	111.0	Bil. US$	2020	Sensor Tower
Worldwide Smartphone Sales	378.0	Mil. Units	Q1 2021	Gartner
Equipment Revenue				
U.S. Exports of Telecommunications Equipment	32.4	Bil. US$	2020	PRE
U.S. Imports of Telecommunications Equipment	102.3	Bil. US$	2020	PRE
TV, Cable & Internet				
Number of High Speed Internet Lines, U.S. (including mobile wireless)	393.4	Mil. Units	Dec-21	PRE
Number of High Speed Internet Lines, U.S. (not including mobile wireless)	107.8	Mil. Units	Dec-21	PRE
Number of Global Internet Users	5.2	Bil. Units	Mar-21	IWS
Fixed (Wired) Broadband Subscriptions per 100 Inhabitants, Worldwide	14.9	Per 100 inhabitants	2019	ITU
Monthly Global Internet Protocol (IP) Traffic	194	EB per Month	2020	Cisco VNI
Projected Monthly Global IP Traffic	396	EB per Month	2022	Cisco VNI
Number of TV households	120.6	Mil. Units	2020	Nielsen
Percent of Households subscribe to some form of pay-TV service	75	%	2019	Leichtman
Employment				
Employment in the Telecommunications Industry, U.S.	680.4	Thous.	May-21	BLS

TIA = Telecommunications Industry Association; FCC = U.S. Federal Communications Commission; ITU = International Telecommunication Union; PRE = Plunkett Research Estimate; NHIS = National Health Interview Survey; IWS = Internetworldstats.com; Cisco VNI = Cisco Visual Networking Index; Leichtman = Leichtman Research Group; BLS = U.S. Bureau of Labor Statistics.

* The actual number of individuals who own cell phones is lower, as some people own more than one "subscription."

** Forecasted or estimated figure.

[1] ICT, or Information and Communication Technologies, is a term used to describe the relationship between the myriad types of goods, services and networks that make up the global information and communications system. Sectors involved in ICT include landlines, data networks, the Internet, wireless communications, (including cellular and remote wireless sensors) and satellites.

Plunkett's Telecommunications Industry Almanac 2022
www.plunkettresearch.com

Quarterly Telecommunications Industry Revenue by Class of Customer, U.S.: 2nd Quarter 2020-1st Quarter 2021

(In Millions of US$)

NAICS Code	Kind of Business	1Q 2021[P]	4Q 2020	3Q 2020	2Q 2020
517	Telecommunications	163,698	167,481	158,967	155,502
	Government	S	5,282	4,921	4,570
	Business	52,601	53,172	50,932	49,996
	Household consumers & individual users	106,080	109,027	103,114	100,936
5171	Wired telecommunications carriers	79,997	80,815	78,465	78,107
	Government	S	2,714	2,606	S
	Business	23,409	23,669	23,301	22,959
	Household consumers & individual users	54,034	54,432	52,558	52,652
5172	Wireless telecommunications carriers (except satellite)	71,492	74,591	68,684	65,534
	Government	1,588	1,707	1,509	1,264
	Business	20,985	21,523	19,683	19,096
	Household consumers & individual users	48,919	51,361	47,492	45,174
517 pt[1]	Other telecommunications	12,209	12,075	11,818	11,861
	Government	875	861	806	810
	Business	8,207	7,980	7,948	7,941
	Household consumers & individual users	3,127	3,234	3,064	3,110

Note: Estimates are not adjusted for seasonal variation or for price changes and are based on data from the Quarterly Services Survey.

[1] Includes NAICS 5174 (satellite telecommunications) and 5179 (other telecommunications).

[P] Preliminary estimate.

S = Estimate does not meet publication standards because of high variability (coefficient of variation greater than 30%), poor response quality (total quantity response rate is less than 50%) or other concerns about the estimate's quality.

Source: U.S. Census Bureau

Plunkett Research, Ltd.

www.plunkettresearch.com

Wired Telecommunications Carriers,
Estimated Sources of Revenue, U.S.: 2016-2020

(In Millions of US$; Latest Year Available)

NAICS Code: 5171[1]	2020	2019	2018	2017	2016	% Chg. 19/18
Total Operating Revenue	316,382	320,681	311,465	315,390	326,119	3.0%
Fixed local		13,865	15,165	17,087	27,386	-8.6%
Fixed long-distance		20,000	20,401	S	10,820	-2.0%
Fixed all distance		3,554	2,761	1,587	1,952	28.7%
Carrier services		14,493	14,279	13,254	S	1.5%
Private network services		8,073	7,598	S	17,607	6.3%
Internet access services		100,371	95,786	88,714	87,250	4.8%
Internet telephony		10,100	9,583	10,244	11,291	5.4%
Telecommunications network installation services		S	1,293	842	818	NA
Reselling services for telecommunications equipment, retail		1,873	802	1,466	1,476	133.5%
Rental of telecommunications equipment		7,327	6,923	4,458	1,701	5.8%
Repair and maintenance services for telecommunications equipment		S	S	858	S	NA
Subscriber line charges		2,312	2,784	2,896	3,222	-17.0%
Basic programming package		61,887	60,321	59,733	63,659	2.6%
Premium programming package		22,954	22,180	22,978	24,394	3.5%
Pay-per-view		1,645	1,986	2,782	2,898	-17.2%
Air time		5,919	6,451	5,607	6,345	-8.2%
Rental and reselling services for program distribution equipment		10,679	11,001	12,049	13,862	-2.9%
Installation services for connections to program distribution networks		S	S	S	S	NA
Website hosting services		S	S	S	S	NA
All other operating revenue		30,709	28,931	33,544	31,271	6.1%

Note: Dollar volume estimates are published in millions of dollars; consequently, results may not be additive.

S = Estimate does not meet publication standards because of high sampling variability (coefficient of variation is greater than 30%) or poor response quality (total quantity response rate is less than 50%) or other concerns about the estimate's quality. Unpublished estimates derived from this table by subtraction are subject to these same limitations and should not be attributed to the U.S. Census Bureau. NA = Not Avaialble.

[1] Includes 2002 NAICS 5171 (Wired Telecommunications Carriers), 2002 NAICS 5175 (Cable and Other Program Distribution), and a portion of 2002 NAICS 518111 (Internet Service Providers). Historical data, 2010 and prior, have been restated to reflect comparable data on the 2007 NAICS basis.

Source: U.S. Census Bureau

Plunkett Research, Ltd.

www.plunkettresearch.com

Wired Telecommunications Carriers, Estimated Breakdown of Revenue by Type of Customer, U.S.: 2016-2019

(In Millions of US$; Latest Year Available)

NAICS 5171* Kind of Business	2019	2018	2017	2016	% Chg. 19/18
Total Operating Revenue	**320,681**	**311,465**	**315,390**	**326,119**	**3.0%**
Household consumers & individual users	209,519	223,043	194,532	200,051	-6.1%
Business firms, not-for-profit organizations & Gov't (Federal, state & local)	111,162	88,422	120,858	126,068	25.7%
Fixed local telephony	13,865	15,165	17,087	27,386	-8.6%
Household consumers & individual users	7,154	7,787	8,628	12,981	-8.1%
Business firms, not-for-profit organizations & Gov't (Federal, state & local)	6,711	7,378	8,459	14,405	-9.0%
Fixed long-distance telephony	20,000	20,401	S	10,820	-2.0%
Household consumers & individual users	11,839	15,422	S	4,096	-23.2%
Business firms, not-for-profit organizations & Gov't (Federal, state & local)	8,161	4,979	S	6,724	63.9%
Subscriber line charges	2,312	2,784	2,896	3,222	-17.0%
Household consumers & individual users	S	1,698	1,760	2,068	NA
Business firms, not-for-profit organizations & Gov't (Federal, state & local)	906	1,086	1,136	1,154	-16.6%

Note: Dollar volume estimates are published in millions of dollars; consequently, results may not be additive.

* Includes 2002 NAICS 5171 (Wired Telecommunications Carriers), 2002 NAICS 5175 (Cable and Other Program Distribution), and a portion of 2002 NAICS 518111 (Internet Service Providers). Historical data, 2010 and prior, have been restated to reflect comparable data on the 2007 NAICS basis.

S = Estimate does not meet publication standards because of high sampling variability (coefficient of variation is greater than 30%) or poor response quality (total quantity response rate is less than 50%). Unpublished estimates derived from this table by subtraction are subject to these same limitations and should not be attributed to the U.S. Census Bureau. NA = Not Available.

Source: U.S. Census Bureau

Plunkett Research, Ltd.

www.plunkettresearch.com

Wired Telecommunications Carriers,
Estimated Sources of Expenses, U.S.: 2016-2019

(In Millions of US$; Latest Year Available)

NAICS Code: 5171*	2018	2017	2016	2015	% Chg. 18/17
Total operating expenses	**268,369**	**249,981**	**262,254**	**262,993**	**-4.7%**
Gross annual payroll	59,907	53,731	54,720	57,469	-1.8%
Health insurance	NA	NA	S	S	NA
Defined benefit pension plans	NA	NA	S	S	NA
Defined contribution plans	NA	NA	1,351	1,368	NA
Payroll taxes, employer paid insurance premiums (except health), and other employer benefits	NA	NA	3,990	4,116	NA
Temporary staff and leased employee expense	S	S	S	S	NA
Expensed equipment	NA	NA	S	S	NA
Expensed purchases of other materials, parts, and supplies	S	S	S	S	NA
Expensed purchases of software	S	S	S	S	NA
Purchased electricity	NA	NA	1,964	1,853	NA
Purchased fuels (except motor fuels)	NA	NA	38	34	NA
Lease and rental payments for machinery, equipment, and other tangible items	NA	NA	S	S	NA
Lease and rental payments for land, buildings, structures, store spaces, and offices	NA	NA	2,596	S	NA
Purchased repairs and maintenance to machinery and equipment	NA	NA	2,373	2,346	NA
Purchased repairs and maintenance to buildings, structures, and offices	NA	NA	716	703	NA
Purchased advertising and promotional services	NA	NA	6,903	7,153	NA
Access charges	8,569	8,295	S	S	NA
Universal service contributions (USC) and other similar charges	S	3,437	3,020	3,285	13.8%
Program and production costs	49,812	48,860	50,577	47,708	-3.4%
Depreciation and amortization charges	53,390	53,734	55,386	54,117	-3.0%
Governmental taxes and license fees	NA	NA	5,836	6,134	NA
Data processing and other purchased computer services	NA	NA	977	966	NA
Purchased communication services	NA	NA	1,443	1,460	NA
Water, sewer, refuse removal, and other utility payments	NA	NA	54	60	NA
Purchased professional and technical services	NA	NA	3,315	3,799	NA
All other operating expenses	56,682	44,652	50,480	50,335	-11.5%

Note: Dollar volume estimates are published in millions of dollars; consequently, results may not be additive.

S = Estimate does not meet publication standards because of high sampling variability (coefficient of variation is greater than 30%) or poor response quality (total quantity response rate is less than 50%). Unpublished estimates derived from this table by subtraction are subject to these same limitations and should not be attributed to the U.S. Census Bureau. NA = Not Available.

* Includes 2002 NAICS 5171 (Wired Telecommunications Carriers), 2002 NAICS 5175 (Cable and Other Program Distribution), and a portion of 2002 NAICS 518111 (Internet Service Providers). Historical data, 2010 and prior, have been restated to reflect comparable data on the 2007 NAICS basis.

Source: U.S. Census Bureau

Plunkett Research, Ltd.

www.plunkettresearch.com

The Baby Bells Then & Now

AT&T's seven Regional Bell Operating Companies (RBOCs, also known as the "Baby Bells") at the time of its breakup on January 1, 1984:

- Ameritech (merged with SBC, SBC is now AT&T, Inc.)
- Bell Atlantic (merged in 2000 with GTE and now called Verizon)
- BellSouth (merged with AT&T in 2006)
- NYNEX (merged in 1997 with Bell Atlantic, now called Verizon)
- Pacific Telesis Group (merged with SBC; SBC is now AT&T, Inc.)
- Southwestern Bell (renamed itself SBC Communications; SBC is now AT&T, Inc)
- US West (acquired in 2000 by Qwest)

Remaining consolidated firms as of July 2021:

- Lumen Technologies, Inc., formally known as Centurylink (acquired Qwest on April 1, 2011)
- Verizon
- AT&T, Inc.
    - Originally Southwestern Bell. Renamed SBC Communications.
    - Acquired AT&T Corp. in November 2005 for $16.5 billion. Renamed AT&T Inc.
    - Acquired BellSouth and Cingular Wireless in December 2006.
    - Acquired satellite TV provider DirecTV in July 2015 for $49 billion.
    - Acquired media company Time Warner, Inc. in 2018.

Total Retail Local Telephone Service Connections, U.S.: 2016-2019

(Figures in Thousands; Latest Year Available)

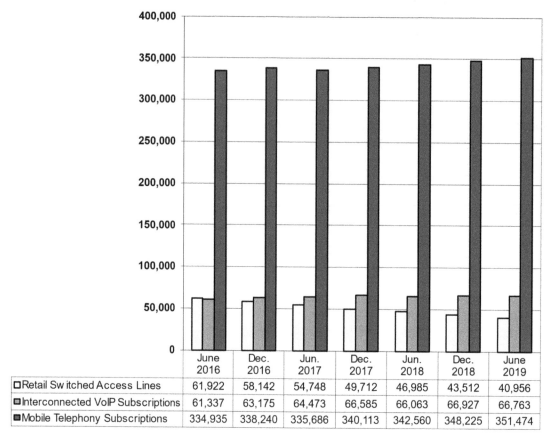

	June 2016	Dec. 2016	Jun. 2017	Dec. 2017	Jun. 2018	Dec. 2018	June 2019
☐ Retail Switched Access Lines	61,922	58,142	54,748	49,712	46,985	43,512	40,956
☐ Interconnected VoIP Subscriptions	61,337	63,175	64,473	66,585	66,063	66,927	66,763
■ Mobile Telephony Subscriptions	334,935	338,240	335,686	340,113	342,560	348,225	351,474

Note: Of the 107 million wireline retail voice telephone service connections (including both switched access lines and interconnected VoIP subscriptions) in June 2019, 55 million (or 50%) were residential connections and 54 million (or 50%) were business connections.

Source: U.S. Federal Communications Commission (FCC)

Plunkett Research, Ltd.

www.plunkettresearch.com

U.S. Households With & Without Telephone Service, including Wireless: November 1983-July 2020

(In Millions; Latest Year Available)

Date	Households	Households w/ Telephones	Percentage w/ Telephones	Households w/o Telephones	Percentage w/o Telephones
Nov-83	85.8	78.4	91.4%	7.4	8.6%
Nov-84	87.4	79.9	91.4%	7.5	8.6%
Nov-85	88.8	81.6	91.9%	7.2	8.1%
Nov-86	89.9	83.1	92.4%	6.8	7.6%
Nov-87	91.3	84.3	92.3%	7.0	7.7%
Nov-88	92.6	85.7	92.5%	6.9	7.5%
Nov-89	93.9	87.3	93.0%	6.6	7.0%
Nov-90	94.7	88.4	93.3%	6.3	6.7%
Nov-91	95.7	89.4	93.4%	6.3	6.6%
Nov-92	97.0	91.0	93.8%	6.0	6.2%
Nov-93	98.8	93.0	94.2%	5.8	5.8%
Nov-94	99.8	93.7	93.8%	6.2	6.2%
Nov-95	100.4	94.2	93.9%	6.2	6.1%
Nov-96	101.3	95.1	93.9%	6.2	6.1%
Nov-97	102.8	96.5	93.8%	6.3	6.2%
Nov-98	104.1	98.0	94.2%	6.1	5.8%
Nov-99	105.4	99.1	94.1%	6.3	5.9%
Mar-00	105.3	99.6	94.6%	5.7	5.4%
Jul-00	105.8	99.8	94.4%	5.9	5.6%
Nov-00	106.5	100.2	94.1%	6.3	5.9%
Mar-01	107.0	101.1	94.6%	5.8	5.4%
Jul-01	106.9	101.7	95.1%	5.2	4.9%
Nov-01	107.7	102.2	94.9%	5.5	5.1%
Mar-02	108.3	103.4	95.5%	4.8	4.5%
Jul-02	108.5	103.2	95.1%	5.3	4.9%
Nov-02	109.0	104.0	95.3%	5.1	4.7%
Mar-03	112.1	107.1	95.5%	5.0	4.5%
Jul-03	112.1	106.8	95.2%	5.3	4.8%
Nov-03	113.1	107.1	94.7%	6.0	5.3%
Mar-04	112.9	106.4	94.2%	6.5	5.8%
Jul-04	113.5	106.5	93.8%	7.1	6.2%
Nov-04	113.8	106.4	93.5%	7.4	6.5%
Mar-05	114.5	105.8	92.4%	8.7	7.6%
Jul-05	114.4	107.5	94.0%	6.8	6.0%
Nov-05	115.2	107.0	92.9%	8.2	7.1%
Mar-06	115.5	107.2	92.8%	8.4	7.2%
Jul-06	116.2	109.9	94.6%	6.3	5.4%
Nov-06	116.4	108.8	93.4%	7.6	6.6%
Mar-07	117.1	110.8	94.6%	6.4	5.4%
Jul-07	117.7	111.7	95.0%	5.9	5.0%
Nov-07	118.2	112.2	94.9%	6.0	5.1%

(Continued on next page)

U.S. Households With & Without Telephone Service, including Wireless: November 1983-July 2020(cont.)

(In Millions; Latest Year Available)

Date	Households	Households w/ Telephones	Percentage w/ Telephones	Households w/o Telephones	Percentage w/o Telephones
Mar-08	117.8	112.2	95.2%	5.6	4.8%
Jul-08	118.0	112.6	95.4%	5.5	4.6%
Nov-08	118.6	112.7	95.0%	5.9	5.0%
Mar-09	118.4	113.2	95.6%	5.2	4.4%
Jul-09	118.4	113.3	95.7%	5.1	4.3%
Nov-09	119.2	114.0	95.7%	5.1	4.3%
Mar-10	118.3	113.6	96.0%	4.7	4.0%
Jul-10	118.3	113.5	96.0%	4.8	4.0%
Nov-10	119.4	114.0	95.5%	5.4	4.5%
Mar-11	119.8	114.9	95.9%	4.9	4.1%
Jul-11	119.3	114.1	95.6%	5.2	4.4%
Nov-11	119.7	114.4	95.6%	5.3	4.4%
Mar-12	121.9	117.0	96.0%	4.9	4.0%
Jul-12	121.7	117.0	96.1%	4.7	3.9%
Nov-12	122.0	116.9	95.8%	5.1	4.2%
Mar-13	123.3	118.3	96.0%	5.0	4.0%
Jul-13	123.1	118.3	96.1%	4.8	3.9%
Nov-13	123.7	118.4	95.7%	5.3	4.3%
Mar-14	124.2	119.5	96.2%	4.7	3.8%
Jul-14	123.9	119.0	96.0%	4.9	4.0%
Nov-14	124.8	119.9	96.1%	4.9	3.9%
Mar-15	125.5	121.1	96.5%	4.4	3.5%
Jul-15	125.8	121.7	96.3%	4.1	3.5%
Nov-15	126.1	122.2	96.3%	3.9	3.1%
Mar-16	127.2	122.7	96.5%	4.5	3.5%
Jul-16	127.0	122.4	96.4%	4.6	3.6%
Nov-16	127.3	122.6	96.3%	4.7	3.7%
Mar-17	127.4	122.6	96.2%	4.8	3.8%
Jul-17	127.5	122.9	96.4%	4.6	3.6%
Nov-17	127.5	122.1	95.8%	5.4	4.2%
Mar-18	128.8	124.2	96.4%	4.6	3.6%
Jul-18	129.1	123.9	96.0%	5.2	4.0%
Nov-18	129.4	124.2	96.0%	5.2	4.0%
Mar-19	129.9	124.9	96.2%	4.9	3.8%
Jul-19	129.9	124.9	96.2%	4.9	3.8%
Nov-19	130.6	125.2	95.8%	5.4	4.2%
Mar-20	129.3	125.4	97.0%	3.9	3.0%
Jul-20	128.5	126.1	98.1%	2.4	1.9%

Note: Penetration rates include wired and/or wireless subscriptions. Details may not add to totals due to rounding.

Source: U.S. Federal Communications Commission (FCC)

Annual Personal Consumption Expenditures on Telecommunications, U.S.: Selected Years, 1980-2019

(In Millions of US$; Latest Year Available)

Year	All Goods & Services[1]	Wireline Telephone Services[2]	Cellular Telephone Services[3]	Total Telephone Services	Telephone Service as a Percentage of All Goods & Services	Wireline as a Percentage of All Telephone Service	Cellular as a Percentage of All Telephone Service
1980	1,754,616	27,574	0	27,574	1.57	100	0
1985	2,722,674	45,877	101	45,978	1.69	99.78	0.22
1990	3,825,630	58,456	2,246	60,702	1.59	96.30	3.70
1995	4,984,178	73,893	11,274	85,167	1.71	86.76	13.24
2000	6,762,144	93,824	32,590	126,414	1.87	74.22	25.78
2001	7,065,634	90,423	40,763	131,187	1.86	68.93	31.07
2002	7,342,686	82,368	48,933	131,301	1.79	62.73	37.27
2003	7,723,109	75,875	54,572	130,446	1.69	58.17	41.83
2004	8,212,662	71,654	61,173	132,828	1.62	53.94	46.05
2005	8,747,118	68,895	68,794	137,689	1.57	50.04	49.96
2006	9,260,345	67,571	77,268	144,838	1.56	46.65	53.35
2007	9,706,431	64,948	84,094	149,042	1.54	43.58	56.42
2008	9,976,330	62,325	89,843	152,168	1.53	40.96	59.04
2009	9,842,209	53,937	92,414	146,352	1.49	36.85	63.15
2010	10,185,836	49,665	97,962	147,627	1.45	33.64	66.36
2011	10,641,109	44,539	105,071	149,609	1.41	29.77	70.23
2012	11,006,814	39,347	106,987	146,333	1.33	26.89	73.11
2013	11,317,210	35,338	110,620	145,959	1.29	24.21	75.79
2014	11,822,753	33,546	119,426	152,972	1.29	21.93	78.07
2015	12,284,281	32,222	120,668	152,890	1.24	21.08	78.92
2016	12,748,483	32,983	122,900	155,883	1.22	21.16	78.84
2017	13,312,060	30,069	122,209	152,278	1.14	19.75	80.25
2018	13,998,666	29,017	129,824	158,842	1.13	18.27	81.73
2019	14,544,600	NA	NA	161,000	1.11	NA	NA

[1] Represents the sum of two series: Goods (Series DGDSRC) and Services (Series DSERRC).

[2] Represents the sum of two series: Local Telephone Service (Series DLOCRC) and Long Distance Telephone Services (Series DLDTRC).

[3] Cellular Telephone Service (Series DCELRC).

Source: U.S. Bureau Of Economic Analysis
Plunkett Research®, Ltd.
www.plunkettresearch.com

Wireless Telecommunications Carriers (except Satellite): Estimated Sources of Revenue & Expenses, U.S.: 2016-2020

(In Millions of US$; Latest Year Available)

NAICS 5172[1]	2020	2019	2018	2017	2016	% Chg. 19/18
Total Operating Revenue	276,145	276,114	272,046	257,778	259,321	1.5%
Messaging (paging) services		S	2,217	S	2,956	NA
Mobile telephony		28,579	47,477	S	45,659	-39.8%
Mobile long-distance		2,585	2,484	2,530	2,441	4.1%
Mobile all distance		59,712	40,031	37,722	S	49.2%
Internet access services		92,179	90,949	96,257	97,296	1.4%
Installation services for telecommunication networks		195	S	192	242	NA
Reselling services for telecommunications equipment, retail		58,217	57,730	46,767	44,367	0.8%
Rental of telecommunications equipment		6,643	6,768	4,714	S	-1.8%
Repair & maintenance svcs. for telecom equipment		1,694	1,684	1,861	2,338	0.6%
All other operating revenue		24,052	22,518	18,092	17,484	6.8%
Total Operating Expenses		182,269	181,197	189,092	188,983	0.6%
Gross annual payroll		18,306	18,052	18,561	18,899	1.4%
Health insurance		NA	NA	2,065	2,067	NA
Defined benefit pension plans		NA	NA	S	196	NA
Defined contribution plans		NA	NA	521	425	NA
Payroll taxes, employer paid insurance premiums (except health), and other employer benefits		NA	NA	2,230	2,213	NA
Temporary staff and leased employee expense		5,421	5,470	S	7,914	-0.9%
Expensed equipment		NA	S	42,766	43,164	NA
Expensed purchases of other materials, parts, and supplies		S	S	1,742	1,673	NA
Expensed purchases of software		D	S	945	921	NA
Purchased electricity		NA	NA	S	1,029	NA
Purchased fuels (except motor fuels)		NA	NA	3	2	NA
Lease and rental payments for machinery, equipment, and other tangible items		NA	NA	S	887	NA
Lease and rental payments for land, buildings, structures, store spaces, and offices		NA	NA	11,059	10,815	NA
Purchased repairs and maintenance to machinery and equipment		NA	NA	188	184	NA
Purchased repairs and maintenance to buildings, structures, and offices		NA	NA	486	310	NA
Purchased advertising and promotional services		NA	NA	8,337	8,145	NA
Access charges		4,775	4,811	5,593	5,147	-0.7%
Universal service contributions (USC) and other similar charges		S	3,586	S	4,571	NA
Depreciation and amortization charges		36,077	37,176	35,634	34,721	-3.0%
Governmental taxes and license fees		NA	NA	2,278	2,353	NA
Data processing and other purchased computer services		NA	NA	1,953	2,035	NA
Purchased communication services		NA	NA	6,605	7,012	NA
Water, sewer, refuse removal, and other utility payments		NA	NA	13	7	NA
Purchased professional and technical services		NA	NA	4,755	4,498	NA
All other operating expenses		D	60,930	S	29,795	NA

Note: Dollar volume estimates are published in millions of dollars; consequently, results may not be additive.

S = Estimate does not meet publication standards because of high sampling variability (coefficient of variation is greater than 30%) or poor response quality (total quantity response rate is less than 50%). Unpublished estimates derived from this table by subtraction are subject to these same limitations and should not be attributed to the U.S. Census Bureau. NA = Not Available. D = Estimate in table is withheld to avoid disclosing data of individual companies; data are included in higher total levels.

[1] Includes 2002 NAICS 517211 (Paging), 2002 NAICS 517212 (Cellular and Other Wireless Telecommunications) and a portion of 2002 NAICS 518111 (Internet Service Providers). Historical data, 2010 and prior, have been restated to reflect comparable data on the 2007 NAICS basis.

Top Mobile Operators by Number of Subscribers, Worldwide

(In Millions)

#	Mobile Operator	Major Operating Regions	Mobile Subscribers	Date
1	China Mobile	China	942.8	May-21
2	Airtel	India, South Asia, Africa	458.0	Dec-21
6	Reliance Jio	India	422.9	Jun-21
5	China Telecom	China	360.7	May-21
3	Vodafone	Europe, Africa, Australia	311.2	Mar-20
4	China Unicom	China	309.7	May-21
7	Vodafone Idea	EMEA, India, APAC	283.7	Mar-21
11	América Móvil	Latin America	280.7	Oct-21
20	MTN Group	Africa, Asia	277.9	May-21
8	Telefónica	Spain, Europe, Latin America	266.3	Mar-20
9	Orange	Europe, Africa, Caribbean	208.5	Mar-20
10	Veon	Asia, Africa, Europe	212.7	Mar-21
13	Deutsche Telekom	Europe, USA	185.5	Mar-20
12	Telenor	Eastern Europe, SE Asia	187.0	Jun-21
14	AT&T Mobility	United States	186.0	Mar-21
15	Telkomsel	Indonesia	169.5	Dec-20
17	Etisalat	Middle East, Asia, Africa	154.0	Dec-20
19	Axiata	South Asia, SE Asia	157.0	Dec-20
18	BSNL	India, SE Asia	121.8	Mar-21
16	Verizon Wireless	United States	120.3	Mar-20

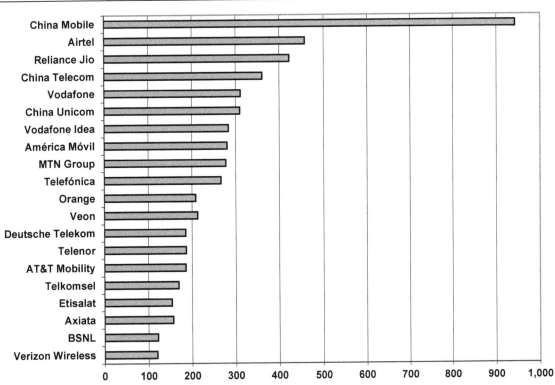

Notes: In some cases, these figures represent proportionate subscribers (adjusted according to percentage of company ownership). Note that some companies listed also have sizeable fixed-line customer bases, in addition to their mobile operations.

Source: Plunkett Research,® Ltd.

Internet Access Technologies Compared
(In Millions of Bits per Second - Mbps)

Type of Access	Maximum Data Rate (In Mbps)	Characteristics
Dialup		
Dialup	.0288, .0336, .056	Analog modems that require dialup connection. Slowest method of Internet access.
ISDN	.064, .128	Integrated Services Digital Network. Digital access that requires dialup connection.
Wired Broadband		
ADSL	1.5 - 24 Downstream .5 - 3.5 Upstream	Asymmetrical Digital Subscriber Line. Highest speeds are on ADSL2+ (ULL).
SDSL	2.3	Symmetric Digital Subscriber Line. Downstream and upstream data transfer rates are similar. Ideal for businesses because of synchronous speed and high-speed router capabilities.
VDSL	24 - 100 Downstream 2.3 - 16 Upstream	Very High bit-Rate DSL.
Cable Modem	4 - 2,000 Downstream .384 - 50 Upstream	2 Gigabyte (2 GB) speeds are possible with DOCSIS 3.1 technology.
FTTH	15 to 1,000 Downstream 5 to 1,000 Upstream	Fiber to the x (Home, Node, Premises, etc). Google Fiber is a leading provider. Google is developing future 10 Gigabyte (10 GB) technologies.
T1/DS1	1.544	Ideal for businesses with high bandwidth requirements.
T3/DS3	44.736	Equivalent to 30 T1 circuits.
E1 (Europe)	2.048	European version of T1.
E3 (Europe)	34.368	European version of T3.
OC3	155.52	High-speed access. Uses optical fiber technology.
OC12	622.08	Offers higher speed access than OC3. Uses optical fiber technology.
OC48	2,488.32	Offers one of the fastest data rates. Uses optical fiber technology. Extremely expensive to setup and maintain.
OC768	39,813.12	Network line used by AT&T, Cisco and others.
Wireless Broadband		
802.15.3 (UWB)	100 - 2,000	UWB stands for ultrawideband. It is useful for high-speed, short distance data transfer.
802.11b-g (Wi-Fi)	11 - 54	Typical home and office wireless networks.
802.11n (MIMO), 802.11ac	100 - 2,000	Faster data transmission rates and broader area coverage than other 802.11 technologies.
802.15 (Bluetooth) versions 1.0 - 2.0	1 - 3	Useful for high-speed, short distance data transfer.
802.15 Bluetooth version 3.0	24	Bluetooth 3.0 offers high speed data transfer at short range of up to 10 meters.
802.16e (WiMAX)	15 - 70	Has the potential to be useful for distances of up to 30 miles.
802.16m (WiMAX2)	110-365 Download 70-376 Upload	Also known as WiMAX Advanced, this technology is classified by the ITU as true 4G.
Satellite	5 to 20	Limited upstream speeds. Low-Earth Orbit satellites may offer faster speeds.
CDMA2000 EV-DO	2.4	Popular cellular technology. EV-DO Rev. A is 3.1 Mbps, Rev. B is 14.7 Mbps
HSPA	14.4	Popular 3G cellular
HSPA+	42 - 168	Advanced cellular, Release 8 is 42 Mbps, Release 9 is 84 Mbps and Release 10 is 168 Mbps.
LTE (3G-4G)	36 to 326	"Long Term Evolution" technology for cellular networks.
LTE Advanced (4G, Release 10)	100-1,000 Download up to 500 Upload	An upgraded version of LTE that is classified by the ITU as 4G. Sometimes called an IMT-Advanced technology.
5G	10,000	A 5G standard is expected to be adopted by 2019 or 2020 at the earliest. Download speeds of as much 10 Gigabytes may be possible.

Note: 1 Mbps = 1,000 Kbps; 1,000 Mbps = 1 Gigabyte (1 GB)

Wireless Standards & Speeds

Approx. theoretical maximum download speeds, with approx. year of first use and generation of technology. (Actual speeds attained in daily use may be substantially lower.)

Gen.	Year	Technology	Max. Data Speed
1	1981	Nordisk MobilTelefoni (NMT-450, NMT-900)	1.2 Kbps
1	1983	Advanced Mobile Phone System (AMPS)	9.6 Kbps
1	1986	Mobitex	8.0 Kbps
1	1990	Cellular Digital Packet Data (CDPD), AMPS standard	19.2 Kbps
1	90s	DataTAC	19.2 Kbps
2	1990	IS-54 (aka Digital AMPS, D-AMPS, TDMA)	13 Kbps
2	1991	Global System for Mobile Communications (GSM)	9.6 Kbps
2	1993	IS-136 (aka D-AMPS, TDMA)	48.6 Kbps
2	1993	Personal Digital Cellular (PDC), Japan, TDMA standard	11.2 Kbps
2	1995	IS-95 (aka cdmaOne, CDMA)	9.6 Kbps
2	1996	Integrated Digital Enhanced Network (iDEN), TDMA standard	19.2 Kbps
2.5	2001	GSM General Packet Radio Service (GPRS)	144 Kbps
2.5	2002	CDMA2000 1x Radio Transmission Technology (1xRTT)	144 Kbps
2.5	2005	Wideband Integrated Dispatch Enhanced Network (WiDEN)	60 Kbps
2.75	2003	GSM Enhanced Data Rates for GSM Evolution (EDGE)	236.8 - 473.6 Kbps
3	2001	Wideband Code Division Multiple Access (W-CDMA)	.384 - 2 Mbps
3	2001	Freedom of Mobile Multimedia Access (FOMA), NTT DoCoMo	7.2 Mbps
3	2003	Universal Mobile Telecommunications System (UMTS)	3.6 Mbps
3	2004	CDMA2000 EV-DO (Evolution-Data Optimization) Rev. 0	2.4 Mbps
3	2006	EV-DO Rev. A	3.1 Mbps
3	2006	EV-DO Rev. B	14.7 Mbps
3	2006	Evolution-Data and Voice (EV-DV)	14.7 Mbps
3+	2006	Worldwide Interoperability for Microwave Access (WiMAX); IEEE 802.16d, 802.16e	144 Mbps fixed, 46 Mbps mobile
4	~2012	WiMax Advanced (WiMax 2) 802.16m	170-300 Mbps mobile
3+	2007	High-Speed Packet Access (HSPA)	14.4 Mbps
3+	~2010	HSPA+ (release 8)	42 Mbps
3+	~2011	HSPA+ (release 9)	84 Mbps
4	~2012	HSPA+ (release 10)	168 Mbps
3+	~2008	Evolved UMTS Terrestrial Radio Access (E-UTRA)	200 Mbps
3+	~2009	3GPP Long Term Evolution (LTE), UMTS Release 8	326 Mbps
4	~2012	LTE Advanced, UMTS Release 10	1,000 Mbps
5	~2019	3GPP New Radio (NR), Massive MIMO, Edge Computing, Small Cell, Beamforming, Radio Convergence, NOMA (Non-Orthogonal Multiple Access)	20 Gbps

Notes: Kbps = kilobits per second; 1 Mbps = 1,000 Kbps; 1 Gbps = 1,000 Mbps. Years and speeds are estimates.

TDMA = Time Division Multiple Access; CDMA = Code Division Multiple Access; 3GPP = 3rd Generation Partnership Project.

Satellite Telecommunications:
Estimated Sources of Revenue & Expenses, U.S.: 2016-2019

(In Millions of US$; Latest Year Available)

NAICS 5174	2019	2018	2017	2016	% Chg. 19/18
Total Operating Revenue	**5,862**	**7,070**	**6,947**	**7,208**	**-17.1%**
Carrier services	1,780	2,068	2,190	2,313	-13.9%
Private network services	S	S	S	1,786	NA
All other operating revenue	2,811	3,396	3,120	3,109	-17.2%
Total Operating Expense	**4,521**	**5,511**	**5,432**	**5,634**	**-18.0%**
Gross annual payroll	973	1089	1165	1,106	-10.7%
Health insurance	NA	NA	102	101	NA
Defined benefit pension plans	NA	NA	3	3	NA
Defined contribution plans	NA	NA	48	45	NA
Payroll taxes, employer paid insurance premiums (except health), and other employer benefits	NA	NA	112	100	NA
Temporary staff and leased employee expense	46	64	61	60	-28.1%
Expensed equipment		NA	83	80	NA
Expensed purchases of other materials, parts, and supplies	S	S	S	S	NA
Expensed purchases of software	S	S	16	14	NA
Purchased electricity	NA	NA	24	23	NA
Purchased fuels (except motor fuels)	NA	NA	S	ZZ	NA
Lease and rental payments for machinery, equipment, and other tangible items	NA	NA	9	10	NA
Lease and rental payments for land, buildings, structures, store spaces, and offices	NA	NA	119	123	NA
Purchased repairs and maintenance to machinery and equipment	NA	NA	72	109	NA
Purchased repairs and maintenance to buildings, structures, and offices	NA	NA	14	14	NA
Purchased advertising and promotional services	NA	NA	35	40	NA
Access charges	13	17	S	S	NA
Depreciation and amortization charges	812	920	767	S	-11.7%
Governmental taxes and license fees	NA	NA	30	33	NA
Data processing and other purchased computer services	NA	NA	13	10	NA
Purchased communication services	NA	NA	1889	1,892	NA
Water, sewer, refuse removal, and other utility payments	NA	NA	1	1	NA
Purchased professional and technical services	NA	NA	248	264	NA
All other operating expenses	2092	2992	2978	3,269	-30.1%

Note: Dollar volume estimates are published in millions of dollars; consequently, results may not be additive. Estimates cover taxable and tax-exempt firms and are not adjusted for price changes.

S = Estimate does not meet publication standards because of high sampling variability (coefficient of variation is greater than 30%) or poor response quality (total quantity response rate is less than 50%). Unpublished estimates derived from this table by subtraction are subject to these same limitations and should not be attributed to the U.S. Census Bureau.

NA = Not Available

Source: U.S. Census Bureau

Plunkett Research,® Ltd.

www.plunkettresearch.com

Number of Business & Residential High Speed Internet Lines, U.S.: 2016-2021

(In Thousands)

Types of Technology	Dec-16	Dec-17	Dec-18	Dec-19	Dec-20*	Dec-21*
ADSL	23,891	21,653	19,691	18,462	16,942	15,547
SDSL	8	9	4	3	2	2
Other Wireline[1]	32	68	74	98	142	206
Cable Modem	59,145	61,567	63,788	65,415	65,415	67,650
FTTP[2]	10,956	12,702	14,621	16,097	18,300	20,804
Satellite	1,676	1,688	1,787	1,826	1,878	1,933
Fixed Wireless	1,099	1,146	1,318	1,400	1,518	1,646
Total Fixed	**96,907**	**98,832**	**101,283**	**101,283**	**104,198**	**107,787**
Mobile Wireless (Smartphone)	253,000	266,208	267,191	272,096	278,777	285,621
Total Lines	**349,607**	**365,040**	**368,473**	**368,473**	**382,975**	**393,408**

Notes: High-speed lines are connections to end-user locations that deliver services at speeds exceeding 200 kbps in at least one direction. Advanced services lines, which are a subset of high-speed lines, are connections that deliver services at speeds exceeding 200 kbps in both directions. Line counts presented in this report are not adjusted for the number of persons at a single end-user location who have access to, or who use, the Internet-access services that are delivered over the high-speed connection to that location.

[1] Power Line and Other are summarized with Other Wireline to maintain firm confidentiality.

[2] Fiber to the premises.

* Plunkett Research Estimate.

Source: U.S. Federal Communications Bureau (FCC)

Plunkett Research, Ltd.

www.plunkettresearch.com

Exports & Imports of Telecommunications Equipment, U.S.: 2015-1st Quarter 2021

(In Thousands of US$)

Exports

Partner	2015	2016	2017	2018	2019	2020	1Q 2020	1Q 2021
World Total	42,157,175	41,542,551	40,777,095	38,351,310	35,896,344	32,446,485	8,671,866	9,000,583
Hong Kong	4,946,287	5,692,071	4,604,774	4,651,895	4,462,929	3,582,930	1,218,808	1,242,563
Canada	5,171,993	4,916,023	5,242,642	5,302,171	4,716,730	4,152,075	1,006,770	1,092,936
Mexico	6,843,682	5,310,740	4,707,371	5,006,096	4,213,339	3,229,103	834,015	858,369
United Arab Emirates	2,109,653	1,573,509	1,829,491	1,688,361	1,662,696	1,870,004	482,880	756,311
Netherlands	2,190,278	1,887,378	2,231,185	2,090,316	2,058,970	2,086,825	487,961	536,531
United Kingdom	1,030,348	1,029,305	1,106,889	1,257,820	1,052,993	972,340	264,151	260,920
China	2,560,847	2,504,620	1,766,070	1,236,369	1,100,626	954,673	208,133	248,145
Japan	1,041,032	1,390,429	1,318,084	1,165,564	1,091,408	1,069,074	291,873	244,820
Paraguay	524,343	793,249	1,195,193	1,083,777	1,086,121	703,272	188,186	229,696
Germany	1,166,467	1,112,224	1,004,908	956,603	1,009,225	804,135	223,416	223,927
Australia	786,575	972,943	795,346	868,642	891,939	856,572	215,367	201,154
Singapore	712,376	755,932	790,486	878,829	873,201	811,991	221,788	173,905
Brazil	1,034,458	1,231,666	927,998	920,475	829,047	736,854	183,183	172,566
Costa Rica	407,709	360,132	281,698	305,703	310,126	362,731	109,075	169,411
Chile	510,632	523,902	563,066	507,588	458,475	407,594	99,947	151,600

Imports

Partner	2015	2016	2017	2018	2019	2020	1Q 2020	1Q 2021
World Total	114,257,343	116,365,960	125,317,129	121,719,538	111,613,563	102,295,171	20,423,859	24,548,595
China	67,380,799	65,739,211	78,236,724	77,486,889	64,574,401	55,583,486	9,729,139	13,309,058
Viet Nam	4,064,150	5,753,419	5,502,287	6,738,052	14,214,290	13,957,289	3,013,308	3,102,187
Mexico	13,344,495	14,454,745	12,499,426	11,550,239	9,149,130	8,813,754	2,218,299	2,424,194
Taiwan	3,740,815	3,669,923	3,723,937	2,900,760	4,007,632	5,099,911	1,074,892	1,113,054
Thailand	3,496,109	3,543,782	3,869,507	3,420,584	2,695,363	3,464,004	645,758	885,194
Malaysia	5,604,034	6,118,530	5,736,698	4,235,548	2,997,279	2,854,814	653,454	668,118
South Korea	7,232,736	7,199,958	6,364,703	4,957,189	4,374,025	1,986,521	504,602	408,298
Canada	1,692,433	1,575,253	1,452,618	1,631,978	1,525,747	1,438,318	352,664	350,503
Japan	1,459,554	1,415,613	1,298,804	1,406,603	1,285,260	1,144,184	289,939	275,718
Estonia	225,380	712,755	251,669	496,748	491,265	591,183	96,788	259,064
India	186,459	167,475	163,894	250,263	373,696	884,055	242,185	228,255
Indonesia	385,708	428,733	345,950	222,131	420,404	975,094	291,944	214,109
Germany	729,475	726,751	678,121	770,389	726,324	566,605	166,986	163,305
Phillipines	221,614	217,101	209,957	218,168	356,324	509,812	101,404	145,851
Israel	494,771	459,383	557,044	566,289	612,382	761,766	148,139	138,767

Note: "Telecommunications Equipment" refers to NAICS (North American Industry Classification System) Code 3342.

Source: Foreign Trade Division, U.S. Census Bureau

Plunkett Research, Ltd.

www.plunkettresearch.com

Employment in the Telecommunications Industry, U.S.: 1990-May 2021

(Annual Estimates in Thousands of Employed Workers)

Year	Telecom (517)	Wired Telecom Carriers (517311)	Wireless Telecom Carriers (except Satellite) (517312)	Other Telecom (5179)	Telecom Resellers (517911)	Cable & Other Subscription Programming (5152)
1990	1,008.5	759.5	35.8	213.2	179.5	51.7
1991	999.9	749.9	41.8	208.3	178.1	52.5
1992	972.9	725.8	47.8	199.3	172.6	53.6
1993	969.5	716.5	56.3	196.7	170.5	55.9
1994	989.5	719.2	71.7	198.6	171.8	59.3
1995	1,009.3	717.6	90.3	201.4	171.2	63.8
1996	1,038.1	722.2	110.1	205.8	171.6	69.8
1997	1,108.0	755.7	132.1	220.2	181.3	71.5
1998	1,167.4	789.8	144.2	233.4	188.7	75.5
1999	1,270.8	853.2	159.9	257.6	200.2	81.8
2000	1,396.6	921.8	185.6	289.3	213.6	90.7
2001	1,423.9	933.8	201.4	288.8	214.1	95.6
2002	1,280.9	837.1	197.3	246.6	179.5	92.9
2003	1,166.8	761.8	189.9	215.1	154.9	85.9
2004	1,115.1	720.4	189.7	205.1	147.3	85.5
2005	1,071.3	689.6	191.3	190.5	135.1	88.9
2006	1,047.6	669.2	200.2	178.1	125.6	90.0
2007	1,030.6	664.5	203.4	162.7	117.2	88.5
2008	1,019.4	666.4	200.5	152.6	108.6	85.6
2009	965.7	635.0	186.9	143.8	100.7	85.3
2010	902.9	602.9	170.2	129.8	91.5	80.4
2011	873.6	585.1	165.5	123.0	87.1	73.6
2012	856.8	589.5	156.8	110.4	75.1	73.3
2013	853.2	605.2	154.6	93.4	57.6	69.1
2014	838.5	600.7	145.9	91.8	54.4	62.8
2015	810.9	593.1	127.9	89.9	54.0	59.3
2016	801.1	592.3	121.4	87.4	51.8	53.8
2017	780.8	575.1	117.1	88.6	51.3	52.7
2018	751.2	547.3	114.3	89.5	49.2	53.6
2019	713.0	519.5	105.8	87.7	48.8	53.0
2020	691.3	500.1	99.6	91.6	49.0	48.6
May-21*	680.4	495.7	98.0	89.1	47.4	47.1

* Preliminary Estimate

Source: U.S. Bureau of Labor Statistics (BLS)

Plunkett Research, Ltd.

www.plunkettresearch.com

Chapter 3

IMPORTANT TELECOMMUNICATIONS INDUSTRY CONTACTS

Addresses, Telephone Numbers and Internet Sites

Contents:

1) Apps Industry Associations
2) Broadcasting, Cable, Radio & TV Associations
3) Canadian Government Agencies-General
4) Canadian Government Agencies-Scientific
5) Careers-Computers/Technology
6) Careers-First Time Jobs/New Grads
7) Careers-General Job Listings
8) Careers-Job Reference Tools
9) Chinese Government Agencies-Science & Technology
10) Computer & Electronics Industry Associations
11) Computer & Electronics Industry Resources
12) Corporate Information Resources
13) Economic Data & Research
14) Engineering Industry Resources
15) Engineering, Research & Scientific Associations
16) Industry Research/Market Research
17) Internet Industry Associations
18) Internet Industry Resources
19) Internet Usage Statistics
20) MBA Resources
21) Outsourcing Industry Resources
22) Patent Organizations

23) Payment, Ecommerce and Data Interchange Technology
24) Research & Development, Laboratories
25) Robotics & Automation Industry Associations
26) Satellite Industry Associations
27) Satellite-Related Professional Organizations
28) Software Industry Associations
29) Software Industry Resources
30) Technology Law Associations
31) Technology Transfer Associations
32) Telecommunications Industry Associations
33) Telecommunications Resources
34) Telecommunications-VOIP Resources
35) Trade Associations-General
36) Trade Associations-Global
37) Trade Resources
38) U.S. Government Agencies
39) Wireless & Cellular Industry Associations
40) Wireless & Cellular Industry Resources

1) Apps Industry Associations

Association for Competitive Technology (ACT)
1401 K St. NW, Ste. 502
Washington, DC 20005 US
Phone: 202-331-2130
Web Address: www.actonline.org

The Association for Competitive Technology (ACT) is an international advocacy and education organization representing more than 3,000 small and mid-size app developers and information technology firms. It has offices in Washington, DC and in Brussels, Belgium.

2)   Broadcasting, Cable, Radio & TV Associations

Cable Center (The)
2000 Buchtel Blvd.
Denver, CO 80210 USA
Phone: 720-502-7500
E-mail Address: info@cablecenter.org
Web Address: www.cablecenter.org
The Cable Center supports communication in the business, technology and programming of cable telecommunications and provides education, training and research for all aspects of the industry.

National Cable and Telecommunications Association (NCTA)
25 Massachusetts Ave. NW, Ste. 100
Washington, DC 20001-1413 USA
Phone: 202-222-2300
Fax: 202-222-2514
E-mail Address: info@ncta.com
Web Address: www.ncta.com
The National Cable and Telecommunications Association (NCTA) is the principal trade association of the cable television industry in the United States. It represents cable operators as well as over 200 cable program networks that produce TV shows.

3)   Canadian Government Agencies-General

Canadian Intellectual Property Office (CIPO)
Place du Portage, 50 Victoria St., Rm. C-229
Gatineau, QC K1A 0C9 Canada
Phone: 819-934-0544
Fax: 819-953-2476
Toll Free: 866-997-1936
Web Address: www.cipo.ic.gc.ca
The Canadian Intellectual Property Office (CIPO) is the agency responsible for the administration and processing of intellectual property in Canada, including patents, trademarks, copyrights, industrial designs and integrated circuit topographies.

4)   Canadian Government Agencies-Scientific

Institute for Microstructural Sciences (IMS)
1200 Montreal Rd., Bldg. M-58
Ottawa, ON K1A 0R6 Canada
Phone: 613-993-9101
Fax: 613-952-9907
Toll Free: 877-672-2672
E-mail Address: info@nrc-cnrc.gc.ca
Web Address: www.nrc-cnrc.gc.ca
The Institute for Microstructural Sciences (IMS) is a branch of Canada's National Research Council (NRC) that focuses its research on the information and telecommunications technology sector.

5)   Careers-Computers/Technology

Dice.com
6465 S. Greenwood Plaza Blvd., Ste. 400
Centennial, CO 80111 USA
Phone: 515-280-1144
Fax: 515-280-1452
Toll Free: 888-321-3423
E-mail Address: techsupport@dice.com
Web Address: www.dice.com
Dice.com provides free employment services for IT jobs. The site includes advanced job searches by geographic location and category, availability announcements and resume postings, as well as employer profiles, a recruiter's page and career links. It is maintained by Dice Holdings, Inc., a publicly traded company.

Institute for Electrical and Electronics Engineers (IEEE) Job Site
445 Hoes Ln.
Piscataway, NJ 08855-1331 USA
Phone: 732-981-0060
Toll Free: 800-678-4333
E-mail Address: candidatejobsite@ieee.org
Web Address: careers.ieee.org
The Institute for Electrical and Electronics Engineers (IEEE) Job Site provides a host of employment services for technical professionals, employers and recruiters. The site offers job listings by geographic area, a resume bank and links to employment services.

Pencom Systems, Inc.
152 Remsen St.
Brooklyn, NY 11201 USA

Phone: 718-923-1111
Fax: 718-923-6065
E-mail Address: tom@pencom.com
Web Address: www.pencom.com
Pencom Systems, Inc., an open system recruiting company, hosts a career web site geared toward high-technology and scientific professionals, featuring an interactive salary survey, career advisor, job listings and technology resources. Its focus is the financial services industry within the New York City area.

6) Careers-First Time Jobs/New Grads

CollegeGrad.com, Inc.
950 Tower Ln., Fl. 6
Foster City, CA 94404 USA
E-mail Address: info@quinstreet.com
Web Address: www.collegegrad.com
CollegeGrad.com, Inc. offers in-depth resources for college students and recent grads seeking entry-level jobs.

National Association of Colleges and Employers (NACE)
62 Highland Ave.
Bethlehem, PA 18017-9085 USA
Phone: 610-868-1421
E-mail Address: customerservice@naceweb.org
Web Address: www.naceweb.org
The National Association of Colleges and Employers (NACE) is a premier U.S. organization representing college placement offices and corporate recruiters who focus on hiring new grads.

7) Careers-General Job Listings

CareerBuilder, Inc.
200 N La Salle Dr., Ste. 1100
Chicago, IL 60601 USA
Phone: 773-527-3600
Fax: 773-353-2452
Toll Free: 800-891-8880
Web Address: www.careerbuilder.com
CareerBuilder, Inc. focuses on the needs of companies and also provides a database of job openings. The site has over 1 million jobs posted by 300,000 employers, and receives an average 23 million unique visitors monthly. The company also operates online career centers for 140 newspapers and 9,000 online partners. Resumes are sent directly to the company, and applicants can set up a special e-mail account for job-seeking purposes. CareerBuilder

is primarily a joint venture between three newspaper giants: The McClatchy Company, Gannett Co., Inc. and Tribune Company.

CareerOneStop
Toll Free: 877-872-5627
E-mail Address: info@careeronestop.org
Web Address: www.careeronestop.org
CareerOneStop is operated by the employment commissions of various state agencies. It contains job listings in both the private and government sectors, as well as a wide variety of useful career resources and workforce information. CareerOneStop is sponsored by the U.S. Department of Labor.

LaborMarketInfo (LMI)
Employment Development Dept.
P.O. Box 826880, MIC 57
Sacramento, CA 94280-0001 USA
Phone: 916-262-2162
Fax: 916-262-2352
Web Address: www.labormarketinfo.edd.ca.gov
LaborMarketInfo (LMI) provides job seekers and employers a wide range of resources, namely the ability to find, access and use labor market information and services. It provides statistics for employment demographics on both a local and regional level, as well as career searching tools for California residents. The web site is sponsored by California's Employment Development Office.

Recruiters Online Network
E-mail Address: rossi.tony@comcast.net
Web Address: www.recruitersonline.com
The Recruiters Online Network provides job postings from thousands of recruiters, Careers Online Magazine, a resume database, as well as other career resources.

USAJOBS
USAJOBS Program Office
1900 E St. NW, Ste. 6500
Washington, DC 20415-0001 USA
Phone: 818-934-6600
Web Address: www.usajobs.gov
USAJOBS, a program of the U.S. Office of Personnel Management, is the official job site for the U.S. Federal Government. It provides a comprehensive list of U.S. government jobs, allowing users to search for employment by location; agency; type of work; or by senior executive positions. It also has special employment sections for individuals with disabilities, veterans and recent college graduates; an information

center, offering resume and interview tips and other information; and allows users to create a profile and post a resume.

8) Careers-Job Reference Tools

Vault.com, Inc.
132 W. 31st St., Fl. 16
New York, NY 10001 USA
Fax: 212-366-6117
Toll Free: 800-535-2074
E-mail Address: customerservice@vault.com
Web Address: www.vault.com
Vault.com, Inc. is a comprehensive career web site for employers and employees, with job postings and valuable information on a wide variety of industries. Its features and content are largely geared toward MBA degree holders.

9) Chinese Government Agencies-Science & Technology

China Ministry of Science and Technology (MOST)
15B Fuxing Rd.
Beijing, 100862 China
Web Address: www.most.gov.cn
The China Ministry of Science and Technology (MOST) is the PRC's official body for science and technology related activities. It drafts laws, policies and regulations regarding science and technology; oversees budgeting and accounting for funds; and supervises research institutes operating in China, among other duties.

10) Computer & Electronics Industry Associations

Asian-Oceanian Computing Industry Organization (ASOCIO)
No. 2, Jalan PJU 8/8A,
c/o PIKOM, Block E1, Empire Damansara E-01-G,
Petaling Jaya, Selangor 47820 Malaysia
Phone: 603-7622-0079
Fax: 603-7622-4879
E-mail Address: secretariat@asocio.org
Web Address: www.asocio.org
The Asian-Oceanian Computing Industry Organization's (ASOCIO) objective is to promote the development of the computing industry in the region.

Association for Information Systems (AIS)
35 Broad St., Ste. 917
Atlanta, GA 30303 USA
Phone: 404-413-7445
Fax: 404-413-7443
E-mail Address: membership@aisnet.org
Web Address: www.aisnet.org
The Association for Information Systems (AIS) is an organization for information system researchers and educators working in colleges and universities worldwide. Its web site offers substantial resources regarding computer systems research and new developments.

Association of Information Technology Professionals (AITP)
3500 Lacey Rd., Ste. 100
Downers Grove, IL 60515 USA
Phone: 630-678-8300
Fax: 630-678-8384
Toll Free: 866-835-8020
E-mail Address: aitp_hq@aitp.org
Web Address: www.aitp.org
The Association of Information Technology Professionals (AITP) is a trade organization that provides training and education through partnerships within the information technology industry.

Association of the Computer and Multimedia Industry of Malaysia (PIKOM)
E1, Empire Damansara, E-01-G
No.2, Jalan PJU 8/8A, Damansara Perdana
Petaling Jaya, Selangor Darul Ehsan 47820 Malaysia
Phone: 603-7622-0079
Fax: 603-7622-4879
E-mail Address: info@pikom.org.my
Web Address: www.pikom.org.my
The Association of the Computer and Multimedia Industry of Malaysia, or, in Malay, Persatuan Industri Komputer dan Multimedia Malaysia (PIKOM), is the national association representing more than 1,000 companies active in the information and communications technology (ICT) industry in Malaysia.

Canadian Advanced Technology Alliances (CATAAlliance)
207 Bank St., Ste. 416
Ottawa, ON K2P 2N2 Canada
Phone: 613-236-6550
E-mail Address: info@cata.ca
Web Address: www.cata.ca

The Canadian Advanced Technology Alliances (CATAAlliance) is one of Canada's leading trade organizations for the research, development and technology sectors.

China Electronic Components Association (CECA)

23 Shijingshan Rd.
ZhongChu Building
Beijing, 100049 China
Phone: 86-10-6887-1587
E-mail Address: icceca@ic-ceca.org.cn
Web Address: www.ic-ceca.org.cn
The China Electronic Components Association (CECA) acts as the representative of the Chinese electronics components industry. Its web site provides consultation services and research reports on components for a wide variety of markets.

China Electronics Chamber of Commerce (CECC)

No. 15 Bldg., Cuiwei Zhongli
Haidian District
Beijing, 100036 China
Phone: 86-10-6825-6762
Fax: 86-10-6825-6764
E-mail Address: ceccinfo@126.com
Web Address: www.cecc.org.cn
China Electronics Chamber of Commerce (CECC), which is led by the Ministry of Information Industry, is the national professional organization for telecommunications and mobile electronics. The group circulates industry information and mediates between its members and the government.

Communications and Information Network Association of Japan (CIAJ)

2-2-12 Hamamatsucho, Minato-ku
Fl. 3, JEI Hamamatsucho Bldg.
Tokyo, 105-0013 Japan
Phone: 81-3-5403-9363
Fax: 81-3-5463-9360
E-mail Address: webmaster@ciaj.or.jp
Web Address: www.ciaj.or.jp/en/
Communications and Information Network Association of Japan (CIAJ) works to help the development of the communication and information network industry in Japan through the promotion of info-communication technologies.

Computer & Communications Industry Association (CCIA)

25 Massachusetts Ave., Ste. 300C
Washington, DC 20001 USA
Phone: 202-783-0070
Fax: 202-783-0534
Web Address: www.ccianet.org
The Computer & Communications Industry Association (CCIA) is a non-profit membership organization for companies and senior executives representing the computer, Internet, information technology (IT) and telecommunications industries.

Computer Technology Industry Association (CompTIA)

3500 Lacey Rd., Ste. 100
Downers Grove, IL 60515 USA
Phone: 630-678-8300
Fax: 630-678-8384
Toll Free: 866-835-8020
Web Address: www.comptia.org
The Computer Technology Industry Association (CompTIA) is the leading association representing the international technology community. Its goal is to provide a unified voice, global advocacy and leadership, and to advance industry growth through standards, professional competence, education and business solutions.

Electronics Technicians Association international (ETA International)

5 Depot St.
Greencastle, IN 46135 USA
Phone: 765-653-8262
Fax: 765-653-4287
Toll Free: 800-288-3824
E-mail Address: eta@eta-i.org
Web Address: www.eta-i.org
The Electronics Technicians Association International (ETA International) is a nonprofit professional association for electronics technicians worldwide. The organization provides recognized professional credentials for electronics technicians.

Federation of Malaysia Manufacturers (FMM)

Wisma FMM, No. 3 Persiaran Dagang, PJU 9
Bandar Sri Damansara
Kuala Lumpur, 52200 Malaysia
Phone: 603-6286-7200
Fax: 603-6274-1266
E-mail Address: webmaster@fmm.org.my
Web Address: www.fmm.org.my
The Federation of Malaysian Manufacturers is an economic organization for the electrical and electronics industry in Malaysia.

Federation of Thai Electrical, Electronics and Allied Industries Club (FTI)
2 Nang Linchi Rd., Fl. 8
Bangkok, 10120 Thailand
Phone: 66-02-345-1000
E-mail Address: information@ft.or.th
Web Address: www.fti.or.th
The Federation of Thai Electrical, Electronics and Allied Industries Club (FTI) represents manufacturers and related firms in these industries within Thailand.

German Association for Information Technology, Telecom and New Media (BITKOM)
Bundersverband Informationswirtschaft
Telekommunikation und neue Medien
Albrechtstr. 10A
Berlin-Mitte, 10117 Germany
Phone: 49-30-27576-0
Fax: 49-30-27576-400
E-mail Address: bitkom@bitkom.org
Web Address: www.bitkom.org
German Association for Information Technology, Telecom and New Media (BITKOM) represents information technology and telecommunications specialists and companies.

German Electrical and Electronic Manufacturers' Association (ZVEI)
Zentralverband Elektrotechnik- und
Elektronikindustrie e.V.
Lyoner St. 9
Frankfurt am Main, 60528 Germany
Phone: 49-69-6302-0
Fax: 49-69-6302-317
E-mail Address: zvei@zvei.org
Web Address: www.zvei.org
The German Electrical and Electronic Manufacturers' Association (ZVEI) represents its members' interests at the national and international level.

Indian Electrical & Electronics Manufacturers Association (IEEMA)
501 Kakad Chambers
132 Dr. Annie Besant Rd., Worli
Mumbai, 400018 India
Phone: 91-22-2493-0532
Fax: 91-22-2493-2705
E-mail Address: mumbai@ieema.org
Web Address: www.ieema.org
The Indian Electrical & Electronics Manufacturers Association (IEEMA) represents all sectors of the electrical and allied products businesses of the Indian electrical industry.

Information Technology Association of Canada (ITAC)
5090 Explorer Dr., Ste. 801
Mississauga, ON L4W 4T9 Canada
Phone: 905-602-8345
Fax: 905-602-8346
E-mail Address: dwhite@itac.ca
Web Address: www.itac.ca
The Information Technology Association of Canada (ITAC) represents the IT, software, computer and telecommunications industries in Canada.

Information Technology Management Association (ITMA)
Robinson Rd.
P.O. Box 3297
Singapore, 905297 Singapore
Phone: 65-8171-4456
Fax: 65-6410-8008
E-mail Address: secretariat@itma.org.sg
Web Address: www.itma.org.sg
Information Technology Management Association (ITMA) represents professionals working in the field of IT management in Singapore.

Institute for Interconnecting and Packaging Electronic Circuits (IPC)
3000 Lakeside Dr., Ste. 105 N
Bannockburn, IL 60015 USA
Phone: 847-615-7100
Fax: 847-615-7105
E-mail Address: answers@ipc.org
Web Address: www.ipc.org
The Institute for Interconnecting and Packaging Electronic Circuits (IPC) is a trade association for companies in the global printed circuit board and electronics manufacturing services industries.

International Microelectronics Assembly and Packaging Society (IMAPS)
P.O. Box 110127
Research Triangle Park, NC 27709-5127 USA
Phone: 919-293-5000
Fax: 919-287-2339
E-mail Address: info@imaps.org
Web Address: www.imaps.org
The International Microelectronics Assembly and Packaging Society (IMAPS) is dedicated to the advancement and growth of the use of microelectronics and electronic packaging through professional education, workshops and conferences.

Korea Association of Information and Telecommunications (KAIT)
NO. 1678-2, 2nd Fl. Dong-Ah Villat 2 Town
Seocho-dong, Seocho-gu
Seoul, 137-070 Korea
Phone: 82-2-580-0582
E-mail Address: webmaster@kait.or.kr
Web Address: www.kait.or.kr/eng
The Korea Association of Information and Telecommunications (KAIT) was created to develop and promote the InfoTech, computer, consumer electronics, wireless, software and telecommunications sectors in Korea.

Korea Semiconductor Industry Association (KSIA)
182, Pangyoyeok-ro, Bundang-gu, Seongnam-si
Fl. 9-12, KSIA Bldg.
Gyeonggi-do, Korea
Phone: 82-2-576-3472
Fax: 82-2-570-5269
E-mail Address: admin@ksia.or.kr
Web Address: www.ksia.or.kr
The Korean Semiconductor Industry Association (KSIA) represents the interests of Korean semiconductor manufacturers.

National Electrical Manufacturers Association (NEMA)
1300 N. 17th St., Ste. 900
Arlington, VA 22209 USA
Phone: 703-841-3200
E-mail Address: press@nema.org
Web Address: www.nema.org
The National Electrical Manufacturers Association (NEMA) develops standards for the electrical manufacturing industry and promotes safety in the production and use of electrical products.

Network Professional Association (NPA)
3517 Camino Del Rio S., Ste. 215
San Diego, CA 92108-4089 USA
Fax: 888-672-6720
Toll Free: 888-672-6720
Web Address: www.npanet.org
The Network Professionals Association (NPA) is a self-regulating, nonprofit association of network computing professionals that sets standards of technical expertise and professionalism.

Semiconductor Equipment and Materials International (SEMI)
673 S. Milpitas Blvd.
Milpitas, CA 95035 USA
Phone: 408-943-6900
Fax: 408-428-9600
E-mail Address: semihq@semi.org
Web Address: www.semi.org
Semiconductor Equipment and Materials International (SEMI) is a trade association serving the global semiconductor equipment, materials and flat-panel display industries.

Semiconductor Industry Association (SIA)
1101 K St. NW, Ste. 450
Washington, DC 20005 USA
Phone: 202-446-1700
Fax: 202-216-9745
Toll Free: 866-756-0715
Web Address: www.semiconductors.org
The Semiconductor Industry Association (SIA) is a trade association representing the semiconductor industry in the U.S. Through its coalition of more than 60 companies, SIA members represent roughly 80% of semiconductor production in the U.S. The coalition aims to advance the competitiveness of the chip industry and shape public policy on issues particular to the industry.

Singapore Computer Society
53/53A Neil Rd.
Singapore, 088891 Singapore
Phone: 65-6226-2567
Fax: 65-6226-2569
E-mail Address: scs.secretariat@scs.org.sg
Web Address: www.scs.org.sg
The Singapore Computer Society is a membership society for infocomm professionals in Singapore.

Surface Mount Technology Association (SMTA)
6600 City West Pkwy., Ste. 300
Eden Prairie, MN 55424 USA
Phone: 952-920-7682
Fax: 952-926-1819
E-mail Address: smta@smta.org
Web Address: www.smta.org
The Surface Mount Technology Association (SMTA) is an international network of professionals whose careers encompass electronic assembly technologies, microsystems, emerging technologies and associated business operations.

Taiwan Electrical and Electronic Manufacturers' Association (TEEMA)
Min Chuan E. Rd., Fl. 6, No. 109, Sec. 6
Taipei, 11490 Taiwan

Phone: 886-2-8792-6666
Fax: 886-2-8792-6088
E-mail Address: teema@teema.org.tw
Web Address: www.teema.org.tw
The Taiwan Electrical and Electronic Manufacturers'
Association (TEEMA) works as an intermediary
between its members and the government to help the
industry to succeed.

Telecom Equipment Manufacturers Association of India (TEMA)
PHD House, 4th Fl.
Khel Gaon Marg, Hauz Khas
New Delhi, 110 0016 India
Phone: 91-11-49545454
E-mail Address: tema@tematelecom.in
Web Address: www.tematelecom.in
The Telecom Equipment Manufacturers Association
of India (TEMA) is national organization for
companies in the telecommunications industry. The
group disseminates and exchanges information with
the Indian government, foreign agencies, embassies,
trade missions, Indian missions abroad and leading
international trade associations.

World Information Technology and Services Alliance (WITSA)
8300 Boone Blvd., Ste. 450
Vienna, VA 22182 USA
Phone: 571-265-5964
Fax: 703-893-1269
E-mail Address: admin@witsa.org
Web Address: www.witsa.org
The World Information Technology and Services
Alliance (WITSA) is a consortium of over 70
information technology (IT) industry associations
from economies around the world. WITSA members
represent over 90% of the world IT market. Founded
in 1978 and originally known as the World
Computing Services Industry Association, WITSA is
an advocate in international public policy issues
affecting the creation of a robust global information
infrastructure.

11) Computer & Electronics Industry Resources

Cisco Cloud Index
170 W. Tasman Dr.
San Jose, CA 95134 USA
Toll Free: 800-553-6387
Web Address: www.cisco.com/go/cloudindex

The Cisco Cloud Index covers three areas focused on
data center and cloud traffic trends and next-
generation service or application adoption. They
include: Data center and cloud traffic forecast;
Workload transition, which provides projections for
workloads moving from traditional IT to cloud-based
architectures; and Cloud readiness, which provides
regional statistics on broadband adoption as a
precursor for cloud services.

Information Technology and Innovation Foundation (ITIF)
700 K St. NW, Ste. 600
Washington, DC 20001 USA
Phone: 202-449-1351
E-mail Address: mail@itif.org
Web Address: www.itif.org
Information Technology and Innovation Foundation
(ITIF) is a non-partisan research and educational
institute (a think tank) with a mission to formulate
and promote public policies to advance technological
innovation and productivity internationally, in
Washington, and in the States. Recognizing the vital
role of technology in ensuring American prosperity,
ITIF focuses on innovation, productivity, and digital
economy issues.

Ministry of Electronics and Information Technology (India)
Electronics Niketan
6 CGO Complex, Lodhi Rd.
New Delhi, 110003 India
Phone: 91-11-2430-1851
E-mail Address: webmaster@deity.gov.in
Web Address: www.meity.gov.in
Ministry of Communications & Information
Technology (MIT) of the Government of India, is
charged with promoting the information technology
and communications industries.

12) Corporate Information Resources

Business Journals (The)
120 W. Morehead St., Ste. 400
Charlotte, NC 28202 USA
Toll Free: 866-853-3661
E-mail Address: gmurchison@bizjournals.com
Web Address: www.bizjournals.com
Bizjournals.com is the online media division of
American City Business Journals, the publisher of
dozens of leading city business journals nationwide.
It provides access to research into the latest news
regarding companies both small and large. The

organization maintains 42 websites and 64 print publications and sponsors over 700 annual industry events.

Business Wire
101 California St., Fl. 20
San Francisco, CA 94111 USA
Phone: 415-986-4422
Fax: 415-788-5335
Toll Free: 800-227-0845
E-mail Address: info@businesswire.com
Web Address: www.businesswire.com
Business Wire offers news releases, industry- and company-specific news, top headlines, conference calls, IPOs on the Internet, media services and access to tradeshownews.com and BW Connect On-line through its informative and continuously updated web site.

Edgar Online, Inc.
35 W. Wacker Dr.
Chicago, IL 60601 USA
Phone: 301-287-0300
Fax: 301-287-0390
Toll Free: 800-823-5304
Web Address: www.edgar-online.com
Edgar Online, Inc. is a gateway and search tool for viewing corporate documents, such as annual reports on Form 10-K, filed with the U.S. Securities and Exchange Commission.

PR Newswire Association LLC
200 Vesey St., Fl. 19
New York, NY 10281 USA
Fax: 800-793-9313
Toll Free: 800-776-8090
E-mail Address: mediainquiries@cision.com
Web Address: www.prnewswire.com
PR Newswire Association LLC provides comprehensive communications services for public relations and investor relations professionals, ranging from information distribution and market intelligence to the creation of online multimedia content and investor relations web sites. Users can also view recent corporate press releases from companies across the globe. The Association is owned by United Business Media plc.

Silicon Investor
E-mail Address: si.admin@siliconinvestor.com
Web Address: www.siliconinvestor.com
Silicon Investor is focused on providing information about technology companies. Its web site serves as a financial discussion forum and offers quotes, profiles and charts.

---

13) Economic Data & Research

Centre for European Economic Research (The, ZEW)
L 7, 1
Mannheim, 68161 Germany
Phone: 49-621-1235-01
Fax: 49-621-1235-224
E-mail Address: empfang@zew.de
Web Address: www.zew.de/en
Zentrum fur Europaische Wirtschaftsforschung, The Centre for European Economic Research (ZEW), distinguishes itself in the analysis of internationally comparative data in a European context and in the creation of databases that serve as a basis for scientific research. The institute maintains a special library relevant to economic research and provides external parties with selected data for the purpose of scientific research. ZEW also offers public events and seminars concentrating on banking, business and other economic-political topics.

Economic and Social Research Council (ESRC)
Polaris House
North Star Ave.
Swindon, SN2 1UJ UK
Phone: 44-01793 413000
E-mail Address: esrcenquiries@esrc.ac.uk
Web Address: www.esrc.ac.uk
The Economic and Social Research Council (ESRC) funds research and training in social and economic issues. It is an independent organization, established by Royal Charter. Current research areas include the global economy; social diversity; environment and energy; human behavior; and health and well-being.

Eurostat
5 Rue Alphonse Weicker
Joseph Bech Bldg.
Luxembourg, L-2721 Luxembourg
Phone: 352-4301-1
E-mail Address: eurostat-pressoffice@ec.europa.eu
Web Address: ec.europa.eu/eurostat
Eurostat is the European Union's service that publishes a wide variety of comprehensive statistics on European industries, populations, trade, agriculture, technology, environment and other matters.

Federal Statistical Office of Germany
Gustav-Stresemann-Ring 11
Wiesbaden, D-65189 Germany
Phone: 49-611-75-2405
Fax: 49-611-72-4000
Web Address: www.destatis.de
Federal Statistical Office of Germany publishes a
wide variety of nation and regional economic data of
interest to anyone who is studying Germany, one of
the world's leading economies. Data available
includes population, consumer prices, labor markets,
health care, industries and output.

India Brand Equity Foundation (IBEF)
Fl. 20, Jawahar Vyapar Bhawan
Tolstoy Marg
New Delhi, 110001 India
Phone: 91-11-43845500
Fax: 91-11-23701235
E-mail Address: info.brandindia@ibef.org
Web Address: www.ibef.org
India Brand Equity Foundation (IBEF) is a public-
private partnership between the Ministry of
Commerce and Industry, the Government of India
and the Confederation of Indian Industry. The
foundation's primary objective is to build positive
economic perceptions of India globally. It aims to
effectively present the India business perspective and
leverage business partnerships in a globalizing
marketplace.

National Bureau of Statistics (China)
57, Yuetan Nanjie, Sanlihe
Xicheng District
Beijing, 100826 China
Fax: 86-10-6878-2000
E-mail Address: info@gj.stats.cn
Web Address: www.stats.gov.cn/english
The National Bureau of Statistics (China) provides
statistics and economic data regarding China's
economy and society.

**Organization for Economic Co-operation and
Development (OECD)**
2 rue Andre Pascal
Cedex 16
Paris, 75775 France
Phone: 33-1-45-24-82-00
Fax: 33-1-45-24-85-00
E-mail Address: webmaster@oecd.org
Web Address: www.oecd.org
The Organization for Economic Co-operation and
Development (OECD) publishes detailed economic,
government, population, social and trade statistics on
a country-by-country basis for over 30 nations
representing the world's largest economies. Sectors
covered range from industry, labor, technology and
patents, to health care, environment and
globalization.

**Statistics Bureau, Director-General for Policy
Planning (Japan)**
19-1 Wakamatsu-cho
Shinjuku-ku
Tokyo, 162-8668 Japan
Phone: 81-3-5273-2020
E-mail Address: toukeisoudan@soumu.go.jp
Web Address: www.stat.go.jp/english
The Statistics Bureau, Director-General for Policy
Planning (Japan) and Statistical Research and
Training Institute, a part of the Japanese Ministry of
Internal Affairs and Communications, plays the
central role of producing and disseminating basic
official statistics and coordinating statistical work
under the Statistics Act and other legislation.

Statistics Canada
150 Tunney's Pasture Driveway
Ottawa, ON K1A 0T6 Canada
Phone: 514-283-8300
Fax: 514-283-9350
Toll Free: 800-263-1136
E-mail Address: STATCAN.infostats-
infostats.STATCAN@canada.ca
Web Address: www.statcan.gc.ca
Statistics Canada provides a complete portal to
Canadian economic data and statistics. Its conducts
Canada's official census every five years, as well as
hundreds of surveys covering numerous aspects of
Canadian life.

14) **Engineering Industry Resources**

Cornell Engineering Library (The)
Engineering Library Cornell University
Carpenter Hall, Fl. 1
Ithaca, NY 14853 USA
Phone: 607-254-6261
E-mail Address: engrref@cornell.edu
Web Address: engineering.library.cornell.edu
Cornell University's Engineering Library web site has
a number of resources concerning engineering
research, as well as links to other engineering
industry information sources.

15) Engineering, Research & Scientific Associations

American Association for the Advancement of Science (AAAS)
1200 New York Ave. NW
Washington, DC 20005 USA
Phone: 202-326-6400
Web Address: www.aaas.org
The American Association for the Advancement of Science (AAAS) is the world's largest scientific society and the publisher of Science magazine. It is an international nonprofit organization dedicated to advancing science around the globe.

American National Standards Institute (ANSI)
1899 L St. NW, Fl. 11
Washington, DC 20036 USA
Phone: 202-293-8020
Fax: 202-293-9287
E-mail Address: info@ansi.org
Web Address: www.ansi.org
The American National Standards Institute (ANSI) is a private, nonprofit organization that administers and coordinates the U.S. voluntary standardization and conformity assessment system. Its mission is to enhance both the global competitiveness of U.S. business and the quality of life by promoting and facilitating voluntary consensus standards and conformity assessment systems and safeguarding their integrity.

American Society for Engineering Education (ASEE)
1818 North St. NW, Ste. 600
Washington, DC 20036-2479 USA
Phone: 202-331-3500
Fax: 202-265-8504
E-mail Address: board@asee.org
Web Address: www.asee.org
The American Society for Engineering Education (ASEE) is nonprofit organization dedicated to promoting and improving engineering and technology education.

Association for Electrical, Electronic & Information Technologies (VDE)
Stresemannallee 15
Frankfurt, 60596 Germany
Phone: 49-69-6308-0
Fax: 49-69-6308-9865
E-mail Address: service@vde.com
Web Address: www.vde.com

The Association for Electrical, Electronic & Information Technologies (VDE) is a German organization with roughly 36,000 members, representing one of the largest technical associations in Europe.

Association of Federal Communications Consulting Engineers (AFCCE)
P.O. Box 19333
Washington, DC 20036 USA
Web Address: www.afcce.org
The Association of Federal Communications Consulting Engineers (AFCCE) is a professional organization of individuals who regularly assist clients on technical issues before the Federal Communications Commission (FCC).

Audio Engineering Society, Inc. (AES)
551 Fifth Ave., Ste. 1225
New York, NY 10176 USA
Phone: 212-661-8528
Web Address: www.aes.org
The Audio Engineering Society (AES) provides information on educational and career opportunities in audio technology and engineering.

Center for Innovative Technology (CIT)
2214 Rock Hill Rd., Ste. 600
Herndon, VA 20170-4228 USA
Phone: 703-689-3000
Fax: 703-689-3041
E-mail Address: info@cit.org
Web Address: www.cit.org
The Center for Innovative Technology is a nonprofit organization designed to enhance the research and development capabilities by creating partnerships between innovative technology start-up companies and advanced technology consumers.

China Association for Science and Technology (CAST)
3 Fuxing Rd.
Beijing, 100863 China
Phone: 8610-6857-1898
Fax: 8610-6857-1897
E-mail Address: cast-liasion@cast.org.cn
Web Address: english.cast.org.cn
The China Association for Science and Technology (CAST) is the largest national non-governmental organization of scientific and technological workers in China. The association has nearly 207 member organizations in the fields of engineering, science and technology.

Engineer's Club (The) (TEC)
1737 Silverwood Dr.
San Jose, CA 95124 USA
Phone: 408-316-0488
E-mail Address: INFO@engineers.com
Web Address: www.engineers.com
The Engineer's Club (TEC) provides a variety of
resources for engineers and technical professionals.

IEEE Communications Society (ComSoc)
3 Park Ave., Fl. 17
New York, NY 10016 USA
Phone: 212-705-8900
Fax: 212-705-8999
Web Address: www.comsoc.org
The IEEE Communications Society (ComSoc) is
composed of industry professionals with a common
interest in advancing communications technologies.

Industrial Research Institute (IRI)
P.O. Box 13968
Arlington, VA 22219 USA
Phone: 703-647-2580
Fax: 703-647-2581
E-mail Address: information@iriweb.org
Web Address: www.iriweb.org
The Innovation Research Interchange (IRI) is a
nonprofit organization of over 200 leading industrial
companies, representing industries such as aerospace,
automotive, chemical, computers and electronics,
which carry out industrial research efforts in the U.S.
manufacturing sector. IRI helps members improve
research and development capabilities.

**Institute of Electrical and Electronics Engineers
(IEEE)**
3 Park Ave., Fl. 17
New York, NY 10016-5997 USA
Phone: 212-419-7900
Fax: 212-752-4929
Toll Free: 800-678-4333
E-mail Address: society-info@ieee.org
Web Address: www.ieee.org
The Institute of Electrical and Electronics Engineers
(IEEE) is a nonprofit, technical professional
association of more than 430,000 individual members
in approximately 160 countries. The IEEE sets global
technical standards and acts as an authority in
technical areas ranging from computer engineering,
biomedical technology and telecommunications to
electric power, aerospace and consumer electronics.

**Institution of Engineering and Technology (The)
(IET)**
Michael Faraday House
Six Hills Way
Stevenage, Herts SG1 2AY UK
Phone: 44-1438-313-311
Fax: 44-1438-765-526
E-mail Address: postmaster@theiet.org
Web Address: www.theiet.org
The Institution of Engineering and Technology (IET)
is an innovative international organization for
electronics, electrical, manufacturing and IT
professionals.

International Electrotechnical Commission (IEC)
3, rue de Varembe
P.O. Box 131
Geneva 20, CH-1211 Switzerland
Phone: 41-22-919-02-11
Fax: 41-22-919-03-00
E-mail Address: info@iec.ch
Web Address: www.iec.ch
The International Electrotechnical Commission
(IEC), based in Switzerland, promotes international
cooperation on all questions of standardization and
related matters in electrical and electronic
engineering.

International Standards Organization (ISO)
Chemin de Blandonnet 8
1214 Vernier
Geneva, CP 401 Switzerland
Phone: 41-22-749-01-11
Fax: 41-22-733-34-30
E-mail Address: central@iso.org
Web Address: www.iso.org
The International Standards Organization (ISO) is a
global consortium of national standards institutes
from 162 countries. The established International
Standards are designed to make products and services
more efficient, safe and clean.

Optical Society of America (OSA)
2010 Massachusetts Ave. NW
Washington, DC 20036-1023 USA
Phone: 202-223-8130
Fax: 202-223-1096
E-mail Address: info@osa.org
Web Address: www.osa.org
The Optical Society of America (OSA) is an
interdisciplinary society offering synergy between all
components of the optics industry, from basic
research to commercial applications such as fiber-

optic networks. It has a membership group of over 16,000 individuals from over 100 countries. Members include scientists, engineers, educators, technicians and business leaders.

Research in Germany, German Academic Exchange Service (DAAD)
Kennedyallee 50
Bonn, 53175 Germany
Phone: 49-228-882-743
Web Address: www.research-in-germany.de
The Research in Germany portal, German Academic Exchange Service (DAAD), is an information platform and contact point for those looking to find out more about Germany's research landscape and its latest research achievements. The portal is an initiative of the Federal Ministry of Education and Research.

Royal Society (The)
6-9 Carlton House Ter.
London, SW1Y 5AG UK
Phone: 44-20-7451-2500
E-mail Address: science.policy@royalsociety.org
Web Address: royalsociety.org
The Royal Society, originally founded in 1660, is the UK's leading scientific organization and the oldest scientific community in continuous existence. It operates as a national academy of science, supporting scientists, engineers, technologists and researchers. Its web site contains a wealth of data about the research and development initiatives of its fellows and foreign members.

Society of Cable Telecommunications Engineers (SCTE)
140 Philips Rd.
Exton, PA 19341-1318 USA
Phone: 610-363-6888
Fax: 610-884-7237
Toll Free: 800-542-5040
E-mail Address: info@scte.org
Web Address: www.scte.org
The Society of Cable Telecommunications Engineers (SCTE) is a nonprofit professional association dedicated to advancing the careers and serving the industry of telecommunications professionals by providing technical training, certification and information resources.

World Federation of Engineering Organizations
Maison de l'UNESCO
1, rue Miollis

Paris, 75015 France
Phone: 33-1-45-68-48-47
Fax: 33-1-45-68-48-65
E-mail Address: secretariat@wfeo.net
Web Address: www.wfeo.org
World Federation of Engineering Organizations (WFEO) is an international non-governmental organization that represents major engineering professional societies in over 90 nations. It has several standing committees including engineering and the environment, technology, communications, capacity building, education, energy and women in engineering.

16) Industry Research/Market Research

Forrester Research
60 Acorn Park Dr.
Cambridge, MA 02140 USA
Phone: 617-613-5730
Toll Free: 866-367-7378
E-mail Address: press@forrester.com
Web Address: www.forrester.com
Forrester Research is a publicly traded company that identifies and analyzes emerging trends in technology and their impact on business. Among the firm's specialties are the financial services, retail, health care, entertainment, automotive and information technology industries.

Gartner, Inc.
56 Top Gallant Rd.
Stamford, CT 06902 USA
Phone: 203-964-0096
E-mail Address: info@gartner.com
Web Address: www.gartner.com
Gartner, Inc. is a publicly traded IT company that provides competitive intelligence and strategic consulting and advisory services to numerous clients worldwide.

MarketResearch.com
6116 Executive Blvd., Ste. 550
Rockville, MD 20852 USA
Phone: 240-747-3093
Fax: 240-747-3004
Toll Free: 800-298-5699
E-mail Address:
customerservice@marketresearch.com
Web Address: www.marketresearch.com
MarketResearch.com is a leading broker for professional market research and industry analysis. Users are able to search the company's database of

research publications including data on global industries, companies, products and trends.

Plunkett Research, Ltd.
P.O. Drawer 541737
Houston, TX 77254-1737 USA
Phone: 713-932-0000
Fax: 713-932-7080
E-mail Address:
customersupport@plunkettresearch.com
Web Address: www.plunkettresearch.com
Plunkett Research, Ltd. is a leading provider of market research, industry trends analysis and business statistics. Since 1985, it has served clients worldwide, including corporations, universities, libraries, consultants and government agencies. At the firm's web site, visitors can view product information and pricing and access a large amount of basic market information on industries such as financial services, InfoTech, ecommerce, health care and biotech.

Portio Research Limited
16 Moss Mead
Chippenham, Wilts SN14 OTN UK
Phone: 44-1249-656-964
Fax: 44-1249-656-967
E-mail Address: info@portioresearch.com
Web Address: www.portioresearch.com
Portio Research Limited is a research firm engaged in the study of the mobile and wireless sector. It provides data-centric reports and database products.

Pyramid Research
179 South St., Ste. 200
Boston, MA 02111 USA
Phone: 617-747-4100
Web Address: www.pyramidresearch.com
Pyramid Research provides international market analysis and advisory services to the global communications, media and technology industries. It advises vendors, equipment manufacturers, service providers and the financial community.

17) Internet Industry Associations

Asia & Pacific Internet Association (APIA)
P.O. Box 1908
Milton, 4064 Australia
E-mail Address: apiasec@apia.org
Web Address: www.apia.org
Asia & Pacific Internet Association (APIA) is a nonprofit trade association whose aim is to promote

the business interests of the Internet-related service industry in the Asia Pacific region. The site contains a list of organizations, standards, regional Internet registries and related Asia Pacific organizations.

Cooperative Association for Internet Data Analysis (CAIDA)
9500 Gilman Dr.
Mail Stop 0505
La Jolla, CA 92093-0505 USA
Phone: 858-534-5000
E-mail Address: info@caida.org
Web Address: www.caida.org
The Cooperative Association for Internet Data Analysis (CAIDA), representing organizations from the government, commercial and research sectors, works to promote an atmosphere of greater cohesion in the engineering and maintenance of the Internet. CAIDA is located at the San Diego Supercomputer Center (SDSC) on the campus of the University of California, San Diego (UCSD).

Federation of Internet Service Providers of the Americas (FISPA)
c/o Jim Hollis
8200 Raintree Ln., Ste. 100
Charlotte, NC 28277 USA
Phone: 704-844-2540
Fax: 704-844-2728
Toll Free: 813-574-2556
E-mail Address: executive.director@fipsa.org
Web Address: www.fispa.org
The Federation of Internet Service Providers of the Americas (FISPA) encourages discussion, education and collective buying power for organizations involved in providing Internet access, web hosting, web design and other Internet products and services.

Internet and Mobile Association of India (IAMAI)
406 Ready Money Terr.
167 Dr. Annie Besant Rd.
Mumbai, 400 018 India
E-mail Address: gaurav@iamai.in
Web Address: www.iamai.in
The Internet & Mobile Association of India (IAMAI) is an industry organization representing the interests of India's online and mobile value-added services industry.

Internet Law & Policy Forum (ILPF)
2440 Western Ave., Ste. 709
Seattle, WA 98121 USA
Phone: 206-727-0700

Fax: 206-374-2263
E-mail Address: admin@ilpf.org
Web Address: www.ilpf.org
The Internet Law & Policy Forum (ILPF) is
dedicated to the global development of the Internet
through legal and public policy initiatives. It is an
international nonprofit organization whose member
companies develop and deploy the Internet in every
aspect of business today.

Internet Society (ISOC)
11710 Plaza America Dr., Ste. 400
Reston, VA 20190 USA
Phone: 703-439-2120
Fax: 703-326-9881
E-mail Address: isoc@isoc.org
Web Address: www.isoc.org
The Internet Society (ISOC) is a nonprofit
organization that provides leadership in public policy
issues that influence the future of the Internet. The
organization is the home of groups that maintain
infrastructure standards for the Internet, such as the
Internet Engineering Task Force (IETF) and the
Internet Architecture Board (IAB).

Internet Systems Consortium, Inc. (ISC)
P.O. Box 360
Newmarket, NH 03857 USA
Phone: 650-423-1300
Fax: 650-423-1355
E-mail Address: info@isc.org
Web Address: www.isc.org
The Internet Systems Consortium, Inc. (ISC) is a
nonprofit organization with extensive expertise in the
development, management, maintenance and
implementation of Internet technologies.

US Internet Service Provider Association (US ISPA)
700 12th St. NW, Ste. 700E
Washington, DC 20005 USA
Phone: 202-904-2351
E-mail Address: kdean@usispa.org
Web Address: www.usispa.org
US Internet Service Provider Association (US ISPA)
is a leading provider of technical, business, policy
and regulatory support to ISPs (Internet service
providers).

World Wide Web Consortium (W3C)
32 Vassar St., Bldg. 32-G515
Cambridge, MA 02139 USA
Phone: 617-253-2613

Fax: 617-258-5999
E-mail Address: susan@w3.org
Web Address: www.w3.org
The World Wide Web Consortium (W3C) develops
technologies and standards to enhance the
performance and utility of the World Wide Web. The
W3C is hosted by three different organizations: the
European Research Consortium for Informatics and
Mathematics (ERICM) handles inquiries about the
W3C in the EMEA region; Keio University handles
W3C's Japanese and Korean correspondence; and the
Computer Science & Artificial Intelligence Lab
(CSAIL) at MIT handles all other countries, include
Australia and the U.S.

18) Internet Industry Resources

American Registry for Internet Numbers (ARIN)
P.O. Box 232290
Centreville, VA 20120 USA
Phone: 703-227-9840
Fax: 703-263-0417
E-mail Address: info@arin.net
Web Address: www.arin.net
The American Registry for Internet Numbers (ARIN)
is a nonprofit organization that administers and
registers Internet protocol (IP) numbers. The
organization also develops policies and offers
educational outreach services.

Berkman Center for Internet & Society
23 Everett St., Fl. 2
Cambridge, MA 02138 USA
Phone: 617-495-7547
Fax: 617-495-7641
E-mail Address: cyber@law.harvard.edu
Web Address: cyber.law.harvard.edu
The Berkman Center for Internet & Society, housed
at Harvard University's law school, focuses on the
exploration of the development and inner-workings
of laws pertaining to the Internet. The center offers
Internet courses, conferences, advising and advocacy.

Congressional Internet Caucus Advisory Committee (CICA)
1440 G St. NW
Washington, DC 20005 USA
Phone: 202-638-4370
E-mail Address: tlordan@netcaucus.org
Web Address: www.netcaucus.org
The Congressional Internet Caucus Advisory
Committee (ICAC) works to educate the public, as

well as a bipartisan group from the U.S. House and Senate about Internet-related policy issues.

Internet Assigned Numbers Authority (IANA)
12025 Waterfront Dr., Ste. 300
Los Angeles, CA 90094 USA
Phone: 424-254-5300
Fax: 424-254-5033
E-mail Address: iana@iana.org
Web Address: www.iana.org
The Internet Assigned Numbers Authority (IANA) serves as the central coordinator for the assignment of parameter values for Internet protocols. IANA is operated by the Internet Corporation for Assigned Names and Numbers (ICANN).

19) Internet Usage Statistics

comScore, Inc.
11950 Democracy Dr., Ste. 600
Reston, VA 20190 USA
Phone: 703-438-2000
Fax: 703-438-2051
Toll Free: 866-276-6972
Web Address: www.comscore.com
comScore, Inc. provides excellent data on consumer behavior and audiences, particularly in terms of how consumers access and use online sites and digital data and entertainment. They are global leaders in Internet usage data.

eMarketer
11 Times Square
New York, NY 10036 USA
Toll Free: 800-405-0844
Web Address: www.emarketer.com
eMarketer is a comprehensive, objective and easy-to-use resource for any person or business interested in online marketing and emerging media. The firm offers news articles, market projections and analytical commentaries.

Nielsen
85 Broad St.
New York, NY 10004 USA
Toll Free: 800-864-1224
Web Address: www.nielsen.com
Nielsen offers detailed, real-time Internet, retail and media research and analysis.

Pew Internet & American Life Project
1615 L St. NW, Ste. 800
Washington, DC 20036 USA

Phone: 202-419-4300
Fax: 202-857-8562
E-mail Address: info@pewinternet.org
Web Address: www.pewinternet.org
The Pew Internet & American Life Project, an initiative of the Pew Research Center, produces reports that explore the impact of the Internet on families, communities, work and home, daily life, education, health care and civic and political life.

20) MBA Resources

MBA Depot
Web Address: www.mbadepot.com
MBA Depot is an online community and information portal for MBAs, potential MBA program applicants and business professionals.

21) Outsourcing Industry Resources

CIO Outsourcing Center
492 Old Connecticut Path
P.O. Box 9208
Framingham, MA 01701-9208 USA
Phone: 508-872-0080
E-mail Address: rhein@cio.com
Web Address: www.cio.com/topic/3195/Outsourcing
CIO Outsourcing Center, a feature on CIO.com, provides data for chief information officers about technology outsourcing. CIO.com and the Outsourcing Center are products of CXO Media Inc., which is itself a division of International Data Group.

22) Patent Organizations

European Patent Office
Bob-van-Benthem-Platz 1
Munich, 80469 Germany
Phone: 49 89 2399-0
Toll Free: 08-800-80-20-20-20
E-mail Address: press@epo.org
Web Address: www.epo.org
The European Patent Office (EPO) provides a uniform application procedure for individual inventors and companies seeking patent protection in up to 38 European countries. It is the executive arm of the European Patent Organization and is supervised by the Administrative Council.

23) Payment, Ecommerce and Data Interchange Technology

RosettaNet
7877 Washington Village Dr., Ste. 300
Dayton, OH 45459 USA
Phone: 937-435-3870
E-mail Address: info@gs1us.org
Web Address: www.resources.gs1us.org/rosettanet
RosettaNet, a subsidiary of GS1 US, is a nonprofit organization whose mission is to develop e-business process standards that serve as a frame of reference for global trading networks. The organization's standards provide a common language for companies within the global supply chain.

24) Research & Development, Laboratories

Advanced Technology Laboratory (ARL)
10000 Burnet Rd.
University of Texas at Austin
Austin, TX 78758 USA
Phone: 512-835-3200
Fax: 512-835-3259
Web Address: www.arlut.utexas.edu
Advanced Technology Laboratory (ARL) at the University of Texas at Austin provides research programs dedicated to improving the military capability of the United States in applications of acoustics, electromagnetic and information technology.

Commonwealth Scientific and Industrial Research Organization (CSRIO)
CSIRO Enquiries
Private Bag 10
Clayton South, Victoria 3169 Australia
Phone: 61-3-9545-2176
Toll Free: 1300-363-400
Web Address: www.csiro.au
The Commonwealth Scientific and Industrial Research Organization (CSRIO) is Australia's national science agency and a leading international research agency. CSRIO performs research in Australia over a broad range of areas including agriculture, minerals and energy, manufacturing, communications, construction, health and the environment.

Electronics and Telecommunications Research Institute (ETRI)
218 Gajeongno
Yuseong-gu
Daejeon, 34129 Korea
Phone: 82-42-860-6114
E-mail Address: k21human@etri.re.kr
Web Address: www.etri.re.kr
Established in 1976, the Electronics and Telecommunications Research Institute (ETRI) is a nonprofit government-funded research organization that promotes technological excellence. The research institute has successfully developed information technologies such as TDX-Exchange, High Density Semiconductor Microchips, Mini-Super Computer (TiCOM), and Digital Mobile Telecommunication System (CDMA). ETRI's focus is on information technologies, robotics, telecommunications, digital broadcasting and future technology strategies.

Fraunhofer-Gesellschaft (FhG) (The)
Fraunhofer-Gesellschaft zur Forderung der angewandten Forschung e.V.
Postfach 20 07 33
Munich, 80007 Germany
Phone: 49-89-1205-0
Fax: 49-89-1205-7531
Web Address: www.fraunhofer.de
The Fraunhofer-Gesellschaft (FhG) institute focuses on research in health, security, energy, communication, the environment and mobility. FhG includes over 80 research units in Germany. Over 70% of its projects are derived from industry contracts.

Helmholtz Association
Anna-Louisa-Karsch-Strasse 2
Berlin, 10178 Germany
Phone: 49-30-206329-0
E-mail Address: info@helmholtz.de
Web Address: www.helmholtz.de/en
The Helmholtz Association is a community of 18 scientific-technical and biological-medical research centers. Helmholtz Centers perform top-class research in strategic programs in several core fields: energy, earth and environment, health, key technologies, structure of matter, aeronautics, space and transport.

Institute for Telecommunication Sciences (ITS)
325 Broadway
Boulder, CO 80305-3337 USA
Phone: 303-497-3571

E-mail Address: info@its.bldrdoc.gov
Web Address: www.its.bldrdoc.gov
The Institute for Telecommunication Sciences (ITS) is the research and engineering branch of the National Telecommunications and Information Administration (NTIA), a division of the U.S. Department of Commerce (DOC). Its research activities are focused on advanced telecommunications and information infrastructure development.

National Research Council Canada (NRC)
1200 Montreal Rd., Bldg. M-58
Ottawa, ON K1A 0R6 Canada
Phone: 613-993-9101
Fax: 613-952-9907
Toll Free: 877-672-2672
E-mail Address: info@nrc-cnrc.gc.ca
Web Address: www.nrc-cnrc.gc.ca
National Research Council Canada (NRC) is comprised of 12 government organization, research institutes and programs that carry out multidisciplinary research. It maintains partnerships with industries and sectors key to Canada's economic development.

SRI International
1100 Wilson Blvd., Ste. 2800
Arlington, VA 22209 USA
Phone: 650-859-2000
Web Address: www.sri.com
SRI International is a nonprofit research organization that offers contract research services to government agencies, as well as commercial enterprises and other private sector institutions. It is organized around broad divisions including biosciences, global partnerships, education, products and solutions division, advanced technology and systems and information and computing sciences division.

25) Robotics & Automation Industry Associations

Singapore Industrial Automation Association (SIAA)
9, Town Hall Rd., Ste. 02-23
Singapore, 609431 Singapore
Phone: 65-6749-1822
Fax: 65-6841-3986
E-mail Address: secretariat@siaa.org
Web Address: www.siaa.org
The Singapore Industrial Automation Association (SIAA) is a non-profit organization which promotes

the application of industrial automation with reference to business, technology & information services.

26) Satellite Industry Associations

Satellite Broadcasting & Communications Association (SBCA)
230 Washington Ave., Ste. 101
Albany, NY 12203 USA
Phone: 202-349-3620
Fax: 202-349-3621
Toll Free: 800-541-5981
E-mail Address: info@sbca.org
Web Address: www.sbca.com
The Satellite Broadcasting & Communications Association (SBCA) is the national trade organization representing all segments of the satellite consumer services industry in America.

World Teleport Association (WTA)
250 Park Ave., Fl. 7
New York, NY 10177 USA
Phone: 212-825-0218
Fax: 212-825-0075
E-mail Address: wta@worldteleport.org
Web Address: www.worldteleport.org
The World Teleport Association (WTA) is a nonprofit trade association representing the key commercial players in satellite communications.

27) Satellite-Related Professional Organizations

Geospatial Information and Technology Association (GITA)
1360 University Ave. W., Ste. 455
St. Paul, MN 55104 USA
Phone: 844-447-4482
Fax: 844-223-8218
E-mail Address: president@gita.org
Web Address: www.gita.org
The Geospatial Information and Technology Association (GITA) is an educational association for geospatial information and technology professionals.

Society of Satellite Professionals International (SSPI)
250 Park Ave., Fl. 7
The New York Information Technology Ctr.
New York, NY 10177 USA
Phone: 212-809-5199

Fax: 212-825-0075
E-mail Address: rbell@sspi.org
Web Address: www.sspi.org
The Society of Satellite Professionals International
(SSPI) is a nonprofit member-benefit society that
serves satellite professionals worldwide.

28) Software Industry Associations

European Software Institute (ESI)
Parque Tecnologico de Bizkaia
Edificio 202
Zamudio, Bizkaia E-48170 Spain
Phone: 34-946-430-850
Fax: 34-901-706-009
Web Address: www.esi.es
The European Software Institute (ESI) is a nonprofit
foundation launched as an initiative of the European
Commission, with the support of leading European
companies working in the information technology
field.

Korea Software Industry Association (KOSA)
IT Venture Tower W., 12F
135 Jung-daero, Songpa-gu
Seoul, 05717 South Korea
Phone: 82-2-2188-6900
Fax: 82-2-2188-6901
E-mail Address: choicy@sw.or.kr
Web Address: www.sw.or.kr
The Korea Software Industry Association (KOSA) is
Korea's nonprofit trade organization representing
more than 1,200 member companies in the software
industry.

National Association of Software and Service Companies of India (NASSCOM)
Plot No. 7-10 NASSCOM Campus
Sector 126
Noida, 201303 India
Phone: 91-120-4990111
Fax: 91-120-4990119
E-mail Address: north@nasscom.in
Web Address: www.nasscom.im
The National Association of Software and Service
Companies (NASSCOM) is the trade body and
chamber of commerce for the IT and business
process outsourcing (BPO) industry in India. The
association's 1,400 members consist of corporations
located around the world involved in software
development, software services, software products,
IT-enabled/BPO services and e-commerce.

Singapore Infocomm Technology Federation (SiTF)
79 Ayer Rajah Crescent, Ste. 02-03/04/05
Singapore, 139955 Singapore
Phone: 65-6325-9700
Fax: 65-6325-4993
E-mail Address: info@sitf.org.sg
Web Address: sitf.org.sg
Singapore Infocomm Technology Federation (SiTF)
is an infocom industry association that has four
chapters: Cloud Computing Chapter, Digital Media
Wireless Chapter, Security and Governance Chapter
and Singapore Enterprise Chapter.

Software & Information Industry Association (SIIA)
1090 Vermont Ave. NW, Fl. 6
Washington, DC 20005-4095 USA
Phone: 202-289-7442
Fax: 202-289-7097
Web Address: www.siia.net
The Software & Information Industry Association
(SIIA) is a principal trade association for the software
and digital content industry.

29) Software Industry Resources

Software Engineering Institute (SEI)-Carnegie Mellon
4500 5th Ave.
Pittsburgh, PA 15213-2612 USA
Phone: 412-268-5800
Fax: 412-268-5758
Toll Free: 888-201-4479
E-mail Address: info@sei.cmu.edu
Web Address: www.sei.cmu.edu
The Software Engineering Institute (SEI) is a
federally funded research and development center at
Carnegie Mellon University, sponsored by the U.S.
Department of Defense through the Office of the
Under Secretary of Defense for Acquisition,
Technology, and Logistics [OUSD (AT&L)]. The
SEI's core purpose is to help users make measured
improvements in their software engineering
capabilities.

30) Technology Law Associations

International Technology Law Association (ITechLaw)
7918 Jones Branch Dr., Ste. 300
McLean, VA 22102 USA

Phone: 703-506-2895
Fax: 703-506-3266
E-mail Address: memberservices@itechlaw.org
Web Address: www.itechlaw.org
The International Technology Law Association
(ITechLaw) offers information concerning Internet
and converging technology law. It represents lawyers
in the field of technology law.

31) Technology Transfer Associations

Association of University Technology Managers (AUTM)
111 W. Jackson Blvd., Ste. 1412
Chicago, IL 60604 USA
Phone: 847-686-2244
Fax: 847-686-2253
E-mail Address: info@autm.net
Web Address: www.autm.net
The Association of University Technology Managers
(AUTM) is a nonprofit professional association
whose members belong to over 300 research
institutions, universities, teaching hospitals,
government agencies and corporations. The
association's mission is to advance the field of
technology transfer and enhance members' ability to
bring academic and nonprofit research to people
around the world.

Licensing Executives Society (USA and Canada), Inc.
11130 Sunrise Valley Dr., Ste. 350
Reston, VA 20191 USA
Phone: 703-234-4058
Fax: 703-435-4390
E-mail Address: info@les.org
Web Address: www.lesusacanada.org
Licensing Executives Society (USA and Canada),
Inc., established in 1965, is a professional association
composed of about 3,000 members who work in
fields related to the development, use, transfer,
manufacture and marketing of intellectual property.
Members include executives, lawyers, licensing
consultants, engineers, academic researchers,
scientists and government officials. The society is
part of the larger Licensing Executives Society
International, Inc. (same headquarters address), with
a worldwide membership of some 12,000 members
from approximately 80 countries.

32) Telecommunications Industry Associations

Alliance for Telecommunications Industry Solutions (ATIS)
1200 G St. NW, Ste. 500
Washington, DC 20005 USA
Phone: 202-628-6380
E-mail Address: moran@atis.org
Web Address: www.atis.org
The Alliance for Telecommunications Industry
Solutions (ATIS) is a U.S.-based body committed to
rapidly developing and promoting technical and
operations standards for the communications and
related information technologies industry worldwide.

Asia-Pacific Telecommunity (APT)
Chaengwattana Rd., 12/49 Soi 5
Bangkok, 10210 Thailand
Phone: 66-2-573-0044
Fax: 66-2-573-7479
E-mail Address: aptmail@apt.int
Web Address: www.aptsec.org
The Asia-Pacific Telecommunity (APT) is an
organization of governments, telecom service
providers, manufacturers of communication
equipment, research & development organizations
and other stakeholders active in the field of
communication and information technology. APT
serves as the focal organization for communication
and information technology in the Asia-Pacific
region.

Association of Telecommunications and Value-added Service Providers (VATM)
Neustadtische Kirchstrasse 8
Berlin, 10117 Germany
Phone: 49-30/50-56-15-38
Fax: 49-30/50-56-15-39
E-mail Address: vatm@vatm.de
Web Address: www.vatm.de
The Association of Telecommunications and Value-
added Service Providers (VATM) represents over 90
private companies in the German telecommunications
industry at the national and international level.

China Communications Standards Association (CCSA)
52 Garden Rd., Haidian District
Beijing, 100083 China
Phone: 86-10-6230-2730
Fax: 86-10-6230-1849
Web Address: www.ccsa.org.cn/english

The China Communications Standards Association (CCSA) is a nonprofit organization that works to standardize the field of communications technology across China. Its membership includes operators, telecom equipment manufacturers and universities and academies from across China.

DigitalEurope
Rue de la Science 14
Brussels, 1040 Belgium
Phone: 32-2-609-5310
Fax: 32-2-609-5339
E-mail Address: info@digitaleurope.org
Web Address: www.digitaleurope.org
DigitalEurope is dedicated to improving the business environment for the European information and communications technology and consumer electronics sector. Its members include 57 leading corporations and 37 national trade associations from across Europe.

European Telecommunications Standards Institute (ETSI)
ETSI Secretariat
650, route des Lucioles
Sophia-Antipolis Cedex, 06921 France
Phone: 33-4-92-94-42-00
Fax: 33-4-93-65-47-16
E-mail Address: info@etsi.org
Web Address: www.etsi.org
The European Telecommunications Standards Institute (ETSI) is a non-profit organization whose mission is to produce the telecommunications standards to be implemented throughout Europe.

Fiber to the Home (FTTH) Council
6841 Elm St., Ste. 843
McLean, VA 22101-0843 USA
Phone: 202-524-9550
E-mail Address: heather.b.gold@ftthcouncil.org
Web Address: www.ftthcouncil.org
The Fiber-to-the-Home (FTTH) Council is a nonprofit organization established in 2001 to educate the public on the opportunities and benefits of FTTH solutions. Its website is an excellent resource for statistics, general reference and trends in the delivery of fiber optic cable directly to the home and office.

INCOMPAS
1100 G St. NW, Ste. 800
Washington, DC 20005 USA
Phone: 202-296-6650
E-mail Address: gnorris@comptel.org

Web Address: www.incompas.org
CompTel is a trade organization representing voice, data and video communications service providers and their supplier partners. Members are supported through education, networking, policy advocacy and trade shows.

International Federation for Information Processing (IFIP)
Hofstrasse 3
Laxenburg, A-2361 Austria
Phone: 43-2236-73616
Fax: 43-2236-73616-9
E-mail Address: ifip@ifip.org
Web Address: www.ifip.org
The International Federation for Information Processing (IFIP) is a multinational, apolitical organization in information & communications technologies and sciences recognized by the United Nations and other world bodies. It represents information technology societies from 56 countries or regions, with over 500,000 members in total.

International Multimedia Telecommunications Consortium (IMTC)
Bishop Ranch 6, 2400 Camino Ramon, Ste. 375
San Ramon, CA 94583 USA
Phone: 925-275-6600
Fax: 925-275-6691
Web Address: www.imtc.org
The International Multimedia Telecommunications Consortium (IMTC) is a non-profit corporation that promotes interoperable multimedia conferencing and telecommunications solutions based on international standards.

International Telecommunications Union (ITU)
Place des Nations
Geneva 20, 1211 Switzerland
Phone: 41-22-730-5111
Fax: 41-22-733-7256
E-mail Address: itumail@itu.int
Web Address: www.itu.int
The International Telecommunications Union (ITU) is an international organization for the standardization of the radio and telecommunications industry. It is an agency of the United Nations (UN).

National Association of Telecommunications Officers and Advisors (NATOA)
3213 Duke St., Ste. 695
Alexandria, VA 22314 USA
Phone: 703-519-8035

Fax: 703-997-7080
E-mail Address: info@natoa.org
Web Address: www.natoa.org
The National Association of Telecommunications
Officers and Advisors (NATOA) works to support
and serve the telecommunications industry's interests
and the needs of local governments.

National Exchange Carrier Association (NECA)
80 S. Jefferson Rd.
Whippany, NJ 07981-1009 USA
Fax: 973-884-8469
Toll Free: 800-228-8597
E-mail Address: necainfo@neca.org
Web Address: www.neca.org
The National Exchange Carrier Association (NECA),
formed by the FCC, helps administer the FCC's
access charge plan. The association helps ensure that
telephone service remains available in all areas of the
country.

**National Telecommunications Cooperative
Association (NTCA)**
4121 Wilson Blvd., Ste. 1000
Arlington, VA 22203 USA
Phone: 703-351-2000
Fax: 703-351-2001
E-mail Address: membership@ntca.org
Web Address: www.ntca.org
The National Telecommunications Cooperative
Association (NTCA) is an association representing
more than 580 small and rural independent local
exchange carriers providing telecommunications
services throughout rural America.

Telecommunications Carriers Association (TCA)
E-mail Address: enq@tca.or.jp
Web Address: www.tca.or.jp
The Telecommunications Carriers Association (TCA)
represents major telecommunications firms within
Japan. It publishes a large amount of research
regarding the telecom industry in Japan.

Telecommunications Industry Association (TIA)
1310 N. Courthouse Rd., Ste. 890
Arlington, VA 22201 USA
Phone: 703-907-7700
Fax: 703-907-7727
E-mail Address: smontgomery@tiaonline.org
Web Address: www.tiaonline.org
The Telecommunications Industry Association (TIA)
is a leading trade association in the information,
communications and entertainment technology
industry. TIA focuses on market development, trade
promotion, trade shows, domestic and international
advocacy, standards development and enabling e-
business.

TeleManagement Forum (TM Forum)
240 Headquarters Plz., E. Twr., 10th Fl.
Morristown, NJ 07960-6628 USA
Phone: 973-944-5100
Fax: 973-944-5110
E-mail Address: info@tmforum.org
Web Address: www.tmforum.org
The TeleManagement Forum (TM Forum) is a
nonprofit global organization that provides
leadership, strategic guidance and practical solutions
to improve the management and operation of
information and communications services.

United States Telecom Association (USTelecom)
601 New Jersey Ave. NW, Ste. 600
Washington, DC 20001 USA
Phone: 202-326-7300
Fax: 202-315-3603
E-mail Address: membership@ustelecom.org
Web Address: www.ustelecom.org
The United States Telecom Association (USTelecom)
is a trade association representing service providers
and suppliers for the telecom industry.

Voice On the Net (VON) Coalition, Inc.
1200 Seventh St. NW
Pillsbury Winthrop Shaw Pittman LLP
Washington, DC 20036-3006 USA
Phone: 202-663-8215
E-mail Address: glenn.richards@pillsburylaw.com
Web Address: www.von.org
Voice On the Net (VON) Coalition, Inc. is an
organization is an advocate for the IP telephony
industry. The VON Coalition supports that the IP
industry should remain free of governmental
regulations. It also serves to educate consumers and
the media on Internet communications technologies.

33) Telecommunications Resources

Call Centers India
Phone: 206-384-4669
E-mail Address: sandy@callcentersindia.com
Web Address: www.callcentersindia.com
Call Centers India provides news and information
concerning offshore call center services in India.

Center for Democracy and Technology (CDT)
1401 K St. NW, Ste. 200
Washington, DC 20005 USA
Phone: 202-637-9800
Fax: 202-637-0968
Web Address: www.cdt.org
The Center for Democracy and Technology (CDT) works to promote democratic values and constitutional liberties in the digital age.

Department of Telecommunication (Gov. of India)
20 Ashoka Rd.
Sanchar Bhawan
New Delhi, 110001 India
Phone: 91-11-2373-9191
Fax: 91-11-2372-3330
E-mail Address: secy-dot@nic.in
Web Address: www.dot.gov.in
The Government of India's Department of Telecommunication web site provides information, directories, guidelines, news and information related to the telecom, Internet, Wi-Fi and wireless communication industries. It is a branch of India's Ministry of Communications & Information Technology.

Infocomm Development Authority of Singapore (IMDA)
10 Pasir Panjang Rd.
#10-01 Mapletree Business City
Singapore, 117438 Singapore
Phone: 65-6211-0888
Fax: 65-6211-2222
E-mail Address: info@imda.gov.sg
Web Address: www.imda.gov.sg
The goal of the Infocomm Media Development Authority of Singapore (IMDA) is to actively seek opportunities to grow infocomm industry in both the domestic and international markets.

International Communications Project (The)
Unit 2, Marine Action
Birdhill Industrial Estate
Birdhill, Co Tipperary Ireland
Phone: 353-86-108-3932
Fax: 353-61-749-801
E-mail Address: robert.alcock@intercomms.net
Web Address: www.intercomms.net
The International Communications Project (InterComms) is an authoritative policy, strategy and reference publication for the international telecommunications industry.

International Customer Management Institute (ICMI)
121 S. Tejon St., Ste. 1100
Colorado Springs, CO 80903 USA
Phone: 719-955-8149
Fax: 719-955-8146
Toll Free: 800-672-6177
E-mail Address: icmi@informa.com
Web Address: www.icmi.com
International Customer Management Institute (ICMI) is a leader in call center consulting, training, publications and membership services. ICMI is a part of UBM, a global marketing and communications company.

Ministry of Communications and Information (Gov. of Singapore)
140 Hill St. #01-01A
Old Hill St. Police Station
Singapore, 179369 Singapore
Fax: 65-6837-9480
Toll Free: 800-837-9655
E-mail Address: MCI_Connects@mci.gov.sg
Web Address: www.mci.gov.sg
The Ministry of Communications and Information, is the department of the Singapore government responsible for the development of the nation as a global hub for information, communication and arts related endeavors through the promotion of creativity in the arts, design, media and infocomm technology sectors.

Ministry of Communications and Information Technology (Gov. of India)
Electronics Niketan, 6
CGO Complex, Lodhi Rd.
New Delhi, 110 003 India
Phone: 91-11-2371-0445
Fax: 91-11-2337-2428
E-mail Address: mocit@nic.in
Web Address: www.mit.gov.in
The Government of India's Ministry of Communications and Information Technology is the department responsible for matters relating to communications and IT issues in India. It oversees three branches: the Department of Telecommunications, the Department of IT and the Department of Posts (the Indian postal service).

Telecom Regulatory Authority of India (TRAI)
Mahanagar Doorsanchar Bhawan
Jawaharlal Nehru Marg (Old Minto Rd.)
New Delhi, 110 002 India

Phone: 91-11-2323-6308
Fax: 91-11-2321-3294
E-mail Address: ap@trai.gov.in
Web Address: www.trai.gov.in
The TRAI publishes frequently updated data
regarding wireless, landline and broadcast industry
usage within India.

Total Telecom
Wren House
43 Hatton Garden
London, EC1N 8 EL UK
Phone: 44-20-7092-100
Fax: 44-20-7242-1508
E-mail Address: info@totaltele.com
Web Address: www.totaltele.com
Total Telecom offers information, news and articles
on the telecommunications industry in the U.K. and
worldwide through its web site and the Total
Telecom Magazine. Total Telecom is owned by
Terrapinn Ltd.

34) Telecommunications-VOIP Resources

VOIP News
28 E. 28th St.
New York, NY 10016 USA
Toll Free: 877-864-7275
E-mail Address: info@ziffdavis.com
Web Address: www.voip-news.com
VOIP News provides extensive news and information
about the VOIP industry, including FAQs,
comparison guides, buyer's guides, a dictionary of
terms, case studies, vendor directories and resources
for providers, users and technicians.

35) Trade Associations-General

**Associated Chambers of Commerce and Industry
of India (ASSOCHAM)**
5, Sardar Patel Marg
Chanakyapuri
New Delhi, 110 021 India
Phone: 91-11-4655-0555
Fax: 91-11-2301-7008
E-mail Address: assocham@nic.in
Web Address: www.assocham.org
The Associated Chambers of Commerce and Industry
of India (ASSOCHAM) has a membership of more
than 300 chambers and trade associations and serves
members from all over India. It works with domestic

and international government agencies to advocate
for India's industry and trade activities.

BUSINESSEUROPE
168 Ave. de Cortenbergh 168
Brussels, 1000 Belgium
Phone: 32-2-237-65-11
Fax: 32-2-231-14-45
E-mail Address: main@businesseurope.eu
Web Address: www.businesseurope.eu
BUSINESSEUROPE is a major European trade
federation that operates in a manner similar to a
chamber of commerce. Its members are the central
national business federations of the 34 countries
throughout Europe from which they come.
Companies cannot become direct members of
BUSINESSEUROPE, though there is a support group
which offers the opportunity for firms to encourage
BUSINESSEUROPE objectives in various ways.

Federation of Hong Kong Industries
8 Cheung Yue St.
Fl. 31, Billion Plz., Cheung Sha Wan
Kowloon, Hong Kong Hong Kong
Phone: 852-2732-3188
Fax: 852-2721-3494
E-mail Address: fhki@fhki.org.hk
Web Address: www.industryhk.org
The Federation of Hong Kong Industries promotes
the trade, investment advancement and development
of opportunities for the industrial and business
communities of Hong Kong. The web site hosts a
trade enquiry on products and services and publishes
research reports and trade publications.

**United States Council for International Business
(USCIB)**
1212 Ave. of the Americas
New York, NY 10036 USA
Phone: 212-354-4480
Fax: 212-575-0327
E-mail Address: azhang@uscib.org
Web Address: www.uscib.org
The United States Council for International Business
(USCIB) promotes an open system of world trade
and investment through its global network. Standard
USCIB members include corporations, law firms,
consulting firms and industry associations. Limited
membership options are available for chambers of
commerce and sole legal practitioners.

36) Trade Associations-Global

World Trade Organization (WTO)
Centre William Rappard
Rue de Lausanne 154
Geneva 21, CH-1211 Switzerland
Phone: 41-22-739-51-11
Fax: 41-22-731-42-06
E-mail Address: enquiries@wto.og
Web Address: www.wto.org
The World Trade Organization (WTO) is a global organization dealing with the rules of trade between nations. To become a member, nations must agree to abide by certain guidelines. Membership increases a nation's ability to import and export efficiently.

37) Trade Resources

Made-in-China.com - China Manufacturers Directory
Block A, Software Bldg. No. 9, Xinghuo Rd.
Nanjing New & High Technology Industry Development Zone
Nanjing, Jiangsu 210032 China
Fax: 86-25-6667-0000
Web Address: www.made-in-china.com
Made-in-China.com - China Manufacturers Directory, one of the largest business to business portals in China, helps to connect Chinese manufacturers, suppliers and traders with international buyers. Made-in-China.com contains additional information on trade shows and important laws and regulations about business with China.

38) U.S. Government Agencies

Bureau of Economic Analysis (BEA)
4600 Silver Hill Rd.
Washington, DC 20233 USA
Phone: 301-278-9004
E-mail Address: customerservice@bea.gov
Web Address: www.bea.gov
The Bureau of Economic Analysis (BEA), is an agency of the U.S. Department of Commerce, is the nation's economic accountant, preparing estimates that illuminate key national, international and regional aspects of the U.S. economy.

Bureau of Labor Statistics (BLS)
2 Massachusetts Ave. NE
Washington, DC 20212-0001 USA
Phone: 202-691-5200

Fax: 202-691-7890
Toll Free: 800-877-8339
E-mail Address: blsdata_staff@bls.gov
Web Address: stats.bls.gov
The Bureau of Labor Statistics (BLS) is the principal fact-finding agency for the Federal Government in the field of labor economics and statistics. It is an independent national statistical agency that collects, processes, analyzes and disseminates statistical data to the American public, U.S. Congress, other federal agencies, state and local governments, business and labor. The BLS also serves as a statistical resource to the Department of Labor.

FCC-Office of Engineering & Technology (OET)
Office of Engineering and Technology
445 12th St. SW
Washington, DC 20554 USA
Fax: 866-418-0232
Toll Free: 888-225-5322
E-mail Address: oetinfo@fcc.gov
Web Address: www.fcc.gov/engineering-%26-technology
The Office of Engineering & Technology (OET) unit of the Federal Communications Commission (FCC) acts as a consultant to the FCC regarding matters of engineering and technology. It also provides evaluations of emerging technologies and equipment.

FCC-VoIP Division
445 12th St. SW
Washington, DC 20554 USA
Fax: 866-418-0232
Toll Free: 888-225-5322
E-mail Address: FOIA@fcc.gov
Web Address: www.fcc.gov/voip
The FCC-VoIP Division is dedicated to the promotion and regulation of the VoIP (Voice over Internet Protocol) industry. It operates as part of the Federal Communications Commission (FCC). VoIP allows users to call from their computer (or adapters) over the Internet to regular telephone numbers.

FCC-Wireline Competition Bureau (WCB)
445 12th St. SW
Washington, DC 20554 USA
Phone: 202-418-1500
Fax: 202-418-2825
Toll Free: 888-225-5322
E-mail Address: FOIA@fcc.gov
Web Address: www.fcc.gov/wcb
The FCC-Wireline Competition Bureau (WCB), formerly the Common Carrier Bureau, is a unit of the

Federal Communications Commission (FCC). It is responsible for administering the FCC's policies concerning companies that provide wireline telecommunications.

Federal Communications Commission (FCC)
445 12th St. SW
Washington, DC 20554 USA
Fax: 866-418-0232
Toll Free: 888-225-5322
E-mail Address: PRA@fcc.gov
Web Address: www.fcc.gov
The Federal Communications Commission (FCC) is an independent U.S. government agency established by the Communications Act of 1934 responsible for regulating interstate and international communications by radio, television, wire, satellite and cable.

Federal Communications Commission (FCC)-International Bureau
445 12th St. SW
Washington, DC 20554 USA
Fax: 866-418-0232
Toll Free: 888-225-5322
E-mail Address: PRA@fcc.gov
Web Address: www.fcc.gov/international
The Federal Communications Commission (FCC)-International Bureau exists to administer the FCC's international telecommunications and satellite policies and obligations, such as licensing and regulatory functions, as well as promotes U.S. interests in international communications arena.

Federal Communications Commission (FCC)-Wireless Telecommunications Bureau
445 12th St. SW
Washington, DC 20554 USA
Phone: 202-418-0600
Fax: 202-418-0787
Toll Free: 888-225-5322
E-mail Address: PRA@fcc.gov
Web Address: www.fcc.gov/wireless-telecommunications#block-menu-block-4
The Federal Communications Commission (FCC)-Wireless Telecommunications Bureau handles nearly all FCC domestic wireless telecommunications programs and policies, including cellular and smarftphones, pagers and two-way radios. The bureau also regulates the use of radio spectrum for businesses, aircraft/ship operators and individuals.

National Institute of Standards and Technology (NIST)
100 Bureau Dr.
Gaithersburg, MD 20899-1070 USA
Phone: 301-975-6478
Toll Free: 800-877-8339
E-mail Address: inquiries@nist.gov
Web Address: www.nist.gov
The National Institute of Standards and Technology (NIST) is an agency of the U.S. Department of Commerce that works with various industries to develop and apply technology, measurements and standards.

National Science Foundation (NSF)
2415 Eisenhower Ave.
Alexandria, VA 22314 USA
Phone: 703-292-5111
Toll Free: 800-877-8339
E-mail Address: info@nsf.gov
Web Address: www.nsf.gov
The National Science Foundation (NSF) is an independent U.S. government agency responsible for promoting science and engineering. The foundation provides colleges and universities with grants and funding for research into numerous scientific fields.

National Telecommunications and Information Administration (NTIA)
1401 Constitution Ave. NW
Herbert C. Hoover Bldg.
Washington, DC 20230 USA
Phone: 202-482-2000
Web Address: www.ntia.doc.gov
The National Telecommunications and Information Administration (NTIA), an agency of the U.S. Department of Commerce, is the Executive Branch's principal voice on domestic and international telecommunications and information technology issues.

U.S. Census Bureau
4600 Silver Hill Rd.
Washington, DC 20233-8800 USA
Phone: 301-763-4636
Toll Free: 800-923-8282
E-mail Address: pio@census.gov
Web Address: www.census.gov
The U.S. Census Bureau is the official collector of data about the people and economy of the U.S. Founded in 1790, it provides official social, demographic and economic information. In addition to the Population & Housing Census, which it

conducts every 10 years, the U.S. Census Bureau numerous other surveys annually.

U.S. Department of Commerce (DOC)
1401 Constitution Ave. NW
Washington, DC 20230 USA
Phone: 202-482-2000
E-mail Address: TheSec@doc.gov
Web Address: www.commerce.gov
The U.S. Department of Commerce (DOC) regulates trade and provides valuable economic analysis of the economy.

U.S. Department of Labor (DOL)
200 Constitution Ave. NW
Washington, DC 20210 USA
Phone: 202-693-4676
Toll Free: 866-487-2365
Web Address: www.dol.gov
The U.S. Department of Labor (DOL) is the government agency responsible for labor regulations. The Department of Labor's goal is to foster, promote, and develop the welfare of the wage earners, job seekers, and retirees of the United States; improve working conditions; advance opportunities for profitable employment; and assure work-related benefits and rights.

U.S. Patent and Trademark Office (PTO)
600 Dulany St.
Madison Bldg.
Alexandria, VA 22314 USA
Phone: 571-272-1000
Toll Free: 800-786-9199
E-mail Address: usptoinfo@uspto.gov
Web Address: www.uspto.gov
The U.S. Patent and Trademark Office (PTO) administers patent and trademark laws for the U.S. and enables registration of patents and trademarks.

U.S. Securities and Exchange Commission (SEC)
100 F St. NE
Washington, DC 20549 USA
Phone: 202-942-8088
Fax: 202-772-9295
Toll Free: 800-732-0330
E-mail Address: help@sec.gov
Web Address: www.sec.gov
The U.S. Securities and Exchange Commission (SEC) is a nonpartisan, quasi-judicial regulatory agency responsible for administering federal securities laws. These laws are designed to protect investors in securities markets and ensure that they have access to disclosure of all material information concerning publicly traded securities. Visitors to the web site can access the EDGAR database of corporate financial and business information.

---

39) Wireless & Cellular Industry Associations

3GPP (The 3rd Generation Partnership Project)
3GPP Mobile Competence Centre, c/o ETSI
650, route des Lucioles
Sophia-Antipolis, Cedex 06921 France
E-mail Address: info@3gpp.org
Web Address: www.3gpp.org
The 3GPP is engaged in study, discussion and information approval through its members, which includes seven telecommunications standard development organizations (ARIB, ETSI, ATIS, CCSA, TTA, TSDSI and TTC) and mainly covers topics, such as cellular telecommunications network technologies, including radio access, the core transport network and service capabilities.

4GAmericas
1750 112th Ave. NE, Ste. B220
Bellevue, WA 98004 USA
Phone: 425-372-8922
Fax: 425-372-8923
Web Address: www.4gamericas.org
4G Americas is an industry trade organization composed of leading telecommunications service providers and manufacturers. The organization's mission is to promote, facilitate and advocate for the deployment and adoption of the 3GPP family of technologies throughout the Americas. The organization aims to develop the expansive wireless ecosystem of networks, devices, and applications enabled by GSM and its evolution to LTE. The organization publishes a significant amount of research and holds important conferences.

Bluetooth Special Interest Group (SIG)
5209 Lake Washington Blvd. NE, Ste. 350
Kirkland, WA 98033 USA
Phone: 425-691-3535
Fax: 425-691-3524
Web Address: www.bluetooth.com
The Bluetooth Special Interest Group (SIG) is a trade association comprised of leaders in the telecommunications, computing, automotive, industrial automation and network industries that is driving the development of Bluetooth wireless technology, a low cost short-range wireless

specification for connecting mobile devices and bringing them to market.

Broadband Wireless Association (BWA)
Phone: 44-7765-250610
E-mail Address: Stephen@thebwa.eu
Web Address: www.thebwa.eu
The Broadband Wireless Association (BWA) provides representation, news and information for the European broadband wireless industry.

Canada Wireless Telecommunications Association (CWTA)
80 Elgin St., Ste. 300
Ottawa, ON K1P 6R2 Canada
Phone: 613-233-4888
Fax: 613-233-2032
E-mail Address: info@cwta.ca
Web Address: www.cwta.ca
The Canada Wireless Telecommunications Association (CWTA) seeks to be the pre-eminent source of input to government policy and public opinion on behalf of the wireless communications industry in Canada, in order to establish and maintain a positive economic environment for the wireless industry.

CDMA Development Group (CDG)
P.O. Box 22249
San Diego, CA 92129-2249 USA
Phone: 714-987-2362
Fax: 714-545-4601
Toll Free: 888-800-2362
E-mail Address: info@mobilitydg.org
Web Address: www.cdg.org
The CDMA Development Group (CDG) is composed of the world's leading code division multiple access (CDMA) service providers and manufacturers that have joined together to lead the adoption and evolution of CDMA wireless systems around the world.

Cellular Telecommunications & Internet Association (CTIA)
1400 16th St. NW, Ste. 600
Washington, DC 20036 USA
Phone: 202-785-0081
Web Address: www.ctia.org
The Cellular Telecommunications & Internet Association (CTIA) is an international nonprofit membership organization that represents a variety of wireless communications sectors including cellular service providers, manufacturers, wireless data and

Internet companies. CTIA's industry committees study spectrum allocation, homeland security, taxation, safety and emerging technology.

Competitive Carrier Association (CCS)
805 15th St. NW, Ste. 401
Washington, DC 20005 USA
Fax: 866-436-1080
Toll Free: 800-722-1872
E-mail Address: administrator@rca-usa.org
Web Address: www.rca-usa.org
The Competitive Carrier Association (CCS), formerly the Rural Cellular Association (RCA) represents rural telecommunications providers in the United States before state and federal legislators. It primarily focuses on two-way wireless providers with a subscriber base less than 500,000.

Global System for Mobile Communication Association (GSMA)
The Wallbrook Bldg.
Fl. 2, 25 Wallbrook
London, EC4N 8AF UK
Phone: 44-207-356-0600
Fax: 44-20-7356-0601
E-mail Address: info@gsma.com
Web Address: www.gsmworld.com
The Global System for Mobile Communications Association (GSMA) is a global trade association representing nearly 800 GSM mobile phone operators from 219 countries.

Hong Kong Wireless Technology Industry Association
16 Cheung Yue St.
Unit B & D, Fl. 11, Gee Hing
Hong Kong, Hong Kong
Phone: 582-2989-9164
E-mail Address: contact@hkwtia.org
Web Address: www.hkwtia.org
The Hong Kong Wireless Technology Industry Association (WTIA), established in 2001, is a nonprofit trade association intended to provide a platform for wireless-related businesses to work together for the development and growth of the wireless industry.

Industrial Internet Consortium
9C Medway Rd., PMB 274
Milford, MA 01757 USA
Phone: 781-444-0404
E-mail Address: info@iiconsortium.org
Web Address: www.iiconsortium.org

The Industrial Internet Consortium was founded in 2014 to further development, adoption and widespread use of interconnected machines, intelligent analytics and people at work. Through an independently-run consortium of technology innovators, industrial companies, academia and government, the goal of the IIC is to accelerate the development and availability of intelligent industrial automation for the public good.

Li-Fi Consortium
E-mail Address: info@lificonsortium.org
Web Address: www.lificonsortium.org
The Li-Fi Consortium is a membership group founded to set standards and promote utilization of next-generation optical wireless networks, which are sometimes referred to as Li-Fi. Li-Fi is somewhat like Wi-Fi, except that it utilizes light as a means to transmit data.

Open Handset Alliance
E-mail Address: press@openhandsetalliance.com
Web Address: www.openhandsetalliance.com
The Open Handset Alliance is a group of about mobile-handset and technology makers, cellular carriers, semiconductor companies and software firms (largely led by Google, Inc.) who are collectively committed to an open system platform for cell phones. The Alliance has developed Android, the first open and free mobile platform.

Open Mobile Alliance (OMA)
2907 Shelter Island, Ste. 105-273
San Diego, CA 92106 USA
Phone: 858-623-0742
Fax: 858-623-0743
E-mail Address: snewberry@omaorg.org
Web Address: www.openmobilealliance.org
The Open Mobile Alliance (OMA) facilitates global user adoption of mobile data services by specifying market driven mobile service enablers that ensure service interoperability across devices, geographies, service providers, operators and networks, while allowing businesses to compete through innovation and differentiation.

Personal Communications Industry Association (PCIA)
500 Montgomery St., Ste. 500
Alexandria, VA 22314 USA
Phone: 703-739-0300
Fax: 703-836-1608
Toll Free: 800-759-0300

E-mail Address: jennifer.blasi@pcia.com
Web Address: www.pcia.com
The Personal Communications Industry Association (PCIA) is an association of companies that own and operate tower, rooftop and other kinds of wireless broadcasting and telecommunications equipment.

Small Cell Forum
P.O. Box 23
Dursley, Gloucestershire GL11 5WA UK
E-mail Address: info@smallcellforum.org
Web Address: www.smallcellforum.org
The Small Cell Forum, formerly the Femto Forum is a not-for-profit membership organization founded in 2007 to promote femtocell deployment worldwide. Comprised of mobile operators, telecoms hardware and software vendors, content providers and innovative start-ups, the group's mission is to advance the development and adoption of femtocell products and services within the residential and small to medium business markets.

Wi-Fi Alliance
10900-B Stonelake Blvd., Ste. 126
Austin, TX 78759 USA
Phone: 512-498-9434
Fax: 512-498-9435
Web Address: www.wi-fi.org
The Wi-Fi Alliance is a non-profit group that promotes wireless interoperability via Wi-Fi (802.11 standards). It also provides consumers with current information about Wi-Fi systems. The alliance currently includes over 350 member organizations.

WiMAX Forum
9009 SE Adams St., Ste. 2259
Clackamas, OR 97015 USA
Phone: 858-605-0978
Fax: 858-461-6041
Web Address: www.wimaxforum.org
The WiMAX Forum supports the implementation and standardization of long-range wireless Internet connections. It is a non-profit organization dedicated to the promotion and certification of interoperability and compatibility of broadband wireless products.

WiMedia Alliance, Inc.
2400 Camino Ramon, Ste. 375
San Ramon, CA 94583 USA
Phone: 925-275-6604
Fax: 925-886-3809
E-mail Address: help@wimedia.org
Web Address: www.wimedia.org

WiMedia Alliance, Inc. is an open, nonprofit wireless industry association that promotes the adoption and standardization of ultrawideband (UWB) worldwide for use in the personal computer, consumer electronics and mobile market segments.

Wireless Communications Alliance (WCA)
1510 Page Mill Rd.
Palo Alto, CA 94304-1125 USA
E-mail Address: promote@wca.org
Web Address: www.wca.org
The Wireless Communications Alliance (WCA) is a non-profit business association for companies and organizations working with wireless technologies. It promotes networking, education and the exchange of information amongst its members.

Wireless Communications Association International (WCAI)
1333 H St. NW, Ste. 700 W
Washington, DC 20005-4754 USA
Phone: 202-452-7823
Web Address: www.wcainternational.com/
The Wireless Communications Association International (WCAI) is a nonprofit trade association representing the wireless broadband industry.

40) Wireless & Cellular Industry Resources

Hong Kong Wireless Development Centre (HKWDC)
31 Wylie Rd.
Room 1814, Fl. 18, Tung Wah College
Homantin, Kowloon Hong Kong
Phone: 852-3190-6630
E-mail Address: po@twc.edu.hk
Web Address: www.hkwdc.org
The Hong Kong Wireless Development Centre (HKWDC) aims to facilitate mobile and wireless application development in Hong Kong.

Wi-Fi Planet
Web Address: www.wi-fiplanet.com
Wi-Fi Planet is a web site devoted to wireless networking protocols. The site features daily news, reviews, tutorials, forums and event and product listings related to the Wi-Fi performance.

Wireless Design Online
5340 Fryling Rd., Ste. 300
Erie, PA 16510 USA
Phone: 814-897-7700
Fax: 814-897-9555
E-mail Address: info@wirelessdesignonline.com
Web Address: www.wirelessdesignonline.com
Wireless Design Online is an Internet resource for technical information covering the wireless industry.

Chapter 4

THE TELECOMMUNICATIONS 350: WHO THEY ARE AND HOW THEY WERE CHOSEN

Includes Indexes by Company Name, Industry & Location

The companies chosen to be listed in PLUNKETT'S TELECOMMUNICATIONS INDUSTRY ALMANAC comprise a unique list. THE TELECOMMUNICATIONS 350 were chosen specifically for their dominance in the many facets of the telecommunications industry in which they operate. Complete information about each firm can be found in the "Individual Profiles," beginning at the end of this chapter. These profiles are in alphabetical order by company name.

THE TELECOMMUNICATIONS 350 companies are from all parts of the United States, Asia, Canada, Europe and beyond. Essentially, THE TELECOMMUNICATIONS 350 includes companies that are deeply involved in the manufacturing, services and technologies that keep the entire industry forging ahead. To be included in our list, the firms had to meet the following criteria:

1) These companies were selected from top firms on a global basis.
2) Prominence, or a significant presence, in telecommunications and supporting fields. (See the following Industry Codes section for a complete list of types of businesses that are covered).
3) The companies in THE TELECOMMUNICATIONS 350 do not have to

be exclusively in the telecommunications industry.
4) Financial data and vital statistics must have been available to the editors of this book, either directly from the company being written about or from outside sources deemed reliable and accurate by the editors. A small number of companies that we would like to have included are not listed because of a lack of sufficient, objective data.

INDEX OF COMPANIES WITHIN INDUSTRY GROUPS

The industry codes shown below are based on the 2012 NAIC code system (NAIC is used by many analysts as a replacement for older SIC codes because NAIC is more specific to today's industry sectors, see www.census.gov/NAICS). Companies are given a primary NAIC code, reflecting the main line of business of each firm.

Industry Group/Company	Industry Code	2020 Sales	2020 Profits
Advertising, Public Relations and Marketing Services			
TTEC Holdings Inc	541800	1,949,248,000	118,648,000
Cloud, Data Processing, Business Process Outsourcing (BPO) and Internet Content Hosting Services			
Cyxtera Technologies Inc	518210	690,000,000	-239,000,000
GoDaddy Inc	518210	3,316,699,904	-495,100,000
Neustar Inc	518210	1,447,556,250	
Newfold Digital Inc	518210	833,250,000	
Sitel Corporation	518210	2,100,000,000	
Computer and Data Systems Design, Consulting and Integration Services			
Kratos Defense & Security Solutions Inc	541512	747,699,968	79,600,000
Sopra Steria Group SA	541512	5,235,880,000	131,176,000
Sykes Enterprises Incorporated	541512	1,710,260,992	56,432,000
Computer Manufacturing, Including PCs, Laptops, Mainframes and Tablets			
Fujitsu Limited	334111	35,233,280,000	1,461,664,256
HP Inc	334111	56,639,000,576	2,844,000,000
MiTAC Holdings Corp	334111	1,463,350,000	101,388,000
Computer Networking & Related Equipment Manufacturing (may incl. Internet of Things, IoT)			
Calix Inc	334210A	541,238,976	33,484,000
Cisco Systems Inc	334210A	49,301,000,192	11,214,000,128
D-Link Corporation	334210A	536,339,000	44,097,900
Extreme Networks Inc	334210A	948,019,008	-126,845,000
Juniper Networks Inc	334210A	4,445,100,032	257,800,000
NETGEAR Inc	334210A	1,255,202,048	58,293,000
Computer Peripherals and Accessories, including Printers, Monitors and Terminals Manufacturing			
Belkin International Inc	334118	1,842,001,875	
Computer Software, Accounting, Banking & Financial			
Calero-MDSL	511210Q		
Computer Software, Business Management & ERP			
Microsoft Corporation	511210H	143,015,002,112	44,280,999,936
Computer Software, E-Commerce, Web Analytics & Applications Management			
Realtime Corporation	511210M		
Computer Software, Network Management, System Testing, & Storage			
F5 Networks Inc	511210B	2,350,821,888	307,440,992
NetScout Systems Inc	511210B	891,820,032	-2,754,000
OPTERNA	511210B	15,006,000	

Industry Group/Company	Industry Code	2020 Sales	2020 Profits
Computer Software, Sales & Customer Relationship Management			
Aspect Software Inc	511210K	505,220,625	
Computer Software, Security & Anti-Virus			
AsiaInfo Technologies Limited	511210E	922,293,000	101,422,000
Axway Inc	511210E	365,076,000	10,413,100
Certicom Corp	511210E		
Cloudflare Inc	511210E	431,059,008	-119,370,000
Entrust Corporation	511210E	840,000,000	
McAfee Corp	511210E	2,905,999,872	-289,000,000
OneSpan Inc	511210E	215,691,008	-5,455,000
VeriSign Inc	511210E	1,265,052,032	814,888,000
Computer Software, Telecom, Communications & VOIP, Internet of Things (IoT)			
BlackBerry Limited	511210C	1,040,000,000	-152,000,000
Skype Technologies Sarl	511210C		
Slack Technologies Inc	511210C	630,422,016	-571,057,984
TeamViewer AG	511210C	372,939,075	
XIUS	511210C	507,385,000	-3,782,000
Zoom Video Communications Inc	511210C	622,657,984	25,305,000
Computers, Peripherals, Software and Accessories Distribution			
Anixter International Inc	423430	9,287,879,731	
Black Box Corporation	423430	874,371,504	
Ingram Micro Mobility	423430	49,100,000,000	644,219,000
ScanSource Inc	423430	3,047,734,016	-192,654,000
TESSCO Technologies Incorporated	423430	540,298,304	-21,568,900
Connectors for Electronics Manufacturing			
Belden Inc	334417		
Construction of Telecommunications Lines and Systems & Electric Power Lines and Systems			
Bouygues SA	237130		
China Communications Services Corporation Limited	237130	19,221,864,448	482,936,832
Dycom Industries Inc	237130	3,339,682,048	57,215,000
Consumer Electronics Manufacturing, Including Audio and Video Equipment, Stereos, TVs and Radios			
AAC Technologies Holdings Inc	334310	2,686,259,968	236,135,056
Koninklijke Philips NV (Royal Philips)	334310	23,867,412,480	1,450,249,344
Panasonic Corporation	334310	68,411,695,104	2,061,383,040
Samsung Electronics Co Ltd	334310	213,877,211,136	23,564,496,896
TCL Technology Group Corporation	334310	11,770,800,000	776,013,000
Contract Electronics Manufacturing Services (CEM) and Printed Circuits Assembly			
Accton Technology Corporation	334418	1,936,970,000	179,555,000
Celestica Inc	334418		
Flex Ltd	334418	24,209,870,848	87,579,000
Foxconn Technology Co Ltd	334418	3,726,840,000	166,662,000
Jabil Inc	334418	27,266,437,120	53,912,000
Sanmina Corporation	334418	6,960,370,176	139,712,992
SMTC Corporation	334418	417,212,329	

Industry Group/Company	Industry Code	2020 Sales	2020 Profits
Copper Rolling, Drawing, Extruding and Alloying			
Bangkok Cable Co Ltd	331420		
Distributors of Telecommunications Equipment, Telephones, Cellphones and Electronics Components (Wholesale Distribution)			
Brightstar Corporation	423690	11,576,250,000	
Simply Inc	423690		
Electric Signal, Electricity, and Semiconductor Test and Measuring Equipment Manufacturing			
Anritsu Corporation	334515	977,441,536	121,971,272
Rohde & Schwarz GmbH & Co KG	334515	2,901,780,000	
Tektronix Inc	334515		
Electrical Contractors and Other Wiring Installation Contractors			
TKH Group NV	238210		
Electricity Control Panels, Circuit Breakers and Power Switches Equipment (Switchgear) Manufacturing			
Broadcom Inc	335313	23,887,998,976	2,960,000,000
Factory Automation, Robots (Robotics) Industrial Process, Thermostat, Flow Meter and Environmental Quality Monitoring and Control Manufacturing (incl. Artificial Intelligence, AI)			
Siemens AG	334513	69,811,109,888	4,923,761,152
Fiber Optic Cable, Connectors and Related Products Manufacturing			
Amphenol Corporation	335921	8,598,899,712	1,203,399,936
CommScope Holding Company Inc	335921	8,435,899,904	-573,400,000
Energy Focus Inc	335921	16,828,000	-5,981,000
Optical Cable Corporation	335921	55,277,400	-6,121,224
Preformed Line Products Company	335921	466,448,992	29,803,000
Iron and Steel Mills and Ferroalloy Manufacturing			
Tata Group	331110	106,000,000,000	
LCD (Liquid-Crystal Display), Radio Frequency (RF, RFID) and Microwave Equipment Manufacturing			
Qisda Corporation	334419	6,817,870,000	226,427,000
Mail Order, Catalogs and Other Direct Marketing, and TV Shopping			
Hello Direct Inc	454113		
Management of Businesses & Enterprises			
LG Corporation	551114	6,206,060,000	1,524,570,000
OJSC JFSC Sistema	551114	9,407,905,792	138,964,064
Medical Imaging and Electromedical (Medical Devices) Equipment, including MRI, Ultrasound, Pacemakers, EKG and CAT			
Aware Inc	334510	11,309,000	-7,614,000
Outsourced Computer Facilities Management and Operations Services			
International Business Machines Corporation (IBM)	541513	73,620,996,096	5,590,000,128
Photographic and Photocopying Equipment Manufacturing			
BenQ Corporation	333316	3,281,118,750	
Kyocera Corporation	333316	14,604,157,952	983,816,384

Industry Group/Company	Industry Code	2020 Sales	2020 Profits
Port and Harbor Operations			
CK Hutchison Holdings Limited	488310	34,332,919,808	3,755,928,320
Pressed and Blown Glass and Glassware (except Glass Packaging Containers) Manufacturing			
Corning Incorporated	327212		
Radar, Navigation, Sonar, Space Vehicle Guidance, Flight Systems and Marine Instrument Manufacturing			
Garmin Ltd	334511	4,186,573,056	992,323,968
TomTom International BV	334511	645,324,224	-314,777,408
Trimble Inc	334511	3,147,699,968	389,900,000
Radio, Television and Other Electronics Stores			
Hikari Tsushin Inc	443142	4,790,900,224	471,902,336
Satellite Telecommunications			
Asia Satellite Telecommunications Holdings Ltd	517410	205,059,460	
Eutelsat Communications SA	517410	1,561,797,504	363,600,832
Gilat Satellite Networks Ltd	517410	165,884,992	34,911,000
Globalstar Inc	517410	128,487,000	-109,639,000
Inmarsat Global Limited	517410	1,444,480,000	
Intelsat SA	517410		
Iridium Communications Inc	517410	583,438,976	-56,054,000
OneWeb Ltd	517410	26,520,760	
Orbsat Corp	517410		
Planet Labs Inc	517410		
SES SA	517410	2,243,182,592	-105,072,816
Thuraya Telecommunications Company	517410	180,017,726	
Semiconductor and Solar Cell Manufacturing, Including Chips, Memory, LEDs, Transistors and Integrated Circuits, Artificial Intelligence (AI), & Internet of Things (IoT)			
Advanced Micro Devices Inc (AMD)	334413	9,763,000,320	2,489,999,872
DSP Group Inc	334413	114,480,000	-6,790,000
Infinera Corporation	334413	1,355,596,032	-206,723,008
Intel Corporation	334413	77,866,999,808	20,899,000,320
Marvell Technology Group Ltd	334413	2,699,161,088	1,584,391,040
Qualcomm Incorporated	334413	23,530,999,808	5,198,000,128
Toshiba Corporation	334413	30,959,708,160	-1,046,943,680
Telecommunications, Telephone and Network Equipment Manufacturing, including PBX, Routers, Switches, Internet of Things (IoT), and Handsets Manufacturing			
ADTRAN Inc	334210	506,510,016	2,378,000
Avaya Holdings Corp	334210	2,872,999,936	-680,000,000
Calient Technologies Inc	334210		
Channell Commercial Corporation	334210		
Ciena Corporation	334210	3,532,156,928	361,291,008
Communications Systems Inc	334210	42,575,544	-171,658
Datang Telecom Technology Co Ltd	334210	215,019,000	
Dialogic Inc	334210	128,750,000	
DZS Inc	334210	300,640,000	-23,082,000
ECI Telecom Ltd	334210	366,600,000	

Industry Group/Company	Industry Code	2020 Sales	2020 Profits
Fujitsu Network Communications Inc	334210		
Harmonic Inc	334210	378,831,008	-29,271,000
Huawei Technologies Co Ltd	334210		
ITI Limited	334210	298,092,000	20,051,000
Lattice Incorporated	334210	8,364,579	
MedTel Services LLC	334210		
Mitel Networks Corporation	334210	1,365,000,000	
Plantronics Inc	334210	1,696,990,000	-827,182,000
Tellabs Inc	334210	1,610,256,375	
VTech Holdings Limited	334210	2,165,499,904	190,700,000
Westell Technologies Inc	334210		
ZTE Corporation	334210	15,899,615,232	667,599,488
Telemarketing Bureaus and Other Contact Centers			
Intrado Corporation	561422	2,730,000,000	
Telephone, Internet Access, Broadband, Data Networks, Server Facilities and Telecommunications Services Industry			
AAPT Limited	517110		
Akamai Technologies Inc	517110	3,198,149,120	557,054,016
Alaska Communications Systems Group Inc	517110	240,568,992	-1,073,000
Altice Portugal SA	517110		
Altice USA Inc	517110	9,894,641,664	436,183,008
Arqiva Limited	517110	1,112,460,000	-397,765,000
AT&T Inc	517110	171,759,992,832	-5,176,000,000
ATN International Inc	517110	455,444,000	-14,122,000
Axtel SAB de CV	517110	618,999,872	18,097,860
B Communications Ltd	517110		
BCE Inc (Bell Canada Enterprises)	517110	18,960,146,432	2,182,450,688
Bell Aliant Inc	517110	3,414,993,750	
Bell MTS Inc	517110	833,490,000	
Bezeq-The Israel Telecommunication Corp Ltd	517110	2,692,957,440	245,740,448
Bharat Sanchar Nigam Limited (BSNL)	517110	2,512,930,000	-2,060,100,000
Boingo Wireless Inc	517110	276,979,500	
BT Global Services plc	517110	143,008,000	809,236
BT Group plc	517110		
Ceske Radiokomunikace as	517110	89,137,125	
Charter Communications Inc	517110	48,097,001,472	3,222,000,128
China Telecom Corporation Limited	517110		
China Unicom (Hong Kong) Limited	517110		
Chorus Limited	517110	691,240,896	37,717,236
Chunghwa Telecom Co Ltd	517110	7,527,028,736	1,211,632,256
Cincinnati Bell Inc	517110	1,559,800,064	-55,600,000
Cisco Webex	517110		
Cogent Communications Group Inc	517110	568,102,976	6,216,000
Colt Technology Services Group Limited	517110	165,830,000	
Comcast Corporation	517110	103,564,001,280	10,533,999,616
Consolidated Communications Holdings Inc	517110	1,304,028,032	36,977,000
Cox Communications Inc	517110	12,600,000,000	
DirecTV LLC (DIRECTV)	517110	26,690,880,207	

Industry Group/Company	Industry Code	2020 Sales	2020 Profits
EarthLink LLC	517110	1,183,644,000	
EchoStar Corporation	517110	1,887,906,944	-40,150,000
eircom Limited	517110	1,384,530,000	24,743,900
Elisa Corporation	517110	2,314,778,624	400,742,848
Embratel Participacoes SA	517110	10,893,251,250	
Emirates Telecommunications Corporation (Etisalat)	517110	14,073,700,000	2,449,970,000
Empresa Nacional de Telecommunications SA (Entel)	517110	2,932,460,000	118,364,000
Equinix Inc	517110	5,998,544,896	369,776,992
FASTWEB SpA	517110	2,829,870,000	190,378,000
Frontier Communications Corporation	517110		
Fusion Connect Inc	517110	137,891,638	
GCI Liberty Inc	517110	873,259,400	
HC2 Holdings Inc	517110	1,005,800,000	-92,000,000
Hellenic Telecommunications Organization SA	517110	3,981,648,896	439,717,536
HKT Trust and HKT Limited	517110	4,174,270,464	683,446,720
iBasis Inc	517110	1,050,000,000	
IDT Corporation	517110	1,345,768,960	21,430,000
Iliad SA	517110	7,173,052,416	521,698,752
Internap Corporation	517110	284,700,000	
Internet Initiative Japan Inc	517110	1,867,457,536	36,593,876
J2 Global Inc	517110	1,489,592,960	150,668,000
KCOM Group Limited	517110	325,735,000	-9,615,410
Koninklijke KPN NV (Royal KPN NV)	517110	6,455,868,928	685,416,896
KT Corporation	517110	22,074,085,376	633,022,656
Liberty Global plc	517110	11,980,099,584	-1,628,000,000
Lumen Technologies Inc	517110	20,711,999,488	-1,232,000,000
Magyar Telekom plc	517110	2,377,715,200	149,661,728
Mahanagar Telephone Nigam Limited	517110	222,846,736	-506,997,472
Maroc Telecom SA	517110	4,173,552,896	615,550,528
Maxis Berhad	517110	2,174,102,784	335,111,520
Mediacom Communications Corporation	517110	2,131,224,000	
Megacable Holdings SAB de CV	517110		
Momentum Telecom	517110	137,550,000	
Net2Phone Inc	517110	50,800,000	
Nippon Telegraph and Telephone Corporation (NTT)	517110	108,677,406,720	7,811,513,856
Nortel Inversora SA	517110	2,975,813,366	
O2 Czech Republic AS	517110	1,440,770,000	271,190,000
Oblong Inc	517110		
Oi SA	517110	1,802,882,176	-2,044,772,096
Orange	517110	51,644,510,208	5,891,408,896
Orange Polska SA	517110	3,153,524,480	12,605,329
Pakistan Telecommunication Company Limited	517110	840,405,824	21,251,078
PCCW Limited	517110	4,903,340,544	-131,456,848
Perusahaan Perseroan PT Telekomunikasi Indonesia Tbk (Telkom)	517110	9,574,220,800	1,477,177,856
PLDT Inc	517110	3,794,155,776	509,034,528
Proximus Group	517110	6,650,131,968	689,082,176
Rackspace Technology Inc	517110	2,707,099,904	-245,800,000
RCN Telecom Services LLC	517110	609,375,000	

Industry Group/Company	Industry Code	2020 Sales	2020 Profits
Rogers Communications Inc	517110	11,530,366,976	1,319,081,984
Rostelecom PJSC	517110	7,439,107,584	317,089,984
Shaw Communications Inc	517110	4,480,072,704	570,055,488
Shenandoah Telecommunications Company	517110	220,775,008	126,723,000
Singapore Technologies Telemedia Pte Ltd	517110	6,055,403,827	
Singapore Telecommunications Limited	517110	12,508,261,376	812,545,792
Singtel Optus Pty Limited	517110	4,768,040,000	1,570,080,000
SK Broadband Co Ltd	517110	3,411,250,000	138,446,000
SoftBank Group Corp	517110	56,488,484,864	-8,782,077,952
Spark New Zealand Limited	517110	2,602,489,344	309,716,544
Speedcast International Limited	517110	685,300,000	
Startec Global Communications Corporation	517110		
Swisscom AG	517110	12,374,858,752	1,705,723,648
Syniverse Technologies LLC	517110	896,718,154	
Tata Communications Limited	517110	2,277,820,000	-11,275,000
Tata Teleservices Limited	517110	144,655,000	-493,567,000
TDC A/S	517110	2,643,760,384	24,812,470
TDS Telecommunications LLC	517110	976,000,000	100,000,000
Tele2 AB	517110	3,212,280,832	896,157,952
Telecom Argentina SA	517110	3,186,875,136	-60,388,704
Telecom Egypt SAE	517110		
Telecom Italia SpA	517110		
Telecomunicaciones de Puerto Rico Inc	517110	926,100,000	
Telefonica Brasil SA	517110	8,374,559,744	926,369,920
Telefonica Chile SA	517110	18,561,080,000	
Telefonica de Argentina SA	517110		
Telefonica del Peru SAA	517110	1,803,670,000	-190,572,000
Telefonica SA	517110	52,629,266,432	1,932,851,200
Telefonos de Mexico SAB de CV (Telmex)	517110		
Telekom Austria AG	517110	5,453,871,616	474,563,808
Telekom Malaysia Berhad	517110	2,628,588,544	246,362,752
Telenet Group NV/SA	517110	3,146,320,128	414,060,224
Telephone and Data Systems Inc (TDS)	517110	5,224,999,936	226,000,000
Telia Company AB	517110	10,789,460,992	-2,771,702,272
Telia Lietuva AB	517110	488,943,000	68,617,100
Telkom SA SOC Limited	517110	3,128,754,688	43,831,496
Telstra Corporation Limited	517110	17,657,858,048	1,410,798,208
TELUS Corporation	517110	12,711,077,888	1,000,082,880
TOT pcl	517110		
TPG Telecom Limited	517110	3,373,816,576	574,712,192
TruConnect Communications Inc	517110	148,050,000	
True Corporation Public Company Limited	517110	4,434,715,136	33,639,156
United Online Inc	517110	189,150,000	
Verizon Communications Inc	517110	128,292,003,840	17,801,000,960
Virgin Media Business Ltd	517110	1,084,820,000	
Vocus Group Limited	517110	1,221,160,000	-122,355,000
Vonage Holdings Corp	517110		
Windstream Holdings Inc	517110	4,987,515,000	

Industry Group/Company	Industry Code	2020 Sales	2020 Profits
Wireless Communications and Radio and TV Broadcasting Equipment Manufacturing, including Cellphones (Handsets) and Internet of Things (IoT)			
Anaren Inc	334220	238,140,000	
ARC Group Worldwide Inc	334220		
Aviat Networks Inc	334220	238,642,000	257,000
Blonder Tongue Laboratories Inc	334220	16,379,000	-7,474,000
CalAmp Corp	334220	366,107,008	-79,304,000
ClearOne Inc	334220	29,069,000	505,000
Comtech Telecommunications Corp	334220	616,715,008	7,020,000
EF Johnson Technologies Inc	334220	150,491,250	
Filtronic plc	334220	24,323,292	-2,767,711
Hitachi Kokusai Electric Inc	334220	622,570,000	
InterDigital Inc	334220	358,991,008	44,801,000
L3Harris Technologies Inc	334220	18,193,999,872	1,119,000,064
Laird Connectivity	334220	1,461,474,000	
LG Electronics Inc	334220	58,120,400,000	1,896,060,000
LG Electronics USA Inc	334220	12,429,400,000	152,231,000
LM Ericsson Telephone Company (Ericsson)	334220	28,112,599,040	2,114,947,200
Loral Space & Communications Inc	334220	0	93,093,000
Lumentum Operations LLC	334220	1,678,600,000	135,500,000
Nokia Corporation	334220	26,698,270,720	-3,073,990,912
Phazar Antenna Corp	334220	13,837,500	
Potevio Corporation	334220	12,618,112,500	
Proxim Wireless Corporation	334220		
Socket Mobile Inc	334220	15,700,036	-3,278,601
Sonim Technologies Inc	334220	63,992,000	-29,932,000
Sony Mobile Communications AB	334220	3,358,360,000	-256,284,000
TCI International Inc	334220	1,449,350,000	
Telular Corporation	334220	160,875,000	
Uniden Corporation	334220	185,786,000	-4,284,380
ViaSat Inc	334220	2,309,238,016	-212,000
Viavi Solutions Inc	334220	1,136,300,032	28,700,000
Wireless Telecommunications Carriers (except Satellite)			
Advanced Info Service plc	517210	5,547,399,168	880,265,664
Altice Europe NV	517210		
America Movil SAB de CV	517210	50,943,152,128	2,347,183,616
AT&T Mexico SAU	517210	2,562,000,000	
AT&T Mobility LLC	517210	72,564,000,000	22,372,000,000
Axiata Group Berhad	517210	5,866,420,736	88,543,888
Bharti Airtel Limited	517210	11,635,100,000	4,931,780,000
Cellcom Israel Ltd	517210		
China Mobile Limited	517210		
COSMOTE Mobile Telephones SA	517210	1,494,530,000	162,988,000
Cricket Wireless LLC	517210	4,630,500,000	
Data Select Limited	517210	144,769,000	909,840
Deutsche Telekom AG	517210		
Digi.com Bhd	517210	1,491,936,640	296,064,256

Industry Group/Company	Industry Code	2020 Sales	2020 Profits
Far EasTone Telecommunications Co Ltd	517210	2,184,530,000	297,115,000
First Pacific Company Limited	517210	7,130,500,096	201,600,000
Freenet AG	517210	3,147,578,368	691,324,160
Global Telecom Holding SAE	517210	2,180,850,000	
Globe Telecom Inc	517210	3,364,766,208	389,433,664
GTT Communications Inc	517210		
Hutchison Telecommunications Hong Kong Holdings Limited	517210	585,756,224	46,525,416
Indosat Ooredoo	517210	1,856,190,000	115,872,000
Jio (Reliance Jio Infocomm Limited)	517210	8,504,180,000	734,478,000
KDDI Corporation	517210	47,831,560,192	5,842,995,200
LG Uplus Corp	517210	12,327,100,000	439,210,000
M1 Limited	517210	807,817,000	58,434,600
Millicom International Cellular SA	517210	4,172,000,000	-344,000,000
Mobilcom-Debitel GmbH	517210		
Mobile Telecommunications Company KSCP (Zain Group)	517210	5,327,040,000	681,749,000
Mobile TeleSystems PJSC	517210	6,732,276,224	835,362,304
NTT DOCOMO Inc	517210	43,150,700,000	5,485,300,000
Ooredoo QPSC	517210	7,865,600,000	387,443,000
Orange Belgium	517210	1,606,475,392	65,951,520
Partner Communications Co Ltd	517210	984,505,344	5,248,226
Purple Communications Inc	517210	160,909,875	
SK Telecom Co Ltd	517210	16,821,246,976	1,358,687,232
SmarTone Telecommunications Holdings Limited	517210	901,407,000	43,818,100
Spok Inc	517210	148,180,000	-44,225,000
Sprint Corporation	517210		
TalkTalk Telecom Group Limited	517210		
Telefonica Deutschland Holding AG	517210	9,202,424,832	400,742,848
Telenor ASA	517210	14,771,981,312	2,085,814,144
TIM SA	517210		
T-Mobile Polska SA	517210	1,784,640,000	106,857,000
T-Mobile US Inc	517210	68,396,998,656	3,064,000,000
Total Access Communication PCL	517210	2,148,911,104	163,868,256
Trilogy International Partners Inc	517210	610,299,008	-47,787,000
Turkcell Iletisim Hizmetleri AS	517210	3,383,486,720	492,587,040
United States Cellular Corporation	517210	4,036,999,936	229,000,000
Veon Ltd	517210	7,980,000,256	-349,000,000
Verio Inc	517210		
Virgin Media Limited	517210	6,963,080,000	53,358,500
Vodafone Group plc	517210	54,948,196,352	-1,124,034,816
WIND Hellas Telecommunications SA	517210	642,369,420	

ALPHABETICAL INDEX

First Pacific Company Limited
Flex Ltd
Foxconn Technology Co Ltd
Freenet AG
Frontier Communications Corporation
Fujitsu Limited
Fujitsu Network Communications Inc
Fusion Connect Inc
Garmin Ltd
GCI Liberty Inc
Gilat Satellite Networks Ltd
Global Telecom Holding SAE
Globalstar Inc
Globe Telecom Inc
GoDaddy Inc
GTT Communications Inc
Harmonic Inc
HC2 Holdings Inc
Hellenic Telecommunications Organization SA
Hello Direct Inc
Hikari Tsushin Inc
Hitachi Kokusai Electric Inc
HKT Trust and HKT Limited
HP Inc
Huawei Technologies Co Ltd
Hutchison Telecommunications Hong Kong Holdings Limited
iBasis Inc
IDT Corporation
Iliad SA
Indosat Ooredoo
Infinera Corporation
Ingram Micro Mobility
Inmarsat Global Limited
Intel Corporation
Intelsat SA
InterDigital Inc
Internap Corporation
International Business Machines Corporation (IBM)
Internet Initiative Japan Inc
Intrado Corporation
Iridium Communications Inc
ITI Limited
J2 Global Inc
Jabil Inc
Jio (Reliance Jio Infocomm Limited)
Juniper Networks Inc
KCOM Group Limited
KDDI Corporation
Koninklijke KPN NV (Royal KPN NV)
Koninklijke Philips NV (Royal Philips)
Kratos Defense & Security Solutions Inc
KT Corporation
Kyocera Corporation
L3Harris Technologies Inc
Laird Connectivity
Lattice Incorporated
LG Corporation

LG Electronics Inc
LG Electronics USA Inc
LG Uplus Corp
Liberty Global plc
LM Ericsson Telephone Company (Ericsson)
Loral Space & Communications Inc
Lumen Technologies Inc
Lumentum Operations LLC
M1 Limited
Magyar Telekom plc
Mahanagar Telephone Nigam Limited
Maroc Telecom SA
Marvell Technology Group Ltd
Maxis Berhad
McAfee Corp
Mediacom Communications Corporation
MedTel Services LLC
Megacable Holdings SAB de CV
Microsoft Corporation
Millicom International Cellular SA
MiTAC Holdings Corp
Mitel Networks Corporation
Mobilcom-Debitel GmbH
Mobile Telecommunications Company KSCP (Zain Group)
Mobile TeleSystems PJSC
Momentum Telecom
Net2Phone Inc
NETGEAR Inc
NetScout Systems Inc
Neustar Inc
Newfold Digital Inc
Nippon Telegraph and Telephone Corporation (NTT)
Nokia Corporation
Nortel Inversora SA
NTT DOCOMO Inc
O2 Czech Republic AS
Oblong Inc
Oi SA
OJSC JFSC Sistema
OneSpan Inc
OneWeb Ltd
Ooredoo QPSC
OPTERNA
Optical Cable Corporation
Orange
Orange Belgium
Orange Polska SA
Orbsat Corp
Pakistan Telecommunication Company Limited
Panasonic Corporation
Partner Communications Co Ltd
PCCW Limited
Perusahaan Perseroan PT Telekomunikasi Indonesia Tbk (Telkom)
Phazar Antenna Corp
Planet Labs Inc
Plantronics Inc

PLDT Inc
Potevio Corporation
Preformed Line Products Company
Proxim Wireless Corporation
Proximus Group
Purple Communications Inc
Qisda Corporation
Qualcomm Incorporated
Rackspace Technology Inc
RCN Telecom Services LLC
Realtime Corporation
Rogers Communications Inc
Rohde & Schwarz GmbH & Co KG
Rostelecom PJSC
Samsung Electronics Co Ltd
Sanmina Corporation
ScanSource Inc
SES SA
Shaw Communications Inc
Shenandoah Telecommunications Company
Siemens AG
Simply Inc
Singapore Technologies Telemedia Pte Ltd
Singapore Telecommunications Limited
Singtel Optus Pty Limited
Sitel Corporation
SK Broadband Co Ltd
SK Telecom Co Ltd
Skype Technologies Sarl
Slack Technologies Inc
SmarTone Telecommunications Holdings Limited
SMTC Corporation
Socket Mobile Inc
SoftBank Group Corp
Sonim Technologies Inc
Sony Mobile Communications AB
Sopra Steria Group SA
Spark New Zealand Limited
Speedcast International Limited
Spok Inc
Sprint Corporation
Startec Global Communications Corporation
Swisscom AG
Sykes Enterprises Incorporated
Syniverse Technologies LLC
TalkTalk Telecom Group Limited
Tata Communications Limited
Tata Group
Tata Teleservices Limited
TCI International Inc
TCL Technology Group Corporation
TDC A/S
TDS Telecommunications LLC
TeamViewer AG
Tektronix Inc
Tele2 AB
Telecom Argentina SA
Telecom Egypt SAE

Telecom Italia SpA
Telecomunicaciones de Puerto Rico Inc
Telefonica Brasil SA
Telefonica Chile SA
Telefonica de Argentina SA
Telefonica del Peru SAA
Telefonica Deutschland Holding AG
Telefonica SA
Telefonos de Mexico SAB de CV (Telmex)
Telekom Austria AG
Telekom Malaysia Berhad
Telenet Group NV/SA
Telenor ASA
Telephone and Data Systems Inc (TDS)
Telia Company AB
Telia Lietuva AB
Telkom SA SOC Limited
Tellabs Inc
Telstra Corporation Limited
Telular Corporation
TELUS Corporation
TESSCO Technologies Incorporated
Thuraya Telecommunications Company
TIM SA
TKH Group NV
T-Mobile Polska SA
T-Mobile US Inc
TomTom International BV
Toshiba Corporation
TOT pcl
Total Access Communication PCL
TPG Telecom Limited
Trilogy International Partners Inc
Trimble Inc
TruConnect Communications Inc
True Corporation Public Company Limited
TTEC Holdings Inc
Turkcell Iletisim Hizmetleri AS
Uniden Corporation
United Online Inc
United States Cellular Corporation
Veon Ltd
Verio Inc
VeriSign Inc
Verizon Communications Inc
ViaSat Inc
Viavi Solutions Inc
Virgin Media Business Ltd
Virgin Media Limited
Vocus Group Limited
Vodafone Group plc
Vonage Holdings Corp
VTech Holdings Limited
Westell Technologies Inc
WIND Hellas Telecommunications SA
Windstream Holdings Inc
XIUS
Zoom Video Communications Inc

INDEX OF U.S. HEADQUARTERS LOCATION BY STATE

To help you locate the firms geographically, the city and state of the headquarters of each company are in the following index.

Trimble Inc; Sunnyvale
TruConnect Communications Inc; Los Angeles
United Online Inc; Woodland Hills
ViaSat Inc; Carlsbad
Zoom Video Communications Inc; San Jose

COLORADO
EchoStar Corporation; Englewood
GCI Liberty Inc; Englewood
Oblong Inc; Conifer
TTEC Holdings Inc; Englewood

CONNECTICUT
Amphenol Corporation; Wallingford
Charter Communications Inc; Stamford
Frontier Communications Corporation; Norwalk

DELAWARE
InterDigital Inc; Wilmington

DISTRICT OF COLUMBIA
Cogent Communications Group Inc; Washington

FLORIDA
ARC Group Worldwide Inc; DeLand
Cyxtera Technologies Inc; Coral Gables
Dycom Industries Inc; Palm Beach Gardens
Hello Direct Inc; Cape Canaveral
Jabil Inc; St. Petersburg
L3Harris Technologies Inc; Melbourne
MedTel Services LLC; Palmetto
Newfold Digital Inc; Jacksonville
Orbsat Corp; Aventura
Simply Inc; Miami
Sykes Enterprises Incorporated; Tampa
Syniverse Technologies LLC; Tampa

GEORGIA
AT&T Mobility LLC; Atlanta
Cox Communications Inc; Atlanta
Cricket Wireless LLC; Atlanta
EarthLink LLC; Atlanta
Fusion Connect Inc; Atlanta
Momentum Telecom; Atlanta

ILLINOIS
Anixter International Inc; Glenview
Consolidated Communications Holdings Inc; Mattoon
OneSpan Inc; Chicago
Telephone and Data Systems Inc (TDS); Chicago
Telular Corporation; Chicago
United States Cellular Corporation; Chicago
Westell Technologies Inc; Aurora

KANSAS
Sprint Corporation; Overland Park

LOUISIANA
Lumen Technologies Inc; Monroe

MARYLAND
Ciena Corporation; Hanover
TESSCO Technologies Incorporated; Hunt Valley

MASSACHUSETTS
Akamai Technologies Inc; Cambridge
Aspect Software Inc; Westford
ATN International Inc; Beverly
Aware Inc; Bedford
iBasis Inc; Lexington
NetScout Systems Inc; Westford
Verio Inc; Burlington
XIUS; North Chelmsford

MINNESOTA
Communications Systems Inc; Minnetonka
Entrust Corporation; Shakopee

MISSOURI
Belden Inc; St. Louis

NEBRASKA
Intrado Corporation; Omaha

NEW JERSEY
Blonder Tongue Laboratories Inc; Old Bridge
Dialogic Inc; Parsippany
IDT Corporation; Newark
Lattice Incorporated; Pennsauken
LG Electronics USA Inc; Englewood Cliffs
Net2Phone Inc; Newark
RCN Telecom Services LLC; Princeton
Vonage Holdings Corp; Holmdel

NEW YORK
Altice USA Inc; Long Island City
Anaren Inc; East Syracuse
Calero-MDSL; Rochester
Comtech Telecommunications Corp; Melville
Corning Incorporated; Corning
HC2 Holdings Inc; New York
International Business Machines Corporation (IBM);
Armonk
Loral Space & Communications Inc; New York
Mediacom Communications Corporation; Middletown
OPTERNA; East Syracuse
Verizon Communications Inc; New York

NORTH CAROLINA
CommScope Holding Company Inc; Hickory

OHIO
Cincinnati Bell Inc; Cincinnati

Energy Focus Inc; Solon
Preformed Line Products Company; Mayfield Village

OREGON

Tektronix Inc; Beaverton

PENNSYLVANIA

Black Box Corporation; Lawrence
Comcast Corporation; Philadelphia

SOUTH CAROLINA

ScanSource Inc; Greenville

TENNESSEE

Sitel Corporation; Nashville

TEXAS

AT&T Inc; Dallas
Aviat Networks Inc; Austin
Brightstar Corporation; Southlake
Channell Commercial Corporation; Rockwall
EF Johnson Technologies Inc; Irving
Fujitsu Network Communications Inc; Richardson
Kratos Defense & Security Solutions Inc; Round Rock
Phazar Antenna Corp; Mineral Wells
Purple Communications Inc; Austin
Rackspace Technology Inc; San Antonio
Sonim Technologies Inc; Austin
Speedcast International Limited; Houston
Startec Global Communications Corporation; Irving
Tellabs Inc; Carrollton

UTAH

ClearOne Inc; Salt Lake City

VIRGINIA

GTT Communications Inc; McLean
Internap Corporation; Renton
Iridium Communications Inc; McLean
Neustar Inc; Reston
Optical Cable Corporation; Roanoke
Shenandoah Telecommunications Company; Edinburg
Spok Inc; Alexandria
VeriSign Inc; Reston

WASHINGTON

F5 Networks Inc; Seattle
Microsoft Corporation; Redmond
T-Mobile US Inc; Bellevue
Trilogy International Partners Inc; Bellevue

WISCONSIN

TDS Telecommunications LLC; Madison

INDEX OF NON-U.S. HEADQUARTERS LOCATION BY COUNTRY

ARGENTINA

Nortel Inversora SA; Buenos Aires
Telecom Argentina SA; Buenos Aires
Telefonica de Argentina SA; Buenos Aires

AUSTRALIA

AAPT Limited; Sydney
Singtel Optus Pty Limited; Macquarie Park
Telstra Corporation Limited; Melbourne
TPG Telecom Limited; Sydney
Vocus Group Limited; Melbourne

AUSTRIA

Telekom Austria AG; Vienna

BELGIUM

Orange Belgium; Brussels
Proximus Group; Brussels
Telenet Group NV/SA; Mechelen

BERMUDA

Marvell Technology Group Ltd; Hamilton

BRAZIL

Embratel Participacoes SA; Rio de Janeiro
Oi SA; Rio de Janeiro
Realtime Corporation; Sao Paulo
Telefonica Brasil SA; Sao Paulo
TIM SA; Rio de Janeiro

CANADA

BCE Inc (Bell Canada Enterprises); Verdun
Bell Aliant Inc; Halifax
Bell MTS Inc; Winnipeg
BlackBerry Limited; Waterloo
Celestica Inc; Toronto
Certicom Corp; Mississauga
Mitel Networks Corporation; Kanata
Rogers Communications Inc; Toronto
Shaw Communications Inc; Calgary
SMTC Corporation; Markham
TELUS Corporation; Vancouver

CHILE

Empresa Nacional de Telecommunications SA (Entel);
Santiago
Telefonica Chile SA; Santiago

CHINA

AAC Technologies Holdings Inc; Shenzhen
AsiaInfo Technologies Limited; Beijing
China Communications Services Corporation Limited;
Beijing

China Telecom Corporation Limited; Beijing
Datang Telecom Technology Co Ltd; Beijing
Huawei Technologies Co Ltd; Shenzhen
Potevio Corporation; Beijing
TCL Technology Group Corporation; Huizhou
ZTE Corporation; Shenzhen

CZECH REPUBLIC
Ceske Radiokomunikace as; Prague
O2 Czech Republic AS; Prague 4-Michle

DENMARK
TDC A/S; Copenhagen

EGYPT
Global Telecom Holding SAE; Cairo
Telecom Egypt SAE; Cairo

FINLAND
Elisa Corporation; Elisa
Nokia Corporation; Espoo

FRANCE
Bouygues SA; Paris
Eutelsat Communications SA; Paris
Iliad SA; Paris
Orange; Paris
Sopra Steria Group SA; Paris

GERMANY
Deutsche Telekom AG; Bonn
Freenet AG; Büdelsdorf
Mobilcom-Debitel GmbH; Budelsdorf
Rohde & Schwarz GmbH & Co KG; Munich
Siemens AG; Munich
TeamViewer AG; Goppingen
Telefonica Deutschland Holding AG; Munich

GREECE
COSMOTE Mobile Telephones SA; Maroussi
Hellenic Telecommunications Organization SA; Marousi
WIND Hellas Telecommunications SA; Athens

HONG KONG
Asia Satellite Telecommunications Holdings Ltd; New Territories
China Mobile Limited; Hong Kong
China Unicom (Hong Kong) Limited; Hong Kong
CK Hutchison Holdings Limited; Hong Kong
First Pacific Company Limited; Hong Kong
HKT Trust and HKT Limited; Quarry Bay
Hutchison Telecommunications Hong Kong Holdings Limited; Hong Kong
PCCW Limited; Hong Kong
SmarTone Telecommunications Holdings Limited; Kowloon

VTech Holdings Limited; Hong Kong

HUNGARY
Magyar Telekom plc; Budapest

INDIA
Bharat Sanchar Nigam Limited (BSNL); New Delhi
Bharti Airtel Limited; New Delhi
ITI Limited; Bengaluru
Jio (Reliance Jio Infocomm Limited); Ambawadi
Mahanagar Telephone Nigam Limited; New Delhi
Tata Communications Limited; Mumbai
Tata Group; Mumbai
Tata Teleservices Limited; Mumbai

INDONESIA
Indosat Ooredoo; Jakarta
Perusahaan Perseroan PT Telekomunikasi Indonesia Tbk (Telkom); Jakarta

IRELAND
eircom Limited; Dublin

ISRAEL
B Communications Ltd; Tel Aviv
Bezeq-The Israel Telecommunication Corp Ltd; Tel Aviv
Cellcom Israel Ltd; Netanya
ECI Telecom Ltd; Petah Tikva
Gilat Satellite Networks Ltd; Petah Tikva
Partner Communications Co Ltd; Rosh Ha'ayin

ITALY
FASTWEB SpA; Milan
Telecom Italia SpA; Milan

JAPAN
Anritsu Corporation; Kanagawa
Fujitsu Limited; Tokyo
Hikari Tsushin Inc; Tokyo
Hitachi Kokusai Electric Inc; Tokyo
Internet Initiative Japan Inc; Tokyo
KDDI Corporation; Tokyo
Kyocera Corporation; Kyoto
Nippon Telegraph and Telephone Corporation (NTT); Tokyo
NTT DOCOMO Inc; Tokyo
Panasonic Corporation; Osaka
SoftBank Group Corp; Tokyo
Toshiba Corporation; Tokyo
Uniden Corporation; Tokyo

KOREA
KT Corporation; Gyeonggi-do
LG Corporation; Seoul
LG Electronics Inc; Seoul
LG Uplus Corp; Seoul
Samsung Electronics Co Ltd; Suwon-si

SK Broadband Co Ltd; Seoul
SK Telecom Co Ltd; Seoul

KUWAIT
Mobile Telecommunications Company KSCP (Zain Group); Safat

LITHUANIA
Telia Lietuva AB; Vilnius

LUXEMBOURG
Intelsat SA; Luxembourg
Millicom International Cellular SA; Luxembourg
SES SA; Luxembourg
Skype Technologies Sarl; Luxembourg

MALAYSIA
Axiata Group Berhad; Kuala Lumpur
Digi.com Bhd; Selangor
Maxis Berhad; Kuala Lumpur
Telekom Malaysia Berhad; Jalan Pantai Baharu, Kuala Lumpur

MEXICO
America Movil SAB de CV; Delegacion Miguel Hidalgo
AT&T Mexico SAU; Delegacion Miguel Hidalgo
Axtel SAB de CV; Unidad San Pedro
Megacable Holdings SAB de CV; Guadalajara
Telefonos de Mexico SAB de CV (Telmex); Mexico City

MOROCCO
Maroc Telecom SA; Rabat

NEW ZEALAND
Chorus Limited; Wellington
Spark New Zealand Limited; Auckland

NORWAY
Telenor ASA; Fornebu

PAKISTAN
Pakistan Telecommunication Company Limited; Islamabad

PERU
Telefonica del Peru SAA; Lima 1

PHILIPPINES
Globe Telecom Inc; Taguig City
PLDT Inc; Makati

POLAND
Orange Polska SA; Warszawa
T-Mobile Polska SA; Warsaw

PORTUGAL
Altice Portugal SA; Lisboa

PUERTO RICO
Telecomunicaciones de Puerto Rico Inc; Guaynabo

QATAR
Ooredoo QPSC; Doha

RUSSIA
Mobile TeleSystems PJSC; Moscow
OJSC JFSC Sistema; Moscow
Rostelecom PJSC; Moscow

SINGAPORE
Flex Ltd; Singapore
M1 Limited; Singapore
Singapore Technologies Telemedia Pte Ltd; Singapore
Singapore Telecommunications Limited; Singapore

SOUTH AFRICA
Telkom SA SOC Limited; Centurion

SPAIN
Telefonica SA; Madrid

SWEDEN
LM Ericsson Telephone Company (Ericsson); Stockholm
Sony Mobile Communications AB; Lund
Tele2 AB; Stockholm
Telia Company AB; Stockholm

SWITZERLAND
Garmin Ltd; Schaffhausen
Swisscom AG; Worblaufen

TAIWAN
Accton Technology Corporation; Hsinchu
BenQ Corporation; Taipei
Chunghwa Telecom Co Ltd; Taipei City
D-Link Corporation; Taipei
Far EasTone Telecommunications Co Ltd; Taipei
Foxconn Technology Co Ltd; Tu-Cheng Dist.
MiTAC Holdings Corp; Taoyuan City
Qisda Corporation; Taoyuan

THAILAND
Advanced Info Service plc; Phayathai, Bangkok
Bangkok Cable Co Ltd; Bangkok
TOT pcl; Bangkok
Total Access Communication PCL; Bangkok
True Corporation Public Company Limited; Bangkok

THE NETHERLANDS
Altice Europe NV; Amsterdam
Koninklijke KPN NV (Royal KPN NV); Rotterdam

Koninklijke Philips NV (Royal Philips); Amsterdam
TKH Group NV; Haaksbergen
TomTom International BV; Amsterdam
Veon Ltd; Amsterdam

TURKEY
Turkcell Iletisim Hizmetleri AS; Maltepe, Istanbul

UNITED ARAB EMIRATES
Emirates Telecommunications Corporation (Etisalat); Abu Dhabi
Thuraya Telecommunications Company; Dubai

UNITED KINGDOM
Arqiva Limited; Winchester
BT Global Services plc; London
BT Group plc; London
Colt Technology Services Group Limited; London
Data Select Limited; Theale, Reading
Filtronic plc; West Yorkshire
Ingram Micro Mobility; Surrey
Inmarsat Global Limited; London
KCOM Group Limited; Hull
Laird Connectivity; Akron
Liberty Global plc; London
OneWeb Ltd; London
TalkTalk Telecom Group Limited; Salford
Virgin Media Business Ltd; Peterborough
Virgin Media Limited; London
Vodafone Group plc; Newbury

Individual Profiles
On Each Of
THE TELECOMMUNICATIONS 350

AAC Technologies Holdings Inc

www.aactechnologies.com

NAIC Code: 334310

TYPES OF BUSINESS:

Audio and Video Equipment Manufacturing
Audio Components
Manufacture
Miniaturized Solutions

BRANDS/DIVISIONS/AFFILIATES:

Ibeo Automotive Systems GmbH

GROWTH PLANS/SPECIAL FEATURES:

AAC Technologies Holdings, Inc. designs, develops and manufactures innovative miniaturized components and solutions. The company's products include speakers, receivers, microphones, haptics vibrators, radio frequency components, antennas and optical lenses. These products and solutions are found in mobile devices such as smartphones, tablets, wearables, ultrabooks, notebooks and electronic book readers. AAC Technologies' global reach includes sales offices, production bases and research and development centers throughout the world. The firm has more than 6,000 patents worldwide. In mid-2021, AAC Technologies announced an investment in Ibeo Automotive Systems GmbH, and entered into a strategic partnership with Ibeo to integrate AAC's expertise in optics and imaging into the development of Ibeo's future generation of products. Ibeo is a technology leader for light detection and ranging systems (LiDAR systems), a key requirement in the automotive industry.

CONTACTS:
Note: Officers with more than one job title may be intentionally listed here more than once.

Pan Benjamin Zhengmin, CEO
Hongjiang Zhang, Chmn.

FINANCIAL DATA:
Note: Data for latest year may not have been available at press time.

In U.S. $	2020	2019	2018	2017	2016	2015
Revenue	2,686,260,000	2,802,789,000	2,841,562,000	3,309,757,000	2,430,271,000	1,839,746,000
R&D Expense	300,947,400	269,132,100	236,989,700	260,734,200	182,686,700	134,620,400
Operating Income	211,566,400	387,357,100	668,349,600	979,873,300	730,732,900	530,749,200
Operating Margin %		.14%	.24%	.30%	.30%	.29%
SGA Expense	150,028,700	143,892,000	151,453,100	152,833,700	119,618,800	125,872,600
Net Income	236,135,100	348,296,400	594,901,100	834,481,900	630,912,800	486,922,100
Operating Cash Flow	563,042,300	602,362,200	1,064,037,000	828,592,000	754,146,000	589,321,900
Capital Expenditure	742,360,100	457,884,100	647,954,600	802,025,200	633,094,300	381,536,700
EBITDA	699,559,000	779,998,800	984,089,300	1,170,455,000	887,352,300	653,283,800
Return on Assets %		.07%	.13%	.19%	.20%	.21%
Return on Equity %		.12%	.21%	.34%	.32%	.30%
Debt to Equity		0.354	0.128	0.111	0.056	0.057

CONTACT INFORMATION:

Phone: 86 755 33972018   Fax: 86 755 33018531
Toll-Free:
Address: Blk. A, No. 6 Yuexing 3rd Rd., South Hi-Tech Indus, Shenzhen, 518057 China

STOCK TICKER/OTHER:

Stock Ticker: AACAY
Employees: 39,385
Parent Company:

Exchange: PINX
Fiscal Year Ends: 12/31

SALARIES/BONUSES:

Top Exec. Salary: $ Bonus: $
Second Exec. Salary: $ Bonus: $

OTHER THOUGHTS:

Estimated Female Officers or Directors:
Hot Spot for Advancement for Women/Minorities:

AAPT Limited

NAIC Code: 517110

www.aapt.com.au

TYPES OF BUSINESS:

Local & Long Distance Service
Internet & Broadband Service
Cloud Services
Voice & Data Services
Media Services

BRANDS/DIVISIONS/AFFILIATES:

TPG Telecom Limited

GROWTH PLANS/SPECIAL FEATURES:

AAPT Limited is the wholesale arm of TPG Telecom Limited, supplying broadband services and backhaul to small, medium, large and international internet service providers (ISPs) as well as government organizations throughout Australia. AAPT owns and operates its own carrier-grade voice, data and internet network. It comprises more than 6,835 miles of fibre optic cables and 410 exchanges, as well as Ethernet capability in over 210 of the exchanges. AAPT also provides cloud services, and broadcast and media services.

CONTACTS: *Note: Officers with more than one job title may be intentionally listed here more than once.*

David Yuile, CEO
Mark Rafferty, Dir.-Sales
Michael Edwards, Gen. Mgr.-Product & Technology
Art Cartwright, Gen. Mgr.-Customer Svc. & Sales

FINANCIAL DATA: *Note: Data for latest year may not have been available at press time.*

In U.S. $	2020	2019	2018	2017	2016	2015
Revenue						
R&D Expense						
Operating Income						
Operating Margin %						
SGA Expense						
Net Income						
Operating Cash Flow						
Capital Expenditure						
EBITDA						
Return on Assets %						
Return on Equity %						
Debt to Equity						

CONTACT INFORMATION:

Phone: 61-2-8314-1700   Fax: 61-2-9009-9999
Toll-Free:
Address: 680 George St., Sydney, NSW 2000 Australia

SALARIES/BONUSES:

Top Exec. Salary: $ Bonus: $
Second Exec. Salary: $ Bonus: $

STOCK TICKER/OTHER:

Stock Ticker: Subsidiary   Exchange:
Employees: 732   Fiscal Year Ends: 06/30
Parent Company: TPG Telecom Limited

OTHER THOUGHTS:

Estimated Female Officers or Directors:
Hot Spot for Advancement for Women/Minorities:

Accton Technology Corporation

www.accton.com

NAIC Code: 334418

TYPES OF BUSINESS:

Contract Electronics Manufacturing
Technical & Communications Outsourcing
IP Network Switches
Semiconductors & Chipsets
Wireless Hardware
Online Portal
VoIP Hardware

BRANDS/DIVISIONS/AFFILIATES:

CONTACTS: Note: Officers with more than one job title may be intentionally listed here more than once.

Edgar Masri, CEO
Meen-Ron Lin, CFO
George Tchaparian, Sr. VP-R&D
Edward Lin, Contact-News & Media Rel.
Fai-Long Kuo, Exec. VP
Kuo-Tai Choiu, Sr. VP
Fai-Long Kuo, Chmn.
Sheng-Shun Liou, VP-Logistics

GROWTH PLANS/SPECIAL FEATURES:

Accton Technology Corporation is a Taiwan-based company that researches, develops, manufactures and markets computer network system products. The company also manufactures network computers and network peripheral equipment. Accton's solutions are divided into five categories: cloud data center, carrier access, campus network, Internet of Things (IoT) integration and SD-WAN. The firm's cloud data center solution comprises high-speed, high-density, standardized OCP-compliant (open compute project) platforms, which provide an open hardware network fabric for cloud data centers. Accton has developed a full range of Top-of-Rack and spine switches that support interface speeds from 1G up to 400G. Carrier access solutions are provided to carrier, service provider and multiple system operator (MS) customers, with products ranging from passive optical networks for residential broadband access to NEBS-compliant (network equipment building system) aggregation switches and routers, as well as 3G/4G mobile and enterprise IP backhaul devices. Campus network solutions consist of flexible wired connectivity and high-density wireless access for campus and enterprise networks. IoT integration solutions cover three main areas: integrating networking protocols and developing service applications; creating a database for big data applications services; and partnership and collaboration with alliances in the IoT ecosystem. By connecting IoT demands from different communities and through virtualized, digitalized solutions, Accton aims to enhance the quality of life with all alliances. Last, SD-WAN solutions include open software-defined network platforms that provide the foundation for next-generation networks, and involve the transformation of WAN networks into SD-WANs. Accton's R&D division is continually engaged in design and development, with more than 1,000 patents related to network product design and manufacturing.

FINANCIAL DATA: Note: Data for latest year may not have been available at press time.

In U.S. $	2020	2019	2018	2017	2016	2015
Revenue	1,936,970,000	1,842,250,000	1,433,710,000	1,180,920,704	951,584,448	808,667,712
R&D Expense						
Operating Income						
Operating Margin %						
SGA Expense						
Net Income	179,555,000	164,602,000	96,409,500	82,924,760	61,170,752	38,125,688
Operating Cash Flow						
Capital Expenditure						
EBITDA						
Return on Assets %						
Return on Equity %						
Debt to Equity						

CONTACT INFORMATION:

Phone: 886 35770270   Fax: 886 35780764
Toll-Free:
Address: No.1 Creation 3rd Rd., Hsinchu Science Park, Hsinchu, 30077 Taiwan

STOCK TICKER/OTHER:

Stock Ticker: 2345   Exchange: TWSE
Employees: 5,200   Fiscal Year Ends: 12/31
Parent Company:

SALARIES/BONUSES:

Top Exec. Salary: $ Bonus: $
Second Exec. Salary: $ Bonus: $

OTHER THOUGHTS:

Estimated Female Officers or Directors:
Hot Spot for Advancement for Women/Minorities:

ADTRAN Inc

NAIC Code: 334210

www.adtran.com

TYPES OF BUSINESS:

Carrier Networks
Network Platforms
Communications Platforms
Broadband Access
Internet of Things
Cloud
Gateways
Fiber Optics

BRANDS/DIVISIONS/AFFILIATES:

CONTACTS: *Note: Officers with more than one job title may be intentionally listed here more than once.*

Thomas Stanton, CEO
Michael Foliano, CFO
Raymond Harris, Chief Information Officer
Roy Nichols, Director Emeritus
James Wilson, Senior VP, Divisional
John Neville, Senior VP, Divisional
Eduard Scheiterer, Senior VP, Divisional
Roger Shannon, Vice President, Divisional

GROWTH PLANS/SPECIAL FEATURES:

ADTRAN, Inc. is a global provider of networking and communications platforms and services, with a focus on the broadband access market. The company operates through two segments: network solutions and services and support. The network solutions segment includes hardware and software products, and the services and support segment includes services that compliment ADTRAN's product portfolio and can be utilized to support other platforms as well. The segments span across three categories: access and aggregation, offering solutions used by service providers to connect their network infrastructure to subscribers; subscriber solutions and experience, offering subscriber solutions that terminate broadband access in the home and/or business; and traditional and other products, offering prior-generation technologies, products and services. ADTRAN's platforms and services enable voice, data and video communications across a variety of network infrastructures, serving millions of end-users worldwide, including North America, Europe, Middle East, Africa and Asia-Pacific regions. Products and services include fiber optic terminals, routers, switches, gateways, Wi-Fi, Internet of Things (IoT) gateways, fiber extensions, cloud, network implementation and more.

ADTRAN offers its employees comprehensive health benefits, life and disability insurance, flexible spending accounts and a variety of employee assistance programs and incentives.

FINANCIAL DATA: *Note: Data for latest year may not have been available at press time.*

In U.S. $	2020	2019	2018	2017	2016	2015
Revenue	506,510,000	530,061,000	529,277,000	666,900,000	636,781,000	600,064,000
R&D Expense	113,287,000	126,200,000	124,547,000	130,434,000	124,804,000	129,876,000
Operating Income	-9,708,000	-37,321,000	-45,422,000	37,737,000	34,735,000	13,479,000
Operating Margin %		- .07%	- .09%	.06%	.05%	.02%
SGA Expense	113,972,000	130,288,000	124,440,000	135,489,000	131,805,000	123,542,000
Net Income	2,378,000	-52,982,000	-19,342,000	23,840,000	35,229,000	18,646,000
Operating Cash Flow	-16,518,000	-2,472,000	55,454,000	-42,379,000	42,000,000	18,547,000
Capital Expenditure	6,413,000	9,494,000	8,110,000	14,720,000	21,441,000	11,753,000
EBITDA	10,386,000	-6,495,000	-16,947,000	60,935,000	61,874,000	40,549,000
Return on Assets %		- .09%	- .03%	.04%	.05%	.03%
Return on Equity %		- .13%	- .04%	.05%	.07%	.04%
Debt to Equity			0.055	0.051	0.056	0.058

CONTACT INFORMATION:

Phone: 256 963-8000   Fax: 256 963-8004
Toll-Free: 800-923-8726
Address: 901 Explorer Blvd., Huntsville, AL 35806-2807 United States

STOCK TICKER/OTHER:

Stock Ticker: ADTN   Exchange: NAS
Employees: 1,405   Fiscal Year Ends: 12/31
Parent Company:

SALARIES/BONUSES:

Top Exec. Salary: $ Bonus: $
Second Exec. Salary: $ Bonus: $

OTHER THOUGHTS:

Estimated Female Officers or Directors:
Hot Spot for Advancement for Women/Minorities:

Advanced Info Service plc

NAIC Code: 517210

TYPES OF BUSINESS:

Cell Phone Service
Phone & Telecom Accessories Distribution
Voice & Data Networks
Internet Service
Broadcast Service
Travel Insurance

BRANDS/DIVISIONS/AFFILIATES:

GROWTH PLANS/SPECIAL FEATURES:

Advanced Info Service plc (AIS) is one of Thailand's largest mobile wireless communication providers, offering coverage to millions of subscribers. The company offers 900-2600 MHz and 26 GHz frequencies through its 2G, 3G WCDMA/HSPA+, LTE (4G and 5G) and NR (5G) networks. AIS' data is sold in time-based, volume-based and unlimited packages, and offers pre-paid services under the 1-2Call brand. Services encompass mobile, fixed broadband and digital. AIS also offers phones, tablets, connection devices and related accessories, as well as television broadcasting services and travel insurance services.

CONTACTS: *Note: Officers with more than one job title may be intentionally listed here more than once.*

Somchai Lertsutiwong, CEO
Suwimol Kaewkoon, Chief Organization Dev. Officer
Vilasinee Puddhikarant, Chief Customer Officer
Allen Lew Yoong Keong, Chmn.-Exec. Committee
Vithit Leenutaphong, Chmn.

FINANCIAL DATA: *Note: Data for latest year may not have been available at press time.*

In U.S. $	2020	2019	2018	2017	2016	2015
Revenue	5,547,399,000	5,804,199,000	5,450,036,000	5,060,701,000	4,881,918,000	4,982,238,000
R&D Expense						
Operating Income	1,210,006,000	1,323,676,000	1,286,829,000	1,295,817,000	1,263,625,000	1,616,057,000
Operating Margin %		.23%	.24%	.26%	.26%	.32%
SGA Expense	780,686,800	890,090,000	843,702,800	804,650,300	955,394,500	644,657,200
Net Income	880,265,700	1,000,756,000	952,389,600	965,068,000	983,974,100	1,256,254,000
Operating Cash Flow	2,747,526,000	2,458,680,000	2,218,177,000	2,102,564,000	1,977,650,000	1,977,456,000
Capital Expenditure	1,761,262,000	867,901,100	1,306,988,000	1,647,770,000	1,784,745,000	1,810,123,000
EBITDA	2,839,229,000	2,545,068,000	2,392,567,000	2,285,345,000	1,981,912,000	2,297,638,000
Return on Assets %		.11%	.10%	.11%	.13%	.25%
Return on Equity %		.49%	.55%	.65%	.67%	.82%
Debt to Equity		0.999	1.60	1.989	2.05	1.087

CONTACT INFORMATION:

Phone: 662-029-5000   Fax:
Toll-Free:
Address: No. 414 Phaholyothin Rd., Samsen Nai, Phayathai, Bangkok, 10400 Thailand

STOCK TICKER/OTHER:

Stock Ticker: AVIFY   Exchange: PINX
Employees: 7,914   Fiscal Year Ends: 12/31
Parent Company:

SALARIES/BONUSES:

Top Exec. Salary: $ Bonus: $
Second Exec. Salary: $ Bonus: $

OTHER THOUGHTS:

Estimated Female Officers or Directors: 4
Hot Spot for Advancement for Women/Minorities: Y

Advanced Micro Devices Inc (AMD)

NAIC Code: 334413

www.amd.com

TYPES OF BUSINESS:

Microprocessors
Semiconductors
Chipsets
Wafer Manufacturing
Multimedia Graphics

BRANDS/DIVISIONS/AFFILIATES:

AMD
ATI
Athlon
EPYC
Radeon
Ryzen
Threadripper

CONTACTS: *Note: Officers with more than one job title may be intentionally listed here more than once.*

Lisa Su, CEO
Devinder Kumar, CFO
Darla Smith, Chief Accounting Officer
Mark Papermaster, Chief Technology Officer
John Caldwell, Director
Sandeep Chennakeshu, Executive VP, Divisional
Forrest Norrod, General Manager, Divisional
Darren Grasby, Other Executive Officer
Harry Wolin, Senior VP

GROWTH PLANS/SPECIAL FEATURES:

Advanced Micro Devices, Inc. (AMD) is a global semiconductor company that provides processing products for the computing, graphics and consumer electronics markets. AMD operates through two segments. The computing and graphics segment primarily includes desktop and notebook processors and chipsets, discrete and integrated graphics processing units (GPUs), data center and professional GPUs and development services. The enterprise, embedded and semi-custom segment primarily includes server and embedded processors, semi-custom system-on-chip (SoC) products, development services and technology for game consoles. The company's x86 microprocessors are primarily offered as standalone devices or as incorporated into an accelerated processing unit (APU), chipsets, discrete/integrated GPUs and professional GPUs. A microprocessor is an integrated circuit (IC) that serves as the CPU of a computer, and generally consists of hundreds of millions or billions of transistors that process date in a serial fashion, and control other devices in the system, acting as the brain of the computer. A GPU is a programmable logic chip that helps render images, animations and video. An APU is a processing unit that integrates a CPU and a GPU onto one chip, along with other special-purpose components. This integration enhances system performance by offloading selected tasks to the best-suited component (the CPU of GPU) to optimize component use, increasing the speed of data flow via shared memory while also improving energy efficiency. AMD's server and embedded processors and semi-custom system-on-a-chip (SoC) products and technology are utilized in game consoles. AMD also license portions of its intellectual property. Trademarks of the firm include AMD, ATI, Athlon, EPYC, Radeon, Ryzen and Threadripper, as well as combinations of these. In October 2020, AMD agreed to acquire rival chip maker Xilinx Inc. for $35 billion. The planned purchase still must pass regulatory scrutiny.

FINANCIAL DATA: *Note: Data for latest year may not have been available at press time.*

In U.S. $	2020	2019	2018	2017	2016	2015
Revenue	9,763,000,000	6,731,000,000	6,475,000,000	5,329,000,000	4,272,000,000	3,991,000,000
R&D Expense	1,983,000,000	1,547,000,000	1,434,000,000	1,160,000,000	1,008,000,000	947,000,000
Operating Income	1,369,000,000	631,000,000	451,000,000	204,000,000	-382,000,000	-352,000,000
Operating Margin %		.09%	.07%	.04%	- .09%	- .09%
SGA Expense	995,000,000	750,000,000	562,000,000	511,000,000	460,000,000	482,000,000
Net Income	2,490,000,000	341,000,000	337,000,000	43,000,000	-497,000,000	-660,000,000
Operating Cash Flow	1,071,000,000	493,000,000	34,000,000	68,000,000	90,000,000	-226,000,000
Capital Expenditure	294,000,000	217,000,000	163,000,000	113,000,000	77,000,000	96,000,000
EBITDA	1,676,000,000	724,000,000	621,000,000	339,000,000	-159,000,000	-319,000,000
Return on Assets %		.06%	.08%	.01%	- .15%	- .19%
Return on Equity %		.17%	.36%	.08%	-248.50%	
Debt to Equity		0.242	0.88	2.169	3.45	

CONTACT INFORMATION:

Phone: 408 749-4000   Fax:
Toll-Free:
Address: 2485 Augustine Dr., Santa Clara, CA 95054 United States

STOCK TICKER/OTHER:

Stock Ticker: AMD
Employees: 12,600
Parent Company:

Exchange: NAS
Fiscal Year Ends: 12/31

SALARIES/BONUSES:

Top Exec. Salary: $ Bonus: $
Second Exec. Salary: $ Bonus: $

OTHER THOUGHTS:

Estimated Female Officers or Directors: 3
Hot Spot for Advancement for Women/Minorities: Y

Akamai Technologies Inc

NAIC Code: 517110

www.akamai.com

TYPES OF BUSINESS:

Online Information Service-Streaming Content
e-Business Software
Web Analytics
Online Content Distribution Support Services
Internet of Things

BRANDS/DIVISIONS/AFFILIATES:

Asavie

CONTACTS: *Note: Officers with more than one job title may be intentionally listed here more than once.*

F. Leighton, CEO
Edward McGowan, CFO
William Wheaton, Chief Strategy Officer
Frederic Salerno, Director
Robert Blumofe, Executive VP, Divisional
Aaron Ahola, Executive VP
Adam Karon, Executive VP
James Gemmell, Executive VP
Rick Mcconnell, President

GROWTH PLANS/SPECIAL FEATURES:

Akamai Technologies, Inc. provides cloud solutions for delivering, optimizing and securing content and business applications over the internet. The company's globally-distributed platform comprises more than 325,000 servers across 130+ countries. Top brands rely on Akamai to help them realize competitive advantage through agile solutions, and its intelligent edge platform surrounds everything, from the enterprise to the cloud. Its portfolio of edge security, web and mobile performance, and over-the-top (OTT) solutions is supported by customer service and 24/7/365 monitoring. In October 2020, Akamai Technologies acquired Asavie, which has a global platform that manages the security, performance and access policies for mobile and internet-connected devices. Asavie's mobile, Internet of Things (IoT) and security solutions became part of Akamai's security and personalization services product line sold to carrier partners that embed the solution within the technology bundle sold to their subscribers.

Akamai offers its employees health and dental care, time off, fitness/wellness options and more.

FINANCIAL DATA: *Note: Data for latest year may not have been available at press time.*

In U.S. $	2020	2019	2018	2017	2016	2015
Revenue	3,198,149,000	2,893,617,000	2,714,474,000	2,502,996,000	2,340,049,000	2,197,448,000
R&D Expense	269,315,000	261,365,000	246,165,000	222,434,000	167,628,000	148,591,000
Operating Income	701,674,000	577,991,000	416,052,000	394,476,000	470,923,000	468,673,000
Operating Margin %		.20%	.15%	.16%	.20%	.21%
SGA Expense	966,696,000	947,545,000	982,775,000	900,087,000	798,840,000	771,218,000
Net Income	557,054,000	478,035,000	298,373,000	218,321,000	316,132,000	321,406,000
Operating Cash Flow	1,215,000,000	1,058,304,000	1,008,327,000	800,983,000	866,298,000	764,151,000
Capital Expenditure	731,872,000	562,077,000	405,741,000	414,778,000	316,289,000	444,983,000
EBITDA	1,163,591,000	1,022,519,000	820,811,000	707,274,000	812,386,000	772,868,000
Return on Assets %		.08%	.06%	.05%	.07%	.08%
Return on Equity %		.14%	.09%	.07%	.10%	.11%
Debt to Equity		0.692	0.274	0.20	0.199	0.20

CONTACT INFORMATION:

Phone: 617 444-3000   Fax:
Toll-Free: 877-425-2624
Address: 145 Broadway, Cambridge, MA 02142 United States

STOCK TICKER/OTHER:

Stock Ticker: AKAM
Employees: 8,368
Parent Company:

Exchange: NAS
Fiscal Year Ends: 12/31

SALARIES/BONUSES:

Top Exec. Salary: $ Bonus: $
Second Exec. Salary: $ Bonus: $

OTHER THOUGHTS:

Estimated Female Officers or Directors: 4
Hot Spot for Advancement for Women/Minorities: Y

Alaska Communications Systems Group Inc

www.alaskacommunications.com

NAIC Code: 517110

TYPES OF BUSINESS:

Telecommunications Services
Local Exchange Carrier
Internet Access
Long-Distance Service

BRANDS/DIVISIONS/AFFILIATES:

ACS of Anchorage LLC
ACS of Alaska LLC
ACS of Fairbanks LLC
ACS of the Northland LLC
ACS Wireless Inc
ACS Long Distance LLC
Alaska Communications Internet LLC
TekMate LLC

CONTACTS: Note: Officers with more than one job title may be intentionally listed here more than once.

Anand Vadapalli, CEO
Laurie Butcher, CFO
William Bishop, COO
Leonard Steinberg, Secretary

GROWTH PLANS/SPECIAL FEATURES:

Alaska Communications Systems Group, Inc. (ACS) is a fiber broadband and managed information technology (IT) services provider. The firm offers technology and service-enabled customer solutions to business and wholesale customers in and out of Alaska. ACS also provides telecommunication services to consumers in very populated communities throughout the state. The company's communication network extends through significant portions of Alaska and connects to the contiguous states via ACS' two diverse undersea fiber optic cable system. ACS operates in a largely two-player terrestrial wireline market, serving an estimated statewide market share of less than 25%. ACS' business segments represent three customer categories: business and wholesale, consumer and regulatory services. The business and wholesale segment provides broadband, voice and managed IT services. The consumer segment provides broadband and voice services. The regulatory segment provides access services, high-cost support and carrier termination services. Primary subsidiaries of the firm include ACS of Anchorage, LLC; ACS of Alaska, LLC; ACS of Fairbanks, LLC; and ACS of the Northland, LLC. Other subsidiaries include: ACS Wireless, Inc; ACS Long Distance, LLC; Alaska Communications Internet, LLC; ACS Messaging, Inc.; ACS Cable Systems, LLC; Crest Communications Corporation; WCI Cable, Inc.; WCI Hillsboro, LLC; Alaska Northstar Communications, LLC; WCI Lightpoint, LLC; WorldNet Communications, Inc.; Alaska Fiber Star LLC; and TekMate, LLC.

ACS offers its employees medical insurance, retirement plans, life and disability insurance, and a variety of employee assistance programs and incentives.

FINANCIAL DATA: Note: Data for latest year may not have been available at press time.

In U.S. $	2020	2019	2018	2017	2016	2015
Revenue	240,569,000	231,694,000	232,468,000	226,905,000	226,866,000	232,817,000
R&D Expense						
Operating Income	21,686,000	22,085,000	24,404,000	18,757,000	19,830,000	-1,562,000
Operating Margin %		.10%	.10%	.08%	.09%	-.01%
SGA Expense	65,773,000	66,718,000	66,647,000	67,227,000	70,209,000	88,389,000
Net Income	-1,073,000	4,928,000	9,080,000	-6,101,000	2,386,000	12,954,000
Operating Cash Flow	57,119,000	58,815,000	56,195,000	30,406,000	37,253,000	12,581,000
Capital Expenditure	50,186,000	45,503,000	40,185,000	32,585,000	40,301,000	48,477,000
EBITDA	56,073,000	56,935,000	58,366,000	47,531,000	53,889,000	76,793,000
Return on Assets %		.01%	.02%	-.01%	.01%	.02%
Return on Equity %		.03%	.06%	-.04%	.02%	.09%
Debt to Equity		1.426	0.995	1.101	1.125	1.211

CONTACT INFORMATION:

Phone: 907 297-3000   Fax: 907 297-3100
Toll-Free:
Address: 600 Telephone Ave., Anchorage, AK 99503-6091 United States

STOCK TICKER/OTHER:

Stock Ticker: ALSK
Employees: 569
Parent Company:

Exchange: NAS
Fiscal Year Ends: 12/31

SALARIES/BONUSES:

Top Exec. Salary: $ Bonus: $
Second Exec. Salary: $ Bonus: $

OTHER THOUGHTS:

Estimated Female Officers or Directors: 3
Hot Spot for Advancement for Women/Minorities: Y

Sales, profits and employees may be estimates. Financial information, benefits and other data can change quickly and may vary from those stated here.

Altice Europe NV

NAIC Code: 517210

www.altice.net

TYPES OF BUSINESS:

Wireless Telecommunications Carriers
Telecommunications
Media
Data Technology
Live Broadcasting
Advertising Solutions
Digital Solutions
Fiber-to-the-Home

BRANDS/DIVISIONS/AFFILIATES:

Altice
Covage by SFR FTTH

GROWTH PLANS/SPECIAL FEATURES:

Altice Europe NV is a multinational fiber, broadband, telecommunications, contents and media company. Its global presence covers France, Israel, the Dominican Republic and Portugal. The firm's activities are divided into three segments: telecom, media and content, and data and advertising. The telecom segment distributes, invests and services high speed broadband. The media and content segment provides original content, high-quality TV shows and international, national and local news channels. The firm delivers live broadcast premium sports events as well as well-known media and entertainment. The data and advertising segment innovates with technology in its labs across the world; links leading brands to audiences through its premium advertising solutions; and provides enterprise digital solutions to businesses. All of the company's products are marketed under the Altice brand name. During 2020, Altice acquired Covage by SFR FTTH, expanding its fiber-to-the-home (FTTH) wholesale operations in Europe.

CONTACTS:
Note: Officers with more than one job title may be intentionally listed here more than once.

Alain Weill, CEO
Armando Pereira, COO
Malo Corbin, CFO
Patrick Drahi, Pres. of the Board

FINANCIAL DATA:
Note: Data for latest year may not have been available at press time.

In U.S. $	2020	2019	2018	2017	2016	2015
Revenue		17,383,571,456	16,747,968,512	25,401,894,912	24,498,884,608	16,109,720,576
R&D Expense						
Operating Income						
Operating Margin %						
SGA Expense						
Net Income		288,312,416	-391,113,312	-590,193,728	-1,838,505,216	-353,520,832
Operating Cash Flow						
Capital Expenditure						
EBITDA						
Return on Assets %						
Return on Equity %						
Debt to Equity						

CONTACT INFORMATION:

Phone: 41-79946 4931   Fax:
Toll-Free:
Address: Prins Bernhardplein 200, Amsterdam, 1097JB Netherlands

STOCK TICKER/OTHER:

Stock Ticker: ALLVF   Exchange: PINX
Employees: 35,328   Fiscal Year Ends:
Parent Company:

SALARIES/BONUSES:

Top Exec. Salary: $ Bonus: $
Second Exec. Salary: $ Bonus: $

OTHER THOUGHTS:

Estimated Female Officers or Directors:
Hot Spot for Advancement for Women/Minorities:

Altice Portugal SA

NAIC Code: 517110

www.telecom.pt

TYPES OF BUSINESS:

Telephony Services
Mobile Services
Cable & Satellite Television Service
Internet Services

BRANDS/DIVISIONS/AFFILIATES:

Altice NV
Altice Group
Altice
MEO
Altice Empresas
SAPO
MOCHE

CONTACTS: Note: Officers with more than one job title may be intentionally listed here more than once.

Alexandre Filipe Fonseca, CEO
Alexander Freese, COO
Alexandre Matos, CFO
Joao Teixeira, CTO

GROWTH PLANS/SPECIAL FEATURES:

Altice Portugal SA is a leading provider of telecommunications and multimedia services in Portugal. The firm develops equipment and solutions in markets such as medicine, education, culture and sports. Altice Portugal's brands include: Altice, offering telecommunications, media, content, data and advertising services, solutions and products; MEO offers telephone, interactive televisions, voice and internet services through its technological infrastructure of fiber optics; Altice Empresas offers business solutions in regards to technology and telecommunication, which are designed for small and medium enterprises, as well as for large corporations and public institutions; SAPO gathers news, shopping services, job opportunities, blogs, weather reports and more and offers the information on its digital platform; and MOCHE is a tactical brand for younger persons engaged in areas such as skateboarding, gaming and nightlife. Altice Portugal develops technology used within its branded products, including television channels with their own content, cloud file storage, payment capabilities via mobile devices, online video games, online radios, the delivery of large volumes of data, applications that allow companies to analyze large amounts of data about their consumer's behavior, a remote diagnosis and medical care tool, the monitoring of health and safety of vulnerable people, a learning management system, Gigabit passive optical network technology, extended reach of television networks to remote locations and much more. Altice Portugal, part of the Altice Group, operates as a wholly-owned subsidiary of Altice NV, a multinational telecommunications company.

FINANCIAL DATA: Note: Data for latest year may not have been available at press time.

In U.S. $	2020	2019	2018	2017	2016	2015
Revenue						
R&D Expense						
Operating Income						
Operating Margin %						
SGA Expense						
Net Income						
Operating Cash Flow						
Capital Expenditure						
EBITDA						
Return on Assets %						
Return on Equity %						
Debt to Equity						

CONTACT INFORMATION:

Phone: 351-21-500-1701   Fax: 351-21-500-0800
Toll-Free:
Address: Avenida Fontes Pereira de Melo, 40, Lisboa, 1250 -133 Portugal

STOCK TICKER/OTHER:

Stock Ticker: Subsidiary
Employees: 14
Parent Company: Altice NV

Exchange:
Fiscal Year Ends: 12/31

SALARIES/BONUSES:

Top Exec. Salary: $ Bonus: $
Second Exec. Salary: $ Bonus: $

OTHER THOUGHTS:

Estimated Female Officers or Directors:
Hot Spot for Advancement for Women/Minorities:

Altice USA Inc

NAIC Code: 517110

www.alticeusa.com

TYPES OF BUSINESS:

Cable Television Service
Professional Sports Teams
Television Programming
Communications Services
Movie Theatres
Voice Over Internet Protocol
High-Speed Internet

BRANDS/DIVISIONS/AFFILIATES:

Optimum
Suddenlink
Altice Mobile
News 12 Networks
Cheddar
i24NEWS
a4
New York Interconnect

CONTACTS: *Note: Officers with more than one job title may be intentionally listed here more than once.*

Dexter Goei, CEO
Charles Stewart, CFO
Patrick Drahi, Chairman of the Board
Layth Taki, Chief Accounting Officer
Abdelhakim Boubazine, Co-President
Colleen Schmidt, Executive VP, Divisional

GROWTH PLANS/SPECIAL FEATURES:

Altice USA, Inc. is a leading media and telecommunications firm. The company delivers broadband, video and telephone service to more than 5 million residential and business customers across 21 states through a hybrid-fiber coaxial broadband network. Through its Optimum brand, Altice serves the New York metropolitan area, and serves markets in the south-central U.S. through its Suddenlink brand. The firm also offers news programming and content, and advertising services. Altice Mobile is a full-service mobile offering. Altice is building a fiber-to-the-home (FTTH) network, which will enable the company to deliver more than 10 gigabits per second (Gbps) broadband speeds to residential and business customers. 1 Gbps broadband services are available in many areas of Altice's footprint and plans to expand it to other areas each year. Altice offers a variety of products and services to large enterprises and small- and medium-sized business customers, including broadband, telephone, networking and video services. News and advertising services are offered through: News 12 Networks, which consists of seven 24-hour local news channels in the New York metro area; Cheddar, consisting of two live networks, Cheddar Business and Cheddar News, covering business, politics, headline news, popular culture and innovative products, technologies and services; i24NEWS, consisting of three 24-hour global channels in New York, Paris and Israel, offering global news, with a focus on the Middle East and Israel; a4, an advanced advertising and data solutions entity that provides IP-authenticated cross-screen advertising solutions to local and national businesses and advertising clients; and New York Interconnect, which sells local advertising in television and digital formats. In April 2021, Altice USA acquired Morris Broadband LLC, which provides high-speed data, video and voice services to approximately 36,500 residential and business customers in western North Carolina.

FINANCIAL DATA: *Note: Data for latest year may not have been available at press time.*

In U.S. $	2020	2019	2018	2017	2016	2015
Revenue	9,894,642,000	9,760,859,000	9,566,608,000	9,326,570,000	6,017,212,000	
R&D Expense						
Operating Income	2,206,362,000	1,896,789,000	1,720,927,000	1,017,785,000	700,061,000	
Operating Margin %		.19%	.18%	.11%	.12%	
SGA Expense						
Net Income	436,183,000	138,936,000	18,833,000	1,520,031,000	-832,030,000	
Operating Cash Flow	2,980,164,000	2,554,169,000	2,508,317,000	2,001,743,000	1,184,455,000	
Capital Expenditure	1,073,955,000	1,359,421,000	1,154,173,000	993,071,000	625,647,000	
EBITDA	4,019,127,000	3,986,832,000	3,920,560,000	3,202,258,000	2,065,702,000	
Return on Assets %		.00%	.00%	.04%	-.02%	
Return on Equity %		.05%	.00%	.40%	-.41%	
Debt to Equity		10.801	6.171	3.885	11.051	

CONTACT INFORMATION:

Phone: 516 803-2300   Fax: 516 803-2273
Toll-Free:
Address: 1 Court Square West, Long Island City, NY 11101 United States

STOCK TICKER/OTHER:

Stock Ticker: ATUS   Exchange: NYS
Employees: 8,900   Fiscal Year Ends: 12/31
Parent Company: Next Alt Sarl

SALARIES/BONUSES:

Top Exec. Salary: $ Bonus: $
Second Exec. Salary: $ Bonus: $

OTHER THOUGHTS:

Estimated Female Officers or Directors: 4
Hot Spot for Advancement for Women/Minorities: Y

America Movil SAB de CV

NAIC Code: 517210

www.americamovil.com

TYPES OF BUSINESS:

Cell Phone Service
Wireless Internet
Local & Long Distance
Satellite & Cable TV

BRANDS/DIVISIONS/AFFILIATES:

Telcel
Telmex
Claro
TracFone
A1
Straight Talk
KPN

CONTACTS: Note: Officers with more than one job title may be intentionally listed here more than once.

Daniel Hajj Aboumrad, CEO
Carlos Garcia Moreno Elizondo, CFO
Patric Slim Domit, Vice Chmn.
Alejandro Cantu Jimenez, General Counsel
Salvador Cortes Gomez, COO-Mexico
Fernando Ocampo Carapia, CFO-Mexico
Juan Antonio Aguilar, CEO-Central America
Enrique Luna Roshard, CFO-Central America
Juan Carlos Archila Cabal, CEO-Colombia
Fernando Gonzalez Apango, CFO-Colombia
Carlos Slim Domit, Chmn.

GROWTH PLANS/SPECIAL FEATURES:

America Movil SAB de CV is a leading provider of integrated telecommunications services, serving 25 countries. As of June 30, 2020, the company had nearly 280 million wireless subscribers, of which the majority came from Mexico and Brazil, with other countries and regions including Colombia, the Southern Cone, the Andean Region, Central America, the Caribbean, the U.S. and Europe. America Movil's telecommunications products include wireless, fixed-line, broadband and Pay TV services. Prepaid plans represent approximately 68% of annual revenues, and fixed voice, data, broadband and IT solutions represent approximately 29%. Value-added services include internet access, messaging and other wireless entertainment and corporate services via GSM/EDGE, 3G and 4G LTE networks. America Movil offers Pay TV via cable and satellite TV subscriptions to both retail and corporate customers under a variety of plans; and the company sells video, audio and other media content delivered through the internet directly from the content provider to the viewer or end user. Subsidiary brands within the company include Telcel, Telmex, Claro, TracFone, A1, Straight Talk, and KPN, among others. In September 2020, America Movil agreed to sell its 100% interest in subsidiary TracFone Wireless, Inc. to Verizon Communications, Inc. The transaction was expected to close during 2021.

FINANCIAL DATA: Note: Data for latest year may not have been available at press time.

In U.S. $	2020	2019	2018	2017	2016	2015
Revenue	50,943,150,000	50,465,300,000	52,011,280,000	51,180,970,000	48,865,420,000	44,797,740,000
R&D Expense						
Operating Income	8,283,816,000	7,757,075,000	6,991,422,000	5,016,898,000	5,491,168,000	7,086,460,000
Operating Margin %		.15%	.13%	.10%	.11%	.16%
SGA Expense	10,627,410,000	10,820,680,000	11,381,700,000	12,055,110,000	11,427,220,000	10,196,020,000
Net Income	2,347,184,000	3,393,127,000	2,633,418,000	1,469,146,000	433,311,900	1,756,145,000
Operating Cash Flow	14,068,670,000	11,736,690,000	12,440,660,000	10,909,780,000	11,812,820,000	8,202,261,000
Capital Expenditure	6,490,340,000	7,607,117,000	7,605,839,000	6,849,471,000	7,766,261,000	7,593,368,000
EBITDA	14,111,960,000	16,423,550,000	14,877,970,000	12,770,980,000	10,642,080,000	10,790,360,000
Return on Assets %		.05%	.04%	.02%	.01%	.03%
Return on Equity %		.36%	.27%	.15%	.05%	.24%
Debt to Equity		3.315	2.769	3.328	2.993	5.02

CONTACT INFORMATION:

Phone: 52-55-2581-4449 Fax: 52-55-2581-4422
Toll-Free:
Address: Lago Zurich 245, Plaza Carso, Delegacion Miguel Hidalgo, 11529 Mexico

STOCK TICKER/OTHER:

Stock Ticker: AMOV
Employees: 186,851
Parent Company:

Exchange: NYS
Fiscal Year Ends: 12/31

SALARIES/BONUSES:

Top Exec. Salary: $ Bonus: $
Second Exec. Salary: $ Bonus: $

OTHER THOUGHTS:

Estimated Female Officers or Directors: 2
Hot Spot for Advancement for Women/Minorities:

Amphenol Corporation

NAIC Code: 335921

www.amphenol.com

TYPES OF BUSINESS:

Cables & Connectors
Fiber Optic Cable
Interconnect Systems

BRANDS/DIVISIONS/AFFILIATES:

MTS Systems Corporation

CONTACTS: *Note: Officers with more than one job title may be intentionally listed here more than once.*

Richard Norwitt, CEO
Craig Lampo, CFO
Martin Loeffler, Director
Lance DAmico, General Counsel
Zachary Raley, General Manager, Divisional
Luc Walter, General Manager, Divisional
William Doherty, General Manager, Divisional
Martin Booker, General Manager, Divisional
Richard Gu, General Manager, Divisional
David Silverman, Senior VP, Divisional
Jean-Luc Gavelle, Vice President
Dieter Ehrmanntraut, Vice President

GROWTH PLANS/SPECIAL FEATURES:

Amphenol Corporation is a leading global designer, manufacturer and marketer of electrical, electronic and fiber optic connectors, interconnect systems and coaxial and flat-ribbon cable. The company has two operating segments: interconnect products and assemblies, and cable products and solutions. Interconnect products and assemblies include connectors, which when attached to an electrical, electronic or fiber optic cable; a printed circuit board; or other device, facilitate transmission of power or signal. Value-add systems generally consist of a system of cable, flexible circuits or printed circuit boards and connectors for linking electronic equipment. The cable products and solutions segment primarily designs, manufacturers and markets cable, value-added products and components for use primarily in the broadband communications and information technology markets as well as certain applications in other markets. Amphenol's interconnect products and assemblies are intended for the following primary industry and end markets, accounting for 96% of 2020 net sales, and include automotive, broadband communications, industrial, information technology, data communications, military, mobile devices and mobile networks. Cable products and solutions account for the remaining 4% of annual net sales, with its primary markets including automotive, broadband communications, industrial, information technology, data communications and mobile networks. Amphenol has international manufacturing and assembly facilities in the Americas, Europe, Asia and Africa. In April 2021, Amphenol acquired MTS Systems Corporation, a global supplier of precision sensors.

FINANCIAL DATA: *Note: Data for latest year may not have been available at press time.*

In U.S. $	2020	2019	2018	2017	2016	2015
Revenue	8,598,900,000	8,225,400,000	8,202,000,000	7,011,300,000	6,286,400,000	5,568,700,000
R&D Expense						
Operating Income	1,649,900,000	1,644,600,000	1,695,400,000	1,431,600,000	1,241,800,000	1,110,400,000
Operating Margin %		.20%	.21%	.20%	.20%	.20%
SGA Expense	1,014,200,000	971,400,000	959,500,000	878,300,000	798,200,000	669,100,000
Net Income	1,203,400,000	1,155,000,000	1,205,000,000	650,500,000	822,900,000	763,500,000
Operating Cash Flow	1,592,000,000	1,502,300,000	1,112,700,000	1,144,200,000	1,077,600,000	1,030,500,000
Capital Expenditure	276,800,000	295,000,000	310,600,000	226,600,000	190,800,000	172,100,000
EBITDA	1,950,100,000	1,925,600,000	1,989,800,000	1,671,500,000	1,430,700,000	1,292,700,000
Return on Assets %		.11%	.12%	.07%	.10%	.11%
Return on Equity %		.27%	.30%	.17%	.24%	.25%
Debt to Equity		0.707	0.699	0.888	0.717	0.869

CONTACT INFORMATION:

Phone: 203 265-8900   Fax: 203 265-8516
Toll-Free: 877-267-4366
Address: 358 Hall Ave., Wallingford, CT 06492 United States

STOCK TICKER/OTHER:

Stock Ticker: APH   Exchange: NYS
Employees: 62,000   Fiscal Year Ends: 12/31
Parent Company:

SALARIES/BONUSES:

Top Exec. Salary: $ Bonus: $
Second Exec. Salary: $ Bonus: $

OTHER THOUGHTS:

Estimated Female Officers or Directors: 1
Hot Spot for Advancement for Women/Minorities:

Anaren Inc

www.anaren.com

NAIC Code: 334220

TYPES OF BUSINESS:

Wireless Telecommunications Components
Radio Frequency
Microwave Microelectronics
Components
Beamforming Networks
Unicircuit
Printed Circuit Board Fabrication
Ceramic Solutions

BRANDS/DIVISIONS/AFFILIATES:

TTM Technologies Inc

CONTACTS: Note: Officers with more than one job title may be intentionally listed here more than once.

Thomas T. Edman, CEO
David M. Ferrara, General Counsel
Timothy P. Ross, Pres., Space & Defense
George A. Blanton, Treas.
Gert Thygesen, Sr. VP-Tech.
Mark Burdick, Pres., Wireless Group

GROWTH PLANS/SPECIAL FEATURES:

Anaren, Inc., a subsidiary of TTM Technologies, Inc., is a global designer and manufacturer of high-frequency radio frequency (RF) and microwave microelectronics, components and assemblies. The firm's engineering expertise and products are utilized by major manufacturers around the world, which are primarily engaged in the space, defense and telecommunications sectors. Anaren's capabilities span beamforming networks, integrated RF solutions, complex build-to-print (unicircuit), high-reliability printed circuit board (PCB) fabrication, thick film substrates, low temperature co-fired ceramic (LTCC) solutions and multi-chip modules. The company's standard RF components include couplers, power dividers, baluns, and radio transceivers, as well as build-to-print complex subassemblies including beamformers, RF modules, hybrid microelectronics, ceramic substrates and more. Products that can be customized include beamforming networks, integrated RF solutions, ceramic circuits and packaging, microelectronics and high-reliability PCB. Anaren's diverse portfolio delivers innovations in design and solutions for military, satellite and telecommunications applications.

Anaren offers its employees health and wealth benefits, as well as a variety of employee assistance programs.

FINANCIAL DATA: Note: Data for latest year may not have been available at press time.

In U.S. $	2020	2019	2018	2017	2016	2015
Revenue	238,140,000	226,800,000	189,000,000	180,000,000	175,000,000	170,000,000
R&D Expense						
Operating Income						
Operating Margin %						
SGA Expense						
Net Income						
Operating Cash Flow						
Capital Expenditure						
EBITDA						
Return on Assets %						
Return on Equity %						
Debt to Equity						

CONTACT INFORMATION:

Phone: 315 432-8909   Fax: 315 432-9121
Toll-Free: 800-544-2414
Address: 6635 Kirkville Rd., East Syracuse, NY 13057 United States

STOCK TICKER/OTHER:

Stock Ticker: Subsidiary   Exchange:
Employees: 1,100   Fiscal Year Ends: 12/31
Parent Company: TTM Technologies Inc

SALARIES/BONUSES:

Top Exec. Salary: $ Bonus: $
Second Exec. Salary: $ Bonus: $

OTHER THOUGHTS:

Estimated Female Officers or Directors: 2
Hot Spot for Advancement for Women/Minorities:

Anixter International Inc

NAIC Code: 423430

TYPES OF BUSINESS:

Wire & Cable Distribution
C Class Inventory Component Distribution
Connectivity Parts Distribution

BRANDS/DIVISIONS/AFFILIATES:

WESCO International Inc

CONTACTS: *Note: Officers with more than one job title may be intentionally listed here more than once.*

William Galvin, CEO
Theodore Dosch, CFO
Rodney Smith, Executive VP, Divisional
Robert Graham, Executive VP, Divisional
William Geary, Executive VP, Divisional
Orlando McGee, Executive VP, Divisional
Justin Choi, Executive VP

GROWTH PLANS/SPECIAL FEATURES:

Anixter International, Inc. is a leading global distributor of data, voice, video and security network communication products and one of the largest North American distributors of specialty wire and cable products. With more than 300 sales and warehouse locations in over 50 countries, the firm sells nearly 600,000 products, such as transmission media (copper and fiber optic cable) and connectivity, support, supply and security surveillance products as well as C-class inventory components (small parts used in manufacturing such as nuts and bolts) to original equipment manufacturers (OEMs). These products, used to connect personal computers, peripheral equipment, mainframe equipment, security equipment and various networks to each other, are incorporated into enterprise networks, physical security networks, central switching offices, web hosting sites and remote transmission sites. In addition, Anixter provides industrial wire and cable products, including electrical and electronic wire and cable, control and instrumentation cable and coaxial cable, used in a wide variety of maintenance, repair and construction-related applications. During 2020, Anixter International was acquired by WESCO International, Inc., and ceased from public trading.

FINANCIAL DATA: *Note: Data for latest year may not have been available at press time.*

In U.S. $	2020	2019	2018	2017	2016	2015
Revenue	9,287,879,731	8,845,599,744	8,400,200,192	7,927,399,936	7,622,799,872	6,190,499,840
R&D Expense						
Operating Income						
Operating Margin %						
SGA Expense						
Net Income		262,900,000	156,300,000	109,000,000	120,500,000	127,600,000
Operating Cash Flow						
Capital Expenditure						
EBITDA						
Return on Assets %						
Return on Equity %						
Debt to Equity						

CONTACT INFORMATION:

Phone: 224-521-8000   Fax: 224-521-8100
Toll-Free: 800-323-8167
Address: 2301 Patriot Blvd., Glenview, IL 60026 United States

SALARIES/BONUSES:

Top Exec. Salary: $ Bonus: $
Second Exec. Salary: $ Bonus: $

STOCK TICKER/OTHER:

Stock Ticker: Subsidiary   Exchange:
Employees: 9,400   Fiscal Year Ends: 12/31
Parent Company: WESCO International Inc

OTHER THOUGHTS:

Estimated Female Officers or Directors: 2
Hot Spot for Advancement for Women/Minorities: Y

Anritsu Corporation

www.anritsu.com

NAIC Code: 334515

TYPES OF BUSINESS:

Test & Measurement Equipment
Communications Applications
Optical Measurement Devices
Industrial Equipment
Internet of Things

BRANDS/DIVISIONS/AFFILIATES:

CONTACTS: Note: Officers with more than one job title may be intentionally listed here more than once.

Hirokazu Hamada, CEO
Akifumi Kubota, CFO
Yoshiyuki Amano, VP-Global Sales
Takashi Sakamoto, Chief Human Resources Officer
Hanako Noda, CTO
Kenji Tanaka, Sr. Exec. VP
Frank Tiernan, Exec. VP
Fumihiro Tsukasa, Sr. VP
Junkichi Shirono, Sr. VP

GROWTH PLANS/SPECIAL FEATURES:

Anritsu Corporation develops, manufactures and sells measurement instruments and systems for a wide array of communications applications. The firm has subsidiaries and operations worldwide, which together offer products and services such as testing, measurement, components, related accessories, service assurance, food equipment, pharmaceutical equipment, optical devices and ultra-high-frequency electronic devices. Anritsu's technologies span 3G/4G/5G testing, base station testing, Bluetooth, broadband stimulus, interference/coverage mapping, common public radio interface (CPRI), Open Base Station Architecture Initiative (OBSAI), Cloud radio access network, Ethernet, FirstNet, interference hunting, Internet of Things (IoT), land mobile radio, long-term evolution (LTE), microwave components, device characterization, optical time-domain reflectometer (OTDR), passive intermodulation, remote spectrum monitoring, shockline non-linear transmission (NLTL), signal integrity, synchronous Ethernet (SyncE), TD-SCDMA, W-CDMA/HSPA/HSPA Evolution and WLAN. Industries served by Anritsu encompass automotive, avionics, aircraft manufacturing, energy, petrochemical, radar, electronic peacekeeping, satellite communications and smart grid. Anritsu is continually engaged in research and development activities to develop advanced solutions for 5G, machine-to-machine, IoT and other emerging and legacy wireline and wireless communication markets.

FINANCIAL DATA: Note: Data for latest year may not have been available at press time.

In U.S. $	2020	2019	2018	2017	2016	2015
Revenue	977,441,500	910,186,100	785,137,000	800,398,300	872,494,200	902,697,100
R&D Expense	118,500,700	106,993,200	92,754,800	99,604,550	117,085,100	118,181,100
Operating Income	159,042,100	102,718,900	44,870,450	38,669,140	53,866,460	99,403,620
Operating Margin %	.16%	.11%	.06%	.05%	.06%	.11%
SGA Expense	256,052,900	255,212,700	242,600,000	248,399,500	270,528,700	270,382,600
Net Income	121,971,300	82,114,840	26,467,450	24,969,640	34,404,030	71,913,280
Operating Cash Flow	134,447,000	111,851,900	72,570,860	84,443,760	93,110,980	69,246,440
Capital Expenditure	25,846,400	19,307,170	22,321,060	18,649,600	70,004,480	45,774,620
EBITDA	207,839,800	146,301,600	87,028,400	78,753,900	91,503,580	142,438,300
Return on Assets %	.10%	.07%	.02%	.02%	.03%	.06%
Return on Equity %	.15%	.11%	.04%	.04%	.05%	.10%
Debt to Equity	0.032	0.128	0.147	0.189	0.27	0.121

CONTACT INFORMATION:

Phone: 81-46-223-1111   Fax:
Toll-Free:
Address: 5-1-1 Onna, Atsugi-shi, Kanagawa, 243-8555 Japan

STOCK TICKER/OTHER:

Stock Ticker: AITUF
Employees: 4,336
Parent Company:

Exchange: GREY
Fiscal Year Ends: 03/31

SALARIES/BONUSES:

Top Exec. Salary: $ Bonus: $
Second Exec. Salary: $ Bonus: $

OTHER THOUGHTS:

Estimated Female Officers or Directors:
Hot Spot for Advancement for Women/Minorities:

ARC Group Worldwide Inc

www.arcw.com

NAIC Code: 334220

TYPES OF BUSINESS:

Telecommunications Equipment
Metal Injection Molding
Plastic Injection Molding
Tooling
Wireless

BRANDS/DIVISIONS/AFFILIATES:

GROWTH PLANS/SPECIAL FEATURES:

ARC Group Worldwide, Inc. is a global advanced manufacturer specializing in metal injection molding (MIM). Complementary services are also offered by ARC, and include precision metal stamping, traditional and clean room plastic injection molding, and advanced rapid and conformal tooling. The firm manufactures highly-engineered precision components for original equipment manufacturers (OEMs) in the medical and dental device, aerospace, defense and automotive industries, among others. ARC's process is highly automated, utilizing advanced robotics and automation to ensure high levels of quality and efficiency. The company's complementary services provide customers with a full suite of custom-component products. During 2021, ARC Group announced that it entered into an ownership investment into Veloxint CIF to enhance the development and commercialization of nanocrystalline metal alloy materials.

CONTACTS: Note: Officers with more than one job title may be intentionally listed here more than once.

Jedidiah Rust, CEO
Eli Davidai, Director

FINANCIAL DATA: Note: Data for latest year may not have been available at press time.

In U.S. $	2020	2019	2018	2017	2016	2015
Revenue		60,060,000	82,438,000	99,069,000	103,840,000	112,505,000
R&D Expense						
Operating Income						
Operating Margin %						
SGA Expense						
Net Income		-24,016,000	-13,180,000	-10,199,000	-2,314,000	-212,000
Operating Cash Flow						
Capital Expenditure						
EBITDA						
Return on Assets %						
Return on Equity %						
Debt to Equity						

CONTACT INFORMATION:

Phone: 386-736-4890   Fax:
Toll-Free:
Address: 810 Flightline Blvd., DeLand, FL 32724 United States

STOCK TICKER/OTHER:

Stock Ticker: ARCW   Exchange: OTC
Employees: 576   Fiscal Year Ends: 06/30
Parent Company:

SALARIES/BONUSES:

Top Exec. Salary: $ Bonus: $
Second Exec. Salary: $ Bonus: $

OTHER THOUGHTS:

Estimated Female Officers or Directors: 1
Hot Spot for Advancement for Women/Minorities:

Arqiva Limited

www.arqiva.com

NAIC Code: 517110

TYPES OF BUSINESS:

Satellite Media Distribution Services
Broadcast Infrastructure
Digital Television
Satellite Television
Radio Distribution
Smart Meter

BRANDS/DIVISIONS/AFFILIATES:

CONTACTS: Note: Officers with more than one job title may be intentionally listed here more than once.

Paul Donovan, CEO
Adrian Twyning, Chief of Operations
Sean West, CFO
Shuja Khan, CCO
Vivian Leinster, Chief People Officer
Clive White, CTO
Doug Umbers, Managing Dir.-Bus. Oper.
Wendy McMillan, Dir.-Strategy & Bus. Dev.
Michael Giles, Group Comm. Dir.
Matthew Brearley, Dir.-People & Organization
Charles Constable, Managing Dir.-Digital Platforms
Steve Holebrook, Managing Dir.-Broadcast & Media
Nicolas Ott, Managing Dir.-Gov't, Mobile & Enterprise

GROWTH PLANS/SPECIAL FEATURES:

Arqiva Limited is a broadcast and machine-to-machine (M2M) infrastructure solutions provider based in the U.K. The company's television distribution platforms include over-the-top media services, digital terrestrial television and satellite television channels and content. Its radio distribution platforms include analogue radio (FM/AM) and digital radio (DAB), with related services including coding, multiplexing, distribution, managed transmission, network access and service management. In addition, Arqiva offers smart metering products and services, offering gas, electricity and water smart metering communications across the U.K.; providing gas and electricity smart meter networks in Scotland and northern England for the Data Communications Company; and providing smart water network in partnership with Anglian Water and Thames Water, two leading water companies in the U.K. In July 2020, Arqiva sold its telecommunications infrastructure to Cellnex, including towers, pylons and masts, across the U.K. As a result of the deal, Cellnex acquired more than 7,000 cellular sites that were operated by Arqiva.

Arqiva offers apprentice, intern and graduate recrutiment progrrams.

FINANCIAL DATA: Note: Data for latest year may not have been available at press time.

In U.S. $	2020	2019	2018	2017	2016	2015
Revenue	1,112,460,000	1,268,350,000	1,281,210,000	1,223,990,000	1,185,050,000	1,347,140,000
R&D Expense						
Operating Income						
Operating Margin %						
SGA Expense						
Net Income	-397,765,000	-478,913,000	-262,503,000	-553,763,000	-334,203,000	-534,077,000
Operating Cash Flow						
Capital Expenditure						
EBITDA						
Return on Assets %						
Return on Equity %						
Debt to Equity						

CONTACT INFORMATION:

Phone: 44-1962 823434   Fax:
Toll-Free:
Address: Crawley Ct., Winchester, SO21 2QA United Kingdom

STOCK TICKER/OTHER:

Stock Ticker: Subsidiary
Employees: 1,864
Parent Company: Arqiva Holdings Limited

Exchange:
Fiscal Year Ends: 06/30

SALARIES/BONUSES:

Top Exec. Salary: $ Bonus: $
Second Exec. Salary: $ Bonus: $

OTHER THOUGHTS:

Estimated Female Officers or Directors: 1
Hot Spot for Advancement for Women/Minorities:

Asia Satellite Telecommunications Holdings Ltd www.asiasat.com

NAIC Code: 517410

TYPES OF BUSINESS:

Satellites
Satellite Services

BRANDS/DIVISIONS/AFFILIATES:

Asia Satellite Telecommunications Company Limited
AsiaSat 5
AsiaSat 6
AsiaSat 7
AsiaSat 8
AsiaSat 9

CONTACTS: *Note: Officers with more than one job title may be intentionally listed here more than once.*

Roger Tong, CEO
William Wade, Pres.
Sue Yeung, CFO
Fred Ho, VP-Technical Oper.

GROWTH PLANS/SPECIAL FEATURES:

Asia Satellite Telecommunications Holdings Ltd. is the parent company of Asia Satellite Telecommunications Company Limited (AsiaSat), a leading provider of satellite transponder capacity in Asia. The firm's satellite services connect countries across the Asia Pacific and bridge communication for over two-thirds of the world's population. The firm operates five in-orbit satellites: AsiaSat 5, AsiaSat 6, AsiaSat 7, AsiaSat 8 and AsiaSat 9. AsiaSat 5 is a Space Systems/Loral 1300 series satellite; its footprint covers more than 53 countries, including New Zealand, Japan and Russia. It also covers the Middle East and parts of Africa. Additionally, the AsiaSat 5 offers two high-power fixed Ku-band beams over East Asia and South Africa. AsiaSat 6 is a Space Systems/Loral 1300 series satellite, and carries 28 C band transponders covering southern Asia, Australia and New Zealand. AsiaSat 7 is also a Space Systems/Loral 1300 series satellite that supports a broad range of applications across its coverage area. The satellite's C-band footprint covers Central Asia, the Middle East and Australia, while its K-beam provides service to South and East Asia. AsiaSat 8 is a Space Systems/Loral 1300 series satellite, and carries 24 Ku band transponders and a Ka band payload, covering southern and south-eastern Asia, China and the Middle East. AsiaSat 9 is a Space Systems Loral 1300 satellite equipped with 28 C-band and 32 Ku-band transponders, and a Ka-band payload, covering Asia and Australia. The satellites are managed by a control center in Hong Kong, and together deliver more than 500 television and radio channels. The firm also offers applications such as broadcast, telecommunications, broadband and mobility, as well as video, streaming and hosting services.

FINANCIAL DATA: *Note: Data for latest year may not have been available at press time.*

In U.S. $	2020	2019	2018	2017	2016	2015
Revenue	205,059,460	195,294,724	185,994,976	174,686,944	163,707,664	167,492,768
R&D Expense						
Operating Income						
Operating Margin %						
SGA Expense						
Net Income		58,161,154	55,391,576	51,179,724	55,316,192	56,183,288
Operating Cash Flow						
Capital Expenditure						
EBITDA						
Return on Assets %						
Return on Equity %						
Debt to Equity						

CONTACT INFORMATION:

Phone: 852-2500-0888   Fax: 852-2500-0895
Toll-Free:
Address: 15 Dai Kwai St., Tai Po Industrial Estate, New Territories, Hong Kong Hong Kong

STOCK TICKER/OTHER:

Stock Ticker: Private
Employees: 133
Parent Company: Bowenvale Limited

Exchange:
Fiscal Year Ends: 12/31

SALARIES/BONUSES:

Top Exec. Salary: $ Bonus: $
Second Exec. Salary: $ Bonus: $

OTHER THOUGHTS:

Estimated Female Officers or Directors: 2
Hot Spot for Advancement for Women/Minorities: Y

AsiaInfo Technologies Limited

www.asiainfo.com

NAIC Code: 511210E

TYPES OF BUSINESS:

Computer Software: Network Security, Managed Access, Digital ID, Cybersecurity & Anti-Virus
Business Operation Support Systems
Business Intelligence Systems
Service and Data Applications
Network Infrastructure Services
Internet of Things
Artificial Intelligence
Big Data

BRANDS/DIVISIONS/AFFILIATES:

AISWare

GROWTH PLANS/SPECIAL FEATURES:

AsiaInfo Technologies Limited is based in Beijing and is a provider of software products, solutions and services. The company's AISWare product series is an artificial intelligence (AI) platform that enables the digital transformation of large enterprises. The AI-based platform includes solutions such as billing, big data, customer relations management, DevOps, intelligent/smart operation, Internet of Things (IoT), global AI, infrastructure foundations and 5G network intelligence. AsiaInfo's products, solutions and services offer operators and enterprises the ability to acquire new customers, promote customers, retain customers and increase business volume based on AI technology. It provides governments with public services and city management and operation services based on big data. AsiaInfo also offers management consulting services, from corporate strategy to organization, and from marketing and service to customer experience. End-to-end hardware and software integration services are provided.

CONTACTS: Note: Officers with more than one job title may be intentionally listed here more than once.

Steve Zhang, Pres.
Ying Huang, CFO
Ye Ouyang, CTO
Alex Hawker, Corp. VP
Jerry Li, VP-Bus. Mgmt. Support
Feng Liu, Gen. Mgr.-Global Delivery Svcs.
Suning Tian, Chmn.
Jason Ong, Managing Dir.-AsiaInfo Int'l Pte Ltd.

FINANCIAL DATA: Note: Data for latest year may not have been available at press time.

In U.S. $	2020	2019	2018	2017	2016	2015
Revenue	922,293,000	818,693,000	757,610,000	759,799,000	650,000,000	635,000,000
R&D Expense						
Operating Income						
Operating Margin %						
SGA Expense						
Net Income	101,422,000	58,529,100	29,688,100	51,468,900		
Operating Cash Flow						
Capital Expenditure						
EBITDA						
Return on Assets %						
Return on Equity %						
Debt to Equity						

CONTACT INFORMATION:

Phone: 86 1082166688   Fax: 86 1082166699
Toll-Free:
Address: AsianInfo Plaza East Area, #10, Xibeiwang East Rd., Beijing, 100193 China

STOCK TICKER/OTHER:

Stock Ticker: 1675
Employees: 13,216
Parent Company: CITIC Capital Partners

Exchange: Hong Kong
Fiscal Year Ends: 12/31

SALARIES/BONUSES:

Top Exec. Salary: $ Bonus: $
Second Exec. Salary: $ Bonus: $

OTHER THOUGHTS:

Estimated Female Officers or Directors:
Hot Spot for Advancement for Women/Minorities:

Aspect Software Inc

www.aspect.com

NAIC Code: 511210K

TYPES OF BUSINESS:

Software-Customer Service Request Processing
Contact Center Automation Systems
Workforce Optimization
Software Applications
Analytics
Professional Services

BRANDS/DIVISIONS/AFFILIATES:

Vector Capital
Aspect Via

CONTACTS: Note: Officers with more than one job title may be intentionally listed here more than once.

Patrick Dennis, CEO
Sherri Moyen, CFO
Michael Harris, CMO
Ed Berndt, Chief Customer Officer
Michael Regan, Sr. VP-R&D
David Funck, CTO
Stephen Beaver, General Counsel
Manish Chandak, VP-Microsoft Professional Svcs.
David Herzog, Sr. VP
Spence Mallder, Gen. Mgr.-Workforce Optimization
Chris Koziol, Pres.
Bryan Sheppeck, Exec. VP-Worldwide Sales

GROWTH PLANS/SPECIAL FEATURES:

Aspect Software, Inc. is a leading provider of contact servers for managing dynamic customer transactions across wired and wireless communication channels. The firm's products and solutions include its capabilities across both contact center and workforce optimization needs, and can be deployed in the contact center environment of choice: Aspect Unified IP, for an on-premises or hosted platform; or Aspect Via, for a cloud-neutral contact center platform. Aspect Software's contact management suite includes call center software applications that support automated and live inbound and outbound communications across voice, short instant messaging (SMS), email, chat and mobile interactions. Its workforce optimization suite provides workforce optimization applications that support both workforce productivity and employee engagement strategies, with workforce, performance and quality management solutions. The company's workforce and interaction analytics are available across these capabilities. Professional services by Aspect Software include consultancy, implementation, business intelligence optimization, workforce automation innovations and customer experience innovations. Headquartered in Boston, Massachusetts, Aspect Software has additional offices in Colorado, Florida, Georgia, Illinois and Tennessee. The company is owned by global private equity firm, Vector Capital.

Aspect Software offers its employees comprehensive health benefits, life and disability insurance, 401(k(and retirement plans, tuition reimbursement and a variety of assistance plans and programs.

FINANCIAL DATA: Note: Data for latest year may not have been available at press time.

In U.S. $	2020	2019	2018	2017	2016	2015
Revenue	505,220,625	518,175,000	493,500,000	470,000,000	468,000,000	462,000,000
R&D Expense						
Operating Income						
Operating Margin %						
SGA Expense						
Net Income						
Operating Cash Flow						
Capital Expenditure						
EBITDA						
Return on Assets %						
Return on Equity %						
Debt to Equity						

CONTACT INFORMATION:

Phone: 978-250-7900   Fax: 978-244-7410
Toll-Free: 888-412-7728
Address: 5 Technology Park Dr., Westford, MA 01886 United States

STOCK TICKER/OTHER:

Stock Ticker: Private   Exchange:
Employees: 1,911   Fiscal Year Ends: 12/31
Parent Company: Vector Capital

SALARIES/BONUSES:

Top Exec. Salary: $ Bonus: $
Second Exec. Salary: $ Bonus: $

OTHER THOUGHTS:

Estimated Female Officers or Directors: 1
Hot Spot for Advancement for Women/Minorities:

AT&T Inc

www.att.com

NAIC Code: 517110

TYPES OF BUSINESS:

Local Telephone Service
Wireless Telecommunications
Long-Distance Telephone Service
Corporate Telecom, Backbone & Wholesale Services
Internet Access
Entertainment & Television via Internet
Satellite TV
VOIP

BRANDS/DIVISIONS/AFFILIATES:

WanerMedia
Xandr
AT&T
Cricket
AT&T PREPAID
Home Box Office Inc (HBO)
Warner Bros Entertainment Inc
Vrio

CONTACTS: Note: Officers with more than one job title may be intentionally listed here more than once.

Brian Lesser, CEO, Divisional
John Stankey, CEO, Subsidiary
John Donovan, CEO, Subsidiary
Lori Lee, CEO, Subsidiary
Randall Stephenson, CEO
John Stephens, CFO
David Huntley, Chief Compliance Officer
David McAtee, General Counsel
William Blase, Senior Executive VP, Divisional

GROWTH PLANS/SPECIAL FEATURES:

AT&T, Inc. is one of the world's largest providers of diversified telecommunications services. The company and its subsidiaries offers communications, digital entertainment services and products to consumers in the U.S., Mexico and Latin America, as well as to businesses and other providers of telecommunications services worldwide. AT&T also owns and operates three regional sports networks. Services and products include wireless communications, data/broadband and internet services, digital video services, local and long-distance telephone services, telecommunications equipment, managed networking and wholesale services. The company operates through four business segments: communication, generating over 75% of operating revenues; WarnerMedia; Latin America; and Xandr. The communications segment provides mobile, broadband, video and other communications services to over 166 million U.S.-based consumers, and products and services are marketed under the AT&T, Cricket, AT&T PREPAID and DIRECTV brand names. The WanerMedia segment consists of the operations of Home Box Office, Inc. (HBO); Turner Broadcasting System, Inc. (Turner); and Warner Bros Entertainment, Inc. Together these firms create premium content, operate one of the largest TV and film studios and own a vast library of entertainment. The Latin America business provides entertainment and wireless services outside the U.S. through its Vrio segment, which provides video services in Latin America, and its Mexico segment, which provides wireless service and equipment to customers in Mexico. The Xandr segment provides advertising services using data (on an anonymous basis) from the firm's more than 170 million customer relationships to develop digital advertising that is more relevant to consumers. In November 2020, AT&T completed its sale of its wireless and wireline operations in Puerto Rico and the U.S. Virgin Islands to Liberty Latin America for $1.95 billion. The following month, the firm agreed to sell its Crunchyroll anime business to Sony's Funimation Global Group, LLC.

FINANCIAL DATA: Note: Data for latest year may not have been available at press time.

In U.S. $	2020	2019	2018	2017	2016	2015
Revenue	171,760,000,000	181,193,000,000	170,756,000,000	160,546,000,000	163,786,000,000	146,801,000,000
R&D Expense						
Operating Income	25,285,000,000	29,413,000,000	26,142,000,000	23,863,000,000	24,708,000,000	24,785,000,000
Operating Margin %		.16%	.15%	.15%	.15%	.17%
SGA Expense	38,039,000,000	39,422,000,000	36,765,000,000	34,917,000,000	36,347,000,000	32,954,000,000
Net Income	-5,176,000,000	13,903,000,000	19,370,000,000	29,450,000,000	12,976,000,000	13,345,000,000
Operating Cash Flow	43,130,000,000	48,668,000,000	43,602,000,000	39,151,000,000	39,344,000,000	35,880,000,000
Capital Expenditure	15,675,000,000	19,435,000,000	20,758,000,000	20,647,000,000	21,516,000,000	19,218,000,000
EBITDA	42,188,000,000	64,694,000,000	65,032,000,000	45,826,000,000	50,569,000,000	46,828,000,000
Return on Assets %		.03%	.04%	.07%	.03%	.04%
Return on Equity %		.08%	.12%	.22%	.11%	.13%
Debt to Equity		0.94	0.903	0.894	0.923	0.966

CONTACT INFORMATION:

Phone: 210 821-4105   Fax:
Toll-Free:
Address: 208 S. Akard St., Dallas, TX 75202 United States

STOCK TICKER/OTHER:

Stock Ticker: T
Employees: 230,000
Parent Company:

Exchange: NYS
Fiscal Year Ends: 12/31

SALARIES/BONUSES:

Top Exec. Salary: $ Bonus: $
Second Exec. Salary: $ Bonus: $

OTHER THOUGHTS:

Estimated Female Officers or Directors: 4
Hot Spot for Advancement for Women/Minorities: Y

AT&T Mexico SAU

NAIC Code: 517210

www.att.com.mx

TYPES OF BUSINESS:

Cell Phone Service
Long-Distance Service
Wireless Local Service
Paging Service
Internet Access
Data Transport Services

BRANDS/DIVISIONS/AFFILIATES:

AT&T Inc

GROWTH PLANS/SPECIAL FEATURES:

AT&T Mexico SAU is a wireless telecommunications and personal communication service (PCS) provider, as well as one of the largest telecom providers in Mexico. Services include 4G LTE, emergency codes, voicemail, sensor observation service (SOS), Google Play music, multimedia messaging service and downloadable apps. The firm's 4G LTE network covers nearly 100 million people all over Mexico, enabling users to browse, download and connect at speeds up to six-times faster than with the 3G network. In addition, the company's high-speed mobile network covers more than 400 million people and businesses in Mexico and the U.S. AT&T Mexico provides mobile phones such as Alcatel, Hisense, Huawei, Lanix, Manzana, Motorola, Samsung, among others. The firm operates as a wholly-owned subsidiary of AT&T, Inc. and has headquarters in Mexico City.

CONTACTS: *Note: Officers with more than one job title may be intentionally listed here more than once.*

Monica Aspe Bernal, CEO
Ricardo B. Salinas Pliego, Pres.
Diego Foyo, Gen. Dir.-Admin.
Francisco Borrego, Gen. Dir.-Legal
Diego Foyo, Gen. Dir.-Oper.
Joaquin Arrangoiz, Dir.-Strategic Svcs.
Tristan Canales, Gen. Dir.-Corp. Comm.
Rodrigo Pliego, Gen. Dir.-Finance
Pedro Padilla, Gen. Dir.
Gustavo Vega, Gen. Dir.-Systems & Telecommunications
Luis J. Echarte, VP-Finance Strategy & Int'l Rel.

FINANCIAL DATA: *Note: Data for latest year may not have been available at press time.*

In U.S. $	2020	2019	2018	2017	2016	2015
Revenue	2,562,000,000	2,869,000,000	2,868,000,000	2,831,000,000	2,472,000,000	1,952,000,000
R&D Expense						
Operating Income						
Operating Margin %						
SGA Expense						
Net Income		-718,000,000	-1,057,000,000	-788,000,000		
Operating Cash Flow						
Capital Expenditure						
EBITDA						
Return on Assets %						
Return on Equity %						
Debt to Equity						

CONTACT INFORMATION:

Phone: 52-55-5109-4400   Fax: 52-55-5109-5925
Toll-Free: 800-333-4321
Address: Montes Urales 460, Colonia Lomas de Chapultepec, Delegacion Miguel Hidalgo, 11000 Mexico

STOCK TICKER/OTHER:

Stock Ticker: Subsidiary
Employees: 9,522
Parent Company: AT&T Inc

Exchange:
Fiscal Year Ends: 12/31

SALARIES/BONUSES:

Top Exec. Salary: $ Bonus: $
Second Exec. Salary: $ Bonus: $

OTHER THOUGHTS:

Estimated Female Officers or Directors:
Hot Spot for Advancement for Women/Minorities:

AT&T Mobility LLC

NAIC Code: 517210

www.att.com/wireless

TYPES OF BUSINESS:
Mobile Phone and Wireless Services
Wireless Data Services
Cell Phone Services

BRANDS/DIVISIONS/AFFILIATES:
AT&T Inc
AT&T Wireless

GROWTH PLANS/SPECIAL FEATURES:
AT&T Mobility, LLC, also referred to as AT&T Wireless, is a leading wireless telecommunications service provider predominantly serving the U.S. The wholly-owned subsidiary of AT&T, Inc. provides wireless voice and data services to consumer and wholesale subscribers. AT&T Mobility offers a comprehensive range of nationwide wireless voice and data communications services in a variety of pricing plans, including postpaid and prepaid service plans. The firm provides 5G services in select locations throughout the U.S., which offers seamless connection and ultra-fast speeds at home, business or on-the-go. AT&T also offers 5G phones and devices for 5G connection and compatibility.

CONTACTS: *Note: Officers with more than one job title may be intentionally listed here more than once.*
John T. Stankey, CEO-Corporate
Ralph de la Vega, Pres.

FINANCIAL DATA: *Note: Data for latest year may not have been available at press time.*

In U.S. $	2020	2019	2018	2017	2016	2015
Revenue	72,564,000,000	71,056,000,000	70,521,000,000	70,259,000,000	72,587,000,000	73,705,000,000
R&D Expense						
Operating Income						
Operating Margin %						
SGA Expense						
Net Income	22,372,000,000	22,321,000,000	21,568,000,000	20,204,000,000	20,743,000,000	19,803,000,000
Operating Cash Flow						
Capital Expenditure						
EBITDA						
Return on Assets %						
Return on Equity %						
Debt to Equity						

CONTACT INFORMATION:
Phone: 404-236-7895   Fax:
Toll-Free:
Address: 1025 Lenox Park Blvd., Atlanta, GA 30319 United States

STOCK TICKER/OTHER:
Stock Ticker: Subsidiary
Employees: 40,000
Parent Company: AT&T Inc

Exchange:
Fiscal Year Ends: 12/31

SALARIES/BONUSES:
Top Exec. Salary: $ Bonus: $
Second Exec. Salary: $ Bonus: $

OTHER THOUGHTS:
Estimated Female Officers or Directors:
Hot Spot for Advancement for Women/Minorities:

ATN International Inc

NAIC Code: 517110

TYPES OF BUSINESS:

Wired & Wireless Telecommunications
Long Distance & International Telecom Services
Local Exchange Telecom Services
Communications Transport Services

BRANDS/DIVISIONS/AFFILIATES:

Choice
Commnet
Geoverse
Fireminds
GTT+
One
Viya
Vibrant Energy

CONTACTS: *Note: Officers with more than one job title may be intentionally listed here more than once.*

Michael Prior, CEO
Justin Benincasa, CFO
Brad Martin, Executive VP, Divisional
Mary Mabey, General Counsel
William Kreisher, Senior VP, Divisional

GROWTH PLANS/SPECIAL FEATURES:

ATN International, Inc. is a holding company that owns and operates telecommunications and renewable energy businesses in North America, India, Bermuda and the Caribbean. The firm also holds controlling positions with respect to some of its investments and minority interests in others. These investments primarily offer a product and service development component in addition to the prospect of generating returns on ATN's invested capital. ATN operates its business in three segments: U.S. telecom, international telecom and renewable energy. The U.S. telecom segment offers wireless and wireline services. Wholesale wireless voice and data roaming services are provided to national, regional, local and select international wireless carriers in rural markets in the southwest and midwest U.S. This division also provides retail wireless, wireline services and wholesale long-distance voice services to telecommunications carriers in the areas in which ATN offers wireline services. Brands within this segment include Choice, Commnet, Geoverse, Essextel, NTUA Wireless and Deploycom. The international telecom segment provides voice and data services to retail customers in Bermuda, Guyana and the U.S. Virgin Islands. International wireline services include voice and data services in Bermuda, the Cayman Islands, Guyana and the U.S. Virgin Islands, as well as video services in Bermuda, the Cayman Islands and the U.S. Virgin Islands. This segment also offers wholesale long-distance voice services to other telecommunications carriers in the countries in which ATN offers international wireline services. Brands within this segment include Fireminds, GTT+, One, Logic and Viya. Last, the renewable energy segment, in India, provides distributed generation solar power to corporate, utility and municipal customers. This division's solutions are marketed under the Vibrant Energy brand name. In mid-2021, ATN acquired Alaska Communications Systems Group, Inc., and merged it into its U.S. telecom segment.

FINANCIAL DATA: *Note: Data for latest year may not have been available at press time.*

In U.S. $	2020	2019	2018	2017	2016	2015
Revenue	455,444,000	438,722,000	451,207,000	481,193,000	457,003,000	355,369,000
R&D Expense						
Operating Income	32,393,000	19,741,000	38,505,000	61,703,000	72,009,000	82,954,000
Operating Margin %		.04%	.09%	.13%	.16%	.23%
SGA Expense	139,011,000	139,264,000	139,474,000	137,318,000	125,343,000	81,356,000
Net Income	-14,122,000	-10,806,000	19,815,000	31,488,000	12,101,000	16,940,000
Operating Cash Flow	86,284,000	87,903,000	115,865,000	145,725,000	111,656,000	139,238,000
Capital Expenditure	75,323,000	72,725,000	185,921,000	179,203,000	135,142,000	64,753,000
EBITDA	93,751,000	100,207,000	147,434,000	143,325,000	126,716,000	116,271,000
Return on Assets %		-.01%	.02%	.03%	.01%	.02%
Return on Equity %		-.02%	.03%	.05%	.02%	.02%
Debt to Equity		0.205	0.124	0.21	0.213	0.039

CONTACT INFORMATION:

Phone: 978 619-1300   Fax:
Toll-Free:
Address: 500 Cummings Ctr., Beverly, MA 01915 United States

STOCK TICKER/OTHER:

Stock Ticker: ATNI   Exchange: NAS
Employees: 1,700   Fiscal Year Ends: 12/31
Parent Company:

SALARIES/BONUSES:

Top Exec. Salary: $ Bonus: $
Second Exec. Salary: $ Bonus: $

OTHER THOUGHTS:

Estimated Female Officers or Directors: 1
Hot Spot for Advancement for Women/Minorities:

Avaya Holdings Corp

www.avaya.com

NAIC Code: 334210

TYPES OF BUSINESS:

Telecommunications Systems
Telecommunications Software
Consulting Services
Networking Systems & Software
Network Maintenance, Management & Security Services
Systems Planning & Integration
Unified Communications Systems

BRANDS/DIVISIONS/AFFILIATES:

Avaya Inc

CONTACTS: Note: Officers with more than one job title may be intentionally listed here more than once.

James Chirico, CEO
Kieran McGrath, CFO
William Watkins, Chairman of the Board
Kevin Speed, Chief Accounting Officer
Shefali Shah, Chief Administrative Officer
Gaurav Passi, President, Divisional
Edward Nalbandian, President, Divisional
Patrick OMalley, Senior VP, Divisional

GROWTH PLANS/SPECIAL FEATURES:

Avaya Holdings Corp. operates as a holding company which, through its subsidiary Avaya Inc., is a leading global provider of unified communications solutions, customer experience management and cloud services. The company's unified communications solutions include conferencing and infrastructure solutions that support real-time engagement by integrating voice, video, data, messaging, conferencing, mobility and more. Its customer experience management solution is designed with a discipline of treating customer relationships as assets in order to transform them into loyal customers via persistent conversation and consistent experience via context. This product offers an omnichannel assisted experience, an omnichannel automated experience and actionable insights. Avaya's cloud services include a subscription-based hosted service in the cloud for high-performance video conferencing, voice over internet protocol (IP), unified communications and remote collaboration. The firm's cloud solutions for partners and service providers enable them to deliver cloud services for every size enterprise, including unified communications, contact center applications and video. The solutions can integrate with other applications by using open standards, APIs and other capabilities. They can be customized for BYOD and deliver standards-based endpoint support. Its multi-tenant capabilities enable partners to optimize their infrastructure for the entire customer base. Partners include channel partners, technology partners, consultants and more.

FINANCIAL DATA: Note: Data for latest year may not have been available at press time.

In U.S. $	2020	2019	2018	2017	2016	2015
Revenue	2,873,000,000	2,887,000,000	2,887,000,000	3,272,000,000	3,702,000,000	4,081,000,000
R&D Expense	207,000,000	204,000,000	204,000,000	229,000,000	275,000,000	338,000,000
Operating Income	199,000,000	208,000,000	208,000,000	284,000,000	331,000,000	434,000,000
Operating Margin %		.07%		.09%	.09%	.11%
SGA Expense	1,013,000,000	1,001,000,000	1,001,000,000	1,282,000,000	1,413,000,000	1,432,000,000
Net Income	-680,000,000	-671,000,000	-671,000,000	-182,000,000	-730,000,000	-168,000,000
Operating Cash Flow	147,000,000	241,000,000	241,000,000	291,000,000	113,000,000	215,000,000
Capital Expenditure	98,000,000	113,000,000	113,000,000	59,000,000	96,000,000	124,000,000
EBITDA	31,000,000	11,000,000	11,000,000	374,000,000	126,000,000	725,000,000
Return on Assets %		-.09%		-.06%	-.11%	-.03%
Return on Equity %		-.40%				
Debt to Equity		2.377				

CONTACT INFORMATION:

Phone: 908-953-6000   Fax:
Toll-Free: 866-462-8292
Address: 4655 Great American Pkwy., Santa Clara, CA 95054 United States

STOCK TICKER/OTHER:

Stock Ticker: AVYA
Employees: 8,266
Parent Company:

Exchange: NYS
Fiscal Year Ends: 09/30

SALARIES/BONUSES:

Top Exec. Salary: $ Bonus: $
Second Exec. Salary: $ Bonus: $

OTHER THOUGHTS:

Estimated Female Officers or Directors: 1
Hot Spot for Advancement for Women/Minorities:

Aviat Networks Inc

www.aviatnetworks.com

NAIC Code: 334220

TYPES OF BUSINESS:

Wireless Transmission Systems
Network Management Services
Network Operations Centers

BRANDS/DIVISIONS/AFFILIATES:

GROWTH PLANS/SPECIAL FEATURES:

Aviat Networks, Inc. designs, manufactures and sells a range of wireless networking solutions and services. The company serves mobile and fixed telephone service providers, private network operators, government agencies, transportation and utility companies, public safety agencies, and broadcast system operators throughout the world. Aviat's products include microwave routers, microwave switches, split mount radio frequency (RF) units, outdoor and indoor radios, network management, antenna stabilization systems, embedded software tools, paperless chart recording, automation software and compliance solutions. Services by Aviat include assessment, network design, engineering, program and project management, network implementation, factory assembly, integration, installation, commissioning, managed network, network optimization, education and support. Based in the U.S., the firm has global offices spanning North America, Asia, Asia-Pacific, Africa, Europe, Latin America and the Middle East. More than 1 million Aviat systems have been sold into 170 countries.

CONTACTS: *Note: Officers with more than one job title may be intentionally listed here more than once.*

Michael Pangia, CEO
Walter Gallagher, CFO
Eric Chang, Chief Accounting Officer
John Mutch, Director
Shaun McFall, Senior VP, Divisional
Heinz Stumpe, Senior VP, Divisional

FINANCIAL DATA: *Note: Data for latest year may not have been available at press time.*

In U.S. $	2020	2019	2018	2017	2016	2015
Revenue	238,642,000	243,858,000	242,506,000	241,874,000	268,690,000	335,900,000
R&D Expense	19,284,000	21,111,000	19,750,000	18,684,000	20,806,000	25,400,000
Operating Income	7,427,000	2,104,000	2,596,000	-396,000	-24,991,000	-21,100,000
Operating Margin %		.01%	.01%	.00%	-.09%	-.06%
SGA Expense	57,985,000	56,055,000	58,157,000	57,184,000	65,902,000	76,000,000
Net Income	257,000	9,738,000	1,845,000	-823,000	-29,907,000	-24,700,000
Operating Cash Flow	17,493,000	2,944,000	8,209,000	9,405,000	-126,000	-9,000,000
Capital Expenditure	4,608,000	5,246,000	6,563,000	4,021,000	1,574,000	3,700,000
EBITDA	8,150,000	6,120,000	6,494,000	5,285,000	-21,791,000	-18,000,000
Return on Assets %		.06%	.01%	-.01%	-.15%	-.10%
Return on Equity %		.15%	.03%	-.02%	-.44%	-.27%
Debt to Equity						

CONTACT INFORMATION:

Phone: 408 941-7100   Fax: 512-582-4605
Toll-Free:
Address: 200 Parker Dr., Ste. C100A, Austin, TX 78728 United States

SALARIES/BONUSES:

Top Exec. Salary: $ Bonus: $
Second Exec. Salary: $ Bonus: $

STOCK TICKER/OTHER:

Stock Ticker: AVNW   Exchange: NAS
Employees: 708   Fiscal Year Ends: 07/01
Parent Company:

OTHER THOUGHTS:

Estimated Female Officers or Directors: 1
Hot Spot for Advancement for Women/Minorities:

Aware Inc

NAIC Code: 334510

www.aware.com

TYPES OF BUSINESS:

Biometric Systems
Seismic Data Storage Software
ADSL Diagnostics
Medical Imaging Software

BRANDS/DIVISIONS/AFFILIATES:

Nexa

CONTACTS: Note: Officers with more than one job title may be intentionally listed here more than once.

David Martin, CFO
Brent Johnstone, Chairman of the Board
Kevin Russell, President

GROWTH PLANS/SPECIAL FEATURES:

Aware, Inc. provides software and services to the biometrics industry. Its software products are used in government and commercial biometrics systems to identify or authenticate people. Principal government applications of biometrics include border control, visitor screening, law enforcement, national defense, secure credentialing, access control and background checks. Principal commercial applications include user authentication for login mobile devices, computers, networks and software programs; user authentication for financial transactions and purchases; physical access control to buildings; and screening and background checks for prospective employees and customers. Aware sells a broad range of software products for fingerprint, facial and iris modalities, including its Nexa line of biometric search and matching products. The company also offers a variety of software engineering services such as project planning and management; system design; software design, development, customization, configuration and testing; and software integration installation. Aware sells its biometric software products and services globally through systems integrators and original equipment manufacturers (OEMs) as well as directly to end-user customers.

The company offers employees health and life insurance as well as a 401(k) plan.

FINANCIAL DATA: Note: Data for latest year may not have been available at press time.

In U.S. $	2020	2019	2018	2017	2016	2015
Revenue	11,309,000	12,204,000	16,131,000	16,282,000	21,566,000	19,621,000
R&D Expense	9,093,000	7,928,000	7,105,000	7,769,000	6,938,000	5,800,000
Operating Income	-9,424,000	-4,178,000	312,000	228,000	5,099,000	3,872,000
Operating Margin %		-.34%	.02%	.01%	.24%	.20%
SGA Expense	10,830,000	7,193,000	7,474,000	7,410,000	7,428,000	7,442,000
Net Income	-7,614,000	-8,340,000	1,233,000	1,282,000	4,103,000	4,614,000
Operating Cash Flow	-5,274,000	-2,945,000	660,000	3,669,000	3,814,000	6,684,000
Capital Expenditure	484,000	111,000	206,000	82,000	87,000	127,000
EBITDA	-8,863,000	-3,737,000	755,000	746,000	5,721,000	4,512,000
Return on Assets %		-.13%	.02%	.02%	.07%	.08%
Return on Equity %		-.14%	.02%	.02%	.07%	.08%
Debt to Equity						

CONTACT INFORMATION:

Phone: 781 276-4000   Fax: 781 276-4001
Toll-Free:
Address: 40 Middlesex Turnpike, Bedford, MA 01730 United States

SALARIES/BONUSES:

Top Exec. Salary: $ Bonus: $
Second Exec. Salary: $ Bonus: $

STOCK TICKER/OTHER:

Stock Ticker: AWRE
Employees: 71
Parent Company:

Exchange: NAS
Fiscal Year Ends: 12/31

OTHER THOUGHTS:

Estimated Female Officers or Directors:
Hot Spot for Advancement for Women/Minorities:

Axiata Group Berhad

www.axiata.com

NAIC Code: 517210

TYPES OF BUSINESS:

Mobile Phone Service
Telecommunications Services

BRANDS/DIVISIONS/AFFILIATES:

Celcom
XL Axiata
Dialog
Robi
Boost
Aspirasi
Axiata Digital Labs
Edotco

CONTACTS: *Note: Officers with more than one job title may be intentionally listed here more than once.*

Dato Izzaddin Idris, CEO
Vivek Sood, CFO
Norlida Azmi, Chief People Officer
Anthony Rodrigo, CIO
Amandeep Singh, Head-Tech.
Tan Gim Boon, Gen. Counsel
Supun Weerasinghe, Chief Strategy Officer
Nik Hasnan Nik Abd Kadir, Chief Internal Auditor
Datin Badrunnisa Mohd Yasin Khan, Chief Talent Officer
Annis Sheikh Mohamad, Head-Corp. Dev.
Suryani Binti Hussein, Sec.
Mohamad Idham Nawawi, Chief Corp. Officer
Ghazzali Shelkh Abdul Khalid, Chmn.

GROWTH PLANS/SPECIAL FEATURES:

Axiata Group Berhad is one of the largest telecommunications providers in Asia, with approximately 150 million subscribers across nine countries. These countries include Malaysia, Indonesia, Sri Lanka, Bangladesh, Cambodia, Nepal, Myanmar, Thailand and Pakistan. Asiata comprises a diverse portfolio in mobile network, communications infrastructure and digital services, and through its subsidiaries, offers a range of innovative telecommunications products and services. The firm has controlling interests in six mobile operators whose brand names include: Celcom, in Malaysia; XL Axiata, in Indonesia; Dialog, in Sri Lanka; Robi, in Bangladesh; Smart, in Cambodia; and NCell in Napal. Axiata also encompasses four digital businesses: Boost and Aspirasi, each offering digital financial services; ADA, offering digital analytics and artificial intelligence services and solutions; and Axiata Digital Labs, offering digital consulting and related solutions. Edotco is Axiata's infrastructure company, operating in five countries to deliver telecommunications infrastructure services. Edotco also operates and manages a regional portfolio of approximately 32,800 towers.

FINANCIAL DATA: *Note: Data for latest year may not have been available at press time.*

In U.S. $	2020	2019	2018	2017	2016	2015
Revenue	5,866,421,000	5,961,036,000	5,791,896,000	5,917,168,000	5,229,241,000	4,821,402,000
R&D Expense						
Operating Income	649,035,600	975,752,900	337,293,900	821,904,200	609,906,400	774,166,800
Operating Margin %		.17%	.07%	.15%	.13%	.17%
SGA Expense	508,978,200	604,626,300	612,807,000	593,876,400	543,329,700	428,091,900
Net Income	88,543,890	353,431,100	-1,220,798,000	220,533,500	122,273,000	619,355,000
Operating Cash Flow						
Capital Expenditure	1,245,922,000	1,745,966,000	1,748,578,000	1,215,670,000	1,592,464,000	1,235,150,000
EBITDA	2,530,349,000	2,679,999,000	985,750,700	2,215,600,000	1,925,215,000	2,023,289,000
Return on Assets %		.02%	-.08%	.01%	.01%	.05%
Return on Equity %		.09%	-.24%	.04%	.02%	.12%
Debt to Equity		1.025	0.838	0.598	0.642	0.597

CONTACT INFORMATION:

Phone: 60 3-2263-8888   Fax: 60 3-2263-8822
Toll-Free:
Address: 9 Jalan Stesen Sentral 5, Kuala Lumpur Sentral, Kuala Lumpur, 50470 Malaysia

STOCK TICKER/OTHER:

Stock Ticker: AXXTF   Exchange: PINX
Employees: 12,600   Fiscal Year Ends: 12/31
Parent Company:

SALARIES/BONUSES:

Top Exec. Salary: $ Bonus: $
Second Exec. Salary: $ Bonus: $

OTHER THOUGHTS:

Estimated Female Officers or Directors: 3
Hot Spot for Advancement for Women/Minorities: Y

Axtel SAB de CV

www.axtelcorp.mx

NAIC Code: 517110

TYPES OF BUSINESS:

Wired Telecommunications Carriers
Information, Communication Technology (ICT)
Data Center Solutions

BRANDS/DIVISIONS/AFFILIATES:

GROWTH PLANS/SPECIAL FEATURES:

Axtel SAB de CV provides information and communication technology (ICT) and data center solutions and services throughout Latin America. The firm primarily serves companies and government entities, and also provides infrastructure solutions to national and foreign operators. Axtel hosts more than 27, 525 miles (44,300 km) of fiber optics, including 14,291.5 miles (23,000 km) of transportation network and 13,236 miles (21,300 km) of metropolitan rings. Through its operation centers, the company integrates functions, processes, tools and people to offer its technology, operation and administration services, solutions, equipment and infrastructure. The operations centers monitors, identifies and diagnoses network events; the administration center ensures continuity of IT services; and the security operation center designs, develops and implements security controls to mitigate risks. Axtel's help desk and systems support provide support to corporate systems.

CONTACTS: Note: Officers with more than one job title may be intentionally listed here more than once.

Rolando Zubiran Shetler, CEO
Adrian De Los Santos Escobedo, Exec. Dir.-Finance

FINANCIAL DATA: Note: Data for latest year may not have been available at press time.

In U.S. $	2020	2019	2018	2017	2016	2015
Revenue	618,999,900	640,424,100	636,204,500	777,162,200	698,220,500	487,202,200
R&D Expense						
Operating Income	38,706,640	41,945,770	20,012,520	44,453,990	31,478,520	9,210,918
Operating Margin %		.07%	.03%	.06%	.05%	.02%
SGA Expense	271,129,200	292,663,600	301,031,700	361,808,500	368,959,100	236,447,200
Net Income	18,097,860	-698,305	54,840,290	3,114,592	-180,313,200	-86,084,740
Operating Cash Flow	210,800,800	148,122,500	271,078,400	220,161,300	195,261,500	156,319,900
Capital Expenditure	107,498,800	88,272,740	93,716,860	152,729,100	207,691,100	100,767,000
EBITDA	292,168,300	227,059,000	217,123,700	291,187,600	-12,088,200	88,636,340
Return on Assets %		.00%	.04%	.00%	- .13%	- .08%
Return on Equity %		.00%	.36%	.03%	-1.10%	- .35%
Debt to Equity		4.178	4.186	7.641	8.535	3.028

CONTACT INFORMATION:

Phone: 52 8181140000   Fax:
Toll-Free:
Address: Blvd. Diaz Ordaz Km. 3.33, L-1, Unidad San Pedro, 66215 Mexico

STOCK TICKER/OTHER:

Stock Ticker: AXTLF
Employees: 4,643
Parent Company:

Exchange: GREY
Fiscal Year Ends: 12/31

SALARIES/BONUSES:

Top Exec. Salary: $ Bonus: $
Second Exec. Salary: $ Bonus: $

OTHER THOUGHTS:

Estimated Female Officers or Directors:
Hot Spot for Advancement for Women/Minorities:

Axway Inc

NAIC Code: 511210E

TYPES OF BUSINESS:

Computer Software, Network Security, Managed Access, Digital ID,
Cybersecurity & Anti-Virus
E-Mail, Firewall & Anti-Spam Software
Secure File Transfer Software
Professional Services
Security Software
Business Processing Management
Tracking Software

BRANDS/DIVISIONS/AFFILIATES:

Axway AMPLIFY

CONTACTS: *Note: Officers with more than one job title may be intentionally listed here more than once.*

Patrick Donovan, CEO
Cecile Allmacher, CFO
Dominique Fougerat, Exec. VP-Human Resources
Vince Padua, CTO
Rohit Khanna, Sr. VP-Consulting & Professional Svcs.
Pierre Pasquier, Chmn.

GROWTH PLANS/SPECIAL FEATURES:

Axway, Inc. is a leading provider of multi-enterprise solutions, serving more than 11,000 enterprises in 100 countries. Its Axway AMPLIFY platform unifies a business' employees, suppliers, partners and developers in order to create a powerful customer experience network that meets consumer demands. The platform's capabilities include analytics, application program interface (API) lifecycle management, app development, community management and integration. For IT and architects, Axway's product offers big data integration, cloud integration, identity federation, identity validation, mobility and Internet of Things (IoT). For developers, it offers cross-platform application, development, API development and DevOps. Businesses and industries served by the firm include automotive, banking/financial services, healthcare, life sciences, manufacturing, consumer packaged goods, retail, U.S. federal government and many more. Axway offers various types of support, including downloads, documentation, contact support, how-to videos, webinars, training courses, resource library, cloud consulting, API management consulting and managed file transfer consulting. Corporately headquartered in Arizona, USA, the firm has global headquarters in France, Singapore and Brazil, and offices throughout North America, Asia-Pacific, Europe and Latin America.

FINANCIAL DATA: *Note: Data for latest year may not have been available at press time.*

In U.S. $	2020	2019	2018	2017	2016	2015
Revenue	365,076,000	395,928,698	377,074,950	359,119,000	317,227,000	310,937,000
R&D Expense						
Operating Income						
Operating Margin %						
SGA Expense						
Net Income	10,413,100	11,565,164	12,581,700	5,270,600	33,187,100	30,481,900
Operating Cash Flow						
Capital Expenditure						
EBITDA						
Return on Assets %						
Return on Equity %						
Debt to Equity						

CONTACT INFORMATION:

Phone: 480-627-1800   Fax: 480-627-1801
Toll-Free: 877-564-7700
Address: 16220 N. Scottsdale Rd., Ste. 500, Scottsdale, AZ 85254
United States

STOCK TICKER/OTHER:

Stock Ticker: AXW
Employees: 1,885
Parent Company:

Exchange: Amsterdam
Fiscal Year Ends: 12/31

SALARIES/BONUSES:

Top Exec. Salary: $ Bonus: $
Second Exec. Salary: $ Bonus: $

OTHER THOUGHTS:

Estimated Female Officers or Directors:
Hot Spot for Advancement for Women/Minorities:

B Communications Ltd

www.bcommunications.co.il

NAIC Code: 517110

TYPES OF BUSINESS:
Wired Telecommunications Carriers
Telecommunications
Mobile Voice
Internet
Pay TV
Fiber Optic
Broadband

BRANDS/DIVISIONS/AFFILIATES:
Eurocom Group
Internet Gold-Golden Lines Ltd
Israeli Telecommunications Corp Ltd
Bezeq

GROWTH PLANS/SPECIAL FEATURES:
B Communications Ltd. is a holding company with a single asset, its 26.72% controlling interest in Israeli Telecommunications Corp., Ltd. (operating as Bezeq), Israel's incumbent telecommunications provider. B Communications is majority-owned by Internet Gold-Golden Lines Ltd., which itself is part of the Eurocom Group. Bezeq provides mobile voice, internet services, international long-distance services, multichannel pay TV and other services. As of mid-2021, Bezeq had approximately 1.8 million active fixed telephone lines in its portfolio, with services including basic telephone on domestic lines as well as value-added services such as voicemail, caller ID, call waiting, call forwarding and conference calling. The company has tens of thousands of fiber optic lines, and has installed over 1.6 million high-speed retail and wholesale broadband lines.

CONTACTS:
Note: Officers with more than one job title may be intentionally listed here more than once.

Tomer Raved, CEO
Itzik Tadmor, CFO
Darren Glatt, Chmn.

FINANCIAL DATA:
Note: Data for latest year may not have been available at press time.

In U.S. $	2020	2019	2018	2017	2016	2015
Revenue		2,623,707,136	2,738,892,800	2,789,779,200	2,919,057,152	2,857,061,376
R&D Expense						
Operating Income						
Operating Margin %						
SGA Expense						
Net Income		-250,646,448	-302,362,496	22,229,316	-68,315,896	60,088,416
Operating Cash Flow						
Capital Expenditure						
EBITDA						
Return on Assets %						
Return on Equity %						
Debt to Equity						

CONTACT INFORMATION:
Phone: 972-3-6796121   Fax: 972-3-6796111
Toll-Free:
Address: 144 Menachem Begin Rd., Tel Aviv, 6492102 Israel

STOCK TICKER/OTHER:
Stock Ticker: BCOM   Exchange: NAS
Employees: 10,212   Fiscal Year Ends: 12/31
Parent Company: Eurocom Group

SALARIES/BONUSES:
Top Exec. Salary: $ Bonus: $
Second Exec. Salary: $ Bonus: $

OTHER THOUGHTS:
Estimated Female Officers or Directors:
Hot Spot for Advancement for Women/Minorities:

Bangkok Cable Co Ltd

www.bangkokcable.com

NAIC Code: 331420

TYPES OF BUSINESS:

Telecommunications & Electrical Wire Manufacturing
Solar Panel Manufacturing

BRANDS/DIVISIONS/AFFILIATES:

Pongtipa Co Ltd
Indra Industrial Park Co Ltd
Bangkok Solar Power Co Ltd
Bangkok Magnet Wire Co Ltd
Bangkok Cable Ventures Co Ltd
HBC Telecom Co Ltd
Tawana Container Co Ltd
Thai Copper Rod Co Ltd

CONTACTS: *Note: Officers with more than one job title may be intentionally listed here more than once.*

Sompong Nakornsri, CEO
AthikomTongnumtago, Sr. Exec. VP
Kantika Prechaharn, Exec. Dir.
Titinan Nakornsri, Exec. Dir.

GROWTH PLANS/SPECIAL FEATURES:

Bangkok Cable Co., Ltd. (BCC), established in 1964, is a Thai manufacturer of aluminum and copper cables and wires for various applications, primarily electrical and telecommunications systems. Aluminum cables principally consist of overhead power distribution lines for low and medium voltages. Copper conductors comprise both power transmission lines for low to high voltages as well as wiring for buildings, household appliances, industrial equipment and other applications. The firm also manufactures specialty cables designed to resist threats such as fire and vermin. These specialty cables are general purpose conductors used in everything from fire alarm systems to general building wiring. BCC also manufactures several wires and cables specifically for the electronics and telecommunications markets, including coaxial cables, automobile wires, heavy-duty transmission cables and light-duty end point wires. Additionally, the company produces photovoltaic interconnection systems, which include photovoltaic cables, junction boxes and connector compliances. BCC maintains three factories, in Samut Prakan, Ban Pho and Chachoengsao, Thailand, which manufacture copper and aluminum wires and cables. Currently, BCC sells its cables domestically and exports them to countries such as India, Bangladesh, Australia and the Philippines. Cable subsidiaries include, but are not limited to: Pongtipa Co. Ltd., Indra Industrial Park Co. Ltd., Bangkok Solar Power Co. Ltd., Bangkok Magnet Wire Co. Ltd. and Bangkok Cable Ventures Co. Ltd. Joint ventures include HBC Telecom Co. Ltd., Tawana Container Co. Ltd., Thai Copper Rod Co. Ltd., Thai Refrigeration Components Co. Ltd., and Hayakawa Electronics (Thailand) Co. Ltd.

FINANCIAL DATA: *Note: Data for latest year may not have been available at press time.*

In U.S. $	2020	2019	2018	2017	2016	2015
Revenue						
R&D Expense						
Operating Income						
Operating Margin %						
SGA Expense						
Net Income						
Operating Cash Flow						
Capital Expenditure						
EBITDA						
Return on Assets %						
Return on Equity %						
Debt to Equity						

CONTACT INFORMATION:

Phone: 66-2254-4550   Fax: 66-2253-6028
Toll-Free:
Address: 187/1 Rajdamri Rd., Lumpinee, Pathumwan, Bangkok, 10330 Thailand

STOCK TICKER/OTHER:

Stock Ticker: Private   Exchange:
Employees: Fiscal Year Ends:
Parent Company:

SALARIES/BONUSES:

Top Exec. Salary: $ Bonus: $
Second Exec. Salary: $ Bonus: $

OTHER THOUGHTS:

Estimated Female Officers or Directors: 3
Hot Spot for Advancement for Women/Minorities: Y

BCE Inc (Bell Canada Enterprises)

www.bce.ca

NAIC Code: 517110

TYPES OF BUSINESS:

Telecommunication Service Provider
Telecommunications
Media
Wireless
Internet
Television Services
Retail

BRANDS/DIVISIONS/AFFILIATES:

CONTACTS: *Note: Officers with more than one job title may be intentionally listed here more than once.*

Glen LeBlanc, CFO
Blaik Kirby, Pres., Subsidiary
Gordon Nixon, Chairman of the Board
Mirko Bibic, COO
George Cope, Director
Bernard le Duc, Executive VP, Divisional
John Watson, Executive VP, Subsidiary
Stephen Howe, Executive VP, Subsidiary
Michael Cole, Executive VP, Subsidiary
Wade Oosterman, President, Divisional
Thomas Little, President, Subsidiary
Rizwan Jamal, President, Subsidiary
Randy Lennox, President, Subsidiary
Martine Turcotte, Vice Chairman, Divisional
Martine Turcotte, Vice Chairman, Divisional

GROWTH PLANS/SPECIAL FEATURES:

BCE, Inc. (which stands for Bell Canada Enterprises) is a telecommunications and media company that provides wireless, wireline, internet and television services to residential, business and wholesale customers in Canada. BCE is also one of Canada's biggest retailers. BCE's media segment provides conventional TV, specialty TV, pay TV, streaming services, digital media services, radio broadcasting services and out-of-home advertising services to customers in Canada. The wireless segment provides integrated digital wireless voice and data communications products and services to residential and business customers. The wireline segment provides data, including internet access and internet protocol television (IPTV), local telephone, long distance, satellite TV service and connectivity, as well as other communications services and products. This division also generates revenues from BCE's wholesale business, which buys and sells local telephone, long distance, data and other services from or to resellers and other carriers.

FINANCIAL DATA: *Note: Data for latest year may not have been available at press time.*

In U.S. $	2020	2019	2018	2017	2016	2015
Revenue	18,960,150,000	19,855,830,000	19,444,860,000	18,824,260,000	17,995,690,000	17,825,840,000
R&D Expense						
Operating Income	4,311,045,000	4,843,815,000	4,508,244,000	4,414,616,000	4,374,844,000	4,251,388,000
Operating Margin %		.24%	.23%	.23%	.24%	.24%
SGA Expense		-114,342,500	66,285,520			
Net Income	2,182,451,000	2,643,964,000	2,426,879,000	2,414,450,000	2,511,393,000	2,218,908,000
Operating Cash Flow	6,424,724,000	6,593,753,000	6,118,154,000	6,096,611,000	5,504,184,000	5,198,442,000
Capital Expenditure	3,552,904,000	3,304,333,000	3,336,648,000	3,342,447,000	3,125,362,000	3,447,676,000
EBITDA	7,312,122,000	8,268,291,000	7,499,378,000	7,362,664,000	7,187,008,000	6,705,610,000
Return on Assets %		.05%	.05%	.05%	.06%	.05%
Return on Equity %		.18%	.18%	.19%	.22%	.21%
Debt to Equity		1.313	1.208	1.202	1.224	1.182

CONTACT INFORMATION:

Phone: 514-870-8777   Fax: 514 766-5735
Toll-Free: 800-339-6353
Address: 1, carrefour Alexander-Graham Bell, Bldg. A, 7/Fl, Verdun, QC H3E 3B3 Canada

STOCK TICKER/OTHER:

Stock Ticker: BCE
Employees: 50,704
Parent Company:

Exchange: NYS
Fiscal Year Ends: 12/31

SALARIES/BONUSES:

Top Exec. Salary: $ Bonus: $
Second Exec. Salary: $ Bonus: $

OTHER THOUGHTS:

Estimated Female Officers or Directors: 4
Hot Spot for Advancement for Women/Minorities: Y

Belden Inc

NAIC Code: 334417

www.belden.com

TYPES OF BUSINESS:
Cable & Wire Connectors Manufacturing
Electronic Products
Broadcasting Equipment
Aerospace & Automotive Electronics
Enclosures

BRANDS/DIVISIONS/AFFILIATES:
OTN Systems NV

CONTACTS: Note: Officers with more than one job title may be intentionally listed here more than once.
John Stroup, CEO
Doug Zink, Chief Accounting Officer
Henk Derksen, CFO
Douglas Zink, Chief Accounting Officer
Dhrupad Trivedi, Chief Technology Officer
Roel Vestjens, Executive VP, Divisional
Glenn Pennycook, Executive VP, Divisional
Brian Anderson, General Counsel
Dean McKenna, Senior VP, Divisional
Ross Rosenberg, Senior VP, Divisional
Leo Kulmaczewski, Senior VP, Divisional
Paul Turner, Senior VP, Divisional

GROWTH PLANS/SPECIAL FEATURES:
Belden, Inc. is an innovative signal transmission solutions company operating through two business segments: enterprise solutions and industrial solutions. Enterprise solutions provides in-network infrastructure solutions, as well as cabling and connectivity solutions for broadcast, commercial audio/video and security applications. This division serves customers in markets such as healthcare, education, financial, government and corporate enterprises, as well as end-markets, including sport venues, broadcast studios and academic campuses and facilities. Enterprise product lines include copper cable and related connectivity solutions, fiber cable and related connectivity solutions, and racks and enclosures. These products are used in applications such as local area networks, data centers, access control and building automation. The industrial solutions segment provides high-performance networking components and machine connectivity products. These products include physical network and fieldbus infrastructure components and on-machine connectivity systems customized to end-user and original equipment manufacturer (OEM) needs. They are used in applications such as network and fieldbus infrastructure, sensor and actuator connectivity; and power, control and data transmission. Belden has manufacturing facilities in the U.S., and manufacturing and other operating facilities in Brazil, Canada, China, India, Japan, Mexico and St. Kitts, as well as in various countries in Europe. Approximately 45% of the firm's 2020 sales were to customers outside the U.S. In February 2020, Belden announced the signing of a definitive agreement to sell its live media business (Grass Valley) to Black Dragon Capital, a private equity firm with a focus on technology investment opportunities in disrupted industries. In early-2021, Belden acquired OTN Systems NV, a Belgium-based provider of automation networking infrastructure solutions..

FINANCIAL DATA: Note: Data for latest year may not have been available at press time.

In U.S. $	2020	2019	2018	2017	2016	2015
Revenue	1,862,716,000	2,131,278,000	2,585,368,000	2,388,643,000	2,356,672,000	2,309,222,000
R&D Expense	107,296,000	94,360,000	140,585,000	134,330,000	140,601,000	148,311,000
Operating Income	125,410,000	207,207,000	243,080,000	234,690,000	247,784,000	138,783,000
Operating Margin %		.10%	.09%	.10%	.11%	.06%
SGA Expense	366,188,000	417,329,000	525,918,000	461,022,000	494,224,000	527,288,000
Net Income	-55,162,000	-377,015,000	160,894,000	93,210,000	128,003,000	66,204,000
Operating Cash Flow	173,364,000	276,893,000	289,220,000	255,300,000	314,794,000	236,410,000
Capital Expenditure	90,215,000	110,002,000	97,847,000	64,261,000	53,974,000	54,969,000
EBITDA	233,702,000	347,483,000	430,521,000	331,899,000	367,104,000	290,895,000
Return on Assets %		-.11%	.03%	.02%	.03%	.02%
Return on Equity %		-.34%	.09%	.04%	.10%	.08%
Debt to Equity		1.558	1.055	1.088	1.109	2.124

CONTACT INFORMATION:
Phone: 314 854-8000   Fax: 314 854-8001
Toll-Free: 800-235-3361
Address: 1 N. Brentwood Blvd., 15/Fl, St. Louis, MO 63105 United States

STOCK TICKER/OTHER:
Stock Ticker: BDC   Exchange: NYS
Employees: 7,000   Fiscal Year Ends: 12/31
Parent Company:

SALARIES/BONUSES:
Top Exec. Salary: $ Bonus: $
Second Exec. Salary: $ Bonus: $

OTHER THOUGHTS:
Estimated Female Officers or Directors: 2
Hot Spot for Advancement for Women/Minorities: Y

Belkin International Inc

www.belkin.com

NAIC Code: 334118

TYPES OF BUSINESS:
Keyboards & Mouse Devices, Computer Peripheral Equipment, Manufacturing
Computer & Networking Accessories
Cables
Adapters
USB Devices
Power Supplies
MP3 Accessories
Energy Conservation

BRANDS/DIVISIONS/AFFILIATES:
Hon Hai Precision Industry Co Ltd
Foxconn Interconnect Technology Limited
Belkin
WeMo

CONTACTS: Note: Officers with more than one job title may be intentionally listed here more than once.
Steve Malony, CEO
Mark Reynoso, Pres.
Romain Cholat, Managing Dir.-Europe Region
Gary Tubb, Managing Dir.-U.K. & Ireland & OEM in EMEA
Chet Pipkin, Chmn.

GROWTH PLANS/SPECIAL FEATURES:
Belkin International, Inc. is a leading designer, manufacturer and supplier of accessories for consumer computers, electronics, phones and mobile products. The company's primary brands include Belkin and WeMo. Products include screen protectors, wireless chargers, speakers, headphones, USB accessories, power banks, cables, cases, armbands, in-car devices and accessories, lightning accessories, mobile accessories, smartwatch accessories, tablet keyboards, tablet cases, smart home, Internet of Things (IoT), networking and more. Belkin's solutions span health, work from home, connect from home, charging smart devices, charging mobile devices and phone protection. Products, solutions and services for businesses include docks, hubs, adapters, cables, keyboards, mice, wrist pads, surge protectors, power strips, multi-device charging, desktop accessories, wireless charging, cyber security, classroom accessories, and more. Based in California, USA, Belkin International has worldwide offices throughout the Americas, Europe, Asia, the Middle East, Australia and New Zealand. Belkin International is privately-held by Foxconn Interconnect Technology Limited, itself a subsidiary of Hon Hai Precision Industry Co., Ltd.

FINANCIAL DATA: Note: Data for latest year may not have been available at press time.

In U.S. $	2020	2019	2018	2017	2016	2015
Revenue	1,842,001,875	1,797,075,000	1,711,500,000	1,630,000,000	1,610,000,000	1,590,000,000
R&D Expense						
Operating Income						
Operating Margin %						
SGA Expense						
Net Income						
Operating Cash Flow						
Capital Expenditure						
EBITDA						
Return on Assets %						
Return on Equity %						
Debt to Equity						

CONTACT INFORMATION:
Phone: 310-751-5100   Fax:
Toll-Free: 800-223-5546
Address: 12045 Waterfront Dr., Playa Vista, CA 90094 United States

STOCK TICKER/OTHER:
Stock Ticker: Subsidiary   Exchange:
Employees: 1,450   Fiscal Year Ends: 12/31
Parent Company: Hon Hai Precision Industry Co Ltd

SALARIES/BONUSES:
Top Exec. Salary: $ Bonus: $
Second Exec. Salary: $ Bonus: $

OTHER THOUGHTS:
Estimated Female Officers or Directors:
Hot Spot for Advancement for Women/Minorities:

Bell Aliant Inc

NAIC Code: 517110

aliant.bell.ca

TYPES OF BUSINESS:

Telecommunications Services
Local, Long-Distance & Cellular Services
System Integration & Software Engineering
Infrastructure Services
IT Consulting & Services
Fiber Optic Cable & Satellite TV Service
Internet Service

BRANDS/DIVISIONS/AFFILIATES:

BCE Inc (Bell Canada Enterprises)
Bell
Bell Aliant

GROWTH PLANS/SPECIAL FEATURES:

Bell Aliant, Inc. provides regional telecommunications services to residential and business customers in the Atlantic region of Canada, including Ontario and Quebec. The company's communications services are offered under the Bell and Bell Aliant brands, and consist of fiber-based internet protocol television (IPTV) and high-speed internet services, 4G and 5G LTE wireless, home phone and business network and communications services (data hosting, cloud computing). Bell Aliant also provides license, hosting and maintenance services. The firm sells devices and related equipment, including mobile phones, landline phones, television receivers (including wireless and satellite) and smart home devices. Bell Aliant is wholly-owned and privatized by its parent BCE, Inc. (Bell Canada Enterprises).

Employee benefits include performance incentives, unit purchase programs, employee discounts and retirement savings plans

CONTACTS: *Note: Officers with more than one job title may be intentionally listed here more than once.*

Stephen Wetmore, CEO
John Watson, Director Nominee
Frederick Crooks, Secretary
Charles Hartlen, Senior VP, Subsidiary
Daniel McKeen, Senior VP, Subsidiary
Mary-Ann Bell, Senior VP, Subsidiary
Rod MacGregor, Vice President, Divisional

FINANCIAL DATA: *Note: Data for latest year may not have been available at press time.*

In U.S. $	2020	2019	2018	2017	2016	2015
Revenue	3,414,993,750	3,252,375,000	3,097,500,000	2,950,000,000	2,972,000,000	2,974,000,000
R&D Expense						
Operating Income						
Operating Margin %						
SGA Expense						
Net Income						
Operating Cash Flow						
Capital Expenditure						
EBITDA						
Return on Assets %						
Return on Equity %						
Debt to Equity						

CONTACT INFORMATION:

Phone: 902 487-4609   Fax: 902 425-0708
Toll-Free: 877-248-3113
Address: 6 S. Maritime Centre, 1505 Barrington St., Halifax, NS B3J 2W3 Canada

STOCK TICKER/OTHER:

Stock Ticker: Subsidiary
Employees: 5,800
Parent Company: BCE Inc

Exchange:
Fiscal Year Ends: 06/30

SALARIES/BONUSES:

Top Exec. Salary: $ Bonus: $
Second Exec. Salary: $ Bonus: $

OTHER THOUGHTS:

Estimated Female Officers or Directors: 4
Hot Spot for Advancement for Women/Minorities: Y

Bell MTS Inc

www.bellmts.ca

NAIC Code: 517110

TYPES OF BUSINESS:

Telephone Service
Internet Service
Smart Home
Business Voice & Data Connectivity
Digital Television Services
Security Monitoring Services

BRANDS/DIVISIONS/AFFILIATES:

BCE Inc
Fibe

CONTACTS: Note: Officers with more than one job title may be intentionally listed here more than once.

Paul Cadieux, CFO
Marvin Boakye, Other Executive Officer
Heather Tulk, Other Executive Officer
Paul Beauregard, Other Executive Officer
Kevin Jessiman, Senior VP, Divisional
Patricia Solman, Senior VP, Divisional
Brenda McInnes, Treasurer

GROWTH PLANS/SPECIAL FEATURES:

Bell MTS, Inc. is a full-service telecommunications company that serves the Manitoba region within Canada. The BCE, Inc. subsidiary provides its services and solutions for residential customers, including mobility, internet, TV, smart home, and connected things. Mobile services encompass long-term evolution (LTE)-A and 5G networks, offering internet, streaming and sharing capabilities. Devices can be purchased through Bell MTS, as well as travel protection insurance and a variety of rate plans and pre-paid options. Bell MTS Fibe TV offers an array of channels and movies and shows on-demand. TV features include 4K picture quality, recording, pausing, rewinding, set-top boxes and Crave and Netflix capabilities. Related accessories and hardware are available, as well as satellite TV and a mobile TV app. Internet services is powered by Bell MTS' fiber optic network, providing whole home smart and wi-fi and internet capability for every room of the home. Business solutions include mobility, internet, phone, TV, security, automation and more.

FINANCIAL DATA: Note: Data for latest year may not have been available at press time.

In U.S. $	2020	2019	2018	2017	2016	2015
Revenue	833,490,000	793,800,000	756,000,000	720,000,000	725,000,000	728,123,000
R&D Expense						
Operating Income						
Operating Margin %						
SGA Expense						
Net Income						
Operating Cash Flow						
Capital Expenditure						
EBITDA						
Return on Assets %						
Return on Equity %						
Debt to Equity						

CONTACT INFORMATION:

Phone: 204 269-4727   Fax: 204 786-4514
Toll-Free: 888-544-5554
Address: 333 Main St., Winnipeg, MB R3C 3V6 Canada

STOCK TICKER/OTHER:

Stock Ticker: Subsidiary
Employees: 2,928
Parent Company: BCE Inc

Exchange:
Fiscal Year Ends: 12/31

SALARIES/BONUSES:

Top Exec. Salary: $ Bonus: $
Second Exec. Salary: $ Bonus: $

OTHER THOUGHTS:

Estimated Female Officers or Directors: 4
Hot Spot for Advancement for Women/Minorities: Y

BenQ Corporation

NAIC Code: 333316

TYPES OF BUSINESS:

Photographic and Photocopying Equipment Manufacturing

BRANDS/DIVISIONS/AFFILIATES:

Qisda Corporation
BenQ America Corporation
BenQ Asia Pacific Corporation
BenQ Latin America Corporation
BenQ China
BenQ Europe BV
ZOWIE
AQCOLOR

CONTACTS: *Note: Officers with more than one job title may be intentionally listed here more than once.*

Conway Lee, CEO
Lars Yoder, Pres., BenQ America
Jeffrey Liang, Pres., BenQ Asia Pacific
Steve Chu, Pres., BenQ Europe
Israel Bedolla, Pres., BenQ Latin America
Michael Tseng, Pres., BenQ China
Tony Yang, Pres., BenQ China
Lars Yoder, Pres., BenQ America
Peter Tan, Pres., BenQ Latin America
Adrian Chang, Pres., BenQ Asia Pacific
K.Y. Lee, Chmn.
Adams Lee, Pres., BenQ Europe

GROWTH PLANS/SPECIAL FEATURES:

BenQ Corporation, a subsidiary of Qisda Corporation, is a Taiwan-based producer of consumer electronics, communication devices and components. The firm operates worldwide, maintaining an active presence in more than 100 countries. BenQ continuously invests and utilizes most of its resources and expertise in product design, visual display, mobile solutions and network convergence technologies. These include digital projectors, professional monitors, interactive large-format displays and panels, imaging solutions, mobile computing devices, speakers, light emitting diode (LED) lighting solutions and accessories/attachments. The firm's products and solutions primarily serve the business, education and e-sports industries. BenQ's AQCOLOR program offers BenQ partners innovative and reliable solutions for professional audio/visual products. All Integrators Choice partners receive access to product assortment, deal registration, preferential pricing, a three-year warranty, access to an exclusive partner portal and more. The company's ZOWIE brand is dedicated to the development of professional eSports equipment, including monitors, mouse products, audio systems and accessories. BenQ is headquartered in Taiwan, with offices in China, the Netherlands and the U.S. Subsidiaries of the firm include BenQ America Corporation, BenQ Asia Pacific Corporation, BenQ Latin America Corporation, BenQ China and BenQ Europe BV.

FINANCIAL DATA: *Note: Data for latest year may not have been available at press time.*

In U.S. $	2020	2019	2018	2017	2016	2015
Revenue	3,281,118,750	3,365,250,000	3,202,500,000	3,050,000,000	3,000,000,000	2,850,000,000
R&D Expense						
Operating Income						
Operating Margin %						
SGA Expense						
Net Income						
Operating Cash Flow						
Capital Expenditure						
EBITDA						
Return on Assets %						
Return on Equity %						
Debt to Equity						

CONTACT INFORMATION:

Phone: 886-2-2727-8899   Fax: 886-2-2797-9288
Toll-Free:
Address: 16 Jihu Rd., Neihu, Taipei, 114 Taiwan

STOCK TICKER/OTHER:

Stock Ticker: Subsidiary   Exchange:
Employees: 1,500   Fiscal Year Ends: 12/31
Parent Company: Qisda Corporation

SALARIES/BONUSES:

Top Exec. Salary: $ Bonus: $
Second Exec. Salary: $ Bonus: $

OTHER THOUGHTS:

Estimated Female Officers or Directors:
Hot Spot for Advancement for Women/Minorities:

Bezeq-The Israel Telecommunication Corp Ltd

ir.bezeq.co.il/phoenix.zhtml?c=159870&p=irol-IRHome

NAIC Code: 517110

TYPES OF BUSINESS:

Telecommunications Provider
Domestic & International Phone Service
Cell Phone Service
Broadband Internet & Data Services
Network Infrastructure Installation
Call Center Services
Internet Portal

BRANDS/DIVISIONS/AFFILIATES:

Eurocom Group
Internet Gold-Golden Lines Ltd
B Communications

GROWTH PLANS/SPECIAL FEATURES:

Bezeq-The Israel Telecommunication Corp., Ltd., together with its subsidiaries, is a leading telecommunications company in Israel. Bezeq provides domestic, international and cellular phone services, broadband internet and other data communications, satellite and internet-based multi-channel TV and corporate networks. The firm's fiber optic network reaches 680,000 homes in Israel, and expects to reach approximately 1 million homes by the end of 2021. As of the first quarter of 2021, Bezeq had approximately 1.63 million active fixed telephone lines in its portfolio, with services including basic telephone on domestic lines as well as value-added services such as voicemail, caller ID, call waiting, call forwarding and conference calling. B Communications Ltd. is a holding company with a single asset, its 26.34% controlling interest in Israeli Telecommunications Corp., Ltd. (Bezeq). B Communications is majority-owned by Internet Gold-Golden Lines Ltd., which itself is part of the Eurocom Group.

CONTACTS: Note: Officers with more than one job title may be intentionally listed here more than once.

Dudu Mizrahi, CEO
Tobi Fischbein, CFO
Gil Sharon, CEO-Telephone Communications Ltd
Ron Eilon, CEO-Yes
Gil Sharon, Chmn.
Isaac Benbenisti, CEO-Bezeq International

FINANCIAL DATA: Note: Data for latest year may not have been available at press time.

In U.S. $	2020	2019	2018	2017	2016	2015
Revenue	2,692,957,000	2,756,553,000	2,877,571,000	3,022,052,000	3,113,124,000	3,082,561,000
R&D Expense						
Operating Income	549,520,100	558,781,700	515,869,700	664,981,100	713,141,300	757,288,100
Operating Margin %		.17%	.18%	.22%	.23%	.25%
SGA Expense	142,628,300	349,778,800	372,932,700	380,033,300	409,361,600	338,973,600
Net Income	245,740,400	-335,577,800	-329,094,600	381,268,200	384,046,600	531,305,700
Operating Cash Flow	994,075,700	902,694,800	1,084,222,000	1,088,235,000	1,088,544,000	1,154,610,000
Capital Expenditure	462,770,000	455,978,200	495,803,000	472,340,300	437,146,300	504,755,800
EBITDA	995,310,600	846,508,000	493,642,000	1,155,844,000	1,224,380,000	1,316,996,000
Return on Assets %		- .07%	-.06%	.08%	.08%	.11%
Return on Equity %			- .83%	.57%	.54%	.71%
Debt to Equity			24.753	4.771	4.143	3.65

CONTACT INFORMATION:

Phone: 972 3626-2600   Fax: 972 3626-2609
Toll-Free:
Address: Azrieli Center 2, 132 Menachem Begin Ave., 27/Fl., Tel Aviv, 61620 Israel

STOCK TICKER/OTHER:

Stock Ticker: BZQIF   Exchange: PINX
Employees: 5,256   Fiscal Year Ends: 12/31
Parent Company: Eurocom Group

SALARIES/BONUSES:

Top Exec. Salary: $ Bonus: $
Second Exec. Salary: $ Bonus: $

OTHER THOUGHTS:

Estimated Female Officers or Directors: 3
Hot Spot for Advancement for Women/Minorities: Y

Bharat Sanchar Nigam Limited (BSNL)

NAIC Code: 517110

www.bsnl.co.in

TYPES OF BUSINESS:

Telecommunications Service Provider
Local & Long-Distance Telephone Service
Cell Phone Service
Internet Services & Internet Telephony
Intelligent Network Services
Satellite Services

BRANDS/DIVISIONS/AFFILIATES:

CONTACTS: *Note: Officers with more than one job title may be intentionally listed here more than once.*

Yojana Das, Dir.-Finance
Rajesh Wadhwa, Dir.-Oper.
Pravin Kumar Purwar, Chmn.

GROWTH PLANS/SPECIAL FEATURES:

Bharat Sanchar Nigam Limited (BSNL) is a government-owned telecommunications company in India. The firm offers fixed landline services, mobile services, broadband, enterprise solutions and more. Landline and data solutions encompass BSNL telephone landline, next generation network (NGN) services such as conference calling, landline broadband (subscription, post- and pre-paid options), Wi-Fi, Bharat fiber-to-the-home (FTTH) broadband and Wi-Max broadband. Mobile and data plans include pre- and post-paid GSM (global system for mobile communication), international roaming, GSM Wi-Fi, Wi-Max (pre- and post-paid) and value-added services. A wide range of corporate services are provided by BSNL, including toll-free numbers, universal access numbers, voice VPN, televoting, video conferencing, Wi-Max, Wi-Fi, DSL/Bharat fiber broadband, managed colocation services, managed hosting, managed IT, cloud, managed network, managed Software-as-a-Service, internet data center, webcare, data services, fleet tracking and much more. In March 2021, the government of Indian deferred the merger plan between BSNL and Mahanagar Telephone Nigam Limited (MTNL) due to financial reasons; but said that close cooperation and service integration between BSNL and MTNL had been undertaken.

FINANCIAL DATA: *Note: Data for latest year may not have been available at press time.*

In U.S. $	2020	2019	2018	2017	2016	2015
Revenue	2,512,930,000	2,777,080,000	3,854,000,000	4,939,320,000	5,116,828,267	4,122,113,891
R&D Expense						
Operating Income						
Operating Margin %						
SGA Expense						
Net Income	-2,060,100,000	-2,147,140,000	-1,229,130,000	-7,507,960,000	-603,077,989	-1,213,483,368
Operating Cash Flow						
Capital Expenditure						
EBITDA						
Return on Assets %						
Return on Equity %						
Debt to Equity						

CONTACT INFORMATION:

Phone: 91-11-2373-4064　　Fax: 91-11-2373-0392
Toll-Free:
Address: Harish Chandra Mathur Ln., New Delhi, 110 001 India

STOCK TICKER/OTHER:

Stock Ticker: Government-Owned　　Exchange:
Employees: 69,824　　Fiscal Year Ends: 03/31
Parent Company:

SALARIES/BONUSES:

Top Exec. Salary: $　　Bonus: $
Second Exec. Salary: $　　Bonus: $

OTHER THOUGHTS:

Estimated Female Officers or Directors:
Hot Spot for Advancement for Women/Minorities:

Bharti Airtel Limited

NAIC Code: 517210

www.airtel.in

TYPES OF BUSINESS:

Cell Phone Service
Telecommunications
Mobile Services
Digital TV
Telephone Services
Broadband Services
ICT Services

BRANDS/DIVISIONS/AFFILIATES:

Bharti Enterprises Limited
Singapore Telecommunications Limited

CONTACTS: *Note: Officers with more than one job title may be intentionally listed here more than once.*

Gopal Vittal, CEO
Jyoti Pawar, Dir.-Legal & Regulatory
Raghunath Mandava, Dir.-Customer Experience
Manoj Kohli, CEO-International
Jagbir Singh, Dir.-Network Svcs. Group
Sunil Bharti Mittal, Chmn.

GROWTH PLANS/SPECIAL FEATURES:

Bharti Airtel Limited is an Indian telecommunications service provider. With customers and operations spanning India, as well as countries across south Asia and Africa, Airtel is one of India's largest telecommunications firms. The company is divided into four business units: mobile services, home services, Airtel business and digital TV services. The mobile services unit offers prepaid and postpaid voice, data (2G, 3G, 4G LTE and 4G+) and other services, including news updates, mobile internet and email. The home services business unit offers fixed-line telephone and broadband services across pan-India. Product offerings include voice connectivity over fixed-line and high-speed broadband on copper and fiber with speeds up to 100 megabits per second. The Airtel business unit provides information and communication technology (ICT) services in India, and offers a portfolio of services to enterprises, governments, carriers and small/medium businesses. Services include voice, data and video, as well as network integration, data centers, managed services, enterprise mobility applications, digital media, international toll free services and short-message-system (SMS) hubbing. The digital TV services business unit offers standard and high-definition (HD) digital TV services with 3D capabilities and Dolby surround sound. This division offers 635 channels, including 80 HD channels, five international channels and three interactive services. The firm is 64%-owned by Bharti Enterprises Limited and 36%-owned by Singapore Telecommunications Limited (SingTel).

Bharti Airtel offers its employees sabbaticals, onsite day care and fitness center, concierge service and maternity leave.

FINANCIAL DATA: *Note: Data for latest year may not have been available at press time.*

In U.S. $	2020	2019	2018	2017	2016	2015
Revenue	11,635,100,000	11,611,000,000	12,865,000,000	14,709,500,000	14,791,625,789	13,575,139,566
R&D Expense						
Operating Income						
Operating Margin %						
SGA Expense						
Net Income	4,931,780,000	58,859,900	168,929,000	585,452,000	840,076,842	763,734,298
Operating Cash Flow						
Capital Expenditure						
EBITDA						
Return on Assets %						
Return on Equity %						
Debt to Equity						

CONTACT INFORMATION:

Phone: 91-11-4666-6100   Fax: 91-11-4166-6137
Toll-Free:
Address: 1 Nelson Mandela Rd., Vasant Kunj, Phase II, New Delhi, 110 070 India

STOCK TICKER/OTHER:

Stock Ticker: 532454
Employees: 20,793
Parent Company: Bharti Enterprises

Exchange: Bombay
Fiscal Year Ends: 03/31

SALARIES/BONUSES:

Top Exec. Salary: $ Bonus: $
Second Exec. Salary: $ Bonus: $

OTHER THOUGHTS:

Estimated Female Officers or Directors: 4
Hot Spot for Advancement for Women/Minorities: Y

Black Box Corporation

NAIC Code: 423430

www.blackbox.com

TYPES OF BUSINESS:

Networking Products, Distribution
Technical Network Services
Data & Voice Infrastructure
Custom Networking Products

BRANDS/DIVISIONS/AFFILIATES:

Essar Group
AGC Networks Ltd
Black Box Commercial Services

CONTACTS: *Note: Officers with more than one job title may be intentionally listed here more than once.*

Sanjeev Verma, CEO
David Russo, CFO
Ronald Basso, Executive VP, Divisional

GROWTH PLANS/SPECIAL FEATURES:

Black Box Corporation is a leading technology solutions provider. The firm helps customers build, manage, optimize and secure their IT infrastructure. As a technology solutions provider, Black Box connects people to devices through a range of products and services. Black Box also develops custom orders for unique applications. Applications the company supports includes classroom (K-12), conference room (for business meeting needs), and control room. Black Box Commercial Services focuses on industry-specific designs, global deployment capabilities, managed services, wireless/mobility, UC&C (unified communications and collaboration) and structured cabling solutions at the intelligent digital edge. Black Box products are grouped into several categories, including cabinets/racks/enclosures, cables, carts/storage, control systems, datacom, digital signage, jacks/panels/hardware, KVM switch (keyboard, video and mouse), networking, power solutions, premises security, testers, tools, video & multimedia, voice communications and USB connectivity. Industries Black Box specializes in include broadcast, media, corporate, education, government, industrial, public safety and transportation. Based in the U.S., Black Box has global locations throughout the Americas, Europe, Asia and Asia Pacific. Black Box is privately-owned by AGC Networks Ltd., part of the Essar Group.

FINANCIAL DATA: *Note: Data for latest year may not have been available at press time.*

In U.S. $	2020	2019	2018	2017	2016	2015
Revenue	874,371,504	832,734,766	774,636,992	855,731,008	912,654,976	992,444,032
R&D Expense						
Operating Income						
Operating Margin %						
SGA Expense						
Net Income		-105,099,750	-100,095,000	-7,051,000	-171,102,000	15,342,000
Operating Cash Flow						
Capital Expenditure						
EBITDA						
Return on Assets %						
Return on Equity %						
Debt to Equity						

CONTACT INFORMATION:

Phone: 724 746-5500   Fax:
Toll-Free: 800-316-7107
Address: 1000 Park Dr., Lawrence, PA 15055 United States

STOCK TICKER/OTHER:

Stock Ticker: Private   Exchange:
Employees: 3,264   Fiscal Year Ends: 03/31
Parent Company: Essar Group

SALARIES/BONUSES:

Top Exec. Salary: $ Bonus: $
Second Exec. Salary: $ Bonus: $

OTHER THOUGHTS:

Estimated Female Officers or Directors: 2
Hot Spot for Advancement for Women/Minorities:

BlackBerry Limited

www.blackberry.com

NAIC Code: 511210C

TYPES OF BUSINESS:

Computer Software: Telecom, Communications & VOIP
Security Software & Services
Internet of Things
Machine Learning
Endpoint Security
Artificial Intelligence
Intelligent Vehicle Solutions

BRANDS/DIVISIONS/AFFILIATES:

BlackBerry Spark
BlackBerry Protect
BlackBerry Persona
BlackBerry QNX
BlackBerry IVY
BlackBerry AtHoc
BlackBerry Alert
Cylance Inc

CONTACTS: *Note: Officers with more than one job title may be intentionally listed here more than once.*

John Chen, CEO
Steven Capelli, CFO
Randall Cook, Chief Legal Officer
Mark Wilson, Chief Marketing Officer
Bryan Palma, COO
Nita White-Ivy, Executive VP, Divisional
Sai Yuen Ho, Executive VP, Divisional
Sandeep Chennakeshu, President, Divisional
Carl Wiese, President, Divisional
Stuart McClure, President, Subsidiary

GROWTH PLANS/SPECIAL FEATURES:

BlackBerry Limited provides intelligent security software and services to enterprises and governments throughout the world. BlackBerry secures more than 500 million endpoints, including 175 million cars. The company leverages artificial intelligence (AI) and machine learning to deliver innovative solutions in the areas of cybersecurity, safety and data privacy, and is a leader in the areas of endpoint security, endpoint management, encryption and embedded systems. The firm's core secure software and services offering is its BlackBerry Spark software platform, which integrates a unified endpoint security layer with BlackBerry unified endpoint management to enable secure endpoint communications in zero-trust environments. The Spark suite offers AI- and machine learning-based cybersecurity solutions, including: BlackBerry Protect, which uses machine learning to prevent suspicious behavior and malicious code on an endpoint; BlackBerry Persona, which provides continuous authentication by validating user identity in real-time; and BlackBerry Spark SDK, which enables enterprise and independent software vendor developers to integrate the security features of BlackBerry Spark into their own mobile and web applications. BlackBerry Internet of Things (IoT) consists of: BlackBerry QNX, a provider of real-time operating systems, middleware, development tools and professional services for connected embedded systems in the automotive, medical, industrial automation and other markets; BlackBerry IVY, an intelligent vehicle data platform that leverages QNX's automotive capabilities and allows automakers to safely access a vehicle's sensor data, normalize it and apply machine learning to generate and share predictive insights and inferences; and BlackBerry AtHoc and BlackBerry Alert, which are secure critical event management solutions that enable people, devices and organizations to exchange critical information in real-time. Wholly-owned subsidiaries include BlackBerry Corporation, BlackBerry UK Limited, and Cylance Inc.

BlackBerry's employee benefits vary by location, but can include comprehensive health benefits, reimbursement programs, stock purchase and savings plans, as well as a variety of employee assistance programs.

FINANCIAL DATA: *Note: Data for latest year may not have been available at press time.*

In U.S. $	2020	2019	2018	2017	2016	2015
Revenue	1,040,000,000	904,000,000	932,000,000	1,309,000,000	2,160,000,000	
R&D Expense	259,000,000	219,000,000	239,000,000	306,000,000	469,000,000	
Operating Income	-183,000,000	-63,000,000	-189,000,000	-428,000,000	-517,000,000	
Operating Margin %	- .18%	- .07%	- .20%	- .33%	- .24%	
SGA Expense	493,000,000	406,000,000	467,000,000	553,000,000	712,000,000	
Net Income	-152,000,000	93,000,000	405,000,000	-1,206,000,000	-208,000,000	
Operating Cash Flow	26,000,000	100,000,000	704,000,000	-224,000,000	257,000,000	
Capital Expenditure	44,000,000	49,000,000	45,000,000	69,000,000	102,000,000	
EBITDA	29,000,000	86,000,000	-12,000,000	-189,000,000	99,000,000	
Return on Assets %	- .04%	.02%	.12%	- .27%	- .03%	
Return on Equity %	- .06%	.04%	.18%	- .46%	- .06%	
Debt to Equity	0.047	0.252	0.312	0.287	0.398	

CONTACT INFORMATION:

Phone: 519 888-7465   Fax: 519 888-7884
Toll-Free:
Address: 2200 University Ave. E., Waterloo, ON N2K 0A7 Canada

STOCK TICKER/OTHER:

Stock Ticker: BB
Employees: 3,497
Parent Company:

Exchange: NYS
Fiscal Year Ends: 02/28

SALARIES/BONUSES:

Top Exec. Salary: $ Bonus: $
Second Exec. Salary: $ Bonus: $

OTHER THOUGHTS:

Estimated Female Officers or Directors:
Hot Spot for Advancement for Women/Minorities: Y

Sales, profits and employees may be estimates. Financial information, benefits and other data can change quickly and may vary from those stated here.

Blonder Tongue Laboratories Inc   www.blondertongue.com
NAIC Code: 334220

TYPES OF BUSINESS:

Digital Video Electronics Manufacturing
Telephone Products
Networking & Broadband Equipment
Receivers & Antennas
Cable TV Equipment
Microwave Products
Technology Development

BRANDS/DIVISIONS/AFFILIATES:

RL Drake Holdings LLC
EdgeQAM Collection

CONTACTS: *Note: Officers with more than one job title may be intentionally listed here more than once.*

Edward Grauch, CEO
Eric Skolnik, CFO
Ronald Alterio, Chief Technology Officer
Steven Shea, Director
Jeffrey Smith, Vice President, Divisional
Allen Horvath, Vice President, Divisional

GROWTH PLANS/SPECIAL FEATURES:

Blonder Tongue Laboratories, Inc., together with subsidiary R.L. Drake Holdings, LLC, is a technology-development and manufacturing company. The firm delivers a wide range of products and services to the cable entertainment and media industry. Customers served include business entities installing private video and data networks for environments such as lodging/hospitality, multi-dwelling units/apartments, broadcast studios/networks, education universities/schools, health care hospitals/fitness centers, government facilities/offices, prisons, airports, sports stadiums/arenas, entertainment venues/casinos, retail stores and small- and medium-sized businesses. Five primary categories define its product portfolio: digital video headend products, analog video headend products, hybrid fiber-coaxial (HFC) distribution products, data products, and consumer premise equipment CPE) products Digital video headend products are used by operators to acquire, process and manipulate digital video signals. Its line of products includes the EdgeQAM Collection, which includes a line of HD, SD, MPEG-2 and H.265 encoders and multiplexers. The analog video headend products allow operators to acquire, process and manipulate analog signals for further transmission. These products include integrated receiver/decoders, modulators, demodulators, channel combiners and processors. The headend is essentially the brain of an analog TV signal distribution system. HFC distribution products facilitate the transfer of signals from the headend to destinations in homes or other terminal locations along a distribution network of fiber optic or coaxial cable. The firm's distribution products include line broadband amplifiers, directional taps, splitters and wall outlets. Data products include high-speed data products, such as cable modems and cable modem termination systems. CPE products include Android-based IPTV set top boxes targeted to the Tier 2 and Tier 3 telecommunications and fiber optics based service providers.

FINANCIAL DATA: *Note: Data for latest year may not have been available at press time.*

In U.S. $	2020	2019	2018	2017	2016	2015
Revenue	16,379,000	19,842,000	21,707,000	23,283,000	22,506,000	20,943,000
R&D Expense	2,524,000	3,066,000	2,576,000	2,452,000	2,741,000	3,331,000
Operating Income	-7,114,000	-7,641,000	-854,000	463,000	-671,000	-6,400,000
Operating Margin %		-.39%	-.04%	.02%	-.03%	-.31%
SGA Expense	7,608,000	8,006,000	6,697,000	6,021,000	6,287,000	7,224,000
Net Income	-7,474,000	-742,000	-1,339,000	-384,000	-1,195,000	-6,771,000
Operating Cash Flow	-3,212,000	-6,538,000	587,000	-237,000	771,000	-798,000
Capital Expenditure	191,000	316,000	101,000	200,000	56,000	641,000
EBITDA	-6,013,000	-6,532,000	-333,000	963,000	301,000	-5,092,000
Return on Assets %		-.04%	-.09%	-.03%	-.08%	-.36%
Return on Equity %		-.10%	-.18%	-.06%	-.17%	-.64%
Debt to Equity		0.355	0.024	0.502	0.568	0.015

CONTACT INFORMATION:

Phone: 732 679-4000   Fax: 732 679-4353
Toll-Free: 800-523-6049
Address: 1 Jake Brown Rd., Old Bridge, NJ 08857 United States

STOCK TICKER/OTHER:

Stock Ticker: BDR   Exchange: ASE
Employees: 85   Fiscal Year Ends: 12/31
Parent Company:

SALARIES/BONUSES:

Top Exec. Salary: $ Bonus: $
Second Exec. Salary: $ Bonus: $

OTHER THOUGHTS:

Estimated Female Officers or Directors: 1
Hot Spot for Advancement for Women/Minorities:

Boingo Wireless Inc

NAIC Code: 517110

www.boingo.com

TYPES OF BUSINESS:

Wi-Fi Internet Access
Software Development
Wireless Internet Service Provider
Mobile Advertising Services

BRANDS/DIVISIONS/AFFILIATES:

Boingo
Boingo Wi-Finder
Boingo Broadband
Cloud 9 Media
Concourse Communications
AWG-WIFI
Digital Colony Management LLC

CONTACTS: *Note: Officers with more than one job title may be intentionally listed here more than once.*

Michael Finley, CEO
Peter Hovenier, CFO
Lance Rosenzweig, Chairman of the Board
Dawn Callahan, Chief Marketing Officer
Derek Peterson, Chief Technology Officer

GROWTH PLANS/SPECIAL FEATURES:

Boingo Wireless, Inc. offers high-speed wireless internet roaming access across a network of over 1.3 million commercial Wi-Fi hotspots in more than 100 countries, including hotels, airports and other public spaces. The firm also operates Wi-Fi and internet protocol television (IPTV) networks at more than 60 U.S. Army, Air Force and Marines bases worldwide. Boingo operates 73 distributed antenna system (DAS) networks containing approximately 38,100 DAS nodes, making it one of the largest indoor DAS providers in the world. Revenue is generated from the firm's wireless networks, including its DAS and wholesale Wi-Fi offerings; wholesale revenue is generated from telecom operators that pay build-out fees and recurring access fees so that their cellular customers may use Boingo's DAS or small cell networks; military revenue is obtained when military personnel purchase broadband and IPTV services on military bases; usage-based Wi-Fi network access and software licensing fees are generated from enterprise customers; and advertising revenue is generated from advertisers seeking to reach consumers via sponsored Wi-Fi access. Registered trademarks include Boingo, Boingo Wi-Finder, Boingo Broadband, Cloud 9 Media, Concourse Communications and AWG-WIFI, among others. In June 2021, the firm was acquired by Digital Colony Management, LLC.

The company offers employees medical, dental and vision coverage; domestic partner benefits; a 401(k) plan; a profit sharing plan; life and AD&D insurance; disability benefits; flexible spending accounts; and phone, transportation and education reimbursem

FINANCIAL DATA: *Note: Data for latest year may not have been available at press time.*

In U.S. $	2020	2019	2018	2017	2016	2015
Revenue	276,979,500	263,790,000	250,820,992	204,368,992	159,344,000	139,626,000
R&D Expense						
Operating Income						
Operating Margin %						
SGA Expense						
Net Income		-10,296,000	-1,220,000	-19,366,000	-27,331,000	-22,292,000
Operating Cash Flow						
Capital Expenditure						
EBITDA						
Return on Assets %						
Return on Equity %						
Debt to Equity						

CONTACT INFORMATION:

Phone: 310 586-5180   Fax: 310 586-4060
Toll-Free: 800-880-4117
Address: 10960 Wilshire Blvd., Ste. 800, Los Angeles, CA 90024 United States

STOCK TICKER/OTHER:

Stock Ticker: Subsidiary   Exchange:
Employees: 411   Fiscal Year Ends: 12/31
Parent Company: Digital Colony Management LLC

SALARIES/BONUSES:

Top Exec. Salary: $ Bonus: $
Second Exec. Salary: $ Bonus: $

OTHER THOUGHTS:

Estimated Female Officers or Directors: 1
Hot Spot for Advancement for Women/Minorities:

Bouygues SA

NAIC Code: 237130

TYPES OF BUSINESS:

Construction & Telecommunications
Construction
Road Building
Property Development
Precasting
Cellular Phone Service
Media Operation
Research & Development

BRANDS/DIVISIONS/AFFILIATES:

Bouygues Construction
Bouygues Immobilier
Colas
Buoygues Telecom
Bbox
TF1
TMC

CONTACTS: *Note: Officers with more than one job title may be intentionally listed here more than once.*

Olivier Roussat, CEO
Pascal Grange, CFO
Jean-Claude Tostivin, Sr. VP-Admin.
Jean Francois Guillemin, Corp. Sec.
Olivier Bouygues, Deputy CEO
Philippe Marien, Chmn.-Bourgues Telecom
Martin Bouygues, Chmn.

GROWTH PLANS/SPECIAL FEATURES:

Buoygues SA, based in Paris, France, was founded in 1952 as a construction and industrial works company. Operating in over 80 countries, the firm currently provides services to three sectors: construction, telecoms and media. The construction sector operates through three subsidiaries: Bouygues Construction, which is dedicated to electrical contracting, building, energy services and civil works; Bouygues Immobilier, committed to property development; and Colas, dedicated to building roads and other complementary activities, such as safety, road marking and signaling services. The telecom sector operates through subsidiary Buoygues Telecom, a mobile telephone operator comprising a 4G+ network. Its Bbox offerings consist of bundled telephone (fixed and mobile), TV and/or Wi-Fi options, combining traditional TV content with apps and content from the web within a highly seamless interface. The media sector operates through TF1, a leading private media group in freeview television within France. TF1 produces five complementary freeview TV channels TF1, TMC, TFX, TF1 Series films and rolling news channel, LCI, that together claimed an average 30% audience share in 2020. Buoygues maintains operations in Europe, Central and South America, North America, Asia, the Middle East and Africa. In April 2021, Buoygues announced that it sold TF1 Games and Dujardin, France's leading toy and game publishers, to Jumbodiset.

FINANCIAL DATA: *Note: Data for latest year may not have been available at press time.*

In U.S. $	2020	2019	2018	2017	2016	2015
Revenue	42,468,970,000	46,439,740,000	43,440,280,000			
R&D Expense						
Operating Income	1,656,730,000	2,702,571,000	2,679,357,000			
Operating Margin %		.06%	.06%			
SGA Expense	9,274,509,000	9,713,127,000	9,584,841,000			
Net Income	850,356,700	1,446,584,000	1,601,750,000			
Operating Cash Flow	4,161,372,000	4,121,054,000	2,707,458,000			
Capital Expenditure	3,235,265,000	2,295,719,000	2,862,623,000			
EBITDA	4,465,595,000	5,118,024,000	4,747,826,000			
Return on Assets %		.03%	.04%			
Return on Equity %		.12%	.14%			
Debt to Equity		0.536	0.522			

CONTACT INFORMATION:

Phone: 33-1-44-20-10-00   Fax: 33-1-30-60-4861
Toll-Free:
Address: 32 Ave. Hoche, Paris, 75008 France

STOCK TICKER/OTHER:

Stock Ticker: BOUYF   Exchange: PINX
Employees: 130,500   Fiscal Year Ends: 12/31
Parent Company:

SALARIES/BONUSES:

Top Exec. Salary: $ Bonus: $
Second Exec. Salary: $ Bonus: $

OTHER THOUGHTS:

Estimated Female Officers or Directors: 5
Hot Spot for Advancement for Women/Minorities: Y

Brightstar Corporation

NAIC Code: 423690

www.brightstar.com

TYPES OF BUSINESS:

Telecommunication Supply Chain & Distribution Services
Wireless Device & Accessories Distribution
Wireless Device Manufacturing
Supply Chain, Marketing and Retail Consultation

BRANDS/DIVISIONS/AFFILIATES:

Brightstar Capital Partners

GROWTH PLANS/SPECIAL FEATURES:

Brightstar Corporation, owned by private equity firm Brightstar Capital Partners, distributes and manages telecommunication devices and accessories globally. The firm serves carrier, retail and enterprise customers across approximately 50 countries worldwide and process millions of devices annually. Brightstar operates at every stage of the device lifecycle to provide an integrated experience with its customer's business, from the moment it is manufactured to the time it is traded in and remarketed. For businesses, Brightstar also operates at every stage of the device lifecycle in order to provide integrated services that link seamlessly. This infrastructure enables businesses to better serve their customers by providing end-to-end service. In December 2020, Brightstar announced plans to sell its 51% stake in Brightstar India to an investment firm in the U.K., to focus on core geographies and streamline operations.

CONTACTS: Note: Officers with more than one job title may be intentionally listed here more than once.

Rod Millar, CEO
Dennis J. Strand, Pres., Brightstar Financial Svcs.
Jack Negro, CFO
Ray Roman, CCO
Catherine Smith, Sr. VP
Bela Lainck, Pres., Buy-Back & Trade-In Solutions
Rafael M. de Guzman, III, VP-Strategy
Oscar J. Fumagali, Chief Treas. Officer
Oscar J. Rojas, Pres., Brightstar Latin America
Arturo A. Osorio, Pres., Asia Pacific, Middle East & Africa
Jeff Gower, Pres., Brightstar U.S. & Canada
David Leach, CEO-eSecuritel
Michael Singer, Sr. VP-Global Strategy & New Bus. Dev.
Ramon Colomina, Pres., Supply Chain Solutions

FINANCIAL DATA: Note: Data for latest year may not have been available at press time.

In U.S. $	2020	2019	2018	2017	2016	2015
Revenue	11,576,250,000	11,025,000,000	10,500,000,000	10,000,000,000	7,750,000,000	7,600,000,000
R&D Expense						
Operating Income						
Operating Margin %						
SGA Expense						
Net Income						
Operating Cash Flow						
Capital Expenditure						
EBITDA						
Return on Assets %						
Return on Equity %						
Debt to Equity						

CONTACT INFORMATION:

Phone: 682-348-0354   Fax:
Toll-Free:
Address: 1900 W. Kirkwood Blvd., Ste. 1600C, Southlake, TX 76092 United States

STOCK TICKER/OTHER:

Stock Ticker: Subsidiary
Employees: 9,000
Parent Company: Brightstar Capital Partners

Exchange:
Fiscal Year Ends: 12/31

SALARIES/BONUSES:

Top Exec. Salary: $ Bonus: $
Second Exec. Salary: $ Bonus: $

OTHER THOUGHTS:

Estimated Female Officers or Directors: 1
Hot Spot for Advancement for Women/Minorities:

Sales, profits and employees may be estimates. Financial information, benefits and other data can change quickly and may vary from those stated here.

Broadcom Inc

NAIC Code: 335313

www.broadcom.com

TYPES OF BUSINESS:

Electrical Switches, Sensors, MEMS, Optomechanicals
Semiconductors
Connectivity Technology
Wireless Applications
Optical Products
Mainframe Software
Enterprise Software
Security Software

BRANDS/DIVISIONS/AFFILIATES:

CONTACTS: Note: Officers with more than one job title may be intentionally listed here more than once.

Hock Tan, CEO
Thomas Krause, CFO
Kirsten Spears, Chief Accounting Officer
Henry Samueli, Chief Technology Officer
Bryan Ingram, General Manager, Divisional
Mark Brazeal, Other Executive Officer
Charles Kawwas, Other Executive Officer

GROWTH PLANS/SPECIAL FEATURES:

Broadcom, Inc. designs, develops and supplies a broad range of semiconductor and infrastructure software solutions, with a focus on connectivity technologies. The firm develops semiconductor devices with a focus on complex digital and mixed signal complementary metal oxide semiconductor (CMOS) based devices and analog III-V based products. Broadcom's applications include data center, enterprise storage, broadband, wired networking, wireless communications, mobile communications, industrial, automotive and software solutions. Broadcom's products are vast and are grouped into the categories of storage and systems, wireless, wired connectivity, optical products, mainframe software, enterprise software, and security. Storage and systems products include storage adapters, controllers, integrated circuits, fiber channel networking, peripheral component interconnect (PCI) switches and bridges. Wireless products include radio frequency (RF) and microwave demo boards, FBAR devices, handset power amplifiers, Bluetooth system-on-a-chip (SoC), GNSS/GPS functionality, wireless LAN/Bluetooth combos, and wireless LAN infrastructure. Wired connectivity products include Ethernet connectivity, switching, broadband digital subscriber lines, passive optical networking, set-top box solutions, embedded and networking processors, and customized SoCs. Optical products include fiber optic modules and components, LEDs and other displays, motion control encoders, optocouplers, opto-isolators and optical sensors. Mainframe software products span application development, testing/quality, identity, access, compliance, data protection, operational analytics, operations management, workload automation, content management, databases and product portfolio. Enterprise software products span business management, artificial intelligence (AI) capabilities, enterprise automation, continuous testing and application programming interface (API) full lifecycle management. Last, security products include cyber security and payment security.

FINANCIAL DATA: Note: Data for latest year may not have been available at press time.

In U.S. $	2020	2019	2018	2017	2016	2015
Revenue	23,888,000,000	22,597,000,000	20,848,000,000	17,636,000,000	13,240,000,000	6,824,000,000
R&D Expense	4,968,000,000	4,696,000,000	3,768,000,000	3,292,000,000	2,674,000,000	1,049,000,000
Operating Income	4,212,000,000	4,180,000,000	5,368,000,000	2,666,000,000	587,000,000	1,769,000,000
Operating Margin %		.18%	.26%	.15%	.04%	.26%
SGA Expense	1,935,000,000	1,709,000,000	1,056,000,000	787,000,000	806,000,000	486,000,000
Net Income	2,960,000,000	2,724,000,000	12,259,000,000	1,692,000,000	-1,739,000,000	1,364,000,000
Operating Cash Flow	12,061,000,000	9,697,000,000	8,880,000,000	6,551,000,000	3,411,000,000	2,318,000,000
Capital Expenditure	463,000,000	432,000,000	635,000,000	1,069,000,000	723,000,000	593,000,000
EBITDA	11,125,000,000	9,478,000,000	9,254,000,000	7,016,000,000	2,520,000,000	2,620,000,000
Return on Assets %		.05%	.23%	.03%	-.06%	.13%
Return on Equity %		.10%	.52%	.09%	-.15%	.34%
Debt to Equity		1.203	0.656	0.859	0.698	0.828

CONTACT INFORMATION:

Phone: 408-433-8000   Fax:
Toll-Free:
Address: 1320 Ridder Park Dr., San Jose, CA 95131 United States

STOCK TICKER/OTHER:

Stock Ticker: AVGO   Exchange: NAS
Employees: 21,000   Fiscal Year Ends: 10/31
Parent Company:

SALARIES/BONUSES:

Top Exec. Salary: $ Bonus: $
Second Exec. Salary: $ Bonus: $

OTHER THOUGHTS:

Estimated Female Officers or Directors: 5
Hot Spot for Advancement for Women/Minorities: Y

BT Global Services plc

www.globalservices.bt.com

NAIC Code: 517110

TYPES OF BUSINESS:

Telecommunications Equipment-Networking
Network Software
Managed Network Services
Consulting Services
Broadcast Transmission Products

BRANDS/DIVISIONS/AFFILIATES:

BT Group plc

GROWTH PLANS/SPECIAL FEATURES:

BT Global Services plc is the international business services and information technology division of BT Group plc, one of the leading telecommunications carriers in the U.K. The firm serves global multinational organizations with security, cloud and networking services. BT Global helps clients move to the cloud, integrates collaboration into part of their workforce culture, improves their contact centers, transforms their customer service and simplifies their network. The company's technologies span the areas of security, cloud infrastructure, cloud collaboration, cloud contact center and networking. In late-2020, BT Global announced the sale of its domestic operations in France to Computacenter.

Employees of BT Group receive benefits including retirement plans, employee discounts and flexible work hours.

CONTACTS:
Note: Officers with more than one job title may be intentionally listed here more than once.

Bas Burger, CEO
Martin Smith, CFO
Rebecca Kilpatrick-Markovits, Chief Human Resources Officer
Hriday Ravindranath, CTO

FINANCIAL DATA:
Note: Data for latest year may not have been available at press time.

In U.S. $	2020	2019	2018	2017	2016	2015
Revenue	143,008,000	150,086,000	152,233,000	158,112,000	159,520,000	172,006,000
R&D Expense						
Operating Income						
Operating Margin %						
SGA Expense						
Net Income	809,236	-359,440	-1,071,990	-473,229	-3,304,560	-1,189,680
Operating Cash Flow						
Capital Expenditure						
EBITDA						
Return on Assets %						
Return on Equity %						
Debt to Equity						

CONTACT INFORMATION:

Phone: 44-20-7356-5000   Fax: 44-20-7356-5520
Toll-Free:
Address: 81 Newgate St., BT Centre, London,   EC1A 7AJ United Kingdom

STOCK TICKER/OTHER:

Stock Ticker: Subsidiary
Employees: 16,800
Parent Company: BT Group plc

Exchange:
Fiscal Year Ends: 03/31

SALARIES/BONUSES:

Top Exec. Salary: $ Bonus: $
Second Exec. Salary: $ Bonus: $

OTHER THOUGHTS:

Estimated Female Officers or Directors:
Hot Spot for Advancement for Women/Minorities: Y

BT Group plc

NAIC Code: 517110

TYPES OF BUSINESS:

Telecommunications Services
Communications Networks
Telecommunications Equipment Distribution
International Broadband Networks
Consulting Services
Internet Service Provider
Local & Long-Distance Phone Service
Networking Services

BRANDS/DIVISIONS/AFFILIATES:

British Telecommunications plc
BT
EE
Plusnet
Openreach

CONTACTS: Note: Officers with more than one job title may be intentionally listed here more than once.

Philip Jansen, CEO
Simon Lowth, CFO
Dan Fitz, General Counsel
Jan du Plessis, Chmn.
Stephen Yeo, CEO-South East Asia

GROWTH PLANS/SPECIAL FEATURES:

BT Group plc is one of the world's largest integrated telecommunications providers. BT operates through four customer-facing lines of business: consumer, enterprise, global and Openreach. The consumer business provides fixed-voice, broadband and mobile services in the U.K., which are marketed under the BT, EE or Plusnet brands. This division comprises over 30 million customers and more than 620 stores. The enterprise business sells communication and IT services in the U.K. and Ireland, serving more than 1 million customers with fixed-voice, networking, cloud and broadband services. This division also provides network products and services to communication providers operating in Great Britain. The global business has customers in 180 countries, providing them business communications services, including digital transformation services. Openreach is a digital network business serving the U.K. It connects homes and businesses in order to build/retain network relationships. Moreover, TB Group's internal networks unit designs, builds and runs the networks and technology platforms that BT and its customers rely on; and its internal digital unit is responsible for BT's digital transformation processes and solutions so that BT can meet its own goals and deliver products and services to support its customer's needs. Wholly-owned British Telecommunications plc encompasses virtually all businesses and assets of the BT Group.

Most BT employees in the UK can receive broadband, BT TV, BT Sport and BT Mobile products either for free or at discounted rates. The firm also offers a retirement savings scheme and optional health benefits.

FINANCIAL DATA: Note: Data for latest year may not have been available at press time.

In U.S. $	2020	2019	2018	2017	2016	2015
Revenue		30,274,004,275	28,832,385,024	29,244,397,568	23,143,206,912	21,851,260,928
R&D Expense						
Operating Income						
Operating Margin %						
SGA Expense						
Net Income		2,593,128,115	2,469,645,824	2,318,939,136	3,145,395,200	2,594,829,568
Operating Cash Flow						
Capital Expenditure						
EBITDA						
Return on Assets %						
Return on Equity %						
Debt to Equity						

CONTACT INFORMATION:

Phone: 44 2073565000   Fax: 44 2073565520
Toll-Free:
Address: 81 Newgate St., London, EC1A 7AJ United Kingdom

STOCK TICKER/OTHER:

Stock Ticker: BTGOF   Exchange: NYS
Employees: 106,000   Fiscal Year Ends: 03/31
Parent Company:

SALARIES/BONUSES:

Top Exec. Salary: $ Bonus: $
Second Exec. Salary: $ Bonus: $

OTHER THOUGHTS:

Estimated Female Officers or Directors: 1
Hot Spot for Advancement for Women/Minorities: Y

CalAmp Corp

www.calamp.com

NAIC Code: 334220

TYPES OF BUSINESS:

Microwave Communications Equipment
Wireless Broadband Access Systems
Satellite Products

BRANDS/DIVISIONS/AFFILIATES:

CONTACTS:
Note: Officers with more than one job title may be intentionally listed here more than once.

Michael Burdiek, CEO
Kurtis Binder, CFO
Albert Moyer, Chairman of the Board

GROWTH PLANS/SPECIAL FEATURES:

CalAmp Corp. is a telematics solutions provider. The company helps reinvent businesses and improves lives worldwide with technology solutions that streamline complex mobile Internet of Things (IoT) deployments through wireless connectivity solutions and data intelligence. CalAmp's software applications, scalable cloud services and intelligent devices collect and assess critical data anywhere in the world, including industrial machines, commercial and passenger vehicles, vehicle drivers and contents. CalAmp operates through two business segments: telematics systems and software and subscription services. The telematics systems segment offers a series of advanced telematics and stolen vehicle recovery (SVR) products for the broader connected vehicle and emerging Internet of Machines marketplace. These products enable customers to optimize operations by collecting, monitoring and reporting information and intelligence from remote and mobile assets. CalAmp's telematics products include asset tracking units, mobile telematics devices, fixed and mobile wireless gateways and routers. The software and subscription services segment offers cloud-based application enablement and telematics service platforms that facilitate the integration of CalAmp applications, as well as those of third parties. This occurs via open application programming interfaces (APIs) to deliver full-featured mobile IoT solutions to a wide range of customers and markets. This division's scalable proprietary applications and other subscription services enable rapid and cost-effective development of high-value solutions for customers all over the world. CalAmp partnerships include: CargoSense, Overhaul, Cryoport and RoviTracker, which are supply chain providers; TransUnion, to work with insurance companies and to provide stolen vehicle recovery services; and AT&T, Verizon, Sprint and Telefonica, mobile network operators

FINANCIAL DATA:
Note: Data for latest year may not have been available at press time.

In U.S. $	2020	2019	2018	2017	2016	2015
Revenue	366,107,000	363,800,000	365,912,000	351,102,000	280,719,000	
R&D Expense	29,436,000	27,656,000	25,761,000	22,005,000	19,803,000	
Operating Income	-16,657,000	27,710,000	7,955,000	123,000	28,085,000	
Operating Margin %	-.05%	.08%	.02%	.00%	.10%	
SGA Expense	118,203,000	80,962,000	102,185,000	106,163,000	48,445,000	
Net Income	-79,304,000	18,398,000	16,617,000	-7,904,000	16,940,000	
Operating Cash Flow	11,544,000	47,740,000	66,894,000	25,796,000	47,400,000	
Capital Expenditure	22,192,000	12,007,000	8,339,000	7,962,000	4,317,000	
EBITDA	-6,237,000	60,597,000	61,946,000	25,182,000	40,144,000	
Return on Assets %	-.14%	.03%	.04%	-.02%	.06%	
Return on Equity %	-.46%	.09%	.09%	-.04%	.10%	
Debt to Equity	1.46	1.342	0.776	0.899	0.738	

CONTACT INFORMATION:

Phone: 949-600-5600   Fax: 805-856-3857
Toll-Free:
Address: 15635 Alton Pkwy, Ste. 250, Irvine, CA 92618 United States

STOCK TICKER/OTHER:

Stock Ticker: CAMP   Exchange: NAS
Employees: 983   Fiscal Year Ends: 02/28
Parent Company:

SALARIES/BONUSES:

Top Exec. Salary: $ Bonus: $
Second Exec. Salary: $ Bonus: $

OTHER THOUGHTS:

Estimated Female Officers or Directors: 1
Hot Spot for Advancement for Women/Minorities:

Calero-MDSL

NAIC Code: 511210Q

TYPES OF BUSINESS:

Financial Software for the Telecommunications Industry
Software
Expense Management
Telecom Solutions
Mobility Solutions
Software-as-a-Service Solutions

BRANDS/DIVISIONS/AFFILIATES:

CONTACTS: *Note: Officers with more than one job title may be intentionally listed here more than once.*

Scott Gilbert, CEO
Andrew Taylor, Pres.
Brian Brady, CFO
David Bliss, Exec. VP-Product Mgmt..
Kris Sleeper, VP-Human Resources
James Jones, Dir.-R&D
Simon Mendoza, CTO
Kristie Shanks, Dir.-Prod. Management & Quality Assurance
Brian Martin, Pres., Telesoft Recovery Corp.
Robert Sullivan, Exec. VP-Telesoft Recovery Corp.
Joan Lara, Dir.-Managed Services
Devin Gentry, Dir.-Implementation
Patrick Mulvehill, Exec. VP-Oper.

GROWTH PLANS/SPECIAL FEATURES:

Calero-MDSL is a software provider, with a focus on expense management for the technology industry. The firm's solutions are designed to offer clarity, control, compliance and cost savings. Solutions are grouped into three categories: telecom, mobility and software-as-a-service (SaaS). The telecom solutions category provides an easy-to-use platform that enables order management, usage analysis, call accounting and expense management for telecom environments, spanning a wide range of applications such as inventory tracking, automating expenses and gaining insight. The mobility solution category offers managed mobility services, which centralizes enterprise mobility across global carriers from a single platform. This division support customer's teams with resources for all mobile hardware, software and carrier-related issues. It prepares and delivers devices for immediate use, including pre-loading of apps, configuration and customized packaging. Calero-MDSL verifies device eligibility and places orders with carriers around the world to keep mobile inventory up-to-date, which also offering a centralized view of everything. The SaaS solution category provides expense management across all unified communications spend, including subscriptions, variable teleconferencing and call usage. Turn-key integrations are provided for enabling end-to-end invoice, subscription (phone, webinar, rooms, etc.), call accounting, contract and renewals management. Based in the U.S., Calero-MDSL has offices worldwide, including North America, Europe and Asia.

FINANCIAL DATA: *Note: Data for latest year may not have been available at press time.*

In U.S. $	2020	2019	2018	2017	2016	2015
Revenue						
R&D Expense						
Operating Income						
Operating Margin %						
SGA Expense						
Net Income						
Operating Cash Flow						
Capital Expenditure						
EBITDA						
Return on Assets %						
Return on Equity %						
Debt to Equity						

CONTACT INFORMATION:

Phone: 866-769-5992   Fax:
Toll-Free:
Address: 1040 University Ave., Ste. 200, Rochester, NY 14607 United States

STOCK TICKER/OTHER:

Stock Ticker: Private   Exchange:
Employees: 140   Fiscal Year Ends: 11/30
Parent Company:

SALARIES/BONUSES:

Top Exec. Salary: $ Bonus: $
Second Exec. Salary: $ Bonus: $

OTHER THOUGHTS:

Estimated Female Officers or Directors: 2
Hot Spot for Advancement for Women/Minorities:

Calient Technologies Inc

www.calient.net

NAIC Code: 334210

TYPES OF BUSINESS:

Fiber-Optic Switches
Photonic Switches & Software
MEMS Technologies
Professional Services

BRANDS/DIVISIONS/AFFILIATES:

Suzhou Chunxing Precision Mechanical Co Ltd
S Series Optical Circuit Switch
LightConnect Fabric Manager
Edge/640 Optical Circuit Switch
Calient Optical Components

CONTACTS: Note: Officers with more than one job title may be intentionally listed here more than once.

Arjun Gupta, CEO
Kevin Walsh, Pres.-Oper.
Rick Santos, CFO
Jitender K. Miglani, VP-Eng.
Kevin Welsh, Sr. VP-Oper.
John Reynolds, Head-Bus. Dev. & OEM Partnerships
Shifu Yuan, Co-CTO
Chris Lee, Co-CTO
Daniel Tardent, VP-Mktg.
Erik Leonard, VP-Sales, Svc. Providers & Digital Entertainment

GROWTH PLANS/SPECIAL FEATURES:

Calient Technologies, Inc. manufactures adaptive photonic switching products and software for global service provider, cloud computing, content delivery and government network clients. Products include the S Series Optical Circuit Switch, a family of scalable optical circuit switches with port densities ranging from 160 to 320 ports. These switches are suited for data center, cloud computing, service provider and government applications. Calient's OEM (original equipment manufacturer) subsystem solutions build on the S Series Optical Circuit Switch family, aiming to bring pure-photonoic layer optical circuit switching to new markets. The subsystem solutions provide white label optical switching system solutions for OEM applications, and can also be integrated into partner router, switching, next generation ROADM, optical transport and cloud computing platforms. The company's LightConnect Fabric Manager provides software management of the dynamic optical layer in Optical Circuit Switch-powered LightConnect Fabric networks. Core functions of the fabric manager include a topology manager, which maintains a database of the data center network topology and a cross-connect manager. The Edge/640 Optical Circuit Switch is a variant of the S-Series and built for reconfiguring connectivity between network or device domains. Subsidiary Calient Optical Components manufactures MEMS (microelectromechanical systems) silicon semiconductor systems on micro- to nano-scale wafers for the biotechnology and nanotechnology industries. Its 3D MEMs switches allow data center operators to dramatically improve utilization rates of expensive compute resources. Partners of Calient include Spirent Communications, ADARA Networks, Phoenix Datacom, Cumulus Networks, Signa Solutions Nordic Oy and Plexxi, Inc.

FINANCIAL DATA: Note: Data for latest year may not have been available at press time.

In U.S. $	2020	2019	2018	2017	2016	2015
Revenue						
R&D Expense						
Operating Income						
Operating Margin %						
SGA Expense						
Net Income						
Operating Cash Flow						
Capital Expenditure						
EBITDA						
Return on Assets %						
Return on Equity %						
Debt to Equity						

CONTACT INFORMATION:

Phone: 805-695-4800   Fax:
Toll-Free:
Address: 25 Castilian Dr., Goleta, CA 93117 United States

STOCK TICKER/OTHER:

Stock Ticker: Subsidiary   Exchange:
Employees: 82   Fiscal Year Ends: 12/31
Parent Company: Suzhou Chunxing Precision Mechanical Co.Ltd

SALARIES/BONUSES:

Top Exec. Salary: $ Bonus: $
Second Exec. Salary: $ Bonus: $

OTHER THOUGHTS:

Estimated Female Officers or Directors:
Hot Spot for Advancement for Women/Minorities:

Sales, profits and employees may be estimates. Financial information, benefits and other data can change quickly and may vary from those stated here.

Calix Inc

NAIC Code: 334210A

www.calix.com

TYPES OF BUSINESS:
Network Access Equipment
Cloud
Software
Real-Time Data
Insights
Customer Acquisition
Technologies
Professional Services

BRANDS/DIVISIONS/AFFILIATES:

GROWTH PLANS/SPECIAL FEATURES:

Calix, Inc. is a provider of cloud and software platforms that enable service providers to innovate and transform. Customers utilize Calix's real-time data and insights platforms to deliver enhanced subscriber experiences, resulting in subscriber acquisition, loyalty and revenue. Calix solutions include passive optical network (PON), Wi-Fi 6, 5G and cloud technologies, as well as customer support, marketing, network and premises operations solutions. Services by Calix span professional, managed, support, education and customer success. Headquartered in California, USA, Calix has domestic offices in Minnesota and Texas, as well as international offices in Russia, Australia, China and United Arab Emirates.

CONTACTS: *Note: Officers with more than one job title may be intentionally listed here more than once.*
Carl Russo, CEO
Cory Sindelar, CFO
Donald Listwin, Chairman of the Board
Michael Weening, Executive VP, Divisional

FINANCIAL DATA: *Note: Data for latest year may not have been available at press time.*

In U.S. $	2020	2019	2018	2017	2016	2015
Revenue	541,239,000	424,330,000	441,320,000	510,367,000	458,787,000	407,463,000
R&D Expense	85,258,000	81,184,000	89,963,000	127,541,000	106,869,000	89,714,000
Operating Income	43,132,000	-12,927,000	-19,513,000	-77,307,000	-32,619,000	-26,510,000
Operating Margin %		-.03%	-.04%	-.15%	-.07%	-.07%
SGA Expense	138,629,000	119,668,000	126,932,000	122,656,000	125,267,000	117,017,000
Net Income	33,484,000	-17,694,000	-19,298,000	-83,032,000	-27,402,000	-26,333,000
Operating Cash Flow	51,409,000	4,654,000	3,560,000	-62,772,000	24,419,000	-5,341,000
Capital Expenditure	7,819,000	13,353,000	10,426,000	8,026,000	9,839,000	7,278,000
EBITDA	49,587,000	-2,611,000	-10,326,000	-66,316,000	-12,346,000	4,169,000
Return on Assets %		-.06%	-.06%	-.26%	-.08%	-.08%
Return on Equity %		-.12%	-.13%	-.46%	-.12%	-.10%
Debt to Equity		0.093				

CONTACT INFORMATION:
Phone: 408-514-3000   Fax:
Toll-Free:
Address: 2777 Orchard Pkwy, San Jose, CA 95131 United States

STOCK TICKER/OTHER:
Stock Ticker: CALX   Exchange: NYS
Employees: 763   Fiscal Year Ends: 12/31
Parent Company:

SALARIES/BONUSES:
Top Exec. Salary: $ Bonus: $
Second Exec. Salary: $ Bonus: $

OTHER THOUGHTS:
Estimated Female Officers or Directors: 2
Hot Spot for Advancement for Women/Minorities:

Sales, profits and employees may be estimates. Financial information, benefits and other data can change quickly and may vary from those stated here.

Celestica Inc

NAIC Code: 334418

www.celestica.com

TYPES OF BUSINESS:

Contract Electronics Manufacturing
Product Design
Engineering and Design
Distribution Services

BRANDS/DIVISIONS/AFFILIATES:

GROWTH PLANS/SPECIAL FEATURES:

Celestica, Inc. provides design, manufacturing and supply chain solutions globally to customers engaged in the communications, enterprise, aerospace/defense, smart energy, healthcare technology, industrial and capital equipment markets. Celestica smart supply chain solutions and services help customers reduce costs, improve speed-to-market and drive innovation. The company's services include design, engineering, hardware platform solutions, manufacturing services, precision machining, supply chain services, logistics, fulfillment, after-market, and product licensing. Based in Ontario, Canada, Celestica has operation throughout the Americas, Europe and Asia.

CONTACTS: Note: Officers with more than one job title may be intentionally listed here more than once.

Robert Mionis, CEO
Mandeep Chawla, CFO
William Etherington, Chairman of the Board
Elizabeth DelBianco, Chief Administrative Officer
Nicolas Pujet, Chief Strategy Officer
Todd Cooper, COO
John Lawless, President, Divisional
Jason Phillips, President, Divisional

FINANCIAL DATA: Note: Data for latest year may not have been available at press time.

In U.S. $	2020	2019	2018	2017	2016	2015
Revenue	5,748,100,000	5,888,300,000	6,633,200,000	6,110,500,000	6,016,500,000	5,639,200,000
R&D Expense	29,900,000	28,400,000	28,800,000	26,200,000	24,900,000	23,200,000
Operating Income	151,400,000	99,400,000	167,300,000	179,500,000	182,200,000	151,200,000
Operating Margin %		.02%	.03%	.03%	.03%	.03%
SGA Expense	230,700,000	227,300,000	219,000,000	203,200,000	211,100,000	207,500,000
Net Income	60,600,000	70,300,000	98,900,000	105,000,000	136,300,000	66,900,000
Operating Cash Flow	239,600,000	345,000,000	33,100,000	127,000,000	173,300,000	196,300,000
Capital Expenditure	52,800,000	80,500,000	82,200,000	102,600,000	64,100,000	62,800,000
EBITDA	252,600,000	284,700,000	195,400,000	219,000,000	246,600,000	183,700,000
Return on Assets %		.02%	.03%	.04%	.05%	.03%
Return on Equity %		.05%	.07%	.08%	.12%	.05%
Debt to Equity		0.412	0.488	0.123	0.152	0.23

CONTACT INFORMATION:

Phone: 416 448-2211   Fax: 416 448-4810
Toll-Free: 888-899-9998
Address: 844 Don Mills Rd., Toronto, ON M3C 1V7 Canada

SALARIES/BONUSES:

Top Exec. Salary: $ Bonus: $
Second Exec. Salary: $ Bonus: $

STOCK TICKER/OTHER:

Stock Ticker: CLS   Exchange: NYS
Employees: 26,400   Fiscal Year Ends: 12/31
Parent Company:

OTHER THOUGHTS:

Estimated Female Officers or Directors: 4
Hot Spot for Advancement for Women/Minorities: Y

Cellcom Israel Ltd

NAIC Code: 517210

www.cellcom.co.il

TYPES OF BUSINESS:

Cell Phone Service
Virtual Private Network Provider
Internet Service Provider

GROWTH PLANS/SPECIAL FEATURES:

Cellcom Israel, Ltd., founded in 1994, is one of Israel's leading cellular providers. The company offers a broad range of cellular services such as basic and advanced cellular telephone services, text and multimedia messaging services and advanced cellular content and data services. International roaming is available via partnerships with operators in 180 countries. Cellcom sells a wide variety of handsets, along with extended warranty and repair and replacement services. It also offers landline telephony services. Cellcom operates an LTE 4 generation network and high-speed packet access (HSPA) 3.5 generation network, which enables high-speed data transmission in addition to GSM/GPRS/EDGE networks. The firm's advanced technological infrastructure allows it to offer subscribers value-added services including nationwide video streaming; Java games; multimedia messages (MMS); prepaid telephone SIM cards; internet television services (over-the-top/OTT); and subscription-based streaming music services. In addition, the company offers a range of wireless communication services to both the private and business sectors, including virtual private network (VPN), global roaming, voice-activated dialing, conference calling, content and media services. The firm offers landline telephone communication services and data communication services through its wholly-owned subsidiary Cellcom Fixed Line Communications LP.

BRANDS/DIVISIONS/AFFILIATES:

Cellcom Fixed Line Communications LP

CONTACTS: Note: Officers with more than one job title may be intentionally listed here more than once.

Avi Gabbay, CEO
Liat Menahemi-Stadler, Gen. Legal Counsel
Eli Nir, Chief Internal Audit
Amos Maor, VP-Sales & Svcs.
Keren Shtevy, VP-Bus. Customers
Itamar Bartov, VP-Exec. & Regulatory Affairs
Galit Tuchterman, Spokeswoman

FINANCIAL DATA: Note: Data for latest year may not have been available at press time.

In U.S. $	2020	2019	2018	2017	2016	2015
Revenue		1,088,401,792	1,082,531,200	1,103,201,024	1,178,043,392	1,196,045,568
R&D Expense						
Operating Income						
Operating Margin %						
SGA Expense						
Net Income		-31,407,494	-18,198,736	31,919,018	43,295,360	27,182,856
Operating Cash Flow						
Capital Expenditure						
EBITDA						
Return on Assets %						
Return on Equity %						
Debt to Equity						

CONTACT INFORMATION:

Phone: 972 529990052   Fax:
Toll-Free:
Address: 10 Hagavish St., Netanya, 42140 Israel

STOCK TICKER/OTHER:

Stock Ticker: CEL
Employees: 3,358
Parent Company:

Exchange: NYS
Fiscal Year Ends: 12/31

SALARIES/BONUSES:

Top Exec. Salary: $ Bonus: $
Second Exec. Salary: $ Bonus: $

OTHER THOUGHTS:

Estimated Female Officers or Directors: 6
Hot Spot for Advancement for Women/Minorities: Y

Certicom Corp

www.certicom.com

NAIC Code: 511210E

TYPES OF BUSINESS:

Computer Software: Network Security, Managed Access, Digital ID, Cybersecurity & Anti-Virus
Cryptography Software
RFID Technology

BRANDS/DIVISIONS/AFFILIATES:

BlackBerry Limited

CONTACTS: Note: Officers with more than one job title may be intentionally listed here more than once.

John Chen, CEO

GROWTH PLANS/SPECIAL FEATURES:

Certicom Corp. manages and protects the value of content, applications and devices with government-approved security solutions. The firm's innovative software solutions encompass encryption technologies for public key infrastructure implementation, device security, anti-counterfeiting, product authentication, asset management and fixed-mobile convergence operations. Certicom has more than 450 patents and patents pending worldwide that cover aspects of elliptic curve cryptography (ECC). Certicom's ECC-based products include asset management systems, which help semiconductor companies secure their manufacturing processes; advanced metering infrastructure and ZigBee power saving technologies; security software for wireless carriers, chip manufacturers, government agencies, telecommunications providers and other companies; and digital rights management (DRM) software for end-user software. Moreover, Certicom has developed key management solutions for automotive gateways and a V2X security credential management system service for vehicle-to-anything communication based on ECC technology innovations. The company's other products include asset management systems, hardware IP cores, gaming security products, security protocols, managed certificate services to secure sensor networks and Internet of Things (IoT) applications, and RFID and 2D barcode solutions. Certicom also provides a suite of professional services, including custom design services; professional services; and consulting services, such as ECC consulting, assessment, planning, architecture and design, implementation, management, cryptographic system and product security consulting services. Certicom provides the core technology for the National Security Agency (NSA) Suite B standard for secure government communications. The company is a member of the ZigBee Alliance, a group of companies globally dedicated to producing cost-effective, low-power monitoring and control products based on an open global standard. Certicom operates as a subsidiary of BlackBerry Limited.

FINANCIAL DATA: Note: Data for latest year may not have been available at press time.

In U.S. $	2020	2019	2018	2017	2016	2015
Revenue						
R&D Expense						
Operating Income						
Operating Margin %						
SGA Expense						
Net Income						
Operating Cash Flow						
Capital Expenditure						
EBITDA						
Return on Assets %						
Return on Equity %						
Debt to Equity						

CONTACT INFORMATION:

Phone: 905-507-4220   Fax: 905-507-4230
Toll-Free: 800-561-6100
Address: 4701 Tahoe Blvd., Fl. 5, Mississauga, ON L4W 0B5 Canada

SALARIES/BONUSES:

Top Exec. Salary: $ Bonus: $
Second Exec. Salary: $ Bonus: $

STOCK TICKER/OTHER:

Stock Ticker: Subsidiary
Employees: 209
Parent Company: BlackBerry Limited

Exchange:
Fiscal Year Ends: 04/30

OTHER THOUGHTS:

Estimated Female Officers or Directors:
Hot Spot for Advancement for Women/Minorities:

Ceske Radiokomunikace as

NAIC Code: 517110

TYPES OF BUSINESS:

Telephone Services
Television Infrastructure
Radio Infrastructure
Internet Infrastructure
Cloud
Streaming
Data Center
Telecommunications

BRANDS/DIVISIONS/AFFILIATES:

Cordiant Digital Infrastructer Limited

GROWTH PLANS/SPECIAL FEATURES:

Ceske Radiokomunikace a.s. (CRA) is a provider of television, radio and internet infrastructure throughout the Czech Republic. CRA's products and services include cloud, streaming, over-the-top (OTT), data centers, telecommunications, infrastructure, Internet of Things (IoT), television broadcasting, radio broadcasting, and corporate network security. The company also offers General Data Protection Regulation (GDPR) data security and cybernetic security solutions. CRA operates as a wholly-owned subsidiary of Cordiant Digital Infrastructer Limited.

CONTACTS: Note: Officers with more than one job title may be intentionally listed here more than once.

Vit Vazan, CEO
Michal Omelka, CFO
Milos Mastnik, CCO
Pavel Kos, CTO
Pavla Tloustova, Legal & Regulatory Dir.
Marie Fianova, Dir.-Comm.

FINANCIAL DATA: Note: Data for latest year may not have been available at press time.

In U.S. $	2020	2019	2018	2017	2016	2015
Revenue	89,137,125	84,892,500	80,850,000	77,000,000	76,000,000	75,828,610
R&D Expense						
Operating Income						
Operating Margin %						
SGA Expense						
Net Income						
Operating Cash Flow						
Capital Expenditure						
EBITDA						
Return on Assets %						
Return on Equity %						
Debt to Equity						

CONTACT INFORMATION:

Phone: 420 2 4241 1111   Fax: 420 2 4241 7595
Toll-Free:
Address: Skokanska 2117/1, Praha 6 SkokanskÃ¡ 2117/1 169 00, Prague, 160 00 Czech Republic

STOCK TICKER/OTHER:

Stock Ticker: Private   Exchange:
Employees: 226   Fiscal Year Ends: 12/31
Parent Company: Cordiant Digital Infrastructer Limited

SALARIES/BONUSES:

Top Exec. Salary: $ Bonus: $
Second Exec. Salary: $ Bonus: $

OTHER THOUGHTS:

Estimated Female Officers or Directors: 3
Hot Spot for Advancement for Women/Minorities: Y

Channell Commercial Corporation

www.channell.com

NAIC Code: 334210

TYPES OF BUSINESS:

Telecommunications Infrastructure Hardware
Thermoplastic & Metal Enclosures
Fiber-Optic Cable Management Systems
Termination & Connection Products
Splice Closures
Terminals
Splitters
Pedestals

BRANDS/DIVISIONS/AFFILIATES:

GROWTH PLANS/SPECIAL FEATURES:

Channell Commercial Corporation, founded in 1922, manufactures and supplies fiber optic solutions, thermoplastic pedestals and grade level vaults for outside plant construction needs. The company specializes in end-to-end, full network solutions. Channell serves the fiber optic, telecommunication, broadband, water, power and utility industries. Channell's products include splice closures, splitters, terminals, pedestals, vaults, grade level boxes, cabinets, covers and self-lock protection systems. Channell's Rockwall, Texas facility is a 280,000-square-foot state-of-the-art plant featuring high-automation robotics and end-to-end material processing. The firm's other manufacturing facilities are located in Canada, the U.K. (which serves Europe, the Middle East and Africa) and Australia (which also services Asia and the Pacific Rim). Channell is headquartered in Texas, USA.

CONTACTS: *Note: Officers with more than one job title may be intentionally listed here more than once.*

William H. Channell, Jr., Pres.
Jacqueline M. Channell, Sec.
Greg Balla, Managing Dir.-Australasia

FINANCIAL DATA: *Note: Data for latest year may not have been available at press time.*

In U.S. $	2020	2019	2018	2017	2016	2015
Revenue						
R&D Expense						
Operating Income						
Operating Margin %						
SGA Expense						
Net Income						
Operating Cash Flow						
Capital Expenditure						
EBITDA						
Return on Assets %						
Return on Equity %						
Debt to Equity						

CONTACT INFORMATION:

Phone: 214-304-7800   Fax:
Toll-Free: 800-423-1863
Address: 1700 Justin Rd., Rockwall, TX 75087 United States

STOCK TICKER/OTHER:

Stock Ticker: Private   Exchange:
Employees: 200   Fiscal Year Ends: 12/31
Parent Company:

SALARIES/BONUSES:

Top Exec. Salary: $ Bonus: $
Second Exec. Salary: $ Bonus: $

OTHER THOUGHTS:

Estimated Female Officers or Directors: 1
Hot Spot for Advancement for Women/Minorities:

Charter Communications Inc

NAIC Code: 517110

www.charter.com

TYPES OF BUSINESS:

Cable TV Service
Internet Access
Advanced Broadband Cable Services
Telephony Services
Voice Over Internet Protocol

BRANDS/DIVISIONS/AFFILIATES:

Spectrum
Spectrum TV
Spectrum Internet Gig
Spectrum Voice
Spectrum Mobile
Spectrum Enterprise Solutions
Spectrum Community Solutions
Spectrum Reach

CONTACTS: *Note: Officers with more than one job title may be intentionally listed here more than once.*

Thomas Rutledge, CEO
James Blackley, Executive VP, Divisional
Christopher Winfrey, CFO
Kevin Howard, Chief Accounting Officer
Jonathan Hargis, Chief Marketing Officer
John Bickham, COO
John Malone, Director Emeritus
Tom Montemagno, Executive VP, Divisional
Paul Marchand, Executive VP, Divisional
Kathleen Mayo, Executive VP, Divisional
Thomas Adams, Executive VP, Divisional
Scott Weber, Executive VP, Divisional
Catherine Bohigian, Executive VP, Divisional
James Nuzzo, Executive VP, Divisional

GROWTH PLANS/SPECIAL FEATURES:

Charter Communications, Inc. operates broadband communications businesses in the U.S., offering traditional cable video programming, high-speed internet access and voice service as well as advanced broadband services. The company serves approximately 29.2 million residential and business customers. In addition, Charter sells video and online advertising inventory to local, regional and national advertising customers, as well as fiber-delivered communications and managed information technology (IT) solutions to larger enterprise customers. The firm owns and operates regional sports networks and local sports, news and lifestyle channels; and sells security and home management services to the residential marketplace. Charter's products and services include subscription-based video services, including video on demand (VOD), high definition (HD) television, and digital video recorder (DVR), internet services and voice services. Video, internet and voice services are offered to residential and commercial customers on a subscription basis, sold as bundled or individually. The firm sells its products and services under the Spectrum brand name, including Spectrum TV, Spectrum Internet Gig, Spectrum Voice, Spectrum Mobile, Spectrum Business, Spectrum Enterprise Solutions, Spectrum Community Solutions, Spectrum Reach and Spectrum en Espanol and Spectrum.net.

Charter Communications offers its employees comprehensive benefits and retirement options.

FINANCIAL DATA: *Note: Data for latest year may not have been available at press time.*

In U.S. $	2020	2019	2018	2017	2016	2015
Revenue	48,097,000,000	45,764,000,000	43,634,000,000	41,581,000,000	29,003,000,000	9,754,000,000
R&D Expense						
Operating Income	8,463,000,000	6,614,000,000	5,456,000,000	4,452,000,000	4,340,000,000	1,203,000,000
Operating Margin %		.14%	.13%	.11%	.15%	.12%
SGA Expense					-899,000,000	
Net Income	3,222,000,000	1,668,000,000	1,230,000,000	9,895,000,000	3,522,000,000	-271,000,000
Operating Cash Flow	14,562,000,000	11,748,000,000	11,767,000,000	11,954,000,000	8,041,000,000	2,359,000,000
Capital Expenditure	7,956,000,000	7,140,000,000	9,595,000,000	7,870,000,000	33,532,000,000	1,812,000,000
EBITDA	17,854,000,000	16,154,000,000	15,544,000,000	14,706,000,000	10,226,000,000	3,100,000,000
Return on Assets %		.01%	.01%	.07%	.04%	-.01%
Return on Equity %		.05%	.03%	.25%	.18%	-5.42%
Debt to Equity		2.435	1.916	1.745	1.488	

CONTACT INFORMATION:

Phone: 203-905-7801   Fax:
Toll-Free:
Address: 400 Atlantic St., Stamford, CT 06901 United States

SALARIES/BONUSES:

Top Exec. Salary: $ Bonus: $
Second Exec. Salary: $ Bonus: $

STOCK TICKER/OTHER:

Stock Ticker: CHTR   Exchange: NAS
Employees: 96,100   Fiscal Year Ends: 12/31
Parent Company:

OTHER THOUGHTS:

Estimated Female Officers or Directors: 1
Hot Spot for Advancement for Women/Minorities:

China Communications Services Corporation Limited

www.chinaccs.com.hk

NAIC Code: 237130

TYPES OF BUSINESS:

Power and Communication Line and Related Structures Construction
Telecommunications
Business Process Outsourcing

BRANDS/DIVISIONS/AFFILIATES:

China Telecom Corporation Limited

CONTACTS: Note: Officers with more than one job title may be intentionally listed here more than once.

Xiaoqing Huang, Pres.
Xu Zhang, CFO
Xiaochu Wang, Chmn.

GROWTH PLANS/SPECIAL FEATURES:

China Communications Services Corporation Limited is a leading service provider in China, serving the information sector. China Communications operates as a subsidiary of China Telecom Corporation Limited, and offers telecommunications infrastructure services, business process outsourcing services, and applications and content services. Telecommunications infrastructure services include design, construction, project supervision and management; business process outsourcing services include management of infrastructure for information technology (IT), general facilities management, supply chain and products distribution; and applications and content services include system integration, software development, system support and value-added services. China Communications comprises more than 100 specialized subsidiaries, which serve all the major telecommunications operators in China, including those within the information, media and technology industries. The firm also provides services to domestic non-telecom operator customers such as government agencies, industrial consumers and small-to-medium-sized businesses. To a lesser extent, China Communications offers various related services to global customers in Africa, the Middle East and Southeast Asia.

FINANCIAL DATA: Note: Data for latest year may not have been available at press time.

In U.S. $	2020	2019	2018	2017	2016	2015
Revenue	19,221,860,000	18,401,290,000	16,640,280,000	14,821,640,000	13,862,010,000	12,688,250,000
R&D Expense						
Operating Income	442,129,900	457,512,300	447,960,600	452,160,600	434,080,100	408,621,500
Operating Margin %		.03%	.03%	.03%	.03%	.03%
SGA Expense	1,853,475,000	1,801,433,000	1,662,995,000	1,549,270,000	1,489,097,000	1,458,484,000
Net Income	482,936,800	477,883,200	454,703,100	425,378,600	397,487,600	365,855,200
Operating Cash Flow	854,684,500	754,094,600	667,790,500	1,091,455,000	825,183,500	734,686,000
Capital Expenditure	553,525,100	184,965,500	154,744,600	158,860,300	132,689,100	127,222,600
EBITDA	768,146,100	754,479,500	672,123,800	643,718,000	619,517,400	583,301,700
Return on Assets %		.04%	.04%	.04%	.04%	.04%
Return on Equity %		.09%	.10%	.10%	.10%	.10%
Debt to Equity		0.02	0.00	0.001	0.001	0.001

CONTACT INFORMATION:

Phone: 8610-58502290   Fax: 8610-58601534
Toll-Free:
Address: Blk. 1, Compound No. 1, Fenghuangzui St., Beijing, 100073 China

STOCK TICKER/OTHER:

Stock Ticker: CUCSF   Exchange: GREY
Employees: 90,003   Fiscal Year Ends: 12/31
Parent Company: China Telecom Corporation Limited

SALARIES/BONUSES:

Top Exec. Salary: $ Bonus: $
Second Exec. Salary: $ Bonus: $

OTHER THOUGHTS:

Estimated Female Officers or Directors:
Hot Spot for Advancement for Women/Minorities:

China Mobile Limited

www.chinamobileltd.com

NAIC Code: 517210

TYPES OF BUSINESS:

Mobile Phone Service
Wireless Music Service
News & Information Service
Instant Messaging Service
Data Services

BRANDS/DIVISIONS/AFFILIATES:

China Mobile Communications Group Co Ltd
Shanghai Pudong Development Bank

CONTACTS: *Note: Officers with more than one job title may be intentionally listed here more than once.*

Xin Dong, CEO
Ronghua Li, CFO
Huang Wnelin, VP
Sha Yuejia, VP
Liu Aili, VP
Jie Yang, Chmn.

GROWTH PLANS/SPECIAL FEATURES:

China Mobile Limited (CML) is a leading provider of mobile telecommunications services in Mainland China. CML is one of the largest wireless communications providers in the world in terms of total subscribers, with more than 945 million customers. The firm is a publicly-traded subsidiary of China Mobile Communications Group Co., Ltd., owning a majority 72.72%. CML provides wireless products and services in all 31 Chinese provinces, regions and municipalities, including Hong Kong, through several wholly-owned subsidiaries. The company offers voice services comprising local calls, domestic long-distance calls, international long-distance calls, intra-provincial roaming, inter-provincial roaming and international roaming, as well as providing voice value-added services such as caller identity display, caller restrictions, call waiting, call forwarding, call holding, voice mail, conference calls and more. The company also offers: SMS (short message services) and other data services; and MMS (multimedia message services), which allows users to combine and deliver several types of messages, including graphics, sounds, text, and motion pictures over wireless networks. In addition, CML provides high-speed internet through wireless local area networks (WLAN) throughout Mainland China. The company's 4G and 5G business is based on the FDD (frequency division duplex) mode long-term evolution (LTE) technology. CML owns a minority interest in Shanghai Pudong Development Bank.

FINANCIAL DATA: *Note: Data for latest year may not have been available at press time.*

In U.S. $	2020	2019	2018	2017	2016	2015
Revenue		110,869,217,280	109,516,939,264	104,327,135,232	104,893,775,872	97,093,730,304
R&D Expense						
Operating Income						
Operating Margin %						
SGA Expense						
Net Income		15,850,562,560	17,506,353,152	16,100,168,704	16,100,953,088	15,768,224,768
Operating Cash Flow						
Capital Expenditure						
EBITDA						
Return on Assets %						
Return on Equity %						
Debt to Equity						

CONTACT INFORMATION:

Phone: 85 231218888　　　　Fax: 85 225119092
Toll-Free:
Address: 99 Queen's Rd. Central, The Center, 60/Fl, Hong Kong, Hong Kong Hong Kong

STOCK TICKER/OTHER:

Stock Ticker: CHL　　　　　　　　Exchange: NYS
Employees: 456,239　　　　　　　Fiscal Year Ends: 12/31
Parent Company: China Mobile Communications Group Co Ltd

SALARIES/BONUSES:

Top Exec. Salary: $　　　　Bonus: $
Second Exec. Salary: $　　　Bonus: $

OTHER THOUGHTS:

Estimated Female Officers or Directors: 1
Hot Spot for Advancement for Women/Minorities: Y

China Telecom Corporation Limited

www.chinatelecom-h.com

NAIC Code: 517110

TYPES OF BUSINESS:

Fixed-Line & Wireless Telecommunications Services
Internet & e-Commerce Services
Outsourcing Services

BRANDS/DIVISIONS/AFFILIATES:

CONTACTS: Note: Officers with more than one job title may be intentionally listed here more than once.

Ruiwen Ke, CEO
Zhengmao Li, Pres.
Min Zhu, CFO
Yung Shun Loy, Jacky, Sec.
Gao Jinxing, Financial Controller
Li Ping, Exec. VP
Zhang Jiping, Exec. VP
Yang Xiaowei, Exec. VP
Sun Kangmin, Exec. VP
Ruiwen Ke, Chmn.

GROWTH PLANS/SPECIAL FEATURES:

China Telecom Corporation Limited is one of the largest telecommunications and broadband service providers in China. With 153 million wireline access lines in service, 336 million mobile subscribers, 153 million broadband subscribers and 111 million access lines in service. China Telecom operates in 31 provinces, municipalities and autonomous regions. The company focuses on government, financial and large enterprise customers. China Telecom's wireline telephone services consist of local telephone; domestic long distance; and international, Hong Kong, Macau and Taiwan long distance and interconnection. Mobile voice services include local calls, domestic long-distance calls, international long-distance calls, intra-provincial roaming, inter-provincial roaming and international roaming. The firm is focused on further developing high speed services. It is a leader in 4G and 5G wireless within China. The firm also provides industry-specific applications for government and enterprise subscribers. Internet access services consist of wireline internet access services, including dial-up and broadband services, and wireless internet access services. Services are offered through integrated and customized plans. The firm's fiber-to-the-home (FTTH) subscribers comprise approximately 110 million. Value added services are offered for the wireline and mobile services, and include caller ID, color ringtone, mobile MMS (multimedia messaging service) and industry-specific applications for government and enterprises. Additionally, the company provides integrated information application services and managed data and leased line services.

FINANCIAL DATA: Note: Data for latest year may not have been available at press time.

In U.S. $	2020	2019	2018	2017	2016	2015
Revenue		55,847,145,472	56,053,747,712	51,596,083,200	52,161,781,760	48,116,047,872
R&D Expense						
Operating Income						
Operating Margin %						
SGA Expense						
Net Income		3,049,539,840	3,152,543,744	2,622,851,584	2,665,798,400	2,913,385,728
Operating Cash Flow						
Capital Expenditure						
EBITDA						
Return on Assets %						
Return on Equity %						
Debt to Equity						

CONTACT INFORMATION:

Phone: 86 10 5850 1800   Fax: 86 10 6601 0728
Toll-Free:
Address: 31 Jinrong St., Xicheng Dist., Beijing, 100033 China

STOCK TICKER/OTHER:

Stock Ticker: CHA
Employees: 281,215
Parent Company:

Exchange: NYS
Fiscal Year Ends: 12/31

SALARIES/BONUSES:

Top Exec. Salary: $ Bonus: $
Second Exec. Salary: $ Bonus: $

OTHER THOUGHTS:

Estimated Female Officers or Directors: 3
Hot Spot for Advancement for Women/Minorities: Y

China Unicom (Hong Kong) Limited

www.chinaunicom.com.hk/en/global/home.php
NAIC Code: 517110

TYPES OF BUSINESS:
Wireless Phone Service
Fixed Line Services
Wireless Services
Communications Technology
Omnichannel

BRANDS/DIVISIONS/AFFILIATES:
China United Network Communications Group Co Ltd

CONTACTS: Note: Officers with more than one job title may be intentionally listed here more than once.
Zhongyue Chen, CEO
Kebing Zhu, CFO
Chu Ka Yee, Sec.
Tong Jilu, Sr. VP
Xiaochu Wang, Chmn.

GROWTH PLANS/SPECIAL FEATURES:
China Unicom (Hong Kong) Limited is an integrated telecommunications operator in China. The company offers value-added services, fixed-line voice services, wireless services, fixed-line broadband and other internet-related services, information and communications technology services, as well as business and data communications services. China Unicom's nationwide cellular communications services are based on Global System for Mobile (GSM) communications technologies. Its mobile business provides a full range of IT and telecommunication services, including mobile broadband (Wideband Code Division Multiple Access-WCDMA, long-term evolution-LTE, frequency division duplex-FDD, time division LTE/TD-LTE, 5G), fixed-line broadband, GSM, fixed-line local access, ICT, data communications and other related value-added services. The mobile division offers products such as mobile Internet, mobile music, mobile TV, video handsets, mobile reading and an app store. China Unicom's fixed-line business includes fixed-line broadband, data communication and traditional fixed-line businesses. This division features public telephone systems, local calls, domestic and international long-distance calls, IP phones and telephone cards. Its value-added services include personalized ring and caller identification services. China Unicom has built an integrated online-to-offline (O2O) business model, bringing physical store products to online consumers, offering an omnichannel retail strategy. China Unicom operates as a subsidiary of China United Network Communications Group Company Limited, which holds a majority, 52.1% share.

FINANCIAL DATA: Note: Data for latest year may not have been available at press time.

In U.S. $	2020	2019	2018	2017	2016	2015
Revenue		43,180,634,112	43,234,443,264	38,719,217,664	40,599,527,424	40,248,860,672
R&D Expense						
Operating Income						
Operating Margin %						
SGA Expense						
Net Income		1,684,032,128	1,515,629,056	257,537,328	92,541,872	1,534,416,000
Operating Cash Flow						
Capital Expenditure						
EBITDA						
Return on Assets %						
Return on Equity %						
Debt to Equity						

CONTACT INFORMATION:
Phone: 852 21213220   Fax: 852 21213232
Toll-Free:
Address: 99 Queens Rd. Central, The Center, 75/Fl, Hong Kong, Hong Kong Hong Kong

STOCK TICKER/OTHER:
Stock Ticker: CHU   Exchange: NYS
Employees: 242,894   Fiscal Year Ends: 12/31
Parent Company: China United Network Communications Group Co Ltd

SALARIES/BONUSES:
Top Exec. Salary: $ Bonus: $
Second Exec. Salary: $ Bonus: $

OTHER THOUGHTS:
Estimated Female Officers or Directors:
Hot Spot for Advancement for Women/Minorities:

Chorus Limited

www.chorus.co.nz

NAIC Code: 517110

TYPES OF BUSINESS:

Wired Telecommunications Carriers
Telecommunications
Open Access Internet Network
Broadband
Telephone Services

BRANDS/DIVISIONS/AFFILIATES:

GROWTH PLANS/SPECIAL FEATURES:

Chorus Limited is a telecommunication business that builds and operates an open access internet network, providing broadband services throughout New Zealand. For residential and business customers, Chorus offers telephone and internet services over copper and fiber infrastructure. Copper connectivity includes asymmetric digital subscriber line (ADSL), ADSL2+, baseband IP, unbundled copper local loop (UCLL) and very high-speed digital subscriber line (VDSL). Fiber connectivity spans home, hyper fiber home, new property development and pre-built fiber.

CONTACTS: *Note: Officers with more than one job title may be intentionally listed here more than once.*

JB Rousselot, CEO
David Collins, CFO
Ed Hyde, CCO
Shaun Philip, Chief People Officer
Ewen Powell, CTO

FINANCIAL DATA: *Note: Data for latest year may not have been available at press time.*

In U.S. $	2020	2019	2018	2017	2016	2015
Revenue	691,240,900	645,545,000	713,000,800	747,816,800	726,782,100	723,880,800
R&D Expense						
Operating Income	174,079,600	118,229,000	187,860,800	240,084,700	189,311,500	195,839,500
Operating Margin %		.18%	.26%	.32%	.26%	.27%
SGA Expense	67,455,830	63,103,840	59,477,180	66,005,160	68,181,160	63,103,840
Net Income	37,717,240	38,442,570	61,653,180	81,962,460	66,005,160	66,005,160
Operating Cash Flow						
Capital Expenditure	492,500,100	584,617,200	555,603,900	462,761,500	412,713,600	427,220,300
EBITDA	478,718,800	468,564,100	478,718,800	480,169,400	435,924,200	442,452,200
Return on Assets %		.01%	.02%	.03%	.02%	.02%
Return on Equity %		.05%	.09%	.12%	.11%	.12%
Debt to Equity		2.03	2.00	1.873	1.924	2.189

CONTACT INFORMATION:

Phone: 649-975-2983   Fax:
Toll-Free:
Address: 1 Willis St., 10/Fl, Wellington, 6140 New Zealand

STOCK TICKER/OTHER:

Stock Ticker: CHRYY   Exchange: PINX
Employees: 870   Fiscal Year Ends: 06/30
Parent Company:

SALARIES/BONUSES:

Top Exec. Salary: $ Bonus: $
Second Exec. Salary: $ Bonus: $

OTHER THOUGHTS:

Estimated Female Officers or Directors:
Hot Spot for Advancement for Women/Minorities:

Chunghwa Telecom Co Ltd

NAIC Code: 517110

www.cht.com.tw/en/home/cht

TYPES OF BUSINESS:

Telephone Service
Cellular Service
Internet & Data Service

BRANDS/DIVISIONS/AFFILIATES:

Ministry of Transportation and Communications
Light Era Development Co Ltd
Chunghwa System Integration Co Ltd
Chunghwa Telecom Global Inc
HiNet

CONTACTS: *Note: Officers with more than one job title may be intentionally listed here more than once.*

Shui-yi Kuo, Pres.
Chi-Mau Sheih, Chmn.

GROWTH PLANS/SPECIAL FEATURES:

Chunghwa Telecom Co., Ltd. is one of the largest telecommunications service providers in Taiwan as well as in Asia (revenue-wise). The Republic of China, through Taiwan's Ministry of Transportation and Communications, has a significant holding in Chunghwa, granting the government significant levels of control over many managerial aspects of the firm. The firm's principal offerings are domestic fixed communications business, mobile communications business, internet business and international fixed communications business. Domestic fixed communication services include local and domestic long-distance voice services, broadband access services, leased line services, multimedia on demand (MOD) and domestic data services. The mobile communications group offers mobile and paging services, mobile handsets, data cards and other mobile phone accessories. Internet services provide internet data center services, asymmetric digital subscriber line (ADSL), FTTx (fiber to the x, meaning any one of many fiber-optic based network architectures), 4G and 5G/LTE mobile services and HiNet (the company's ISP). Because FTTx uses fiber-optic cables, it can offer increased speed over traditional ADSL service. International fixed communications services include international long-distance telephone services, international leased line services, data services and satellite services. Among Chunghwa's many wholly-owned subsidiaries are included Light Era Development Co. Ltd., a developer of eco-friendly and intelligent structures; Chunghwa System Integration Co. Ltd., a provider of advanced business solutions so financial, public/government, telecom and high-tech manufacturing industries; and Chunghwa Telecom Global, Inc., which oversees the firm's international telecommunications facilities and provides network/communications integration services.

FINANCIAL DATA: *Note: Data for latest year may not have been available at press time.*

In U.S. $	2020	2019	2018	2017	2016	2015
Revenue	7,527,029,000	7,523,802,000	7,812,507,000	8,248,700,000	8,338,506,000	8,403,911,000
R&D Expense	139,584,800	142,884,100	135,052,800	140,890,000	137,228,200	131,137,200
Operating Income	1,478,004,000	1,478,257,000	1,578,360,000	1,697,061,000	1,762,068,000	1,829,685,000
Operating Margin %		.20%	.20%	.21%	.21%	.22%
SGA Expense	939,713,900	978,108,800	1,006,425,000	1,087,057,000	1,089,595,000	1,072,664,000
Net Income	1,211,632,000	1,194,520,000	1,361,659,000	1,413,541,000	1,467,816,000	1,524,157,000
Operating Cash Flow	2,699,461,000	2,625,898,000	2,406,152,000	2,571,696,000	2,354,886,000	2,767,224,000
Capital Expenditure	2,578,367,000	889,318,300	1,053,158,000	1,384,246,000	862,851,600	1,285,775,000
EBITDA	2,878,638,000	2,797,026,000	2,787,055,000	2,899,049,000	2,970,002,000	3,097,477,000
Return on Assets %		.07%	.08%	.09%	.09%	.09%
Return on Equity %		.09%	.10%	.11%	.11%	.12%
Debt to Equity		0.022	0.004	0.004	0.004	0.005

CONTACT INFORMATION:

Phone: 886 223445488   Fax: 886 233938188
Toll-Free:
Address: No.21-3, Sec. 1, Xinyi Rd., Zhongzheng Dist.,, Taipei City, 100 Taiwan

STOCK TICKER/OTHER:

Stock Ticker: CHT   Exchange: NYS
Employees: 32,218   Fiscal Year Ends: 12/31
Parent Company:

SALARIES/BONUSES:

Top Exec. Salary: $ Bonus: $
Second Exec. Salary: $ Bonus: $

OTHER THOUGHTS:

Estimated Female Officers or Directors: 3
Hot Spot for Advancement for Women/Minorities: Y

Ciena Corporation

www.ciena.com

NAIC Code: 334210

TYPES OF BUSINESS:

Communications Networking Equipment
Software & Support Services
Consulting Services
Switching Platforms
Packet Interworking Products
Access Products
Network & Service Management Tools

BRANDS/DIVISIONS/AFFILIATES:

Blue Planet Automation
Adaptive Network

CONTACTS: *Note: Officers with more than one job title may be intentionally listed here more than once.*

Gary Smith, CEO
James Moylan, CFO
Patrick Nettles, Chairman of the Board
Andrew Petrik, Chief Accounting Officer
Stephen Alexander, Chief Technology Officer
David Rothenstein, General Counsel
James Frodsham, Other Executive Officer
Scott McFeely, Senior VP, Divisional
Jason Phipps, Senior VP, Divisional
Rick Hamilton, Senior VP, Divisional

GROWTH PLANS/SPECIAL FEATURES:

Ciena Corporation provides communications networking equipment, software and services that support the transport, switching, aggregation and management of voice, video and data traffic. The firm's solutions include its portfolio of networking platforms, including the converged packet optical and packet networking products, that can be applied from the network core to end user access points, and that allow network operators to scale capacity, increase transmission speeds, allocate traffic and adapt dynamically to changing end-user service demands. Additionally, Ciena offers platform software that provides management and domain control of our hardware solutions and automates network lifecycle operations, including provisioning equipment and services. Through the Blue Planet Automation Software, the firm enables network providers to use network data, analytics and policy-based assurance to achieve closed loop automation across multi-vendor and multi-domain network environments, streamlining key business and network processes. To complement these hardware and software products, Ciena offers a broad range of services that help customers build, operate and improve their networks and associated operational environments. The firm refers to the complete portfolio vision as the Adaptive Network. The Adaptive Network emphasizes a programmable network infrastructure, software control and automation capabilities, and network analytics and intelligence. By transforming network infrastructures into a dynamic, programmable environment driven by automation and analytics, network operators can realize greater business agility, dynamically adapt to changing end user service demands and rapidly introduce new revenue-generating services. They can also gain valuable real-time network insights, allowing them to optimize network operation and maximize the return on their network infrastructure investment. In November 2019, Ciena closed on its acquisition of Centina Systems, a provider of service assurance analytics and network performance management solutions.

FINANCIAL DATA: *Note: Data for latest year may not have been available at press time.*

In U.S. $	2020	2019	2018	2017	2016	2015
Revenue	3,532,157,000	3,572,131,000	3,094,286,000	2,801,687,000	2,600,573,000	2,445,669,000
R&D Expense	529,888,000	548,139,000	491,564,000	475,329,000	451,794,000	414,201,000
Operating Income	513,647,000	374,674,000	253,196,000	238,655,000	165,715,000	134,613,000
Operating Margin %		.10%	.08%	.09%	.06%	.06%
SGA Expense	585,973,000	597,445,000	554,193,000	498,773,000	482,559,000	457,238,000
Net Income	361,291,000	253,434,000	-344,690,000	1,261,953,000	72,584,000	11,667,000
Operating Cash Flow	493,654,000	413,140,000	229,261,000	234,882,000	289,520,000	262,112,000
Capital Expenditure	82,667,000	62,579,000	67,616,000	94,600,000	107,185,000	62,109,000
EBITDA	619,809,000	473,354,000	314,050,000	334,880,000	285,066,000	210,710,000
Return on Assets %		.07%	-.09%	.37%	.03%	.00%
Return on Equity %		.12%	-.17%	.87%	.10%	.04%
Debt to Equity		0.343	0.391	0.308	1.371	2.07

CONTACT INFORMATION:

Phone: 410 694-5700   Fax: 410 694-5750
Toll-Free: 800-921-1144
Address: 7035 Ridge Rd., Hanover, MD 21076 United States

SALARIES/BONUSES:

Top Exec. Salary: $ Bonus: $
Second Exec. Salary: $ Bonus: $

STOCK TICKER/OTHER:

Stock Ticker: CIEN   Exchange: NYS
Employees: 7,032   Fiscal Year Ends: 10/31
Parent Company:

OTHER THOUGHTS:

Estimated Female Officers or Directors: 2
Hot Spot for Advancement for Women/Minorities:

Cincinnati Bell Inc

www.cincinnatibell.com

NAIC Code: 517110

TYPES OF BUSINESS:

Local Telephone Service
Wireless Local Phone Service
Long-Distance Service
Data Services
Internet Access
Digital Services
Payphone Services
IT Consulting

BRANDS/DIVISIONS/AFFILIATES:

Cincinnati Bell Telephone Company LLC
Cincinnati Bell Extended Territories LLC
Hawaiian Telecom Holdco Inc

CONTACTS: Note: Officers with more than one job title may be intentionally listed here more than once.

Andrew Kaiser, CFO
Suzanne Maratta, Controller
Thomas Simpson, COO
Leigh Fox, Director
Christi Cornette, Other Executive Officer
Shannon Mullen, Vice President, Divisional
Joshua Duckworth, Vice President, Divisional
Christopher Wilson, Vice President

GROWTH PLANS/SPECIAL FEATURES:

Cincinnati Bell, Inc. provides integrated communications and information technology (IT) solutions to residential and business customers. The company operates through two business segments: entertainment and communications and IT services and hardware. The entertainment and communications segment provides high-speed data, video and voice solutions over an expanding fiber network, as well as a copper network. Subsidiary Cincinnati Bell Telephone Company, LLC, is the incumbent local exchange carrier for a geography that covers about 25 miles around Cincinnati, and includes parts of northern Kentucky and southeastern Indiana. This segment also provides voice and data services in Dayton and Mason, Ohio, through Cincinnati Bell Extended Territories, LLC, a subsidiary of Cincinnati Bell Telephone; and provides full-service communications on all of Hawaii's major islands through subsidiary Hawaiian Telcom Holdco, Inc. The IT services and hardware segment sells and services end-to-end communications and IT systems and solutions, as well as hybrid cloud services. These products and services are categorized into: consulting, offering IT staffing and application services; cloud, offering virtual data centers, storage, backup, network management/monitoring, security, and cloud consulting; communications, offering unified communications-as-a-services, contact center, software-defined wide area networking, networking solutions, multi-protocol label switching and network-as-a-service; and infrastructure solutions, offering hardware, software licenses and maintenance. During 2020, Cincinnati Bell agreed to be acquired by Macquarie Infrastructure Partners V, a fund managed by Macquarie Infrastructure and Real Assets. The transaction was expected to close by mid-2021, and would cease from being publicly traded.

FINANCIAL DATA: Note: Data for latest year may not have been available at press time.

In U.S. $	2020	2019	2018	2017	2016	2015
Revenue	1,559,800,000	1,536,700,000	1,378,200,000	1,288,500,000	1,185,800,000	1,167,800,000
R&D Expense						
Operating Income	117,900,000	92,800,000	114,100,000	89,300,000	104,900,000	136,500,000
Operating Margin %		.06%	.08%	.07%	.09%	.12%
SGA Expense	346,500,000	354,400,000	313,400,000	240,900,000	218,700,000	219,100,000
Net Income	-55,600,000	-66,600,000	-69,800,000	35,100,000	102,100,000	353,700,000
Operating Cash Flow	206,100,000	259,100,000	214,700,000	203,400,000	173,200,000	110,900,000
Capital Expenditure	230,000,000	223,800,000	220,600,000	210,500,000	286,400,000	283,600,000
EBITDA	346,500,000	367,300,000	323,100,000	344,200,000	420,800,000	723,900,000
Return on Assets %		- .03%	- .03%	.01%	.06%	.21%
Return on Equity %						
Debt to Equity						

CONTACT INFORMATION:

Phone: 513 397-9900   Fax: 513 784-1613
Toll-Free: 800-345-6301
Address: 221 E. Fourth St., Cincinnati, OH 45202 United States

STOCK TICKER/OTHER:

Stock Ticker: CBB   Exchange: NYS
Employees: 4,600   Fiscal Year Ends: 12/31
Parent Company:

SALARIES/BONUSES:

Top Exec. Salary: $ Bonus: $
Second Exec. Salary: $ Bonus: $

OTHER THOUGHTS:

Estimated Female Officers or Directors:
Hot Spot for Advancement for Women/Minorities: Y

Cisco Systems Inc

www.cisco.com

NAIC Code: 334210A

TYPES OF BUSINESS:

Computer Networking Equipment
Routers & Switches
Real-Time Conferencing Technology
Server Virtualization Software
Data Storage Products
Security Products
Teleconference Systems and Technology
Unified Communications Systems

BRANDS/DIVISIONS/AFFILIATES:

AppDynamics Inc
Cicsco Talos
Fluidmesh Networks LLC

CONTACTS: Note: Officers with more than one job title may be intentionally listed here more than once.

Charles Robbins, CEO
Prat Bhatt, Chief Accounting Officer
Geraldine Elliott, Chief Marketing Officer
Kelly Kramer, Executive VP
David Goeckeler, Executive VP
Maria Martinez, Executive VP
Mark Chandler, Executive VP
Irving Tan, Senior VP, Divisional

GROWTH PLANS/SPECIAL FEATURES:

Cisco Systems, Inc. designs and sells a broad range of technologies that power the internet. The company's products and services are grouped into the categories of infrastructure platforms, applications and security. Infrastructure platforms consist of Cisco's core networking technologies of switching, routing, data center products, and wireless that are designed to work together to deliver networking capabilities and transport and/or store data. These technologies consist of both hardware and software that help customers build networks, automate, orchestrate, integrate and digitize data. The firm is moving to software and subscriptions across its core networking portfolio. The applications category primarily includes network security, cloud and email security, identity and access management, advanced threat protection, and unified threat management products. These offerings encompass hardware- and software, including licenses and software-as-a-service (SaaS). Applications include collaboration products/solutions such as unified communications, telepresence and conferencing; and the Internet of Things (IoT) and analytics software from subsidiary AppDynamics, an application intelligence software company. Last, the security category includes Cisco's network security, cloud and email security, identity and access management, advanced threat protection and unified threat management products. Offerings in this category are powered by cloud-delivered threat intelligence based on our Cisco Talos technology. Other products offered primarily consists of Cisco's cloud and system management products. In July 2020, Cisco acquired Fluidmesh Networks, LLC, which has expertise in wireless backhaul systems. As of January 2021, Cisco Systems announced that it was seeking confirmation from the Delaware Court of Chancery that it had met all conditions for closing its acquisition of Acacia Communications, Inc., a public fabless semiconductor company.

FINANCIAL DATA: Note: Data for latest year may not have been available at press time.

In U.S. $	2020	2019	2018	2017	2016	2015
Revenue	49,301,000,000	51,904,000,000	49,330,000,000	48,005,000,000	49,247,000,000	49,161,000,000
R&D Expense	6,347,000,000	6,577,000,000	6,332,000,000	6,059,000,000	6,296,000,000	6,207,000,000
Operating Income	14,101,000,000	14,541,000,000	12,667,000,000	12,729,000,000	12,928,000,000	11,254,000,000
Operating Margin %		.28%	.26%	.27%	.26%	.23%
SGA Expense	11,094,000,000	11,398,000,000	11,386,000,000	11,177,000,000	11,433,000,000	11,861,000,000
Net Income	11,214,000,000	11,621,000,000	110,000,000	9,609,000,000	10,739,000,000	8,981,000,000
Operating Cash Flow	15,426,000,000	15,831,000,000	13,666,000,000	13,876,000,000	13,570,000,000	12,552,000,000
Capital Expenditure	770,000,000	909,000,000	834,000,000	964,000,000	1,146,000,000	1,227,000,000
EBITDA	16,363,000,000	17,327,000,000	16,174,000,000	15,434,000,000	15,746,000,000	14,209,000,000
Return on Assets %		.11%	.00%	.08%	.09%	.08%
Return on Equity %		.30%	.00%	.15%	.17%	.15%
Debt to Equity		0.431	0.471	0.389	0.385	0.359

CONTACT INFORMATION:

Phone: 408 526-4000   Fax: 408 526-4100
Toll-Free: 800-553-6387
Address: 170 W. Tasman Dr., San Jose, CA 95134 United States

STOCK TICKER/OTHER:

Stock Ticker: CSCO   Exchange: NAS
Employees: 77,500   Fiscal Year Ends: 07/31
Parent Company:

SALARIES/BONUSES:

Top Exec. Salary: $ Bonus: $
Second Exec. Salary: $ Bonus: $

OTHER THOUGHTS:

Estimated Female Officers or Directors: 10
Hot Spot for Advancement for Women/Minorities: Y

Sales, profits and employees may be estimates. Financial information, benefits and other data can change quickly and may vary from those stated here.

Cisco Webex
NAIC Code: 517110

www.webex.com

TYPES OF BUSINESS:
Videoconferencing Services
Online Conferencing Services & Software

BRANDS/DIVISIONS/AFFILIATES:
Cisco Systems Inc

CONTACTS: *Note: Officers with more than one job title may be intentionally listed here more than once.*
Chuck Robbins, CEO

GROWTH PLANS/SPECIAL FEATURES:
Cisco Webex, a subsidiary of Cisco Systems, Inc., provides on-demand collaboration, online meeting, online training, web conferencing and video conferencing software applications. The company's services scale to business needs in order to reach and deliver anywhere in the world. Staff meetings, presentations and trainings do not have to be rescheduled or delayed, because they can be accessed anywhere in the world on any device, even mobile. Cisco Webex products are cloud-based and therefore designed to integrate with the rest of a business' IT investments. Cisco Webex products also include cloud calling, a video support platform for providing real-time technical help, an agile contact center focused on customer experience, and artificial intelligence (AI) and machine learning capabilities for enhanced collaboration experiences. Cisco Webex also offers devices, including an all-in-one wireless whiteboard, intelligent video conferencing devices for meeting rooms of all sizes and compact desk video conferencing devices, as well as related accessories such as sound bars, headsets, screen stands and other room kits. Price plans include: Free, for up to 50 participants in each meeting, with meetings lasting up to 40 minutes and 1 gigabytes (GB) of cloud storage; Starter for $13.50 per month for up to 50 participants, 5GB of cloud storage, unlimited time for meetings and other features; Plus for $17.95 per month for up to 100 people per meeting, 5GB of cloud storage, an administrative portal and other features; and Business for $26.95 per month for up to 200 people per meeting, 10GB of cloud storage, branding and customizations and other features.

FINANCIAL DATA: *Note: Data for latest year may not have been available at press time.*

In U.S. $	2020	2019	2018	2017	2016	2015
Revenue						
R&D Expense						
Operating Income						
Operating Margin %						
SGA Expense						
Net Income						
Operating Cash Flow						
Capital Expenditure						
EBITDA						
Return on Assets %						
Return on Equity %						
Debt to Equity						

CONTACT INFORMATION:
Phone: 408-435-7048   Fax:
Toll-Free: 877-509-3239
Address: 855 E. Tasman Dr., San Jose, CA 95035 United States

STOCK TICKER/OTHER:
Stock Ticker: Subsidiary   Exchange:
Employees: 229   Fiscal Year Ends: 12/31
Parent Company: Cisco Systems Inc

SALARIES/BONUSES:
Top Exec. Salary: $ Bonus: $
Second Exec. Salary: $ Bonus: $

OTHER THOUGHTS:
Estimated Female Officers or Directors:
Hot Spot for Advancement for Women/Minorities:

CK Hutchison Holdings Limited
www.ckh.com.hk/en/global/home.php

NAIC Code: 488310

TYPES OF BUSINESS:

Port Operations
Port Operations
Terminal Operator
Retail
Manufacturing
Telecommunications
Investments
Biopharmaceuticals

BRANDS/DIVISIONS/AFFILIATES:

Hutchison Port Holdings Limited
AS Watson Group (HK) Limited
CK Hutchison Group Telecom
Hutchison Telecommunications Hong Kong Holdings
Hutchison Whampoa
Hutchison China MediTech
Cenovus Energy Inc
Hutchison Water

CONTACTS: Note: Officers with more than one job title may be intentionally listed here more than once.

Kin-ning Fok, Group Co-Managing Dir.
Tzar Kuoi (Victor) Li, Group Co-Managing Dir.
Frank J. Sixt, Group Dir.-Finance
Tzar Kuoi Li, Deputy Chmn.
Mo Fong Chow Woo, Deputy Group Managing Dir.
Tzar Kuoi (Victor) Li, Chmn.

GROWTH PLANS/SPECIAL FEATURES:

CK Hutchison Holdings Limited is a Hong Kong-based holding company with operations in over 50 countries. Its five core businesses are: ports and related services, retail, infrastructure, telecommunications, and finance and investments and others. The ports and related services segment, managed through Hutchison Port Holdings Limited, operates 53 ports located in 27 countries. Its operations include Hongkong International Terminals Limited, one of the largest independently owned container terminal operators, as well as distribution centers, ship repair facilities, rail services and cruise ship terminals. The firm's retail activities are conducted by A.S. Watson Group (HK), Limited, an international retail and manufacturing company with over 16,100 retail stores in 23 countries focusing on health and beauty, food, electrical appliances and other consumer goods and the manufacture and distribution of beverages. Retail stores include Watsons, ParknShop, Drogas, Rossmann and Savers, among others. The infrastructure unit consists of a diverse portfolio of investments in energy infrastructure, transportation infrastructure, water infrastructure, waste management, energy-from-waste, household infrastructure and infrastructure-related businesses. The telecommunications business is a global operator of mobile telecommunications and data services, serving more than 110 million customers. CK Hutchison Group Telecom operates networks in Italy, the U.K., Sweden, Denmark, Austria and Ireland, and holds a majority interest in Hutchinson Telecommunications Hong Kong Holdings Limited, a telecommunications operator and mobile services provider. Last, the finance and investments and others business includes returns earned on the group's holdings of cash as liquid investments, Hutchison Whampoa (China), Hutchison China MediTech, Cenovus Energy Inc., TOM Group, Marionnaud, CK Life Sciences and Hutchison Water. These companies are engaged in activities such as venture investments, biopharmaceuticals, energy production, media technology, retail of perfumes and cosmetics, agriculture, water technologies and solutions, digital health devices and more.

FINANCIAL DATA: Note: Data for latest year may not have been available at press time.

In U.S. $	2020	2019	2018	2017	2016	2015
Revenue	34,332,920,000	38,537,610,000	35,716,180,000	32,028,430,000	33,488,240,000	21,491,910,000
R&D Expense						
Operating Income	4,782,838,000	6,657,387,000	5,796,087,000	4,561,681,000	4,808,743,000	3,180,998,000
Operating Margin %		.17%	.16%	.14%	.14%	.15%
SGA Expense	2,550,649,000	3,634,138,000	3,306,269,000	2,132,307,000	2,470,616,000	1,593,463,000
Net Income	3,755,928,000	5,133,261,000	5,026,291,000	4,523,662,000	4,254,047,000	15,281,210,000
Operating Cash Flow	9,430,225,000	8,927,468,000	7,182,957,000	6,907,413,000	5,198,732,000	5,741,443,000
Capital Expenditure	3,811,475,000	4,677,415,000	4,838,901,000	3,082,148,000	3,163,471,000	3,284,101,000
EBITDA	12,102,410,000	13,678,470,000	10,228,890,000	9,387,307,000	9,275,699,000	8,133,442,000
Return on Assets %		.03%	.03%	.03%	.03%	.16%
Return on Equity %		.09%	.08%	.08%	.08%	.29%
Debt to Equity		0.799	0.712	0.682	0.555	0.642

CONTACT INFORMATION:

Phone: 852 21281188   Fax: 852 21281705
Toll-Free:
Address: 48/F, Cheung Kong Center, 2 Queen's Road Central, Hong Kong, Hong Kong Hong Kong

STOCK TICKER/OTHER:

Stock Ticker: CKHUY
Employees: 300,000
Parent Company:

Exchange: PINX
Fiscal Year Ends: 12/31

SALARIES/BONUSES:

Top Exec. Salary: $ Bonus: $
Second Exec. Salary: $ Bonus: $

OTHER THOUGHTS:

Estimated Female Officers or Directors: 2
Hot Spot for Advancement for Women/Minorities:

Sales, profits and employees may be estimates. Financial information, benefits and other data can change quickly and may vary from those stated here.

ClearOne Inc

NAIC Code: 334220

www.clearone.com

TYPES OF BUSINESS:

Teleconferencing Products & Services
Tabletop Conferencing Phones
Installed Audio Systems
Microphones
Conference Furniture
Streaming A/V Equipment
Digital Signage

BRANDS/DIVISIONS/AFFILIATES:

CONTACTS: *Note: Officers with more than one job title may be intentionally listed here more than once.*

Zeynep Hakimoglu, CEO
Narsi Narayanan, CFO

GROWTH PLANS/SPECIAL FEATURES:

ClearOne, Inc. designs, develops and sells conferencing, collaboration and networked streaming solutions for audio/voice and visual communication purposes. The company's global network of audio/visual and information technology experts specify, install and support ClearOne's hardware, software, apps and cloud solutions. Audio conferencing solutions encompass microphones, digital signal processing (DSP) mixers, amplifiers, phones and speakerphones. Visual collaboration solutions encompass cloud-based and on-premise video products, including cameras, connectivity devices, speakers, microphones, web conferencing capabilities and unified messaging/calling. Audio/visual streaming solutions include video on walls, network streaming devices, audio distribution devices, sound reinforcement devices and more. Conference and collaboration spaces range from ad-hoc work spaces and mobile conferences to large meeting venues and boardrooms. ClearOne's solutions and services serve global organizations worldwide, whether a Fortune 500, a small/medium business or an institution. ClearOne is an option for any industry or organization that relies on teamwork and collaboration to be successful. Headquartered in Utah, USA, ClearOne has domestic locations in Florida and Texas, and international locations in Spain, India and the United Arab Emirates.

Employees receive flexible spending accounts; medical, dental and vision coverage; insurance protection; and flexible time-off.

FINANCIAL DATA: *Note: Data for latest year may not have been available at press time.*

In U.S. $	2020	2019	2018	2017	2016	2015
Revenue	29,069,000	25,042,000	28,156,000	41,804,000	48,637,000	57,796,000
R&D Expense	5,512,000	5,775,000	7,840,000	9,342,000	8,584,000	8,318,000
Operating Income	-5,567,000	-8,562,000	-10,327,000	-3,490,000	3,546,000	10,262,000
Operating Margin %		-.34%	-.37%	-.08%	.07%	.18%
SGA Expense	12,614,000	13,980,000	15,858,000	18,157,000	17,357,000	18,139,000
Net Income	505,000	-8,408,000	-16,687,000	-14,172,000	2,444,000	6,776,000
Operating Cash Flow	-982,000	-4,656,000	-6,621,000	-9,271,000	7,834,000	7,594,000
Capital Expenditure	7,217,000	5,367,000	5,135,000	3,205,000	891,000	359,000
EBITDA	-2,612,000	-6,087,000	-8,737,000	-1,959,000	5,419,000	12,320,000
Return on Assets %		-.15%	-.26%	-.18%	.03%	.07%
Return on Equity %		-.17%	-.31%	-.21%	.03%	.09%
Debt to Equity		0.095				

CONTACT INFORMATION:

Phone: 801 975-7200   Fax: 801 977-0087
Toll-Free: 800-945-7730
Address: 5225 Wiley Post Way, Ste. 500, Salt Lake City, UT 84116 United States

STOCK TICKER/OTHER:

Stock Ticker: CLRO
Employees: 126
Parent Company:

Exchange: NAS
Fiscal Year Ends: 12/31

SALARIES/BONUSES:

Top Exec. Salary: $ Bonus: $
Second Exec. Salary: $ Bonus: $

OTHER THOUGHTS:

Estimated Female Officers or Directors: 1
Hot Spot for Advancement for Women/Minorities:

Cloudflare Inc

www.cloudflare.com

NAIC Code: 511210E

TYPES OF BUSINESS:

Computer Software, Network Security, Managed Access, Digital ID,
Cybersecurity & Anti-Virus
Web Content Delivery
Cloud

BRANDS/DIVISIONS/AFFILIATES:

Linc

CONTACTS: Note: Officers with more than one job title may be intentionally listed here more than once.

Matthew Prince, CEO
Lee Holloway, Lead Engineer
Michelle Zatlyn, Head-User Experience

GROWTH PLANS/SPECIAL FEATURES:

Cloudflare, Inc. has built a global cloud platform that delivers a broad range of network services to businesses of all sizes. These services offer web infrastructure and website security, enhance the performance of business-critical applications, and eliminate the complexity of managing individual network hardware. Cloudflare's platform is scalable and easy to use, and its unified control plane delivers security and reliability across the client's on-premise, hybrid, cloud and software-as-a-service (SaaS) applications. For developers, Cloudflare products address serverless applications, domain registration and website development. For infrastructure, its products span application/network security, bot management, SSL/TLS, network interconnect, CDN, DNS, smart routing, load balancing, stream delivery and more. Cloudflare serves data from more than 200 cities in over 100 countries worldwide. In January 2021, Cloudflare acquired Australian web front-end delivery platform, Linc.

Cloudflare offers health benefits and other employee assistance programs.

FINANCIAL DATA: Note: Data for latest year may not have been available at press time.

In U.S. $	2020	2019	2018	2017	2016	2015
Revenue	431,059,000	287,022,000	192,674,000	134,915,000	84,791,000	
R&D Expense	127,144,000	90,669,000	54,463,000	33,650,000	23,663,000	
Operating Income	-106,768,000	-107,946,000	-84,899,000	-9,730,000	-17,029,000	
Operating Margin %		-.38%	-.44%	-.07%	-.20%	
SGA Expense	309,628,000	240,876,000	179,573,000	82,207,000	54,195,000	
Net Income	-119,370,000	-105,828,000	-87,164,000	-10,748,000	-17,334,000	
Operating Cash Flow	-17,129,000	-38,917,000	-43,281,000	3,167,000	-13,318,000	
Capital Expenditure	74,962,000	57,279,000	34,839,000	22,975,000	18,558,000	
EBITDA	-50,622,000	-74,122,000	-66,190,000	3,321,000	-8,256,000	
Return on Assets %		-.19%	-.38%	-.07%		
Return on Equity %		-.35%				
Debt to Equity		0.014				

CONTACT INFORMATION:

Phone: 888-993-5273   Fax:
Toll-Free:
Address: 101 Townsend St., San Francisco, CA 94107 United States

STOCK TICKER/OTHER:

Stock Ticker: NET
Employees: 1,788
Parent Company:

Exchange: NYS
Fiscal Year Ends: 12/31

SALARIES/BONUSES:

Top Exec. Salary: $ Bonus: $
Second Exec. Salary: $ Bonus: $

OTHER THOUGHTS:

Estimated Female Officers or Directors: 1
Hot Spot for Advancement for Women/Minorities:

Cogent Communications Group Inc

www.cogentco.com

NAIC Code: 517110

TYPES OF BUSINESS:

Facilities-Based Internet Service Provider
VoIP Service

BRANDS/DIVISIONS/AFFILIATES:

CONTACTS: *Note: Officers with more than one job title may be intentionally listed here more than once.*

Robert Beury, Assistant Secretary
David Schaeffer, CEO
Thaddeus Weed, CFO
R. Kummer, Chief Technology Officer
James Bubeck, Other Executive Officer
Timothy ONeill, Vice President, Divisional
Bryant Banks, Vice President, Divisional
Henry Kilmer, Vice President, Divisional

GROWTH PLANS/SPECIAL FEATURES:

Cogent Communications Group, Inc. is a facilities-based provider of low-cost, high-speed internet access and internet protocol (IP) communications services. The firm's network is specifically designed and optimized to transmit data using IP. Cogent delivers its services primarily to small- and medium-sized businesses, communications service providers and other bandwidth-intensive organizations in North America, Europe and Asia. The company offers on-net internet access at speeds ranging from 100 megabits per second to 100 gigabits per second. This on-net service is offered via Cogent's own facilities, which run all the way to its customers' premises. Corporate customers are located in multi-tenant office buildings and in Cogent's data centers and typically include law firms, financial services firms, advertising and marketing firms and other professional services businesses. Bandwidth-intensive customers include universities, other internet service providers, telephone companies, cable television companies, web hosting companies, content delivery networks and commercial content and application service providers. Cogent delivers its internet, ethernet and colocation services to over 88,500 enterprise and net-centric customers. The firm serves more than 205 markets in 47 countries across its facilities-based, all-optical IP network.

FINANCIAL DATA: *Note: Data for latest year may not have been available at press time.*

In U.S. $	2020	2019	2018	2017	2016	2015
Revenue	568,103,000	546,159,000	520,193,000	485,175,000	446,900,000	404,234,000
R&D Expense						
Operating Income	106,993,000	99,198,000	85,576,000	72,056,000	56,890,000	46,094,000
Operating Margin %		.18%	.16%	.15%	.13%	.11%
SGA Expense	158,476,000	146,913,000	133,858,000	127,915,000	120,709,000	113,103,000
Net Income	6,216,000	37,520,000	28,667,000	5,876,000	14,929,000	4,896,000
Operating Cash Flow	140,320,000	148,809,000	133,921,000	111,702,000	107,967,000	83,809,000
Capital Expenditure	55,952,000	46,958,000	49,937,000	45,801,000	45,234,000	35,582,000
EBITDA	156,275,000	190,374,000	173,671,000	155,511,000	140,298,000	124,519,000
Return on Assets %		.04%	.04%	.01%	.02%	.01%
Return on Equity %						.14%
Debt to Equity						

CONTACT INFORMATION:

Phone: 202 295-4200   Fax:
Toll-Free: 877-875-4432
Address: 2450 N St. NW, Washington, DC 20037 United States

STOCK TICKER/OTHER:

Stock Ticker: CCOI   Exchange: NAS
Employees: 1,083   Fiscal Year Ends: 12/31
Parent Company:

SALARIES/BONUSES:

Top Exec. Salary: $ Bonus: $
Second Exec. Salary: $ Bonus: $

OTHER THOUGHTS:

Estimated Female Officers or Directors:
Hot Spot for Advancement for Women/Minorities:

Colt Technology Services Group Limited

www.colt.net

NAIC Code: 517110

TYPES OF BUSINESS:

Business Voice & Data Services
Data Center & Managed Services
Fiber Optics
Internet
Ethernet
Cybersecurity
Cloud
Data Center

BRANDS/DIVISIONS/AFFILIATES:

Fidelity Investments Inc
Colt IQ Network

GROWTH PLANS/SPECIAL FEATURES:

Colt Technology Services Group Limited is a business communications solutions and services provider. The company offers its services to midsize and major businesses and wholesale customers across Europe, Asia and North America. Colt enables the digital transformation of businesses through its intelligent, purpose-built, cloud-integrated network, known as the Colt IQ Network. Colt's solutions include optical network services, business internet, virtual private network (VPN), Ethernet, voice, cybersecurity, cloud connectivity and data centers. Colt Group connects over 900 data centers worldwide, with more than 29,000 on-net buildings. The firm is owned by Fidelity Investments, Inc., a multinational financial services corporation based in Massachusetts. Based in the U.K., Colt has offices in Austria, Belgium, China, Denmark, France, Germany, Hong Kong, India, Ireland, Italy, Japan, Netherlands, Portugal, Romania, Singapore, South Korea, Spain, Sweden, Switzerland, and the U.S.

CONTACTS:
Note: Officers with more than one job title may be intentionally listed here more than once.

Keri Gilder, CEO
Rajiv Datta, COO
Gary Carr, CFO
Andrew Edison, Exec. VP-Mktg. & Sales
Tessa Raum, Exec. VP-Human Resources
Ashish Surti, Exec. VP-IT & Security
Simon Walsh, Exec. VP-Enterprise Solutions
Caroline Griffin Pain, Sec.
Richard Oosterom, Exec. VP-Bus. Dev. & Strategy
Francois Eloy, Exec. VP-Colt Comm. Svcs.
Morten Singleton, VP-Investor Rel.
Mark Leonard, Exec. VP-Infrastructure Svcs.
Jurgen Hernichel, Exec. VP-Bus. Svcs. Unit
Bernard Geoghegan, Exec. VP-Data Center Svcs.
Adriaan Oosthoek, Exec. VP-Data Center Svcs.
Robin Farnan, Exec. VP-Oper. & Engineering
Andy Kankan, Managing Dir.-COLT India

FINANCIAL DATA:
Note: Data for latest year may not have been available at press time.

In U.S. $	2020	2019	2018	2017	2016	2015
Revenue	165,830,000	161,000,000	1,598,000,000	1,556,000,000	1,550,000,000	1,500,000,000
R&D Expense						
Operating Income						
Operating Margin %						
SGA Expense						
Net Income						
Operating Cash Flow						
Capital Expenditure						
EBITDA						
Return on Assets %						
Return on Equity %						
Debt to Equity						

CONTACT INFORMATION:

Phone: 4420-7390-3900 Fax:
Toll-Free:
Address: 20 Great Eastern St., London, EC2A 3EH United Kingdom

STOCK TICKER/OTHER:

Stock Ticker: Subsidiary
Employees: 5,438
Parent Company: Fidelity Investments Inc

Exchange:
Fiscal Year Ends: 12/31

SALARIES/BONUSES:

Top Exec. Salary: $ Bonus: $
Second Exec. Salary: $ Bonus: $

OTHER THOUGHTS:

Estimated Female Officers or Directors: 1
Hot Spot for Advancement for Women/Minorities: Y

Comcast Corporation

NAIC Code: 517110

corporate.comcast.com

TYPES OF BUSINESS:

Cable Television
VoIP Service
Cable Network Programming
High-Speed Internet Service
Video-on-Demand
Advertising Services
Streaming TV Programming
Wireless Services

BRANDS/DIVISIONS/AFFILIATES:

Sky Limited
XFINITY
Universal Pictures
Sky News
Sky Sports
Philadelphia Flyers
Universal Studios
Peacock

CONTACTS: Note: Officers with more than one job title may be intentionally listed here more than once.

Stephen Burke, CEO, Subsidiary
Dave Watson, CEO, Subsidiary
Brian Roberts, CEO
Michael Cavanagh, CFO
Daniel Murdock, Chief Accounting Officer
Joseph Collins, Director Emeritus
Judith Rodin, Director Emeritus
Arthur Block, Executive VP
David Cohen, Senior Executive VP

GROWTH PLANS/SPECIAL FEATURES:

Comcast Corporation is a global media and technology company with three primary businesses: Comcast Cable, NBCUniversal and Sky. Comcast Cable is a leading provider of high-speed internet, video, voice, wireless and security and automation services to residential customers in the U.S. under the Xfinity brand and to commercial customers as well. NBCUniversal operates in four business segments: Cable Networks, Broadcast Television, Filmed Entertainment and Theme Parks. The Cable Networks segment consists primarily of national cable networks that provide a variety of entertainment, news and information and sports content; regional sports and news networks; international cable networks; cable television studio production operations; and various digital properties. Broadcast Television consists of the NBC and Telemundo broadcast networks; NBC and Telemundo owned local broadcast television stations; the NBC Universo national cable network; broadcast television studio production operations; and various digital properties. Filmed Entertainment consists of the operation of Universal Pictures which produces, acquires, markets and distributes filmed entertainment worldwide (films are also produced under the Illumination, DreamWorks Animation and Focus Features names). Theme Parks consists of Universal Studios theme parks in Orlando, Florida; Hollywood, California; and Osaka Japan. A theme park in Beijing, China is under development in partnership with a consortium of Chinese state-owned companies and a fully owned new park is also under development in Orlando. Sky is a leading European entertainment company which includes a direct-to-consumer business providing video, high-speed internet, voice and wireless phone services and a content business which operates the Sky News broadcast network and Sky Sports networks. Other business interests consist primarily of the operations of Comcast Spectacor, which owns the Philadelphia Flyers and the Wells Fargo Center arena in Philadelphia, Pennsylvania. Peacock, is a direct-to-consumer online streaming service that features NBCUniversal content.

FINANCIAL DATA: Note: Data for latest year may not have been available at press time.

In U.S. $	2020	2019	2018	2017	2016	2015
Revenue	103,564,000,000	108,942,000,000	94,507,000,000	84,526,000,000	80,403,000,000	74,510,000,000
R&D Expense						
Operating Income	17,493,000,000	21,125,000,000	19,009,000,000	17,987,000,000	16,859,000,000	15,998,000,000
Operating Margin %		.19%	.20%	.21%	.21%	.21%
SGA Expense	39,850,000,000	40,424,000,000	35,130,000,000	31,330,000,000	29,523,000,000	27,282,000,000
Net Income	10,534,000,000	13,057,000,000	11,731,000,000	22,714,000,000	8,695,000,000	8,163,000,000
Operating Cash Flow	24,737,000,000	25,697,000,000	24,297,000,000	21,403,000,000	19,240,000,000	18,778,000,000
Capital Expenditure	11,634,000,000	12,428,000,000	11,709,000,000	11,297,000,000	10,821,000,000	9,869,000,000
EBITDA	31,753,000,000	34,516,000,000	29,801,000,000	28,675,000,000	26,853,000,000	24,754,000,000
Return on Assets %		.05%	.05%	.12%	.05%	.05%
Return on Equity %		.17%	.17%	.37%	.16%	.16%
Debt to Equity		1.182	1.499	0.866	1.03	0.937

CONTACT INFORMATION:

Phone: 215 286-1700   Fax:
Toll-Free: 800-266-2278
Address: One Comcast Center, Philadelphia, PA 19103 United States

STOCK TICKER/OTHER:

Stock Ticker: CMCSA   Exchange: NAS
Employees: 168,000   Fiscal Year Ends: 12/31
Parent Company:

SALARIES/BONUSES:

Top Exec. Salary: $ Bonus: $
Second Exec. Salary: $ Bonus: $

OTHER THOUGHTS:

Estimated Female Officers or Directors: 16
Hot Spot for Advancement for Women/Minorities: Y

Sales, profits and employees may be estimates. Financial information, benefits and other data can change quickly and may vary from those stated here.

CommScope Holding Company Inc

www.commscope.com

NAIC Code: 335921

TYPES OF BUSINESS:

Cable-Coaxial & Fiber Optic
Broadband Networks
Outdoor Wireless Networks
Venue Networks
Campus Networks
Home Networks

BRANDS/DIVISIONS/AFFILIATES:

CommScope NEXT

CONTACTS: *Note: Officers with more than one job title may be intentionally listed here more than once.*

Alexander Pease, CFO
Frank Drendel, Chairman of the Board
Brooke Clark, Chief Accounting Officer
Bruce McClelland, COO
Morgan Kurk, Executive VP
Frank Wyatt, General Counsel
Robyn Mingle, Other Executive Officer
Marvin Edwards, President
Peter Karlsson, Senior VP, Divisional

GROWTH PLANS/SPECIAL FEATURES:

CommScope Holding Company, Inc., along with its subsidiaries, operate in four business segments: broadband networks, outdoor wireless networks, venue and campus networks, and home networks. The broadband networks segment provides an end-to-end product portfolio serving the telecommunications and cable provider broadband market. This division includes converged cable access, passive optical networking, video systems, access technologies, fiber and coaxial cable, fiber and copper connectivity and hardened closures. The outdoor wireless networks segment focuses on the macro and metro cell markets, and includes base station antennas, radio frequency filters, tower connectivity, microwave antennas, metro cell products, cabinets, steel, accessories, access systems and search solutions. The venue and campus networks segment provides public and private networks for campuses, venues, data centers and buildings. This division combines Wi-Fi and switching, distributed antenna systems, licensed and unlicensed small cells and enterprise fiber and copper infrastructure. Last, the home networks segment includes subscriber-based solutions that support broadband and video applications. In early-2021, CommScope announced and began implementing a business transformation initiative called CommScope NEXT, with plans to spin off its home networks business.

FINANCIAL DATA: *Note: Data for latest year may not have been available at press time.*

In U.S. $	2020	2019	2018	2017	2016	2015
Revenue	8,435,900,000	8,345,100,000	4,568,507,000	4,560,582,000	4,923,621,000	3,807,828,000
R&D Expense	703,300,000	578,500,000	185,696,000	185,222,000	200,715,000	135,964,000
Operating Income	243,300,000	-44,700,000	508,993,000	521,392,000	656,177,000	301,865,000
Operating Margin %		-.01%	.11%	.11%	.13%	.08%
SGA Expense	1,170,700,000	1,277,100,000	729,032,000	794,291,000	879,495,000	687,389,000
Net Income	-573,400,000	-929,500,000	140,217,000	193,764,000	222,838,000	-70,875,000
Operating Cash Flow	436,200,000	596,400,000	494,144,000	586,286,000	606,225,000	302,060,000
Capital Expenditure	121,200,000	104,100,000	82,347,000	68,721,000	68,314,000	56,501,000
EBITDA	746,600,000	274,100,000	770,187,000	844,803,000	949,156,000	476,160,000
Return on Assets %		-.09%	.02%	.03%	.03%	-.01%
Return on Equity %		-.75%	.08%	.13%	.17%	-.06%
Debt to Equity		11.719	2.269	2.652	3.263	4.278

CONTACT INFORMATION:

Phone: 828-324-2200   Fax:
Toll-Free: 800-982-1708
Address: 1100 CommScope Place SE, Hickory, NC 28602 United States

STOCK TICKER/OTHER:

Stock Ticker: COMM
Employees: 30,000
Parent Company:

Exchange: NAS
Fiscal Year Ends: 12/31

SALARIES/BONUSES:

Top Exec. Salary: $ Bonus: $
Second Exec. Salary: $ Bonus: $

OTHER THOUGHTS:

Estimated Female Officers or Directors: 2
Hot Spot for Advancement for Women/Minorities:

Communications Systems Inc

www.commsystems.com

NAIC Code: 334210

TYPES OF BUSINESS:

Telecommunications Equipment-Voice, Data & Video Communications
Renewable Energy
Solar Power
Solar Storage
Battery Storage
Grid Services

BRANDS/DIVISIONS/AFFILIATES:

Pineapple Energy LLC

GROWTH PLANS/SPECIAL FEATURES:

Communications Systems, Inc. (CSI) has operated as an Internet of Things (IoT) intelligent edge products and services company, but began a merger process with Pineapple Energy, LLC in early 2021. Pineapple Energy would become a wholly-owned subsidiary of CSI, and is a U.S. operator and consolidator of residential solar, battery storage and grid services solutions. As part of the transaction, in July (2021) CSI's shareholders approved the sale of CSI's transition networks and Net2Edge businesses to Lantronix, Inc. After the Pineapple merger, CSI would be positioned to grow organically and would acquire and grow leading local and regional solar, storage and energy services companies nationwide. The new direction of CSI is to power the energy transition through growth of solar electricity paired with battery storage on consumers' homes.

CONTACTS: Note: Officers with more than one job title may be intentionally listed here more than once.

Roger Lacey, CEO
Roger Lacey, CEO
Mark Fandrich, CFO
Curtis Sampson, Chairman Emeritus
Kristin Hlavka, Chief Accounting Officer
Scott Fluegge, General Manager, Subsidiary
Scott Otis, General Manager, Subsidiary

FINANCIAL DATA: Note: Data for latest year may not have been available at press time.

In U.S. $	2020	2019	2018	2017	2016	2015
Revenue	42,575,540	50,906,180	65,762,940	82,322,620	99,352,940	107,669,500
R&D Expense						
Operating Income	-2,012,494	9,214	-6,194,442	-7,862,899	-4,456,547	-10,505,870
Operating Margin %		.00%	-.09%	-.10%	-.04%	-.10%
SGA Expense	19,218,920	22,176,600	27,501,690	28,699,140	31,038,090	42,052,030
Net Income	-171,658	6,469,049	-6,791,735	-11,825,630	-8,113,548	-9,648,308
Operating Cash Flow	-4,683,529	10,231,140	-4,722,732	3,649,920	1,215,361	840,292
Capital Expenditure	249,727	424,988	763,627	773,367	2,286,027	2,394,261
EBITDA	-784,511	1,306,587	-4,133,265	-8,602,249	-4,053,962	-6,968,701
Return on Assets %		.12%	-.12%	-.18%	-.10%	-.10%
Return on Equity %		.15%	-.15%	-.22%	-.12%	-.12%
Debt to Equity		0.005				

CONTACT INFORMATION:

Phone: 952 996-1674   Fax: 320 848-2702
Toll-Free:
Address: 10900 Red Circle Dr., Minnetonka, MN 55543 United States

STOCK TICKER/OTHER:

Stock Ticker: JCS
Employees: 150   Exchange: NAS
Parent Company: Fiscal Year Ends: 12/31

SALARIES/BONUSES:

Top Exec. Salary: $ Bonus: $
Second Exec. Salary: $ Bonus: $

OTHER THOUGHTS:

Estimated Female Officers or Directors: 2
Hot Spot for Advancement for Women/Minorities:

Comtech Telecommunications Corp

www.comtechtel.com

NAIC Code: 334220

TYPES OF BUSINESS:

Communications Equipment-Microwave & RF
Satellite Equipment & Technologies
Communication Solutions
Next-Generation 911 Solutions

BRANDS/DIVISIONS/AFFILIATES:

UHP Networks Inc

CONTACTS: Note: Officers with more than one job title may be intentionally listed here more than once.

Fred Kornberg, CEO
Michael Bondi, CFO
Michael Porcelain, COO
John Branscum, President, Subsidiary
Richard Burt, President, Subsidiary
Nancy Stallone, Secretary

GROWTH PLANS/SPECIAL FEATURES:

Comtech Telecommunications Corp. is a provider of advanced communication solutions for both commercial and government customers worldwide. The company's solutions fulfill the needs for secure wireless communications in demanding environments, including areas where traditional communications are unavailable or cost-prohibitive, and in mission-critical situations where performance is critical. Comtech operates its business through two segments: commercial solutions and government solutions. The commercial solutions segment derives more than half of annual net sales (2019) and offers two solution categories: satellite ground station technologies, such as single channel per carrier and modems that facilitate the transmission of voice, video and data over satellite links, and solid-state and traveling wave tube amplifiers used to amplify signals from satellite ground stations; and public safety and location technologies, such as wireless/voice-over-internet-protocol (VoIP) 911 service for network operators, next-generation (NG) 911 solutions, emergency services IP network technologies, call handling applications for public safety answering points (PSAPs), and software and equipment for location-based and messaging infrastructure. The government solutions segment derives approximately 47% of annual net sales and offers two solution categories: mission-critical technologies, such as tactical satellite-based communications, field support and end-to-end integration, satellite-based mobile communications and tracking systems, procurement of satellite-based space components, satellite-based antenna systems and high-reliability electrical, electronic and electromechanical (EEE) parts; and high-performance transmission technologies, such as over-the-horizon microwave equipment that can transmit digitalized voice, video and data over distances from 20 to 200 miles using the troposphere; and solid-state, high-power amplifiers designed for radar, electronic warfare, jamming, medical and aviation applications. In March 2021, Comtech acquired UHP Networks, Inc., a provider of innovative and disruptive satellite ground station technology solutions.

FINANCIAL DATA: Note: Data for latest year may not have been available at press time.

In U.S. $	2020	2019	2018	2017	2016	2015
Revenue	616,715,000	671,797,000	570,589,000	550,368,000	411,004,000	307,289,000
R&D Expense	52,180,000	56,407,000	53,869,000	54,260,000	42,190,000	35,916,000
Operating Income	35,928,000	44,074,000	35,075,000	25,022,000	20,700,000	34,077,000
Operating Margin %		.07%	.06%	.05%	.05%	.11%
SGA Expense	117,130,000	128,639,000	113,922,000	116,080,000	94,932,000	62,680,000
Net Income	7,020,000	25,041,000	29,769,000	15,827,000	-7,738,000	23,245,000
Operating Cash Flow	52,764,000	68,031,000	50,344,000	66,655,000	14,970,000	21,726,000
Capital Expenditure	7,225,000	8,785,000	8,642,000	8,150,000	5,667,000	3,362,000
EBITDA	47,520,000	68,437,000	69,805,000	74,287,000	22,803,000	47,218,000
Return on Assets %		.03%	.04%	.02%	-.01%	.05%
Return on Equity %		.05%	.06%	.03%	-.02%	.06%
Debt to Equity		0.308	0.294	0.371	0.519	

CONTACT INFORMATION:

Phone: 631 962-7000   Fax: 631 777-8877
Toll-Free:
Address: 68 S. Service Rd., Ste. 230, Melville, NY 11747 United States

STOCK TICKER/OTHER:

Stock Ticker: CMTL
Employees: 2,034
Parent Company:

Exchange: NAS
Fiscal Year Ends: 07/31

SALARIES/BONUSES:

Top Exec. Salary: $ Bonus: $
Second Exec. Salary: $ Bonus: $

OTHER THOUGHTS:

Estimated Female Officers or Directors:
Hot Spot for Advancement for Women/Minorities:

Consolidated Communications Holdings Inc www.consolidated.com

NAIC Code: 517110

TYPES OF BUSINESS:

Telephone Service Provider
Internet Service Provider
Internet Protocol Digital TV
VoIP Telephony

BRANDS/DIVISIONS/AFFILIATES:

GROWTH PLANS/SPECIAL FEATURES:

Consolidated Communications Holdings, Inc. (CCH), through its subsidiaries, provide integrated communications services. CCH serves the consumer, commercial and carrier channels across a 23-state service area. As of March 31, 2021, CCH had approximately 768,000 voice connections, 794,000 data connections and 74,000 video connections, and its advanced fiber network spanned approximately 47,400 fiber route miles. As an integrated company, CCH operates both as an incumbent local exchange carrier and a competitive local exchange carrier, depending on the territory serviced. Services include local and long-distance service, high-speed broadband internet access, video services, voice over internet protocol (VoIP), custom calling features, private line services, carrier grade access services, network capacity services over the company's regional fiber optic networks, data center & managed services, directory publishing, video advertising, equipment sales, and cloud data services.

CONTACTS: Note: Officers with more than one job title may be intentionally listed here more than once.

C. Udell, CEO
Steven Childers, CFO
Robert Currey, Chairman of the Board

FINANCIAL DATA: Note: Data for latest year may not have been available at press time.

In U.S. $	2020	2019	2018	2017	2016	2015
Revenue	1,304,028,000	1,336,542,000	1,399,074,000	1,059,574,000	743,177,000	775,737,000
R&D Expense						
Operating Income	143,159,000	81,281,000	20,929,000	72,304,000	89,264,000	89,188,000
Operating Margin %		.06%	.01%	.07%	.12%	.11%
SGA Expense	275,361,000	299,088,000	333,605,000	249,332,000	157,111,000	178,227,000
Net Income	36,977,000	-20,383,000	-50,834,000	64,945,000	14,931,000	-881,000
Operating Cash Flow	364,980,000	339,096,000	357,321,000	210,027,000	218,233,000	219,179,000
Capital Expenditure	217,563,000	232,203,000	244,816,000	181,185,000	125,192,000	133,934,000
EBITDA	468,023,000	462,518,000	453,597,000	364,177,000	263,274,000	269,110,000
Return on Assets %		-.01%	-.01%	.02%	.01%	.00%
Return on Equity %		-.06%	-.11%	.17%	.07%	.00%
Debt to Equity		6.603	5.622	4.068	8.053	5.609

CONTACT INFORMATION:

Phone: 217 235-3311   Fax: 217 258-7883
Toll-Free:
Address: 2116 S. 17th ST., Mattoon, IL 61938 United States

STOCK TICKER/OTHER:

Stock Ticker: CNSL   Exchange: NAS
Employees: 3,200   Fiscal Year Ends: 12/31
Parent Company:

SALARIES/BONUSES:

Top Exec. Salary: $ Bonus: $
Second Exec. Salary: $ Bonus: $

OTHER THOUGHTS:

Estimated Female Officers or Directors: 1
Hot Spot for Advancement for Women/Minorities:

Corning Incorporated

NAIC Code: 327212

www.corning.com

TYPES OF BUSINESS:

Glass & Optical Fiber Manufacturing
Glass Substrates for LCDs
Optical Switching Products
Photonic Modules & Components
Networking Devices
Semiconductor Materials
Laboratory Supplies
Emissions Control Products

BRANDS/DIVISIONS/AFFILIATES:

Eagle XG
Iris
Vascade
LEAF
ClearCurve
InfiniCor
Gorilla

CONTACTS: Note: Officers with more than one job title may be intentionally listed here more than once.

Wendell Weeks, CEO
Martin Curran, Executive VP
R. Tripeny, CFO
Edward Schlesinger, Chief Accounting Officer
Jeffrey Evenson, Chief Strategy Officer
David Morse, Chief Technology Officer
Clark Kinlin, Executive VP
Christine Pambianchi, Executive VP, Divisional
James Clappin, Executive VP, Divisional
Eric Musser, Executive VP, Divisional
Lewis Steverson, Executive VP
Lawrence McRae, Other Corporate Officer

GROWTH PLANS/SPECIAL FEATURES:

Corning Incorporated, established in 1851, is an international technology-based corporation. The firm operates in five business segments: display technologies, optical communications, specialty materials, environmental technologies and life sciences. The display technologies segment manufactures glass substrates for active matrix liquid crystal displays (LCDs), used in notebook computers, flat panel desktop monitor and LCD televisions. Its Eagle XG glass is an LCD glass substrate free of heavy metals; and its Eagle XG slim glass and Iris glass products enables lighter-weight portable devices and thinner televisions and monitors. The optical communications segment is divided into carrier network and enterprise network. The carrier network products include: Vascade submarine optical fibers for use in submarine networks; LEAF optical fiber for long-haul, regional and metropolitan networks; SMF-28e single mode optical fiber for additional transmission wavelengths in metropolitan and access networks; and ClearCurve fiber for use in multiple dwelling units. Enterprise network products include ClearCurve ultra-bendable multimode fiber for data centers and other enterprise network applications; InfiniCor fibers for local area networks; and ClearCurve VSDN ultra-bendable optical fiber designed to support emerging high-speed interconnects between computers and other consumer electronics devices. The specialty materials segment offers products such as glass windows for space shuttles and optical components for high-tech industries and includes the firm's Gorilla glass product line of protective cover glass for portable display devices. The environmental technologies segment produces ceramic products for emissions and pollution control, such as gasoline/diesel substrate and filter products. The life sciences segment manufactures laboratory products such as consumables (plastic vessels, specialty surfaces and media), as well as general labware and equipment used for cell culture research, bioprocessing, genomics, drug discovery, microbiology and chemistry. Corning manufactures products at 122 plants in 15 countries.

FINANCIAL DATA: Note: Data for latest year may not have been available at press time.

In U.S. $	2020	2019	2018	2017	2016	2015
Revenue	11,303,000,000	11,503,000,000	11,290,000,000	10,116,000,000	9,390,000,000	9,111,000,000
R&D Expense	1,154,000,000	1,031,000,000	993,000,000	860,000,000	742,000,000	769,000,000
Operating Income	509,000,000	1,306,000,000	1,575,000,000	1,630,000,000	1,468,000,000	1,307,000,000
Operating Margin %		.11%	.14%	.16%	.16%	.14%
SGA Expense	1,747,000,000	1,585,000,000	1,799,000,000	1,467,000,000	1,472,000,000	1,523,000,000
Net Income	512,000,000	960,000,000	1,066,000,000	-497,000,000	3,695,000,000	1,339,000,000
Operating Cash Flow	2,180,000,000	2,031,000,000	2,919,000,000	2,004,000,000	2,521,000,000	2,809,000,000
Capital Expenditure	1,377,000,000	1,987,000,000	2,310,000,000	1,804,000,000	1,130,000,000	1,250,000,000
EBITDA	2,419,000,000	2,940,000,000	2,987,000,000	2,970,000,000	5,046,000,000	2,810,000,000
Return on Assets %		.03%	.04%	-.02%	.13%	.04%
Return on Equity %		.08%	.08%	-.04%	.22%	.07%
Debt to Equity		0.771	0.522	0.354	0.234	0.237

CONTACT INFORMATION:

Phone: 607 974-9000   Fax: 607 974-8688
Toll-Free:
Address: 1 Riverfront Plaza, Corning, NY 14831 United States

STOCK TICKER/OTHER:

Stock Ticker: GLW
Employees: 40,700
Parent Company:

Exchange: NYS
Fiscal Year Ends: 12/31

SALARIES/BONUSES:

Top Exec. Salary: $ Bonus: $
Second Exec. Salary: $ Bonus: $

OTHER THOUGHTS:

Estimated Female Officers or Directors: 1
Hot Spot for Advancement for Women/Minorities: Y

COSMOTE Mobile Telephones SA

www.cosmote.gr

NAIC Code: 517210

TYPES OF BUSINESS:

Mobile Phone Service
Mobile Services
Telecommunication
Technology
Ecommerce
Television Production
Electronic Payment Solutions

BRANDS/DIVISIONS/AFFILIATES:

Deutsche Telekom AG
Hellenic Telecommunications Organization SA
COSMOTE eValue
CsomoONE
COSMOTE Payments

CONTACTS: *Note: Officers with more than one job title may be intentionally listed here more than once.*

Konstantinos Apostolidis, VP
George Tsonis, General Technical Dir.
Irini Nikolaidi, Chief Exec. Legal & Regulatory Affairs Officer
Deppie Tzimea, Group Corporate Communications Officer

GROWTH PLANS/SPECIAL FEATURES:

COSMOTE Mobile Telephones SA (formerly COSMOTE Mobile Telecommunications SA) is a leading mobile telecommunications company in Greece. Together with its subsidiary in Romania, COSMOTE offers mobile services to over 15 million customers. The firm utilizes state-of-the-art technologies, offering 4G and 4G+ networks and related services. COSMOTE e-Value is the company's 24/7/365 customer service division, offering telephone service solutions, sales development solutions, technical assistance, consulting, service client services and more. CosmoONE offers ecommerce services between businesses (B2B), and specializes in eProcurement solutions, applications and services for electronic bids, electronic tenders, electronic auctions, electronic orders, invoice transfer and more. COSMOTE's television productions division produces and distributes programs and audiovisual content intended for payTV and televised broadcasting. COSMOTE Payments is an electronic money services division. COSMOTE operates as a wholly-owned subsidiary of Hellenic Telecommunications Organization SA (OTE SA), which is majority-owned by Deutsche Telekom AG. During 2021, COSMOTE Mobile Telecommunications SA was renamed as COSMOTE Mobile Telephones SA.

FINANCIAL DATA: *Note: Data for latest year may not have been available at press time.*

In U.S. $	2020	2019	2018	2017	2016	2015
Revenue	1,494,530,000	1,272,400,000	1,278,320,000	1,336,820,000	1,181,040,000	1,586,335,898
R&D Expense						
Operating Income						
Operating Margin %						
SGA Expense						
Net Income	162,988,000	601,579,000	716,463,000	-493,520,000	129,588,000	102,314,203
Operating Cash Flow						
Capital Expenditure						
EBITDA						
Return on Assets %						
Return on Equity %						
Debt to Equity						

CONTACT INFORMATION:

Phone: 30-210-61-77-777   Fax: 30-210-61-77-999
Toll-Free:
Address: 99 Kifissias Ave., Maroussi, 151 24 Greece

STOCK TICKER/OTHER:

Stock Ticker: Subsidiary   Exchange:
Employees: 1,941   Fiscal Year Ends: 12/31
Parent Company: Deutsche Telekom AG

SALARIES/BONUSES:

Top Exec. Salary: $ Bonus: $
Second Exec. Salary: $ Bonus: $

OTHER THOUGHTS:

Estimated Female Officers or Directors: 4
Hot Spot for Advancement for Women/Minorities: Y

Cox Communications Inc

www.cox.com/residential/home.cox

NAIC Code: 517110

TYPES OF BUSINESS:

Cable TV Service and Internet Access
Broadband
Internet
TV
Streaming
Smart Home
Security
Telephone Service

BRANDS/DIVISIONS/AFFILIATES:

Cox Enterprises Inc

GROWTH PLANS/SPECIAL FEATURES:

Cox Communications, Inc., owned by Cox Enterprises, Inc., is a broadband communications and entertainment company, serving millions of customers throughout the U.S. Cox Communications' products and services include internet, TV, streaming, smart home, security, home phone and bundled deals. The company serves both residential and business customers.

CONTACTS: *Note: Officers with more than one job title may be intentionally listed here more than once.*

Patrick J. Esser, Pres.
Len Barlik, Exec. VP-Prod. Mgmt. & Dev.
Asheesh Saksena, Chief Strategy Officer
Joseph J. Rooney, Sr. VP-Social Media, Advertising & Brand Mktg.
William (Bill) J. Fitzsimmons, Chief Acct. Officer
Philip G. Meeks, Sr. VP-Cox Bus.
Jennifer W. Hightower, Sr. VP-Law & Policy
David Pugliese, Sr. VP-Product Mktg.
Mark A. Kaish, Sr. VP-Tech. Oper.
George Richter, VP-Supply Chain Mgmt.

FINANCIAL DATA: *Note: Data for latest year may not have been available at press time.*

In U.S. $	2020	2019	2018	2017	2016	2015
Revenue	12,600,000,000	12,300,000,000	12,000,000,000	11,550,000,000	11,000,000,000	10,650,000,000
R&D Expense						
Operating Income						
Operating Margin %						
SGA Expense						
Net Income						
Operating Cash Flow						
Capital Expenditure						
EBITDA						
Return on Assets %						
Return on Equity %						
Debt to Equity						

CONTACT INFORMATION:

Phone: 404-843-5000   Fax: 404-843-5939
Toll-Free: 888-566-7751
Address: 6205-B Peachtree Dunwoody Rd., Atlanta, GA 30328 United States

STOCK TICKER/OTHER:

Stock Ticker: Subsidiary   Exchange:
Employees: 18,000   Fiscal Year Ends: 12/31
Parent Company: Cox Enterprises Inc

SALARIES/BONUSES:

Top Exec. Salary: $ Bonus: $
Second Exec. Salary: $ Bonus: $

OTHER THOUGHTS:

Estimated Female Officers or Directors: 3
Hot Spot for Advancement for Women/Minorities: Y

Cricket Wireless LLC

NAIC Code: 517210

TYPES OF BUSINESS:

Mobile Phone and Wireless Services
Retail Sales
Wireless Services
Mobile Phones
Telecommunications
Lease-to-own

BRANDS/DIVISIONS/AFFILIATES:

AT&T Inc
Cricket

CONTACTS: Note: Officers with more than one job title may be intentionally listed here more than once.

John Dwyer, Pres.
Colin E. Holland, Sr. VP - Eng. & Tech. Oper.
Robert J. Irving, Jr., Sr. VP-Gen. Counsel
William D. Ingram, Exec. VP-Strategy
Anne M. Liu, Sr. VP
John H. Casey III, Sr. VP -Customer Experience & Growth
David B. Davis, Sr. VP
Annette M. Jacobs, Sr. VP
Aaron P. Maddox, Sr. VP-Finance
Catherine Shackleford, Sr.VP-Supply Chain & Procurement

GROWTH PLANS/SPECIAL FEATURES:

Cricket Wireless, LLC provides mobile wireless services targeted to meet the needs of younger and lower-income customers underserved by traditional communications companies. Its 4G LTE (long-term evolution) network covers more than 99% of Americans (based on overall coverage in U.S.-licensed areas). Cricket Wireless serves approximately 10 million subscribers. The company offers smartphones under brands such as LG, Motorola, iPhone, Alcatel, Samsung, Nokia and Cricket. Cricket Wireless comprises Cricket-branded retail stores nationwide. Cricket stores are either dealer-owned or company-owned. Cricket's rate plans offer unlimited talk and text, and data access; data-only plans feature 2GB, 5GB and unlimited data for a monthly fee; and add-on features include device protection, international, individual country, additional 1GB of high-speed and mobile hotspot, each for an additional monthly fee. Monthly taxes are included with each plan. There are no annual contracts and no overage fees with unlimited talk, text and data access cell phone plans. Cricket Wireless operates as a subsidiary of AT&T, Inc.

FINANCIAL DATA: Note: Data for latest year may not have been available at press time.

In U.S. $	2020	2019	2018	2017	2016	2015
Revenue	4,630,500,000	4,410,000,000	4,200,000,000	4,000,000,000	3,900,000,000	3,776,000,000
R&D Expense						
Operating Income						
Operating Margin %						
SGA Expense						
Net Income						
Operating Cash Flow						
Capital Expenditure						
EBITDA						
Return on Assets %						
Return on Equity %						
Debt to Equity						

CONTACT INFORMATION:

Phone: Fax:
Toll-Free: 800=274-2538
Address: 1025 Lenox Park Blvd. NE, Atlanta, GA 30319 United States

STOCK TICKER/OTHER:

Stock Ticker: Subsidiary   Exchange:
Employees: 3,820   Fiscal Year Ends: 12/31
Parent Company: AT&T Inc

SALARIES/BONUSES:

Top Exec. Salary: $ Bonus: $
Second Exec. Salary: $ Bonus: $

OTHER THOUGHTS:

Estimated Female Officers or Directors:
Hot Spot for Advancement for Women/Minorities: Y

Cyxtera Technologies Inc

www.cyxtera.com

NAIC Code: 518210

TYPES OF BUSINESS:

Hosting & Collocation Services
Data Centers
Networking
Digital Computing
Artificial Intelligence
Machine Learning

BRANDS/DIVISIONS/AFFILIATES:

Medina Capital
BC Partners LLP

GROWTH PLANS/SPECIAL FEATURES:

Cyxtera Technologies, Inc., founded by private equity firms Medina Capital and BC Partners LLP, houses servers and networking equipment in its data centers, also referred to as colocation. The data centers interconnects businesses with customers, partners and employees via digital technology. Cyxtera's continuous delivery experience (CDX) platform provides accurate, real-time data and enhanced customer experience services. The firm has 62 data centers 29 global markets across North America, Europe and Asia Pacific. Services by Cyxtera include structured cabling, secure cabinet and cage, on-demand cabinets, enterprise metal nodes, artificial intelligence (AI), machine learning, compute-as-a-service and CDX. The company provides services to more than 2,000 leading enterprises, as well as U.S. federal government agencies. In February 2021, Cyxtera announced it was going public via a $3.4 billion merger with the special-purpose acquisition company Starboard Value Acquisition Corp.

CONTACTS: Note: Officers with more than one job title may be intentionally listed here more than once.

Nelson Fonseca, CEO
Randy Rowland, Pres.
Carlos Sagasta, CFO
Russell Cozart, Sr. VP-Mktg. & Product Strategy
Frank Barnett, Chief Human Resources Officer
Leo Taddeo, CIO
Andrew Higginbotham, Sr. VP-Cloud & Tech.
Pete Bazil, General Counsel
Pete Bazil, Chief Commercial Officer
Marc Capri, Sr. VP-Global Advanced Svcs.
Jason Lochhead, CTO
Mark Smith, Managing Dir.-Asia

FINANCIAL DATA: Note: Data for latest year may not have been available at press time.

In U.S. $	2020	2019	2018	2017	2016	2015
Revenue	690,000,000	679,000,000	685,755,000	653,100,000	622,000,000	626,000,000
R&D Expense						
Operating Income						
Operating Margin %						
SGA Expense						
Net Income	-239,000,000	-295,000,000				
Operating Cash Flow						
Capital Expenditure						
EBITDA						
Return on Assets %						
Return on Equity %						
Debt to Equity						

CONTACT INFORMATION:

Phone: 305-537-9500 Fax:
Toll-Free: 855-699-8372
Address: BAC Colonnade Office Twr., 2333 Ponce De Leon Blvd, Coral Gables, FL 33134 United States

STOCK TICKER/OTHER:

Stock Ticker: Private
Employees: 110
Parent Company: Medina Capital

Exchange:
Fiscal Year Ends: 12/31

SALARIES/BONUSES:

Top Exec. Salary: $ Bonus: $
Second Exec. Salary: $ Bonus: $

OTHER THOUGHTS:

Estimated Female Officers or Directors: 1
Hot Spot for Advancement for Women/Minorities:

Sales, profits and employees may be estimates. Financial information, benefits and other data can change quickly and may vary from those stated here.

Data Select Limited

www.dataselect.com

NAIC Code: 517210

TYPES OF BUSINESS:

Mobile Phone Sales & Distribution
Marketing
Business-to-Business Solutions
Retail Solutions
Ecommerce Solutions
Mobile Network Solutions
Telecommunications

BRANDS/DIVISIONS/AFFILIATES:

Westcoast Holdings Limited

GROWTH PLANS/SPECIAL FEATURES:

Data Select Limited provides a marketing platform for mobile telecommunication brands to engage with U.K. business-to-business (B2B) resellers, retailers, ecommerce businesses and mobile network operators. The company's portfolio helps customers leverage advanced mobile technologies to bring their products and services to market. Data Select offers mobile B2B resellers access to: a broad smartphone, tablet, drone and accessories portfolio; mobile solutions; and a B2B loyalty program. The firm offers retailers an end-to-end mobile supply chain solution across a variety of shopping channels, including ecommerce, home shopping and stores. Data Select also manages multiple sales channel and network marketing promotions to help deliver product and sales support for retailers and network operators alike. Data Select serves more than 400 active customers, spanning 30+ brands. Data Select is privately-owned by Westcoast Holdings Limited.

CONTACTS: *Note: Officers with more than one job title may be intentionally listed here more than once.*

Peter Jones, CEO

FINANCIAL DATA: *Note: Data for latest year may not have been available at press time.*

In U.S. $	2020	2019	2018	2017	2016	2015
Revenue	144,769,000	209,857,000	215,119,000	201,940,000	194,508,000	185,659,000
R&D Expense						
Operating Income						
Operating Margin %						
SGA Expense						
Net Income	909,840	2,456,622	2,339,640	2,461,560	986,396	2,888,270
Operating Cash Flow						
Capital Expenditure						
EBITDA						
Return on Assets %						
Return on Equity %						
Debt to Equity						

CONTACT INFORMATION:

Phone: 0844-249-0792   Fax:
Toll-Free:
Address: Arrowhead Rd., Theale, Reading, RG7 4AH United Kingdom

STOCK TICKER/OTHER:

Stock Ticker: Subsidiary   Exchange:
Employees: 60   Fiscal Year Ends: 04/30
Parent Company: Westcoast Holdings Limited

SALARIES/BONUSES:

Top Exec. Salary: $ Bonus: $
Second Exec. Salary: $ Bonus: $

OTHER THOUGHTS:

Estimated Female Officers or Directors:
Hot Spot for Advancement for Women/Minorities:

Datang Telecom Technology Co Ltd

www.datang.com

NAIC Code: 334210

TYPES OF BUSINESS:

Telecommunications Equipment
Mobile Communications Products
Optical Communications Products
Digital Microwave Products
Software
Integrated Circuits
Internet of Things
Microelectronics

BRANDS/DIVISIONS/AFFILIATES:

CONTACTS: Note: Officers with more than one job title may be intentionally listed here more than once.

Xincheng Lei, Managing Dir.
Gui Xue, CFO
Xiubin Qi, Corp. Sec.
Desheng Zhou, Vice Chmn.
Kun Jiang, Deputy Gen. Mgr.
Hongyan Wang, Deputy Gen. Mgr.
Pengfei Wang, Deputy Gen. Mgr.
Bin Cao, Chmn.

GROWTH PLANS/SPECIAL FEATURES:

Datang Telecom Technology Co., Ltd., owned by the Chinese government, is principally engaged in integrated circuit (IC) design, terminal design, software, applications, mobile internet services, communication devices and Internet of Things. Datang's IC design solutions include security chips and mobile terminal security chips. The firm implements hardware system-level terminal security solutions that comply with GP International Standards and UnionPay specifications. They can be used for enterprise applications, industrial applications, financial payments, digital rights, personal privacy and more. Terminal design products and services include smartphones, data terminals and industry terminals. Software solutions include wireless access, operation support systems, information security and platform products. Related applications include smart city, smart business, smart traffic, tourism, energy conservation, government information and more. Mobile internet products and services include custom-designed terminals, custom services and mobile applications. Datang's communication devices offer wired access, wireless access and optical communication. Its Internet of Things (IoT) and smart device products and solutions include smart cards, smart cities, car networking, sensor networks, information security, converged communication systems and video surveillance. In addition, Datang offers a core cloud integrated security+ solution based on loading a domestic cryptographic algorithm security chip, expanding the IoT category to include solutions such as smart door locks.

FINANCIAL DATA: Note: Data for latest year may not have been available at press time.

In U.S. $	2020	2019	2018	2017	2016	2015
Revenue	215,019,000	204,780,000	340,788,000	667,468,000	1,052,584,806	1,293,674,576
R&D Expense						
Operating Income						
Operating Margin %						
SGA Expense						
Net Income		-128,650,000	81,998,400	-406,745,000	-258,531,837	4,210,494
Operating Cash Flow						
Capital Expenditure						
EBITDA						
Return on Assets %						
Return on Equity %						
Debt to Equity						

CONTACT INFORMATION:

Phone: 86-10-5891-9000   Fax: 86-10 58919131
Toll-Free:
Address: Yongjia N. Rd., No. 6, Haidian Dist., Beijing, 100094 China

STOCK TICKER/OTHER:

Stock Ticker: 600198   Exchange: Shanghai
Employees: 2,997   Fiscal Year Ends: 12/31
Parent Company:

SALARIES/BONUSES:

Top Exec. Salary: $ Bonus: $
Second Exec. Salary: $ Bonus: $

OTHER THOUGHTS:

Estimated Female Officers or Directors:
Hot Spot for Advancement for Women/Minorities:

Deutsche Telekom AG

NAIC Code: 517210

www.telekom.com

TYPES OF BUSINESS:

Local & Long-Distance Telephone Service
Mobile Telephone Service
Fixed Network Provider
Information Technology Services

BRANDS/DIVISIONS/AFFILIATES:

Deutsche Telekom (UK) Ltd
T-Systems South Africa (Pty) Limited
T-Systems PR China Ltd
T-Systems North America Inc
T-Systems Argentina SA
T-Systems do Brasil Ltda
T-Mobile

CONTACTS: *Note: Officers with more than one job title may be intentionally listed here more than once.*

Timotheus Hottges, CEO
Thomas Kremer, Dir.-Legal Affairs, Compliance & Data Privacy
Claudia Nemat, Dir.-Europe & Technology
Reinhard Clemens, Dir.-T-Systems
Niek Jan van Damme, Dir.-Germany

GROWTH PLANS/SPECIAL FEATURES:

Deutsche Telekom AG (DT) is one of the world's largest telecommunications companies, with roughly 235.8 million mobile customers, 27.3 million fixed-network lines and 21.3 million broadband lines. It offers its products and services in approximately 50 countries around the world while operating domestically out of Germany. The firm generally operates under the T-Mobile brand. It offers a complete range of global telecom services through its global subsidiaries and affiliates located in Europe, Africa, Asia, North America and South America. Various national companies offer ICT (information communication technology) info solutions to business customers. DT's systems solution division operates under the T-Systems brand, offering bundled ICT products and business solutions to larger multinational corporations. T-Systems' integrated solutions include the transformation to cloud-based services as well as new strategies regarding data analytics, the Internet of Things, machine-to-machine communication and Industrial Internet. Just a few of DT's many subsidiaries include: wholly-owned European firms, Deutsche Telekom (UK) Ltd. and T-Systems Austria GesmbH; 70%-owned South African firm, T-Systems South Africa (Pty) Limited; wholly-owned Asian firms, T-Systems PR China Ltd. and T-Systems Singapore Pte. Ltd.; wholly-owned North American firms, T-Systems Canada, Inc. and T-Systems North America, Inc.; and wholly-owned South American firms, T-Systems Argentina SA and T-Systems do Brasil Ltda. The German government holds a 14.5%-stake in DT's stock directly, and another 17.4% through the government bank, KfW. The remaining stock is free float. During 2020, Sprint merged with the T-Mobile brand in the US, with SoftBank Group holding up to 24% of the combined T-Systems North America shares, while Deutsche Telekom holds up to 43% and the remainder is held by public shareholders.

FINANCIAL DATA: *Note: Data for latest year may not have been available at press time.*

In U.S. $	2020	2019	2018	2017	2016	2015
Revenue		86,675,243,008	81,449,975,808	81,013,276,672	80,808,132,608	76,647,481,344
R&D Expense						
Operating Income						
Operating Margin %						
SGA Expense						
Net Income		4,179,998,208	2,341,317,888	3,741,136,128	2,957,271,552	3,602,746,112
Operating Cash Flow						
Capital Expenditure						
EBITDA						
Return on Assets %						
Return on Equity %						
Debt to Equity						

CONTACT INFORMATION:

Phone: 49 2281814949   Fax: 49 2281819400
Toll-Free:
Address: Friedrich-Ebert-Allee 140, Bonn, GM 53113 Germany

STOCK TICKER/OTHER:

Stock Ticker: DTEGF   Exchange: OTC
Employees: 210,533   Fiscal Year Ends: 12/31
Parent Company:

SALARIES/BONUSES:

Top Exec. Salary: $ Bonus: $
Second Exec. Salary: $ Bonus: $

OTHER THOUGHTS:

Estimated Female Officers or Directors: 6
Hot Spot for Advancement for Women/Minorities: Y

Dialogic Inc

www.dialogic.com

NAIC Code: 334210

TYPES OF BUSINESS:

Internet Protocol Products
Cloud Solutions
Communications
Voice Over Solutions
Internet of Things
Software
Gateways

BRANDS/DIVISIONS/AFFILIATES:

Enghouse Systems Limited

CONTACTS: *Note: Officers with more than one job title may be intentionally listed here more than once.*

Bill Crank, CEO
John Hanson, CFO
Anthony Housefather, Executive VP, Divisional

GROWTH PLANS/SPECIAL FEATURES:

Dialogic, Inc. is a cloud-optimized solutions provider for real-time communications media, applications and infrastructure. The company serves service providers, enterprises and developers throughout the world, and works with world-leading mobile operators. Dialogic's solutions include applications for service providers and enterprises, NFV and cloud enablement, IP multimedia subsystem (IMS) for voice over long-term evolution (VoLTE) and voice over WiFi, web real-time communication (WebRTC), multimedia value-added services, VoLTE mobile data roaming, internetwork packet exchange (IPX) enablement, diameter and SS7 signaling, IP networking transformation, and Internet of Things (IoT). Products by Dialogic include unified communications, real-time communication apps, load balancer software, media server software, fax boards and related software, control switch systems, session border controllers, media gateways, SS7 components, and more. Dialogic has authorized distributors throughout the Americas, Asia Pacific, Europe, Middle East and Africa. Dialogic operates as a subsidiary of Enghouse Systems Limited.

FINANCIAL DATA: *Note: Data for latest year may not have been available at press time.*

In U.S. $	2020	2019	2018	2017	2016	2015
Revenue	128,750,000	125,000,000	115,000,000	110,000,000	105,000,000	100,000,000
R&D Expense						
Operating Income						
Operating Margin %						
SGA Expense						
Net Income						
Operating Cash Flow						
Capital Expenditure						
EBITDA						
Return on Assets %						
Return on Equity %						
Debt to Equity						

CONTACT INFORMATION:

Phone: 973-967-6000   Fax: 973-285-1832
Toll-Free:
Address: 4 Gatehall Dr., Parsippany, NJ 07054 United States

STOCK TICKER/OTHER:

Stock Ticker: Private   Exchange:
Employees: 1,000   Fiscal Year Ends: 12/31
Parent Company: Enghouse Systems Limited

SALARIES/BONUSES:

Top Exec. Salary: $ Bonus: $
Second Exec. Salary: $ Bonus: $

OTHER THOUGHTS:

Estimated Female Officers or Directors: 1
Hot Spot for Advancement for Women/Minorities:

Digi.com Bhd
NAIC Code: 517210

www.digi.com.my

TYPES OF BUSINESS:
Mobile Phone Services
Mobile Voice Services
Internet Services
Digital Services
Broadband Services
Mobile Applications

GROWTH PLANS/SPECIAL FEATURES:
Digi.com Bhd is part of the Telenor Group, and provides mobile voice, internet and digital services to 11.3 million customers in Malaysia, under the DiGi brand line. Of those customers, 9.4 million are subscribed to Digi's internet data services. Digi.com provides mobile phones such as Samsung, iPhone, Huawei, Lenovo and more through its ecommerce website. Payment plans include postpaid, prepaid, and monthly plans; broadband services (18GB, 40GB and 100GB); and roaming and international direct dialing (IDD) services. The company maintains a 4G LTE network that reaches the majority of Malaysia's population. DiGi also provides applications for music, video, games, cloud and visual voice mail through MusicFreedom, VideoFreedom and MyDigi. In June 2021, Digi.com announced that it signed a conditional share purchase agreement with Axiata Group Berhad to pave the way for a proposed merger of telecommunications operations between Digi Telecommunications Sdn Bhd and Celcom Axiata Berhad. At completion, Axiata and Telenor will hold equal ownership of 33.1% each in the new merged company, which will be named Celcom Digi Berhad.

BRANDS/DIVISIONS/AFFILIATES:
Telenor Group
Digi Telecommunications Sdn Bhd
DiGi
MusicFreedom
VideoFreedom
MyDigi

CONTACTS: *Note: Officers with more than one job title may be intentionally listed here more than once.*
Albern Murty, CEO
Eugene The, Chief Business Officer
Otto Risbakk, CFO
Praveen Rajan, CMO
Elisabeth Melander Stene, Chief Human Resources Officer
Kesavan Sivabalan, CTO
Christian Thrane, Head-Strategy & Bus. Transformation
Chan Nam Kiong, Head-Customer & Channels
Haakon Bruaset Kjoel, Chmn.

FINANCIAL DATA: *Note: Data for latest year may not have been available at press time.*

In U.S. $	2020	2019	2018	2017	2016	2015
Revenue	1,491,937,000	1,527,002,000	1,582,714,000	1,537,457,000	1,599,685,000	1,676,524,000
R&D Expense						
Operating Income	619,421,600	683,070,300	718,654,900	656,569,100	730,174,300	735,432,100
Operating Margin %		.45%	.45%	.43%	.46%	.44%
SGA Expense	98,104,020	110,077,800	118,765,000	135,282,000	138,817,200	140,354,000
Net Income	296,064,300	347,465,800	373,614,900	358,074,200	395,891,800	417,689,100
Operating Cash Flow	589,732,800	499,913,200	527,663,400	624,787,100	371,561,300	539,539,700
Capital Expenditure	174,643,300	182,034,900	198,460,700	325,953,700	188,090,200	217,394,500
EBITDA	750,988,100	808,771,600	731,047,000	703,942,000	719,554,500	729,078,500
Return on Assets %		.20%	.26%	.26%	.32%	.38%
Return on Equity %		2.15%	2.59%	2.85%	3.14%	2.86%
Debt to Equity		6.759	3.733	5.189	3.464	0.049

CONTACT INFORMATION:
Phone: 60 357211800   Fax:
Toll-Free:
Address: Jalan Delima 1/1, Subang Industrial Park, Lot 10, Selangor, 40000 Malaysia

STOCK TICKER/OTHER:
Stock Ticker: DIGBF   Exchange: GREY
Employees: 1,535   Fiscal Year Ends:
Parent Company: Telenor Group

SALARIES/BONUSES:
Top Exec. Salary: $ Bonus: $
Second Exec. Salary: $ Bonus: $

OTHER THOUGHTS:
Estimated Female Officers or Directors: 3
Hot Spot for Advancement for Women/Minorities: Y

DirecTV LLC (DIRECTV)

www.directv.com

NAIC Code: 517110

TYPES OF BUSINESS:

Satellite Broadcasting
Satellite TV
Streaming
Bundled Services
Internet
Fiber Network
Wireless

BRANDS/DIVISIONS/AFFILIATES:

AT&T Inc
Movie Extra Pack
DIRECTV Cinema

CONTACTS: Note: Officers with more than one job title may be intentionally listed here more than once.

Michael White, CEO
Patrick Doyle, CFO
Romulo Pontual, Chief Technology Officer
Larry Hunter, Executive VP
Joseph Bosch, Executive VP
Bruce Churchill, Executive VP
Steven Adams, Senior VP
Fazal Merchant, Senior VP

GROWTH PLANS/SPECIAL FEATURES:

DirecTV, LLC (DIRECTV), a wholly-owned subsidiary of AT&T, Inc., is a leading provider of satellite TV and streaming TV services via televisions, online or mobile app. DIRECTV offers premium networks such as HBO, Cinemax, STARZ and SHOWTIME, as well as DogTV and MBC Drama HD. For those who enjoy movies, the company offers a Movie Extra Pack with eight niche movie channels. DIRECTV subscribers can watch recent blockbuster movies via DIRECTV Cinema, and offers international packages for multi-language programming. Premium sports entertainment is also provided. DIRECTV offers several TV packages, including DIRECTV Entertainment, Choice, Ultimate and Premier, which differ in price depending on what the package offers. Packages can be bundled with AT&T internet, AT&T fiber and AT&E wireless plans (based on location availability). DIRECTV services are provided for consumers and/or businesses.

DIRECTV employees receive medical, dental and vision coverage; flexible spending accounts; wellness plans; employee assistance programs; and a 401(k) savings plan with a matching contribution opportunity.

FINANCIAL DATA: Note: Data for latest year may not have been available at press time.

In U.S. $	2020	2019	2018	2017	2016	2015
Revenue	26,690,880,207	29,656,533,563	30,416,957,500	32,017,850,000	33,703,000,000	34,000,000,000
R&D Expense						
Operating Income						
Operating Margin %						
SGA Expense						
Net Income				4,305,000,000	32,000,000	-100,000
Operating Cash Flow						
Capital Expenditure						
EBITDA						
Return on Assets %						
Return on Equity %						
Debt to Equity						

CONTACT INFORMATION:

Phone: 310-964-5000   Fax:
Toll-Free:
Address: 2260 E. Imperial Hwy., El Segundo, CA 90245 United States

STOCK TICKER/OTHER:

Stock Ticker: Subsidiary   Exchange:
Employees: 30,000   Fiscal Year Ends: 12/31
Parent Company: AT&T Inc

SALARIES/BONUSES:

Top Exec. Salary: $ Bonus: $
Second Exec. Salary: $ Bonus: $

OTHER THOUGHTS:

Estimated Female Officers or Directors: 3
Hot Spot for Advancement for Women/Minorities: Y

D-Link Corporation

NAIC Code: 334210A

www.dlinktw.com.tw

TYPES OF BUSINESS:

Networking Equipment Manufacturing & Distribution
Broadband Products
Modems
Telephony Products
Security Products
Software
Switches & Routers
Media Converters

BRANDS/DIVISIONS/AFFILIATES:

CONTACTS: *Note: Officers with more than one job title may be intentionally listed here more than once.*

An-Ping Chen, Pres.
Benedict Lee, VP-Oper.
Jui-Hsu Chen, Exec. VP
John Lee, Chmn.
Bendict Lee, Pres., Latin America

GROWTH PLANS/SPECIAL FEATURES:

D-Link Corporation is a leading global designer, developer, manufacturer and distributor of networking, broadband, digital, voice and data communications products for mass consumer and small- to medium-sized business market segments. The company is one of the largest networking hardware vendors in the distribution channel, including value-added resellers, online retailers, retail chains, service providers and direct market resellers. Its products are sold through independent distributors worldwide, with emerging markets and the Asia Pacific region responsible for a majority of global revenues. D-Link manufactures ADSL (asymmetric digital subscriber line) broadband products, cable modems, wireless local area network (LAN), IP telephony products, remote router and security products, network attached storage, LAN switches, print servers, LAN hubs, network management software, LAN cards and network kits, media converters, transceivers, KVM switches, home phone line networks, analog modems, USB devices, audio/video converters, broadband internet video phones and home plug power lines. The company implements and supports unified network solutions that integrate capabilities in switching, wireless, broadband, IP surveillance and cloud-based network management. D-Link holds the patents and copyrights on several technological platforms, including application specific integrated circuit (ASIC) computer chips, hardware technology designs and software applications. The company is also a key contributor to the Digital Living Network Alliance (DLNA), a group that works to maintain industry standards in consumer electronics. D-Link is a global brand with employees in 60 countries.

FINANCIAL DATA: *Note: Data for latest year may not have been available at press time.*

In U.S. $	2020	2019	2018	2017	2016	2015
Revenue	536,339,000	549,600,000	632,998,000	650,070,000	758,781,167	823,325,913
R&D Expense						
Operating Income						
Operating Margin %						
SGA Expense						
Net Income	44,097,900	4,892,572	4,750,070	-15,380,000	-31,585,848	-57,880,919
Operating Cash Flow						
Capital Expenditure						
EBITDA						
Return on Assets %						
Return on Equity %						
Debt to Equity						

CONTACT INFORMATION:

Phone: 886-2-6600-0123   Fax: 886-2-6600-9898
Toll-Free:
Address: No. 289, Xinhu Third Rd., Neihu Dist., Taipei, 114 Taiwan

STOCK TICKER/OTHER:

Stock Ticker: 2332   Exchange: TWSE
Employees: 2,725   Fiscal Year Ends: 12/31
Parent Company:

SALARIES/BONUSES:

Top Exec. Salary: $ Bonus: $
Second Exec. Salary: $ Bonus: $

OTHER THOUGHTS:

Estimated Female Officers or Directors: 1
Hot Spot for Advancement for Women/Minorities:

DSP Group Inc

www.dspg.com

NAIC Code: 334413

TYPES OF BUSINESS:

Integrated Circuits-Digital Signal Processors
Wireless Chipsets
Voice Recognition

BRANDS/DIVISIONS/AFFILIATES:

HDClear
DBM10

CONTACTS: *Note: Officers with more than one job title may be intentionally listed here more than once.*

Ofer Elyakim, CEO
Dror Levy, CFO
Kenneth Traub, Chairman of the Board

GROWTH PLANS/SPECIAL FEATURES:

DSP Group, Inc. produces wireless chipsets for a wide range of smart-enabled devices. Founded in 1987 on the principles of experience, insight and continuous advancement enables DSP to consistently deliver next-generation solutions in the areas of voice, audio, video and data connectivity across diverse mobile, consumer and enterprise products. The group delivers semiconductor system solutions with software and hardware reference designs, enabling original equipment manufacturers (OEMs), original design manufacturers (ODMs), consumer electronics manufacturers and service providers to cost-effectively develop new revenue-generating products with fast time-to-market. DSP's broad portfolio of wireless chipsets integrate digital enhanced cordless telecommunications (DECT), cordless advanced technology-internet and quality (CAT-iq), ultra-low energy (ULE), WiFi, public switched telephone network (PSTN), HDClear, video and voice-over-internet-protocol (VoIP) technologies. HDClear is DSP's own technology and is incorporated into its smart voice product line for mobile, wearables and always-one Internet of Things (IoT) devices. HDClear capitalizes on the voice user interface by incorporating voice command, voice activation, proprietary noise cancellation, acoustic echo cancellation and beam-forming algorithms for the purpose of improving user experience and delivering voice and speech recognition. Recently (2021), DSP Group launched its DBM10 low-power Edge artificial intelligence/machine learning (AI/ML) system on chip (SoC), which comprises a digital signal processor (DSP) and the company's nNetLite neural network processor, both optimized for low-power voice and sensor processing in battery-operated devices. Based in California, USA, the firm has international offices in Israel, Germany, the U.K., Hong Kong, China, Japan, South Korea and India. Export sales account for the majority (approximately 95%) of DSP's total annual revenues.

FINANCIAL DATA: *Note: Data for latest year may not have been available at press time.*

In U.S. $	2020	2019	2018	2017	2016	2015
Revenue	114,480,000	117,613,000	117,438,000	124,753,000	137,869,000	144,271,000
R&D Expense	35,511,000	35,552,000	36,109,000	36,655,000	34,885,000	35,483,000
Operating Income	-8,101,000	-4,404,000	-5,640,000	-4,764,000	4,180,000	1,114,000
Operating Margin %		-.04%	-.05%	-.04%	.03%	.01%
SGA Expense	29,715,000	27,982,000	25,278,000	24,104,000	22,873,000	21,979,000
Net Income	-6,790,000	-1,190,000	-1,957,000	-3,003,000	4,813,000	1,562,000
Operating Cash Flow	14,571,000	10,472,000	8,691,000	8,503,000	16,515,000	12,224,000
Capital Expenditure	973,000	5,638,000	1,181,000	838,000	2,103,000	2,297,000
EBITDA	-4,118,000	546,000	-517,000	400,000	8,584,000	4,541,000
Return on Assets %		-.01%	-.01%	-.02%	.03%	.01%
Return on Equity %		-.01%	-.01%	-.02%	.03%	.01%
Debt to Equity		0.068				

CONTACT INFORMATION:

Phone: 408 986-4300   Fax: 408 986-4323
Toll-Free:
Address: 2055 Gateway Pl., Ste. 480, San Jose, CA 95110 United States

STOCK TICKER/OTHER:

Stock Ticker: DSPG
Employees: 352
Parent Company:

Exchange: NAS
Fiscal Year Ends: 12/31

SALARIES/BONUSES:

Top Exec. Salary: $ Bonus: $
Second Exec. Salary: $ Bonus: $

OTHER THOUGHTS:

Estimated Female Officers or Directors: 2
Hot Spot for Advancement for Women/Minorities:

Sales, profits and employees may be estimates. Financial information, benefits and other data can change quickly and may vary from those stated here.

Dycom Industries Inc

www.dycomind.com

NAIC Code: 237130

TYPES OF BUSINESS:

Construction, Maintenance & Installation Services
Engineering Services
Utility Maintenance Services

BRANDS/DIVISIONS/AFFILIATES:

CONTACTS: *Note: Officers with more than one job title may be intentionally listed here more than once.*

Steven Nielsen, CEO
H. Deferrari, CFO
Sharon Villaverde, Chief Accounting Officer
Timothy Estes, Executive VP
Scott Horton, Other Executive Officer

GROWTH PLANS/SPECIAL FEATURES:

Dycom Industries, Inc. is a leading provider of specialty contracting services. The firm provides services throughout the U.S., and on a limited basis, in Canada. Services include engineering, construction, maintenance and installation services to telecommunications providers; underground locating services to various utilities including telecommunications providers; and other construction and maintenance services to electric utilities. Dycom's top five customers accounted for approximately 74.1% of its fiscal 2021 revenue, and received 18.8% of its revenue from Verizon Communications Inc., 16.9% from Lumen Technologies Inc., 16.7% from AT&T Inc., 16.7% from Comcast Corporation, and 5% from Windstream Holdings Inc. Dycom provides outside plant engineers and drafters to telecommunication providers who design aerial, underground and buried fiber optic, copper and coaxial cable systems that extend from the telephone company's central office, or cable operator headend, to the consumer's home or business. Engineering services the firm provides to telephone companies include fiber cable routing and design; the design of service area concept boxes, terminals, drops and transmission and central office equipment; and the proper administration of feeder and distribution cable pairs. For cable television multiple system operators, Dycom performs make-ready studies, strand mapping, field walk-out, computer-aided radio frequency design and fiber cable routing and design. The firm's construction, maintenance and installation services include placing and splicing fiber, copper and coaxial cables; excavating trenches in which to place cables; placing related structures such as poles, anchors, conduits, manholes, cabinets and closures; placing drop lines from main distribution lines to the consumer's home or business; and maintaining and removing these facilities. It also provides premise wiring services to various corporations and state and local governments, predominantly limited to the installation, repair and maintenance of telecommunications infrastructure within improved structures.

FINANCIAL DATA: *Note: Data for latest year may not have been available at press time.*

In U.S. $	2020	2019	2018	2017	2016	2015
Revenue	3,339,682,000	3,127,700,000	1,411,348,000	3,066,880,000	2,672,542,000	
R&D Expense						
Operating Income	117,806,000	116,565,000	59,885,000	275,009,000	246,874,000	
Operating Margin %	.04%	.04%		.09%	.09%	
SGA Expense	254,590,000	269,140,000	124,930,000	239,231,000	217,149,000	
Net Income	57,215,000	62,907,000	68,835,000	157,217,000	128,740,000	
Operating Cash Flow	57,999,000	124,447,000	160,533,000	256,443,000	261,488,000	
Capital Expenditure	120,574,000	164,963,000	87,839,000	201,197,000	186,011,000	
EBITDA	316,951,000	312,010,000	151,163,000	435,695,000	365,987,000	
Return on Assets %	.03%	.03%		.09%	.08%	
Return on Equity %	.07%	.08%		.26%	.24%	
Debt to Equity	1.022	1.079		1.099	1.267	

CONTACT INFORMATION:

Phone: 561 627-7171   Fax: 561 627-7709
Toll-Free:
Address: 11780 U.S. Highway 1, Ste. 600, Palm Beach Gardens, FL 33408 United States

STOCK TICKER/OTHER:

Stock Ticker: DY   Exchange: NYS
Employees: 14,276   Fiscal Year Ends: 01/27
Parent Company:

SALARIES/BONUSES:

Top Exec. Salary: $ Bonus: $
Second Exec. Salary: $ Bonus: $

OTHER THOUGHTS:

Estimated Female Officers or Directors:
Hot Spot for Advancement for Women/Minorities:

DZS Inc

NAIC Code: 334210

dasanzhone.com

TYPES OF BUSINESS:

Telecommunications Infrastructure Equipment
Broadband Access Solutions
Mobile Transport

BRANDS/DIVISIONS/AFFILIATES:

DASAN Zhone Solutions Inc
RIFT

CONTACTS: Note: Officers with more than one job title may be intentionally listed here more than once.

Il Yung Kim, CEO
Michael Golomb, CFO
Min Woo Nam, Chairman of the Board
Philip Yim, COO

GROWTH PLANS/SPECIAL FEATURES:

DZS, Inc. (formerly DASAN Zhone Solutions, Inc.) is a global provider of packet-based mobile transport and broadband access converged-edge solutions deployed by advanced Tier 1, 2 and regional service providers and enterprise customers. DZS' solutions are deployed by more than 1,000 customers in over 100 countries. The company researches, develops, tests, sells, manufactures and supports platforms in relation to mobile transport and fixed broadband access. DZS' mobile transport products provide a scalable solution for mobile operators that enable them to upgrade their mobile fronthaul/midhaul/backhaul systems and migrate to 5G wireless technologies and beyond. These products may be collocated at the radio access node base station and can aggregate multiple radio access node base stations into a single backhaul for delivery of mobile traffic to the radio access node network controller. They support pure Ethernet switching as well as layer 3 IP and multiprotocol label switching (MPLS). This division interoperates with other vendors in these markets. DZS' fixed broadband access products offer a variety of solutions for carriers and service providers to connect residential and business customers, either using high-speed fiber or leveraging their existing deployed copper networks to offer broadband services to customer premises. Once the broadband access products are deployed, the service provider can offer voice, high-definition and ultra-high-definition video, high-speed internet access and business class services to their customers. This division's connected premises portfolio consists of indoor/outdoor ONT gateways that deliver data throughout to support fiber-to-the-everything (FTTx) applications. In late-2020, DASAN Zhone Solutions, Inc. changed its corporate name to DZS, Inc. In March 2021, DZS acquired network orchestration and automation solutions innovator, RIFT.

FINANCIAL DATA: Note: Data for latest year may not have been available at press time.

In U.S. $	2020	2019	2018	2017	2016	2015
Revenue	300,640,000	306,882,000	282,348,000	247,114,000	150,304,000	100,756,000
R&D Expense	37,459,000	38,516,000	35,306,000	35,437,000	25,396,000	15,449,000
Operating Income	-6,053,000	-1,118,000	7,180,000	722,000	-13,353,000	-1,748,000
Operating Margin %		.00%	.03%	.00%	-.09%	-.02%
SGA Expense	64,041,000	61,206,000	48,321,000	43,888,000	27,348,000	25,066,000
Net Income	-23,082,000	-13,457,000	2,767,000	1,071,000	-15,326,000	-2,017,000
Operating Cash Flow	5,064,000	-22,702,000	-12,218,000	1,902,000	3,496,000	3,703,000
Capital Expenditure	2,270,000	2,314,000	1,182,000	1,162,000	1,372,000	818,000
EBITDA	-12,403,000	-582,000	9,000,000	3,937,000	-9,838,000	-974,000
Return on Assets %		-.06%	.02%	.01%	-.15%	-.03%
Return on Equity %		-.15%	.04%	.02%	-.30%	-.06%
Debt to Equity		0.349	0.183	0.134	0.102	

CONTACT INFORMATION:

Phone: 510 777-7000   Fax: 510 777-7001
Toll-Free: 877-946-6320
Address: 1350 S. Loop Rd., Ste. 130, Alameda, CA 94502 United States

STOCK TICKER/OTHER:

Stock Ticker: DZSI
Employees: 830
Parent Company: DASAN Networks Inc

Exchange: NAS
Fiscal Year Ends: 12/31

SALARIES/BONUSES:

Top Exec. Salary: $ Bonus: $
Second Exec. Salary: $ Bonus: $

OTHER THOUGHTS:

Estimated Female Officers or Directors: 1
Hot Spot for Advancement for Women/Minorities:

Sales, profits and employees may be estimates. Financial information, benefits and other data can change quickly and may vary from those stated here.

EarthLink LLC

NAIC Code: 517110

TYPES OF BUSINESS:

Internet Service Provider (ISP)
Web Hosting Services
Voice Services
Managed IT & Data Hosting
Value-Added Services
Internet Service Provider
Hyperlink

BRANDS/DIVISIONS/AFFILIATES:

Trive Capital

GROWTH PLANS/SPECIAL FEATURES:

EarthLink LLC is a leading next-generation internet service provider. With access available across the U.S., the firm offers fast and reliable connectivity, customer support and customizable features. Internet access offerings include dial-up, high-speed digital subscriber line (DSL), free-standing DSL hyperlink internet, and a hyperlink and Apple TV option. Website tools and services include site design, domain and email hosting and solutions for businesses. Software and tools include security, WiFi privacy and access solutions. EarthLinks is owned by private equity firm Trive Capital.

EarthLink offers its employees health plan options, 401(k), life and disability insurance, and a variety of assistance plans and company perks.

CONTACTS: Note: Officers with more than one job title may be intentionally listed here more than once.

Glenn Goad, CEO
Michael Toplisek, Pres.
Julie Shimer, Chairman of the Board
Michael Borellis, CFO
Scott Klinger, Sr. VP-Mktg. & Human Resources
Leon Hounshell, Chief Product Officer
Bradley Ferguson, Executive VP, Divisional
Louis Alterman, Executive VP
Samuel Desimone, Executive VP
John Dobbins, Executive VP
Gerard Brossard, Executive VP
Rick Froehlich, Executive VP
Valerie Benjamin, Senior VP, Divisional
R. Thurston, Vice President
Brian McLaughline, COO

FINANCIAL DATA: Note: Data for latest year may not have been available at press time.

In U.S. $	2020	2019	2018	2017	2016	2015
Revenue	1,183,644,000	1,212,750,000	1,155,000,000	1,100,000,000	1,099,800,000	1,097,251,968
R&D Expense						
Operating Income						
Operating Margin %						
SGA Expense						
Net Income						
Operating Cash Flow						
Capital Expenditure						
EBITDA						
Return on Assets %						
Return on Equity %						
Debt to Equity						

CONTACT INFORMATION:

Phone: 404 815-0770   Fax:
Toll-Free: 888-327-8454
Address: 980 Hammond Dr. NE, Ste. 400, Atlanta, GA 30328 United States

STOCK TICKER/OTHER:

Stock Ticker: Private
Employees: 2,138
Parent Company: Trive Capital

Exchange:
Fiscal Year Ends: 12/31

SALARIES/BONUSES:

Top Exec. Salary: $ Bonus: $
Second Exec. Salary: $ Bonus: $

OTHER THOUGHTS:

Estimated Female Officers or Directors: 5
Hot Spot for Advancement for Women/Minorities: Y

Sales, profits and employees may be estimates. Financial information, benefits and other data can change quickly and may vary from those stated here.

EchoStar Corporation

www.echostar.com

NAIC Code: 517110

TYPES OF BUSINESS:
Digital Set-Top Boxes & Related Products
Fixed Satellite Services

BRANDS/DIVISIONS/AFFILIATES:
Hughes
ESS

CONTACTS: *Note: Officers with more than one job title may be intentionally listed here more than once.*
Michael Dugan, CEO
David Rayner, CFO
Charles Ergen, Chairman of the Board
Anders Johnson, Chief Strategy Officer
Pradman Kaul, Director
Dean Manson, Executive VP

GROWTH PLANS/SPECIAL FEATURES:
EchoStar Corporation is a global provider of broadband satellite technologies, broadband internet services and satellite services. The firm also delivers network technologies, managed services and communications solution for enterprise customers, including aeronautical and government enterprises. EchoStar operates through two business segments: Hughes and ESS. Hughes provides broadband satellite technologies and broadband internet services to consumer customers, and broadband network technologies, managed services, hardware, satellite services and communications solutions to both consumer and enterprise customers. This division also designs, provides and installs gateway and terminal equipment to customers for other satellite system; and designs, develops, constructs and provides telecommunication networks comprising satellite ground segment systems and terminals to mobile system operators and EchoStar enterprise customers. The ESS segment provides satellite services on a full-time and/or occasional-use basis to U.S. government service providers, internet service providers, broadcast news organizations, content providers and private enterprise customers. This division primarily uses the EchoStar IX satellite and the EchoStar 105/SES-11 satellite and related infrastructure. Other satellite fleet either owned or leased by EchoStar include: SPACEWAY 3, EchoStar XVII, EchoStar XIX, Al Yah 3, EchoStar XXI and EUTELSAT 10A (owned); and Eutelsat 65 West A, Telesat T19V and EchoStar 105/SES-11 (leased).

EchoStar offers employees medical, dental, vision, life, AD&D and disability insurance; various assistance programs; 401(k) and other retirement/savings plans; paid vacation/holidays; tuition reimbursement and more.

FINANCIAL DATA: *Note: Data for latest year may not have been available at press time.*

In U.S. $	2020	2019	2018	2017	2016	2015
Revenue	1,887,907,000	1,886,081,000	2,091,363,000	1,885,508,000	3,056,730,000	3,143,714,000
R&D Expense	29,448,000	25,739,000	27,570,000	31,745,000	76,024,000	78,287,000
Operating Income	114,158,000	73,077,000	248,463,000	207,069,000	364,398,000	358,433,000
Operating Margin %		.04%	.12%	.11%	.12%	.11%
SGA Expense	474,912,000	509,145,000	436,247,000	366,007,000	385,634,000	374,116,000
Net Income	-40,150,000	-62,917,000	-40,475,000	392,561,000	179,930,000	153,357,000
Operating Cash Flow	534,388,000	656,322,000	734,522,000	726,892,000	803,343,000	776,451,000
Capital Expenditure	447,453,000	482,341,000	586,780,000	610,231,000	721,506,000	729,275,000
EBITDA	645,103,000	746,051,000	838,786,000	851,783,000	905,542,000	871,796,000
Return on Assets %		-.01%	.00%	.04%	.02%	.02%
Return on Equity %		-.02%	-.01%	.10%	.05%	.05%
Debt to Equity		0.678	0.622	0.863	0.924	0.592

CONTACT INFORMATION:
Phone: 303 706-4000   Fax:
Toll-Free:
Address: 100 Inverness Terrace E., Englewood, CO 80112-5308 United States

STOCK TICKER/OTHER:
Stock Ticker: SATS
Employees: 2,500
Parent Company:

Exchange: NAS
Fiscal Year Ends: 12/31

SALARIES/BONUSES:
Top Exec. Salary: $ Bonus: $
Second Exec. Salary: $ Bonus: $

OTHER THOUGHTS:
Estimated Female Officers or Directors: 1
Hot Spot for Advancement for Women/Minorities:

ECI Telecom Ltd

NAIC Code: 334210

www.ecitele.com

TYPES OF BUSINESS:

Digital Communications Equipment Manufacturing
Optical Networking Equipment
Broadband Access Equipment
Data Encryption Services

BRANDS/DIVISIONS/AFFILIATES:

Ribbon Communications Inc
Muse
Elastic Services Platform
Apollo OPT
Neptune
Mercury NFV

CONTACTS: *Note: Officers with more than one job title may be intentionally listed here more than once.*

Darryl Edwards, CEO
Giora Bitan, CFO
Fernando Valdivielso, VP- Global Sales & Mktg.
Adi Bildner, VP-Global Human Resources
Tali Rosenwaks, Head-R&D
Hayim Porat, CTO
Tali Rosenwaks, Head-Eng.
Arnie Taragin, General Counsel
Hezi Basok, Exec. VP-Global Bus. Oper.
Eran Dariel, Gen. Mgr.-Portfolio Bus.
Eran Talmon, Head-Global Svcs. Div.
Shaul Shani, Chmn.

GROWTH PLANS/SPECIAL FEATURES:

ECI Telecom Ltd., based in Israel, delivers elastic network solutions to service providers, utilities and data center/cloud providers worldwide. The company's elastic network solutions ensure open, future-proof and secure communications. ECI's products include the following: the Elastic Services Platform, which simplifies service delivery and lifecycle management, and offers network assurance, optimization and automation; Apollo OPT, a family of optical transport and switching platforms that work seamlessly to provide scalable, high-density and energy-efficient solutions from access to core; Neptune, a family of elastic multiprotocol label switching products; Mercury NFV solutions (network functions virtualization), providing end-users with low-latency experiences, deploying NFV at the mobile edge, the customer premises and in the network as an edge cloud; and Muse, a modular suite of applications that enables ECI customers to create and turn up new services rapidly, and to ensure the network is optimized. ECI also offers cyber security solutions and provides management, insights and professional services. Industries served by ECI products, solutions and services include service providers, critical industries and data center interconnect service providers. ECI has offices located in the Americas, Europe, Africa and Asia. In late 2019, ECI was acquired by Ribbon Communications Inc., a U.S. software and cloud communications firm, for $324 million.

FINANCIAL DATA: *Note: Data for latest year may not have been available at press time.*

In U.S. $	2020	2019	2018	2017	2016	2015
Revenue	366,600,000	376,000,000	399,000,000	380,000,000	785,000,000	774,000,000
R&D Expense						
Operating Income						
Operating Margin %						
SGA Expense						
Net Income						
Operating Cash Flow						
Capital Expenditure						
EBITDA						
Return on Assets %						
Return on Equity %						
Debt to Equity						

CONTACT INFORMATION:

Phone: 972-3-926-6555   Fax: 972-3-926-6500
Toll-Free:
Address: 30 Hasivim St., Petah Tikva, 49517 Israel

STOCK TICKER/OTHER:

Stock Ticker: Subsidiary   Exchange:
Employees: 1,700   Fiscal Year Ends: 09/30
Parent Company: Ribbon Communications Inc

SALARIES/BONUSES:

Top Exec. Salary: $ Bonus: $
Second Exec. Salary: $ Bonus: $

OTHER THOUGHTS:

Estimated Female Officers or Directors: 1
Hot Spot for Advancement for Women/Minorities:

EF Johnson Technologies Inc

www.efjohnson.com

NAIC Code: 334220

TYPES OF BUSINESS:

Voice Communication Security Products
Secure Wireless Communications Systems
Land Mobile Radio Systems

BRANDS/DIVISIONS/AFFILIATES:

JVCKENWOOD Corporation
KENWOOD Viking
Viking P25
ATLAS P25
NEXEDGE
KAIROS

CONTACTS: Note: Officers with more than one job title may be intentionally listed here more than once.

Duane Anderson, CEO
Rich Cagle, Sr. VP-Sales
Brandon Romero, VP-Systems Engineering
Karthik Rangarajan, Sr. VP-Product & Strategy
Timi Jackson, VP
Karthik Rangarajan, VP-Mktg.

GROWTH PLANS/SPECIAL FEATURES:

EF Johnson Technologies, Inc., owned by JVCKENWOOD Corporation, is a provider of secure wireless technologies primarily for the homeland security marketplace. The firm designs, develops, markets and supports private wireless communications, including wireless radios and wireless communications infrastructure and systems for digital and analog platforms. EF's products are grouped into two categories-radios and systems-and serve the fire, law enforcement, public works/utilities federal, military, business, industrial and education industries. KENWOOD Viking radios combine Viking P25 software and KENWOOD's hardware, and are used throughout the world. Radio sets come in portables and mobiles. The KENWOOD Viking portable radios encompass advanced technology such as Armada fleet management and programming software, and TrueVoice software-based noise cancellation. The systems category consists of land mobile radio (LMR) communications systems, which are used for critical communication purposes and keeps teams connected 24/7. ATLAS P25 features patented latitude technology to offer increased transport flexibility in comparison with traditional LMR systems in various aspects of its operations. Latitude technology offers auto-discovery and self-healing sites, distributed call control and simulcast control. NEXEDGE NXDN is one of the largest two-way radio networks in the U.S., and deploys NEXEDGE technology, which incorporates frequency division multiple access (FDMA) for maximum bandwidth utilization and reducing the risk of interference. NEXEDGE comes in a variety of configurations, including conventional, conventional IP, conventional simulcast, Gen1 Trunked and Gen2 Trunked. Last, KAIROS is a digital mobile radio that keeps teams safe and connected via simulcast repeaters. KAIROS features multi-protocol switching, IP multisite multicasting/simulcasting, UHF linking, system redundancy, soft diversity reception, and SIP/RTP integration. EF services encompass support services, training, field service bulletins and repair request processing. Headquartered in Texas, EF Johnson has office locations in Nebraska and California.

FINANCIAL DATA: Note: Data for latest year may not have been available at press time.

In U.S. $	2020	2019	2018	2017	2016	2015
Revenue	150,491,250	143,325,000	136,500,000	130,000,000	128,800,000	125,000,000
R&D Expense						
Operating Income						
Operating Margin %						
SGA Expense						
Net Income						
Operating Cash Flow						
Capital Expenditure						
EBITDA						
Return on Assets %						
Return on Equity %						
Debt to Equity						

CONTACT INFORMATION:

Phone: 972-819-0700   Fax: 972-819-0639
Toll-Free: 800-328-3911
Address: 1440 Corporate Dr., Irving, TX 75038 United States

STOCK TICKER/OTHER:

Stock Ticker: Private   Exchange:
Employees: 200   Fiscal Year Ends: 03/31
Parent Company: JVCKENWOOD Corporation

SALARIES/BONUSES:

Top Exec. Salary: $ Bonus: $
Second Exec. Salary: $ Bonus: $

OTHER THOUGHTS:

Estimated Female Officers or Directors: 2
Hot Spot for Advancement for Women/Minorities:

eircom Limited

NAIC Code: 517110

www.eir.ie

TYPES OF BUSINESS:

Local & Long-Distance Services
Cellular Phone Service
Internet Service Provider
Data Storage & Networking Services
Wholesale Telecommunications Services
Payphones
Directory Services

BRANDS/DIVISIONS/AFFILIATES:

NJJ Group
NJJ Telecom Europe
Open eir
eir Mobile

CONTACTS: *Note: Officers with more than one job title may be intentionally listed here more than once.*

Carolan Lennon, CEO
Brendan Lynch, Managing Dir.-Group Tech.
Ann Marie Kearney, Chief Legal Officer
Pat Galvin, Dir.-Regulation & Public Affairs
Ronan Kneafsey, Managing Dir.-eircom Business
Chris Hutchings, Managing Dir.-eircom Wholesale
Tony Mealy, Dir.-Program Execution
Kevin White, Managing Dir.-Consumer
David McRedmond, Chmn.

GROWTH PLANS/SPECIAL FEATURES:

eircom Limited (eir)is the principal provider of fixed-line telecommunications and mobile telecommunications services in Ireland, serving approximately 2.1 million customers. The firm has the most extensive telecommunications network in Ireland both in terms of capacity and geographic reach. Services provided by eir include a comprehensive range of advanced voice, data, broadband and TV services to the residential, small business, enterprise and government markets. Open eir is a leading wholesale operator in Ireland with approximately 820,000 fiber connections. The company's smart WiFi hub mesh extender enables customers to enjoy ultrafast broadband in every part of the house. The mobile division operates under the eir Mobile brand and serves approximately 20% of Ireland's mobile market, and is the third largest mobile operator in the country. The service offers general packet radio services (GPRS), 3G mobile services and high-speed 4G mobile broadband network services. 5G network is being rolled out, and available in nearly 300 towns and cities throughout the country (as of May 2021), and 5G outdoor population coverage was over 57%. NJJ Telecom Europe, part of NJJ Group, owns a majority stake in eir.

FINANCIAL DATA: *Note: Data for latest year may not have been available at press time.*

In U.S. $	2020	2019	2018	2017	2016	2015
Revenue	1,384,530,000	1,399,830,000	1,479,270,000	1,482,070,000	1,451,810,000	1,403,440,000
R&D Expense						
Operating Income						
Operating Margin %						
SGA Expense						
Net Income	24,743,900	34,100,100	-68,722,000	-257,850,000	-175,104,000	-105,397,000
Operating Cash Flow						
Capital Expenditure						
EBITDA						
Return on Assets %						
Return on Equity %						
Debt to Equity						

CONTACT INFORMATION:

Phone: 353-1-701-5000   Fax: 353-1-671-6916
Toll-Free:
Address: 2022 Bianconi Ave., Dublin, D24 HX03 Ireland

STOCK TICKER/OTHER:

Stock Ticker: Subsidiary   Exchange:
Employees: 3,264   Fiscal Year Ends: 06/30
Parent Company: NJJ Group

SALARIES/BONUSES:

Top Exec. Salary: $ Bonus: $
Second Exec. Salary: $ Bonus: $

OTHER THOUGHTS:

Estimated Female Officers or Directors: 2
Hot Spot for Advancement for Women/Minorities:

Elisa Corporation

NAIC Code: 517110

www.elisa.com

TYPES OF BUSINESS:
Voice & Data Services
Mobile Phone Service
Internet Services
Data Security Software Development
Cable TV

BRANDS/DIVISIONS/AFFILIATES:
Elisa Videra
Elisa Smart Factory
Enia Oy
Elisa Saunalahti
Elisa Estonia
Elisa Santa Monica
Elisa Automate

CONTACTS: *Note: Officers with more than one job title may be intentionally listed here more than once.*
Veli-Matti Mattila, CEO
Jari Kinnunen, CFO
Timo Katajisto, Exec. VP-Prod.
Sami Ylikortes, Exec. VP-Admin.
Katiye Vuorela, Exec. VP-Corp. Comm.
Vesa Sahivirta, Dir.-Investor Relations
Pasi Maenpaa, Exec. VP-Corp. Customers
Asko Kansala, Exec. VP-Consumer Customers
Anssi Vanjoki, Chmn.

GROWTH PLANS/SPECIAL FEATURES:
Elisa Corporation is the one of the largest telecommunications and digital services companies in Finland. Founded in 1882, the firm hosted the world's first global system for mobile communication (GSM) wireless call in 1991, and launched 5G network for mobile, smart home and business customers in 2020. Elisa provides a range of wired and wireless voice and data services, including internet, broadband, data security software, business and residential telephone, mobile phone, mobile internet and messaging. The firm serves approximately 2.8 million mobile consumers in Finland, Estonia and internationally, including corporate and public administration organization customers. Elisa's core markets are Finland and Estonia, but the company also provides digital services for international markets, with services including visual communication services, entertainment services and cloud-based IT services. The firm's brands include Elisa, Elisa Saunalahti, Elisa Videra, Elisa Santa Monica, Elisa Automate and Elisa Smart Factory. Elisa Videra is a subsidiary that provides visual communications through products such as video conferencing and digital signage systems, no matter how large or complex. Elisa Smart Factory provides industrial solutions that are driven by Internet of Things (IoT) and artificial intelligence (AI). It connects the customers' data sources with these solutions in order to reveal insights via complex data, making it easy for employees to understand and therefore make better business decisions. Subsidiary Enia Oy is a telemarketing company responsible for selling Elisa's and Elisa Saunalahti's services to consumer customers together with other sales channels. Enia targets new and existing customers (for upgrades) in Finland. Elisa Estonia serves the Estonian market.

Elisa offers employees occupational health services, staff dining, discounts on telecom services, timeshares in Finland and St. Petersburg and private hospital services including coverage for dependents.

FINANCIAL DATA: *Note: Data for latest year may not have been available at press time.*

In U.S. $	2020	2019	2018	2017	2016	2015
Revenue	2,314,779,000	2,252,468,000	2,237,807,000	2,183,804,000	1,998,461,000	1,917,579,000
R&D Expense						
Operating Income	494,575,300	475,759,900	485,534,200	454,867,600	409,417,500	375,696,400
Operating Margin %		.21%	.22%	.21%	.20%	.20%
SGA Expense				733,066	733,066	733,066
Net Income	400,742,800	370,198,400	385,837,200	411,250,100	314,118,800	297,014,000
Operating Cash Flow	733,066,200	676,742,300	629,703,900	611,865,900	594,394,500	565,438,400
Capital Expenditure	304,466,800	282,963,600	287,850,700	311,308,800	255,229,200	244,111,000
EBITDA	845,591,800	806,861,500	782,548,100	800,141,700	691,770,100	654,017,200
Return on Assets %		.11%	.12%	.13%	.11%	.11%
Return on Equity %		.27%	.29%	.33%	.27%	.27%
Debt to Equity		0.944	0.765	0.904	0.852	0.741

CONTACT INFORMATION:
Phone: 358 10804400   Fax: 358 1026060
Toll-Free:
Address: Ratavartijankatu 5, Helsinki PL 1, Elisa, 00061 Finland

STOCK TICKER/OTHER:
Stock Ticker: ELMUF   Exchange: PINX
Employees: 5,171   Fiscal Year Ends: 12/31
Parent Company:

SALARIES/BONUSES:
Top Exec. Salary: $ Bonus: $
Second Exec. Salary: $ Bonus: $

OTHER THOUGHTS:
Estimated Female Officers or Directors: 3
Hot Spot for Advancement for Women/Minorities: Y

Embratel Participacoes SA

www.embratel.com.br

NAIC Code: 517110

TYPES OF BUSINESS:

Local & Long-Distance Telephone Services
Internet & Data Service
Satellite Services
TV & Radio Broadcasting
Free Dial-up Internet Access
Network Outsourcing
Call Centers
Wi-Fi 6

BRANDS/DIVISIONS/AFFILIATES:

America Movil SAB de CV
Empresa Brasileira de Telecomunicacoes SA
Star One SA (Embratel Star One)

CONTACTS: *Note: Officers with more than one job title may be intentionally listed here more than once.*

Jose Formoso Martinez, Pres.
Isaac Berensztejn, Dir.-Investor Rel.
Jose Formoso Martinez, VP

GROWTH PLANS/SPECIAL FEATURES:

Embratel Participacoes SA is the holding company for Empresa Brasileira de Telecomunicacoes SA (Embratel), which offers voice, data, internet, television and other services in Brazil and internationally. The firm is owned by America Movil SAB de CV. The company is one of the largest providers of telecommunications services in Brazil, offering the entire Brazilian market solutions including local telephone, data and internet services; domestic and international long distance; and TV and radio broadcasting. In addition, Embratel provides IT integration solutions, cloud computing, data center, customer experience, security solutions, Internet of Things (IoT), video services/solutions and energy efficiency solutions, as well as corporate mobile/fixed-line solutions. Subsidiary Star One SA, also known as Embratel Star One, operates one of the largest satellite networks in South America. It provides satellite capacity covering the entire continent for voice, data, internet, TV and radio signals through seven satellites, with two currently under construction. In mid-2021, Embratel Participacoes announced the use of Wi-Fi 6 technology for the development of its projects in various segments, including industry and retail. The company stated Wi-Fi 6 is a next-generation of Wi-Fi offering enhanced efficiency and capacity as well as low latency, increased simultaneous traffic capacity and performance, supporting connected devices without loss of speed.

FINANCIAL DATA: *Note: Data for latest year may not have been available at press time.*

In U.S. $	2020	2019	2018	2017	2016	2015
Revenue	10,893,251,250	10,374,525,000	9,880,500,000	9,410,000,000	9,948,200,000	10,000,000,000
R&D Expense						
Operating Income						
Operating Margin %						
SGA Expense						
Net Income						
Operating Cash Flow						
Capital Expenditure						
EBITDA						
Return on Assets %						
Return on Equity %						
Debt to Equity						

CONTACT INFORMATION:

Phone: 55-21-2121-6474   Fax: 55-21-2121-6388
Toll-Free:
Address: Rua Reg Feijo 166 Sala 1687B Centro, Rio de Janeiro, RJ 20060060 Brazil

STOCK TICKER/OTHER:

Stock Ticker: Subsidiary   Exchange:
Employees: 7,466   Fiscal Year Ends: 12/31
Parent Company: America Movil SAB de CV

SALARIES/BONUSES:

Top Exec. Salary: $ Bonus: $
Second Exec. Salary: $ Bonus: $

OTHER THOUGHTS:

Estimated Female Officers or Directors:
Hot Spot for Advancement for Women/Minorities:

Emirates Telecommunications Corporation (Etisalat)

www.etisalat.ae

NAIC Code: 517110

TYPES OF BUSINESS:

Local Telephone Service
Internet Services
Wireless Services
Digital Cable Service
Underwater Cable Installation

BRANDS/DIVISIONS/AFFILIATES:

Etisalat
Etisalat Software Solutions (P) Ltd
E-Vision
Thuraya
Etihad Etisalat Company
Mobily
Itissalat Al-Maghrib
Etisalat Sri Lanka

CONTACTS: Note: Officers with more than one job title may be intentionally listed here more than once.

Hatem Dowidar, CEO
Paul Werne, Group General Counsel
Daniel Ritz, Chief Strategy Officer
Nasser bin Obood, Chief Gov't Rel. & Corp. Comm. Officer
Javier Garcia, Chief Internal Auditor
Kamal Shehadi, Chief Legal & Regulatory Officer
Jamal Aljarwan, Chief Regional Officer Asis Cluster
Rainer Rathgeber, Chief Commercial Officer
John Wilkes, Chief Internal Control Officer
Essa Al Haddad, Chief Regional Officer-Africa
Obaid Bokisha, Chief Procurement Officer

GROWTH PLANS/SPECIAL FEATURES:

Emirates Telecommunications Corporation (Etisalat), which is 60%-owned by the government of United Arab Emirates, provides telecommunications services to more than 150 million users in 16 countries across the Middle East, Asia and Africa. The firm has a wide coverage of 3G, 4G and 5G mobile technologies, as well as an extensive fiber-to-the-home (FTTH) network. Etisalat offers fixed-line, wireless and internet services to customers spread across Asia and Africa and the Middle East. The company's 4G+ LTE (long-term evolution) network provides mobile broadband speeds of up to 300Mbps. The company launched its commercial 5G wireless network in 2018, becoming the first telecom operator in the Middle East and North Africa region to achieve the technological feat. Etisalat offers post-paid, pre-paid and control/visitor mobile lines, as well as data add-on features. Wholly-owned Etisalat Software Solutions (P) Ltd. (ESSPL), based in Bangalore, develops software for IT solutions and offers its services to other telecommunications companies in the region. Devices sold by the company include smartphones, tablets, routers, gaming devices, smart living and related accessories. Wholly-owned E-Vision offers a turnkey end-to-end over-the-top (OTT) platform that includes video on-demand, a content delivery network (CDN), content aggregation, TV channels hosting (more than 600), advertising sales, creative services and more. Thuraya is a regional mobile satellite service provider, operating two geostationary satellites which provide telecommunications coverage in more than 160 countries. Etihad Etisalat Company is a telecommunications services company that offers its products under the Mobily brand name. Itissalat Al-Maghrib offers telecommunications services in Morocco; and Etisalat Sri Lanka is a mobile telecommunications network in Sri Lanka.

FINANCIAL DATA: Note: Data for latest year may not have been available at press time.

In U.S. $	2020	2019	2018	2017	2016	2015
Revenue	14,073,700,000	14,205,700,000	14,263,600,000	14,072,900,000	14,266,458,109	14,075,880,258
R&D Expense						
Operating Income						
Operating Margin %						
SGA Expense						
Net Income	2,449,970,000	2,584,520,000	2,843,010,000	2,659,980,000	2,287,044,517	2,259,764,142
Operating Cash Flow						
Capital Expenditure						
EBITDA						
Return on Assets %						
Return on Equity %						
Debt to Equity						

CONTACT INFORMATION:

Phone: 971 400444101   Fax: 971 400444105
Toll-Free:
Address: Etisalat Bldg. 1, Sheikh Rashid Bin Saeed Al Maktoum, Abu Dhabi, United Arab Emirates

STOCK TICKER/OTHER:

Stock Ticker: ETISALAT
Employees: 39,600
Parent Company:

Exchange: Abu Dhabi
Fiscal Year Ends: 12/31

SALARIES/BONUSES:

Top Exec. Salary: $ Bonus: $
Second Exec. Salary: $ Bonus: $

OTHER THOUGHTS:

Estimated Female Officers or Directors:
Hot Spot for Advancement for Women/Minorities:

Empresa Nacional de Telecommunications SA (Entel)

www.entel.cl

NAIC Code: 517110

TYPES OF BUSINESS:

Telecommunications Services
Mobile Services
Internet Services
Telephony Services

BRANDS/DIVISIONS/AFFILIATES:

Entel Phone Local Telephone
Entel Telefonia Personal
Entel PCS
Entel Movil

CONTACTS: Note: Officers with more than one job title may be intentionally listed here more than once.

Antonio Buchi Buc, CEO
Juan Baraqui Anania, Dir.-Admin.
Cristian Maturana Miquel, Dir.-Legal
Alfredo Parot Donoso, VP-Oper.
Sebastian Dominguez Philippi, Dir.-Strategy & Innovation
Carmen Luz De La Cerda C., Investor Rel. Officer
Felipe Ureta Prieto, Mgr.-Corp. Finance
Manuel Araya Arroyo, Dir.-Regulation & Corp. Affairs
Luis Ceron Puelam, Dir.-Internal Audit
Juan Jose Hurtado Vicuna, Chmn.
Eduardo Bobenrieth Giglio, Gen. Mgr.-Peru Americatel SA

GROWTH PLANS/SPECIAL FEATURES:

Empresa Nacional de Telecommunications SA (Entel) is a leading telecommunications company in Chile. The firm provides mobile services and fixed network services, including data, IT (information technology) integration, internet, local telephone, long distance and related services. The firm provides 3.5G, 4G, advanced HSPA+ (high speed packet access evolution) and fiber optic network systems, and has engaged in applying technological trends such as 5G, Internet of Things (IoT), analytics, video recognition, augmented reality, virtual reality and more. Entel additionally has a fixed network and call center in Peru. The company offers its products and services in three areas: residential, business and corporate. Residential solutions offered by Entel include mobile solutions, long distance, value added services, calling cards, broadband Internet, dial-up Internet and broadband telephony services. This division also offers hardware for purchase such as new and refurbished phones and Internet equipment. Entel's business offerings include mobile solutions, traditional and IP (Internet protocol) telephony, long distance, broadband Internet, broadband telephony, data networks and IT solutions. Its long-distance business offerings include international calling, calling cards and ISDN (integrated services digital network) videoconferencing. The firm's broadband Internet solutions for businesses include ADSL (asymmetrical digital subscriber line), wireless and dedicated options. Entel's corporate solutions include mobile services, fixed solutions, IT solutions, cloud computing services and data center solutions. Corporate value-added services include infrastructure, network administration, security and studies. Wholly-owned subsidiaries of Entel include Entel Phone Local Telephone, Entel Telefonia Personal, Entel PCS and Entel Movil.

FINANCIAL DATA: Note: Data for latest year may not have been available at press time.

In U.S. $	2020	2019	2018	2017	2016	2015
Revenue	2,932,460,000	2,652,470,000	2,768,160,000	3,157,300,000	2,871,786,398	2,733,572,079
R&D Expense						
Operating Income						
Operating Margin %						
SGA Expense						
Net Income	118,364,000	206,633,000	-33,991,600	70,536,200	51,060,600	-1,553,630
Operating Cash Flow						
Capital Expenditure						
EBITDA						
Return on Assets %						
Return on Equity %						
Debt to Equity						

CONTACT INFORMATION:

Phone: 56-2-3600-123   Fax: 56-2-360-3424
Toll-Free:
Address: Ave. Andres Bello 2687, Fl. 14, Las Condes, Santiago, Casilla 4254 Chile

STOCK TICKER/OTHER:

Stock Ticker: ENTEL
Employees: 8,985
Parent Company:

Exchange: Santiago
Fiscal Year Ends: 12/31

SALARIES/BONUSES:

Top Exec. Salary: $ Bonus: $
Second Exec. Salary: $ Bonus: $

OTHER THOUGHTS:

Estimated Female Officers or Directors: 1
Hot Spot for Advancement for Women/Minorities: Y

Energy Focus Inc

www.energyfocus.com

NAIC Code: 335921

TYPES OF BUSINESS:

Fiber Optic Cable Manufacturing
Lighting Systems
Manufacture
Development
Light-Emitting Diode Products

BRANDS/DIVISIONS/AFFILIATES:

Intellitube

CONTACTS: Note: Officers with more than one job title may be intentionally listed here more than once.

James Tu, CEO

GROWTH PLANS/SPECIAL FEATURES:

Energy Focus, Inc. designs, develops, manufactures, markets and sells energy-efficient lighting systems. The firm's light-emitting diode (LED) lighting products are primarily sold to the general commercial, industrial and military maritime markets. Energy Focus aims to replace fluorescent lamps in institutional buildings and high-intensity discharge lighting in low-bay and high-bay applications with its innovative commercial, military tubular LED (TLED) products, and other LED, ultraviolet light disinfection (UVCD) and lighting control products. The company's LED technology solutions enable customers to run their facilities with greater energy efficiency, productivity and employee wellness. Its lighting solutions are flicker-free, long-lived and mercury-free TLED. Energy Focus' commercial products include: direct-wire TLED replacements for linear fluorescent lamps, commercial Intellitube TLED replacements for linear fluorescent lamps, LED fixtures and panels for low- and high-bay applications, LED down-lights, LED dock lights, LED wall-packs, LED vapor tight lighting fixtures and LED retrofit kits. Military maritime LED lighting products serve the U.S. Navy and allied foreign navies, and include: Military Intellitube, military globe lights, military berth lights and military fixtures. All products are backed by a 10-year warranty, and many qualify for federal and state tax and rebate incentives for commercial consumers (only available in certain states).

FINANCIAL DATA: Note: Data for latest year may not have been available at press time.

In U.S. $	2020	2019	2018	2017	2016	2015
Revenue	16,828,000	12,705,000	18,107,000	19,846,000	30,998,000	64,403,000
R&D Expense	1,415,000	1,284,000	2,597,000	2,940,000	3,537,000	2,810,000
Operating Income	-4,130,000	-6,759,000	-8,974,000	-9,434,000	-15,973,000	9,652,000
Operating Margin %		-.53%	-.50%	-.48%	-.52%	.15%
SGA Expense	7,900,000	7,449,000	9,789,000	11,315,000	20,113,000	16,830,000
Net Income	-5,981,000	-7,373,000	-9,111,000	-11,267,000	-16,887,000	8,780,000
Operating Cash Flow	-2,451,000	-6,624,000	-6,795,000	-5,874,000	-16,553,000	4,446,000
Capital Expenditure	223,000	132,000	57,000	162,000	1,624,000	2,242,000
EBITDA	-5,321,000	-6,720,000	-8,570,000	-10,699,000	-16,043,000	9,971,000
Return on Assets %		-.49%	-.45%	-.39%	-.37%	.23%
Return on Equity %		-.98%	-.60%	-.46%	-.45%	.32%
Debt to Equity		0.297				

CONTACT INFORMATION:

Phone: 440 715-1300   Fax: 440 715-1314
Toll-Free:
Address: 32000 Aurora Rd., Ste. B, Solon, OH 44139 United States

STOCK TICKER/OTHER:

Stock Ticker: EFOI   Exchange: NAS
Employees: 57   Fiscal Year Ends: 12/31
Parent Company:

SALARIES/BONUSES:

Top Exec. Salary: $ Bonus: $
Second Exec. Salary: $ Bonus: $

OTHER THOUGHTS:

Estimated Female Officers or Directors:
Hot Spot for Advancement for Women/Minorities:

Entrust Corporation

NAIC Code: 511210E

www.entrust.com

TYPES OF BUSINESS:

Computer Software, Network Security, Managed Access, Digital ID,
Cybersecurity & Anti-Virus
Digital Identification & Certificates
Digital Security

BRANDS/DIVISIONS/AFFILIATES:

Entrust
Entrust Datacard Corporation

CONTACTS: *Note: Officers with more than one job title may be intentionally listed here more than once.*

Todd Wilkinson, CEO
Jeff Smolinksi, Sr. VP-Operations
Kurt Ishaug, CFO
Karen Kaukol, CMO
Beth Klehr, Chief Human Resources Officer
Anudeep Parhar, CIO
Robert (Bob) VanKirk, Sr. VP-American Sales
Mark Reeves, Sr. VP-Int'l Sales

GROWTH PLANS/SPECIAL FEATURES:

Entrust Corporation (formerly Entrust Datacard Corporation) is a global provider of security applications that protect and secure digital identities and information. The firm designs, produces and sells security, policy and access management software products and related services. Solutions include financial cards, passports, identification cards, authentication solutions (cloud-based, mobile, hybrid), digital certificates, border control, credential lifecycle management and transaction technologies. Entrust products consist of categories such as SSL certificates, qualified certificates, digital signing certificates, passport systems, identification card printers, financial card printers, central card issuance, software, short message service (SMS) passcode, authentication, Internet of Things (IoT) security, public key infrastructure, nCipher hardware security modules, related supplies and related accessories. Supplies include print ribbons, overlays, laminates, tactile impression solutions, cleaning supplies, topping foils, card delivery stickers/labels and more. Accessories include devices such as pin pads, magnetic strip encoders and digital signature pads. Entrust serves financial, corporate, government, education, healthcare, and retail clients located throughout the world. The company is based in Minnesota, USA, and has additional office locations in the U.S., Asia Pacific, Canada, Europe, Latin America, the Caribbean and the Middle East. During 2020, Entrust Datacard rebranded its corporate name to Entrust Corporation, and its brand to Entrust, reflecting its strategy to include digital security along with physical credential issuance.

FINANCIAL DATA: *Note: Data for latest year may not have been available at press time.*

In U.S. $	2020	2019	2018	2017	2016	2015
Revenue	840,000,000	800,000,000	700,000,000	600,000,000	570,000,000	400,000,000
R&D Expense						
Operating Income						
Operating Margin %						
SGA Expense						
Net Income						
Operating Cash Flow						
Capital Expenditure						
EBITDA						
Return on Assets %						
Return on Equity %						
Debt to Equity						

CONTACT INFORMATION:

Phone: 952-933-1223   Fax:
Toll-Free: 800-621-6972
Address: 1187 Park Place, Shakopee, MN 55379 United States

STOCK TICKER/OTHER:

Stock Ticker: Private   Exchange:
Employees: 2,500   Fiscal Year Ends: 12/31
Parent Company:

SALARIES/BONUSES:

Top Exec. Salary: $ Bonus: $
Second Exec. Salary: $ Bonus: $

OTHER THOUGHTS:

Estimated Female Officers or Directors:
Hot Spot for Advancement for Women/Minorities:

Equinix Inc

NAIC Code: 517110

www.equinix.com

TYPES OF BUSINESS:

Data Networks
Internet Exchange Services

BRANDS/DIVISIONS/AFFILIATES:

International Business Exchange (IBX)
xScale
Equinix Internet Exchange
Equinix Fabric
Equinix SmartKey
Bare Metal

CONTACTS: *Note: Officers with more than one job title may be intentionally listed here more than once.*

Charles Meyers, CEO
Keith Taylor, CFO
Peter Van Camp, Chairman of the Board
Simon Miller, Chief Accounting Officer
Brandi Morandi, Chief Legal Officer
Eric Schwartz, Chief Strategy Officer
Michael Campbell, Other Executive Officer
Karl Strohmeyer, Other Executive Officer
Samuel Lee, President, Geographical

GROWTH PLANS/SPECIAL FEATURES:

Equinix, Inc. provides network neutral co-location, interconnection and managed services to enterprises. The company operates data centers in more than 60 markets across the Americas, Europe, Middle East, Africa and Asia Pacific. The firm's proprietary Equinix platform incorporates International Business Exchange (IBX) data centers with unique ecosystems and a global footprint to offer customers accelerated business growth by safeguarding the client's infrastructure, housing their applications and assets closer to the user for improved overall performance and enabling the client to collaborate with numerous customers and partners. The xScale data centers serve the unique core workload deployment needs of a targeted group of hyperscale companies, including cloud service providers. Interconnection solutions connect businesses directly within and between Equinix's data centers across its global platform. Interconnection solutions include: cross connects, providing point-to-point cable link between two customers in the same IBX data center; fabric, offering flexible, on-demand global connection; metro connect, connecting to multiple data centers within a metropolitan area; and Equinix Internet Exchange, which enables networks, content providers and enterprises to exchange internet traffic through a global peering solution. The firm's edge services help businesses deploy-as-a-service networking, security and hardware across its global data footprint as an alternative to buying, owning and managing the physical infrastructure. Edge services include: network edge, allowing customers to modernize networks by deploying network functions virtualization (NFV) from multiple vendors across Equinix metros; Equinix SmartKey, which simplifies data protection across cloud architecture through a global Software-as-a-Service (SaaS)-based, hardware security module management and cryptography service that provides on-premises and hybrid multi-cloud cloud encryption key management; and Bare Metal, which helps enterprises more seamlessly deploy hybrid multi-cloud architectures on the Equinix platform. Equinix also offers remote support and professional services.

Equinix offers its employees health and financial benefit options, depending on location.

FINANCIAL DATA: *Note: Data for latest year may not have been available at press time.*

In U.S. $	2020	2019	2018	2017	2016	2015
Revenue	5,998,545,000	5,562,140,000	5,071,654,000	4,368,428,000	3,611,989,000	2,725,867,000
R&D Expense						
Operating Income	1,114,868,000	1,165,892,000	1,005,783,000	847,649,000	657,816,000	609,065,000
Operating Margin %		.21%	.20%	.19%	.18%	.22%
SGA Expense	1,809,337,000	1,586,064,000	1,460,396,000	1,327,630,000	1,133,303,000	825,296,000
Net Income	369,777,000	507,450,000	365,359,000	232,982,000	126,800,000	187,774,000
Operating Cash Flow	2,309,826,000	1,992,728,000	1,815,426,000	1,439,233,000	1,016,580,000	894,793,000
Capital Expenditure	2,282,504,000	2,079,521,000	2,096,174,000	1,378,725,000	1,113,365,000	868,120,000
EBITDA	2,346,060,000	2,457,118,000	2,182,021,000	1,808,010,000	1,389,222,000	1,035,633,000
Return on Assets %		.02%	.02%	.01%	.01%	.02%
Return on Equity %		.06%	.05%	.04%	.04%	.07%
Debt to Equity		1.396	1.507	1.451	1.51	2.027

CONTACT INFORMATION:

Phone: 650 598-6000   Fax: 650 513-7900
Toll-Free: 800-322-9280
Address: 1 Lagoon Dr., Redwood City, CA 94065 United States

STOCK TICKER/OTHER:

Stock Ticker: EQIX   Exchange: NAS
Employees: 8,378   Fiscal Year Ends: 12/31
Parent Company:

SALARIES/BONUSES:

Top Exec. Salary: $ Bonus: $
Second Exec. Salary: $ Bonus: $

OTHER THOUGHTS:

Estimated Female Officers or Directors: 3
Hot Spot for Advancement for Women/Minorities: Y

Sales, profits and employees may be estimates. Financial information, benefits and other data can change quickly and may vary from those stated here.

Eutelsat Communications SA

www.eutelsat-communications.com

NAIC Code: 517410

TYPES OF BUSINESS:

Satellite Telecommunications

BRANDS/DIVISIONS/AFFILIATES:

Eutelsat SA

GROWTH PLANS/SPECIAL FEATURES:

Eutelsat Communications SA designs and operates satellites. The firm is the holding company of Eutelsat SA. The company's fleet of 39 satellites serve broadcasters, video service providers, telecom operators, internet service providers (ISPs) and government agencies across Europe, Africa, Asia and the Americas. The satellites are used for video broadcasting, satellite news gathering, broadband services, data connectivity, connecting airplanes and ships, enabling mission-critical government and non-government organization (NGO) needs, and more. Eutelsat's fully-owned and partner teleport network (ground network) enables customers to have access to its satellites from almost any geographical location around the globe, from which they can connect to their own customer audiences. Eutelsat delivers TV channels to over 274 million homes, including HDTV and Ultra HD.

CONTACTS: *Note: Officers with more than one job title may be intentionally listed here more than once.*

Rodolphe Belmer, CEO
Sandrine Teran, CFO
Philippe Oliva, CCO
Marie-Sophie Rouzaud, Chief Human Resources Officer
Yohann Leroy, CTO
Dominique d-Hinnin, Chmn.

FINANCIAL DATA: *Note: Data for latest year may not have been available at press time.*

In U.S. $	2020	2019	2018	2017	2016	2015
Revenue	1,561,798,000	1,614,090,000	1,720,140,000	1,805,664,000	1,868,097,000	1,803,832,000
R&D Expense						
Operating Income	595,127,600	642,899,000	674,909,600	751,026,400	808,816,300	808,205,500
Operating Margin %		.40%	.39%	.42%	.43%	.45%
SGA Expense	252,541,300	241,911,800	285,407,100	299,824,100	315,340,600	293,226,500
Net Income	363,600,800	415,892,900	354,437,500	429,821,100	425,789,300	433,975,200
Operating Cash Flow	951,764,200	1,036,311,000	1,076,141,000	1,200,884,000	1,094,346,000	1,264,050,000
Capital Expenditure	269,157,500	257,550,600	365,066,900	480,158,300	476,737,400	557,985,500
EBITDA	1,277,368,000	1,303,636,000	1,299,849,000	1,402,356,000	1,444,629,000	1,445,118,000
Return on Assets %		.04%	.04%	.04%	.04%	.05%
Return on Equity %		.13%	.11%	.13%	.14%	.16%
Debt to Equity		1.261	0.914	1.177	1.244	1.481

CONTACT INFORMATION:

Phone: 33 153983700   Fax:
Toll-Free:
Address: 70 rue Balard, Paris, 75015 France

STOCK TICKER/OTHER:

Stock Ticker: ETLN   Exchange: MEX
Employees: 1,014   Fiscal Year Ends: 06/30
Parent Company:

SALARIES/BONUSES:

Top Exec. Salary: $ Bonus: $
Second Exec. Salary: $ Bonus: $

OTHER THOUGHTS:

Estimated Female Officers or Directors:
Hot Spot for Advancement for Women/Minorities:

Extreme Networks Inc

www.extremenetworks.com

NAIC Code: 334210A

TYPES OF BUSINESS:

Computer Networking & Related Equipment, Manufacturing
Network Management
Software
Technology
Access Controls
Switches
Wireless
Routing

BRANDS/DIVISIONS/AFFILIATES:

CONTACTS: Note: Officers with more than one job title may be intentionally listed here more than once.

Edward Meyercord, CEO
Remi Thomas, CFO
John Shoemaker, Chairman of the Board
Cheryl Burton, Other Corporate Officer
Robert Gault, Other Executive Officer
Matt Cleaver, Vice President, Divisional

GROWTH PLANS/SPECIAL FEATURES:

Extreme Networks, Inc., together with its subsidiaries, provides software-driven networking solutions for enterprise customers. The firm designs and develops wired and wireless network infrastructure equipment and develops the software for network management, policy, analytics, security and access controls. With more than 50,000 customers globally, Extreme Networks serves industries such as primary and secondary education (K-12), retail, service providers, federal government, manufacturing, higher education, healthcare, hospitality, state and local government, sports and public venues. Infrastructure products offered by Extreme Networks include: switching, offering end-to-end fabric networking; routing, offering adaptive connectivity from the data center to the branch; and wireless, offering Wi-Fi 6th Generation (IoT optimized). Applications products include: management and automation, for streamlining network operations from the edge to the data center; analytics and visibility, enable the unlocking of new information technology (IT), business insights and intelligence; and security and access control, enabling the control of corporate, guest, bring your own device (BYOD) and Internet of Things (IoT) access. Extreme Networks' technologies span remote, cloud, security, machine learning, network fabrics, IoT and Wi-Fi 6. Based in California, USA, the firm has domestic corporate offices throughout the country as well as in Canada, India, Ireland, Taiwan, Brazil, Mexico, Italy, France, Germany, Netherlands, Russia, Spain, the U.K., the UAE, Australia, China, Hong Kong, South Korea, Singapore and Malaysia.

FINANCIAL DATA: Note: Data for latest year may not have been available at press time.

In U.S. $	2020	2019	2018	2017	2016	2015
Revenue	948,019,000	995,789,000	983,142,000	598,118,000	528,389,000	552,940,000
R&D Expense	209,606,000	210,132,000	183,877,000	93,724,000	78,721,000	93,447,000
Operating Income	-44,815,000	-6,192,000	23,830,000	21,268,000	-13,415,000	-42,970,000
Operating Margin %		-.01%	.02%	.04%	-.03%	-.08%
SGA Expense	344,623,000	340,949,000	318,095,000	200,791,000	188,481,000	211,391,000
Net Income	-126,845,000	-25,853,000	-46,792,000	-8,517,000	-31,884,000	-71,643,000
Operating Cash Flow	35,884,000	104,945,000	19,043,000	59,283,000	30,366,000	37,423,000
Capital Expenditure	15,268,000	22,730,000	40,411,000	10,425,000	5,327,000	7,774,000
EBITDA	-32,921,000	39,596,000	16,332,000	26,249,000	18,722,000	-14,876,000
Return on Assets %		-.03%	-.07%	-.02%	-.08%	-.15%
Return on Equity %		-.23%	-.43%	-.09%	-.33%	-.55%
Debt to Equity		1.463	1.674	0.754	0.417	0.532

CONTACT INFORMATION:

Phone: 408 579-2800   Fax: 408 579-3000
Toll-Free: 888-257-3000
Address: 6480 Via Del Oro, San Jose, CA 95119 United States

SALARIES/BONUSES:

Top Exec. Salary: $ Bonus: $
Second Exec. Salary: $ Bonus: $

STOCK TICKER/OTHER:

Stock Ticker: EXTR   Exchange: NAS
Employees: 2,584   Fiscal Year Ends: 06/30
Parent Company:

OTHER THOUGHTS:

Estimated Female Officers or Directors: 1
Hot Spot for Advancement for Women/Minorities: Y

F5 Networks Inc

NAIC Code: 511210B

www.f5.com

TYPES OF BUSINESS:

Computer Software: Network Management (IT), System Testing & Storage
Multi-Cloud
Security
Managed Services
Software
Hardware

BRANDS/DIVISIONS/AFFILIATES:

Shape Security Inc

CONTACTS: *Note: Officers with more than one job title may be intentionally listed here more than once.*

Francis Pelzer, CFO
Ryan Kearny, CTO
Alan Higginson, Director
Francois Locoh-Donou, Director
Steve McMillan, Executive VP, Divisional
Chad Whalen, Executive VP, Divisional
Scot Rogers, Executive VP
Ana White, Executive VP
Tom Fountain, Executive VP
Kara Sprague, General Manager, Divisional

GROWTH PLANS/SPECIAL FEATURES:

F5 Networks, Inc. is a multi-cloud application security and delivery company. The firm's enterprise-grade solutions are available in a range of consumption models, from on-premises to managed services, optimized for multi-cloud environments. In connection with its solutions, F5 Networks offers a broad range of professional services, including consulting, training, installation, maintenance and other technical support services. Products by F5 Networks span traffic management, application security, infrastructure security, automation, visibility, centralized management, cloud services, cloud software, hardware, application firewall and more. Based in the U.S. F5 Networks has office located in more than 40 countries worldwide. Over 45 of the Fortune 50 rely on F5's products, solutions and services. In early-2020, F5 Networks acquired Shape Security, Inc., a provider of application security against fraud and abuse. In January 2021, F5 Networks agreed to acquire Volterra, a provider of distributed cloud services for deploying, networking and securing applications across multi-cloud and the edge.

F5 Networks offers its employees comprehensive health benefits and a variety of assistance programs.

FINANCIAL DATA: *Note: Data for latest year may not have been available at press time.*

In U.S. $	2020	2019	2018	2017	2016	2015
Revenue	2,350,822,000	2,242,447,000	2,161,407,000	2,090,041,000	1,995,034,000	1,919,823,000
R&D Expense	441,324,000	408,058,000	366,084,000	350,365,000	334,227,000	296,583,000
Operating Income	400,067,000	518,463,000	609,325,000	577,065,000	556,428,000	552,899,000
Operating Margin %		.23%	.28%	.28%	.28%	.29%
SGA Expense	1,101,544,000	959,349,000	824,517,000	809,126,000	767,174,000	738,080,000
Net Income	307,441,000	427,734,000	453,689,000	420,761,000	365,855,000	365,014,000
Operating Cash Flow	660,898,000	747,841,000	761,068,000	740,281,000	711,535,000	684,541,000
Capital Expenditure	59,940,000	103,542,000	53,465,000	42,681,000	68,238,000	67,086,000
EBITDA	495,924,000	586,970,000	668,816,000	638,213,000	613,204,000	605,482,000
Return on Assets %		.14%	.18%	.18%	.16%	.16%
Return on Equity %		.28%	.36%	.35%	.29%	.27%
Debt to Equity						

CONTACT INFORMATION:

Phone: 206 272-5555 Fax: 206 272-5556
Toll-Free: 888-882-4447
Address: 801 5th Ave., Seattle, WA 98104 United States

SALARIES/BONUSES:

Top Exec. Salary: $ Bonus: $
Second Exec. Salary: $ Bonus: $

STOCK TICKER/OTHER:

Stock Ticker: FFIV Exchange: NAS
Employees: 6,109 Fiscal Year Ends: 09/30
Parent Company:

OTHER THOUGHTS:

Estimated Female Officers or Directors: 3
Hot Spot for Advancement for Women/Minorities: Y

Far EasTone Telecommunications Co Ltd   www.fareastone.com.tw

NAIC Code: 517210

TYPES OF BUSINESS:

Wireless Telecommunications Carriers (except Satellite)
Telecommunications
Digital Applications
Internet
5G

BRANDS/DIVISIONS/AFFILIATES:

New Century InfoComm Tech
Arcoa
Data Express
Qware Systems

CONTACTS: Note: Officers with more than one job title may be intentionally listed here more than once.

Chee Ching, Pres.
Douglas Hsu, Chmn.

GROWTH PLANS/SPECIAL FEATURES:

Far EasTone Telecommunications Co., Ltd. provides telecommunications and digital application services in Taiwan. The company offers triple bandwidths of 700/1800/2600 MHz through its 4.5G mobile internet service, the first to do so in the Asian market. Far EasTone's dual-band system (GSM900 and GSM1800) automatically switches frequency to track the strongest signal for connected devices. Its design of highly-sensitive base stations with hexagonal cells reduces the dead space of reception, making signal delivery more flexible and less susceptible to interference. And as an all-region service, the firm is a provider of enhanced full-rate communication, in which the processing of digital sound delivers voice and speech clarity. Far EasTone is engaged in the development of Internet of Things applications, as well as in 5G roll-out. During 2021, Far EasTone announced that it applied the core technology of 5G in providing a multi-angle viewing through a video app, utilized 5G speed to user experience surveys, introduced 5G telemedicine, built a 5G smart factory in Taiwan (with Data Electronics and Microsoft), and signed a memorandum of understanding with Ericsson to foster cooperation on the development of a 5G communication network. Companies such as New Century InfoComm Tech, Arcoa, Data Express and Qware Systems were established by the firm to further connect the upper and lower streams of the ICT (information and communications technology) industry. Far EasTone offers its services to enterprises, businesses and consumers, providing integrated mobile telecommunications, fixed network and IT services and solutions. The company has successfully established the infrastructure of telecommunications and related applications for more than 100 enterprises, including computer, law, accounting, consulting, news/public relations, finance, manufacturing, transportation, warehousing, security, public, private, retail, wholesale and IT sectors.

FINANCIAL DATA: Note: Data for latest year may not have been available at press time.

In U.S. $	2020	2019	2018	2017	2016	2015
Revenue	2,184,530,000	2,934,117,120	3,030,996,224	3,080,077,568	3,233,182,464	3,123,678,976
R&D Expense						
Operating Income						
Operating Margin %						
SGA Expense						
Net Income	297,115,000	305,600,672	328,214,368	363,196,928	390,380,480	368,757,664
Operating Cash Flow						
Capital Expenditure						
EBITDA						
Return on Assets %						
Return on Equity %						
Debt to Equity						

CONTACT INFORMATION:

Phone: 886 277235000   Fax:
Toll-Free:
Address: 468 Ruei Guang Rd., Nei Hu Dist., Taipei, 11492 Taiwan

STOCK TICKER/OTHER:

Stock Ticker: 4904   Exchange: TWSE
Employees: 5,841   Fiscal Year Ends: 12/31
Parent Company:

SALARIES/BONUSES:

Top Exec. Salary: $ Bonus: $
Second Exec. Salary: $ Bonus: $

OTHER THOUGHTS:

Estimated Female Officers or Directors:
Hot Spot for Advancement for Women/Minorities:

FASTWEB SpA
NAIC Code: 517110

www.fastweb.it

TYPES OF BUSINESS:
Internet Telecommunications Services
Telephony Services
Broadband Internet Access
Video Communications Services
Virtual Private Networks
Digital & Interactive TV
Video-on-Demand Services

BRANDS/DIVISIONS/AFFILIATES:
Swisscom AG
Swisscom Italia Srl

CONTACTS: *Note: Officers with more than one job title may be intentionally listed here more than once.*
Alberto Calcagno, CEO
Walter Renna, COO
Peter Gruter, CFO
Roberto Chieppa, CMO
Matteo Melchiorri Roberto Biazzi, Chief Human Resources Officer
Andrea Lasagna, CTO
Giovanni Moglia, Dir.-Legal & Regulatory Affairs
Federico Ciccone, Chief Strategy Officer
Roberto Biazzi, Dir.-Human Capital
Massimo Mancini, Dir.-Enterprise
Sergio Scalpelli, Dir.-Institutional & External Relations
Danilo Vivarelli, Dir.-Consumer & Micro Bus.
Urs Schaeppi, Chmn.

GROWTH PLANS/SPECIAL FEATURES:
FASTWEB SpA is a leading telecommunications operator based in Italy. The firm has 2.7 million wireline customers and 2 million mobile customers. FASTWEB offers a wide range of voice and data services, fixed communication and mobile, to households and businesses. The company has always focused on innovation and network infrastructure to provide quality ultra-broadband services. Ultra broadband connections can be obtained via personal computers, smartphones and tablets. FASTWEB has developed a national fiber optic network infrastructure of approximately 34,800 miles (56,000 kilometers) with over 2.48 million miles (4 million kilometers) of fiber. Connection speeds range up to 1 Gigabit (Gb). The firm offers customers new generation mobile services based on 4G technology and 4G Plus, and 5G in 2020, with plans to reach 20 million families and businesses by 2024. FASTWEB has 20 retail stores nationwide, enabling consumers to purchase products and services and receive commercial, administrative and technical information. The company has 17 offices, 16 throughout Italy and one in Bruxelles. Swisscom AG owns 100% of FASTWEB through its indirect subsidiary, Swisscom Italia Srl.

FINANCIAL DATA: *Note: Data for latest year may not have been available at press time.*

In U.S. $	2020	2019	2018	2017	2016	2015
Revenue	2,829,870,000	2,483,850,000	2,406,540,000	2,328,650,000	2,061,820,000	2,039,770,000
R&D Expense						
Operating Income						
Operating Margin %						
SGA Expense						
Net Income	190,378,000	156,781,000				
Operating Cash Flow						
Capital Expenditure						
EBITDA						
Return on Assets %						
Return on Equity %						
Debt to Equity						

CONTACT INFORMATION:
Phone: 39-02-4545-1   Fax: 39-02-4545-4811
Toll-Free:
Address: Piazza Adriano Olivetti, 1, Milan, 20139 Italy

STOCK TICKER/OTHER:
Stock Ticker: Subsidiary   Exchange:
Employees: 2,703   Fiscal Year Ends: 12/31
Parent Company: Swisscom AG

SALARIES/BONUSES:
Top Exec. Salary: $ Bonus: $
Second Exec. Salary: $ Bonus: $

OTHER THOUGHTS:
Estimated Female Officers or Directors:
Hot Spot for Advancement for Women/Minorities:

Filtronic plc

NAIC Code: 334220

filtronic.com

TYPES OF BUSINESS:
Telecommunications Equipment-Cellular & Broadband Components
Wireless Infrastructure Products
Microwave Components
Radio Frequency

BRANDS/DIVISIONS/AFFILIATES:

CONTACTS: Note: Officers with more than one job title may be intentionally listed here more than once.
Richard Gibbs, CEO
Michael Tyerman, CFO
Maura Moynihan, General Counsel
Reg Gott, Chmn.

GROWTH PLANS/SPECIAL FEATURES:
Filtronic plc, based in the U.K., designs and manufactures a broad range of customized radio frequency (RF), microwave and millimeter-wave (mmWave) cellular and broadband components and subsystems. Its products, which can be found in over 60 countries worldwide, are used primarily in wireless and point-to-point communication systems. Filtronic operates in two segments: wireless and broadband. With a focus on original equipment manufacturers (OEMs) and network operators, the wireless segment designs and manufactures RF filters, microwave subsystems and combiners for the mobile telecommunications industry. Products in this segment include interference mitigation filters, small cell filters and base station antennas and line equipment such as in-band and cross-band combiners, tower mounted amplifiers, blocking protection filters and interference suppression filters. Products are made and sold to operators with 3G, 4G and 5G networks. The broadband segment designs and manufactures 60-110GHz millimeter-wave products for mobile broadband backhaul and defense applications. Its broadband products have the capacity to cover the frequency range from 4GHz to 110GHz in the V-, E- and W-bands. Filtronic serves the aerospace, defense, critical communications, telecommunications infrastructure, space, test and measurement, and train trackside markets. During 2021, Filtronic announced that it signed an agreement with WTG Marketing, a wireless telecom equipment specialist in Texas, USA, to expand Filtronic's sales channel in North America, covering the states of Texas, Oklahoma, Louisiana and Arkansas.

FINANCIAL DATA: Note: Data for latest year may not have been available at press time.

In U.S. $	2020	2019	2018	2017	2016	2015
Revenue	24,323,290	22,555,070	33,969,930	50,077,870	19,225,330	24,808,880
R&D Expense						
Operating Income	665,383	331,276	2,510,052	2,409,536	-9,574,438	-15,112,690
Operating Margin %		.01%	.07%	.05%	-.50%	-.61%
SGA Expense						
Net Income	-2,767,711	-1,858,826	1,742,738	4,412,765	-7,244,182	-14,876,270
Operating Cash Flow	-3,734,640	-28,314	2,478,906	5,473,130	-7,149,330	-5,209,809
Capital Expenditure	1,759,726	1,496,404	1,499,236	1,148,140	648,395	511,071
EBITDA	746,079	1,272,722	2,788,946	4,467,977	-8,933,122	-10,184,610
Return on Assets %		-.07%	.06%	.17%	-.31%	-.51%
Return on Equity %		-.11%	.11%	.33%	-.61%	-.82%
Debt to Equity		0.011	0.026			

CONTACT INFORMATION:
Phone: 44 174 0625163   Fax:
Toll-Free:
Address: 3 Airport W., Lancaster Way, Leeds, West Yorkshire, LS19 7ZA United Kingdom

STOCK TICKER/OTHER:
Stock Ticker: FLTCF
Employees: 167
Parent Company:

Exchange: PINX
Fiscal Year Ends: 05/31

SALARIES/BONUSES:
Top Exec. Salary: $ Bonus: $
Second Exec. Salary: $ Bonus: $

OTHER THOUGHTS:
Estimated Female Officers or Directors: 1
Hot Spot for Advancement for Women/Minorities:

First Pacific Company Limited

www.firstpacco.com

NAIC Code: 517210

TYPES OF BUSINESS:

Wireless Telecommunications Carriers
Infrastructure
Consumer Food Products
Exploration, Development and Management of Mineral and Energy
Resources
Telecommunications

BRANDS/DIVISIONS/AFFILIATES:

PT Indofood Sukses Makmur Tbk
Indofood CBP
Metro Pacific Investments Corporation
Global Business Power Corporation
Philex Mining Corporation
PXP Energy
PLDT Inc
Smart Communications Inc

CONTACTS: *Note: Officers with more than one job title may be intentionally listed here more than once.*

Manuel V. Pangilinan, Managing Dir.
Christopher H. Young, CFO
Anthoni Salim, Chmn.

GROWTH PLANS/SPECIAL FEATURES:

First Pacific Company Limited is a Hong Kong-based investment management and holding company, with operations in the Asia-Pacific. The firm's primary business segments include consumer food products, infrastructure, natural resources and telecommunications. The consumer food products segment is comprised of two joint ventures: 50.1%-owned PT Indofood Sukses Makmur Tbk and 40.3%-owned Indofood CBP, which produce instant noodles, sauces, seasonings, snacks, biscuits, baby food, dairy products, cereals, flour, pasta, oil, margarine and beverage products. The infrastructure segment is comprised of: 43.1%-owned Metro Pacific Investments Corporation, which provides water, sanitation and sewage services, operates in real estate and infrastructure projects, and invests in some hospitals; 19.6%-owned Global Business Power Corporation, a leading energy company that produces power through subsidiaries which operate power generation facilities; 19.6%-owned Meralco, an electric distribution company in the Philippines; 47.5%-owned PacificLight, a Singapore-based power generator and electricity retailer; 22.8%-owned Maynilad Water Services, a water and wastewater services provider in the Philippines; and 43.1%-owned Metro Pacific Tollways Corporation, which engages in the tollways business in the Philippines. The natural resources segment is comprised of: 31.2%-owned Philex Mining Corporation, a producer of copper and concentrates that contain copper, gold and silver; 42.4%-owned PXP Energy, an upstream oil and gas company in the Philippines; 35.9%-owned Indofood Agri Resources, which is engaged in oil palm seed breeding, cultivation and milling; and 50.8%-owned Roxas Holdings, Inc., an integrated sugar business and ethanol producer in the Philippines. Last, the telecommunications segment is comprised of: 25.6%-owned PLDT, Inc., a provider of long-distance telephone, telecommunications and digital services; and PLDT's wholly-owned Smart Communications, Inc., a wireless communications and digital services firm based in the Philippines.

FINANCIAL DATA: *Note: Data for latest year may not have been available at press time.*

In U.S. $	2020	2019	2018	2017	2016	2015
Revenue	7,130,500,000	8,054,700,000	7,742,400,000	7,296,800,000	6,779,000,000	6,437,000,000
R&D Expense						
Operating Income	1,065,000,000	1,168,900,000	1,003,400,000	1,000,100,000	909,600,000	815,100,000
Operating Margin %		.08%	.12%	.14%	.13%	.10%
SGA Expense	1,223,900,000	1,279,400,000	1,174,400,000	1,152,400,000	1,095,100,000	1,006,600,000
Net Income	201,600,000	-253,900,000	131,800,000	120,900,000	103,200,000	85,100,000
Operating Cash Flow	1,036,600,000	1,455,500,000	734,100,000	776,100,000	731,400,000	650,000,000
Capital Expenditure	1,065,600,000	1,376,500,000	1,236,000,000	1,063,000,000	696,700,000	753,600,000
EBITDA	1,935,600,000	1,598,600,000	1,784,700,000	1,691,900,000	1,516,100,000	1,316,700,000
Return on Assets %		-.01%	.01%	.01%	.01%	.00%
Return on Equity %		-.08%	.04%	.04%	.03%	.03%
Debt to Equity		2.277	2.023	2.017	1.551	1.703

CONTACT INFORMATION:

Phone: 852 28424388   Fax: 852 28459243
Toll-Free:
Address: Fl. 24, Two Exchange Square, 8 Connaught Pl., Hong Kong, Hong Kong Hong Kong

STOCK TICKER/OTHER:

Stock Ticker: FPAFF   Exchange: PINX
Employees: 103,127   Fiscal Year Ends: 12/31
Parent Company:

SALARIES/BONUSES:

Top Exec. Salary: $ Bonus: $
Second Exec. Salary: $ Bonus: $

OTHER THOUGHTS:

Estimated Female Officers or Directors:
Hot Spot for Advancement for Women/Minorities:

Sales, profits and employees may be estimates. Financial information, benefits and other data can change quickly and may vary from those stated here.

Flex Ltd

www.flextronics.com

NAIC Code: 334418

TYPES OF BUSINESS:

Printed Circuit Assembly (Electronic Assembly) Manufacturing
Telecommunications Equipment Manufacturing
Engineering, Design & Testing Services
Logistics Services
Camera Modules
Medical Devices
LCD Displays
Original Design Manufacturing (ODM)

BRANDS/DIVISIONS/AFFILIATES:

CONTACTS: Note: Officers with more than one job title may be intentionally listed here more than once.

Revathi Advaithi, CEO
Francois Barbier, Pres.
Christopher Collier, CFO
Phil Ulrich, Chief Human Resources Officer
Mark Kemp, Pres., Medical
Gus Shahin, CIO
Erik Volkerink, CTO
Christopher Obey, Pres., Automotive
Christopher Cook, Pres., Power Solutions
Jeannine Sargent, Pres., Energy
Jonathan Hoak, General Counsel
Francois Barbier, Pres., Global Oper. & Components
David Mark, Chief Strategy Officer
Renee Brotherton, VP-Corp. Comm.
Christopher Collier, Chief Accounting Officer
Paul Humphries, Pres., High Reliability Solutions
Caroline Dowling, Pres., Integrated Network Solutions
Doug Britt, Pres., Industrial & Emerging Solutions
Mike Dennison, Pres., High Velocity Solutions
Tom Linton, Chief Procurement & Supply Chain Officer

GROWTH PLANS/SPECIAL FEATURES:

Flex Ltd. is a provider of innovative design, engineering, manufacturing and supply chain services and solutions that span from conceptual sketch to full-scale production. The company offers packaged consumer electronics and industrial products for original equipment manufacturers (OEMs) through its four business segments: high reliability solutions (HRS), consumer technologies group (CTG), industrial and emerging industries (IEI) and communications and enterprise compute (CEC). HRS is comprised of Flex's medical business, including consumer health, digital health, disposables, drug delivery, diagnostics, life sciences and imaging equipment; automotive business, including vehicle electronics, connectivity and clean technologies; and defense and aerospace businesses, which focus on commercial aviation, defense and military. CTG includes Flex's mobile devices, consumer electronics and connectivity devices. IEI is comprised of semiconductor and capital equipment, office solutions, household industrial and lifestyle, industrial automation and kiosks, energy and metering and lighting. Last, CEC includes radio access base stations, remote radio heads and small cells for wireless infrastructure; optical, routing, broadcasting and switching products for the data and video networks; server and storage platforms for both enterprise and cloud-based deployments; next generation storage and security appliance products; and rack level solutions, converged infrastructure and software-defined product solutions. Flex is headquartered in Singapore, with locations established throughout the U.S., South America, Europe, the U.K., India, Australia, Japan, Indonesia, Philippines, South Korea, Israel, China and more.

FINANCIAL DATA: Note: Data for latest year may not have been available at press time.

In U.S. $	2020	2019	2018	2017	2016	2015
Revenue	24,209,870,000	26,210,510,000	25,441,130,000	23,862,930,000	24,418,890,000	
R&D Expense						
Operating Income	439,745,000	490,302,000	497,843,000	502,210,000	587,206,000	
Operating Margin %	.02%	.02%	.02%	.02%	.02%	
SGA Expense	834,105,000	953,077,000	1,019,399,000	937,339,000	954,890,000	
Net Income	87,579,000	93,399,000	428,534,000	319,564,000	444,081,000	
Operating Cash Flow	-1,533,276,000	-2,971,024,000	753,598,000	1,149,909,000	1,136,445,000	
Capital Expenditure	461,745,000	725,606,000	561,997,000	525,111,000	510,634,000	
EBITDA	1,052,513,000	1,092,736,000	1,199,080,000	1,080,040,000	1,054,835,000	
Return on Assets %	.01%	.01%	.03%	.03%	.04%	
Return on Equity %	.03%	.03%	.15%	.12%	.18%	
Debt to Equity	1.137	0.815	0.96	1.093	1.054	

CONTACT INFORMATION:

Phone: 65 6890-7188   Fax: 65 6543-1888
Toll-Free:
Address: 2 Changi South Ln., Singapore, 486123 Singapore

SALARIES/BONUSES:

Top Exec. Salary: $ Bonus: $
Second Exec. Salary: $ Bonus: $

STOCK TICKER/OTHER:

Stock Ticker: FLEX   Exchange: NAS
Employees: 167,201   Fiscal Year Ends: 03/31
Parent Company:

OTHER THOUGHTS:

Estimated Female Officers or Directors: 4
Hot Spot for Advancement for Women/Minorities: Y

Foxconn Technology Co Ltd

www.foxconntech.com.tw

NAIC Code: 334418

TYPES OF BUSINESS:

Contract Electronics Manufacturing
Original Design Manufacturer (ODM)
Electronics Manufacturing & Design
Research and Engineering Services
Outsourcing

BRANDS/DIVISIONS/AFFILIATES:

Future Mobility Corporation
Belkin International Inc

CONTACTS: Note: Officers with more than one job title may be intentionally listed here more than once.

Han-Ming Li, Pres.
Tzu-Hung Li, Dir.-Finance
Guangyao Li, Chmn.

GROWTH PLANS/SPECIAL FEATURES:

Foxconn Technology Co., Ltd., a worldwide leader in computer components manufacturing, is an original design manufacturer (ODM) and a provider of computer, communication and consumer electronic products. Foxconn is one of the world's leading exporters of electronics, with major clients including Apple, Cisco, Hewlett-Packard, Microsoft, Dell, Nintendo and Sony. The company's services include research and development, product design, assembly, processing and after-sales services. The firm develops strategic alliances with leading brands in the industries it serves, addressing the current needs of its customers while also conducting new product research to anticipate industry trends. Foxconn groups its products and services under three broad categories: magnesium alloys, thermal modules and consumer electronics products. The magnesium alloy category includes the design and production of products made from magnesium alloys; the surface application of magnesium alloy to products such as portable computer enclosures; and magnesium alloy recycling. The thermal modules category includes heat insulating products as well as cooling systems for various product applications. The consumer electronic products category includes mobile phones, computers, projectors, eBook readers, digital cameras, servers and video game controllers. Additionally, the company produces a wide array of PC components and peripherals, including motherboards, graphic cards, chassis, card readers and power supplies. Foxconn, together with Tencent and luxury car dealer Harmony New Energy Auto Limited, founded Future Mobility Corporation, an automobile startup that plans to sell all-electric, fully-autonomous premium cars beginning in 2020. Foxconn also owns Belkin International, Inc., a manufacturer of consumer electronics, specializing in connectivity devices.

FINANCIAL DATA: Note: Data for latest year may not have been available at press time.

In U.S. $	2020	2019	2018	2017	2016	2015
Revenue	3,726,840,000	3,491,660,288	4,969,997,312	4,944,989,184	2,745,389,312	3,192,141,056
R&D Expense						
Operating Income						
Operating Margin %						
SGA Expense						
Net Income	166,662,000	249,442,000	320,003,456	333,379,680	367,412,896	391,634,656
Operating Cash Flow						
Capital Expenditure						
EBITDA						
Return on Assets %						
Return on Equity %						
Debt to Equity						

CONTACT INFORMATION:

Phone: 886 222680970   Fax: 886 222687176
Toll-Free:
Address: No. 3-2 Chung-Shan Rd., Tu-Cheng Dist., 236 Taiwan

STOCK TICKER/OTHER:

Stock Ticker: 2354
Employees: 700,000
Parent Company:

Exchange: TWSE
Fiscal Year Ends: 12/31

SALARIES/BONUSES:

Top Exec. Salary: $ Bonus: $
Second Exec. Salary: $ Bonus: $

OTHER THOUGHTS:

Estimated Female Officers or Directors:
Hot Spot for Advancement for Women/Minorities:

Sales, profits and employees may be estimates. Financial information, benefits and other data can change quickly and may vary from those stated here.

Freenet AG

NAIC Code: 517210

www.freenet-group.de

TYPES OF BUSINESS:

Mobile Phone Service
Digital Services
Telecommunications
Internet
Mobile Telephone
IPTV
Business Communications

BRANDS/DIVISIONS/AFFILIATES:

Freenet TV
Mobilcom Debitel GmbH
Klarmobil GmbH
Freenet Digital GmbH
GRAVIS-Computervertriebsgesellschaft mbH
Freenet Energy GmbH
waipu.tv

CONTACTS: Note: Officers with more than one job title may be intentionally listed here more than once.

Ingo Arnold, CFO
Rickmann Platen, CCO
Stephan Esch, CTO
Christoph Vilanek, Chmn.

GROWTH PLANS/SPECIAL FEATURES:

Freenet AG is a digital services provider in Germany. The firm offers telecommunications, internet access, landline, mobile telephone and internet protocol television (IPTV) services, applications and devices to approximately 8.6 million subscribers. In addition, Freenet provides web portals and business-to-business (B2B) communications services. As a mobile service provider, the company does not maintain any network infrastructure; instead, Freenet markets wireless services under its own brands for the various network operators in Germany. Freenet provides its services through 520 directly-controlled Mobil-Debitel branded shops, approximately 40 stores operated under the GRAVIS brand via stationary retail points in stores, and through 400 consumer electronics stores via exclusive distribution rights. The firm's portal services consist of ecommerce and advertising services such as online shopping and marketing banners on websites, while its B2B services include value-added services, IT and communication services for corporate clients. Services related to IPTV include planning, project management, installation, operation, services and marketing of broadcast-related solutions for business clients in the radio and media sectors, as well as for end users. Freenet TV and waipu.tv services offer digital motion picture entertainment, payment services and various entertainment formats for downloading, displaying and use on mobile devices. Additional subsidiaries include Mobilcom Debitel GmbH, Klarmobil GmbH, Freenet Digital GmbH, GRAVIS-Computervertriebsgesellschaft mbH, Freenet Energy GmbH, among many others.

FINANCIAL DATA: Note: Data for latest year may not have been available at press time.

In U.S. $	2020	2019	2018	2017	2016	2015
Revenue	3,147,578,000	3,582,915,000	3,540,057,000	4,285,093,000	4,108,111,000	3,809,369,000
R&D Expense						
Operating Income	363,439,600	378,083,800	381,179,700	318,935,100	339,430,400	365,047,400
Operating Margin %		.11%	.11%	.07%	.08%	.10%
SGA Expense	111,738,800	132,253,700	143,413,400	165,222,100		
Net Income	691,324,200	233,236,000	272,624,900	350,245,600	279,080,700	269,974,800
Operating Cash Flow	436,244,000	445,010,300	451,418,500	470,819,100	476,064,200	384,784,000
Capital Expenditure	60,943,460	55,169,340	69,877,090	74,672,570	76,717,820	38,344,250
EBITDA	520,497,800	550,152,700	509,709,500	635,039,400	515,673,000	451,778,900
Return on Assets %		.04%	.05%	.07%	.07%	.08%
Return on Equity %		.15%	.17%	.21%	.17%	.17%
Debt to Equity		1.449	1.536	1.164	1.231	0.165

CONTACT INFORMATION:

Phone: 49-43-31-69-1000   Fax:
Toll-Free:
Address: Hollerstrasse 126, Büdelsdorf, 24782 Germany

STOCK TICKER/OTHER:

Stock Ticker: FRTAF   Exchange: GREY
Employees: 4,004   Fiscal Year Ends: 12/31
Parent Company:

SALARIES/BONUSES:

Top Exec. Salary: $ Bonus: $
Second Exec. Salary: $ Bonus: $

OTHER THOUGHTS:

Estimated Female Officers or Directors:
Hot Spot for Advancement for Women/Minorities:

Frontier Communications Corporation

www.frontier.com

NAIC Code: 517110

TYPES OF BUSINESS:

Telecommunications
Internet Services
Long-Distance Phone Services
Directory Service
Access Services
Wireless Internet Services

BRANDS/DIVISIONS/AFFILIATES:

FiOS
Vantage

GROWTH PLANS/SPECIAL FEATURES:

Frontier Communications Corporation provides communication services to rural, small- and medium-sized towns in 25 U.S. states. The firm's FiOS and Vantage fiber plans use a 100% fiber-optic network to provide fiber-to-the-home (FTTH) service. Frontier's broadband connection offers a range of internet speeds, along with related 24/7 technical support. Besides high-speed internet, Frontier offers video, TV and phone services as well as a broad range of complex communication services to residential and business customers.

CONTACTS: *Note: Officers with more than one job title may be intentionally listed here more than once.*

Bernard L. Han, CEO
Kenneth W. Arndt, COO
Sheldon Bruha, CFO
Elisa Bannon-Jones, Chief Human Resources Officer
Steve Gable, CTO
John Maduri, Executive VP, Divisional
John Lass, Executive VP
Elisa Bannon-Jones, Executive VP

FINANCIAL DATA: *Note: Data for latest year may not have been available at press time.*

In U.S. $	2020	2019	2018	2017	2016	2015
Revenue		8,100,000,000	8,611,000,320	9,127,999,488	8,896,000,000	5,576,000,000
R&D Expense						
Operating Income						
Operating Margin %						
SGA Expense						
Net Income		-6,000,000,000	-643,000,000	-1,804,000,000	-373,000,000	-196,000,000
Operating Cash Flow						
Capital Expenditure						
EBITDA						
Return on Assets %						
Return on Equity %						
Debt to Equity						

CONTACT INFORMATION:

Phone: 203 614-5600   Fax: 203 614-4602
Toll-Free:
Address: 401 Merritt 7, Norwalk, CT 06851 United States

SALARIES/BONUSES:

Top Exec. Salary: $ Bonus: $
Second Exec. Salary: $ Bonus: $

STOCK TICKER/OTHER:

Stock Ticker: FTRCQ   Exchange: NAS
Employees: 28,300   Fiscal Year Ends: 12/31
Parent Company:

OTHER THOUGHTS:

Estimated Female Officers or Directors: 7
Hot Spot for Advancement for Women/Minorities: Y

Fujitsu Limited

NAIC Code: 334111

www.fujitsu.com

TYPES OF BUSINESS:

Computer Manufacturing
Information Technology
Internet of Things
Artificial Intelligence
Cyber Security
Digital Workplace
Hybrid IT
Digital Transformation

BRANDS/DIVISIONS/AFFILIATES:

CONTACTS: Note: Officers with more than one job title may be intentionally listed here more than once.

Takahito Tokita, Pres.
Masami Fujita, Sr. Exec. VP
Hideyuki Saso, Sr. Exec. VP
Masahiro Koezuka, Vice Chmn.
Kazuhiko Kato, Exec. VP

GROWTH PLANS/SPECIAL FEATURES:

Fujitsu Limited is a leading provider of IT products and services globally, with solutions focused on infrastructure, business and technology for both private and public sector customers. The company operates through eight divisions. The Internet of Things (IoT) division offers related software products and solutions so that businesses can become more agile, adaptable and efficient with IoT. The artificial intelligence (AI) division enables the creation of real-time dialogue between people, things and information within hyper-connected environments. The cyber security division offers intelligent security solutions for protecting business information. The digital workplace division offers tools and solutions that empower people to work productively anywhere, anytime on any device. The multi-cloud division offers products and solutions in which clients can personalize their multi-cloud ecosystem, seamlessly connecting its people, data, business operations and more. The hybrid IT infrastructure division offers solutions that enable businesses to run workloads across a variety of infrastructure and still be seamlessly integrated, giving control of on-premises deployment for some workloads and cloud for others, for example. The co-creation division offers solutions to help solve business challenges via business collaboration, digital transformation for the co-creation of experience design, working with customers, exchanging perspectives and ideas within industries, etc. Last, the data-driven transformation division applies digital transformation solutions so that enterprises can assess hidden opportunities via data, technology innovation, artificial intelligence and data science across many locations, from edge to multiple clouds.

FINANCIAL DATA: Note: Data for latest year may not have been available at press time.

In U.S. $	2020	2019	2018	2017	2016	2015
Revenue	35,233,280,000	36,097,630,000	37,430,510,000	41,187,060,000	43,283,990,000	43,411,090,000
R&D Expense						
Operating Income	1,931,475,000	1,189,364,000	1,666,673,000	1,176,888,000	1,101,550,000	1,631,410,000
Operating Margin %	.05%	.03%	.04%	.03%	.03%	.04%
SGA Expense	7,897,172,000	8,524,436,000	9,220,571,000	9,603,555,000	9,928,690,000	10,059,980,000
Net Income	1,461,664,000	954,965,200	1,546,583,000	808,170,400	792,406,900	1,278,840,000
Operating Cash Flow	3,171,555,000	907,966,800	1,830,391,000	2,286,274,000	2,311,490,000	2,558,602,000
Capital Expenditure	1,214,416,000	1,101,778,000	1,233,001,000	1,812,874,000	1,733,170,000	1,818,463,000
EBITDA	4,088,801,000	2,969,295,000	3,851,954,000	3,020,020,000	3,195,364,000	3,631,748,000
Return on Assets %	.05%	.03%	.05%	.03%	.03%	.04%
Return on Equity %	.13%	.09%	.17%	.11%	.11%	.21%
Debt to Equity	0.166	0.164	0.245	0.402	0.496	0.514

CONTACT INFORMATION:

Phone: 81 362522220   Fax:
Toll-Free:
Address: Shiodome City Center, 1-5-2 Higashi-Shimbashi, Tokyo, 105-7123 Japan

STOCK TICKER/OTHER:

Stock Ticker: FJTSY   Exchange: PINX
Employees: 145,845   Fiscal Year Ends: 03/31
Parent Company:

SALARIES/BONUSES:

Top Exec. Salary: $ Bonus: $
Second Exec. Salary: $ Bonus: $

OTHER THOUGHTS:

Estimated Female Officers or Directors: 1
Hot Spot for Advancement for Women/Minorities:

Fujitsu Network Communications Inc

www.fujitsu.com/us/services/telecom

NAIC Code: 334210

TYPES OF BUSINESS:

Telecommunications Equipment & Software
Ethernet Technology
Optical Transport Technology
Optical Networking
Manufacture

BRANDS/DIVISIONS/AFFILIATES:

Fujitsu Limited
FLASHWAVE

GROWTH PLANS/SPECIAL FEATURES:

Fujitsu Network Communications, Inc. (FNC), a subsidiary of Fujitsu Limited, is an innovator in connection-oriented Ethernet and optical transport technologies. The firm is also a provider of synchronous optical networking (SONET), wavelength division multiplexing (WDM) and packet optical networking solutions. FNC supports network operators and enterprise customers of all types and sizes with its services solutions, including optical and wireless networking solutions, end-to-end customized professional services, responsive customer relationships, manufacturing expertise, and local/global support. FNC helped pioneer the development of multi-service provisioning platforms (MSPPs) and reconfigurable optical add-drop multiplexers (ROADMs). FNC's network elements have been deployed by all major carriers throughout North America. The company's FLASHWAVE Packet Optical Networking platforms carry the Fujitsu name forward into next-generation wireline and wireless communications networks.

CONTACTS: Note: Officers with more than one job title may be intentionally listed here more than once.

Doug Moore, CEO

FINANCIAL DATA: Note: Data for latest year may not have been available at press time.

In U.S. $	2020	2019	2018	2017	2016	2015
Revenue						
R&D Expense						
Operating Income						
Operating Margin %						
SGA Expense						
Net Income						
Operating Cash Flow						
Capital Expenditure						
EBITDA						
Return on Assets %						
Return on Equity %						
Debt to Equity						

CONTACT INFORMATION:

Phone: 972-690-6000   Fax: 972-479-4647
Toll-Free: 800-777-3278
Address: 2801 Telecom Pkwy., Richardson, TX 75082 United States

SALARIES/BONUSES:

Top Exec. Salary: $ Bonus: $
Second Exec. Salary: $ Bonus: $

STOCK TICKER/OTHER:

Stock Ticker: Subsidiary   Exchange:
Employees: 1,358   Fiscal Year Ends: 03/31
Parent Company: Fujitsu Limited

OTHER THOUGHTS:

Estimated Female Officers or Directors:
Hot Spot for Advancement for Women/Minorities:

Sales, profits and employees may be estimates. Financial information, benefits and other data can change quickly and may vary from those stated here.

Fusion Connect Inc

www.fusionconnect.com

NAIC Code: 517110

TYPES OF BUSINESS:

Wired Telecommunications Carriers
Internet Technology
Business Connection Solutions
Cloud Communication
Network Security Solutions
Network Management Platforms
Artificial Intelligence

BRANDS/DIVISIONS/AFFILIATES:

GROWTH PLANS/SPECIAL FEATURES:

Fusion Connect, Inc. manages, orchestrates and secures critical internet technology that keeps businesses connected. The company tailors its cloud communication, collaboration, security and network management platforms to meet unique business needs. Its management systems are artificial intelligence (AI)-based. Fusion Connect optimizes business communications, costs and collaboration from any place or device, including remote workers. The firm's leading-edge technology seamlessly integrates solutions across virtual and fixed platforms. Fusion Connect's U.S.-based tech support is available 24/7, and its proactive monitoring system is designed to automatically respond to issues before they impact their customer's business. Other services by Fusion Connect include hosted voice, UCaaS, calling services for Microsoft Teams, contact/call center solutions, SIP trunking, dedicated internet access, broadband, wireless access, SD-WAN, MPLS, remote access VPN, unified threat management and a range of managed IT. In early-2021, to focus on core U.S. business operations, Fusion Connect sold wholly-owned subsidiary Primus, in Canada, to Distributel.

CONTACTS: *Note: Officers with more than one job title may be intentionally listed here more than once.*

Brian Crotty, CEO
John Dobbins, COO
Keith Soldan, CFO
Brian George, CTO
Michael Miller, CIO
Jan Sarro, Executive VP, Divisional
James Prenetta, Executive VP
Jonathan Kaufman, Other Executive Officer
Russell Markman, President, Divisional
Timothy J. Bernlohr, Chmn.

FINANCIAL DATA: *Note: Data for latest year may not have been available at press time.*

In U.S. $	2020	2019	2018	2017	2016	2015
Revenue	137,891,638	135,853,831	143,004,032	150,530,560	122,045,320	101,694,512
R&D Expense						
Operating Income						
Operating Margin %						
SGA Expense						
Net Income		-15,451,011	-14,715,249	-14,014,523	-12,716,323	-8,229,825
Operating Cash Flow						
Capital Expenditure						
EBITDA						
Return on Assets %						
Return on Equity %						
Debt to Equity						

CONTACT INFORMATION:

Phone: Fax:
Toll-Free: 888 301-1721
Address: 210 Interstate N. Pkwy., Ste. 200, Atlanta, GA 30339 United States

STOCK TICKER/OTHER:

Stock Ticker: Private
Employees: 306
Parent Company:

Exchange:
Fiscal Year Ends: 12/31

SALARIES/BONUSES:

Top Exec. Salary: $ Bonus: $
Second Exec. Salary: $ Bonus: $

OTHER THOUGHTS:

Estimated Female Officers or Directors:
Hot Spot for Advancement for Women/Minorities:

Garmin Ltd

NAIC Code: 334511

www.garmin.com

TYPES OF BUSINESS:

Communications Equipment-GPS-Based
Aviation Electronics
Marine Electronics
Automotive Electronics
Recreation & Fitness Electronics
Navigational Equipment

BRANDS/DIVISIONS/AFFILIATES:

Garmin Connect
Connect IQ
GEOS Worldwide Limited

CONTACTS: Note: Officers with more than one job title may be intentionally listed here more than once.

Clifton A. Pemble, CEO
Andrew Etkind, VP-Gen. Counsel
Doug Boessen, CFO
Frank McLoughlin, VP-Aviation Eng.
Andrew Etkind, General Counsel
Brian J. Pokorny, VP-Oper.
Dawn Iddings, VP-Bus. Dev. & Customer Care
Jon Cassat, VP-Comm. Affairs
Patrick Desbois, VP-Exec. Office
Matthew Munn, VP
Philip Straub, VP
Michael Wiegers, VP-Consumer Eng.
Min Kao, Exec. Chmn.

GROWTH PLANS/SPECIAL FEATURES:

Garmin Ltd. designs, manufactures and markets hand-held, portable and fixed-mount navigation and communications equipment based on global positioning system (GPS) technology. Garmin's products are sold in approximately 100 countries through independent dealers and distributors, including Best Buy, Amazon.com, Walmart and Decathlon. The company's products are divided into five categories: aviation, marine, automotive, outdoor and sports/fitness. The aviation segment includes GPS-enabled navigation, VHF communications transmitters/receivers, multi-function displays, electronic flight instrumentation systems, automatic flight control systems, traffic advisory systems, traffic collision avoidance systems, terrain awareness and warning systems, instrument landing system receivers, weather radar, surveillance products and more. The marine segment offers a broad range of products designed for use in the recreational marine industry, including chartplotters, fishfinders, sounders, autopilot systems, radar systems, VHF communication radios and handheld/wrist-worn marine-friendly GPS devices. The automotive segment offers auto navigation products such as personal navigation devices, cameras and original equipment manufacturer solutions. The outdoor segment offers products designed for use in outdoor activities, including outdoor handheld navigation devices, adventure watches, golf devices, dog tracking and training devices, Garmin Connect web and mobile platforms and Connect IQ, an application development platform enables third parties to create a variety of experiences that run on a wide assortment of Garmin devices. The sports/fitness segment offers fitness and activity tracking products such as sport watches, cycling computers, cycling power meters and safety awareness devices. Incorporated in Switzerland, Garmin and its principal subsidiaries are located in the U.S., Taiwan and the U.K. In January 2021, Garmin acquired GEOS Worldwide Limited and its subsidiaries, which provide emergency monitoring and incident response services.

FINANCIAL DATA: Note: Data for latest year may not have been available at press time.

In U.S. $	2020	2019	2018	2017	2016	2015
Revenue	4,186,573,000	3,757,505,000	3,347,444,000	3,087,004,000	3,018,665,000	2,820,270,000
R&D Expense	705,685,000	605,366,000	567,805,000	511,634,000	467,960,000	427,043,000
Operating Income	1,054,240,000	945,586,000	778,343,000	668,860,000	623,909,000	549,581,000
Operating Margin %		.25%	.23%	.22%	.21%	.19%
SGA Expense	721,411,000	683,024,000	633,571,000	602,670,000	587,701,000	562,080,000
Net Income	992,324,000	952,486,000	694,080,000	694,955,000	510,814,000	456,227,000
Operating Cash Flow	1,135,267,000	698,549,000	919,520,000	660,842,000	705,682,000	280,467,000
Capital Expenditure	187,466,000	120,408,000	160,355,000	151,928,000	96,675,000	84,481,000
EBITDA	1,180,955,000	1,051,761,000	874,537,000	755,112,000	710,249,000	627,941,000
Return on Assets %		.16%	.13%	.15%	.11%	.10%
Return on Equity %		.21%	.17%	.19%	.15%	.14%
Debt to Equity		0.01				

CONTACT INFORMATION:

Phone: 41 526301600   Fax:
Toll-Free:
Address: Muhlentalstrasse 2, Schaffhausen, 8200 Switzerland

STOCK TICKER/OTHER:

Stock Ticker: GRMN   Exchange: NAS
Employees: 16,000   Fiscal Year Ends: 12/31
Parent Company:

SALARIES/BONUSES:

Top Exec. Salary: $ Bonus: $
Second Exec. Salary: $ Bonus: $

OTHER THOUGHTS:

Estimated Female Officers or Directors: 2
Hot Spot for Advancement for Women/Minorities: Y

GCI Liberty Inc

NAIC Code: 517110

www.gci.com

TYPES OF BUSINESS:

Local Telephone Service
Long-Distance Services
Cable Television Services
Wireless Communications Services
Video-on-Demand Services
Network Management
Satellite-Based Services
Internet Services

BRANDS/DIVISIONS/AFFILIATES:

GCI Holdings LLC
Liberty Broadband Corporation
Skyhook Holding Inc
Charter Communications Inc
GCI
Spectrum
Evite
Lending Tree

CONTACTS: Note: Officers with more than one job title may be intentionally listed here more than once.

Gregory Maffei, CEO
Mark Carleton, CFO
John Malone, Chairman of the Board
Richard Baer, Chief Legal Officer
Albert Rosenthaler, Other Executive Officer

GROWTH PLANS/SPECIAL FEATURES:

GCI Liberty, Inc. is a U.S.-based communications provider. The firm's two primary subsidiaries include: GCI Holdings, LLC and Liberty Broadband Corporation. GCI Holdings provides a full range of wireless, data, video, voice and managed services to residential customers, businesses, governmental entities and educational and medical institutions primarily in Alaska under the GCI brand. Liberty Broadband consists of its wholly-owned subsidiary Skyhook Holding, Inc. and an interest in Charter Communications, Inc. Skyhook provides mobile positioning and contextual location intelligence solutions; and Charter is a leading cable operator and broadband communications services company. Charter provides video, internet and voice services to approximately 29.2 million residential and small/medium business customers. Charter also offers its Spectrum brand of mobile services to residential customers; sells video and online advertising inventory to local, regional and national advertising customers; sells fiber-based communications and managed information technology solutions to large enterprise customers; and owns and operates regional sports networks and local sports, news and community channels. Other GCI Liberty assets include: Evite, a digital invitation platform that offers thousands of free and premium customizable designs which can be sent by email or text message; and 26.5%-owned Lending Tree, which operates an online loan marketplace for consumers seeking loans and other credit-based offerings. In May 2020, GCI sold its NBC affiliates in southeast Alaska to Gray Television, including KATH and KSCT stations in the Juneau and Sitka markets. That same year, GCI launched 5G service in Alaska. In December 2020, the firm was acquired by Liberty Broadband Corporation via a stock-for-stock merger.

FINANCIAL DATA: Note: Data for latest year may not have been available at press time.

In U.S. $	2020	2019	2018	2017	2016	2015
Revenue	873,259,400	894,732,992	739,761,984	23,000,000	428,000,000	20,307,000
R&D Expense						
Operating Income						
Operating Margin %						
SGA Expense						
Net Income		1,938,697,984	-873,302,976	1,232,999,936	762,000,000	229,000,000
Operating Cash Flow						
Capital Expenditure						
EBITDA						
Return on Assets %						
Return on Equity %						
Debt to Equity						

CONTACT INFORMATION:

Phone: 720-875-5900   Fax:
Toll-Free:
Address: 12300 Liberty Blvd., Englewood, CO 80112 United States

STOCK TICKER/OTHER:

Stock Ticker: Subsidiary
Employees: 2,051
Parent Company: Liberty Broadband Corporation

Exchange:
Fiscal Year Ends: 12/31

SALARIES/BONUSES:

Top Exec. Salary: $ Bonus: $
Second Exec. Salary: $ Bonus: $

OTHER THOUGHTS:

Estimated Female Officers or Directors: 1
Hot Spot for Advancement for Women/Minorities:

Gilat Satellite Networks Ltd

NAIC Code: 517410

www.gilat.com

TYPES OF BUSINESS:

Satellite-Based Internet Service
Satellite-Based Communication Services
VSAT Technology
Cloud-Based Satellite Network

BRANDS/DIVISIONS/AFFILIATES:

CONTACTS: *Note: Officers with more than one job title may be intentionally listed here more than once.*

Adi Sfadia, CEO
Yuval Shani, COO
Bosmat Halpern-Levy, CFO
Ron Levin, VP-Global Accounts & Mobility
Lior Moyal, VP-Human Resources
Gai Berkovich, VP-R&D
Alik Shimelmits, CTO
Alon Levy, General Counsel
Yair Shahrabany, VP-Global Oper. & Customer Svcs.
Doron Elinav, VP-Strategic Accounts
Ari Krashin, VP-Finance
Glenn Katz, CEO-Spacenet, Inc.
Assaf Eyal, VP-Commercial Div.
Moshe Tamir, VP-Defense & Homeland Security
Isaac Angel, Chmn.
Danny Fridman, CEO-Gilat Peru & Colombia

GROWTH PLANS/SPECIAL FEATURES:

Gilat Satellite Networks, Ltd., based in Israel, is a global provider of satellite-based broadband communication technologies and solutions. The firm's solutions span cellular, mobility, residential broadband, enterprise and government defense, including cellular backhaul, 5G, network backup, in-flight/train/maritime connectivity, emergency response, public safety, homeland security and unmanned aircraft systems (UAS). Gilat's portfolio comprises of a cloud-based very small aperture terminal (VSAT) network platform, high-speed modems, high-performance on-the-move antennas and high-power solid-state amplifiers and block upconverters. The company's technologies are developed to support a wide variety of applications, including: cloud-based, software-defined (SDN) X-architecture; 5G cellular backhaul (CBH)-ready modems; low Earth orbit (LEO) satellites; embedded acceleration techniques that enable mobile network operators to achieve long-term emitting (LTE) speeds while overcoming inherent delay in satellite communications; and a virtual network for global networks bandwidth management. In late-2020, Comtech Telecommunications Corp. and Gilat announced that they terminated their merger agreement first announced in January 2020.

FINANCIAL DATA: *Note: Data for latest year may not have been available at press time.*

In U.S. $	2020	2019	2018	2017	2016	2015
Revenue	165,885,000	263,492,000	266,391,000	282,756,000	279,551,000	197,543,000
R&D Expense	26,303,000	30,184,000	33,023,000	28,014,000	24,853,000	22,412,000
Operating Income	-16,022,000	25,572,000	21,284,000	10,861,000	755,000	-21,791,000
Operating Margin %		.10%	.08%	.04%	.00%	-.11%
SGA Expense	30,934,000	40,121,000	39,730,000	43,620,000	49,882,000	43,467,000
Net Income	34,911,000	36,538,000	18,409,000	6,801,000	-5,340,000	-52,334,000
Operating Cash Flow	43,160,000	34,782,000	32,017,000	20,800,000	10,778,000	-14,787,000
Capital Expenditure	4,716,000	7,982,000	10,759,000	3,692,000	4,307,000	3,930,000
EBITDA	46,190,000	34,328,000	30,749,000	20,538,000	10,118,000	-34,333,000
Return on Assets %		.09%	.05%	.02%	-.01%	-.14%
Return on Equity %		.15%	.08%	.03%	-.03%	-.26%
Debt to Equity		0.029	0.034	0.058	0.081	0.121

CONTACT INFORMATION:

Phone: 972 39252000   Fax:
Toll-Free:
Address: 21 Yegia Kapayim St., Kiryat Arie, Petah Tikva, 49130 Israel

STOCK TICKER/OTHER:

Stock Ticker: GILT   Exchange: NAS
Employees: 779   Fiscal Year Ends: 12/31
Parent Company:

SALARIES/BONUSES:

Top Exec. Salary: $ Bonus: $
Second Exec. Salary: $ Bonus: $

OTHER THOUGHTS:

Estimated Female Officers or Directors: 3
Hot Spot for Advancement for Women/Minorities: Y

Global Telecom Holding SAE

NAIC Code: 517210

www.gtelecom.com

TYPES OF BUSINESS:

Mobile Phone Service
International Long-Distance
Value Added Services
Internet Operations

GROWTH PLANS/SPECIAL FEATURES:

Global Telecom Holding SAE (GTH) is an international telecommunications company operating a mobile network in Algeria under the Djezzy brand, having a total population under license of more than 43 million. Djezzy provides a range of pre-paid and post-paid voice, data and multimedia telecommunications services. Global Telecom operates as a subsidiary of the VEON Ltd., a multinational telecommunication services company based in Netherlands.

BRANDS/DIVISIONS/AFFILIATES:

VEON Ltd
Djezzy

CONTACTS: Note: Officers with more than one job title may be intentionally listed here more than once.

Hesham Shoukry, Dir.-Admin.
David Dobbie, Chief Legal & Regulatory Affairs Officer
Murat Kirkgoz, Chmn.

FINANCIAL DATA: Note: Data for latest year may not have been available at press time.

In U.S. $	2020	2019	2018	2017	2016	2015
Revenue	2,180,850,000	2,077,000,000	2,827,000,000	3,014,700,000	2,955,500,000	2,894,400,000
R&D Expense						
Operating Income						
Operating Margin %						
SGA Expense						
Net Income		1,301,000,000	-252,000,000	-79,100,000	193,900,000	-142,700,000
Operating Cash Flow						
Capital Expenditure						
EBITDA						
Return on Assets %						
Return on Equity %						
Debt to Equity						

CONTACT INFORMATION:

Phone: 20 224619654   Fax: 20 224615054
Toll-Free:
Address: 2005A Nile City Towers, Cornish El Nile RamletBeau, Cairo, 11221 Egypt

STOCK TICKER/OTHER:

Stock Ticker: Subsidiary   Exchange:
Employees: 12,500   Fiscal Year Ends: 12/31
Parent Company: VEON Ltd

SALARIES/BONUSES:

Top Exec. Salary: $ Bonus: $
Second Exec. Salary: $ Bonus: $

OTHER THOUGHTS:

Estimated Female Officers or Directors:
Hot Spot for Advancement for Women/Minorities:

Globalstar Inc

NAIC Code: 517410

www.globalstar.com

TYPES OF BUSINESS:

Satellite Phone & Data Service
Satellite Network Operations
Satellite Communications Equipment
Logistics & Transportation Data Services
Shipping Container Data Services

BRANDS/DIVISIONS/AFFILIATES:

Thermo Capital Partners LLC
Globalstar System
SPOT
SmartOne
STX-3
STINGR

CONTACTS: *Note: Officers with more than one job title may be intentionally listed here more than once.*

Rebecca Clary, CFO
James Monroe, Chairman of the Board
L. Ponder, General Counsel
David Kagan, President

GROWTH PLANS/SPECIAL FEATURES:

Globalstar, Inc., majority-owned by Thermo Capital Partners, LLC, provides mobile satellite services, including voice, data and Internet of Things (IoT) communications services, globally via satellite. The company's wireless communications services reach areas not served or underserved by terrestrial wireless and wireline networks. In circumstances where terrestrial networks are not operational due to natural or man-made disasters, Globalstar seeks to meet its customer's need for connectivity. The firm's network of in-orbit satellites and active ground stations (gateways) is collectively referred to as the Globalstar System. The company's services are available only with equipment designed to work on the Globalstar System network, and include: two-way voice communication and data transmission using mobile or fixed devices; one-way data transmission using a mobile or fixed device that transmits its location and other information to a central monitoring station, including the SPOT family of products, which transmit messages and the location of the device; and one-way data transmission using mobile or fixed device that transmits its location and other information to a central monitoring station, including Globalstar's commercial IoT products, such as its battery- and solar-powered SmartOne, STX-3 and STINGR products. The SPOT product family has initiated approximately 7,500 rescues since its 2007 launch, averaging nearly two rescues per day. Globalstar owns and operates gateways in the U.S., Canada, Ireland, Nicaragua, Venezuela, Argentina, Brazil, Panama, Puerto Rico, France, Singapore and Botswana. During 2020, Globalstar announced the deployment of a new ground station with second-generation technology in Cordoba, Argentina, enabling voice calls, two-way data communication and internet connection throughout South America.

FINANCIAL DATA: *Note: Data for latest year may not have been available at press time.*

In U.S. $	2020	2019	2018	2017	2016	2015
Revenue	128,487,000	131,718,000	130,113,000	112,660,000	96,861,000	90,490,000
R&D Expense						
Operating Income	-58,747,000	-62,922,000	-67,857,000	-51,746,000	-63,326,000	-66,604,000
Operating Margin %		-.48%	-.52%	-.46%	-.65%	-.74%
SGA Expense	41,738,000	45,233,000	55,443,000	39,099,000	40,982,000	37,418,000
Net Income	-109,639,000	15,324,000	-6,516,000	-89,074,000	-132,646,000	72,322,000
Operating Cash Flow	22,215,000	3,048,000	5,920,000	13,857,000	8,813,000	2,162,000
Capital Expenditure	7,219,000	8,149,000	10,369,000	9,321,000	11,381,000	8,043,000
EBITDA	38,068,000	174,105,000	127,659,000	23,385,000	-25,847,000	186,815,000
Return on Assets %		.02%	-.01%	-.08%	-.11%	.06%
Return on Equity %		.04%	-.02%	-.39%	-.66%	.46%
Debt to Equity		1.176	1.023	1.493	3.094	2.557

CONTACT INFORMATION:

Phone: 408 933-4000   Fax: 409 933-4100
Toll-Free:
Address: 1351 Holiday Sqare Blvd., Covington, CA 70433 United States

STOCK TICKER/OTHER:

Stock Ticker: GSAT
Employees: 346
Parent Company:

Exchange: ASE
Fiscal Year Ends: 12/31

SALARIES/BONUSES:

Top Exec. Salary: $ Bonus: $
Second Exec. Salary: $ Bonus: $

OTHER THOUGHTS:

Estimated Female Officers or Directors: 1
Hot Spot for Advancement for Women/Minorities:

Globe Telecom Inc

www.globe.com.ph

NAIC Code: 517210

TYPES OF BUSINESS:

Wireless Telecommunications Carriers (except Satellite)
Telecommunications
Digital
Mobile
Broadband

BRANDS/DIVISIONS/AFFILIATES:

GROWTH PLANS/SPECIAL FEATURES:

Globe Telecom, Inc. is a telecommunications company headquartered in the Philippines. The firm provides digital mobile communication services using a fully-digital network based on a global system for mobile (GSM) communication technology to individual customers, small- and medium-sized businesses, as well as corporate and enterprise clients. These services include cellular, broadband and mobile data, and are offered in pre-paid and post-paid plans. Globe Telecom serves retailers, distributors, suppliers and business partners, as well as mobile subscribers (including fully mobile broadband), home broadband customers and landline subscribers. Class radio frequencies used by Globe Telecom include 2G, 3G, 4G and 5G. The company's principal shareholders include Ayala Corporation and Singtel. Globe Telecom is a member of Bridge Alliance, an alliance of mobile carriers in Asia, Australia, Africa and the Middle East. The firm's international mobile operations has hundreds of roaming partners in over 230 destinations worldwide.

CONTACTS: Note: Officers with more than one job title may be intentionally listed here more than once.

Ernest L. Cu, CEO
Rosemarie Maniego-Eala, CFO
Maria Louisa Guevarra-Cabreira, CCO
Renato M. Jiao, Chief Human Resources Officer
Carlomagno E. Malana, CIO
Jaime Augusto Zobel de Ayala, Chmn.

FINANCIAL DATA: Note: Data for latest year may not have been available at press time.

In U.S. $	2020	2019	2018	2017	2016	2015
Revenue	3,364,766,000	3,493,488,000	3,168,843,000	2,835,717,000	2,645,018,000	2,514,761,000
R&D Expense						
Operating Income	887,388,000	937,465,800	789,198,800	635,000,800	606,312,000	574,276,000
Operating Margin %		.27%	.25%	.22%	.23%	.23%
SGA Expense	620,134,100	646,875,200	563,552,600	589,549,300	598,288,000	572,641,200
Net Income	389,433,700	466,803,700	390,742,000	315,804,700	332,839,000	345,798,100
Operating Cash Flow	1,365,866,000	1,552,053,000	1,212,647,000	1,054,464,000	785,280,600	753,620,200
Capital Expenditure	1,264,024,000	1,069,546,000	906,778,200	891,737,500	770,240,400	673,510,400
EBITDA	1,441,052,000	1,535,393,000	1,341,764,000	1,133,974,000	1,031,211,000	993,046,200
Return on Assets %		.07%	.06%	.06%	.07%	.09%
Return on Equity %		.30%	.29%	.27%	.30%	.34%
Debt to Equity		1.584	2.034	2.122	1.734	1.261

CONTACT INFORMATION:

Phone: 63 27302000   Fax: 63 27390072
Toll-Free:
Address: Globe Telecom Plz, Fl. 5, Pioneer corner Madison St., Taguig City, 1634 Philippines

STOCK TICKER/OTHER:

Stock Ticker: GTMEF
Employees: 8,339
Parent Company:

Exchange: PINX
Fiscal Year Ends: 12/31

SALARIES/BONUSES:

Top Exec. Salary: $ Bonus: $
Second Exec. Salary: $ Bonus: $

OTHER THOUGHTS:

Estimated Female Officers or Directors:
Hot Spot for Advancement for Women/Minorities:

GoDaddy Inc

NAIC Code: 518210

www.godaddy.com

TYPES OF BUSINESS:

Domain Name Registration
Domain Name Reselling
Research & Development, Internet Services

BRANDS/DIVISIONS/AFFILIATES:

Poynt

CONTACTS: Note: Officers with more than one job title may be intentionally listed here more than once.

Scott Wagner, CEO
Ray Winborne, CFO
Charles Robel, Chairman of the Board
Rebecca Morrow, Chief Accounting Officer
Arne Josefsberg, Chief Information Officer
Nima Kelly, Chief Legal Officer
Ah Kee Low, COO
James Carroll, Executive VP, Divisional

GROWTH PLANS/SPECIAL FEATURES:

GoDaddy, Inc. provides domain name registration and related services. The company has approximately 19 million customers made up of individuals and organizations. GoDaddy operates the world's largest domain marketplace where customers can find a domain name to match their concept, with nearly 80 million domains under management. The firm is a leading technology provider to small businesses, web design professionals and individuals, offering easy-to-use cloud-based products. GoDaddy provides website building, hosting and security tools to construct and protect each customer's online presence. Products are developed internally, and include shared website hosting, website hosting on virtual dedicated servers and dedicated services, managed hosting services, cloud services, cloud applications, website builder, ecommerce solutions, search engine visibility, email accounts, office solutions, email marketing solutions and payment solutions. GoDaddy provides localized solutions in over 50 markets, with approximately 32% of its total bookings attributable to customers outside the U.S. During 2020, GoDaddy completed its acquisition of Neustar Inc.'s registry business, which features a high-performance backend registry technology platform and enhanced domain security systems that enable people and brands to seamlessly connect and transact online with speed, security and reliability. In February 2021, GoDaddy acquired Poynt, expanding GoDaddy's ecommerce services to help small businesses grow, online and offline, through a single platform.

GoDaddy offers its employees 100% paid medical and dental premiums, employee appreciation outings, a 401(k) plan, life and disability insurance, maternity and paternity leave, adoption assistance, subsidized lunches and employee discounts.

FINANCIAL DATA: Note: Data for latest year may not have been available at press time.

In U.S. $	2020	2019	2018	2017	2016	2015
Revenue	3,316,700,000	2,988,100,000	2,660,100,000	2,231,900,000	1,847,900,000	1,607,300,000
R&D Expense	560,400,000	492,600,000	434,000,000	355,800,000	287,800,000	270,200,000
Operating Income	-358,900,000	211,300,000	164,500,000	190,100,000	37,600,000	-31,000,000
Operating Margin %		.07%	.06%	.03%	.03%	-.02%
SGA Expense	762,300,000	707,700,000	625,400,000	535,600,000	450,000,000	421,900,000
Net Income	-495,100,000	137,000,000	77,100,000	136,400,000	-16,500,000	-75,600,000
Operating Cash Flow	764,600,000	723,400,000	559,800,000	475,600,000	386,500,000	259,400,000
Capital Expenditure	81,500,000	92,300,000	97,000,000	135,200,000	62,800,000	79,300,000
EBITDA	-201,400,000	428,200,000	405,500,000	395,600,000	195,800,000	107,400,000
Return on Assets %		.02%	.01%	.03%	.00%	-.01%
Return on Equity %		.18%	.12%	.26%	-.03%	-.11%
Debt to Equity		3.329	3.02	4.955	1.841	2.442

CONTACT INFORMATION:

Phone: 480-505-8800   Fax: 480-505-8844
Toll-Free:
Address: 2155 E. GoDaddy Way, Tempe, AZ 85284 United States

STOCK TICKER/OTHER:

Stock Ticker: GDDY   Exchange: NYS
Employees: 7,024   Fiscal Year Ends: 12/31
Parent Company:

SALARIES/BONUSES:

Top Exec. Salary: $ Bonus: $
Second Exec. Salary: $ Bonus: $

OTHER THOUGHTS:

Estimated Female Officers or Directors: 3
Hot Spot for Advancement for Women/Minorities: Y

GTT Communications Inc

www.gtt.net/us-en

NAIC Code: 517210

TYPES OF BUSINESS:

Wireless Telecommunications Carriers (except Satellite)
Network Solutions
Digital Business
Cloud Application
Advanced Solutions
Wide Area Networking
Enterprise Voice
Internet

BRANDS/DIVISIONS/AFFILIATES:

GROWTH PLANS/SPECIAL FEATURES:

GTT Communications, Inc. is a network solutions provider that enables digital business and cloud application optimization across six continents, reaching more than 140 countries. The company serves thousands of multinational and national enterprise, government and carrier customers with a portfolio of advanced connectivity and security services. GTT's services are grouped into six categories: transport and infrastructure, consisting of wavelengths, low latency, Ethernet direct, colocation and dark fiber; advanced solutions, such as advanced security, hybrid cloud and advanced services; wide area networking (WAN), consisting of SD-WAN, MPLS, VPLS, uCPE, Ethernet, managed network services and cloud connect; enterprise voice, including SIP trunking; and internet, including IP transit, dedicated internet and broadband. GTT's industry solutions span financial markets, manufacturing, retail, ecommerce, media, broadcast and event services.

CONTACTS: Note: Officers with more than one job title may be intentionally listed here more than once.

Richard Calder, CEO
Michael Bauer, CFO
H. Thompson, Chairman of the Board
Christopher McKee, Executive VP, Divisional

FINANCIAL DATA: Note: Data for latest year may not have been available at press time.

In U.S. $	2020	2019	2018	2017	2016	2015
Revenue		1,727,800,000	1,490,800,000	827,900,000	521,688,000	369,250,000
R&D Expense						
Operating Income						
Operating Margin %						
SGA Expense						
Net Income		-105,900,000	-243,400,000	-71,500,000	5,260,000	19,304,000
Operating Cash Flow						
Capital Expenditure						
EBITDA						
Return on Assets %						
Return on Equity %						
Debt to Equity						

CONTACT INFORMATION:

Phone: 703 442-5500   Fax:
Toll-Free:
Address: 7900 Tysons One Pl., Ste. 1450, McLean, VA 22102 United States

STOCK TICKER/OTHER:

Stock Ticker: GTTN
Employees: 1,257
Parent Company:

Exchange: OTC
Fiscal Year Ends: 12/31

SALARIES/BONUSES:

Top Exec. Salary: $ Bonus: $
Second Exec. Salary: $ Bonus: $

OTHER THOUGHTS:

Estimated Female Officers or Directors:
Hot Spot for Advancement for Women/Minorities:

Harmonic Inc

NAIC Code: 334210

www.harmonicinc.com

TYPES OF BUSINESS:

Networking Equipment
Video Stream Processing
Cable Edge & Access
Software

BRANDS/DIVISIONS/AFFILIATES:

CONTACTS: *Note: Officers with more than one job title may be intentionally listed here more than once.*

Patrick Harshman, CEO
Sanjay Kalra, CFO
Patrick Gallagher, Chairman of the Board
Nimrod Ben-Natan, General Manager, Divisional
Eric Louvet, Senior VP, Divisional
Neven Haltmayer, Senior VP, Divisional

GROWTH PLANS/SPECIAL FEATURES:

Harmonic, Inc. develops and sells high-performance video delivery software, products, system solutions and services. These offerings enable customers to create, prepare, store, playout and deliver a full-range of high-quality broadcast and over-the-top (OTT) video services to consumer devices, including TVs, personal computers, laptops, tablets and smartphones. Harmonic also develops and sells cable access solutions that enable cable operators to deploy high-speed internet, voice and video services to consumers' homes. The company operates its business in two segments: video and cable access. The video business segment provides video processing and production and playout solutions and services worldwide to cable operators and satellite and telecommunications pay-TV service providers, and to broadcast and media companies, including streaming media companies. The cable access business segment provides cable access solutions and related services, including CableOS software-based cable access, primarily to cable operators globally. Across these two segments, Harmonic generated approximately 58% of 2020 revenue from the Americas; 31% from Europe, the Middle East and Africa; and 11% from Asia Pacific regions.

FINANCIAL DATA: *Note: Data for latest year may not have been available at press time.*

In U.S. $	2020	2019	2018	2017	2016	2015
Revenue	378,831,000	402,874,000	403,558,000	358,246,000	405,911,000	377,027,000
R&D Expense	82,494,000	84,614,000	89,163,000	95,978,000	98,401,000	87,545,000
Operating Income	-10,127,000	16,224,000	-2,093,000	-65,570,000	-52,434,000	-11,576,000
Operating Margin %		.04%	-.01%	-.18%	-.13%	-.03%
SGA Expense	119,611,000	119,035,000	118,952,000	136,270,000	144,381,000	120,960,000
Net Income	-29,271,000	-5,924,000	-21,035,000	-82,955,000	-72,314,000	-15,661,000
Operating Cash Flow	39,163,000	31,295,000	12,284,000	3,064,000	438,000	6,351,000
Capital Expenditure	32,205,000	10,328,000	7,044,000	11,399,000	15,107,000	14,356,000
EBITDA	999,000	24,661,000	15,791,000	-50,708,000	-36,147,000	4,008,000
Return on Assets %		-.01%	-.04%	-.16%	-.13%	-.03%
Return on Equity %		-.02%	-.09%	-.34%	-.24%	-.04%
Debt to Equity		0.49	0.559	0.568	0.433	0.30

CONTACT INFORMATION:

Phone: 408 542-2500   Fax:
Toll-Free: 800-788-1330
Address: 2590 Orchard Pkwy., San Jose, CA 95131 United States

SALARIES/BONUSES:

Top Exec. Salary: $ Bonus: $
Second Exec. Salary: $ Bonus: $

STOCK TICKER/OTHER:

Stock Ticker: HLIT   Exchange: NAS
Employees: 1,169   Fiscal Year Ends: 12/31
Parent Company:

OTHER THOUGHTS:

Estimated Female Officers or Directors: 1
Hot Spot for Advancement for Women/Minorities:

HC2 Holdings Inc

www.hc2.com

NAIC Code: 517110

TYPES OF BUSINESS:

International & Long-Distance Telephone Service
Industrial Construction Services
Structural Steel
Water Pipes
Digital Engineering
Healthcare Product Development
Medical Technologies
Over-the-Air Broadcasting Stations

BRANDS/DIVISIONS/AFFILIATES:

DBM Global Inc
GrayWolf
Panseed Life Sciences LLC
HC2 Broadcasting Holdings Inc
Azteca America
INNOVATE Corp

CONTACTS: Note: Officers with more than one job title may be intentionally listed here more than once.

Philip Falcone, CEO
Michael Sena, CFO
Suzi Herbst, Chief Administrative Officer
Joseph Ferraro, Other Executive Officer

GROWTH PLANS/SPECIAL FEATURES:

HC2 Holdings, Inc. is a diversified holding company that operates through three core business segments: infrastructure, life sciences and spectrum. The infrastructure segment is comprised of DBM Global Inc. and its subsidiaries, which offer fully-integrated industrial construction, structural steel and facility maintenance services and solutions. It provides 3D building information modeling, detailing, fabrication and erection of structural steel and heavy plate. These services are provided on commercial, industrial and infrastructure construction projects such as high- and low-rise buildings and office complexes, hotels, casinos, convention centers, sports arenas and girders. This segment specializes in the fabrication and erection of large-diameter water pipe and water storage tanks, and through GrayWolf provides integrated solutions for digital engineering, modeling and detailing to a range of end markets. The life sciences segment is comprised of Pansend Life Sciences LLC, which through its subsidiaries develops products to treat early osteoarthritis of the knee, and develops aesthetic and medical technologies for the skin. This division also invests in early-stage or developmental stage healthcare companies. The spectrum segment is comprised of HC2 Broadcasting Holdings Inc. and its subsidiaries, which acquire and operate over-the-air broadcasting stations across the U.S. This division operates Azteca America, a Spanish-language broadcast network offering Hispanic content throughout the U.S. In July 2021, HC2 Holdings announced it will change its name to INNOVATE Corp., which was to become effective by year's end.

FINANCIAL DATA: Note: Data for latest year may not have been available at press time.

In U.S. $	2020	2019	2018	2017	2016	2015
Revenue	1,005,800,000	1,984,100,000	1,976,700,000	1,634,123,000	1,558,126,000	1,120,806,000
R&D Expense						
Operating Income	9,400,000	84,100,000	-55,800,000	-1,132,000	3,520,000	4,131,000
Operating Margin %		.04%	-.03%	.00%	.00%	.00%
SGA Expense	181,100,000	214,300,000	218,400,000	182,880,000	152,890,000	108,527,000
Net Income	-92,000,000	-31,500,000	162,000,000	-46,911,000	-94,549,000	-35,565,000
Operating Cash Flow	41,700,000	110,500,000	341,400,000	6,142,000	79,148,000	-32,561,000
Capital Expenditure	17,800,000	41,400,000	39,700,000	31,925,000	29,048,000	21,324,000
EBITDA	57,500,000	79,500,000	296,700,000	51,916,000	26,445,000	23,333,000
Return on Assets %		.00%	.03%	-.02%	-.04%	-.02%
Return on Equity %		-.14%	1.72%	-.85%	-1.52%	-.43%
Debt to Equity		2.399	8.444	8.107	9.691	3.955

CONTACT INFORMATION:

Phone: 212-235-2690   Fax:
Toll-Free:
Address: 295 Madison Ave. Fl. 12, New York, NY 10017 United States

STOCK TICKER/OTHER:

Stock Ticker: HCHC   Exchange: NYS
Employees: 2,803   Fiscal Year Ends: 12/31
Parent Company:

SALARIES/BONUSES:

Top Exec. Salary: $ Bonus: $
Second Exec. Salary: $ Bonus: $

OTHER THOUGHTS:

Estimated Female Officers or Directors:
Hot Spot for Advancement for Women/Minorities:

Hellenic Telecommunications Organization SA

www.cosmote.gr/cs/otegroup/en/corp_homepage.html

NAIC Code: 517110

TYPES OF BUSINESS:

Local Telephone Service
Long-Distance Service
Internet Service
Mobile Phone Service
Equipment Sales
Hosting Services
Payphones

BRANDS/DIVISIONS/AFFILIATES:

Deutsche Telekom AG
COSMOTE
CosmoOne
OTE Rural
OTEGlobe
OTE SAT-MARITEL
COSMOTE TV PRODUCTIONS
OTE Estate

CONTACTS: Note: Officers with more than one job title may be intentionally listed here more than once.

Michael Tsamaz, CEO
Eirini Nikolaidi, Exec. Dir.-Legal & Regulatory Affairs
Ioannis Konstantinidis, Chief Strategic Planning & Transformation Officer
Deppie Tzimea, Dir.-Corp. Comm.
Maria Rontogianni, Chief Internal Audit Officer
Aris Dimitriadis, Chief Compliance, ERM & Insurance Officer
Konstantinos Liamidis, Chief Intl Oper. Officer

GROWTH PLANS/SPECIAL FEATURES:

Hellenic Telecommunications Organization SA (OTE), along with its subsidiaries, is a leading provider of telecommunications services throughout Greece and Southeastern Europe. The company operates as a majority-owned subsidiary of Deutsche Telekom AG. OTE provides fixed-line, broadband, data, leased line and mobile telephony services through the COSMOTE brand, as well as satellite communications, real estate and professional training services. OTE's international activities includes the firm's 54% stake in Telekom Romania, a telecommunications operator that provides integrated fixed-line services and satellite TV services to local markets. OTE's mobile telecommunications subsidiary, COSMOTE, is a leader in the Greek mobile market. Business-to-business electronic transactions are managed by CosmoOne. OTE Rural North and OTE Rural South each focus on the development of new generation broadband infrastructure in rural areas of northern and southern Greece. International telecommunications wholesale services to high-capacity carriers and multi-site organizations in SE Europe are operated by OTE Globe; wireless and satellite communications, including maritime services, are operated by OTE SAT-MARITEL; and COSMOTE TV PRODUCTIONS, which is active in the production and exploitation of program and audiovisual content in Greece and abroad, intended for payTV and television operators that broadcast encrypted programs. Additionally, OTE Estate develops and manages real estate assets; OTE Academy trains OTE Group employees; and Germanos SA is a retail distribution network in telecoms and technology related products in SE Europe.

FINANCIAL DATA: Note: Data for latest year may not have been available at press time.

In U.S. $	2020	2019	2018	2017	2016	2015
Revenue	3,981,649,000	4,774,216,000	4,641,164,000	4,712,516,000	4,774,826,000	4,768,473,000
R&D Expense						
Operating Income	401,720,300	177,524,200	536,848,800	340,509,200	430,554,200	433,242,100
Operating Margin %		.04%	.12%	.07%	.09%	.09%
SGA Expense	77,582,840	90,044,960	102,262,700	117,901,500	127,675,700	138,793,900
Net Income	439,717,500	250,586,400	213,811,000	82,103,410	171,048,800	185,587,900
Operating Cash Flow	1,524,655,000	1,408,465,000	1,216,279,000	978,154,600	1,252,444,000	1,152,380,000
Capital Expenditure	815,902,700	808,572,000	879,557,200	1,123,913,000	797,820,400	804,417,900
EBITDA	1,432,534,000	1,752,150,000	1,533,574,000	1,528,321,000	1,567,784,000	1,506,818,000
Return on Assets %		.03%	.03%	.01%	.02%	.02%
Return on Equity %		.09%	.07%	.03%	.06%	.07%
Debt to Equity		0.649	0.549	0.544	0.824	0.778

CONTACT INFORMATION:

Phone: 30 2106111000   Fax: 30 2106111030
Toll-Free:
Address: 99 Kifissias Ave., Marousi, 151 24 Greece

SALARIES/BONUSES:

Top Exec. Salary: $ Bonus: $
Second Exec. Salary: $ Bonus: $

STOCK TICKER/OTHER:

Stock Ticker: HLTOF   Exchange: PINX
Employees: 16,291   Fiscal Year Ends: 12/31
Parent Company: Deutsche Telekom AG

OTHER THOUGHTS:

Estimated Female Officers or Directors: 5
Hot Spot for Advancement for Women/Minorities: Y

Hello Direct Inc

www.hellodirect.com

NAIC Code: 454113

TYPES OF BUSINESS:

Telephone Products & Equipment Interface Solutions Marketing
Telephones & Accessories

BRANDS/DIVISIONS/AFFILIATES:

Synercy Communications Management

GROWTH PLANS/SPECIAL FEATURES:

Hello Direct, Inc. is a provider and direct marketer of innovative, hands-free devices for businesses and governments in the U.S. Hands-free devices include headsets, speakerphones, webcams and conferencing solutions. Hello Direct is a business-to-business leader in telecommunications solutions, with nearly 2 million customers. The company has also developed special services and pricing exclusively for corporate and public-sector customers, with all of the support necessary for a successful implementation. Hello Direct offers more than 1,500 high-quality solutions, including headsets from Jabra, Plantronics, Sennheiser and VXi, as well as business communication products from manufacturers such as Polycom, Logitech, AT&T and Panasonic. The firm offers an extensive line of unified communication (UC) devices compatible with all the leading UC platforms. Hello Direct is privately-owned by Synergy Communications Management.

CONTACTS:
Note: Officers with more than one job title may be intentionally listed here more than once.

Lou Desiderio, Pres.-Synergy
E. Alexander Glover, Pres.
Dean Witter III, Secretary

FINANCIAL DATA:
Note: Data for latest year may not have been available at press time.

In U.S. $	2020	2019	2018	2017	2016	2015
Revenue						
R&D Expense						
Operating Income						
Operating Margin %						
SGA Expense						
Net Income						
Operating Cash Flow						
Capital Expenditure						
EBITDA						
Return on Assets %						
Return on Equity %						
Debt to Equity						

CONTACT INFORMATION:

Phone: Fax:
Toll-Free: 800-435-5634
Address: 400 Imperial Blvd., Cape Canaveral, FL 32920 United States

STOCK TICKER/OTHER:

Stock Ticker: Private   Exchange:
Employees: Fiscal Year Ends: 12/31
Parent Company: Synergy Communications Management

SALARIES/BONUSES:

Top Exec. Salary: $ Bonus: $
Second Exec. Salary: $ Bonus: $

OTHER THOUGHTS:

Estimated Female Officers or Directors: 1
Hot Spot for Advancement for Women/Minorities:

Hikari Tsushin Inc
NAIC Code: 443142

www.hikari.co.jp

TYPES OF BUSINESS:
Cell Phone Retail Sales
Mobile Phone Distribution
Office Automation Equipment Sales
Insurance
Advertising
Venture Capital

BRANDS/DIVISIONS/AFFILIATES:
FT Group Co ltd
Premium Water Holdings Co Ltd
NFC Holdings Inc
CHIC Holdings Inc
IE Group Inc
Members Mobile Inc
Telecom Service Co Ltd
J-Communication Inc

CONTACTS: Note: Officers with more than one job title may be intentionally listed here more than once.
Hideaki Wada, Pres.
Koh Gidoh, Chief Dir.-Admin.

GROWTH PLANS/SPECIAL FEATURES:
Hikari Tsushin, Inc. is a Japanese telecommunications company that operates through various subsidiaries that sell and service goods and provides other services. FT Group Co., Ltd. provides information communication services, environment and energy-saving services, and electricity retailing services. Premium Water Holdings Co., Ltd. is a mineral water delivery business that sells its products and services under the Premium Water brand name. NFC Holdings, Inc. offers insurance services, worker dispatch services, IT services, water serving services and alternative power services. CHIC Holdings, Inc. provides emergency rush services that handles various equipment issues, and offers call center services that connect real estate companies with residents. IE Group, Inc. provides office consulting services in areas such as original equipment manufacturing of phones and network equipment, as well as broadband access, light-emitting diode (LED) lighting and commercial air conditioners. Member's Mobile, Inc. offers corporate mobile and landline services, as well as information and communication technology (ICT) lifecycle services. Telecom Service Co., Ltd. provides mobile and telecommunication integration services, with devices including smartphones, tablet terminals, wearable terminals and related accessories. J-Communication, Inc. is a telecommunications company that provides subscription telecommunications services, telecommunications equipment (for sale and for lease), manufacturing devices, importing/exporting and training. Last, EPARK, Inc. provides a hub that matches users with stores and facilities, and offers information such as when best to visit the store, what the store has in stock, where stores are located, etc.

FINANCIAL DATA: Note: Data for latest year may not have been available at press time.

In U.S. $	2020	2019	2018	2017	2016	2015
Revenue	4,790,900,000	4,423,900,000	3,904,725,000	3,917,264,000	5,247,121,000	5,137,397,000
R&D Expense						
Operating Income	666,745,900	587,042,100	451,928,500	379,586,000	336,505,500	293,032,400
Operating Margin %	.14%	.13%	.12%	.10%	.06%	.06%
SGA Expense	2,250,811,000	2,147,827,000	2,100,253,000	2,106,482,000	2,184,587,000	
Net Income	471,902,300	452,513,000	382,325,900	356,497,700	228,516,900	189,628,600
Operating Cash Flow	795,283,800	577,936,500	254,253,700	156,174,400	94,709,260	144,210,100
Capital Expenditure	169,079,300	151,918,400	121,560,300	82,370,570	67,748,620	48,523,650
EBITDA	966,089,300	803,320,800	657,147,100	647,173,800	558,848,600	477,765,700
Return on Assets %	.06%	.07%	.07%	.08%	.06%	.06%
Return on Equity %	.19%	.21%	.21%	.22%	.15%	.14%
Debt to Equity	1.197	1.011	1.049	0.734	0.241	0.224

CONTACT INFORMATION:
Phone: 81 359513718   Fax: 81 359513709
Toll-Free:
Address: Hikari W. Gate Bldg, 1-4-10 Nishi-Ikebukuro Toshim, Tokyo, 171-0021 Japan

STOCK TICKER/OTHER:
Stock Ticker: HKTGF   Exchange: GREY
Employees: 7,572   Fiscal Year Ends:
Parent Company:

SALARIES/BONUSES:
Top Exec. Salary: $ Bonus: $
Second Exec. Salary: $ Bonus: $

OTHER THOUGHTS:
Estimated Female Officers or Directors:
Hot Spot for Advancement for Women/Minorities:

Hitachi Kokusai Electric Inc

www.hitachi-kokusai.co.jp

NAIC Code: 334220

TYPES OF BUSINESS:

Radio and Television Broadcasting and Wireless Communications
Equipment Manufacturing
Information Communication Systems
Wireless Communication Solutions
Film Processing Solutions
CATV Equipment
Manufacturing
Innovation

BRANDS/DIVISIONS/AFFILIATES:

Hitachi Kokusai Electric America Ltd
Hitachi Kokusai Electric Europe GmbH
Goyo Electronics Co Ltd
Hitachi Kokusai Electric Asia (Singapore) Pte Ltd
HYS Engineering Service Inc
Hitachi Kokusai Electric Comark LLC
Hitachi Kokusai Linear Equip. Eletronicos S/A
Hitachi Kokusai Electric Turkey

CONTACTS: Note: Officers with more than one job title may be intentionally listed here more than once.

Kaichiro Sakuma, CEO

GROWTH PLANS/SPECIAL FEATURES:

Hitachi Kokusai Electric, Inc., part of the Hitachi Group, is a Japanese global provider of information communication systems that offer capabilities through compatibility with global standards on which the next generation of mobile communication systems will be based. The firm is actively engaged in creating new value in the areas of wireless communications, information, broadcasting and video, as well as in the area of eco- and thin-film processing solutions (semiconductor manufacturing equipment). Hitachi Kokusai's products and systems include wireless communications and information systems, financial/stock exchange information systems, broadcasting and video systems, community antenna TV (CATV) equipment and antennas, security and surveillance systems, industrial video cameras and semiconductor manufacturing systems. In addition, Hitachi Kokusai's defense electronics division produces aircraft communication systems, shipboard communication systems and wireless telephone systems for air traffic control purposes. The company has manufacturing plants worldwide, and its subsidiaries include Hitachi Kokusai Electric America Ltd.; Hitachi Kokusai Electric Europe GmbH; Goyo Electronics Co., Ltd.; Hitachi Kokusai Electric Asia (Singapore) Pte. Ltd.; HYS Engineering Service, Inc.; Hitachi Kokusai Electric Comark LLC; Hitachi Kokusai Linear Equipamentos Eletronicos S/A; and Hitachi Kokusai Electric Turkey Elektronik UrUnleri Sanayi ve Ticaret A.S.

FINANCIAL DATA: Note: Data for latest year may not have been available at press time.

In U.S. $	2020	2019	2018	2017	2016	2015
Revenue	622,570,000	774,944,000	1,532,865,360	1,572,169,600	1,653,432,320	1,694,059,136
R&D Expense						
Operating Income						
Operating Margin %						
SGA Expense						
Net Income				68,235,872	118,907,344	159,826,928
Operating Cash Flow						
Capital Expenditure						
EBITDA						
Return on Assets %						
Return on Equity %						
Debt to Equity						

CONTACT INFORMATION:

Phone: 81 3-5510-5931   Fax: 81 3-3502-2502
Toll-Free:
Address: 2-15-12, Nishi-shimbashi, 6/Fl, Hitachi Atago Bldg, Tokyo, 105-8039 Japan

STOCK TICKER/OTHER:

Stock Ticker: Subsidiary   Exchange:
Employees: 1,505   Fiscal Year Ends: 03/31
Parent Company: Hitachi Group

SALARIES/BONUSES:

Top Exec. Salary: $ Bonus: $
Second Exec. Salary: $ Bonus: $

OTHER THOUGHTS:

Estimated Female Officers or Directors:
Hot Spot for Advancement for Women/Minorities:

HKT Trust and HKT Limited

www.hkt.com

NAIC Code: 517110

TYPES OF BUSINESS:

Wired Telecommunications Carriers
Telecommunications Services
Telephone Services
Broadband
Mobile Services

BRANDS/DIVISIONS/AFFILIATES:

PCCW Limited
NETVIGATOR
PCCW Global
PCCW Teleservices

CONTACTS: Note: Officers with more than one job title may be intentionally listed here more than once.

Hanqing Xu, Managing Dir.
Tzar Kai (Richard) Li, Chmn.

GROWTH PLANS/SPECIAL FEATURES:

HKT Trust and HKT Limited (HKT) is a premier telecommunications service provider that serves the Hong Kong public and local and international businesses with a wide range of telecommunications services. Services include local telephone, local data and broadband, international telecommunications, mobile and other telecommunications businesses such as customer premises equipment sale, outsourcing, consulting and contact centers. Local telephony services consist of fixed-line local telecommunications services, multimedia services and wholesale interconnection services provided to other telecommunications carriers and service providers. HKT's local data services consist primarily of data transmission services such as private or virtual private IP network services for private and public sector organizations and business and residential local broadband services in Hong Kong through the NETVIGATOR brand. International telecommunications services consist primarily of wholesale and retail international services to multinational enterprises and telecommunications service providers through the PCCW Global brand. Mobile services provides comprehensive mobile voice and data services via 1O1O and csl, as well as a number of prepaid service brands. Mobile offerings are carried by a unique combination of 4G LTE, DC-HSPA+ and Wi-Fi networks, as well as its LTE-A 600 megabits-per-second mobile network. Together with the media business of its parent company, PCCW Limited, HKT offers innovative media content and services across the PCCW group's quadruple-play platforms, fixed-line, broadband internet access, TV and mobile. Through PCCW Teleservices, HKT offers world-class global contact center and BPO services in all facets of voice and non-voice customer services, technical support, sales, retention and other business processes. HKT is headquartered in Hong Kong, and maintains a presence in mainland China as well as other parts of the world.

FINANCIAL DATA: Note: Data for latest year may not have been available at press time.

In U.S. $	2020	2019	2018	2017	2016	2015
Revenue	4,174,270,000	4,266,290,000	4,534,875,000	4,286,267,000	4,362,177,000	4,475,848,000
R&D Expense						
Operating Income	963,501,400	1,022,399,000	929,992,800	942,236,300	879,601,000	760,774,300
Operating Margin %		.24%	.21%	.22%	.20%	.17%
SGA Expense	317,558,500	333,539,500	1,287,633,000	1,518,971,000	1,613,955,000	1,712,419,000
Net Income	683,446,700	672,363,100	621,842,400	656,897,600	630,090,700	508,944,200
Operating Cash Flow	1,358,387,000	1,428,498,000	1,373,724,000	1,564,852,000	1,580,317,000	1,465,228,000
Capital Expenditure	614,496,300	661,021,800	602,252,800	948,164,800	913,625,100	875,992,400
EBITDA	1,650,943,000	1,654,423,000	1,619,884,000	1,658,547,000	1,616,919,000	1,545,391,000
Return on Assets %		.05%	.05%	.05%	.05%	.04%
Return on Equity %		.14%	.13%	.13%	.13%	.10%
Debt to Equity		1.109	1.12	1.003	0.977	0.862

CONTACT INFORMATION:

Phone: 852 28882888   Fax: 852 28778877
Toll-Free:
Address: 979 Kings Rd., PCCW Tower, Fl. 39, Quarry Bay, Hong Kong
Hong Kong

STOCK TICKER/OTHER:

Stock Ticker: HKTTF   Exchange: PINX
Employees: 17,500   Fiscal Year Ends: 12/31
Parent Company: PCCW Limited

SALARIES/BONUSES:

Top Exec. Salary: $ Bonus: $
Second Exec. Salary: $ Bonus: $

OTHER THOUGHTS:

Estimated Female Officers or Directors:
Hot Spot for Advancement for Women/Minorities:

HP Inc

NAIC Code: 334111

TYPES OF BUSINESS:

Computer Manufacturing
Computer Software
Printers & Supplies
Scanners

BRANDS/DIVISIONS/AFFILIATES:

HP Labs

CONTACTS: Note: Officers with more than one job title may be intentionally listed here more than once.

Steve Fieler, CFO
Charles Bergh, Chairman of the Board
Marie Myers, Chief Accounting Officer
Claire Bramley, Controller
Tracy Keogh, Other Executive Officer
Kim Rivera, President, Divisional
Enrique Lores, President, Divisional
Alex Cho, President, Divisional
Dion Weisler, President

GROWTH PLANS/SPECIAL FEATURES:

HP, Inc. is a global provider of personal computing devices and other access devices. The company operates in three segments: personal systems, printing and corporate investments. The personal systems segment offers the following products and services to the commercial and consumer markets: commercial personal computers (PCs), consumer PCs, workstations, desktops, notebooks, commercial tablets and mobility devices; and retail point-of-sale systems, displays and other related accessories. The printing segment provides consumer and commercial printer hardware, supplies, solutions and services, as well as scanning devices. These include: office printing solutions, home printing solutions, graphics solutions, 3D printing and digital manufacturing, commercial hardware, consumer hardware and supplies. The corporate investments segment includes HP Labs and certain business incubation projects. HP's products and services are available worldwide. As of October 31, 2020, HP's worldwide patent portfolio included over 28,000 patents.

FINANCIAL DATA: Note: Data for latest year may not have been available at press time.

In U.S. $	2020	2019	2018	2017	2016	2015
Revenue	56,639,000,000	58,756,000,000	58,472,000,000	52,056,000,000	48,238,000,000	103,355,000,000
R&D Expense	1,478,000,000	1,499,000,000	1,404,000,000	1,190,000,000	1,209,000,000	3,502,000,000
Operating Income	3,727,000,000	3,001,000,000	3,664,000,000	4,058,000,000	3,933,000,000	8,141,000,000
Operating Margin %		.07%	.07%	.08%	.08%	.08%
SGA Expense	5,120,000,000	5,368,000,000	4,859,000,000	4,376,000,000	3,840,000,000	12,185,000,000
Net Income	2,844,000,000	3,152,000,000	5,327,000,000	2,526,000,000	2,496,000,000	4,554,000,000
Operating Cash Flow	4,316,000,000	4,654,000,000	4,528,000,000	3,677,000,000	3,230,000,000	6,490,000,000
Capital Expenditure	580,000,000	671,000,000	546,000,000	402,000,000	433,000,000	3,603,000,000
EBITDA	4,259,000,000	3,509,000,000	3,853,000,000	3,939,000,000	4,265,000,000	12,202,000,000
Return on Assets %		.09%	.16%	.08%	.04%	.04%
Return on Equity %					.21%	.17%
Debt to Equity						0.784

CONTACT INFORMATION:

Phone: 650 857-1501   Fax:
Toll-Free:
Address: 1501 Page Mill Rd., Palo Alto, CA 94304 United States

STOCK TICKER/OTHER:

Stock Ticker: HPQ   Exchange: NYS
Employees: 53,000   Fiscal Year Ends: 10/31
Parent Company:

SALARIES/BONUSES:

Top Exec. Salary: $ Bonus: $
Second Exec. Salary: $ Bonus: $

OTHER THOUGHTS:

Estimated Female Officers or Directors: 6
Hot Spot for Advancement for Women/Minorities: Y

Huawei Technologies Co Ltd

www.huawei.com

NAIC Code: 334210

TYPES OF BUSINESS:

Telecommunications Equipment Manufacturing
Network Equipment
Software
Wireless Technology
Smartphones
5G Wireless Technology

BRANDS/DIVISIONS/AFFILIATES:

Union of Huawei Investment & Holding Co
Huaewi Matebook
MatePad
Huawei

CONTACTS: *Note: Officers with more than one job title may be intentionally listed here more than once.*

Ren Zhengfei, Pres.
Ding Yun (Ryan Ding), Chief Prod. & Solutions Officer
Yu Chengdong (Richard Yu), Chief Strategy Officer
Chen Lifang, Corp. Sr. VP-Public Affairs & Comm. Dept.
Guo Ping, Chmn.-Finance Committee
Zhang Ping'an (Alex Zhang), CEO-Huawei Symantec
Hu Houkun (Ken Hu), Chmn.-Huawei USA
Liang Hua, Chmn.
Wan Biao, Pres., Russia

GROWTH PLANS/SPECIAL FEATURES:

Huawei Technologies Co., Ltd., founded in 1987, is a leading global information and communications technology (ICT) solutions provider. Huawei is one of the world's leading manufacturers of smartphones. The company's ICT portfolio of end-to-end solutions in telecom, enterprise networks, and consumers are used in more than 170 countries and regions, serving more than one-third of the world's population. Huawei's consumer products include the Huawei brand of mobile smart phones, the Huawei Matebook line of laptops, MatePad line of tablets, the Huawei Watch, the Huawei Band watch (including the TalkBand and Color Band lines), ear buds, speakers, Wi-Fi connection devices and more. The company's business products include switches, routers, WLAN (wireless local area network), servers, storage, cloud computing, network energy services and more. Its carrier products include cloud data centers, wireless network, fixed network, cloud core network, carrier software, IT infrastructure and network energy global services. Huawei Technologies has rolled out 53 NB-IoT city-aware network using a one network/one platform/N-tier applications model. NB-IoT stands for NarrowBand Internet of Things, and is a low-power, wide-area network radio technology standard that enables a wide range of devices and services to be connected using cellular telecommunications bands. Huawei's smart city solutions senses, processes and delivers informed decisions for improving the environment for citizens, with recent information and communications technology (ICT) offering real-time situation reporting and analysis, empowered by a combination of cloud computing, IoT technologies, big data analytics and artificial intelligence (AI). The company has global joint innovation centers and research and development centers and offices. It has invested very heavily in 5G wireless technologies. Huawei Technologies operates as a subsidiary of the Union of Huawei Investment & Holding Co., Ltd.

FINANCIAL DATA: *Note: Data for latest year may not have been available at press time.*

In U.S. $	2020	2019	2018	2017	2016	2015
Revenue						
R&D Expense						
Operating Income						
Operating Margin %						
SGA Expense						
Net Income						
Operating Cash Flow						
Capital Expenditure						
EBITDA						
Return on Assets %						
Return on Equity %						
Debt to Equity						

CONTACT INFORMATION:

Phone: 86-755-28780808   Fax: 86-755-28789251
Toll-Free:
Address: Section H, Bantian, Longgang District, Shenzhen, Guangdong 518129 China

STOCK TICKER/OTHER:

Stock Ticker: Subsidiary   Exchange:
Employees: 200,000   Fiscal Year Ends: 12/31
Parent Company: Union of Huawei Investment & Holding Co Ltd

SALARIES/BONUSES:

Top Exec. Salary: $ Bonus: $
Second Exec. Salary: $ Bonus: $

OTHER THOUGHTS:

Estimated Female Officers or Directors: 3
Hot Spot for Advancement for Women/Minorities: Y

Hutchison Telecommunications Hong Kong Holdings Limited

www.hthkh.com

NAIC Code: 517210

TYPES OF BUSINESS:

Mobile Telecommunication Service Provider
Fixed-Line Operations
Internet Services

BRANDS/DIVISIONS/AFFILIATES:

CK Hutchison Holdings Limited
Hutchison Telephone Company Limited
Hutchison 3G Hong Kong Holdings Limited
Hutchison Telecom Macau
3

CONTACTS: *Note: Officers with more than one job title may be intentionally listed here more than once.*

Wai Sin Cheng, CFO
Edith Shih, Sec.
Kin Ning Fok, Chmn.

GROWTH PLANS/SPECIAL FEATURES:

Hutchison Telecommunications Hong Kong Holdings Limited (HTHKH) is a leading telecommunications operator in Hong Kong and Macau, with a focus on providing mobile services. In Hong Kong, HTHKH provides 5G, 4G LTE (long-term evolution), 3G and GSM (global system for mobile communication) dual-band mobile telecommunications services under the 3 brand. These operations are operated through Hutchison Telephone Company Limited and Hutchison 3G Hong Kong Holdings Limited. Products and services include data-centric services that converge with internet and PC services. Mobile communications services include local voice, mobile messaging (short and multimedia), international direct dialing (IDD) and international roaming, as well as advanced broadband-based data services and applications including direct carrier billing offerings, mobile device security management, eBooks, music downloads, movies-on-demand, mobile social networking applications and stock trading. In Macau, HTHKH provides 4G LTE, 3G and GSM dual-band mobile telecommunications services under the 3 brand through Hutchison Telecom Macau. Products and services include local, IDD, international roaming, wireless internet access, mobile messaging and downloadable infotainment. Through a co-operative commercial relationship, HGC Global Communications Limited is a key supplier of fixed line services to HTHKH. HTHKH is a subsidiary of CK Hutchison Holdings Limited.

FINANCIAL DATA: *Note: Data for latest year may not have been available at press time.*

In U.S. $	2020	2019	2018	2017	2016	2015
Revenue	585,756,200	719,404,100	1,019,693,000	870,192,800	1,549,644,000	2,840,757,000
R&D Expense						
Operating Income	49,747,400	49,876,280	41,112,480	-231,853,800	134,936,600	184,941,800
Operating Margin %		.11%	.06%	- .27%	.09%	.07%
SGA Expense	14,563,360	21,780,600	21,780,600	17,785,340	28,095,680	36,859,470
Net Income	46,525,420	55,289,200	52,067,220	614,238,600	90,344,370	117,924,500
Operating Cash Flow	167,156,400	191,385,700	66,630,580	250,412,400	305,959,400	319,362,800
Capital Expenditure	102,459,000	90,988,760	66,115,060	130,554,700	369,239,100	134,678,800
EBITDA	218,837,000	227,471,900	165,609,800	231,209,400	314,078,800	354,031,400
Return on Assets %		.03%	.02%	.22%	.03%	.04%
Return on Equity %		.03%	.03%	.35%	.06%	.08%
Debt to Equity		0.011			0.386	0.344

CONTACT INFORMATION:

Phone: 852-2128-1188   Fax: 852-2128-1778
Toll-Free:
Address: Fl. 22, Hutchison House, 10 Harcourt Rd., Hong Kong, Hong Kong Hong Kong

STOCK TICKER/OTHER:

Stock Ticker: HTCTF
Employees: 990
Parent Company: CK Hutchison Holdings Limited

Exchange: PINX
Fiscal Year Ends: 12/31

SALARIES/BONUSES:

Top Exec. Salary: $ Bonus: $
Second Exec. Salary: $ Bonus: $

OTHER THOUGHTS:

Estimated Female Officers or Directors: 1
Hot Spot for Advancement for Women/Minorities: Y

iBasis Inc
NAIC Code: 517110

www.ibasis.com

TYPES OF BUSINESS:
International Long Distance Service
Wholesale Voice Services
Prepaid Calling Cards
VoIP Service

BRANDS/DIVISIONS/AFFILIATES:
Tofane Global

CONTACTS: *Note: Officers with more than one job title may be intentionally listed here more than once.*
Alexandre Pebereau, CEO
John Treece, COO
Ardjan Konijnenberg, CFO
Edwin van Ierland, CCO
Ajay Joseph, CTO
Gert-Jan Huizer, Sr. VP-Prod. Mgmt.
Ellen W. Schmidt, General Counsel
Brad Guth, Sr. VP-Oper.
Chris Ward, Sr. Dir.-Corp. Comm.
Edwin van Ierland, Global Sales Officer

GROWTH PLANS/SPECIAL FEATURES:
IBasis, Inc. provides telecommunications services that enable operators and digital players worldwide to perform and transform. The firm offers services such as managed voice, mobile data, Internet of Things (IoT) connectivity, 5G roaming, cloud, eSIM (electronic subscriber identity module) technology, fraud prevention and business intelligence. IBasis has more than 1.5 billion long-term evolution (LTE)-enabled subscribers, over 2,000 fixed and mobile destinations and over 700 LTE destinations, as well as 700+ mobile operator partnerships. The company provides a single point for its customer's local access needs in Asia, the Middle East, Europe, North America and Latin America, as well as select areas within Africa, the Caribbean and French-/Portuguese-speaking markets. The Paris-based telecommunications and digital player specializing in international carrier services firm, Tofane Global, owns iBasis.

iBasis employees are offered health and dental insurance, life insurance and disability coverage.

FINANCIAL DATA: *Note: Data for latest year may not have been available at press time.*

In U.S. $	2020	2019	2018	2017	2016	2015
Revenue	1,050,000,000	1,000,000,000	886,718,700	844,494,000	913,437,000	1,060,000,000
R&D Expense						
Operating Income						
Operating Margin %						
SGA Expense						
Net Income						
Operating Cash Flow						
Capital Expenditure						
EBITDA						
Return on Assets %						
Return on Equity %						
Debt to Equity						

CONTACT INFORMATION:
Phone: 781-430-7500   Fax: 781-505-7300
Toll-Free:
Address: 10 Maguire Rd., Bldg. 3, Lexington, MA 02421 United States

STOCK TICKER/OTHER:
Stock Ticker: Subsidiary   Exchange:
Employees: 300   Fiscal Year Ends: 12/31
Parent Company: Tofane Global

SALARIES/BONUSES:
Top Exec. Salary: $ Bonus: $
Second Exec. Salary: $ Bonus: $

OTHER THOUGHTS:
Estimated Female Officers or Directors: 2
Hot Spot for Advancement for Women/Minorities:

IDT Corporation

NAIC Code: 517110

TYPES OF BUSINESS:

Local & Long-Distance Service
Telecommunication Services
Payment Services

BRANDS/DIVISIONS/AFFILIATES:

IDT Carrier Services
BOSS Revolution
net2phone
National Retail Solutions

CONTACTS: Note: Officers with more than one job title may be intentionally listed here more than once.

Samuel Jonas, CEO
Bill Pereira, CEO, Subsidiary
Marcelo Fischer, CFO
Howard Jonas, Chairman of the Board
Mitch Silberman, Chief Accounting Officer
Menachem Ash, Executive VP, Divisional
Joyce Mason, Executive VP
Anthony Davidson, Senior VP, Divisional

GROWTH PLANS/SPECIAL FEATURES:

IDT Corporation is a worldwide holding company with operations in the telecommunications and payment industries. IDT leverages its expertise to provide consumers and businesses with innovative communications and payments services through its four flagship brands IDT, BOSS Revolution, net2phone and National Retail Solutions. IDT Carrier Services is a leading carrier of international voice calls and strategic outsource partnerships with fixed and mobile operators. BOSS Revolution unites families via telecommunications and payment services. net2phone provides businesses with unified communications, SIP trunking and other communications solutions. National Retail Solutions provides point-of-sale terminal-based services, including advertising, data analytics and payment processing. Headquartered in the U.S., IDT Corporation has international locations in Argentina, Belarus, Brazil, Canada, Colombia, Finland, Guatemala, Hong Kong, Mexico, Spain and the U.K.

IDT offers its employee health, medical, dental, life and disability coverage; flexible spending accounts; tuition reimbursement; and 401(k).

FINANCIAL DATA: Note: Data for latest year may not have been available at press time.

In U.S. $	2020	2019	2018	2017	2016	2015
Revenue	1,345,769,000	1,409,172,000	1,547,495,000	1,501,729,000	1,496,261,000	1,596,777,000
R&D Expense						1,656,000
Operating Income	22,020,000	433,000	13,008,000	5,612,000	24,151,000	24,549,000
Operating Margin %		.00%	.01%	.00%	.02%	.02%
SGA Expense	215,877,000	204,366,000	203,251,000	188,293,000	204,655,000	222,239,000
Net Income	21,430,000	134,000	4,208,000	8,177,000	23,514,000	84,490,000
Operating Cash Flow	-29,591,000	85,137,000	6,894,000	19,014,000	49,054,000	30,534,000
Capital Expenditure	16,041,000	18,681,000	20,567,000	22,949,000	18,370,000	28,556,000
EBITDA	42,426,000	23,065,000	35,809,000	27,316,000	44,686,000	42,967,000
Return on Assets %		.00%	.01%	.02%	.05%	.17%
Return on Equity %		.00%	.05%	.06%	.18%	.72%
Debt to Equity						

CONTACT INFORMATION:

Phone: 973 438-1000   Fax:
Toll-Free:
Address: 520 Broad St., Newark, NJ 07102 United States

STOCK TICKER/OTHER:

Stock Ticker: IDT   Exchange: NYS
Employees: 1,256   Fiscal Year Ends: 07/31
Parent Company:

SALARIES/BONUSES:

Top Exec. Salary: $ Bonus: $
Second Exec. Salary: $ Bonus: $

OTHER THOUGHTS:

Estimated Female Officers or Directors: 1
Hot Spot for Advancement for Women/Minorities:

Iliad SA
NAIC Code: 517110

TYPES OF BUSINESS:
Fixed-Line Telecommunications & Broadband Internet
Broadband Services
Telephony Services

BRANDS/DIVISIONS/AFFILIATES:
Free
Freebox
Free Mobile Plan
Iliad
Scaleway
Jaguar Network
Free Pro

CONTACTS: *Note: Officers with more than one job title may be intentionally listed here more than once.*
Thomas Reynaud, CEO
Nicolas Jaeger, CFO
Camille Perrin, CMO
Celine Polo, Chief Human Resources Officer
Xavier Niel, Chief Strategy Officer
Angelique Berge, Dir.-Client Support
Thomas Reynaud, Head-Bus. Dev.
Xavier Niel, Deputy Chmn.
Xavier Niel, Chmn.
Patrick Fouqueriere, Dir.-Supplier Rel.

GROWTH PLANS/SPECIAL FEATURES:
Iliad SA is a French holding company active in the integrated telecommunications sector. The firm's Free subsidiary developed the Freebox, a multiservice box on asymmetric digital subscriber line (ADSL). Other services by Free include voice on internet protocol (VoIP), internet protocol television (IPTV), flat-rate calling plans and more. Free offers mobile phone usage within France's reach with straightforward, no-commitment contracts at affordable prices. The Free Mobile Plan includes roaming communications all year round from more than 35 countries, and includes unlimited calls, texts and multimedia messaging service (MMS). Free also includes unlimited 4G in a premium plan for Freebox subscribers. Free Pro offers business-to-business (B2B) fiber internet, automatic 4G backup, Wi-Fi, phone usage and data protection. As of mid-2021, Free had approximately 20 million subscribers in France, consisting of broadband, ultra-fast broadband and mobile subscribers. Iliad's mobile network in Italy operates under the Iliad brand and had over 6.8 million subscribers (mid-2021). Scaleway is a business-to-business (B2B) brand and subsidiary of Iliad that supplies a range of cloud infrastructure services for public and private business customers in over 150 countries. Scaleway relies on seven data centers located in France and one in the Netherlands. Jaguar Network offers managed hosting services in the cloud, offering business-to-business (B2B) support. During 2021, Iliad began to roll out 5G services under the Free brand, and launched its B2B Free Pro service.

FINANCIAL DATA: *Note: Data for latest year may not have been available at press time.*

In U.S. $	2020	2019	2018	2017	2016	2015
Revenue	7,173,052,000	6,514,514,000	5,975,711,000	6,093,575,000	5,769,306,000	5,393,440,000
R&D Expense						
Operating Income	676,864,400	263,903,800	854,022,100	1,105,966,000	934,972,200	901,137,500
Operating Margin %		.04%	.14%	.18%	.16%	.17%
SGA Expense	799,042,100	642,654,700	707,408,800	509,675,300	417,934,500	352,482,700
Net Income	521,698,800	2,100,235,000	394,634,000	486,112,100	490,029,100	409,186,600
Operating Cash Flow	2,571,841,000	2,125,892,000	1,732,480,000	1,648,470,000	1,698,392,000	1,490,178,000
Capital Expenditure	2,464,324,000	2,740,446,000	2,989,688,000	2,526,403,000	2,171,431,000	1,509,200,000
EBITDA	3,573,698,000	5,023,947,000	2,116,118,000	2,166,104,000	2,041,406,000	1,815,779,000
Return on Assets %		.12%	.03%	.05%	.05%	.05%
Return on Equity %		.39%	.09%	.13%	.14%	.14%
Debt to Equity		1.112	0.945	0.645	0.464	0.366

CONTACT INFORMATION:
Phone: 33 173502000   Fax:
Toll-Free:
Address: 8 Rue de la Ville l'Eveque, Paris, 75008 France

STOCK TICKER/OTHER:
Stock Ticker: ILIAF   Exchange: PINX
Employees: 10,076   Fiscal Year Ends: 12/31
Parent Company:

SALARIES/BONUSES:
Top Exec. Salary: $ Bonus: $
Second Exec. Salary: $ Bonus: $

OTHER THOUGHTS:
Estimated Female Officers or Directors: 4
Hot Spot for Advancement for Women/Minorities: Y

Indosat Ooredoo

indosatooredoo.com

NAIC Code: 517210

TYPES OF BUSINESS:

Mobile Telephone Service
Fixed Wireless Services
Local & Long-Distance Services
Corporate Network Services
IT Services
Internet Services
Satellite Services

BRANDS/DIVISIONS/AFFILIATES:

Ooredoo QPSC
IM3 Ooredoo

CONTACTS: *Note: Officers with more than one job title may be intentionally listed here more than once.*

Ahmad Al-Neama, CEO
Vikram Sinha, COO
Eyas Naif Assaf, CFO
Ritesh Kumar Singh, CCO
Irsyad Sahroni, Chief Human Resources Officer
Medhat ElHusseiny, CTO
Fadzri Santosa, Chief Wholesale & Infrastructure Officer

GROWTH PLANS/SPECIAL FEATURES:

Indosat Ooredoo is a fully integrated Indonesian digital telecommunications network and service provider. The firm is a leading cellular operators and provider of international long-distance services in the country. Indosat offers 4G Plus network coverage via pre-paid and post-paid plans. Other products by the company include text messaging, data rollover services, payment services, international coverage, international roaming covering, security services, and an array of entertainment content such as music, movies, games, sports, religion, information, kids, education and ecommerce. Indosat Ooredoo is also referred to as IM3 Ooredoo. It is a subsidiary of Ooredoo QPSC. In mid-2021, Indosat Ooredo began to roll out its 5G service, which first launched in the city of Solo to accelerate economic recovery and to help businesses and smart city goals. The company announced plans to extend the commercial roll-out of 5G services to other major cities in Indonesia, including Jakarta, Surabaya and Makassar.

FINANCIAL DATA: *Note: Data for latest year may not have been available at press time.*

In U.S. $	2020	2019	2018	2017	2016	2015
Revenue	1,856,190,000	1,767,420,928	1,565,895,552	2,015,401,984	1,970,258,432	1,889,765,248
R&D Expense						
Operating Income						
Operating Margin %						
SGA Expense						
Net Income	115,872,000	106,176,472	-162,604,768	76,490,408	74,601,552	-92,481,536
Operating Cash Flow						
Capital Expenditure						
EBITDA						
Return on Assets %						
Return on Equity %						
Debt to Equity						

CONTACT INFORMATION:

Phone: 62 213802615   Fax: 62 213458155
Toll-Free:
Address: Indosat Bldg., Jalan Medan Merdeka Barat, 21, Jakarta, IO 10110 Indonesia

STOCK TICKER/OTHER:

Stock Ticker: ISAT
Employees: 3,104
Parent Company: Ooredoo QPSC

Exchange: Jakarta
Fiscal Year Ends: 12/31

SALARIES/BONUSES:

Top Exec. Salary: $ Bonus: $
Second Exec. Salary: $ Bonus: $

OTHER THOUGHTS:

Estimated Female Officers or Directors:
Hot Spot for Advancement for Women/Minorities:

Infinera Corporation

www.infinera.com

NAIC Code: 334413

TYPES OF BUSINESS:

Optical-Electronic Conversion Equipment
Optical Network Infrastructure Equipment
Network Design & Engineering

BRANDS/DIVISIONS/AFFILIATES:

CONTACTS: *Note: Officers with more than one job title may be intentionally listed here more than once.*

Thomas Fallon, CEO
Brad Feller, CFO
Kambiz Hooshmand, Chairman of the Board
David Welch, Co-Founder
David Heard, COO
James Laufman, General Counsel
Robert Jandro, Senior VP, Divisional

GROWTH PLANS/SPECIAL FEATURES:

Infinera Corporation is a global supplier of networking solutions comprised of networking equipment, software and services. The firm's solutions include optical transport platforms, converged packet-optical transport platforms, optical line systems, disaggregated router platforms, a suite of networking and automation software offerings and support and professional services. Infinera customers include telecommunications service providers, internet content providers, cable providers, wholesale carriers, research and education institutions, large enterprises and government entities. The company's networking solutions enable customers to deliver business and consumer communications services, and enables them to scale their transport networks as end-user services. These end-user services and applications include, but are not limited to, high-speed internet access, business Ethernet, 4G/5G mobile broadband, cloud-based services, high-definition video streaming services, virtual and augmented reality (VR/AR) and the Internet of Things (IoT). Infinera's products are designed to be managed by a suite of software solutions that enable end-to-end common network management, multi-layer service orchestration and automated operations.

Infinera offers its employees medical, dental, vision and life insurance, stock options and more.

FINANCIAL DATA: *Note: Data for latest year may not have been available at press time.*

In U.S. $	2020	2019	2018	2017	2016	2015
Revenue	1,355,596,000	1,298,865,000	943,379,000	740,739,000	870,135,000	886,714,000
R&D Expense	265,634,000	287,977,000	244,302,000	224,299,000	232,291,000	180,703,000
Operating Income	-117,480,000	-267,946,000	-157,637,000	-166,981,000	-25,774,000	59,736,000
Operating Margin %		-.21%	-.17%	-.23%	-.03%	.07%
SGA Expense	241,844,000	277,774,000	205,195,000	186,682,000	187,201,000	163,038,000
Net Income	-206,723,000	-386,618,000	-214,295,000	-194,506,000	-23,927,000	51,413,000
Operating Cash Flow	-112,300,000	-167,350,000	-99,083,000	-21,925,000	38,377,000	133,176,000
Capital Expenditure	39,009,000	30,202,000	37,692,000	58,041,000	43,335,000	42,018,000
EBITDA	-53,820,000	-232,174,000	-92,407,000	-115,922,000	44,380,000	98,979,000
Return on Assets %		-.23%	-.15%	-.17%	-.02%	.05%
Return on Equity %		-.71%	-.31%	-.27%	-.03%	.08%
Debt to Equity		1.01	0.654		0.175	0.165

CONTACT INFORMATION:

Phone: 408 572-5200   Fax: 408 572-5343
Toll-Free:
Address: 6373 San Ignacio Ave., San Jose, CA 95119 United States

STOCK TICKER/OTHER:

Stock Ticker: INFN   Exchange: NAS
Employees: 3,261   Fiscal Year Ends: 12/31
Parent Company:

SALARIES/BONUSES:

Top Exec. Salary: $ Bonus: $
Second Exec. Salary: $ Bonus: $

OTHER THOUGHTS:

Estimated Female Officers or Directors: 1
Hot Spot for Advancement for Women/Minorities:

Ingram Micro Mobility

corp.ingrammicro.com/mobility

NAIC Code: 423430

TYPES OF BUSINESS:

Cell Phone Distribution
Outsourced Logistics & Management Services
Customized Logistics

BRANDS/DIVISIONS/AFFILIATES:

Platinum Equity
Ingram Micro Inc
Shipwire
BlueIQ

CONTACTS: Note: Officers with more than one job title may be intentionally listed here more than once.

Alain Monie, CEO-Ingram Micro Corporate
Craig M. Carpenter, General Counsel
Bashar Nejdawi, Pres., North American Mobility
R. Bruce Thomlinson, Pres., Asia Pacific Mobility
Jac Currie, Pres., Europe Mobility

GROWTH PLANS/SPECIAL FEATURES:

Ingram Micro Mobility (IMM), a subsidiary of Ingram Micro, Inc., provides logistics, commerce enablement and device lifecycle services. IMM's services address the full commerce lifecycle of any product. Services include marketplace connectivity, order management, fulfillment, transportation management, reverse logistics, repair, recycling and resale. Combined with an open technology platform and global infrastructure, IMM helps customers to deliver on their brand promises. The company's technologies encompass: Shipwire, is an order management platform designed to connect supply to demand, and provides connectivity, global fulfillment and hundreds of integrations to shopping carts, retailers, marketplaces, small parcel carriers and more; BlueIQ, a global IT asset tracking and control system that drives internal processes and ensures compliance and detailed reporting for every asset touched, from receipt through disposition; and warehouse management systems, which are multiple systems to serve customers' global needs, from end-to-end serialization to apparel size, color and style. Ingram Micro, Inc. itself is owned by private equity company Platinum Equity.

FINANCIAL DATA: Note: Data for latest year may not have been available at press time.

In U.S. $	2020	2019	2018	2017	2016	2015
Revenue	49,100,000,000	47,196,948,000	50,436,670,000	46,674,792,000	41,928,799,000	43,025,852,000
R&D Expense						
Operating Income						
Operating Margin %						
SGA Expense						
Net Income	644,219,000	505,139,000	352,186,000	198,958,000	100,426,000	215,105,000
Operating Cash Flow						
Capital Expenditure						
EBITDA						
Return on Assets %						
Return on Equity %						
Debt to Equity						

CONTACT INFORMATION:

Phone: 44-1784-227000   Fax:
Toll-Free:
Address: Two Pines Trees, Chertsey Ln., Surrey, TW18 3HR United Kingdom

STOCK TICKER/OTHER:

Stock Ticker: Private
Employees: 33,000
Parent Company: Platinum Equity

Exchange:
Fiscal Year Ends: 12/31

SALARIES/BONUSES:

Top Exec. Salary: $ Bonus: $
Second Exec. Salary: $ Bonus: $

OTHER THOUGHTS:

Estimated Female Officers or Directors:
Hot Spot for Advancement for Women/Minorities: Y

Inmarsat Global Limited

NAIC Code: 517410

www.inmarsat.com

TYPES OF BUSINESS:

Satellite Carrier & Equipment
Mobile Satellite Communications
Broadband
Satellite Launch Operations
Remote Connectivity
Satellites
Internet of Things

BRANDS/DIVISIONS/AFFILIATES:

Connect Bidco Limited
Global Xpress
European Aviation Network

CONTACTS: Note: Officers with more than one job title may be intentionally listed here more than once.

Rajeev Suri, CEO
Jason Smith, COO
Tony Bates, CFO
Barry French, CMO
Natasha Dillon, Chief People Officer
Peter Hadinger, CTO
Richard Denny, Sr. VP-Eng. & Global Networks
Alison Horrocks, Corp. Sec.
Diane Cornell, VP-Govt Affairs

GROWTH PLANS/SPECIAL FEATURES:

Inmarsat Global Limited is a world-leading provider of global mobile satellite communications. The firm's broadband global area network (BGAN) offers seamless global coverage, and satellite and ground network availability 99.9% of the time. Through its L-band services, Inmarsat connects people and machines in remote locations (on ships and in airplanes), enabling the global Internet of Things (IoT), voice calls and internet access. L-band service capabilities span email and web browsing to high bandwidth applications such as live streaming and telemedicine. The company's Global Xpress (GX) is a mobile high-speed broadband network from a single provider. Its Ka-band service offers content-rich applications from certified developers. Inmarsat's European Aviation Network (EAN) is an integrated satellite and air-to-ground connectivity network, developed to meet the particular requirements of European skies. The EAN combines S-band satellite coverage with a long-term evolution (LTE)-based terrestrial network to deliver cost-effective, scalable capacity across all 28 member states of the European Union, as well as Switzerland and Norway. Developed in partnership with Deutsche Telekom, EAN gives European aviation cutting-edge inflight connectivity. Inmarsat's sixth generation (I-6) of satellites will feature dual-payload satellites, each supporting L-band and Ka-band services. The I-6 satellites will support advanced global safety services, very low cost mobile services and Internet of Things (IoT) applications. The Ka-band payload will further extend GX capacity in regions of greatest demand. Inmarsat has locations across every continent, offering 24/7/365 customer support. In Inmarsat is a private company owned by Connect Bidco Limited, a consortium consisting of Apax Partners, Warburg Pincus, the CPP Investment Board and the Ontario Teachers' Pension Plan.

FINANCIAL DATA: Note: Data for latest year may not have been available at press time.

In U.S. $	2020	2019	2018	2017	2016	2015
Revenue	1,444,480,000	1,480,000,000	1,465,200,000	1,400,199,936	1,328,999,936	1,274,099,968
R&D Expense						
Operating Income						
Operating Margin %						
SGA Expense						
Net Income		130,410,000	124,200,000	181,700,000	242,800,000	281,400,000
Operating Cash Flow						
Capital Expenditure						
EBITDA						
Return on Assets %						
Return on Equity %						
Debt to Equity						

CONTACT INFORMATION:

Phone: 44 2077281000   Fax: 44 2077281044
Toll-Free:
Address: 99 City Rd., London, EC1Y 1AX United Kingdom

STOCK TICKER/OTHER:

Stock Ticker: Private
Employees: 1,842
Parent Company: Connect Bidco Limited

Exchange:
Fiscal Year Ends: 12/31

SALARIES/BONUSES:

Top Exec. Salary: $ Bonus: $
Second Exec. Salary: $ Bonus: $

OTHER THOUGHTS:

Estimated Female Officers or Directors: 3
Hot Spot for Advancement for Women/Minorities: Y

Intel Corporation

NAIC Code: 334413

www.intel.com

TYPES OF BUSINESS:

Microprocessors
Semiconductors
Circuit Boards
Flash Memory Products
Software Development
Home Network Equipment
Digital Imaging Products
Healthcare Products

BRANDS/DIVISIONS/AFFILIATES:

Intel Neural Compute Stick 2
Moovit

CONTACTS: Note: Officers with more than one job title may be intentionally listed here more than once.

Robert Swan, CEO
George Davis, CFO
Andy Bryant, Chairman of the Board
Kevin McBride, Chief Accounting Officer
Steven Rodgers, Executive VP
Navin Shenoy, Executive VP
Venkata Renduchintala, Executive VP
Todd Underwood, Other Corporate Officer

GROWTH PLANS/SPECIAL FEATURES:

Intel Corporation designs and manufactures products and technologies that power the cloud and smart connectivity. The company produces computer, networking and communications platforms to a broad set of customers, including original equipment manufacturers (OEMs), original design manufacturers (ODMs), cloud and communications service providers, as well as industrial, communications and automotive equipment manufacturers. Intel's business across the cloud and data center are focused on memory and field-programmable gate array technologies. Its devices include everything smart: personal computers (PCs), sensors, consoles and other edge devices that are connected to the cloud. Memory and programmable solutions make possible new classes of products for the data center and Internet of Things (IoT). Its Intel Neural Compute Stick 2 (Intel NCS 2) is designed to build smarter artificial intelligence (AI) algorithms and for prototyping computer vision at the network edge. Intel is a leader in silicon manufacturing process technology, of which its products are manufactured in the company's own facilities. Its intellectual property can be shared across its platforms and operating segments, providing cost reduction and seamless production capabilities. Intel also offers software and services for consumer and corporate environments, as well as for assisting software developers in creating software applications via Intel platforms. Its client computing product group includes platforms for notebooks, 2-in-1 systems, desktops, tablets, phones, wired/wireless connectivity products and mobile communications components. The firm's non-volatile memory solutions (NAND) flash memory products are primarily used in solid-state drives. In May 2020, Intel acquired Moovit, a mobility-as-a-service solutions company, for approximately $900 million. In October of the same year, the firm announced that it will acquire SigOpt, a provider of a platform for the optimization of AI software models at scale.

FINANCIAL DATA: Note: Data for latest year may not have been available at press time.

In U.S. $	2020	2019	2018	2017	2016	2015
Revenue	77,867,000,000	71,965,000,000	70,848,000,000	62,761,000,000	59,387,000,000	55,355,000,000
R&D Expense	13,556,000,000	13,362,000,000	13,543,000,000	13,098,000,000	12,740,000,000	12,128,000,000
Operating Income	23,876,000,000	22,428,000,000	23,244,000,000	18,320,000,000	14,760,000,000	14,356,000,000
Operating Margin %		.31%	.33%	.29%	.25%	.26%
SGA Expense	6,180,000,000	6,150,000,000	6,750,000,000	7,474,000,000	8,397,000,000	7,930,000,000
Net Income	20,899,000,000	21,048,000,000	21,053,000,000	9,601,000,000	10,316,000,000	11,420,000,000
Operating Cash Flow	35,384,000,000	33,145,000,000	29,432,000,000	22,110,000,000	21,808,000,000	19,017,000,000
Capital Expenditure	14,453,000,000	16,213,000,000	15,181,000,000	11,778,000,000	9,625,000,000	7,446,000,000
EBITDA	37,946,000,000	35,373,000,000	32,870,000,000	29,127,000,000	21,459,000,000	23,260,000,000
Return on Assets %		.16%	.17%	.08%	.10%	.12%
Return on Equity %		.28%	.29%	.14%	.16%	.19%
Debt to Equity		0.326	0.335	0.358	0.308	0.323

CONTACT INFORMATION:

Phone: 408 765-8080   Fax: 408 765-2633
Toll-Free: 800-628-8686
Address: 2200 Mission College Blvd., Santa Clara, CA 95054 United States

STOCK TICKER/OTHER:

Stock Ticker: INTC
Employees: 110,600
Parent Company:

Exchange: NAS
Fiscal Year Ends: 12/31

SALARIES/BONUSES:

Top Exec. Salary: $ Bonus: $
Second Exec. Salary: $ Bonus: $

OTHER THOUGHTS:

Estimated Female Officers or Directors: 10
Hot Spot for Advancement for Women/Minorities: Y

Intelsat SA

NAIC Code: 517410

TYPES OF BUSINESS:

Satellite Carrier
Global Network
Broadband
Satellites
Terrestrial Infrastructure
Video Broadcasting
Mobility
Communications

BRANDS/DIVISIONS/AFFILIATES:

Intelsat General Communications LLC
IntelsatOne

CONTACTS: Note: Officers with more than one job title may be intentionally listed here more than once.

Stephen Spengler, CEO
David Tolley, CFO
Samer Halawi, CCO
Bruno Fromont, CTO
Michelle Bryan, Chief Admin. Officer
Michelle Bryan, General Counsel
David McGlade, Chmn.

GROWTH PLANS/SPECIAL FEATURES:

Intelsat SA operates a globalized network that delivers high-quality video and broadband services worldwide. The network combines satellites with terrestrial infrastructure, managed services and an open, interoperable architecture to enable its customers to offer next-generation network services. Intelsat provides broadband connectivity, multi-format video broadcasting, secure satellite communications and seamless mobility services. All of these capabilities are combined into a single ecosystem, including Intelsat's fleet of satellites plus teleports, next-gen satellite technology, the IntesalOne terrestrial network, managed services that simplify satellite-based communications, and strategic partnership to support a wide range of market segments. Intelsat's network solutions are designed for enterprise networks, internet service providers and mobile network operators. Its media services include distribution, contribution and disaster recovery. Its mobility services include aviation and maritime. Solutions and services are also provided for global governments. Wholly-owned Intelsat General Communications, LLC operates the group's globalized network, providing government and commercial customers with communications solutions via Intelsat's satellite backbone and terrestrial infrastructure. After filing a proposed plan of reorganization in its Chapter 11 proceedings in May 2020, Intelsat announced in February 2021 that it filed a plan of reorganization with the support of key creditor groups, which would enable the company to reduce its debt from nearly $15 billion to $7 billion.

FINANCIAL DATA: Note: Data for latest year may not have been available at press time.

In U.S. $	2020	2019	2018	2017	2016	2015
Revenue		2,061,464,960	2,161,189,888	2,148,612,096	2,188,047,104	2,352,520,960
R&D Expense						
Operating Income						
Operating Margin %						
SGA Expense						
Net Income		-913,595,008	-599,604,992	-178,728,000	990,196,992	-3,923,386,880
Operating Cash Flow						
Capital Expenditure						
EBITDA						
Return on Assets %						
Return on Equity %						
Debt to Equity						

CONTACT INFORMATION:

Phone: 352-27-84-1600   Fax: 352-27-84-1690
Toll-Free:
Address: 4 rue Albert Borschette, Luxembourg, 1246 Luxembourg

STOCK TICKER/OTHER:

Stock Ticker: I   Exchange: NYS
Employees: 1,195   Fiscal Year Ends: 12/31
Parent Company:

SALARIES/BONUSES:

Top Exec. Salary: $ Bonus: $
Second Exec. Salary: $ Bonus: $

OTHER THOUGHTS:

Estimated Female Officers or Directors: 1
Hot Spot for Advancement for Women/Minorities:

InterDigital Inc

NAIC Code: 334220

www.interdigital.com

TYPES OF BUSINESS:

Technologies Engineering for Wireless Communications
Research and Development
Connected Technologies
Communications
Wireless
Video Coding
Artificial Intelligence

BRANDS/DIVISIONS/AFFILIATES:

GROWTH PLANS/SPECIAL FEATURES:

InterDigital, Inc. is a research and development company that licenses its innovations to the global wireless and consumer electronics industries. The firm designs and develops advanced technologies that enable connected, immersive experiences in a broad range of communications and entertainment products and services. Since its founding in 1972, InterDigital has designed and developed a wide range of innovations. As of December 31, 2020, the company's wholly-owned subsidiaries held a portfolio of approximately 28,000 patents and patent applications related wireless communications, video coding, display technology and other areas relevant to the wireless and consumer electronics industries. As a leader in video processing, encoding/decoding and display technology, InterDigital's artificial intelligence (AI) research effort intersects with both wireless and visual technologies.

CONTACTS: Note: Officers with more than one job title may be intentionally listed here more than once.

William Merritt, CEO
Richard Brezski, CFO
S. Hutcheson, Chairman of the Board
Jannie Lau, Chief Legal Officer
Kai Oistamo, COO

FINANCIAL DATA: Note: Data for latest year may not have been available at press time.

In U.S. $	2020	2019	2018	2017	2016	2015
Revenue	358,991,000	318,924,000	307,404,000	532,938,000	665,854,000	441,435,000
R&D Expense	84,646,000	74,860,000	69,698,000	70,708,000	68,733,000	72,702,000
Operating Income	55,168,000	37,835,000	62,595,000	301,495,000	437,306,000	208,549,000
Operating Margin %		.12%	.20%	.57%	.66%	.47%
SGA Expense	48,999,000	51,289,000	51,030,000	49,578,000	46,271,000	39,783,000
Net Income	44,801,000	20,928,000	63,868,000	174,293,000	309,001,000	119,225,000
Operating Cash Flow	163,467,000	89,433,000	146,792,000	315,800,000	430,778,000	114,499,000
Capital Expenditure	42,408,000	37,990,000	36,895,000	37,004,000	43,440,000	53,466,000
EBITDA	153,133,000	143,991,000	134,122,000	367,288,000	496,150,000	259,225,000
Return on Assets %		.01%	.04%	.10%	.19%	.09%
Return on Equity %		.02%	.07%	.22%	.49%	.24%
Debt to Equity		0.46	0.342	0.333	0.368	0.508

CONTACT INFORMATION:

Phone: 302 281-3600   Fax: 302 281-3763
Toll-Free:
Address: 200 Bellevue Pkwy., Ste. 300, Wilmington, DE 19809 United States

STOCK TICKER/OTHER:

Stock Ticker: IDCC
Employees: 487
Parent Company:

Exchange: NAS
Fiscal Year Ends: 12/31

SALARIES/BONUSES:

Top Exec. Salary: $ Bonus: $
Second Exec. Salary: $ Bonus: $

OTHER THOUGHTS:

Estimated Female Officers or Directors: 1
Hot Spot for Advancement for Women/Minorities:

Internap Corporation

NAIC Code: 517110

www.internap.com

TYPES OF BUSINESS:

Internet Access Provider
Hybrid Infrastructure Solutions
Multi-platform Cloud Solutions
Data Centers
Intelligent Managed Services
Network Solutions

BRANDS/DIVISIONS/AFFILIATES:

INAP

GROWTH PLANS/SPECIAL FEATURES:

Internap Corporation, branded as INAP, is a global provider of performance-driven, secure hybrid infrastructure solutions. INAP's suite of multi-platform cloud, modern data center, optimized network and intelligent managed services solutions help businesses flexibly move workloads, and thus reducing risk and maximizing value. Cloud solutions include bare metal and multi-cloud, as well as cloud backup for data protection. Network solutions include performance internet protocol (IP) and connectivity solutions. Managed services include intelligent monitoring, managed security, managed storage and managed backups. INAP's data centers are located throughout North America, as well as in Amsterdam, Frankfurt, London, Hong Kong, Singapore, Sydney and Tokyo/Osaka.

CONTACTS: *Note: Officers with more than one job title may be intentionally listed here more than once.*

Michael T. Sicoli, CEO
Mike Higgins, Sr. VP-Oper.
Lisa Mayr, CFO
Warren Greenberg, Sr. VP-Sales
Jackie Coats, Sr. VP-Human Resources
Jennifer Curry, Sr. VP-Product & Technology
Richard Diegnan, Executive VP
Richard Ramlall, Other Executive Officer
Joseph DuFresne, Vice President, Divisional

FINANCIAL DATA: *Note: Data for latest year may not have been available at press time.*

In U.S. $	2020	2019	2018	2017	2016	2015
Revenue	284,700,000	292,000,000	317,372,992	280,718,016	298,296,992	318,292,992
R&D Expense						
Operating Income						
Operating Margin %						
SGA Expense						
Net Income		-138,000,000	-62,500,000	-45,343,000	-124,742,000	-48,443,000
Operating Cash Flow						
Capital Expenditure						
EBITDA						
Return on Assets %						
Return on Equity %						
Debt to Equity						

CONTACT INFORMATION:

Phone: 404 302-9700   Fax: 404 475-0520
Toll-Free: 877-843-7627
Address: 12120 Sunset Hills Rd., Ste. 330, Renton, VA 20190 United States

STOCK TICKER/OTHER:

Stock Ticker: Private   Exchange:
Employees: 530   Fiscal Year Ends: 12/31
Parent Company:

SALARIES/BONUSES:

Top Exec. Salary: $ Bonus: $
Second Exec. Salary: $ Bonus: $

OTHER THOUGHTS:

Estimated Female Officers or Directors: 4
Hot Spot for Advancement for Women/Minorities: Y

International Business Machines Corporation (IBM)

www.ibm.com
NAIC Code: 541513

TYPES OF BUSINESS:

Computer Facilities and Business Process Outsourcing
Supercomputing
Business & Management Consulting
Software & Hardware
Cloud-Based Computer Services
IT Consulting & Outsourcing
Financial Services
Data Analytics and Health Care Analytics

BRANDS/DIVISIONS/AFFILIATES:

Watson

CONTACTS: *Note: Officers with more than one job title may be intentionally listed here more than once.*

Virginia Rometty, CEO
James Kavanaugh, CFO
Robert Del Bene, Chief Accounting Officer
John Kelly, Executive VP
Diane Gherson, Other Executive Officer
Martin Schroeter, Senior VP, Divisional
Kenneth Keverian, Senior VP, Divisional
Erich Clementi, Senior VP, Divisional
Michelle Browdy, Senior VP, Divisional

GROWTH PLANS/SPECIAL FEATURES:

International Business Machines Corporation (IBM) is a global leader in computer facilities management services, business process outsourcing, supercomputing services and advanced computer hardware and software. It is one of the largest technology consulting and services businesses in the world. IBM operates in primary segments that include: cognitive solutions (data analytics, health care analytics, supercomputing, artificial intelligence and machine learning), global business services (offering application management, consulting and business process management), technology services & cloud platforms (including technical support, infrastructure services, integration software and the operation of one of the world's most advanced cloud services systems), systems (including IBM's proprietary hardware and software), global financing, and IBM worldwide organizations. The systems units provide IBM's clients with infrastructure technologies to help meet the requirements of hybrid cloud and workloads. The global financing provides loans and leases for that assist in the marketing of IBM computer systems. For future growth, the firm has developed world-class capabilities in supercomputing (including its Watson computer), artificial intelligence (AI), machine learning and data analytics, particularly the analysis of massive amounts of health care data and patient outcomes information. In late 2020, the company announced that it will spin-off the Managed Infrastructure Services unit of its Global Technology Services unit as a free-standing company, probably by the end of 2021. This will help IBM to refocus on its rapidly growing cloud services offerings for the future.

IBM offers employees medical, vision, dental and disability insurance; a flexible spending account; and 401(k) and stock purchase options.

FINANCIAL DATA: *Note: Data for latest year may not have been available at press time.*

In U.S. $	2020	2019	2018	2017	2016	2015
Revenue	73,621,000,000	77,147,000,000	79,590,000,000	79,139,000,000	79,920,000,000	81,742,000,000
R&D Expense	6,333,000,000	5,989,000,000	5,379,000,000	5,787,000,000	5,751,000,000	5,247,000,000
Operating Income	6,895,000,000	10,631,000,000	13,285,000,000	11,855,000,000	13,192,000,000	15,921,000,000
Operating Margin %		.14%	.17%	.15%	.17%	.19%
SGA Expense	21,850,000,000	19,754,000,000	18,863,000,000	19,555,000,000	20,479,000,000	19,894,000,000
Net Income	5,590,000,000	9,431,000,000	8,728,001,000	5,753,000,000	11,872,000,000	13,190,000,000
Operating Cash Flow	18,197,000,000	14,770,000,000	15,247,000,000	16,724,000,000	16,958,000,000	17,008,000,000
Capital Expenditure	3,230,000,000	2,907,000,000	3,964,000,000	3,773,000,000	4,150,000,000	4,151,000,000
EBITDA	12,620,000,000	17,569,000,000	16,545,000,000	16,556,000,000	17,341,000,000	20,268,000,000
Return on Assets %		.07%	.07%	.05%	.10%	.12%
Return on Equity %		.50%	.51%	.32%	.73%	1.01%
Debt to Equity		2.782	2.12	2.264	1.899	2.344

CONTACT INFORMATION:

Phone: 914-499-1900   Fax: 800-314-1092
Toll-Free: 800-426-4968
Address: 1 New Orchard Rd., Armonk, NY 10504-1722 United States

STOCK TICKER/OTHER:

Stock Ticker: IBM
Employees: 365,000
Parent Company:

Exchange: NYS
Fiscal Year Ends: 12/31

SALARIES/BONUSES:

Top Exec. Salary: $ Bonus: $
Second Exec. Salary: $ Bonus: $

OTHER THOUGHTS:

Estimated Female Officers or Directors: 6
Hot Spot for Advancement for Women/Minorities: Y

Internet Initiative Japan Inc

NAIC Code: 517110

www.iij.ad.jp

TYPES OF BUSINESS:

Internet Service Provider
Internet Access
Wide Area Network
Systems Integration
Outsourcing Services

BRANDS/DIVISIONS/AFFILIATES:

Trust Networks Inc
PTC Systems Pte Ltd

CONTACTS: *Note: Officers with more than one job title may be intentionally listed here more than once.*

Koichi Suzuki, CEO
Eijiro Katsu, Pres.
Kazuhiro Tokita, Sr. Exec. Officer
Masayoshi Tobita, Exec. Managing Officer
Junichi Shimagami, Exec. Managing Officer
Kiyoshi Ishida, Exec. Managing Officer

GROWTH PLANS/SPECIAL FEATURES:

Internet Initiative Japan, Inc. (IIJ) provides internet access and services to consumers, corporations and other internet service providers primarily throughout Japan, focusing on premium services for high-end corporate customers. The firm offers customers internet connectivity, wide area network (WAN), systems integration and outsourcing services. IIJ's connectivity services are for corporate and residential use, and include access such as asymmetric digital subscriber line (ADSL), fiber optic, worldwide interoperability for microwave access (WiMAX), next-generation and long-term evolution (LTE) wireless data connection. IIJ also provides LTE SIM (subscriber identity module) cards with voice call function. For corporate customers, the firm primarily offers services such as: internet protocol (IP) and data center connectivity; IIJ mobile, broadband internet connectivity; IIJ ISDN/F, which provides internet access for integrated services digital network (ISDN) lines; mobile virtual network enabler (MVNE), for generating subscriptions; and IIJ Line Management/F services, which procures FLETS connected services. For residential customers, IIJ provides internet connectivity from its point-of-presence (POP) locations via leased lines and dial-up connections over local exchange facilities. It operates 30 primary POPs for dedicated access and one universal POP for nationwide dial-up access. The firm's WAN service is primarily marketed to corporate customers and features a closed network service that uses dedicated lines. Systems integration services span systems construction, operation and maintenance. Outsourcing services include outsourcing relating to security, networks, servers and businesses; maintenance, monitoring and provision of network equipment; email and web servers; and unauthorized access prevention. In addition, IIJ sells prepaid SIM cards, called Japan Travel SIM, for foreign visitors, which are primarily sold in stores located in the country's train stations. Subsidiary Trust Networks, Inc. operates ATMs and their corresponding network systems. In April 2021, IIJ acquired PTC Systems Pte. Ltd., which operates systems integration business in Singapore.

FINANCIAL DATA: *Note: Data for latest year may not have been available at press time.*

In U.S. $	2020	2019	2018	2017	2016	2015
Revenue	1,867,458,000	1,757,466,000	1,607,871,000	1,441,088,000	1,284,539,000	1,123,817,000
R&D Expense		4,451,893	4,258,894	4,157,326	4,030,660
Operating Income	75,120,540	55,007,960	61,759,220	46,891,650	56,079,880	46,352,170
Operating Margin %	.04%	.03%	.04%	.03%	.04%	.04%
SGA Expense	219,884,000	206,881,100	191,643,600	179,427,600	164,938,700	151,206,300
Net Income	36,593,880	32,153,350	46,660,060	28,919,750	36,881,650	30,340,580
Operating Cash Flow	304,985,300	229,716,500	121,119,700	67,289,160	110,067,200	117,928,800
Capital Expenditure	108,124,900	113,986,800	144,032,800	97,028,980	99,536,350	74,498,970
EBITDA	331,432,100	200,043,100	187,959,000	151,831,600	149,378,900	137,493,600
Return on Assets %	.02%	.02%	.04%	.02%	.04%	.03%
Return on Equity %	.05%	.05%	.07%	.05%	.06%	.05%
Debt to Equity	0.154	0.184	0.361	0.283	0.12	0.069

CONTACT INFORMATION:

Phone: 81 352056500   Fax: 81 352596311
Toll-Free:
Address: Iidabashi Grand Bloom, 2-10-2 Fujimi, Chiyoda-ku, Tokyo, 102-0071 Japan

STOCK TICKER/OTHER:

Stock Ticker: IIJIF   Exchange: GREY
Employees: 3,402   Fiscal Year Ends: 03/31
Parent Company:

SALARIES/BONUSES:

Top Exec. Salary: $ Bonus: $
Second Exec. Salary: $ Bonus: $

OTHER THOUGHTS:

Estimated Female Officers or Directors:
Hot Spot for Advancement for Women/Minorities:

Intrado Corporation

www.intrado.com

NAIC Code: 561422

TYPES OF BUSINESS:

Call Centers
Voice Transaction Services
Business Process Outsourcing
Conferencing Communications
Receivables Management

BRANDS/DIVISIONS/AFFILIATES:

Apollo Global Management Inc

CONTACTS:
Note: Officers with more than one job title may be intentionally listed here more than once.

John Shlonsky, CEO
Steve Cadden, COO
Nancy Disman, CFO
Anup Nair, CIO
David Treinen, Executive VP, Divisional
David Mussman, Executive VP
Nicole Theophilus, Executive VP
Ronald Beaumont, President, Divisional
Jon Hanson, President, Divisional
J. Etzler, President, Divisional

GROWTH PLANS/SPECIAL FEATURES:

Intrado Corporation provides communication and network infrastructure services, helping clients to more efficiently communicate, collaborate and connect with their audiences. The firm does this through its portfolio of services, which include digital media, enterprise collaboration, life and safety, and health and wellness solutions. Digital media solutions span internal communications, marketing, investor relations and public relations, offering end-to-end services that enables the ability to listen, create, connect, deliver, amplify and measure. Enterprise collaboration solutions are cloud-based, connecting the entire organization (even globally), and include Unified-Communications-as-a-Service (UCaaS), hosted voice, video meetings, collaboration and contact center services. Life and safety solutions consist of a next-generation emergency response infrastructure that connects clients to sources of protection, providing the ability to locate, route, transport and deliver emergency communications for safety purposes. Intrado's health and wellness solutions consist of clinical and administrative services as well as behavioral health and wellness programs, which are supported by medical claims data science and a technology platform that uses machine learning so people can be engaged in their health and overall wellbeing. Intrado has sales and/or operations in the U.S., Canada, Europe, the Middle East, Asia Pacific, Latin America and South America. The firm is controlled by affiliates of certain funds managed by Apollo Global Management, Inc.

FINANCIAL DATA:
Note: Data for latest year may not have been available at press time.

In U.S. $	2020	2019	2018	2017	2016	2015
Revenue	2,730,000,000	2,600,000,000	2,156,000,000	2,300,000,000	2,291,962,880	2,280,259,072
R&D Expense						
Operating Income						
Operating Margin %						
SGA Expense						
Net Income						
Operating Cash Flow						
Capital Expenditure						
EBITDA						
Return on Assets %						
Return on Equity %						
Debt to Equity						

CONTACT INFORMATION:

Phone: 402-571-7700   Fax:
Toll-Free: 800-841-9000
Address: 11808 Miracle Hills Dr., Omaha, NE 68154 United States

STOCK TICKER/OTHER:

Stock Ticker: Private   Exchange:
Employees: 9,659   Fiscal Year Ends: 12/31
Parent Company: Apollo Global Management LLC

SALARIES/BONUSES:

Top Exec. Salary: $ Bonus: $
Second Exec. Salary: $ Bonus: $

OTHER THOUGHTS:

Estimated Female Officers or Directors: 1
Hot Spot for Advancement for Women/Minorities:

Iridium Communications Inc

www.iridium.com

NAIC Code: 517410

TYPES OF BUSINESS:

Satellite Communications Services
Satellites
Mobile Voice
Data Communications
Surveillance
Telecommunications

BRANDS/DIVISIONS/AFFILIATES:

Iridium NEXT

CONTACTS: *Note: Officers with more than one job title may be intentionally listed here more than once.*

Matthew J. Desch, CEO
Thomas Fitzpatrick, CFO
Robert Niehaus, Chairman of the Board
Timothy Kapalka, Chief Accounting Officer
Suzanne McBride, COO
Bryan Hartin, Executive VP, Divisional
Scott Scheimreif, Executive VP, Divisional
Thomas Hickey, Other Executive Officer

GROWTH PLANS/SPECIAL FEATURES:

Iridium Communications, Inc. is a leading provider of mobile voice and data communications via satellite. With an architecture of 66 operational satellites with in-orbit spares and related ground infrastructure, the company provides communications in areas where wireline networks do not exist or are limited. Iridium's commercial end-user base includes emergency services, maritime, government, utilities, oil and gas, mining, recreation, forestry, construction and transportation markets, among others. Iridium developed Iridium NEXT through its Thales Alenia Space France partners. Iridium NEXT is a next-generation satellite constellation that replaces Iridium's first-generation satellites and supports higher data speeds for new products, including broadband service. The Iridium constellation also hosts the Aireon system, which provides global air traffic surveillance through a series of automatic dependent surveillance-broadcast receivers on its satellites. The U.S. government is the firm's single largest customer, accounting for 22% of its revenue. Iridium offers a wide variety of products relating to telecommunications, navigation and remote monitoring via satellite, such as satellite handsets, WiFi accessories, voice and data modems, broadband data devices and machine-to-machine (M2M) data devices. Accessories range from extended-life batteries to USB data cables and charging units.

Employee benefits include medical, dental and vision coverage, and a 401(k).

FINANCIAL DATA: *Note: Data for latest year may not have been available at press time.*

In U.S. $	2020	2019	2018	2017	2016	2015
Revenue	583,439,000	560,444,000	523,008,000	448,046,000	433,640,000	411,378,000
R&D Expense	12,037,000	14,310,000	22,429,000	15,247,000	16,079,000	16,144,000
Operating Income	35,483,000	10,120,000	41,653,000	115,476,000	176,371,000	160,842,000
Operating Margin %		.02%	.08%	.26%	.41%	.39%
SGA Expense	90,052,000	93,165,000	97,846,000	84,405,000	82,552,000	81,445,000
Net Income	-56,054,000	-161,999,000	-13,384,000	233,856,000	111,032,000	7,123,000
Operating Cash Flow	249,767,000	198,143,000	263,709,000	259,621,000	225,199,000	217,479,000
Capital Expenditure	38,689,000	117,819,000	391,390,000	400,107,000	405,687,000	494,810,000
EBITDA	308,481,000	307,825,000	259,860,000	237,742,000	225,765,000	212,676,000
Return on Assets %		-.04%	-.01%	.06%	.03%	.00%
Return on Equity %		-.11%	-.01%	.15%	.07%	-.01%
Debt to Equity		1.21	1.142	1.014	1.233	1.239

CONTACT INFORMATION:

Phone: 703 287-7400   Fax: 703 287-7450
Toll-Free:
Address: 1750 Tysons Blvd., Ste. 1400, McLean, VA 22102 United States

STOCK TICKER/OTHER:

Stock Ticker: IRDM
Employees: 522
Parent Company:

Exchange: NAS
Fiscal Year Ends: 12/31

SALARIES/BONUSES:

Top Exec. Salary: $ Bonus: $
Second Exec. Salary: $ Bonus: $

OTHER THOUGHTS:

Estimated Female Officers or Directors:
Hot Spot for Advancement for Women/Minorities:

ITI Limited

NAIC Code: 334210

www.itiltd.in

TYPES OF BUSINESS:

Telecommunications Equipment Manufacturing
Telecommunications Infrastructure
Telecommunications Switching
Phone Call Transmission

BRANDS/DIVISIONS/AFFILIATES:

Indian Telephone Industries

CONTACTS: *Note: Officers with more than one job title may be intentionally listed here more than once.*

Rakesh Mohan Agarwal, Managing Dir.
Rajeev Srivastava, CFO
K.K. Gupta, Dir.-Prod.
K.T.Mayuranathan, Sec.
Rakesh Mohan Agarwal, Chmn.

GROWTH PLANS/SPECIAL FEATURES:

ITI Limited is an India-based telecommunications company and a wing of the Indian Government's Department of Telecommunications. The ITI stands for Indian Telephone Industries. The company offers a complete range of telecom products and services covering the spectrum of switching, transmission, access and subscriber premises equipment. ITI manufactures its mobile infrastructure equipment based on GSM (global system for mobile) and CDMA (code division multiple access) technology. The firm also manufactures switching, transmission, broadband equipment, customer premises equipment, IT and convergence equipment, power plant, network management systems, SIM cards, banking automation equipment, Internet of Things (IoT) products and non-conventional energy system products. ITI has a dedicated network systems business unit for carrying out network planning, engineering, implementation and maintenance services as well as consultancy services. The company also carries out in-house research and development activities focused on specialized areas of encryption, network management, satellite, wireless, system engineering and IT and access products to provide customized solutions to the firm's various customers. ITI is involved in the construction of the Army Static Switched Communication Network (ASCON), a strategic communication network that supports the Indian Army. Additionally, the company entered into the information and communication technology (ICT) market by deploying its telecom expertise and vast infrastructure with initiatives such as network management systems, encryption and networking solutions for internet connectivity. ITI has manufacturing facilities in five locations across the country. The company's regional offices are further supported by area located throughout India, including Bangalore, Naini, Rae Bareli, Mankapur, Palakkad and Srinagar. In-house research and development work is focused on the design and development of encryption solutions to Indian Defense forces.

FINANCIAL DATA: *Note: Data for latest year may not have been available at press time.*

In U.S. $	2020	2019	2018	2017	2016	2015
Revenue	298,092,000	288,168,000	278,492,000	293,356,000	252,628,000	112,319,000
R&D Expense						
Operating Income						
Operating Margin %						
SGA Expense						
Net Income	20,051,000	43,350,600	35,443,600	46,992,700	37,858,300	-47,384,600
Operating Cash Flow						
Capital Expenditure						
EBITDA						
Return on Assets %						
Return on Equity %						
Debt to Equity						

CONTACT INFORMATION:

Phone: 91-80-2561-4466   Fax: 91-80-2561-7525
Toll-Free:
Address: F29, Ground Floor, Doorvaninagar, Bengaluru, 560 016 India

STOCK TICKER/OTHER:

Stock Ticker: 523610   Exchange: Bombay
Employees: 2,876   Fiscal Year Ends: 03/31
Parent Company:

SALARIES/BONUSES:

Top Exec. Salary: $ Bonus: $
Second Exec. Salary: $ Bonus: $

OTHER THOUGHTS:

Estimated Female Officers or Directors:
Hot Spot for Advancement for Women/Minorities:

J2 Global Inc

NAIC Code: 517110

www.j2global.com

TYPES OF BUSINESS:

Unified Messaging & Communication Services
Internet-Based Faxing
Internet Conferencing
Cloud-Based Communications Services
Customer Relationship Management Solutions

BRANDS/DIVISIONS/AFFILIATES:

MyFax
eVoice
LiveDrive
IPVanish
Campaigner
IGN
Mashable
Everyday Health

CONTACTS: *Note: Officers with more than one job title may be intentionally listed here more than once.*

Vivek Shah, CEO
R. Turicchi, CFO
Richard Ressler, Chairman of the Board
Steve Dunn, Chief Accounting Officer
Jeremy Rossen, General Counsel

GROWTH PLANS/SPECIAL FEATURES:

J2 Global, Inc. is a global provider of internet information and services. Through its cloud services division, the company provides cloud services to consumers and businesses (any size), and licenses intellectual property (IP) to third parties. This segment's cloud-based eFax, MyFax and sFax online fax services enable users to receive faxes in their email inboxes and to send faxes via the internet. eVoice and Line2 provide customers a virtual phone system with various available enhancements. LiveDrive enables customers to back up data and dispose tape or other physical systems. IPVanish and Encrypt.me provide virtual private networks that encrypt customers' data and activity on the internet. Campaigner, iContact and SMTP provide enhanced email marketing and delivery solutions. J2's digital media division operates a portfolio of web properties that provide reviews of technology, gaming and lifestyle products and services; news and commentary related to their vertical markets; professional networking tools, targeted emails and white papers for IT professionals; speed testing for internet and mobile network connections; online deals and discounts for consumers; interactive tools and mobile applications that enable consumers to manage an array of health and wellness needs, such as medical conditions, pregnancy, diet and fitness news; and tools and information for healthcare professionals to stay informed about industry, legislative and regulatory developments in major medical specialties. This division's web properties and apps include IGN, Mashable, PC Mag, Humble Bundle, Speedtest, Offers, Black Friday, MedPageToday, Everyday Health, and What to Expect, among others. During the first half of 2021, J2 Global completed two acquisitions that provide access to new markets and expand J2's product line, they include Moz Inc. and Daily OM. J2 Global also announced plans to separate into two independent publicly-traded companies, J2 Global Inc. and Consensus, through a spin-off.

FINANCIAL DATA: *Note: Data for latest year may not have been available at press time.*

In U.S. $	2020	2019	2018	2017	2016	2015
Revenue	1,489,593,000	1,372,054,000	1,207,295,000	1,117,838,000	874,255,000	720,815,000
R&D Expense	64,295,000	54,396,000	48,370,000	46,004,000	38,046,000	34,329,000
Operating Income	334,611,000	277,080,000	244,280,000	245,708,000	242,566,000	199,382,000
Operating Margin %		.20%	.20%	.22%	.28%	.28%
SGA Expense	858,905,000	803,255,000	713,571,000	653,813,000	446,543,000	364,146,000
Net Income	150,668,000	218,806,000	128,687,000	139,425,000	152,439,000	133,636,000
Operating Cash Flow	480,079,000	412,539,000	401,325,000	264,419,000	282,387,000	229,061,000
Capital Expenditure	95,670,000	70,634,000	57,048,000	41,835,000	29,067,000	18,752,000
EBITDA	591,111,000	522,595,000	426,748,000	429,784,000	374,900,000	292,590,000
Return on Assets %		.07%	.05%	.06%	.08%	.08%
Return on Equity %		.18%	.12%	.14%	.17%	.15%
Debt to Equity		0.89	0.978	0.982	0.658	0.675

CONTACT INFORMATION:

Phone: 323 860-9200   Fax: 323 860-9201
Toll-Free:
Address: 700 S. Flower St., Fl. 15, Los Angeles, CA 90017 United States

STOCK TICKER/OTHER:

Stock Ticker: JCOM   Exchange: NAS
Employees: 3,090   Fiscal Year Ends: 12/31
Parent Company:

SALARIES/BONUSES:

Top Exec. Salary: $ Bonus: $
Second Exec. Salary: $ Bonus: $

OTHER THOUGHTS:

Estimated Female Officers or Directors: 2
Hot Spot for Advancement for Women/Minorities:

Jabil Inc

www.jabil.com

NAIC Code: 334418

TYPES OF BUSINESS:

Contract Electronics Manufacturing
Electronic Manufacturing Services
Engineering Solutions

BRANDS/DIVISIONS/AFFILIATES:

CONTACTS: Note: Officers with more than one job title may be intentionally listed here more than once.

Michael Loparco, CEO, Divisional
Alessandro Parimbelli, CEO, Divisional
Steven Borges, CEO, Divisional
Kenneth Wilson, CEO, Divisional
Brenda Chamulak, CEO, Divisional
Mark Mondello, CEO
Meheryar Dastoor, CFO
Timothy Main, Chairman of the Board
Thomas Sansone, Director
Courtney Ryan, Executive VP, Divisional
Robert Katz, Executive VP
Bruce Johnson, Other Executive Officer
Daryn Smith, Senior VP, Divisional
Sergio Cadavid, Senior VP

GROWTH PLANS/SPECIAL FEATURES:

Jabil, Inc. is a provider of worldwide electronic manufacturing services and solutions. Through its 100 locations in 30 countries, the firm develops and manufactures products that help to connect people, advance technology and more. Jabil divides its operations into two segments: diversified manufacturing services (DMS) and electronics manufacturing services (EMS). DMS is focused on providing engineering solutions and on material sciences and technologies. This segment includes customers primarily in the consumer lifestyles and wearable technologies, defense & aerospace, emerging growth, healthcare, mobility and packaging industries. EMS is focused around leveraging information technology, supply chain design and engineering, technologies largely centered on core electronics, sharing of Jabil's large-scale manufacturing infrastructure and the ability to serve a broad range of end markets. This segment includes customers primarily in the automotive, digital home, industrial and energy, networking and telecommunications, point of sale, printing and storage industries. As of fiscal 2020, Jabil's five largest accounted for approximately 47% of net revenue and 73 customers accounted for approximately 90% of net revenue, Apple, Inc. alone accounted for 20%.

FINANCIAL DATA: Note: Data for latest year may not have been available at press time.

In U.S. $	2020	2019	2018	2017	2016	2015
Revenue	27,266,440,000	25,282,320,000	22,095,420,000	19,063,120,000	18,353,090,000	17,899,200,000
R&D Expense	44,143,000	42,861,000	38,531,000	29,680,000	31,954,000	27,645,000
Operating Income	656,432,000	727,270,000	579,055,000	572,737,000	534,202,000	588,477,000
Operating Margin %		.03%	.03%	.03%	.03%	.03%
SGA Expense	1,174,694,000	1,111,347,000	1,050,716,000	907,702,000	924,427,000	862,647,000
Net Income	53,912,000	287,111,000	86,330,000	129,090,000	254,095,000	284,019,000
Operating Cash Flow	1,257,275,000	1,193,066,000	933,850,000	1,256,643,000	916,207,000	1,240,282,000
Capital Expenditure	983,035,000	1,005,480,000	1,036,651,000	716,485,000	924,239,000	963,145,000
EBITDA	1,229,196,000	1,411,267,000	1,296,107,000	1,154,712,000	1,220,333,000	1,088,913,000
Return on Assets %		.02%	.01%	.01%	.03%	.03%
Return on Equity %		.15%	.04%	.05%	.11%	.12%
Debt to Equity		1.124	1.279	0.694	0.851	0.582

CONTACT INFORMATION:

Phone: 727 577-9749   Fax: 727 579-8529
Toll-Free:
Address: 10560 Dr. Martin Luther King Jr. St. N., St. Petersburg, FL 33716 United States

STOCK TICKER/OTHER:

Stock Ticker: JBL   Exchange: NYS
Employees: 240,000   Fiscal Year Ends: 08/31
Parent Company:

SALARIES/BONUSES:

Top Exec. Salary: $ Bonus: $
Second Exec. Salary: $ Bonus: $

OTHER THOUGHTS:

Estimated Female Officers or Directors:
Hot Spot for Advancement for Women/Minorities: Y

Jio (Reliance Jio Infocomm Limited)

www.jio.com

NAIC Code: 517210

TYPES OF BUSINESS:

Wireless Telecommunications Carriers (except Satellite)
LTE Network
Mobile
Fiber-to-the-Home
Internet

BRANDS/DIVISIONS/AFFILIATES:

Reliance Industries Limited
Jio
JioFi
JioFiber

CONTACTS: *Note: Officers with more than one job title may be intentionally listed here more than once.*

Mukesh D. Ambani, Chmn.

GROWTH PLANS/SPECIAL FEATURES:

Reliance Jio Infocomm Limited (popularly known as Jio), a subsidiary of Reliance Industries Limited, is an Indian mobile network operator and fiber-to-the-home (FTTH) provider serving the India market. Jio operates a national long-term evolution (LTE) network with coverage across all telecommunication circles. The firm has built a world-class, all-IP data network with 4G LTE technology, which utilizes voice over LTE (VoLTE) to provide voice service on its network. The company's future-ready network can be easily upgraded to support even more data as technologies advance on to 5G, 6G and beyond. Its 4G data routers and phones are marketed under the JioFi and Jio brand names. Jio apps enable users to manage their Jio accounts and related devices, connect to Wi-Fi, chat, watch entertainment, listen to music, read online magazines and news, browse the web, secure data, file into the cloud, make payments, make calls, make online purchases, and connect with doctors and health test results. Devices can be purchased in-store (in the Mumbai area), as well as online at www.jio.com or via mobile app. Jio has the ability to offer free calls and very cheap internet access by relying on advertising and content revenues. JioFiber offers FTTH broadband with speeds up to 1 gigabytes per second (Gbps) throughout a home or business, separate Wi-Fi identifications for guests, Norton's mobile security for a select number of devices, high-definition (HD) voice calls throughout India, TV video calling and conferencing, integrated TV, home networking, security and surveillance solutions, a multi-player platform and more.

FINANCIAL DATA: *Note: Data for latest year may not have been available at press time.*

In U.S. $	2020	2019	2018	2017	2016	2015
Revenue	8,504,180,000	6,889,980,000	3,645,450,000	17,797,100	5,699,870	218,575
R&D Expense						
Operating Income						
Operating Margin %						
SGA Expense						
Net Income	734,478,000	426,095,000	111,143,000	-5,235,450	-6,276,040	-6,190,310
Operating Cash Flow						
Capital Expenditure						
EBITDA						
Return on Assets %						
Return on Equity %						
Debt to Equity						

CONTACT INFORMATION:

Phone: 91-1800-899999   Fax:
Toll-Free:
Address: Off-101, Saffron, Nr. Cntr. Point Panchwati 5 Rast, Ambawadi, Ahmedabad 380006 India

STOCK TICKER/OTHER:

Stock Ticker: Subsidiary   Exchange:
Employees: Fiscal Year Ends: 03/31
Parent Company: Reliance Industries Limited

SALARIES/BONUSES:

Top Exec. Salary: $ Bonus: $
Second Exec. Salary: $ Bonus: $

OTHER THOUGHTS:

Estimated Female Officers or Directors:
Hot Spot for Advancement for Women/Minorities:

Juniper Networks Inc

www.juniper.net

NAIC Code: 334210A

TYPES OF BUSINESS:

Networking Equipment
IP Networking Systems
Internet Routers
Network Security Products
Internet Software
Intrusion Prevention
Application Acceleration

BRANDS/DIVISIONS/AFFILIATES:

ACX
MX
PTX
EX
SRX
Juniper
Netrounds

CONTACTS: Note: Officers with more than one job title may be intentionally listed here more than once.

Rami Rahim, CEO
Kenneth Miller, CFO
Scott Kriens, Chairman of the Board
Terrance Spidell, Chief Accounting Officer
Bikash Koley, Chief Technology Officer
Manoj Leelanivas, Executive VP
Anand Athreya, Executive VP
Brian Martin, Senior VP

GROWTH PLANS/SPECIAL FEATURES:

Juniper Networks, Inc. designs, develops and sells products and services for high-performance networks. These products help customers build highly scalable, reliable, secure and cost-effective networks for their businesses. Juniper sells its products in more than 150 countries across three geographic regions: Americas; Europe, Middle East and Africa (EMEA); and Asia Pacific. The company's offerings address high-performance network requirements for global service providers, cloud environments, enterprises, governments and research and public-sector organizations who view the network as critical to its business success. Routing products include the firm's ACX universal metro routers, MX universal routing platform, PTX packet transport routers, CTP circuit to pack platforms and JRR200 route reflector appliance. Switching products include the EX ethernet and QFX series switches, as well as data center switching architectures. Security products include the SRX series firewalls; vSRX firewalls for private, hybrid or public cloud environments; cSRX container firewall; next-generation firewall services; Juniper advanced threat prevention products; Juniper security intelligence (SecIntel); Junos space security director; a policy enforcer; Juniper secure analytics; integrate real-time threat intelligence; and Juniper identity management service. Other products include cloud services, network automation, network Edge, network operating system, packet optical, SDN and related management/operations, wireless access points and more. Juniper Networks owns nearly 4,000 issued or pending technology patents. In late-2021, Juniper Networks acquired Netrounds, which provides a programmable, software-based active test and service platform for fixed and mobile networks; and agreed to acquire 128 Technology, Inc. and Apstra, Inc.

Juniper Networks offers medical, dental, prescription and vision insurance; paid time off; and stock/savings plans.

FINANCIAL DATA: Note: Data for latest year may not have been available at press time.

In U.S. $	2020	2019	2018	2017	2016	2015
Revenue	4,445,100,000	4,445,400,000	4,647,500,000	5,027,200,000	4,990,100,000	4,857,800,000
R&D Expense	958,400,000	955,700,000	1,003,200,000	980,700,000	1,013,700,000	994,500,000
Operating Income	421,100,000	477,500,000	579,500,000	913,700,000	893,000,000	911,400,000
Operating Margin %		.11%	.12%	.18%	.18%	.19%
SGA Expense	1,194,200,000	1,183,600,000	1,158,500,000	1,177,700,000	1,197,800,000	1,172,700,000
Net Income	257,800,000	345,000,000	566,900,000	306,200,000	592,700,000	633,700,000
Operating Cash Flow	612,000,000	528,900,000	861,100,000	1,260,100,000	1,106,000,000	892,500,000
Capital Expenditure	100,400,000	109,600,000	147,400,000	151,200,000	214,700,000	210,300,000
EBITDA	554,600,000	713,400,000	846,400,000	1,138,600,000	1,131,800,000	1,112,000,000
Return on Assets %		.04%	.06%	.03%	.06%	.07%
Return on Equity %		.07%	.12%	.06%	.12%	.13%
Debt to Equity		0.40	0.371	0.456	0.43	0.36

CONTACT INFORMATION:

Phone: 408 745-2000   Fax: 408 745-2100
Toll-Free: 888-586-4737
Address: 1133 Innovation Way, Sunnyvale, CA 94089 United States

STOCK TICKER/OTHER:

Stock Ticker: JNPR
Employees: 9,950
Parent Company:

Exchange: NYS
Fiscal Year Ends: 12/31

SALARIES/BONUSES:

Top Exec. Salary: $ Bonus: $
Second Exec. Salary: $ Bonus: $

OTHER THOUGHTS:

Estimated Female Officers or Directors: 3
Hot Spot for Advancement for Women/Minorities: Y

Sales, profits and employees may be estimates. Financial information, benefits and other data can change quickly and may vary from those stated here.

KCOM Group Limited

NAIC Code: 517110

www.kcom.com

TYPES OF BUSINESS:

Voice & Data Services
Fiber Broadband Services
Retail Broadband
Wholesale Broadband

BRANDS/DIVISIONS/AFFILIATES:

Macquarie Group Limited
Macquarie Infrastructure and Real Assets
Macquarie European Infrastructure Fund 6

GROWTH PLANS/SPECIAL FEATURES:

KCOM Group Limited is a regional provider of full fiber broadband services to retail and wholesale customers. The company serves customers across Hull, East Yorkshire and North Lincolnshire. KCOM is owned by Macquarie European Infrastructure Fund 6, an investment fund managed by Macquarie Infrastructure and Real Assets, which itself is owned by Macquarie Group Limited. In August 2021, KCOM sold its national information and communication technology (ICT) business to managed services specialist Nasstar, refocusing its business to regional broadband services and developing its wholesale business.

KCOM offers its employees health and pension benefits, life assurance and a variety of employee assistance programs and ocmpany perks.

CONTACTS: Note: Officers with more than one job title may be intentionally listed here more than once.

Dale Raneberg, CEO
Sam Booth, CFO
Kathy Smith, Sec.
Nathan Luckey, Chmn.

FINANCIAL DATA: Note: Data for latest year may not have been available at press time.

In U.S. $	2020	2019	2018	2017	2016	2015
Revenue	325,735,000	366,781,000	423,602,000	453,017,280	467,380,480	465,723,584
R&D Expense						
Operating Income						
Operating Margin %						
SGA Expense						
Net Income	-9,615,410	-44,152,600	38,555,200	33,140,166	95,202,024	16,788,234
Operating Cash Flow						
Capital Expenditure						
EBITDA						
Return on Assets %						
Return on Equity %						
Debt to Equity						

CONTACT INFORMATION:

Phone: 44 1482607000   Fax: 44 1482219289
Toll-Free:
Address: 37 Carr Ln., Hull, HU1 3RE United Kingdom

SALARIES/BONUSES:

Top Exec. Salary: $ Bonus: $
Second Exec. Salary: $ Bonus: $

STOCK TICKER/OTHER:

Stock Ticker: Subsidiary   Exchange:
Employees: 1,500   Fiscal Year Ends: 03/31
Parent Company: Macquarie Group Limited

OTHER THOUGHTS:

Estimated Female Officers or Directors: 1
Hot Spot for Advancement for Women/Minorities:

KDDI Corporation

www.kddi.com

NAIC Code: 517210

TYPES OF BUSINESS:

Mobile Phone Service
Telecommunications
Communication Technology
Internet of Things
Business Services
Internet Service

BRANDS/DIVISIONS/AFFILIATES:

au Data MAX Plan
au Data MAX Plan Netflix Pack
au Flat Plan 7 Plus
World Data FLAT
Chubu Telecommunications Co Inc
BIGLOBE Inc
ARISE analytics Inc
KDDI Russia LLC

CONTACTS: Note: Officers with more than one job title may be intentionally listed here more than once.

Makoto Takahashi, CEO
Makoto Takahashi, Sr. VP
Kanichiro Aritomi, Vice Chmn.
Hirofumi Morozumi, Exec. VP
Hideo Yuasa, Associate Sr. VP

GROWTH PLANS/SPECIAL FEATURES:

KDDI Corporation is a Japanese telecommunications firm with more than 100 offices in 28 countries worldwide, and a global network covering over 190 countries. KDDI provides complete information and communication technology (ICT) solutions to meet the business needs of its customers, from creating IT environments to operating and maintaining them. Products and services include data centers, network management, 5G, IT solutions, Internet of Things (IoT) solutions, cloud and software-as-a-service solutions, robotic process automation solutions, security solutions, IT outsourcing and wholesale carrier solutions. Additional business services and solutions offered by KIDDI encompass office expansion, office relocation, global communication, global network, building a cloud system, strengthening global office governance and enhancing the business' security system. KDDI also offers many wireless data plans for its personal customers, including: the au Data MAX Plan, with unlimited data; the au Data MAX Plan Netflix Pack, which includes a Netflix; the au Flat Plan 7 Plus, with 7 gigabytes of data and no data consumption charges for popular SNS services; and World Data FLAT, available in select countries. Domestic subsidiaries include Chubu Telecommunications Co., Inc.; BIGLOBE Inc.; Jupiter Telecommunications Co., Ltd.; and ARISE analytics Inc. Global subsidiaries include BRACNet Limited; KDDI China Corporation; KDDI India Private Limited; KDDI Russia LLC; KDDI AMERICA, Inc.; and Ubik do Brasil Solucoes em Tecnologia Ltda.

FINANCIAL DATA: Note: Data for latest year may not have been available at press time.

In U.S. $	2020	2019	2018	2017	2016	2015
Revenue	47,831,560,000	46,398,890,000	46,048,410,000	43,365,870,000	40,789,230,000	41,766,510,000
R&D Expense						59,857,710
Operating Income	9,333,758,000	9,214,735,000	8,751,245,000	8,313,061,000	7,563,845,000	6,770,342,000
Operating Margin %	.20%	.20%	.19%	.19%	.19%	.16%
SGA Expense	11,868,380,000	11,055,230,000	11,610,010,000	10,718,150,000	10,108,390,000	4,351,256,000
Net Income	5,842,995,000	5,641,174,000	5,228,901,000	4,992,630,000	4,515,951,000	3,908,296,000
Operating Cash Flow	12,086,220,000	9,403,405,000	9,693,817,000	10,604,090,000	8,078,490,000	8,788,225,000
Capital Expenditure	5,656,106,000	5,499,329,000	5,122,501,000	4,745,253,000	4,893,464,000	4,759,857,000
EBITDA	15,727,070,000	14,454,710,000	13,826,880,000	13,282,710,000	12,520,300,000	11,461,170,000
Return on Assets %	.08%	.09%	.09%	.09%	.09%	.08%
Return on Equity %	.15%	.16%	.16%	.16%	.16%	.15%
Debt to Equity	0.323	0.249	0.187	0.256	0.289	0.274

CONTACT INFORMATION:

Phone: 81 333470077   Fax:
Toll-Free:
Address: Garden Air Tower, 3-10-10, Iidabashi, Chiyoda-ku, Tokyo, 102-8460 Japan

STOCK TICKER/OTHER:

Stock Ticker: KDDIY
Employees: 78,337
Parent Company:

Exchange: PINX
Fiscal Year Ends: 03/31

SALARIES/BONUSES:

Top Exec. Salary: $ Bonus: $
Second Exec. Salary: $ Bonus: $

OTHER THOUGHTS:

Estimated Female Officers or Directors:
Hot Spot for Advancement for Women/Minorities:

Koninklijke KPN NV (Royal KPN NV)

www.kpn.com

NAIC Code: 517110

TYPES OF BUSINESS:

Wired Telecommunications Carriers
Telecommunications
Information Technology
Mobile Networks
Data
Television

BRANDS/DIVISIONS/AFFILIATES:

KPN
XS4ALL
Simyo
KPN Security
Ortel Mobile
Cam IT Solutions
Solcon
Inspark

CONTACTS: *Note: Officers with more than one job title may be intentionally listed here more than once.*

Joost Farwerck, CEO
Chris Figee, CFO
Hilde Garssen, Chief People Officer
Babak Fouladic, CTO

GROWTH PLANS/SPECIAL FEATURES:

Koninklijke KPN NV (Royal KPN NV) supplies telecommunications and information technology (IT) to customers throughout the Netherlands and abroad. Royal KPN NV serves private and business customers with its fixed and mobile networks to provide telephone, data and television services. The firm also offers telecommunication providers access to its networks. Royal KPN NV markets products under nine primary brands. KPN, the firm's principal brand, develops products, technologies and services that make telecommunications accessible. XS4ALL focuses on professionals and demanding consumers for whom an internet connection is essential. Simyo produces smart telecom cookies that enable users to customize their mobile devices so they can locate the best deals and manage subscriptions online. KPN Security offers digital security for small and large organizations. Ortel Mobile is a pre-paid provider of discount national and international calling cards. Cam IT Solutions is a knowledge organization aimed at unburdening ICT infrastructure. Solcon offers secure internet solutions. Inspark provides digital transformation services. Last, the KPN Partner Network works with business partners in order to offer telecommunications, information technology and security services throughout the Netherlands.

FINANCIAL DATA: *Note: Data for latest year may not have been available at press time.*

In U.S. $	2020	2019	2018	2017	2016	2015
Revenue	6,455,869,000	6,718,551,000	6,882,270,000	7,937,885,000	8,309,305,000	8,559,770,000
R&D Expense						
Operating Income	1,124,035,000	1,021,406,000	955,429,600	1,076,386,000	1,165,575,000	932,215,800
Operating Margin %		.15%	.14%	.14%	.14%	.11%
SGA Expense						
Net Income	685,416,900	764,832,400	329,879,800	590,118,300	968,869,100	779,493,700
Operating Cash Flow	2,496,090,000	2,450,885,000	2,405,679,000	2,382,465,000	2,342,146,000	2,709,901,000
Capital Expenditure	1,910,859,000	1,361,060,000	1,352,507,000	1,392,826,000	1,489,346,000	1,593,197,000
EBITDA	2,979,914,000	3,051,999,000	2,718,454,000	2,937,152,000	2,968,918,000	3,315,902,000
Return on Assets %		.05%	.02%	.03%	.05%	.03%
Return on Equity %		.28%	.08%	.12%	.17%	.12%
Debt to Equity		2.596	3.592	2.257	2.193	1.777

CONTACT INFORMATION:

Phone: 31 703434343   Fax:
Toll-Free:
Address: Wilhelminakade 123, Rotterdam, 3072 AP Netherlands

STOCK TICKER/OTHER:

Stock Ticker: KKPNF   Exchange: PINX
Employees: 11,248   Fiscal Year Ends: 12/31
Parent Company:

SALARIES/BONUSES:

Top Exec. Salary: $ Bonus: $
Second Exec. Salary: $ Bonus: $

OTHER THOUGHTS:

Estimated Female Officers or Directors:
Hot Spot for Advancement for Women/Minorities:

Koninklijke Philips NV (Royal Philips)

www.philips.com/global

NAIC Code: 334310

TYPES OF BUSINESS:

Manufacturing-Electrical & Electronic Equipment
Consumer Electronics & Appliances
Lighting Systems
Medical Imaging Equipment
Semiconductors
Consulting Services
Nanotech Research
MEMS

BRANDS/DIVISIONS/AFFILIATES:

GROWTH PLANS/SPECIAL FEATURES:

Koninklijke Philips NV (Royal Philips) is a health technology company. The firm focuses on improving people's health and enabling better outcomes across the health continuum, from wellness and prevention to diagnosis, treatment and home care. Royal Philips leverages advanced technology and clinical and consumer insights to deliver integrated solutions. The company is a leader in diagnostic imaging, image-guided therapy, patient monitoring and health informatics, as well as in consumer health and home care. Royal Philips plans to further invest and explore in artificial intelligence (AI) technological solutions, not for the purpose of replacing doctors and nurses, but for supporting them in their work. In December 2020, Royal Philips agreed to acquire BioTelemetry, Inc., a U.S.-based provider of remote cardiac diagnostics and monitoring. The transaction was expected to close during the first quarter of 2021.

CONTACTS: Note: Officers with more than one job title may be intentionally listed here more than once.

Frans van Houten, CEO
Sophie Bechu, COO
Abhijit Bhattacharya, CFO
Daniela Seabrook, Chief Human Resources Officer
Jeroen Tas, Exec. VP-Innovation & Strategy
Eric Coutinho, Chief Legal Officer
Jim Andrew, Chief Strategy & Innovation Officer
Deborah DiSanzo, Exec. VP
Pieter Nota, CEO-Phillips Consumer Lifestyle
Eric Rondolat, Exec. VP
Jeroen van der Veer, Chmn.
Patrick Kung, CEO-Greater China

FINANCIAL DATA: Note: Data for latest year may not have been available at press time.

In U.S. $	2020	2019	2018	2017	2016	2015
Revenue	23,867,410,000	23,801,440,000	22,139,820,000	21,723,200,000	29,953,080,000	29,620,760,000
R&D Expense	2,339,703,000	2,301,828,000	2,149,106,000	2,155,215,000	2,469,211,000	2,354,364,000
Operating Income	2,029,372,000	2,014,710,000	2,003,714,000	1,854,657,000	2,303,049,000	1,212,003,000
Operating Margin %		.08%	.09%	.09%	.08%	.04%
SGA Expense	6,443,652,000	6,491,301,000	6,268,937,000	6,078,341,000	8,226,225,000	8,581,762,000
Net Income	1,450,249,000	1,425,814,000	1,331,737,000	2,024,484,000	1,769,133,000	788,046,100
Operating Cash Flow	3,392,874,000	2,481,429,000	2,174,763,000	2,284,723,000	2,326,263,000	1,425,814,000
Capital Expenditure	1,150,914,000	1,237,660,000	1,029,958,000	1,049,506,000	1,061,724,000	1,169,241,000
EBITDA	3,888,916,000	3,819,275,000	3,396,540,000	3,256,036,000	3,940,231,000	2,896,833,000
Return on Assets %		.04%	.04%	.06%	.05%	.02%
Return on Equity %		.09%	.09%	.13%	.12%	.06%
Debt to Equity		0.392	0.283	0.337	0.319	0.351

CONTACT INFORMATION:

Phone: 31 402791111   Fax:
Toll-Free: 877-248-4237
Address: Philips Center, Amstelplein 2, Amsterdam, 1096 BC Netherlands

STOCK TICKER/OTHER:

Stock Ticker: PHG
Employees: 78,392
Parent Company:

Exchange: NYS
Fiscal Year Ends: 12/31

SALARIES/BONUSES:

Top Exec. Salary: $ Bonus: $
Second Exec. Salary: $ Bonus: $

OTHER THOUGHTS:

Estimated Female Officers or Directors: 3
Hot Spot for Advancement for Women/Minorities: Y

Kratos Defense & Security Solutions Inc   www.kratosdefense.com

NAIC Code: 541512

TYPES OF BUSINESS:

IT Consulting
System Design & Engineering Services
Consulting Services
Network Management

BRANDS/DIVISIONS/AFFILIATES:

CONTACTS: Note: Officers with more than one job title may be intentionally listed here more than once.

Eric Demarco, CEO
Deanna Lund, CFO
William Hoglund, Chairman of the Board
Maria Cervantes de Burgreen, Controller
Thomas Mills, President, Divisional
Jonah Adelman, President, Divisional
Phillip Carrai, President, Divisional
David Carter, President, Divisional
Steve Fendley, President, Divisional
Stacey Rock, President, Divisional
Benjamin Goodwin, Senior VP, Divisional
Marie Mendoza, Vice President

GROWTH PLANS/SPECIAL FEATURES:

Kratos Defense & Security Solutions, Inc. is a mid-tier government contractor for the U.S. Department of Defense. The firm develops strategic weapon systems to address peer and near peer threats, with a focus on the U.S. and its allies' national security. Kratos operates through two business segments: government solutions and unmanned systems. The government solutions segment includes the company's microwave electronic products, space and satellite communications, modular systems and defense and rocket support services. Microwave electronics include radio frequency (RF) and microwave assemblies and subassemblies to support high-end requirements of radar, simulators, communications, test and other equipment for various platforms such as fighter aircraft, missiles, smart munition and naval. Space and satellite communication products offer the reliability and security of satellite and terrestrial networks and boost the readiness of human teams via simulations, game-based and full-fidelity training solutions. Modular systems and subsystems encompass missile and radar systems, combat systems, unmanned systems and related technical services. Defense and rocket support services include logistics, engineering, target operations support, international programs, rocket program services and advanced weapon system research and engineering. The unmanned systems segment consists of two divisions: unmanned aerial systems, offering high-performance aerial targets, aerial target services, ancillary target equipment and advanced composite solutions; and unmanned ground and seaborne systems, offering avionics, transponders, payloads, advanced command and control (C2) systems, ground vehicle automation solutions, flight termination systems and autonomous impact protection solutions.

Kratos offers its employees benefits including a 401(k) plan and a stock purchase program.

FINANCIAL DATA: Note: Data for latest year may not have been available at press time.

In U.S. $	2020	2019	2018	2017	2016	2015
Revenue	747,700,000	717,500,000	618,000,000	751,900,000	668,700,000	657,100,000
R&D Expense	27,000,000	18,000,000	15,600,000	17,800,000	13,900,000	16,200,000
Operating Income	31,700,000	41,200,000	34,300,000	18,900,000	-6,600,000	-5,100,000
Operating Margin %		.06%	.06%	.03%	-.01%	-.01%
SGA Expense	144,500,000	130,800,000	119,800,000	160,600,000	146,300,000	150,700,000
Net Income	79,600,000	12,500,000	-3,500,000	-42,700,000	-60,500,000	19,800,000
Operating Cash Flow	46,600,000	30,000,000	10,400,000	-27,000,000	-12,300,000	-26,900,000
Capital Expenditure	35,900,000	26,300,000	22,600,000	26,500,000	9,200,000	11,300,000
EBITDA	64,400,000	74,300,000	48,200,000	800,000	5,200,000	16,900,000
Return on Assets %		.01%	.00%	-.04%	-.07%	.02%
Return on Equity %		.02%	-.01%	-.11%	-.23%	.08%
Debt to Equity		0.58	0.567	0.574	1.559	1.747

CONTACT INFORMATION:

Phone: 512-238-9840   Fax:
Toll-Free:
Address: 1 Chisholm Trail, Ste. 3200, Round Rock, TX 78681 United States

STOCK TICKER/OTHER:

Stock Ticker: KTOS   Exchange: NAS
Employees: 3,200   Fiscal Year Ends: 12/31
Parent Company:

SALARIES/BONUSES:

Top Exec. Salary: $ Bonus: $
Second Exec. Salary: $ Bonus: $

OTHER THOUGHTS:

Estimated Female Officers or Directors: 4
Hot Spot for Advancement for Women/Minorities: Y

KT Corporation

www.kt.com

NAIC Code: 517110

TYPES OF BUSINESS:

Local Telephone Service
Mobile Phone Service
Internet Access & Portal Services
Undersea Cable Construction, Maintenance & Repair
IT Consulting & Outsourcing
Online Billing Services
Security Services
e-Commerce Services

BRANDS/DIVISIONS/AFFILIATES:

BC Card Co Ltd

CONTACTS: Note: Officers with more than one job title may be intentionally listed here more than once.

Hyeon-Mo Ky, CEO
Sang-Bong Nam, Exec. VP-Group Legal & Ethics
Young-Soo Woo, Sr. VP-Corp. Center Strategy & Planning Office
Eun-Hye Kim, Exec. VP-Comm. Office
Hyun-Myung Pyo, Pres., Telecom & Convergence Group
Il Yung Kim, Pres., KT Corp. Center
Seong-Mok Oh, Exec. VP-Network Group
Se-Hyun Oh, Exec. VP-New Bus. Unit

GROWTH PLANS/SPECIAL FEATURES:

KT Corporation (KTC) is a leading telecommunications service provider in Korea. As an integrated telecommunications service provider, the firm's principal services encompass mobile telecom services; fixed-line telephone services, including local, domestic long-distance and international long-distance telephone services, voice over internet protocol (VoIP) services and interconnection services to other telecommunications companies; broadband internet access service and other internet-related services, including IPTV services; and various other services, including leased line service and other data communication services, satellite service and IT and network services. The company owns a large portion of the domestic public exchanges, the nationwide network of local telephone lines, the principal public long-distance telephone transmission facilities and the principal data communications network in Korea. KTC's mobile voice and data telecommunications services are based on 3G W-CDMA technolog, 4G LTE technology and 5G technology. The firm also offers big data, cloud Internet of Things (IoT), blockchain and other transformative technologies. KTC maintains numerous subsidiaries operating both within telecommunications and other industries, including credit card and other financial services via BC Card Co., Ltd.

FINANCIAL DATA: Note: Data for latest year may not have been available at press time.

In U.S. $	2020	2019	2018	2017	2016	2015
Revenue	22,074,090,000	22,488,230,000	21,166,760,000	21,266,910,000	20,882,110,000	20,501,850,000
R&D Expense	141,743,700	149,048,500	159,642,700	152,306,300	151,625,300	166,021,800
Operating Income	923,341,600	921,391,700	994,264,900	965,572,900	1,210,051,000	972,776,600
Operating Margin %		.04%	.05%	.05%	.06%	.05%
SGA Expense	3,289,735,000	3,483,653,000	3,355,023,000	3,615,315,000	3,510,366,000	3,388,561,000
Net Income	633,022,700	586,256,400	583,061,100	416,866,800	639,772,000	493,457,500
Operating Cash Flow	4,280,875,000	3,382,532,000	3,622,135,000	3,502,271,000	4,308,803,000	3,820,382,000
Capital Expenditure	3,363,846,000	3,432,365,000	2,715,919,000	2,759,891,000	2,908,309,000	3,174,741,000
EBITDA	4,482,275,000	4,487,021,000	4,241,102,000	4,115,879,000	4,409,417,000	4,278,025,000
Return on Assets %		.02%	.02%	.02%	.02%	.02%
Return on Equity %		.05%	.05%	.04%	.06%	.05%
Debt to Equity		0.449	0.402	0.438	0.551	0.646

CONTACT INFORMATION:

Phone: 82-31-727-0114   Fax:
Toll-Free:
Address: 90, Buljeong-ro, Gundang-gu, Seongnam-si, Gyeonggi-do, 03155 South Korea

STOCK TICKER/OTHER:

Stock Ticker: KT
Employees: 23,372
Parent Company:

Exchange: NYS
Fiscal Year Ends:

SALARIES/BONUSES:

Top Exec. Salary: $ Bonus: $
Second Exec. Salary: $ Bonus: $

OTHER THOUGHTS:

Estimated Female Officers or Directors:
Hot Spot for Advancement for Women/Minorities:

Kyocera Corporation

NAIC Code: 333316

global.kyocera.com

TYPES OF BUSINESS:

Photographic and Photocopying Equipment Manufacturing
Cell Phone Manufacturing
Semiconductor Components
Optoelectronic Products
Consumer Electronics

BRANDS/DIVISIONS/AFFILIATES:

CONTACTS:
Note: Officers with more than one job title may be intentionally listed here more than once.

Hideo Tanimoto, Pres.
Tatsumi Maeda, Vice Chmn.
Goro Yamaguchi, Chmn.

GROWTH PLANS/SPECIAL FEATURES:

Kyocera Corporation is engaged in a number of high-tech fields, including fine ceramic components, electronic devices, telecom equipment, services and networks. The company operates in six segments: industrial & automotive components, semiconductor components, electronic devices, communications, document solutions and life & environment. Principal products and services offered in each of these segments are represented below. The industrial & automotive components segment offers fine ceramic components, automotive components, liquid crystal displays and industrial tools, which are mainly supplied to the industrial, automotive and construction markets. The semiconductor components segment manufactures and sells ceramic packages and organic multi-layer substrates and boards for various electronic components and devices for the communication infrastructure and automotive markets. The electronic devices segment offers capacitors, crystal devices, connectors, power semiconductor devices, printing devices and more to diverse sectors that include automotive, information and communications equipment, and industrial equipment. The communications segment develops, manufactures and sells mobile phones, mobile-to-mobile modules, information systems and telecommunications systems. The document solutions segment supplies printers, multifunctional products that provide long life cycle and low-running costs, document software solutions, document management systems, document outsourcing services and enterprise contents management. Last, the life & environment segment develops, manufactures and sells solar power generating system products (such as solar modules), medical devices (prosthetics), jewelry and ceramic knives. Kyocera has manufacturing and sales channels in Japan, as well as in the U.S., Europe and Asia (which includes China and Vietnam). Kyocera's Minato Mirai Research Center in Yokohama, Japan, is active in the innovation of artificial intelligence (AI) and Internet of Things (IoT) technologies.

FINANCIAL DATA:
Note: Data for latest year may not have been available at press time.

In U.S. $	2020	2019	2018	2017	2016	2015
Revenue	14,604,160,000	14,829,350,000	14,403,100,000	12,994,020,000	13,513,440,000	13,941,860,000
R&D Expense						
Operating Income	915,063,200	866,018,900	872,886,900	954,782,600	975,395,700	853,278,300
Operating Margin %	.06%	.06%	.06%	.07%	.07%	.06%
SGA Expense	3,114,181,000	3,371,905,000	2,562,292,000	2,454,404,000	2,551,405,000	2,703,105,000
Net Income	983,816,400	942,617,400	746,979,300	948,398,600	995,926,700	1,058,287,000
Operating Cash Flow	1,960,217,000	2,009,489,000	1,451,718,000	1,499,923,000	1,772,168,000	1,194,296,000
Capital Expenditure	1,102,664,000	1,082,763,000	834,656,200	664,069,900	701,460,400	577,836,000
EBITDA	2,220,480,000	1,879,024,000	1,973,323,000	1,974,510,000	2,046,195,000	1,795,311,000
Return on Assets %	.03%	.03%	.03%	.03%	.04%	.04%
Return on Equity %	.05%	.04%	.04%	.04%	.05%	.06%
Debt to Equity	0.032	0.003	0.009	0.007	0.008	0.008

CONTACT INFORMATION:

Phone: 81-75-604-3500   Fax: 81-75-604-3501
Toll-Free:
Address: 6, Takeda Tobadono-cho, Fushimi-ku,, Kyoto, 612-8501 Japan

STOCK TICKER/OTHER:

Stock Ticker: KYOCY   Exchange: PINX
Employees: 70,153   Fiscal Year Ends: 03/31
Parent Company:

SALARIES/BONUSES:

Top Exec. Salary: $ Bonus: $
Second Exec. Salary: $ Bonus: $

OTHER THOUGHTS:

Estimated Female Officers or Directors:
Hot Spot for Advancement for Women/Minorities:

L3Harris Technologies Inc
NAIC Code: 334220

www.l3harris.com

TYPES OF BUSINESS:
Communications Equipment Manufacturing
Aerospace and Defense Technology
Communication Systems
Electronic Systems
Space Systems
Intelligence Systems

BRANDS/DIVISIONS/AFFILIATES:

GROWTH PLANS/SPECIAL FEATURES:

L3Harris Technologies, Inc. is an agile global aerospace and defense technology innovator that designs and builds systems for safety purposes. The company anticipates and mitigates risk with end-to-end solutions that meet its customers' mission-critical needs across air, land, sea, space and cyber domains. L3Harris serves customers in more than 100 countries. During 2020, L3Harris sold its security and detection systems, its MacDonald Humfrey automation solutions business, its applied kilovolts and analytical instruments business, and its EOTech holographic sighting systems, magnified field optics and related accessories business.

CONTACTS:
Note: Officers with more than one job title may be intentionally listed here more than once.

William Brown, CEO
Christopher E. Kubasik, Pres.
Jesus Malave Jr., CFO
James P. Girard, VP-Human Resources
Scott Mikuen, General Counsel
Dana Mehnert, Other Executive Officer
Christopher Young, President, Divisional
Edward Zoiss, President, Divisional
William Gattle, President, Divisional
Robert Duffy, Senior VP, Divisional
Sheldon Fox, Senior VP, Divisional

FINANCIAL DATA:
Note: Data for latest year may not have been available at press time.

In U.S. $	2020	2019	2018	2017	2016	2015
Revenue	18,194,000,000	9,263,000,000	6,182,000,000	5,900,000,000	7,467,000,000	
R&D Expense						
Operating Income	1,993,000,000	610,000,000	1,122,000,000	1,073,000,000	1,149,000,000	
Operating Margin %			.18%	.18%	.15%	
SGA Expense	3,315,000,000	1,927,000,000	1,129,000,000	1,016,000,000	1,186,000,000	
Net Income	1,119,000,000	822,000,000	718,000,000	553,000,000	324,000,000	
Operating Cash Flow	2,790,000,000	939,000,000	751,000,000	569,000,000	924,000,000	
Capital Expenditure	368,000,000	173,000,000	136,000,000	119,000,000	152,000,000	
EBITDA	2,624,000,000	1,485,000,000	1,355,000,000	1,388,000,000	1,155,000,000	
Return on Assets %			.07%	.05%	.03%	
Return on Equity %			.23%	.18%	.10%	
Debt to Equity			1.026	1.16	1.348	

CONTACT INFORMATION:
Phone: 321 727-9100   Fax: 321 724-3973
Toll-Free: 800-442-7747
Address: 1025 West NASA Blvd., Melbourne, FL 32919 United States

STOCK TICKER/OTHER:
Stock Ticker: LHX   Exchange: NYS
Employees: 48,000   Fiscal Year Ends: 06/30
Parent Company:

SALARIES/BONUSES:
Top Exec. Salary: $ Bonus: $
Second Exec. Salary: $ Bonus: $

OTHER THOUGHTS:
Estimated Female Officers or Directors: 2
Hot Spot for Advancement for Women/Minorities: Y

Laird Connectivity

www.lairdconnect.com

NAIC Code: 334220

TYPES OF BUSINESS:

Antennas, Transmitting and Receiving, Manufacturing
Wireless Modules
Internet of Things Devices
Radio Frequency Antennas
Product Development
Wearable Design
Electromagnetic Compatibility Testing

BRANDS/DIVISIONS/AFFILIATES:

Advent International

CONTACTS: Note: Officers with more than one job title may be intentionally listed here more than once.

Scott Lordo, CEO
Bob Sallmann, CFO
Jen Sarto, VP-Sales
Melanie Curtis, VP-Human Resources
Gene Vena, VP-Engineering

GROWTH PLANS/SPECIAL FEATURES:

Laird Connectivity manufactures and sells innovative solutions for the integration of wireless connectivity. The firm's products are grouped into three categories: wireless modules, including Wi-Fi and Bluetooth modules, low-power wide area networking protocol (LoRaWAN) solutions, cellular solutions, RAMP ISM (industrial, scientific and medical) modules and related programming kits; Internet of Things (IoT) devices, including IoT gateways, IoT sensors, IoT starter kits and related programming kits; and radio frequency antennas, including Wi-Fi, Bluetooth, cellular, internal, LoRaWAN, global positioning system (GPS) and GNSS, RFID, IoT, machine-to-machine, public safety and custom antennas, along with related accessories. Services offered by Laird Connectivity include product development, antenna design, wearable design and electromagnetic compatibility (EMC) testing. Laird Connectivity has offices and manufacturing facilities worldwide, including the U.S., the U.K., Malaysia and Taiwan. The company is privately-owned by Advent International, an American private equity firm focused on buyouts of companies in Western and Central Europe, North America, Latin America and Asia.

FINANCIAL DATA: Note: Data for latest year may not have been available at press time.

In U.S. $	2020	2019	2018	2017	2016	2015
Revenue	1,461,474,000	1,391,880,000	1,325,600,000	1,241,796,224	1,062,805,760	835,819,328
R&D Expense						
Operating Income						
Operating Margin %						
SGA Expense						
Net Income				94,931,256	-148,098,064	-11,004,601
Operating Cash Flow						
Capital Expenditure						
EBITDA						
Return on Assets %						
Return on Equity %						
Debt to Equity						

CONTACT INFORMATION:

Phone: 330-434-7929   Fax:
Toll-Free:
Address: 50 S. Main St. #1100, Akron, OH 44308 United Kingdom

STOCK TICKER/OTHER:

Stock Ticker: Private   Exchange:
Employees: 10,132   Fiscal Year Ends: 12/31
Parent Company: Advent International

SALARIES/BONUSES:

Top Exec. Salary: $ Bonus: $
Second Exec. Salary: $ Bonus: $

OTHER THOUGHTS:

Estimated Female Officers or Directors:
Hot Spot for Advancement for Women/Minorities:

Lattice Incorporated

www.latticeinc.com

NAIC Code: 334210

TYPES OF BUSINESS:

Call Control Technology
Inmate Call Control Systems
Calling Cards
Secure Network Applications

BRANDS/DIVISIONS/AFFILIATES:

Corrections Operating Platform
Nexus
NetVisit
CellMate
InTouch

CONTACTS: Note: Officers with more than one job title may be intentionally listed here more than once.

Paul Burgess, CEO
Joseph Noto, CFO

GROWTH PLANS/SPECIAL FEATURES:

Lattice Incorporated provides innovative inmate management and communications solutions to correctional facilities. The company's Corrections Operating Platform (COP) provides benefits to Lattice clients, their inmates and the family and friends of the inmates through a range of secure, integrated inmate management and communications products and services. COP consists of three primary categories: deposit solutions, providing on-site deposit kiosks, online/phone/money-order deposits, commissary integration, Java message service (JMS) integration, payment processing and billing; products and solutions, such as the Nexus inmate phone system, the NetVisit video visitation and video arraignment system, and the CellMate mobile device; and support services and solutions, including the InTouch inmate hotline, billing and technical support, and handling account funding transactions. Lattice's related services span seamless installation, corrections staff training, and system maintenance and technical support.

FINANCIAL DATA: Note: Data for latest year may not have been available at press time.

In U.S. $	2020	2019	2018	2017	2016	2015
Revenue	8,364,579	7,966,266	7,771,967	7,582,407	7,397,471	7,587,150
R&D Expense						
Operating Income						
Operating Margin %						
SGA Expense						
Net Income						
Operating Cash Flow						
Capital Expenditure						
EBITDA						
Return on Assets %						
Return on Equity %						
Debt to Equity						

CONTACT INFORMATION:

Phone: 856 910-1166   Fax: 856 910-1811
Toll-Free: 800-910-1316
Address: 7150 N. Park Dr., Ste. 500, Pennsauken, NJ 08109 United States

STOCK TICKER/OTHER:

Stock Ticker: Private
Employees: 23
Parent Company:

Exchange:
Fiscal Year Ends: 12/31

SALARIES/BONUSES:

Top Exec. Salary: $ Bonus: $
Second Exec. Salary: $ Bonus: $

OTHER THOUGHTS:

Estimated Female Officers or Directors:
Hot Spot for Advancement for Women/Minorities:

LG Corporation

NAIC Code: 551114

lgcorp.com

TYPES OF BUSINESS:

Corporate, Subsidiary, and Regional Managing Offices
Electronics
Technology
Mobile Communications
Vehicle Components
Commercial Displays
Energy Storage

BRANDS/DIVISIONS/AFFILIATES:

LG Electronics Inc
LG Signature
LG ThinQ

CONTACTS: *Note: Officers with more than one job title may be intentionally listed here more than once.*

Seok Kwon Bong, Chmn.

GROWTH PLANS/SPECIAL FEATURES:

LG Corporation is a South Korean firm that operates in the electronics, chemicals and communication & services segments. The electronics division consists of four subsidiaries: LG Electronics, which manufactures and markets home appliances, TVs and mobile communications for consumers, and manufactures and markets commercial air conditioners and car parts for businesses; LG Display, a manufacturer of innovative displays, utilizing technologies such as organic light-emitting diodes (OLEDs) and in-plane switching (IPS); LG Innotek, a developer and producer of materials parts in the fields of vehicles, mobile devices, Internet of Things (IoT), displays, semiconductors and LEDs; and Silicon Works, a fabless company that utilizes its system semiconductors technology. The chemicals division consists of four subsidiaries: LG Chem, a chemical, business-to-business company that produces basic materials and chemicals, battery solutions, IT materials, electronics materials, advanced materials, pharmaceuticals and fine chemicals; LG Household & Health Care, a consumer goods company that manages cosmetics, household goods and beverages businesses; LG Hausys, which specializes in architectural decorative materials, automobile material parts and other high-functional materials; and LG MMA, a joint venture with Sumitomo Chemical and Japan Catalyst, and is a chemical supplier in Japan, primarily methyl methacrylate. Last, the communication & services segment comprises seven subsidiaries: LG U+, a telecommunications service company; GIIR, an advertising and marketing holding company; LG HelloVision Corp., a cable TV company that provides cable TV, internet services, and operates a mobile virtual network; LG International, which trades (imports/exports) textiles and household goods, and is engaged in plant construction projects; LG CNS, a global IT service company; S&I Corporation, a space solution company for construction, leisure and other industry clients; LG Management Development Institute, which specializes in management consulting and research for future LG businesses; and LG Sports, a professional sports management company in Korea.

FINANCIAL DATA: *Note: Data for latest year may not have been available at press time.*

In U.S. $	2020	2019	2018	2017	2016	2015
Revenue	6,206,060,000	5,494,190,000	6,862,430,000	11,088,100,000	8,018,680,000	8,477,950,000
R&D Expense						
Operating Income						
Operating Margin %						
SGA Expense						
Net Income	1,524,570,000	955,782,000	1,685,530,000	2,280,680,000	904,544,000	802,681,000
Operating Cash Flow						
Capital Expenditure						
EBITDA						
Return on Assets %						
Return on Equity %						
Debt to Equity						

CONTACT INFORMATION:

Phone: 822-3773-1114　　　Fax: 822-3773-2292
Toll-Free:
Address: LG Twin Towers, 128 Yeoui-daero, Yeongdeungpo-gu, Seoul, 150-721 South Korea

STOCK TICKER/OTHER:

Stock Ticker: 3550　　　　　　　　Exchange: Seoul
Employees: 222,000　　　　　　　Fiscal Year Ends: 12/31
Parent Company:

SALARIES/BONUSES:

Top Exec. Salary: $　　　Bonus: $
Second Exec. Salary: $　　　Bonus: $

OTHER THOUGHTS:

Estimated Female Officers or Directors:
Hot Spot for Advancement for Women/Minorities:

Sales, profits and employees may be estimates. Financial information, benefits and other data can change quickly and may vary from those stated here.

LG Electronics Inc

www.lg.com

NAIC Code: 334220

TYPES OF BUSINESS:

Manufacturing-Electronics
Technology
Home Appliances
Home Entertainment
Mobile Communications
Vehicle Component Solutions
Commercial Displays
Energy Management

BRANDS/DIVISIONS/AFFILIATES:

LG Corporation
LG Signature
LG ThinQ

GROWTH PLANS/SPECIAL FEATURES:

LG Electronics, Inc. is a global innovator in technology and manufacturing. LG Electronics has operations in more than 140 countries worldwide. It comprises five segments: home appliance and air solutions, home entertainment, mobile communications, vehicle component solutions, and business solutions. LG produces TVs, refrigerators, air conditioners, washing machines and mobile devices, as well as premium LG Signature products and LG ThinQ artificial intelligence technology. Vehicle component solutions span in-vehicle infotainment technology and systems, motor and vehicle engineering components, and vehicle HVAC components. For businesses, LG offers commercial display solutions, solar solutions, energy storage systems and energy management solutions. LG Electronics operates as a subsidiary of LG Corporation.

CONTACTS: Note: Officers with more than one job title may be intentionally listed here more than once.

Seok Kwon Bong, CEO
Hyun-Hoi Ha, Pres.

FINANCIAL DATA: Note: Data for latest year may not have been available at press time.

In U.S. $	2020	2019	2018	2017	2016	2015
Revenue	58,120,400,000	55,760,000,000	52,877,099,008	52,924,182,528	47,726,907,392	47,634,264,064
R&D Expense						
Operating Income						
Operating Margin %						
SGA Expense						
Net Income	1,896,060,000	1,122,462,230	1,069,011,648	1,487,633,664	66,270,432	104,857,912
Operating Cash Flow						
Capital Expenditure						
EBITDA						
Return on Assets %						
Return on Equity %						
Debt to Equity						

CONTACT INFORMATION:

Phone: 82 237771114   Fax:
Toll-Free: 800-243-0000
Address: LG Twin Towers, 128 Yeoui-daero, Yeongdeungpo-gu, Seoul, 073-36 South Korea

STOCK TICKER/OTHER:

Stock Ticker: 66570
Employees: 100,000
Parent Company: LG Corporation

Exchange: Seoul
Fiscal Year Ends: 12/31

SALARIES/BONUSES:

Top Exec. Salary: $ Bonus: $
Second Exec. Salary: $ Bonus: $

OTHER THOUGHTS:

Estimated Female Officers or Directors:
Hot Spot for Advancement for Women/Minorities:

LG Electronics USA Inc

NAIC Code: 334220

www.lg.com/us

TYPES OF BUSINESS:
Consumer Electronics
Mobile Phones & Accessories
Home Appliances
Computer Products

BRANDS/DIVISIONS/AFFILIATES:
LG Corporation
LG Electronics Inc

CONTACTS: *Note: Officers with more than one job title may be intentionally listed here more than once.*
Thomas Yoon, CEO

GROWTH PLANS/SPECIAL FEATURES:
LG Electronics USA, Inc., a subsidiary of South Korea-based LG Electronics, Inc., sells consumer electronics, home appliances, mobile phones and digital applications in the U.S., Canada and Mexico. Products are grouped into five categories: mobile phones; television, audio and video; appliances; computer products; and solar. The mobile phone segment works in conjunction with service providers, developing a wide range of phones including Android powered smartphones, quad core processors, 4G, 5G, touch screens and more. Additionally, the company sells an array of mobile phone accessories including batteries, cables, chargers, hands-free headsets and Bluetooth products. The television, audio and video category includes organic light-emitting diode (OLED) and nanocell TVs, sound bars, projectors, Blu-ray players, speakers and more. The appliances segment sells washers, dryers, refrigerators, built-in ovens, cooktops, dishwashers, microwave ovens, air conditioners, vacuums, dehumidifiers and accessories. The computer products segment offers consumer and commercial laptops, monitors, burners/drives and related accessories. Last, the solar segment manufactures and installs solar cells and solar panels, which come with a 25-year guarantee. Headquartered in Englewood Cliffs, New Jersey, the firm operates additional training facilities in California and Georgia and a R&D center in Illinois. LG Electronics is itself a subsidiary of holding company LG Corporation.

FINANCIAL DATA: *Note: Data for latest year may not have been available at press time.*

In U.S. $	2020	2019	2018	2017	2016	2015
Revenue	12,429,400,000	8,941,270,432	8,515,495,650	8,473,130,000	6,984,197,082	6,101,401,884
R&D Expense						
Operating Income						
Operating Margin %						
SGA Expense						
Net Income	152,231,000	-74,658,681	-78,588,085	-82,724,300	-105,207,004	45,549,348
Operating Cash Flow						
Capital Expenditure						
EBITDA						
Return on Assets %						
Return on Equity %						
Debt to Equity						

CONTACT INFORMATION:
Phone: 201-816-2000   Fax: 201-816-0636
Toll-Free: 800-243-0000
Address: 1000 Sylvan Ave., Englewood Cliffs, NJ 60654 United States

STOCK TICKER/OTHER:
Stock Ticker: Subsidiary
Employees: 2,500
Parent Company: LG Corporation

Exchange:
Fiscal Year Ends: 12/31

SALARIES/BONUSES:
Top Exec. Salary: $ Bonus: $
Second Exec. Salary: $ Bonus: $

OTHER THOUGHTS:
Estimated Female Officers or Directors:
Hot Spot for Advancement for Women/Minorities:

LG Uplus Corp

www.uplus.co.kr/com/main/pemain/PeMain.hpi

NAIC Code: 517210

TYPES OF BUSINESS:

Mobile Telephone Services
Wireless Internet Service
Mobile Commerce Services
Consulting Services
Internet Data Center Services

BRANDS/DIVISIONS/AFFILIATES:

LG Corporation
LG U+
U+ homeBoy

CONTACTS: Note: Officers with more than one job title may be intentionally listed here more than once.

Hyun-sik Hwang, CEO

GROWTH PLANS/SPECIAL FEATURES:

LG Uplus Corp. offers mobile telecommunications and wireless internet solutions primarily marketed under the LG U+ brand. The firm offers three primary types of services: mobile, home and corporate. Mobile services include mobile phone plans; mobile internet service (including national 4G and 5G coverage), which offers full internet browsing, search, email, file viewing and video capabilities; and roaming service, which offers voice over long-term evolution (VoLTE) roaming, LTE data roaming, WCDMA/GSM auto roaming in about 240 countries worldwide, CDMA auto roaming in 10 countries, and rental roaming. Home services are divided into three sections: residential, artificial intelligence (AI) and Internet of Things (IoT). Residential offerings include internet, internet protocol TV (IPTV), video on demand (VOD) and other channels, U+ homeBoy smart pad/speaker dock combination, internet phone, and bundled options. Home AI provides five major services: the ability to search U+ tv VOD video content by a single key word; turning the home IoT on or off by saying a single word; searching NAVER via voice; foreign language education by native-speakers available 24/7; and shopping, from order to payment, via voice. Home IoT is the technology for hyper-connected environments, connecting things with the internet and allowing homeowners to keep an eye of their properties from anywhere, anytime via smart devices. Last, corporate services include products and solutions such as smart drones, customized telecommunications packages, marketing management devices, business phone services, internet, payments/funds management, business information technology (IT), smart sensor devices for facility monitoring and remote control of company vehicles/assets, and industrial Internet of Things (IIoT). LG Uplus is based in Korea and operates as a subsidiary of LG Corporation.

FINANCIAL DATA: Note: Data for latest year may not have been available at press time.

In U.S. $	2020	2019	2018	2017	2016	2015
Revenue	12,327,100,000	11,396,805,000	10,854,100,000	11,498,500,000	10,202,652,290	9,250,098,447
R&D Expense						
Operating Income						
Operating Margin %						
SGA Expense						
Net Income	439,210,000	452,708,550	431,151,000	512,216,000	438,126,013	301,142,677
Operating Cash Flow						
Capital Expenditure						
EBITDA						
Return on Assets %						
Return on Equity %						
Debt to Equity						

CONTACT INFORMATION:

Phone: 82-070-4080-1114   Fax:
Toll-Free:
Address: 32, Hangang-daero, Yongsan-gu, Seoul,   South Korea

STOCK TICKER/OTHER:

Stock Ticker: 32640
Employees: 8,446
Parent Company: LG Corporation

Exchange: Seoul
Fiscal Year Ends: 12/31

SALARIES/BONUSES:

Top Exec. Salary: $ Bonus: $
Second Exec. Salary: $ Bonus: $

OTHER THOUGHTS:

Estimated Female Officers or Directors:
Hot Spot for Advancement for Women/Minorities:

Liberty Global plc

NAIC Code: 517110

www.libertyglobal.com

TYPES OF BUSINESS:

Video, Voice & Broadband Internet Access Services
Telephony Services
VoIP Services
Mobile Telephony Services
Video on Demand Services

BRANDS/DIVISIONS/AFFILIATES:

Virgin Media
Telenet
UPC
Vodafone Ziggo
ITV
All3Media
ITI Neovision
Sunrise Communications AG

CONTACTS: *Note: Officers with more than one job title may be intentionally listed here more than once.*

Michael Fries, CEO
John Malone, Chairman of the Board
Charlie Bracken, CFO
Amy Blair, Sr. VP
Enrique Rodriguez, Exec. VP
Bryan Hall, Executive VP
Diederik Karsten, Executive VP
Leonard Stegman, Managing Director
John C. Malone, Chmn.

GROWTH PLANS/SPECIAL FEATURES:

Liberty Global plc is a leading converged video, broadband and communications company, with operations in six European countries under the Virgin Media, Telenet and UPC brand names. The firm invests in the infrastructure and digital platforms, which enables Liberty Global to develop market-leading products delivered through next-generation networks that connect 11 million customers subscribing to 25 million TV, broadband, internet and telephone services. Liberty Global also serve 6 million mobile subscribers and offers WiFi service through millions of access points across its network footprint. The company also owns 50% of VodafoneZiggo, a joint venture in the Netherlands with 4 million customers subscribing to 10 million fixed-line and 5 million mobile services. Other investments include ITV, All3Media, ITI Neovision, LionsGate, the Formula E racing series and several regional sports networks. During 2020, Liberty Global agreed to form a 50-50 joint venture with Telefonica SA, merging Virgin Media's U.K. telecommunications business and certain other Liberty Global subsidiaries with Telefonica's mobile business in the U.K., creating a nationwide integrated communications provider. That November, Liberty Global acquired Swiss telecommunications provider, Sunrise Communications AG, which serves nearly 3 million customers.

FINANCIAL DATA: *Note: Data for latest year may not have been available at press time.*

In U.S. $	2020	2019	2018	2017	2016	2015
Revenue	11,980,100,000	11,541,500,000	11,957,900,000	15,048,900,000	17,285,000,000	17,062,700,000
R&D Expense						
Operating Income	2,216,300,000	901,500,000	1,087,300,000	2,054,700,000	2,676,900,000	2,255,400,000
Operating Margin %		.08%	.09%	.14%	.15%	.13%
SGA Expense	2,225,900,000	2,107,800,000	2,049,100,000	2,476,000,000	3,027,700,000	2,973,500,000
Net Income	-1,628,000,000	11,521,400,000	725,300,000	-2,778,100,000	1,960,800,000	-1,196,400,000
Operating Cash Flow	4,185,800,000	4,585,400,000	5,963,100,000	5,708,500,000	5,467,300,000	5,399,300,000
Capital Expenditure	1,350,200,000	1,243,100,000	1,453,000,000	1,953,100,000	2,153,900,000	2,272,300,000
EBITDA	1,796,200,000	3,882,100,000	5,498,700,000	5,190,600,000	8,185,700,000	7,116,600,000
Return on Assets %		.23%	.01%	-.05%	.03%	-.02%
Return on Equity %		1.26%	.13%	-.34%	.19%	-.10%
Debt to Equity		1.786	5.594	5.591	3.669	4.039

CONTACT INFORMATION:

Phone: 44-208-483-6300   Fax:
Toll-Free:
Address: Griffin House, 161 Hammersmith Rd., London, W6 8BS United Kingdom

STOCK TICKER/OTHER:

Stock Ticker: LBTYA
Employees: 20,200
Parent Company:

Exchange: NAS
Fiscal Year Ends: 12/31

SALARIES/BONUSES:

Top Exec. Salary: $ Bonus: $
Second Exec. Salary: $ Bonus: $

OTHER THOUGHTS:

Estimated Female Officers or Directors: 3
Hot Spot for Advancement for Women/Minorities: Y

LM Ericsson Telephone Company (Ericsson)   www.ericsson.com

NAIC Code: 334220

TYPES OF BUSINESS:

Wireless Telecommunications Equipment
Information Technology
Communications
Networks
Digital
Internet of Things
Telecommunications
Artificial Intelligence

BRANDS/DIVISIONS/AFFILIATES:

Cradlepoint

CONTACTS: Note: Officers with more than one job title may be intentionally listed here more than once.

Borje Ekholm, CEO
Carl Mellander, Sr. VP
Stella Medlicott, Sr. VP
MajBritt Arfert, Chief People Officer
Erik Ekudden, Sr. VP
Nina Macpherson, General Counsel
Douglas L. Gilstrap, Sr. VP-Function Strategy
Helena Norrman, Sr. VP-Comm..
Jan Frykhammar, Head-Group Function Finance
Angel Ruiz, Head-North America
Magnus Mandersson, Head-Global Svcs.
Rima Qureshi, Sr. VP-Strategic Projects
Johan Wibergh, Exec. VP-Networks
Ronnie Leten, Chmn.
Mats H. Olsson, Head-Asia Pacific

GROWTH PLANS/SPECIAL FEATURES:

LM Ericsson Telephone Company (Ericsson) is a leading global supplier of information and communication technology (ICT) to service providers. Ericsson's comprehensive portfolio spans networks, digital services, managed services and emerging business, each of which are powered by 5G and Internet of Things (IoT) platforms. The networks business develops and manages telecommunication networks by providing hardware, software and services that enable connectivity. The digital services business offers digital transformation services and solutions, covering network management and operations, revenue and customer management, communication services, core network and network function virtualization, infrastructure, and application development and maintenance. The managed services business aims to create value and business differentiation by taking an integrated approach. It manages and optimizes telecom networks and IT operations with industrialized processes and utilizes a global delivery model for the purpose of enhancing the operators' ability to meet and exceed consumer expectations. Last, the emerging business division accelerates new businesses via technologies such as 5G, artificial intelligence (AI), automation, virtual reality/augmented reality (VR/AR) and edge computing. Ericsson's current emerging businesses target high-growth markets where its technology is relevant, such as Industry 4.0 and smart manufacturing, IoT connectivity, connected vehicles, security and edge computing. In late-2020, Ericsson acquired Cradlepoint, a U.S.-based leader in wireless WAN Edge 4G and 5G solutions for the enterprise market.

FINANCIAL DATA: Note: Data for latest year may not have been available at press time.

In U.S. $	2020	2019	2018	2017	2016	2015
Revenue	28,112,600,000	27,486,690,000	25,505,420,000	24,351,950,000	26,929,250,000	29,870,320,000
R&D Expense	4,804,268,000	4,695,514,000	4,706,886,000	4,583,252,000	3,826,938,000	4,215,136,000
Operating Income	3,395,069,000	1,131,085,000	252,951,700	-3,066,752,000	753,774,300	2,623,512,000
Operating Margin %		.04%	.01%	-.13%	.03%	.09%
SGA Expense	3,228,007,000	3,161,836,000	3,329,019,000	3,952,869,000	3,491,967,000	3,542,654,000
Net Income	2,114,947,000	268,920,000	-789,944,800	-4,258,928,000	207,587,300	1,639,045,000
Operating Cash Flow	3,500,072,000	2,041,155,000	1,130,117,000	1,161,449,000	1,694,813,000	2,491,653,000
Capital Expenditure	642,359,400	806,034,000	592,761,000	643,690,100	1,283,751,000	1,408,110,000
EBITDA	4,449,821,000	2,335,237,000	872,931,400	-3,602,173,000	1,725,902,000	3,813,389,000
Return on Assets %		.01%	-.02%	-.13%	.01%	.05%
Return on Equity %		.03%	-.07%	-.29%	.01%	.09%
Debt to Equity		0.434	0.355	0.306	0.133	0.155

CONTACT INFORMATION:

Phone: 46 87190000   Fax: 46 87191976
Toll-Free:
Address: Torshamnsgatan 21, Kista, Stockholm, 164 83 Sweden

SALARIES/BONUSES:

Top Exec. Salary: $ Bonus: $
Second Exec. Salary: $ Bonus: $

STOCK TICKER/OTHER:

Stock Ticker: ERIC   Exchange: NAS
Employees: 100,824   Fiscal Year Ends: 12/31
Parent Company:

OTHER THOUGHTS:

Estimated Female Officers or Directors: 10
Hot Spot for Advancement for Women/Minorities: Y

Loral Space & Communications Inc

www.loral.com

NAIC Code: 334220

TYPES OF BUSINESS:

Satellite Equipment
Satellites
Communications
Telecommunications

BRANDS/DIVISIONS/AFFILIATES:

Telesat Canada
XTAR

CONTACTS: *Note: Officers with more than one job title may be intentionally listed here more than once.*

Avi Katz, CEO
John Capogrossi, CFO
Ravinder Girgla, Chief Accounting Officer
Mark Rachesky, Director
Michael Targoff, Director

GROWTH PLANS/SPECIAL FEATURES:

Loral Space & Communications, Inc. is a leader in satellite communications. Loral's business is primarily operated through 62.7%-owned Telesat Canada. Telesat operates satellites that provide communications services worldwide to broadcast, telecom, corporate and government customers. Telesat's fleet consists of 14 satellites, plus the Canadian payload on ViaSat-1 with another satellite under construction. Telesat also manages the operations of additional satellites for third parties. Loral also majority-owns (56%) XTAR, a joint venture with HISDESAT, a consortium comprised of Spanish telecommunications companies, including Hispasat SA and agencies of the Spanish government. Through its XTAR-EUR satellite, XTAR provides X-band services to government users in the U.S., Spain and other allied countries, including the U.S. Department of State, the Spanish Ministry of Defence and Danish armed forces. XTAR's headquarters are in Ashburn, Virginia. In November 2020, Loral entered into a transaction agreement with Public Sector Pension Investment Board (PSP) and Telesat to combine Loral and Telesat into a new Canadian public company. The merger is expected to close by the end of 2021.

FINANCIAL DATA: *Note: Data for latest year may not have been available at press time.*

In U.S. $	2020	2019	2018	2017	2016	2015
Revenue						
R&D Expense						
Operating Income	-863,000	-6,612,000	-6,534,000	-7,935,000	-6,726,000	-6,530,000
Operating Margin %						
SGA Expense	6,717,000	6,612,000	6,534,000	7,935,000	6,726,000	6,530,000
Net Income	93,093,000	89,755,000	9,614,000	134,464,000	47,200,000	-70,282,000
Operating Cash Flow	-10,907,000	2,126,000	1,812,000	-24,700,000	-21,249,000	-28,754,000
Capital Expenditure		6,000	4,000	50,000	5,000	102,000
EBITDA	-10,707,000	-5,456,000	-5,207,000	-8,705,000	-7,921,000	-10,130,000
Return on Assets %		.25%	.03%	.42%	.20%	- .27%
Return on Equity %		.28%	.03%	.58%	.34%	- .49%
Debt to Equity		0.001				

CONTACT INFORMATION:

Phone: 212 697-1105   Fax: 212 338-5662
Toll-Free:
Address: 600 Fifth Ave., New York, NY 10020 United States

STOCK TICKER/OTHER:

Stock Ticker: LORL   Exchange: NAS
Employees: 12   Fiscal Year Ends: 12/31
Parent Company:

SALARIES/BONUSES:

Top Exec. Salary: $ Bonus: $
Second Exec. Salary: $ Bonus: $

OTHER THOUGHTS:

Estimated Female Officers or Directors:
Hot Spot for Advancement for Women/Minorities:

Lumen Technologies Inc

www.lumen.com

NAIC Code: 517110

TYPES OF BUSINESS:

Local Telephone Service
Enterprise Technology
Industry 4.0
Advanced Architecture
Machine Learning
Artificial Intelligence
Internet of Things

BRANDS/DIVISIONS/AFFILIATES:

Lumen
CenturyLink Inc

CONTACTS: Note: Officers with more than one job title may be intentionally listed here more than once.

Jeffrey Storey, CEO
Neel Dev, CFO
Shaun Andrews, CMO
Scott A. Trezise, Exec. VP-Human Resources
Andrew Dugan, CTO
W. Hanks, Director
Scott Trezise, Executive VP, Divisional
Stacey Goff, Executive VP

GROWTH PLANS/SPECIAL FEATURES:

Lumen Technologies, Inc. (formerly CenturyLink Inc.) offers Lumen, an enterprise technology platform that enables companies to capitalize on emerging applications. Lumen's advanced application delivery architecture is designed specifically to handle complex and data-intensive workloads of next-generation technology and businesses. It integrates network assets, cloud connectivity, security solutions and voice and collaboration tools into one platform, enabling businesses to leverage their data and adopt advanced technologies. Lumen brings together talent, experience, infrastructure and capabilities of CenturyLink, Level 3 and many other technology companies to create a single entity for addressing the dynamic data and application needs of what Lumen calls the 4th Industrial Revolution, commonly referred to as Industry 4.0. The 4th Industrial Revolution is the ongoing automation of traditional manufacturing and industrial practices that analyze and diagnose issues without the need for human intervention, but through modern smart technology such as machine learning, artificial intelligence (AI), Internet of Things (IoT), machine-to-machine communication and more. Lumen's solutions include adaptive networking, collaboration, connected security, Edge computing and hybrid cloud. Industries served by the company's products and solutions include energy, financial services, gaming network, healthcare, manufacturing, media/entertainment, pharmaceuticals, public sector, retail, technology and wholesale. In September 2020, CenturyLink, Inc. launched the Lumen brand, and subsequently began to change its legal name to Lumen Technologies, Inc. Lumen Technologies trades under the ticker symbol LUMN. Over time, the CenturyLink brand will be changed to Lumen.

Lumen offers its employees health coverage, life and disability insurance, 401(k) and many other benefits.

FINANCIAL DATA: Note: Data for latest year may not have been available at press time.

In U.S. $	2020	2019	2018	2017	2016	2015
Revenue	20,712,000,000	22,401,000,000	23,443,000,000	17,656,000,000	17,470,000,000	17,900,000,000
R&D Expense						
Operating Income	3,604,000,000	3,780,000,000	3,296,000,000	2,009,000,000	2,331,000,000	2,605,000,000
Operating Margin %						
SGA Expense	3,464,000,000	3,715,000,000	4,165,000,000	3,508,000,000	3,449,000,000	3,328,000,000
Net Income	-1,232,000,000	-5,269,000,000	-1,733,000,000	1,389,000,000	626,000,000	878,000,000
Operating Cash Flow	6,524,000,000	6,680,000,000	7,032,000,000	3,878,000,000	4,608,000,000	5,152,000,000
Capital Expenditure	3,729,000,000	3,628,000,000	3,175,000,000	3,106,000,000	2,981,000,000	2,872,000,000
EBITDA	5,596,000,000	2,084,000,000	5,734,000,000	5,957,000,000	6,254,000,000	6,817,000,000
Return on Assets %						
Return on Equity %						
Debt to Equity						

CONTACT INFORMATION:

Phone: 318 388-9000   Fax: 318 789-8656
Toll-Free:
Address: 100 CenturyLink Dr., Monroe, LA 71203 United States

STOCK TICKER/OTHER:

Stock Ticker: LUMN   Exchange: NYS
Employees: 39,000   Fiscal Year Ends: 12/31
Parent Company:

SALARIES/BONUSES:

Top Exec. Salary: $ Bonus: $
Second Exec. Salary: $ Bonus: $

OTHER THOUGHTS:

Estimated Female Officers or Directors: 5
Hot Spot for Advancement for Women/Minorities: Y

Sales, profits and employees may be estimates. Financial information, benefits and other data can change quickly and may vary from those stated here.

Lumentum Operations LLC

www.lumentum.com

NAIC Code: 334220

TYPES OF BUSINESS:

Optical Components & Modules
Telecommunications Equipment
Lasers

BRANDS/DIVISIONS/AFFILIATES:

Lumentum Holdings Inc

CONTACTS: *Note: Officers with more than one job title may be intentionally listed here more than once.*

Alan Lowe, CEO
Wajid Ali, CFO
Jason Reinhardt, Exec. VP-Global Sales
Sharon Parker, Sr. VP-Human Resources
Ralph Loura, CIO
Harold Covert, Chmn.

GROWTH PLANS/SPECIAL FEATURES:

Lumentum Operations, LLC designs and manufactures innovative photonics for the purpose of accelerating the speed and scale of cloud, networking, advanced manufacturing and 3D sensing applications. The company's products are categorized into three groups: optical communications, commercial lasers and diode lasers. Optical communications products include dense wavelength division multiplexing (DWDM) and coherent optical transceivers, DWDM transmission components, reconfigurable optical add-drop multiplexers (ROADMs) and wavelength management, software-defined networking (SDN) elements, optical amplifiers, passive components and modules, pump lasers, source lasers and photodiodes, and submarine components. Commercial lasers include kW fiber and direct-diode lasers, ultra-fast lasers, Q-switched lasers, and low power continuous wave lasers. Diode lasers include edge-emitting diode lasers and fiber-coupled diode lasers. Based in California, USA, the firm has additional offices in North America, Europe and Asia. Lumentum operates as a subsidiary of Lumentum Holdings, Inc.

Lumentum offers its employees benefits programs and wellness initiatives, as well as performance incentives.

FINANCIAL DATA: *Note: Data for latest year may not have been available at press time.*

In U.S. $	2020	2019	2018	2017	2016	2015
Revenue	1,678,600,000	1,565,300,000	1,247,700,000	1,001,600,000	903,000,000	837,100,000
R&D Expense						
Operating Income						
Operating Margin %						
SGA Expense						
Net Income	135,500,000	-36,400,000	248,100,000	-102,500,000	9,300,000	-3,400,000
Operating Cash Flow						
Capital Expenditure						
EBITDA						
Return on Assets %						
Return on Equity %						
Debt to Equity						

CONTACT INFORMATION:

Phone: 408-546-5483   Fax: 408-546-4300
Toll-Free:
Address: 1001 Ridder Park Dr., San Jose, CA 95131 United States

SALARIES/BONUSES:

Top Exec. Salary: $ Bonus: $
Second Exec. Salary: $ Bonus: $

STOCK TICKER/OTHER:

Stock Ticker: Subsidiary   Exchange:
Employees: 5,473   Fiscal Year Ends: 06/30
Parent Company: Lumentum Holdings Inc

OTHER THOUGHTS:

Estimated Female Officers or Directors:
Hot Spot for Advancement for Women/Minorities:

M1 Limited

www.m1.com.sg

NAIC Code: 517210

TYPES OF BUSINESS:

Cell Phone Service
Telecommunications
Mobile
Broadband
Digital

BRANDS/DIVISIONS/AFFILIATES:

Keppel Corporation

CONTACTS: *Note: Officers with more than one job title may be intentionally listed here more than once.*

Manjot Singh Mann, CEO
Nathan Bell, Chief Digital Officer
Lee Kok Chew, CFO
Mustafa Kapasi, CCO
Chan Sock Leng, Dir.-Human Resources
Denis Seek, CTO
Alex Tan, Dir.-Enterprise Svcs. & Prod.
Anil Sachdev, Dir.-Legal Svcs.
Lim Sock Leng, Dir.-Corp. Dev.
Ivan Lim, Dir.-Corp. Comm.
Ivan Lim, Dir.-Investor Rel.
Lee Kok Chew, Chief Commercial Officer
Terence Teo, Dir.-Customer Svcs.
Chan Weng Keong, Dir.-Mgmt. Assurance Svcs.
Loh Chin Hua, Chmn.

GROWTH PLANS/SPECIAL FEATURES:

M1 Limited, a subsidiary of Keppel Corporation, is a leading mobile and fixed telecommunications provider in Singapore, with over 2 million customers. The firm uses 3G, 4G and 5G networks, as well as ultra-high-speed fixed broadband, fixed voice and other services on its next-generation nationwide broadband network. M1 offers a wide range of mobile and fixed communication services to consumers, and delivers an extensive suite of services and solutions to corporate customers. These services include symmetrical connectivity solutions of up to 10 gigabits per second (Gbps), managed services, cloud solutions, cybersecurity solutions, Internet of Things (IoT) and data center services. Mobile plans include SIM-only and flexible phone and payment options. The home broadband division offers devices, fixed voice, special benefits and a variety of plans. The travel division offers pre- and post-paid roaming services as well as tourist SIM services. Digital services include entertainment, security, finance/payment, utilities and direct carrier billing. During 2021, M1 Limited, Continental Automotive Singapore and JTC announced a collaboration to conduct autonomous transport systems 5G standalone trials for autonomous robot operations, with a focus on growing 5G use cases in Singapore.

FINANCIAL DATA: *Note: Data for latest year may not have been available at press time.*

In U.S. $	2020	2019	2018	2017	2016	2015
Revenue	807,817,000	815,253,000	800,596,000	790,200,128	782,705,088	853,748,288
R&D Expense						
Operating Income						
Operating Margin %						
SGA Expense						
Net Income	58,434,600			97,769,712	110,408,512	131,679,240
Operating Cash Flow						
Capital Expenditure						
EBITDA						
Return on Assets %						
Return on Equity %						
Debt to Equity						

CONTACT INFORMATION:

Phone: 65 6655-1111   Fax: 65 6655-1977
Toll-Free:
Address: 10 International Business Park, Singapore, 609928 Singapore

STOCK TICKER/OTHER:

Stock Ticker: Subsidiary   Exchange:
Employees: 1,384   Fiscal Year Ends: 12/31
Parent Company: Keppel Corporation

SALARIES/BONUSES:

Top Exec. Salary: $ Bonus: $
Second Exec. Salary: $ Bonus: $

OTHER THOUGHTS:

Estimated Female Officers or Directors: 1
Hot Spot for Advancement for Women/Minorities: Y

Magyar Telekom plc

www.telekom.hu/lakossagi/english

NAIC Code: 517110

TYPES OF BUSINESS:

Local & Long-Distance Telephone Services
Internet & Data Services
Wireless Telephone & Internet Services
Network Infrastructure
Wholesale Services
Telecommunications Equipment

BRANDS/DIVISIONS/AFFILIATES:

Deutsche Telekom AG
T-Mobile
Telekom Hotel Balatonkenese

CONTACTS: *Note: Officers with more than one job title may be intentionally listed here more than once.*

Tibor Rekasi, CEO
Daria Dodonova, CFO
Melinda Szabo, CCO
Zsuzsanna Friedl, Chief People Officer
Zabor Zatko, CTO
Balazs Mathe, Chief Legal & Corp. Affairs Officer
Robert Pataki, Chief Bus. Dev. Officer
Robert Budafoki, Chief Commercial Officer-Enterprise
Attila Keszeg, Chief Commercial Officer-Residential
Peter Lakatos, Chief Commercial Officer-SMB

GROWTH PLANS/SPECIAL FEATURES:

Magyar Telekom plc is a full-service information and communication technologies (ICT) provider based in Hungary. Magyar Telekom operates as a subsidiary of German telecommunications company, Deutsche Telekom AG, and markets its products under the T-Mobile brand and logo. Magyar Telekom provides phone, broadband, TV, digital and IT services and solutions for public and business customers throughout Hungary and internationally. The firm's 5G service is available in more than 20 locations, as of mid-2021. Mobile services encompass voice, text messaging, internet, data and content; and fixed line services consist of voice, data, internet and TV. Magyar Telekom also sells related equipment for using fixed lines and mobile services, including phones, tablets, notebooks, TV sets and more. The firm supports the digitalization of enterprises with the up-to-date ICT, ranging from the entire IT infrastructure to application-side solutions. Beyond ICT, Magyar Telekom provides electricity and natural gas services, as well as a hotel, the Telekom Hotel Balatonkenese, which encompasses a conference center, language labs, an open-air fitness training course, a wellness facility and more.

FINANCIAL DATA: *Note: Data for latest year may not have been available at press time.*

In U.S. $	2020	2019	2018	2017	2016	2015
Revenue	2,377,715,200	2,126,620,544	2,096,159,104	1,887,515,648	1,981,817,856	2,229,952,768
R&D Expense						
Operating Income						
Operating Margin %						
SGA Expense						
Net Income	149,661,728	131,290,672	138,184,256	144,385,360	178,496,512	94,163,024
Operating Cash Flow						
Capital Expenditure						
EBITDA						
Return on Assets %						
Return on Equity %						
Debt to Equity						

CONTACT INFORMATION:

Phone: 36-1-458-0332   Fax:
Toll-Free:
Address: Konyves Kalman krt. 36, Budapest, 1097 Hungary

STOCK TICKER/OTHER:

Stock Ticker: MYTAY   Exchange: GREY
Employees: 7,132   Fiscal Year Ends: 12/31
Parent Company: Deutsche Telekom AG

SALARIES/BONUSES:

Top Exec. Salary: $ Bonus: $
Second Exec. Salary: $ Bonus: $

OTHER THOUGHTS:

Estimated Female Officers or Directors: 1
Hot Spot for Advancement for Women/Minorities:

Mahanagar Telephone Nigam Limited

www.mtnl.net.in

NAIC Code: 517110

TYPES OF BUSINESS:

Telephone Service
Local & Long-Distance Service
Mobile Phone Service
Internet Services

GROWTH PLANS/SPECIAL FEATURES:

Mahanagar Telephone Nigam Limited (MTNL) is a primary provider of telecommunications and broadband services for Delhi and Mumbai, the two largest metropolitan areas in India. MTNL offers landline, broadband, fiber-to-the-home (FTTH) and mobile services to individuals and businesses. Other services include multi-protocol label switching, leased circuits, web hosting, integrated services digital networking (ISDN), industrial training, toll-free solutions, universal access numbers, and virtual card calling. MTNL is also present in Nepal through joint venture United Telecom Limited, and in Mauritius through wholly-owned subsidiary Mahanagar Telephone Mauritius Limited.

BRANDS/DIVISIONS/AFFILIATES:

United Telecom Limited
Mahanagar Telephone Mauritius Limited

CONTACTS: Note: Officers with more than one job title may be intentionally listed here more than once.

Pravin Kumar Purwar, Managing Dir.
Suresh Kumar Gupta, Dir.-Finance
Ashok Kumar Garg, Exec. Dir.-Tech.
S.R. Sayal, Corp. Sec.
Peeyush Aggarwal, Exec. Dir.-MTNL Mumbai
B.K.Mittal, Exec. Dir.-MTNL Delhi

FINANCIAL DATA: Note: Data for latest year may not have been available at press time.

In U.S. $	2020	2019	2018	2017	2016	2015
Revenue	222,846,700	286,239,800	325,567,200	407,572,600	453,441,800	479,931,400
R&D Expense						
Operating Income	-309,871,600	-298,737,200	-273,930,400	-288,003,600	-233,999,000	-232,913,300
Operating Margin %		-1.04%	-.84%	-.71%	-.52%	-.49%
SGA Expense	2,078,100	2,098,689	1,879,075	2,143,985	54,360,030	54,602,980
Net Income	-506,997,500	-465,042,900	-408,074,900	-402,999,100	-276,197,900	-398,210,100
Operating Cash Flow	-165,484,900	-101,288,900	16,247,340	-140,605,300	39,481,160	-160,183,900
Capital Expenditure	19,566,260	40,546,290	67,435,310	57,293,250	70,030,880	40,995,130
EBITDA	-107,856,700	-97,646,010	-63,489,120	-55,945,370	-52,454,880	-39,459,200
Return on Assets %		-.22%	-.18%	-.13%	-.08%	-.11%
Return on Equity %					-1.94%	-.82%
Debt to Equity					473.053	4.862

CONTACT INFORMATION:

Phone: 011 24310212   Fax:
Toll-Free:
Address: Fl. 5, Mahanagar Doorsanchar Sadan, 9, CGO Complex,, New Delhi, Delhi 110003 India

STOCK TICKER/OTHER:

Stock Ticker: MTENY
Employees: 4,185
Parent Company:

Exchange: PINX
Fiscal Year Ends: 03/31

SALARIES/BONUSES:

Top Exec. Salary: $ Bonus: $
Second Exec. Salary: $ Bonus: $

OTHER THOUGHTS:

Estimated Female Officers or Directors:
Hot Spot for Advancement for Women/Minorities:

Maroc Telecom SA
NAIC Code: 517110

TYPES OF BUSINESS:
Telephony & Internet Service Provider
Mobile Service Provider
Business Support Services

BRANDS/DIVISIONS/AFFILIATES:
Mauritel SA
Sotelma
Gabon Telecom
Casanet
Onatel
Moov Benin
Moov Ivory Coast
Moov Togo

CONTACTS: Note: Officers with more than one job title may be intentionally listed here more than once.
Laurent Mairot, Dir.-Gen. Admin
Janie Letrot, Gen. Dir.-Regulatory & Legal Affairs
Larbi Guedira, Dir.-General Svcs.
Rachid Mechahouri, Gen. Dir.-Networks & Systems
Abdeslam Ahizoune, Chmn.

GROWTH PLANS/SPECIAL FEATURES:
Maroc Telecom SA is a leading telecommunications provider in Morocco and other parts of Africa, offering mobile, fixed-line telephone and internet access. The company also offers business support, networking and administration and finance services. Maroc Telecom is the domestic leader in mobile telecommunications and also offers value-added services such as 4G+ internet, customized ringtones, mobile instant messaging and address book backup. The firm's fixed telecommunications services include voice communication, data transmission, internet access via fiber optics and TV via ADSL (asymmetric digital subscriber line) network. Administrative services include monitoring solutions for investment, budgeting, financial reporting and treasury as well as procurement, planning, strategy and economic study support. The company's products and services are marketed through an extensive distribution network of direct and indirect retailers. Products also include smartphones, routers, modems and more. Maroc Telecom operates directly and through a number of wholly- and partially-owned subsidiaries, including: Mauritel SA, operating in Mauritania; Sotelma, operating in Mali; Gabon Telecom, operating in Gabon; Casanet, operating in Morocco; Onatel, operating in Burkina Faso; Moov Benin, serving the Beninese market; Moov Ivory Coast, operating in Cote d'Ivoire; Moov Togo, serving the Togolese market; and Moov Niger, serving the Nigerian market.

FINANCIAL DATA: Note: Data for latest year may not have been available at press time.

In U.S. $	2020	2019	2018	2017	2016	2015
Revenue	4,173,553,000	4,144,949,000	4,089,898,000	3,968,672,000	4,001,362,000	3,874,347,000
R&D Expense						
Operating Income	1,392,622,000	944,835,400	1,272,077,000	1,190,692,000	1,199,319,000	1,199,092,000
Operating Margin %		.23%	.31%	.30%	.30%	.31%
SGA Expense	89,216,800	106,242,900	314,528,900	302,724,200	289,897,800	277,298,500
Net Income	615,550,500	309,421,100	682,179,300	647,673,100	635,414,300	635,073,700
Operating Cash Flow	1,258,570,000	1,734,506,000	1,648,127,000	1,692,508,000	1,530,420,000	1,653,689,000
Capital Expenditure	470,034,000	902,270,100	916,572,000	950,056,700	709,534,600	948,013,600
EBITDA	2,050,057,000	2,145,857,000	2,095,573,000	1,917,821,000	1,913,053,000	1,928,263,000
Return on Assets %		.04%	.10%	.09%	.09%	.11%
Return on Equity %		.20%	.38%	.36%	.36%	.36%
Debt to Equity		0.346	0.222	0.265	0.301	0.394

CONTACT INFORMATION:
Phone: 212 537 719000   Fax: 212 537 710600
Toll-Free:
Address: Ave. Annakhil Hay Riad, Rabat, 10100 Morocco

STOCK TICKER/OTHER:
Stock Ticker: MAOTF   Exchange: PINX
Employees: 10,123   Fiscal Year Ends:
Parent Company:

SALARIES/BONUSES:
Top Exec. Salary: $ Bonus: $
Second Exec. Salary: $ Bonus: $

OTHER THOUGHTS:
Estimated Female Officers or Directors: 1
Hot Spot for Advancement for Women/Minorities:

Marvell Technology Group Ltd

www.marvell.com

NAIC Code: 334413

TYPES OF BUSINESS:

Semiconductor Manufacturing
Storage Technology
Broadband Technology
Wireless Technology
Power Management Technology
Switching Technology

BRANDS/DIVISIONS/AFFILIATES:

OCTEON
OCTEON Fusion-M
NITROX
LiquidIO Server Adapter
ThunderX

CONTACTS: Note: Officers with more than one job title may be intentionally listed here more than once.

Matt Murphy, CEO
Andy Micallef, COO
Jean Hu, CFO
Dean Jarnac, Sr. VP-Global Sales
Janice Hall, Sr. VP-Human Resources
Pantas Sutardja, Chief R&D Officer
Chris Koopmans, Exec. VP-Mktg.& Bus. Oper.
Gani Jusuf, VP-Prod. Dev., Comm., & Consumer Bus. Group
Yosef Meyouhas, VP-Enterprise Bus. Unit Eng., Marvell Israel
Tom Savage, VP-Worldwide Legal Affairs
James Laufman, General Counsel
Albert Wu, VP-Oper.
Sukhi Nagesh, VP-Investor Rel.
Chris Chang, VP-Greater China Bus.
Bouchung Lin, VP
Renu Bhatia, VP-Sales, Strategic Partnerships
Gaurav Shah, Gen. Mgr.-Digital Entertainment Bus.
Hoo Kuong, VP

GROWTH PLANS/SPECIAL FEATURES:

Marvell Technology Group Ltd. is a global fabless semiconductor provider of high-performance analog, mixed-signal, digital signal processing and embedded microprocessor integrated circuits (ICs). Marvell manufactures products for computers, communications-related equipment and consumer devices that require the benefits of integrated mixed-signal devices for high-speed data storage, transmission and management. It also markets a broad range of electronic products that can utilize its power management solutions and support cost-effective green technology. The firm produces System-on-a-Chip (SoC) devices and has four key markets: storage solutions, connectivity, networking and other. The storage market, including hard disk drive controllers and other drive controller solutions, was the original focus of the company. Marvell's development of solid state drive controllers target toward the growing market for flash-based storage systems, for the enterprise, consumer and mobile computing markets, as well as for smartphones and tablets. The networking market includes products such as wired and wireless Ethernet-switching solutions and its embedded processor lines. The OCTEON multi-core processor families provide integrated Layer 4 through 7 data and security processing with additional capabilities at Layers 2 and 3 at line speeds. The OCTEON Fusion-M family of wireless baseband processors is a highly scalable product family for multiple wireless protocols including 5G. The NITROX processor family offers stand-alone security processors that provide the functionality required for Layer 3 to Layer 5 secure communication in a single chip. The LiquidIO Server Adapter family is a high-performance, general-purpose programmable adapter platform that enables cloud service providers to offload any functionality in the datacenter. The ThunderX processor family is a highly integrated, scalable family of multi-core SoC processors optimized for cloud and datacenter servers. In late-2020, Marvell Technology agreed to acquire Inphi Corporation, a leader in high-speed data movement.

FINANCIAL DATA: Note: Data for latest year may not have been available at press time.

In U.S. $	2020	2019	2018	2017	2016	2015
Revenue	2,699,161,000	2,865,791,000	2,409,170,000	2,317,674,000	2,725,828,000	
R&D Expense	1,080,391,000	914,009,000	714,444,000	831,398,000	1,054,257,000	
Operating Income	-188,030,000	120,023,000	509,330,000	205,180,000	-108,821,000	
Operating Margin %	- .07%	.04%	.21%	.09%	- .04%	
SGA Expense	464,580,000	424,360,000	238,166,000	243,193,000	274,908,000	
Net Income	1,584,391,000	-179,094,000	520,831,000	21,151,000	-811,400,000	
Operating Cash Flow	360,297,000	596,744,000	571,113,000	-358,435,000	205,352,000	
Capital Expenditure	86,633,000	87,461,000	45,138,000	54,819,000	55,731,000	
EBITDA	1,408,753,000	363,016,000	538,946,000	235,876,000	-685,484,000	
Return on Assets %	.15%	- .02%	.11%	.00%	- .14%	
Return on Equity %	.20%	- .03%	.13%	.01%	- .17%	
Debt to Equity	0.179	0.237				

CONTACT INFORMATION:

Phone: 441 2966395   Fax: 441 2924720
Toll-Free:
Address: Victoria Place, 5/Fl, 31 Victoria St., Hamilton, HM 10 Bermuda

STOCK TICKER/OTHER:

Stock Ticker: MRVL
Employees: 5,340
Parent Company:

Exchange: NAS
Fiscal Year Ends: 01/31

SALARIES/BONUSES:

Top Exec. Salary: $ Bonus: $
Second Exec. Salary: $ Bonus: $

OTHER THOUGHTS:

Estimated Female Officers or Directors: 2
Hot Spot for Advancement for Women/Minorities:

Maxis Berhad

NAIC Code: 517110

www.maxis.com.my

TYPES OF BUSINESS:

Wired Telecommunications Carriers
Telecommunications
Digital Services
Internet
Cloud
Security Solutions

BRANDS/DIVISIONS/AFFILIATES:

ONERetail
MaxisONE

CONTACTS: *Note: Officers with more than one job title may be intentionally listed here more than once.*

Gokhan Ogut, CEO
Mark Dioguardi, Exec. VP-Tech. & Network
Stephen John Mead, General Counsel
Tan Lay Han, VP-Bus. Transformation
Mariam Bevi Batcha, VP-Corp. Affairs
Chow Chee Yan, Sr. VP-Internal Audit
Mohamed Fitri bin Abdullah, Sr. VP-Bus. Svcs.
Maurice Tan, Sr. VP-Personal Svcs.
Harold Quek, Sr. VP-Home Svcs.
Kala Kularajah Sundram, Chief Talent Officer

GROWTH PLANS/SPECIAL FEATURES:

Maxis Berhad provides a suite of converged telecommunications, digital and related services and solutions in Malaysia and internationally. The company offers prepaid and postpaid mobile; fixed voice telephone products and services; internet; cloud, data protection and security solutions; and satellite services. Maxis provides a range of ecommerce, payment, inventory and marketing solutions to help retail businesses reach more customers, expand into digital channels and make smart data-driven decisions. These services are offered to sole proprietors, small- and medium-sized enterprises and even corporate clients. Maxis sells phones, including the iPhone, Huawei and Samsung brands, as well as its own NeXT line of phones, among others. Maxis' broadband offers up to 100 megabits per second (Mbps) internet, as well as 4G LTE and WiFi hotspot capabilities through its extensive fiber optic network. Nearly all of Malaysia has access to Maxis' 4G coverage. The firm also provides 3G service in select locations and is engaged in the development of high fiber and 5G network coverage. Maxis' website enables consumers to purchase phones and plans, find a store location or service center, chat live with a service representative and pay their bills. In July 2021, Maxis acquired Peering One Sdn Bhd., a Malaysian-based cloud solutions company specializing in hybrid and private cloud managed services.

FINANCIAL DATA: *Note: Data for latest year may not have been available at press time.*

In U.S. $	2020	2019	2018	2017	2016	2015
Revenue	2,174,103,000	2,258,244,000	2,229,010,000	2,108,738,000	2,088,214,000	2,085,493,000
R&D Expense						
Operating Income	609,602,300	616,391,900	685,141,300	816,326,800	762,185,700	694,516,500
Operating Margin %		.27%	.31%	.39%	.36%	.33%
SGA Expense	34,432,590	41,949,560	51,277,400	38,898,880	455,017,000	428,542,900
Net Income	335,111,500	368,331,700	431,551,600	531,414,700	488,157,300	421,666,300
Operating Cash Flow	882,395,700	819,350,100	807,368,300	926,961,700	751,719,900	987,727,200
Capital Expenditure	338,506,300	332,444,200	342,510,900	472,284,400	450,541,500	456,000,500
EBITDA	922,647,900	911,008,700	950,387,700	1,078,465,000	1,051,994,000	991,736,900
Return on Assets %		.07%	.09%	.11%	.10%	.09%
Return on Equity %		.21%	.25%	.37%	.45%	.39%
Debt to Equity		1.117	1.04	1.057	1.856	2.10

CONTACT INFORMATION:

Phone: 60 323307000　　　Fax: 60 323300008
Toll-Free:
Address: Level 18, Menara Maxis, Kuala Lumpur City Centre, Kuala Lumpur, 50088 Malaysia

STOCK TICKER/OTHER:

Stock Ticker: MAXSF　　　　　　　Exchange: GREY
Employees: 3,748　　　　　　　　　Fiscal Year Ends:
Parent Company:

SALARIES/BONUSES:

Top Exec. Salary: $　　　　Bonus: $
Second Exec. Salary: $　　　Bonus: $

OTHER THOUGHTS:

Estimated Female Officers or Directors: 4
Hot Spot for Advancement for Women/Minorities: Y

McAfee Corp

www.mcafee.com

NAIC Code: 511210E

TYPES OF BUSINESS:

Computer Software: Network Security, Managed Access, Digital ID,
Cybersecurity & Anti-Virus
Virus Protection Software
Network Management Software
Cybersecurity
Malware Protection

BRANDS/DIVISIONS/AFFILIATES:

Thoma Bravo LLC
Intel Corporation
Foundation Technology Worldwide LLC
McAfee LLC
McAfee Global Threat Intelligence
MVISION Device

CONTACTS: Note: Officers with more than one job title may be intentionally listed here more than once.

Peter Leav, CEO
Venkat Bhamidipati, CFO
Lynne Doherty, Exec. VP-Global Sales & Mktg.
Chatelle Lynch, Chief Human Resources Officer
Steven Grobman, CTO
Bryan Reed Barney, Exec. VP-Prod. Dev.
Ari Jaaksi, Sr. VP
Louis Riley, General Counsel
Tom Fountain, Sr. VP
Edward Hayden, Sr. VP-Finance & Acct.
Steve Redman, Exec. VP-Global Sales
Ken Levine, Sr. VP
Gert-Jan Schenk, Pres., EMEA
Barry McPherson, Exec. VP-Worldwide Delivery & Support Svcs.
Jean-Claude Broido, Pres., McAfee Japan
Barry McPherson, Exec. VP-Supply Chain & Facilities

GROWTH PLANS/SPECIAL FEATURES:

McAfee Corp. is engaged in designing and delivering global computer security software and is the holding company of Foundation Technology Worldwide, LLC (FTW) and its subsidiaries. FTW wholly-owns McAfee LLC, a cybersecurity company that provides advanced security solutions to consumers, small- and medium-sized businesses, large enterprises and governments. Security technologies from McAfee use a predictive capability powered by McAfee Global Threat Intelligence, which enables home users and businesses to stay ahead of fileless attacks, viruses, malware and other online threats. McAfee's products protect over 600 million devices. The company's personal protection services cover device security, online privacy, comprehensive internet security and identity protection. For enterprises and governments, McAfee offers the MVISION Device, which offers next-generation endpoint solutions offering comprehensive threat detection and data protection for both modern and legacy devices, such as traditional endpoints, mobile and fixed-function systems. McAfee Corp. is a joint venture between Thoma Bravo, LLC and Intel Corporation. In late-2020, McAfee filed a registration statement with the U.S. Securities and Exchange Commission to a proposed initial public offering of its Class A common stock. The firm was approved and is listed on Nasdaq under ticker symbol MCFE.

FINANCIAL DATA: Note: Data for latest year may not have been available at press time.

In U.S. $	2020	2019	2018	2017	2016	2015
Revenue	2,906,000,000	2,635,000,000	2,409,000,000			
R&D Expense	475,000,000	380,000,000	406,000,000			
Operating Income	178,000,000	148,000,000	-137,000,000			
Operating Margin %						
SGA Expense	1,158,000,000	1,042,000,000	1,068,000,000			
Net Income	-289,000,000	-236,000,000	-512,000,000			
Operating Cash Flow	760,000,000	496,000,000	319,000,000			
Capital Expenditure	42,000,000	56,000,000	61,000,000			
EBITDA	540,000,000	682,000,000	400,000,000			
Return on Assets %						
Return on Equity %						
Debt to Equity						

CONTACT INFORMATION:

Phone: 866-622-3911   Fax:
Toll-Free:
Address: 6220 America Center Dr., San Jose, CA 95002 United States

STOCK TICKER/OTHER:

Stock Ticker: MCFE
Employees: 6,916
Parent Company:

Exchange: NAS
Fiscal Year Ends: 12/31

SALARIES/BONUSES:

Top Exec. Salary: $ Bonus: $
Second Exec. Salary: $ Bonus: $

OTHER THOUGHTS:

Estimated Female Officers or Directors: 3
Hot Spot for Advancement for Women/Minorities: Y

Mediacom Communications Corporation   www.mediacomcc.com

NAIC Code: 517110

TYPES OF BUSINESS:

Cable TV Service
Internet Service
Digital Cable
Telephone Service

BRANDS/DIVISIONS/AFFILIATES:

Xtream
Home Controller

CONTACTS: *Note: Officers with more than one job title may be intentionally listed here more than once.*

Rocco B. Commisso, CEO
John G. Pascarelli, VP-Operations
Mark E. Stephan, CFO
David M. McNaughton, Sr. VP-Mktg.
Italia Commisso Weinand, Sr. VP-Human Resources & Programming
Peter Lyons, Sr. VP-IT
Joseph E. Young, General Counsel
John G. Pascarelli, Exec. VP-Oper.
Jack Griffin, Dir.-Corp. Finance
Edward S. Pardini, Sr. VP-Divisional Oper.-North Central Division
Brian M. Walsh, Sr. VP
Tapan Dandnaik, Sr. VP-Customer Service & Financial Oper.
Steve Litwer, Sr. VP-Advertising Sales, OnMedia Div.
Rocco B. Commisso, Chmn.

GROWTH PLANS/SPECIAL FEATURES:

Mediacom Communications Corporation, a leading cable company, supplies an array of broadband products and services to more than 1,500 communities in 22 U.S. states, reaching approximately 1.4 million homes. The firm offers customers a full array of traditional video services such as basic service, digital video service, pay-per-view service, high definition television, digital video recorders and video-on-demand. Xtream is the company's all-in-one integrated platform where TV and internet work together to deliver TV, Wi-Fi, caller ID (without interrupting the show), TiVo, On-Demand and apps. In addition, the company offers three types of high-speed internet access: Internet 60, allows for download speeds up to 60 Mbps (megabits per second); Internet 100, speeds up to 100 Mbps; and Xtreme 1 GIG, which allows for up to 1,000 gigabits of download speeds and upload speeds to 50 Mbps. The firm's phone package offers customers unlimited local, regional and long-distance calling within the U.S., Puerto Rico, U.S. Virgin Islands and Canada. It is delivered over voice over internet protocol (VoIP) that digitizes voice signals and routes them as data packets through Mediacom's controlled broadband cable systems. It includes features such as Caller ID with name and number, call waiting, three-way calling and enhanced Emergency 911 dialing. Mediacom also offers video, HSD (high speed data), phone, network and transport services to commercial and large enterprise customers. It offers large enterprise customers who require high-bandwidth connections solutions such as the point-to-point circuits required by wireless communications providers. Additionally, Mediacom offers a home security product, Home Controller, which provides 24-hour-a-day monitoring from a UL-approved facility.

FINANCIAL DATA: *Note: Data for latest year may not have been available at press time.*

In U.S. $	2020	2019	2018	2017	2016	2015
Revenue	2,131,224,000	1,971,428,550	1,877,551,000	1,810,255,000		
R&D Expense						
Operating Income						
Operating Margin %						
SGA Expense						
Net Income						
Operating Cash Flow						
Capital Expenditure						
EBITDA						
Return on Assets %						
Return on Equity %						
Debt to Equity						

CONTACT INFORMATION:

Phone: 845-695-2600   Fax: 845-698-4069
Toll-Free: 800-479-2082
Address: 100 Crystal Run Rd., Middletown, NY 10941 United States

STOCK TICKER/OTHER:

Stock Ticker: Private   Exchange:
Employees: 7,000   Fiscal Year Ends: 12/31
Parent Company:

SALARIES/BONUSES:

Top Exec. Salary: $ Bonus: $
Second Exec. Salary: $ Bonus: $

OTHER THOUGHTS:

Estimated Female Officers or Directors: 1
Hot Spot for Advancement for Women/Minorities:

MedTel Services LLC

www.medtelservices.com

NAIC Code: 334210

TYPES OF BUSINESS:

Telecommunications Hardware & Software
Telecommunications Software Applications
Contract Manufacturing
Digital & VOIP Switches

BRANDS/DIVISIONS/AFFILIATES:

Cerato

CONTACTS: Note: Officers with more than one job title may be intentionally listed here more than once.

Ewen R. Cameron, Pres.
Robert B. Ramey, Sr. VP-Mfg. Oper.
Angela L. Marvin, VP-Finance
Richard W. Begando, Sr. VP-Int'l Sales

GROWTH PLANS/SPECIAL FEATURES:

MedTel Services, LLC designs, installs, develops, manufactures and markets electronic hardware and application software products primarily for more than 20,000 businesses, including correctional facilities and government agencies. The firm's offerings include business phone systems, unified communication systems, contact center solutions and cloud hosted solutions. MedTel's communication server supports its SIP (session initiation protocol) phones and endpoints; its customer interface management software connects customers to the right resource, manages the interaction and provides reports needed for optimizing contact center operations; its services alarms management solutions provides intelligent monitoring and management through a single source for visibility and control of all related monitored systems; and its voice cyber call recording solution allows businesses to record multimedia interactions, including chat and email, across fixed and mobile devices over a wide-range of network configurations from an unlimited number of locations. Products by the company include the Cerato brand of voice communication servers, voice over internet protocol (VoIP) phones, hosted cloud systems, cloud softphones, unified communication systems, monitoring solutions and remote agent appliances. MedTel offers training and support services. Its partners include AT&T, Verizon, Telus, Marriott, FixAFone, Waterford Crystal, Black Box Network Devices, Carousel Industries, St. Alexius Hospital and many more.

FINANCIAL DATA: Note: Data for latest year may not have been available at press time.

In U.S. $	2020	2019	2018	2017	2016	2015
Revenue						
R&D Expense						
Operating Income						
Operating Margin %						
SGA Expense						
Net Income						
Operating Cash Flow						
Capital Expenditure						
EBITDA						
Return on Assets %						
Return on Equity %						
Debt to Equity						

CONTACT INFORMATION:

Phone: 941-753-5000   Fax: 941-758-8469
Toll-Free:
Address: 2511 Corporate Way, Palmetto, FL 34221 United States

STOCK TICKER/OTHER:

Stock Ticker: Private   Exchange:
Employees: 180   Fiscal Year Ends: 12/31
Parent Company:

SALARIES/BONUSES:

Top Exec. Salary: $ Bonus: $
Second Exec. Salary: $ Bonus: $

OTHER THOUGHTS:

Estimated Female Officers or Directors: 1
Hot Spot for Advancement for Women/Minorities:

Megacable Holdings SAB de CV

www.megacable.com.mx

NAIC Code: 517110

TYPES OF BUSINESS:

Wired Telecommunications Carriers
Cable Television
Internet Services
Telephone Services
Digital Services

BRANDS/DIVISIONS/AFFILIATES:

GROWTH PLANS/SPECIAL FEATURES:

Megacable Holdings SAB de CV offers cable television, internet and telephone services in Mexico. The company's services also include digital television, high-definition television, digital video recording, On Demand, pay-per-view and premium channels. Packages include single service offerings, double service offerings and triple service offerings. Megacable's services are offered to both consumers as well as to small- and medium-sized businesses and enterprises. The firm has more than 3.4 million video subscribers, 3.5 million internet subscribers and 2.7 million telephone subscribers (as of April 2021).

CONTACTS: Note: Officers with more than one job title may be intentionally listed here more than once.

Enrique Yamuni Robles, Managing Dir.

FINANCIAL DATA: Note: Data for latest year may not have been available at press time.

In U.S. $	2020	2019	2018	2017	2016	2015
Revenue		903,642,560	816,644,672	720,653,504	906,834,752	760,681,664
R&D Expense						
Operating Income						
Operating Margin %						
SGA Expense						
Net Income		179,355,984	189,879,776	158,877,376	206,604,704	163,267,264
Operating Cash Flow						
Capital Expenditure						
EBITDA						
Return on Assets %						
Return on Equity %						
Debt to Equity						

CONTACT INFORMATION:

Phone: 52 3337500010   Fax:
Toll-Free:
Address: Lazaro Cardenas 1694, Guadalajara, 44900 Mexico

STOCK TICKER/OTHER:

Stock Ticker: MEGA CPO   Exchange: MEX
Employees: 18,513   Fiscal Year Ends: 12/31
Parent Company:

SALARIES/BONUSES:

Top Exec. Salary: $ Bonus: $
Second Exec. Salary: $ Bonus: $

OTHER THOUGHTS:

Estimated Female Officers or Directors:
Hot Spot for Advancement for Women/Minorities:

Microsoft Corporation

www.microsoft.com

NAIC Code: 511210H

TYPES OF BUSINESS:

Computer Software, Operating Systems, Languages & Development Tools
Enterprise Software
Game Consoles
Operating Systems
Software as a Service (SAAS)
Search Engine and Advertising
E-Mail Services
Instant Messaging

BRANDS/DIVISIONS/AFFILIATES:

Office 365
Exchange
SharePoint
Microsoft Teams
Skype for Business
Outlook.com
OneDrive
LinkedIn

CONTACTS: Note: Officers with more than one job title may be intentionally listed here more than once.

Satya Nadella, CEO
Amy Hood, CFO
John Thompson, Chairman of the Board
Frank Brod, Chief Accounting Officer
Christopher Capossela, Chief Marketing Officer
William Gates, Co-Founder
Kathleen Hogan, Executive VP, Divisional
Margaret Johnson, Executive VP, Divisional
Jean-Philippe Courtois, Executive VP
Bradford Smith, Other Executive Officer

GROWTH PLANS/SPECIAL FEATURES:

Microsoft Corporation develops, license and supports software products, services and devices. Microsoft's services include cloud-based solutions that provide customers with software, services, platforms and content, and it provides solution support and consulting services. The company also delivers online advertising on a global scale. Microsoft's products include operating systems, cross-device productivity applications, server applications, business solution applications, desktop and server management tools, software development tools, and video games. The firm designs, manufactures and sells personal computers, tablets, gaming and entertainment consoles, and other intelligent devices and related accessories. Microsoft operates through three business segments: productivity and business processes, intelligent cloud, and personal computing. The productivity and business processes segment primarily comprises the following products and services: office commercial, including Office 365 subscriptions and Office licensed on-premises (Office, Exchange, SharePoint, Microsoft Teams, Office 365 Security and Compliance, and Skype for Business; office consumer, including Office 365 subscriptions and Office licensed on-premises, and Skype, Outlook.com and OneDrive; LinkedIn, including talent solutions, marketing solutions and premium subscriptions; and dynamic business solutions such as cloud-based applications across enterprise resource planning (ERP) and customer relationship management (CRM). The intelligent cloud segment offers digital technology products, solutions and services to businesses and organizations for empowering employees, customer engagement and optimizing operations. The personal computing segment offers products and solutions that enable users to interact with technology in intuitive, engaging and dynamic ways. Windows 10 offers artificial-intelligence-first interfaces such as voice-activated commands, inking, immersive 3D content storytelling and mixed reality experiences. In September 2020, Microsoft agreed to acquire ZeniMax Media and its game publisher Bethesda Softworks for $7.5 billion

Microsoft offers its employees comprehensive benefits, a 401(k) and employee stock purchase plans; and employee assistance programs.

FINANCIAL DATA: Note: Data for latest year may not have been available at press time.

In U.S. $	2020	2019	2018	2017	2016	2015
Revenue	143,015,000,000	125,843,000,000	110,360,000,000	89,950,000,000	85,320,000,000	93,580,000,000
R&D Expense	19,269,000,000	16,876,000,000	14,726,000,000	13,037,000,000	11,988,000,000	12,046,000,000
Operating Income	52,959,000,000	42,959,000,000	35,058,000,000	22,632,000,000	21,292,000,000	28,172,000,000
Operating Margin %	.37%	.34%	.32%	.25%	.25%	.30%
SGA Expense	24,709,000,000	23,098,000,000	22,223,000,000	20,020,000,000	19,260,000,000	20,324,000,000
Net Income	44,281,000,000	39,240,000,000	16,571,000,000	21,204,000,000	16,798,000,000	12,193,000,000
Operating Cash Flow	60,675,000,000	52,185,000,000	43,884,000,000	39,507,000,000	33,325,000,000	29,080,000,000
Capital Expenditure	15,441,000,000	13,925,000,000	11,632,000,000	8,129,000,000	8,343,000,000	5,944,000,000
EBITDA	68,423,000,000	58,056,000,000	49,468,000,000	34,149,000,000	27,616,000,000	25,245,000,000
Return on Assets %	.15%	.14%	.07%	.10%	.09%	.07%
Return on Equity %	.40%	.42%	.21%	.29%	.22%	.14%
Debt to Equity	0.568	0.712	0.941	1.051	0.566	0.347

CONTACT INFORMATION:

Phone: 425 882-8080   Fax: 425 936-7329
Toll-Free: 800-642-7676
Address: One Microsoft Way, Redmond, WA 98052 United States

SALARIES/BONUSES:

Top Exec. Salary: $ Bonus: $
Second Exec. Salary: $ Bonus: $

STOCK TICKER/OTHER:

Stock Ticker: MSFT   Exchange: NAS
Employees: 163,000   Fiscal Year Ends: 06/30
Parent Company:

OTHER THOUGHTS:

Estimated Female Officers or Directors: 4
Hot Spot for Advancement for Women/Minorities: Y

Sales, profits and employees may be estimates. Financial information, benefits and other data can change quickly and may vary from those stated here.

Millicom International Cellular SA

NAIC Code: 517210

www.millicom.com

TYPES OF BUSINESS:

Cell Phone Service
Telecommunications
Cable TV
Satellite TV
Broadband
Cloud
Financial Services

BRANDS/DIVISIONS/AFFILIATES:

Tigo
Tigo Business

CONTACTS: *Note: Officers with more than one job title may be intentionally listed here more than once.*

Mauricio Ramos, CEO
Tim Pennington, CFO
Susy Bobenrieth, Chief Human Resources Officer
Xavier Rocoplan, CIO
Mario Zanotti, Sr. Exec. VP-Oper.
Martin Weiss, Exec. VP-Strategy & Corp. Dev.
Justine Dimovic, Head-Investor Rel.
Arthur Bastings, Exec. VP-Africa
Martin Lewerth, Exec. VP-Home & Digital Media
Anders Nilsson, Exec. VP-Commerce & Svcs.
Marc Zagar, Exec. VP-Controlling & Analytics
Jose Antonio Rios Garcia, Chmn.

GROWTH PLANS/SPECIAL FEATURES:

Millicom International Cellular SA is a global mobile telecommunications operator selling products and services through its brand Tigo. The company offers a wide range of services in nine Latin American markets, including fixed and mobile, communications, cable TV, satellite TV, mobile financial and local content (music and sports). Tigo has approximately 55 million mobile subscribers. Tigo Business helps businesses transform and grow via high-speed broadband services in data center, cloud and co-location. Tigo ONEtv is an integrated linear and nonlinear TV option that brings next-generation TV to Latin America. Tigo Sports is a sports broadcast business that offers self-coverage and exclusive rights to key fixtures, sponsorship deals and production facilities. Tigo Money offers a range of mobile financial services. Tigo Music offers music streaming capabilities in partnership with Deezer, which sponsors leading music festivals and concerts that feature international artists.

FINANCIAL DATA: *Note: Data for latest year may not have been available at press time.*

In U.S. $	2020	2019	2018	2017	2016	2015
Revenue	4,172,000,000	4,336,000,000	4,075,000,000	4,133,000,000	4,374,000,000	6,730,000,000
R&D Expense						
Operating Income	285,000,000	430,000,000	425,000,000	432,000,000	367,000,000	791,000,000
Operating Margin %		.10%	.11%	.11%	.08%	.12%
SGA Expense	874,000,000	899,000,000	1,073,000,000	1,046,000,000	1,146,000,000	1,680,000,000
Net Income	-344,000,000	149,000,000	-10,000,000	85,000,000	-32,000,000	-559,000,000
Operating Cash Flow	821,000,000	801,000,000	792,000,000	820,000,000	878,000,000	1,651,000,000
Capital Expenditure	824,000,000	907,000,000	780,000,000	783,000,000	862,000,000	1,205,000,000
EBITDA	1,479,000,000	1,834,000,000	1,285,000,000	1,350,000,000	1,397,000,000	1,610,000,000
Return on Assets %		.01%	.00%	.01%	.00%	-.05%
Return on Equity %		.06%	.00%	.03%	-.01%	-.19%
Debt to Equity		2.802	1.622	1.162	1.207	1.09

CONTACT INFORMATION:

Phone: 352 27759021   Fax: 352 27759359
Toll-Free:
Address: 2, Rue du Fort Bourbon, Luxembourg, L-1249 Luxembourg

STOCK TICKER/OTHER:

Stock Ticker: TIGO   Exchange: NAS
Employees: 21,419   Fiscal Year Ends: 12/31
Parent Company:

SALARIES/BONUSES:

Top Exec. Salary: $ Bonus: $
Second Exec. Salary: $ Bonus: $

OTHER THOUGHTS:

Estimated Female Officers or Directors: 1
Hot Spot for Advancement for Women/Minorities: Y

MiTAC Holdings Corp

www.mic-holdings.com/Index.html

NAIC Code: 334111

TYPES OF BUSINESS:

Computer Manufacturing
Server Products
Mobile Communications Products
Storage Products
Tablet PCs & All-in-One PCs

BRANDS/DIVISIONS/AFFILIATES:

MiTAC Computing Technology Corp
MiTAC Digital Technology Corp
MiTAC International Corp
Mio
Magellan
Navman
TYAN

GROWTH PLANS/SPECIAL FEATURES:

MiTAC Holdings Corp. is a leading information technology (IT) and service group. The firm has developed into a multi-national organization of manufacturers (JDM, ODM, OEM and OPM), designers, research and developers, testers, assemblers, marketers and servicers in its years of business. With headquarters in Taiwan, and manufacturing and logistics centers in China, Taiwan and USA, MiTAC sells products in more than 30 countries worldwide with its leading brands include Mio, Magellan and Navman for auto electronics, and TYAN for servers. Subsidiary MiTAC Computing Technology Corp. offers hyper-scale data centers, high-performance computing (HPC), graphics processing unit (GPU) and embedded inter-process communication (IPC) products and services. MiTAC Digital Technology Corp. offers auto electronics, auto-related Internet of Things (IoT) and more. MiTAC International Corp. offers smart environment control products and services, smart service and Smart Factory 4.0.

CONTACTS:
Note: Officers with more than one job title may be intentionally listed here more than once.

Billy Ho, Pres.
Ting Hui-Yuan, Head-Acct.
C.J. Lin, Sr. Vice Gen. Mgr.
Michael Lin, Sr. Vice Gen. Mgr.
Alice Fang, Vice Gen. Mgr.
Doris Huang, VP-Financial Center
Matthew Miau, Chmn.

FINANCIAL DATA:
Note: Data for latest year may not have been available at press time.

In U.S. $	2020	2019	2018	2017	2016	2015
Revenue	1,463,350,000	1,191,520,000	1,004,260,000	1,640,990,000	1,602,922,379	1,550,458,630
R&D Expense						
Operating Income						
Operating Margin %						
SGA Expense						
Net Income	101,388,000	92,236,800	107,646,000	86,861,900	90,144,905	54,330,325
Operating Cash Flow						
Capital Expenditure						
EBITDA						
Return on Assets %						
Return on Equity %						
Debt to Equity						

CONTACT INFORMATION:

Phone: 886-3-3289000   Fax:
Toll-Free:
Address: No. 202, Wnehua 2nd Rd., Guishan Dist., Taoyuan City, 33383 Taiwan

STOCK TICKER/OTHER:

Stock Ticker: 3706
Employees: 7,000
Parent Company:

Exchange: TWSE
Fiscal Year Ends: 12/31

SALARIES/BONUSES:

Top Exec. Salary: $ Bonus: $
Second Exec. Salary: $ Bonus: $

OTHER THOUGHTS:

Estimated Female Officers or Directors:
Hot Spot for Advancement for Women/Minorities: Y

Mitel Networks Corporation

www.mitel.com

NAIC Code: 334210

TYPES OF BUSINESS:

Telephony Products & Services
Security Monitoring Products
Network Management Products
Messaging Products
Conferencing Products
Call Recording Products
Wireless Platforms & Phones
Emergency Response Software

BRANDS/DIVISIONS/AFFILIATES:

Searchlight Capital Partners LP
MiCloud Connect CX
MiContact Center
Mitel Teamwork

CONTACTS: Note: Officers with more than one job title may be intentionally listed here more than once.

Mary T. McDowell, CEO
James Yersh, CFO
Dave Silke, CMO
Billie Hartless, Chief Human Resources Officer
Jamshid Rezaei, CIO
Todd Abbott, Executive VP, Divisional
Graham Bevington, Executive VP, Divisional
Robert Dale, Executive VP
Tarun Loomba, Chief Product Officer

GROWTH PLANS/SPECIAL FEATURES:

Mitel Networks Corporation provides communication solutions. The firm's products are grouped into four categories: contact center, collaboration, business phone systems and phones & accessories. Mitel's contact center portfolio includes the MiCloud Connect CX (customer experience) solution that delivers personalized customer experiences via cloud architecture; and the MiContact Center, an enterprise-grade, omnichannel CX management platform created for customer-centric organizations. The collaboration product category encompasses software that enables employees to remain fluid and connected by sharing information via voice, video and instant messaging. This division's Mitel Teamwork collaborative web and mobile application is designed for the MiCloud Connect user, offering integrated tools ranging from real-time messaging to audio/video conferencing to desktop sharing. The business phone systems product category offers a range of business phone systems and solutions, including a targeted call center, unified communications and cloud communications solutions. This division's business phone systems can be arranged on-site, in the cloud and integrated with third-party applications. The phones & accessories product category offers a range of internet protocol (IP) and digital phones, consoles, conference phones and peripherals tailored for executives and/or employees. Mitel's solutions for business needs include cloud migration, on-site strategies and next-generation applications. The firm serves businesses of all sizes, whether small, medium or an enterprise. Industries served by Mitel primarily include healthcare, hospitality, government, education, field services, manufacturing, retail and sports/entertainment. Mitel is owned by Searchlight Capital Partners LP. The firm has global operations throughout North and South America, Europe, the Middle East, Africa, Asia and Asia Pacific.

FINANCIAL DATA: Note: Data for latest year may not have been available at press time.

In U.S. $	2020	2019	2018	2017	2016	2015
Revenue	1,365,000,000	1,300,000,000	1,112,055,033	1,059,100,032	987,600,000	1,157,699,968
R&D Expense						
Operating Income						
Operating Margin %						
SGA Expense						
Net Income				-49,700,000	-217,300,000	-20,700,000
Operating Cash Flow						
Capital Expenditure						
EBITDA						
Return on Assets %						
Return on Equity %						
Debt to Equity						

CONTACT INFORMATION:

Phone: 613-592-2122   Fax: 613-592-4784
Toll-Free:
Address: 4000 Innovation Dr., Kanata, ON L2K 3K1 Canada

STOCK TICKER/OTHER:

Stock Ticker: Private
Employees: 3,300
Parent Company: Searchlight Capital Partners LP

Exchange:
Fiscal Year Ends: 04/30

SALARIES/BONUSES:

Top Exec. Salary: $ Bonus: $
Second Exec. Salary: $ Bonus: $

OTHER THOUGHTS:

Estimated Female Officers or Directors:
Hot Spot for Advancement for Women/Minorities:

Mobilcom-Debitel GmbH

www.mobilcom-debitel.de

NAIC Code: 517210

TYPES OF BUSINESS:

Cell Phone Service
Broadband Internet Services
Pay TV Services

BRANDS/DIVISIONS/AFFILIATES:

Freenet AG
CallMobile GmbH
Klarmobil GmbH
Mobilcom-Debitel Shop GmbH
debitel light

CONTACTS: Note: Officers with more than one job title may be intentionally listed here more than once.

Rickmann von Platen, Managing Dir.
Hubert Kluske, Managing Dir.-Mobilcom-Debitel Shop GmbH

GROWTH PLANS/SPECIAL FEATURES:

Mobilcom-Debitel GmbH is a German telecommunications provider and one of Europe's largest network-independent telephone companies. Because parent Freenet AG does not own network infrastructure, the firm utilizes a range of partnership agreements to provide customer access to its services through networks operated by other German telecom firms. The company offers mobile telecommunications services in a variety of pre- and post-paid plans which provide various unlimited services for a flat monthly fee. In addition to the primary Mobilcom-Debitel brand, which focuses on contract subscribers, the firm offers mobile services through two niche market subsidiaries: CallMobile GmbH, focusing on the voice and prepaid customer segment; and Klarmobil GmbH, serving the German discount sector. Mobilcom-Debitel's debitel light brand was designed to attract no-frills wireless subscribers. Through wholly-owned Mobilcom-Debitel Shop GmbH, the company operates a network of storefronts that sell mobile handsets and other telecom devices and services. The firm also offers products and services to the enterprise market, with mobile plans tailored for the business world, as well as data and fixed network solutions, vehicle tracking, aerial television broadcasts, video broadcasts, eBooks, eMagazines, smart home, apps and more.

FINANCIAL DATA: Note: Data for latest year may not have been available at press time.

In U.S. $	2020	2019	2018	2017	2016	2015
Revenue						
R&D Expense						
Operating Income						
Operating Margin %						
SGA Expense						
Net Income						
Operating Cash Flow						
Capital Expenditure						
EBITDA						
Return on Assets %						
Return on Equity %						
Debt to Equity						

CONTACT INFORMATION:

Phone: 49-43-31-69-1000   Fax:
Toll-Free:
Address: Hollerstrasse 124-126, Budelsdorf, 24782 Germany

SALARIES/BONUSES:

Top Exec. Salary: $ Bonus: $
Second Exec. Salary: $ Bonus: $

STOCK TICKER/OTHER:

Stock Ticker: Subsidiary
Employees:
Parent Company: Freenet AG

Exchange:
Fiscal Year Ends: 12/31

OTHER THOUGHTS:

Estimated Female Officers or Directors:
Hot Spot for Advancement for Women/Minorities:

Mobile Telecommunications Company KSCP (Zain Group)
www.zain.com
NAIC Code: 517210

TYPES OF BUSINESS:
Mobile Telecommunications Services
Mobile Services
Data Telecommunications Services
Investment

BRANDS/DIVISIONS/AFFILIATES:
Kuwait Investment Authority
Omantel
MADA Bahrain
Zain Ventures

CONTACTS: Note: Officers with more than one job title may be intentionally listed here more than once.
Bader AlpKharafi, CEO
Saud Al-Zaid, Chief Corp. Affairs Officer
Omar Al Omar, CEO-Zain Kuwait
Wael Ghanayem, COO
Fraser Curley, CEO-Zain Saudi Arabia

GROWTH PLANS/SPECIAL FEATURES:
Mobile Telecommunications Company KSCP, operating as Zain Group, provides mobile and data telecommunications services in seven Middle Eastern and African countries. The company provides mobile voice and data services to more than 48.3 million individual and business customers through its 4G LTE and 5G network (as of June 30, 2021). Zain Group also purchases, delivers, installs, manages and maintains mobile telephones and paging systems. Wholly-owned MADA Bahrain offers data and voice technology services. Within the Middle East and North Africa region (MENA), Zain Group has established a corporate entity focused on the delivery of drone-powered solutions. Approximately 24.6% of Zain Group is owned by Kuwait Investment Authority, and 21.9% is owned by Omantel, each of which are the company's largest shareholders. In August 2021, Zain Group created Zain Ventures, which invested in Pipe.com and swvl.com to accelerate company growth across the Middle East and beyond.

FINANCIAL DATA: Note: Data for latest year may not have been available at press time.

In U.S. $	2020	2019	2018	2017	2016	2015
Revenue	5,327,040,000	4,537,249,500	4,321,190,000	3,400,260,000	3,549,480,000	3,741,690,000
R&D Expense						
Operating Income						
Operating Margin %						
SGA Expense						
Net Income	681,749,000	776,365,800	739,396,000	542,141,000	517,963,000	546,405,000
Operating Cash Flow						
Capital Expenditure						
EBITDA						
Return on Assets %						
Return on Equity %						
Debt to Equity						

CONTACT INFORMATION:
Phone: 965-2-464-4444   Fax: 965-2-464-1111
Toll-Free:
Address: Airport Rd., Shuwaikh, Safat, 13083 Kuwait

STOCK TICKER/OTHER:
Stock Ticker: ZAIN   Exchange: Kuwait
Employees: 6,000   Fiscal Year Ends: 12/31
Parent Company:

SALARIES/BONUSES:
Top Exec. Salary: $ Bonus: $
Second Exec. Salary: $ Bonus: $

OTHER THOUGHTS:
Estimated Female Officers or Directors: 1
Hot Spot for Advancement for Women/Minorities:

Mobile TeleSystems PJSC

www.mtsgsm.com

NAIC Code: 517210

TYPES OF BUSINESS:

Mobile Telephone Service
Broadband Internet Services
Pay TV Services
Fixed-Line Telephone Services
Value-Added Services

BRANDS/DIVISIONS/AFFILIATES:

MTS Bank
MTS
JUST AI Limited
SWIPGLOBAL Limited

CONTACTS: Note: Officers with more than one job title may be intentionally listed here more than once.

Vyacheslav Nikolaev, CEO
Ilya V. Filatov, VP-Financial Srvcs.
Olga Ziborova, VP-Mktg.
Pavel Voronin, VP-Technology
Ruslan Ibragimov, VP-Corp. & Legal Matters
Michael Hecker, VP-Strategy & Corp. Dev.
Vadim Savchenko, VP-Sales & Customer Svcs.
Konstantin Markov, Dir.
Felix Evtushenkov, Chmn.
Ivan Zolochevskiy, CEO
Valery Shorzhin, Dir.-Procurement Mgmt.

GROWTH PLANS/SPECIAL FEATURES:

Mobile TeleSystems PJSC (MTS) is a leading telecommunications provider, offering a wide range of mobile and fixed-line voice and data services. MTS serves more than 80 million mobile subscribers in Russia, Armenia and Belarus, and approximately 9 million fixed-line customers in Russia. Fixed line communications services include fixed voice, broadband internet and payTV in Russia. Mobile connectivity is MTS' core business, offering 3G and 4G/LTE networks and a range of tariff plans adapted to suit each regional market. MTS offers financial services to individual and corporate clients. The firm's eWallet division provides customers with a convenient way to manage the majority of their day-to-day financial needs. Through MTS Bank, the company has developed a suite of complex financial products, including cash management solutions, payroll services and overdraft and loan programs. And in cooperation with MTS Bank, MTS has developed and sells a range of smartphones that combine the functionality of a tablet, camera, music player and eBook, as well as a payment device and a window of medical services. These phones are marketed under the MTS brand. MTS' data division offers subscribers (individuals and corporations) high-speed 4G LTE and Internet of Things (IoT)-oriented networks. Its digital division encompasses digital commerce, IoT and system integration; financial technologies, mobile applications and big data; and eTicketing, cloud storage and computing. In July 2021, MTS acquired GDTs Energy Group LLC, the owner of the GreenBush facility in Moscow, one of the largest data center projects in Russia. When fully completed GreenBush is planned to have a gross capacity of 19 MW to power 2,280 racks in 24 server rooms.

FINANCIAL DATA: Note: Data for latest year may not have been available at press time.

In U.S. $	2020	2019	2018	2017	2016	2015
Revenue	6,732,276,000	6,476,275,000	6,533,229,000	6,024,737,000	5,926,540,000	5,865,872,000
R&D Expense						
Operating Income	1,656,524,000	1,594,401,000	1,516,539,000	1,314,894,000	1,150,153,000	1,195,913,000
Operating Margin %		.25%	.23%	.22%	.19%	.20%
SGA Expense	1,141,026,000	1,162,981,000	1,102,952,000	1,114,447,000	1,103,823,000	1,087,826,000
Net Income	835,362,300	737,818,200	93,150,540	762,316,400	659,372,000	673,178,600
Operating Cash Flow	2,115,298,000	1,450,744,000	2,100,104,000	1,967,479,000	1,776,022,000	1,959,970,000
Capital Expenditure	1,325,015,000	1,247,847,000	1,251,561,000	1,039,660,000	1,171,850,000	1,449,179,000
EBITDA	2,965,093,000	2,950,470,000	3,097,745,000	2,425,995,000	2,372,442,000	2,291,111,000
Return on Assets %		.06%	.01%	.10%	.08%	.08%
Return on Equity %		1.10%	.07%	.43%	.32%	.30%
Debt to Equity		12.449	7.81	1.99	1.703	1.825

CONTACT INFORMATION:

Phone: 7 4952232025   Fax: 7 4959116567
Toll-Free:
Address: 4, Marksistskaya St., Moscow, 109147 Russia

STOCK TICKER/OTHER:

Stock Ticker: MBT
Employees: 58,415
Parent Company: Sistema JSGC

Exchange: NYS
Fiscal Year Ends: 12/31

SALARIES/BONUSES:

Top Exec. Salary: $ Bonus: $
Second Exec. Salary: $ Bonus: $

OTHER THOUGHTS:

Estimated Female Officers or Directors: 1
Hot Spot for Advancement for Women/Minorities:

Momentum Telecom

www.momentumtelecom.com

NAIC Code: 517110

TYPES OF BUSINESS:

Local Exchange Carrier
Cloud Voice
Cloud-based Applications
Business Communication Services
Wholesale Services
Telecommunication Security Services

BRANDS/DIVISIONS/AFFILIATES:

GROWTH PLANS/SPECIAL FEATURES:

Momentum Telecom develops and integrates cloud voice and cloud-based applications for enhanced business communication purposes. The company's solutions span unified communications, Microsoft Teams, managed network, mobility, collaboration, contact center and more. Momentum's voice solution architecture interconnects with more than 15 major carriers. Wholesale services include white label cloud voice, broadband management, customer service, realtime subscriber provisioning and management portal, cable diagnostic expansion, fiber expansion, WiFi expansion, network maintenance, bandwidth management and more. Momentum operates one of the most advanced telecommunication platforms in the world and uses state-of-the-art technology to detect and prevent attacks at the network, host and service levels.

CONTACTS: *Note: Officers with more than one job title may be intentionally listed here more than once.*

Todd Zittrouer, CEO
William Birnie, Chief Marketing Officer
Robert Hagan, CFO
Chuck Piazza, Exec. VP-Sales & Mktg.
Heather Dromgoole, VP-Human Resources
Brian Kelley, Director
Mark Marquez, Exec. VP-IT
Andrea McHugh, Vice President

FINANCIAL DATA: *Note: Data for latest year may not have been available at press time.*

In U.S. $	2020	2019	2018	2017	2016	2015
Revenue	137,550,000	131,000,000	124,000,000	99,300,000	30,510,000	30,300,000
R&D Expense						
Operating Income						
Operating Margin %						
SGA Expense						
Net Income						
Operating Cash Flow						
Capital Expenditure						
EBITDA						
Return on Assets %						
Return on Equity %						
Debt to Equity						

CONTACT INFORMATION:

Phone: 877-251-5554   Fax:
Toll-Free:
Address: 1 Concourse Pkwy. NE, Ste. 600, Atlanta, GA 30328 United States

STOCK TICKER/OTHER:

Stock Ticker: Private
Employees: 391
Parent Company: MBS Holdings Inc

Exchange:
Fiscal Year Ends: 12/31

SALARIES/BONUSES:

Top Exec. Salary: $ Bonus: $
Second Exec. Salary: $ Bonus: $

OTHER THOUGHTS:

Estimated Female Officers or Directors: 2
Hot Spot for Advancement for Women/Minorities: Y

Net2Phone Inc

www.net2phone.com

NAIC Code: 517110

TYPES OF BUSINESS:

VoIP Service Providers
Outsourced Telecommunications Services
Calling Card Services
ISP Solutions

BRANDS/DIVISIONS/AFFILIATES:

IDT Corporation
Huddle
N2P Remote

CONTACTS: *Note: Officers with more than one job title may be intentionally listed here more than once.*

Jonah Fink, Pres.
Zali Ritholtz, COO
Dovey Forman, Dir.-Operations
George Longyear, Dir.-Sales
Denise D'Arienzo, Dir.-Mktg.
Jeffrey Skelton, CTO
Andreea Cojocariu, Dir.-Digital Mktg.

GROWTH PLANS/SPECIAL FEATURES:

Net2Phone, Inc. is a provider of retail voice over internet protocol (VoIP) cloud telephone products and services. The firm enables businesses to handle 450,000 simultaneous calls, but serves businesses of any size, whether small or large. Net2Phone's onboarding and implementation team sets up each customer's phone system as needed/required, and provides ongoing support services. The company offers products such as hosted PBX cloud phone systems, Huddle, N2P Remote, Microsoft Teams and SIP (session initiation protocol) trunking for business and call centers. Hosted business PBX (private branch exchange) is a phone system that is completely hosted, managed and maintained by Net2Phone. It features VoIP solutions for a fully-featured cloud PBX, and has a single platform that enables businesses to transfer calls, set up auto-attendant to answer and route calls, manage multiple offices and keep businesses connected even while on-the-go. The hosted PBX phone service includes unlimited calls, both domestic and international, for one low monthly price. Huddle enables virtual face-to-face communications globally. N2P Remote enables work-from-home, work-from-anywhere (remote) connectivity. Microsoft Teams offers a direct routing phone application for productivity, collaboration and content sharing. SIP trunking is a VoIP technology and streaming media service by which internet telephone service providers deliver telephone services and unified communications to customers equipped with SIP-based PBX facilities. This allows businesses and call centers to use their existing internet connection as a phone line, instead of physical leased line, providing cost-savings. Net2Phone's plans offer unlimited calling to/from over 30 countries and virtual phone numbers in over 50 countries. Net2Phone is a subsidiary of IDT Corporation, a holding company with strong interest in telecommunications.

FINANCIAL DATA: *Note: Data for latest year may not have been available at press time.*

In U.S. $	2020	2019	2018	2017	2016	2015
Revenue	50,800,000	47,264,000	34,857,000	29,450,000		
R&D Expense						
Operating Income						
Operating Margin %						
SGA Expense						
Net Income						
Operating Cash Flow						
Capital Expenditure						
EBITDA						
Return on Assets %						
Return on Equity %						
Debt to Equity						

CONTACT INFORMATION:

Phone: 973-438-3111   Fax:
Toll-Free: 866-978-8260
Address: 520 Broad St., Newark, NJ 07102 United States

STOCK TICKER/OTHER:

Stock Ticker: Subsidiary
Employees: 1,800
Parent Company: IDT Corporation

Exchange:
Fiscal Year Ends: 07/31

SALARIES/BONUSES:

Top Exec. Salary: $ Bonus: $
Second Exec. Salary: $ Bonus: $

OTHER THOUGHTS:

Estimated Female Officers or Directors:
Hot Spot for Advancement for Women/Minorities:

NETGEAR Inc

NAIC Code: 334210A

TYPES OF BUSINESS:

Networking Equipment
Wireless Networking Products
Broadband Products
Entertainment Management Software
Security Products
Wi-Fi Phones
Gaming Router

BRANDS/DIVISIONS/AFFILIATES:

Orbi Voice
Meural
Nighthawk

CONTACTS: Note: Officers with more than one job title may be intentionally listed here more than once.

Patrick Lo, CEO
Bryan Murray, CFO
Mark Merrill, Co-Founder
Michael Falcon, COO
Andrew Kim, General Counsel
Michael Werdann, Senior VP, Divisional
John McHugh, Senior VP, Divisional
Tamesa Rogers, Senior VP, Divisional
David Henry, Senior VP, Divisional

GROWTH PLANS/SPECIAL FEATURES:

NETGEAR, Inc. designs, develops and markets internet connected products for consumers and growing businesses. The company operates through two segments: connected home and small and medium business (SMB). The connected home segment focuses on consumers, and consists of high-performance, easy-to-use 4G/5G mobile, 4G and 5G wireless solutions, Wi-Fi internet networking solutions and smart devices such as Orbi Voice smart speakers and Meural digital platforms for visual/canvas art. This division also offers the Nighthawk line of gaming routers. The SMB segment focuses on small- and medium-sized businesses and consists of business networking, storage, wireless LAN and security solutions that bring enterprise-class functionality at an affordable price. NETGEAR's products are sold through multiple sales channels worldwide, including wholesale distributors, traditional and online retailers, direct market resellers, value-added resellers and broadband service providers. Product offerings include remote video security systems, broadband modems, Wi-Fi gateways, Wi-Fi Hotspots, routers, range extenders, powerline adapters, powerline bridges, Wi-Fi network adapters, Ethernet switches, wireless controllers, wireless access points, unified storage and internet security appliances.

FINANCIAL DATA: Note: Data for latest year may not have been available at press time.

In U.S. $	2020	2019	2018	2017	2016	2015
Revenue	1,255,202,000	998,763,000	1,058,816,000	1,406,920,000	1,328,298,000	1,300,695,000
R&D Expense	88,788,000	77,982,000	82,416,000	94,603,000	89,367,000	86,499,000
Operating Income	75,544,000	26,188,000	41,856,000	86,850,000	117,981,000	89,073,000
Operating Margin %		.03%	.04%	.06%	.09%	.07%
SGA Expense	209,002,000	187,582,000	217,426,000	214,589,000	204,837,000	192,107,000
Net Income	58,293,000	25,791,000	-9,162,000	19,436,000	75,851,000	48,584,000
Operating Cash Flow	181,150,000	13,525,000	-103,211,000	87,524,000	115,173,000	110,391,000
Capital Expenditure	10,296,000	14,230,000	12,251,000	13,674,000	10,972,000	14,000,000
EBITDA	94,475,000	45,594,000	60,707,000	112,944,000	149,974,000	124,923,000
Return on Assets %		.03%	-.01%	.02%	.07%	.05%
Return on Equity %		.04%	-.01%	.03%	.10%	.07%
Debt to Equity		0.042				

CONTACT INFORMATION:

Phone: 408 907-8000   Fax: 408 907-8097
Toll-Free: 888-638-4327
Address: 350 E. Plumeria Dr., San Jose, CA 95134 United States

SALARIES/BONUSES:

Top Exec. Salary: $ Bonus: $
Second Exec. Salary: $ Bonus: $

STOCK TICKER/OTHER:

Stock Ticker: NTGR   Exchange: NAS
Employees: 809   Fiscal Year Ends: 12/31
Parent Company:

OTHER THOUGHTS:

Estimated Female Officers or Directors: 4
Hot Spot for Advancement for Women/Minorities: Y

NetScout Systems Inc

www.netscout.com

NAIC Code: 511210B

TYPES OF BUSINESS:

Computer Software, Network Management (IT), System Testing & Storage Application Management Solutions

BRANDS/DIVISIONS/AFFILIATES:

Adaptive Service Intelligence
nGeniusONE
INSG
NetScout Arbor

CONTACTS: Note: Officers with more than one job title may be intentionally listed here more than once.

Anil Singhal, CEO
Jean Bua, CFO
Michael Szabados, COO
John Downing, Executive VP, Divisional

GROWTH PLANS/SPECIAL FEATURES:

NetScout Systems, Inc. designs, develops, manufactures, markets, sells and supports a family of products that assures the performance and availability of critical business applications and services in complex, high-speed networks. Powered by NetScout's proprietary Adaptive Service Intelligence technology, its solutions are used to monitor customers' service delivery environment in order to identify performance issues and provide insight into network-based security threats. The firm markets its core service assurance and cybersecurity solutions into two primary markets: enterprise and service provider. Within the enterprise market, NetScout's nGeniusONE and INSG technologies enable IT and government organizations to improve service issues and security threats before they become serious and affect large numbers of users. These products are based on real-time analytic information platforms that can be managed across both virtual and physical environments. The service provider market serves customers categorized into three groups: mobile operators, fixed-line and cable operators, and internet service providers. For mobile operators, NetScout products monitor radio access networks, and provide analytics that present insight into subscriber trends and their customer experiences. For fixed-line and cable operators, products and solutions enable them to monitor and manage their local area WiFi connectivity services as well as broadband and telephone services targeting small- and medium-sized businesses. These products and solutions provide comprehensive insight into IP services, service usage, service availability, application awareness, traffic load, network availability and network performance. Last, for internet service providers, products and solutions help protect their networks against distributed denial of service (DDos) attacks and assist in rapidly locating and isolating advanced network threats. This division provides a range of network security solutions under the NetScout Arbor brand.

FINANCIAL DATA: Note: Data for latest year may not have been available at press time.

In U.S. $	2020	2019	2018	2017	2016	2015
Revenue	891,820,000	909,918,000	986,787,000	1,162,112,000	955,419,000	
R&D Expense	188,294,000	203,588,000	215,076,000	232,701,000	208,630,000	
Operating Income	20,312,000	-7,544,000	1,151,000	66,065,000	-25,082,000	
Operating Margin %	.02%	-.01%	.00%	.06%	-.03%	
SGA Expense	376,517,000	385,442,000	422,015,000	447,066,000	411,049,000	
Net Income	-2,754,000	-73,324,000	79,812,000	33,291,000	-28,369,000	
Operating Cash Flow	225,023,000	149,838,000	222,454,000	227,809,000	95,285,000	
Capital Expenditure	19,922,000	23,526,000	16,594,000	32,148,000	30,370,000	
EBITDA	138,625,000	71,109,000	147,477,000	222,232,000	113,961,000	
Return on Assets %	.00%	-.02%	.02%	.01%	-.01%	
Return on Equity %	.00%	-.04%	.04%	.01%	-.02%	
Debt to Equity	0.269	0.266	0.29	0.123	0.123	

CONTACT INFORMATION:

Phone: 978 614-4000   Fax: 978 614-4004
Toll-Free: 800-357-7666
Address: 310 Littleton Rd., Westford, MA 01886 United States

STOCK TICKER/OTHER:

Stock Ticker: NTCT   Exchange: NAS
Employees: 2,421   Fiscal Year Ends: 03/31
Parent Company:

SALARIES/BONUSES:

Top Exec. Salary: $ Bonus: $
Second Exec. Salary: $ Bonus: $

OTHER THOUGHTS:

Estimated Female Officers or Directors: 2
Hot Spot for Advancement for Women/Minorities:

Neustar Inc
NAIC Code: 518210

www.home.neustar

TYPES OF BUSINESS:
Clearinghouse Services
Marketing Services
Software
Risk Solutions
Communications Solutions
Security Solutions
Domain Name Services

BRANDS/DIVISIONS/AFFILIATES:
Golden Gate Capital

CONTACTS: *Note: Officers with more than one job title may be intentionally listed here more than once.*
Charles E. Gottdiener, CEO
Dorean Kass, Chief Sales Officer
Carey Pellock, Chief Human Resources Officer
Venkat Achanta, CTO
Leonard Kennedy, General Counsel
Brian Foster, Senior VP, Divisional
Venkat Achanta, Senior VP, Divisional
Steve Edwards, Senior VP, Divisional
Henry (Hank) Skorny, Senior VP, Divisional

GROWTH PLANS/SPECIAL FEATURES:
Neustar, Inc., owned by private equity firm Golden Gate Capital, provides data analytics and modeling software that help marketers send timely and relevant messages to target audiences. The firm's solutions are grouped into four categories: marketing, risk, communications and security. Marketing solutions encompass customer analytics, customer experience and customer intelligence. Risk solutions address compliance intelligence, fraud intelligence and operational intelligence. Communications solutions include branded content management, caller intelligence, global numbering insights, number management and order management. Security solutions include application security, domain name service (DNS), security intelligence and website performance management. Neustar helps organizations across a diverse set of industries understand their customers, personalize their marketing and protect themselves from cyber crime. Industries served by the firm primarily include retail, consumer packaged goods, quick service restaurants, financial services, insurance, automotive, travel, hospitality, communications, technology and government. Its solutions can also be incorporated into the pharmaceutical/biosciences, media/advertising and healthcare industries, among others. Headquartered in Virginia, Neustar has additional offices throughout the U.S., as well as in India, Costa Rica, Germany, India, and the U.K. In late-2020, Neustar completed the divestiture of its registry business to GoDaddy, Inc.

FINANCIAL DATA: *Note: Data for latest year may not have been available at press time.*

In U.S. $	2020	2019	2018	2017	2016	2015
Revenue	1,447,556,250	1,412,250,000	1,345,000,000	1,270,339,392	1,209,847,040	1,049,958,016
R&D Expense						
Operating Income						
Operating Margin %						
SGA Expense						
Net Income						
Operating Cash Flow						
Capital Expenditure						
EBITDA						
Return on Assets %						
Return on Equity %						
Debt to Equity						

CONTACT INFORMATION:
Phone: 571 434-5400   Fax: 571 434-5401
Toll-Free: 855-683-2677
Address: 1906 Reston Metro Plz., Ste. 500, Reston, VA 20190 United States

STOCK TICKER/OTHER:
Stock Ticker: Private   Exchange:
Employees: 1,988   Fiscal Year Ends: 12/31
Parent Company: Golden Gate Capital

SALARIES/BONUSES:
Top Exec. Salary: $ Bonus: $
Second Exec. Salary: $ Bonus: $

OTHER THOUGHTS:
Estimated Female Officers or Directors: 3
Hot Spot for Advancement for Women/Minorities: Y

Newfold Digital Inc

newfold.com

NAIC Code: 518210

TYPES OF BUSINESS:

Web Hosting Products & Services
Web Design Services
Search Engine
eCommerce
Advertising
Domain Name

BRANDS/DIVISIONS/AFFILIATES:

Siris Capital Group LLC
Clearlake Capital Group LP
Web.com Online Marketing
Web.com Contractor Services
Network Solutions
Register.com
Name Jet
bluehost inc.

CONTACTS: *Note: Officers with more than one job title may be intentionally listed here more than once.*

Sharon Rowlands, CEO
Christine Barry, COO
Christina Clohecy, CFO
Paula Drum, CMO
Deb Myers, Chief People Officer
Michael Bouchet, CIO
Roseann Duran, Executive VP

GROWTH PLANS/SPECIAL FEATURES:

Newfold Digital Inc, a result of the combination of Web.com Group, Inc. and Endurance Web Presence, is a web technology company servicing millions of customers worldwide. The firm's portfolio of brands include Web.com, Network Solutions, Register.com, Name Jet, bluehost inc. Web.com Online Marketing Agency offers search engine optimization and placement solutions. Web.com Contractor Services is a online networking platform that displays over 3,000 remodeling contractors who carry out bathroom remodeling, kitchen remodeling, attic remodeling and basement remodeling projects, from which homeowners can locate and hire. Network Solutions helps small businesses to start and market their businesses on the web, offering a full range of web-related services. Register.com is a leading provider of global domain name registration, website design and management services. The platform is also a business web hosting provider. NameJet is the premier aftermarket domain name service. Bluehost inc. is a web hosting solutions company. In February 2021, Siris Capital Group, LLC and Clearlake Capital Group, L.P. announced the formation of Newfold Digital through the combination of Endurance Web Presence and Web.com Group, Inc.

FINANCIAL DATA: *Note: Data for latest year may not have been available at press time.*

In U.S. $	2020	2019	2018	2017	2016	2015
Revenue	833,250,000	825,000,000	798,000,000	749,260,992	710,505,024	543,460,992
R&D Expense						
Operating Income						
Operating Margin %						
SGA Expense						
Net Income		55,795,611	54,701,580	53,629,000	3,990,000	89,961,000
Operating Cash Flow						
Capital Expenditure						
EBITDA						
Return on Assets %						
Return on Equity %						
Debt to Equity						

CONTACT INFORMATION:

Phone: 904 680-6600   Fax: 904 880-0350
Toll-Free:
Address: 5335 Gate Pkwy., Jacksonville, FL 32256 United States

STOCK TICKER/OTHER:

Stock Ticker: Private   Exchange:
Employees: 3,600   Fiscal Year Ends: 12/31
Parent Company: Siris Capital Group LLC

SALARIES/BONUSES:

Top Exec. Salary: $ Bonus: $
Second Exec. Salary: $ Bonus: $

OTHER THOUGHTS:

Estimated Female Officers or Directors: 3
Hot Spot for Advancement for Women/Minorities: Y

Nippon Telegraph and Telephone Corporation (NTT)

www.ntt.co.jp

NAIC Code: 517110

TYPES OF BUSINESS:

Local Telephone Service
Long-Distance Service
Internet Service
Information Technology Services
Cellular Phone Service
Wireless Internet

BRANDS/DIVISIONS/AFFILIATES:

NTT East
NTT West
NTT Communications Corporation
NTT Ltd
NTT Data Corporation
NTT DoCoMo Inc
NTT Urban Solutions Inc
NTT Anode Energy Corporation

CONTACTS: *Note: Officers with more than one job title may be intentionally listed here more than once.*

Jun Sawada, CEO
Takashi Hiroi, CFO
Hiromichi Shinohara, Dir.-R&D Planning
Hiroki Watanabe, Chief Compliance Officer
Mitsuyoshi Kobayashi, Sr. VP-Strategic Bus. Dev. Div.
Yoshikiyo Sakai, Sr. VP-Finance & Acct.
Akira Shimada, Sr. VP-Gen. Affairs & Internal Control
Hiroshi Tsujigami, Sr. VP-Corp. Strategy
Hiromichi Shinohara, Chmn.
Tsunehisa Okuno, Sr. VP-Global Bus. Office

GROWTH PLANS/SPECIAL FEATURES:

Nippon Telegraph and Telephone Corporation (NTT), which is owned in part by the Japanese government, is one of the world's top telecommunications firms. NTT operates mainly through a variety of affiliate organizations and support groups. NTT East and NTT West operate regional communications businesses, with a support group consisting of other regional communications firms, engineering firms, a telemarketing business and other companies. NTT Communications Corporation and various other international communications companies operate a long-distance and international communications business, with a support group consisting of internet-related business and others, including NTT Ltd. NTT Data Corporation runs a data communications business, with its support group consisting of system integration, network system service and other NTT Data subsidiaries. NTT DoCoMo, Inc., along with its subsidiaries and affiliates, runs an extensive mobile communications business, offering cell phone-based internet access, long-term evolution (LTE) mobile phone services and telecommunications technical solutions. Other business activities within NTT include real estate, finance, construction, electric power, system development, advanced technology development and more, via NTT Urban Solutions, Inc. and NTT Anode Energy Corporation. NTT, Inc. is a global holding company whose business activities include strategic planning, governance and execution for the support of global businesses within the NTT group.

FINANCIAL DATA: *Note: Data for latest year may not have been available at press time.*

In U.S. $	2020	2019	2018	2017	2016	2015
Revenue	108,677,400,000	108,498,600,000	107,765,700,000	104,034,200,000	105,404,000,000	101,333,600,000
R&D Expense						
Operating Income	14,419,240,000	16,624,180,000	16,485,180,000	14,737,390,000	12,611,490,000	10,290,790,000
Operating Margin %	.15%	.15%	.15%	.14%	.12%	.10%
SGA Expense			26,665,850,000	25,452,040,000	25,277,970,000	26,088,040,000
Net Income	7,811,514,000	7,804,709,000	8,308,249,000	7,307,582,000	6,737,765,000	4,731,499,000
Operating Cash Flow	27,355,280,000	21,975,440,000	24,088,730,000	26,644,240,000	24,767,290,000	21,844,430,000
Capital Expenditure	16,954,060,000	15,273,580,000	15,624,030,000	15,542,610,000	14,955,710,000	16,467,960,000
EBITDA	28,181,750,000	27,781,410,000	28,561,050,000	27,652,590,000	28,652,550,000	26,838,640,000
Return on Assets %	.04%	.04%	.04%	.04%	.04%	.03%
Return on Equity %	.09%	.09%	.10%	.09%	.08%	.06%
Debt to Equity	0.281	0.309	0.313	0.353	0.405	0.429

CONTACT INFORMATION:

Phone: 81 352055581   Fax: 81 352055589
Toll-Free:
Address: 5-1 Otemachi 1-Chome, Chiyoda-ku, Tokyo, 100-8116 Japan

STOCK TICKER/OTHER:

Stock Ticker: NPPXF   Exchange: PINX
Employees: 274,850   Fiscal Year Ends: 03/31
Parent Company:

SALARIES/BONUSES:

Top Exec. Salary: $ Bonus: $
Second Exec. Salary: $ Bonus: $

OTHER THOUGHTS:

Estimated Female Officers or Directors:
Hot Spot for Advancement for Women/Minorities:

Nokia Corporation

www.nokia.com

NAIC Code: 334220

TYPES OF BUSINESS:
Smartphones and Cellphones
Network Systems & Services
Internet Software & Services
Multimedia Equipment
Brand Licensing
Collaboration Devices
5G
Innovation

BRANDS/DIVISIONS/AFFILIATES:
Nokia Bell Labs

GROWTH PLANS/SPECIAL FEATURES:
Nokia Corporation is a leading supplier of services and software for the converging internet and communications industries. For consumers, Nokia offers phones, home Wi-Fi, smart TVs, laptops, streaming devices and headphones. For businesses, the company offers solutions for service providers, for the industry and public sectors, licensing opportunities, brand licensing, digital automation cloud, business phones, and audio collaboration. Nokia Bell Labs engages in innovative technology, continually moving forward to improve, innovate and propel communication. Nokia Bell Labs is a leader in the development and deployment of 5G networks. Nokia Corporation's communications services customers support more than 6.4 billion subscriptions with Nokia's radio networks, and the firm's enterprise customers have deployed over 1,300 industrial networks worldwide.

CONTACTS: Note: Officers with more than one job title may be intentionally listed here more than once.
Pekka Lundmark, CEO
Marco Wiren, CFO
Stephanie Werner-Dietz, Chief People Officer
Nishant Batra, CTO
Louise Pentland, Chief Legal Officer
Juha Rutkiranta, Exec. VP-Oper.
Kai Oistamo, Chief Dev. Officer
Stephen Elop, Exec. VP-Devices & Svcs.
Timo Toikkanen, Exec. VP-Mobile Phones
Jo Harlow, Exec. VP-Smart Devices

FINANCIAL DATA: Note: Data for latest year may not have been available at press time.

In U.S. $	2020	2019	2018	2017	2016	2015
Revenue	26,698,270,000	28,485,730,000	27,566,950,000	28,280,470,000	28,851,040,000	15,270,990,000
R&D Expense	4,993,402,000	5,389,258,000	5,644,610,000	6,006,255,000	5,991,594,000	2,597,498,000
Operating Income	1,253,543,000	1,172,906,000	408,073,500	799,042,100	-356,758,900	2,114,896,000
Operating Margin %		.04%	.01%	.03%	- .01%	.14%
SGA Expense	3,540,709,000	3,788,730,000	4,231,014,000	4,416,724,000	4,665,966,000	2,018,376,000
Net Income	-3,073,991,000	8,552,439	-415,404,200	-1,825,335,000	-935,881,200	3,012,902,000
Operating Cash Flow	2,149,106,000	476,493,000	439,839,700	2,212,638,000	-1,776,464,000	619,440,900
Capital Expenditure						
EBITDA	2,577,949,000	2,595,054,000	1,682,387,000	1,942,625,000	662,203,100	2,442,332,000
Return on Assets %		.00%	- .01%	- .03%	- .02%	.12%
Return on Equity %		.00%	- .02%	- .08%	- .05%	.26%
Debt to Equity		0.31	0.185	0.214	0.182	0.193

CONTACT INFORMATION:
Phone: 358-10-44-88-000   Fax: 358-10-44-81-002
Toll-Free:
Address: Karakaari 7A, Espoo, FI-02610 Finland

STOCK TICKER/OTHER:
Stock Ticker: NOK
Employees: 92,039
Parent Company:

Exchange: NYS
Fiscal Year Ends: 12/31

SALARIES/BONUSES:
Top Exec. Salary: $ Bonus: $
Second Exec. Salary: $ Bonus: $

OTHER THOUGHTS:
Estimated Female Officers or Directors: 4
Hot Spot for Advancement for Women/Minorities: Y

Sales, profits and employees may be estimates. Financial information, benefits and other data can change quickly and may vary from those stated here.

Nortel Inversora SA

NAIC Code: 517110

www.nortelsa.com.ar

TYPES OF BUSINESS:

Wired Telecommunications Carriers
Telecommunications Services
Telephone Services

BRANDS/DIVISIONS/AFFILIATES:

Fintech Telecom LLC
Telecom Argentina SA
Telecom Personal SA
Personal Envios SA
Micro Sistemas SA
Telecom Argentina USA Inc
Nucleo SA

CONTACTS: *Note: Officers with more than one job title may be intentionally listed here more than once.*

Baruki Luis Alberto Gonzalez, Chmn.

GROWTH PLANS/SPECIAL FEATURES:

Nortel Inversora SA is a stock corporation organized by a consortium of Argentinian and international investors to acquire a controlling interest in the common stock of Telecom Argentina SA. Nortel owns a 54.74% stake in Telecom Argentina, which provides fixed-link public telecommunications services, as well as basic telephone services to Iran (via a roaming mobile services agreement with Mobile Company of Iran (MCI). Telecom's international telecommunications services agreements with international carriers (fixed services) covers delivery of traffic to Iran through non-Iranian carriers. MCI allows its mobile customers to use their mobile device on a network outside their subscriber's home network. Additional subsidiaries owned by the firm include Telecom Personal SA, Personal Envios SA and Micro Sistemas SA, each of which provide mobile telecommunication services in Argentina; Telecom Argentina USA, Inc., which provides fixed line services in the U.S.; and Nucleo SA, which provides mobile telecommunication services in Paraguay. Nortel operates as a majority-owned subsidiary of Fintech Telecom, LLC.

FINANCIAL DATA: *Note: Data for latest year may not have been available at press time.*

In U.S. $	2020	2019	2018	2017	2016	2015
Revenue	2,975,813,366	3,048,989,105	3,123,964,247	3,200,783,040	3,048,364,800	2,317,573,632
R&D Expense						
Operating Income						
Operating Margin %						
SGA Expense						
Net Income						
Operating Cash Flow						
Capital Expenditure						
EBITDA						
Return on Assets %						
Return on Equity %						
Debt to Equity						

CONTACT INFORMATION:

Phone: 541 49683631   Fax: 54 1143131298
Toll-Free:
Address: Alicia Moreau de Justo 50, Buenos Aires, AG 1107 Argentina

STOCK TICKER/OTHER:

Stock Ticker: Private
Employees: 15,500
Parent Company: Fintech Telecom LLC

Exchange:
Fiscal Year Ends: 12/31

SALARIES/BONUSES:

Top Exec. Salary: $ Bonus: $
Second Exec. Salary: $ Bonus: $

OTHER THOUGHTS:

Estimated Female Officers or Directors:
Hot Spot for Advancement for Women/Minorities:

NTT DOCOMO Inc

NAIC Code: 517210

www.nttdocomo.co.jp/english

TYPES OF BUSINESS:

Mobile Telephone Service
Mobile
5G
Telecommunications
Tablets
Data Communication

BRANDS/DIVISIONS/AFFILIATES:

Nippon Telegraph and Telephone Corporation (NTT)
NTT Group
docomo

GROWTH PLANS/SPECIAL FEATURES:

NTT DOCOMO, Inc. is a leading telecommunications company in Japan. The firm serves more than 73 million customers in Japan via advanced wireless networks, including long-term evolution (LTE) and LTE-advanced networks. NTT DOCOMO is a world-leading developer of 5G networks, deploying the network and network function virtualization (NFV) and other related technologies during the 2020s. Outside Japan, NTT DOCOMO provides technical and operational expertise to mobile operators and other partner companies, and contributes to the global standardization of new mobile technologies. Products by NTT DOCOMO include iPhones, iPads, docomo 4G and 5G smartphones, docomo tablets and other phones, watches, data communications products, drivers support products and more. The parent company of the firm is Nippon Telegraph and Telephone Corporation, the holding company of the NTT Group.

CONTACTS: *Note: Officers with more than one job title may be intentionally listed here more than once.*

Motoyuki Ii, CEO
Seizo Onoe, CTO
Fumio Iwasaki, Sr. Exec. VP
Tsutomu Shindou, Exec. VP
Takashi Tanaka, Exec. VP
Kazuhiro Yoshizawa, Exec. VP

FINANCIAL DATA: *Note: Data for latest year may not have been available at press time.*

In U.S. $	2020	2019	2018	2017	2016	2015
Revenue	43,150,700,000	46,076,108,800	45,396,140,032	42,620,825,600	43,089,641,472	40,281,174,016
R&D Expense						
Operating Income						
Operating Margin %						
SGA Expense						
Net Income	5,485,300,000	6,339,808,768	7,086,691,328	6,066,396,160	5,219,565,568	3,768,544,512
Operating Cash Flow						
Capital Expenditure						
EBITDA						
Return on Assets %						
Return on Equity %						
Debt to Equity						

CONTACT INFORMATION:

Phone: 81 351561111   Fax: 81 351560271
Toll-Free:
Address: 2-11-1, Nagata-cho, Chiyoda-ku, Tokyo, 100-6150 Japan

STOCK TICKER/OTHER:

Stock Ticker: Subsidiary   Exchange:
Employees: 38,000   Fiscal Year Ends: 03/31
Parent Company: Nippon Telegraph and Telephone Corporation (NTT)

SALARIES/BONUSES:

Top Exec. Salary: $ Bonus: $
Second Exec. Salary: $ Bonus: $

OTHER THOUGHTS:

Estimated Female Officers or Directors:
Hot Spot for Advancement for Women/Minorities:

O2 Czech Republic AS

NAIC Code: 517110

www.o2.cz/osobni/

TYPES OF BUSINESS:

Local & Long-Distance Telephone Service
Mobile Phone Service
Internet Access

BRANDS/DIVISIONS/AFFILIATES:

PPF Group

GROWTH PLANS/SPECIAL FEATURES:

O2 Czech Republic AS is a leading provider of telecommunications services on the Czech market. The firm provides services through nearly 8 million mobile and fixed lines. O2 Czech offers state-of-the-art high-speed packet access (HSPA) and long-term evolution (LTE) technologies to mobile customers. Information and communication technology (ICT) services include hosting and cloud services in data centers, consisting of a total area 78,576 in square footage (7,300 sm). O2 also offers TV services, stating it is the largest operator of internet television broadcasting in the nation. O2 operates as a subsidiary of PPF Group NV.

CONTACTS: *Note: Officers with more than one job title may be intentionally listed here more than once.*

Jindrich Fremuth, CEO
Tomas Kouril, CFO
Richard Siebenstich, CCO
Pavel Milec, Dir.-Human Resources
Jan Hruska, CTO
Jakub Chytil, Dir.-Legal Affairs
Petr Slovacek, Dir.-Oper. Div.
Felix Geyr, Dir.-Strategy & Bus. Dev.
Dana Dvorakova, Dir.-Corp. Comm.
Martin Bek, Dir.-Support Units
Frantisek Schneider, Dir.-Bus. Div.
Jindrich Fremuth, Dir.-Consumer Div.
Jindrich Fremuth, Chmn.

FINANCIAL DATA: *Note: Data for latest year may not have been available at press time.*

In U.S. $	2020	2019	2018	2017	2016	2015
Revenue	1,440,770,000	1,339,520,000	1,685,650,000	1,765,900,000	1,462,680,000	1,532,109,070
R&D Expense						
Operating Income						
Operating Margin %						
SGA Expense						
Net Income	271,190,000	235,510,000	241,694,000	261,637,000	205,006,000	274,785,000
Operating Cash Flow						
Capital Expenditure						
EBITDA						
Return on Assets %						
Return on Equity %						
Debt to Equity						

CONTACT INFORMATION:

Phone: 420-840-114-114   Fax:
Toll-Free:
Address: Za Brumlovkou 266/2, Prague 4-Michle, 140 22 Czech Republic

STOCK TICKER/OTHER:

Stock Ticker: TELEC   Exchange: Prague
Employees: 4,993   Fiscal Year Ends: 12/31
Parent Company: PPF Group NV

SALARIES/BONUSES:

Top Exec. Salary: $ Bonus: $
Second Exec. Salary: $ Bonus: $

OTHER THOUGHTS:

Estimated Female Officers or Directors: 1
Hot Spot for Advancement for Women/Minorities:

Oblong Inc

www.oblong.com

NAIC Code: 517110

TYPES OF BUSINESS:

Videoconferencing Services
Collaboration Technologies
Managed Services
Video Collaboration
Network Applications
Cloud-based Services

BRANDS/DIVISIONS/AFFILIATES:

Mezzanine

CONTACTS: Note: Officers with more than one job title may be intentionally listed here more than once.

Peter Holst, CEO
David Clark, CFO

GROWTH PLANS/SPECIAL FEATURES:

Oblong, Inc. is a provider of patented multi-stream collaboration technologies and managed services for video collaboration and network applications. The company's flagship product, Mezzanine, enables dynamic and immersive visual collaboration across multi-users, multi-screens, multi-devices and multi-locations. Mezzanine allows multiple people to share, control and arrange content simultaneously, from any location. Applications by Oblong include video telepresence, laptop and application sharing, whiteboard sharing and slides. Spatial input allows content to be spread across screens, spanning different walls, scalable to an arbitrary number of displays and interaction with Oblong's proprietary wand device. Mezzanine's product family includes the 200 Series (two display screen), 300 Series (three screen) and 600 Series (six screen). Oblong also sells maintenance and support contracts and license agreements. Customers of Oblong include Fortune 1000 companies, along with small and medium enterprises in a variety of industries. Video conferencing services include managed video-conferencing and remote service management. Network services can be tailored to each customer's need, and include cloud-connected video, multi-protocol label switching (MPLS) solutions for those with a converged network, and cloud cross-connection for the extension of a Layer 2 private line to Oblong's data center. Professional services by the company include onsite support or dispatch, as well as configuration or customization of equipment or software on behalf of a customer.

FINANCIAL DATA: Note: Data for latest year may not have been available at press time.

In U.S. $	2020	2019	2018	2017	2016	2015
Revenue		12,827,000	12,557,000	14,799,000	19,218,000	25,541,000
R&D Expense						
Operating Income						
Operating Margin %						
SGA Expense						
Net Income		-7,761,000	-7,168,000	5,785,000	-3,533,000	-2,143,000
Operating Cash Flow						
Capital Expenditure						
EBITDA						
Return on Assets %						
Return on Equity %						
Debt to Equity						

CONTACT INFORMATION:

Phone: 303-640-3838   Fax:
Toll-Free: 866-456-9764
Address: 25587 Conifer Rd., Ste. 105-231, Conifer, CO 80433 United States

STOCK TICKER/OTHER:

Stock Ticker: OBLG
Employees: 99
Parent Company:

Exchange: ASE
Fiscal Year Ends: 12/31

SALARIES/BONUSES:

Top Exec. Salary: $ Bonus: $
Second Exec. Salary: $ Bonus: $

OTHER THOUGHTS:

Estimated Female Officers or Directors: 2
Hot Spot for Advancement for Women/Minorities:

Oi SA

NAIC Code: 517110

TYPES OF BUSINESS:

Telecommunications
Fixed & Mobile Telephony Services
Data Transmission Services
Voice Services
Remote Access
Television Services
Internet Portal

BRANDS/DIVISIONS/AFFILIATES:

Oi TV

CONTACTS: *Note: Officers with more than one job title may be intentionally listed here more than once.*

Rodrigo Modesto de Abreu, CEO
Eurico Telles, Exec. Officer-Legal
Fabiano Castello, Internal Audit

GROWTH PLANS/SPECIAL FEATURES:

Oi SA is a leading integrated telecommunications service provider in Brazil. The firm offers a range of services, including residential, mobile and business-to-business (B2B). Residential services include local and long-distance fixed-line voice, broadband and PayTV. As of early-2021, this division had more than 10.5 million fixed lines in service, and owned more than 248,548 miles (400,000 km) of installed fiber optic cable. It offers a variety of high-speed broadband services, serving over 4 million digital subscriber lines. PayTV services are offered under the Oi TV brand, are delivered throughout residential areas using DTH satellite technology. The personal mobile service division offers mobile telecommunications services throughout Brazil, covering areas in which most of the population lives and works. The B2B division provides voice, broadband, PayTV, data transmission and other telecommunications services to small- and medium-sized enterprises, corporations and government agencies throughout Brazil. It also provides wholesale interconnection, network usage services and traffic transportation services to other telecommunications providers.

FINANCIAL DATA: *Note: Data for latest year may not have been available at press time.*

In U.S. $	2020	2019	2018	2017	2016	2015
Revenue	1,802,882,000	3,910,166,000	4,283,747,000	4,619,619,000	5,048,061,000	5,311,720,000
R&D Expense						
Operating Income	-399,054,100	-666,825,000	-184,602,600	-176,063,600	55,537,210	97,139,440
Operating Margin %		-.17%	-.04%	-.04%	.01%	.02%
SGA Expense	964,380,200	1,229,195,000	1,393,521,000	1,449,441,000	1,481,834,000	1,676,212,000
Net Income	-2,044,772,000	-1,747,759,000	5,314,760,000	-725,579,700	-1,348,428,000	-1,778,617,000
Operating Cash Flow	855,720,300	448,887,900	555,864,600	854,760,100	602,038,900	-204,608,200
Capital Expenditure	670,939,300	1,441,931,000	1,018,747,000	843,590,500	633,740,000	714,892,900
EBITDA	-441,982,800	431,880,700	6,840,744,000	615,807,900	1,504,942,000	1,135,516,000
Return on Assets %		-.13%	.40%	-.05%	-.08%	-.09%
Return on Equity %		-.42%	5.07%		-.60%	-.63%
Debt to Equity		1.39	0.635			4.229

CONTACT INFORMATION:

Phone: 55 2131311211   Fax: 55 614151315
Toll-Free:
Address: Rua General Polidoro, No. 99, Fl. 5, Rio de Janeiro, RJ 22280-001 Brazil

STOCK TICKER/OTHER:

Stock Ticker: OIBR.C   Exchange: NYS
Employees: 46,624   Fiscal Year Ends: 12/31
Parent Company:

SALARIES/BONUSES:

Top Exec. Salary: $ Bonus: $
Second Exec. Salary: $ Bonus: $

OTHER THOUGHTS:

Estimated Female Officers or Directors:
Hot Spot for Advancement for Women/Minorities:

OJSC JFSC Sistema

www.sistema.com

NAIC Code: 551114

TYPES OF BUSINESS:

Corporate, Subsidiary, and Regional Managing Offices
Investments
Telecommunications
Ecommerce
Real Estate
Industrial Production
Information Technology
Biotechnology

BRANDS/DIVISIONS/AFFILIATES:

GROWTH PLANS/SPECIAL FEATURES:

OJSC JFSC Sistema is a joint stock financial corporation that invests in and manages a range of companies that have value growth potential exceeding $1 billion. The corporation's diversified portfolio of assets mainly consists of Russian companies representing various industries and operating throughout Russia and abroad. These industries include telecommunications, ecommerce, real estate, industrial production, medicine, agriculture, pharmaceutical, hospitality, retail, energy, microelectronics, information technology, biotechnology and financial services. Sistema manages its own and third-party capital to develop its assets.

CONTACTS: *Note: Officers with more than one job title may be intentionally listed here more than once.*

Vladimir Chirakhov, CEO
Vladimir Travkov, CFO
Vladimir Evtushenkov, Chmn.

FINANCIAL DATA: *Note: Data for latest year may not have been available at press time.*

In U.S. $	2020	2019	2018	2017	2016	2015
Revenue	9,407,906,000	8,935,011,000	10,574,720,000	9,583,719,000	9,490,596,000	9,639,354,000
R&D Expense						
Operating Income	1,458,796,000	1,488,776,000	1,825,209,000	1,387,437,000	1,221,839,000	1,083,759,000
Operating Margin %		.17%	.17%	.14%	.13%	.11%
SGA Expense	1,825,141,000	1,754,911,000	1,926,195,000	2,102,117,000	2,135,648,000	2,035,437,000
Net Income	138,964,100	388,993,300	-624,304,500	-1,286,846,000	-159,939,300	456,938,200
Operating Cash Flow	1,861,202,000	1,445,534,000	1,205,570,000	1,341,243,000	1,423,987,000	2,122,984,000
Capital Expenditure	1,738,112,000	1,599,964,000	1,687,265,000	1,420,709,000	1,671,459,000	1,893,794,000
EBITDA	3,243,756,000	3,257,372,000	3,431,539,000	1,297,456,000	2,670,161,000	2,260,343,000
Return on Assets %		.02%	-.04%	-.08%	-.01%	.03%
Return on Equity %		.98%	-1.41%	-.91%	-.07%	.19%
Debt to Equity		15.492	45.312	8.224	2.481	2.198

CONTACT INFORMATION:

Phone: 7-495-737-0101   Fax: 7-495-730-0330
Toll-Free:
Address: 13/1 Mokhovaya St., Moscow, 125009 Russia

STOCK TICKER/OTHER:

Stock Ticker: JSFCF   Exchange: GREY
Employees: 158,000   Fiscal Year Ends: 12/31
Parent Company:

SALARIES/BONUSES:

Top Exec. Salary: $ Bonus: $
Second Exec. Salary: $ Bonus: $

OTHER THOUGHTS:

Estimated Female Officers or Directors:
Hot Spot for Advancement for Women/Minorities:

OneSpan Inc

NAIC Code: 511210E

www.vasco.com

TYPES OF BUSINESS:

Computer Software, Network Security, Managed Access, Digital ID,
Cybersecurity & Anti-Virus
Identity Security
Authentication
Anti-Fraud Services
Agreement Automation

BRANDS/DIVISIONS/AFFILIATES:

CONTACTS: Note: Officers with more than one job title may be intentionally listed here more than once.

Scott Clements, CEO
Mark Hoyt, CFO
John Fox, Chairman of the Board
T. Hunt, Director

GROWTH PLANS/SPECIAL FEATURES:

OneSpan, Inc. designs, develops, markets and supports digital solutions for identity, security and business productivity that protect and facilitate electronic transactions via mobile and connected devices. The company's products are grouped into five categories: authentication, including intelligent adaptive authentication, mobile authenticators, hardware authenticators, authentication servers and multifactor authentication; fraud analysis, including risk analytics; eSignatures, including electronic and mobile applications; mobile app security; and identity verification. Solutions span opening accounts, application fraud, frictionless authentication, account takeover, regulatory compliance, enterprise security, transaction signing, lending and financing. Industries served by OneSpan primarily include financial services, insurance, government and healthcare. OneSpan has operations in Austria, Australia, Belgium, Brazil, Canada, China, France, Japan, Netherlands, Singapore, Switzerland, the United Arab Emirates, the U.K. and the U.S. More than 10,000 customers, including over half of the top 100 global banks, rely on OneSpan solutions to protect business relationships and business processes.

FINANCIAL DATA: Note: Data for latest year may not have been available at press time.

In U.S. $	2020	2019	2018	2017	2016	2015
Revenue	215,691,000	254,570,000	212,280,000	193,291,000	192,304,000	241,443,000
R&D Expense	41,194,000	42,463,000	32,197,000	23,119,000	23,214,000	18,538,000
Operating Income	-5,258,000	15,275,000	24,000	6,192,000	9,599,000	50,453,000
Operating Margin %		.06%	.00%	.03%	.05%	.21%
SGA Expense	107,194,000	105,400,000	105,394,000	96,394,000	88,995,000	72,159,000
Net Income	-5,455,000	8,789,000	3,846,000	-22,399,000	10,514,000	42,151,000
Operating Cash Flow	14,922,000	18,244,000	1,226,000	17,627,000	28,415,000	68,792,000
Capital Expenditure	3,101,000	7,453,000	3,685,000	3,195,000	2,187,000	1,451,000
EBITDA	6,745,000	26,820,000	12,162,000	16,793,000	20,376,000	56,755,000
Return on Assets %		.02%	.01%	-.07%	.03%	.15%
Return on Equity %		.03%	.02%	-.09%	.04%	.19%
Debt to Equity		0.043				

CONTACT INFORMATION:

Phone: 312-766-4001   Fax:
Toll-Free:
Address: 121 West Wacker Dr., Ste. 2050, Chicago, IL 60601 United States

STOCK TICKER/OTHER:

Stock Ticker: OSPN
Employees: 870
Parent Company:

Exchange: NAS
Fiscal Year Ends: 12/31

SALARIES/BONUSES:

Top Exec. Salary: $ Bonus: $
Second Exec. Salary: $ Bonus: $

OTHER THOUGHTS:

Estimated Female Officers or Directors:
Hot Spot for Advancement for Women/Minorities:

OneWeb Ltd

www.oneweb.world

NAIC Code: 517410

TYPES OF BUSINESS:

Satellite Internet Access Services
Satellites
Global Communications Network
Internet
User Terminals
5G

BRANDS/DIVISIONS/AFFILIATES:

UK Department for Business, Energy and Industrial

CONTACTS: *Note: Officers with more than one job title may be intentionally listed here more than once.*

Adrian Steckel, CEO
Larry Alder, COO
Tom Whayne, CFO
Nicolas Zibell, CCO
Heidi Dillard, Chief Human Resources Officer
Vikas Grover, CIO
Greg Wyler, Chmn.

GROWTH PLANS/SPECIAL FEATURES:

OneWeb Ltd. is building a global communications network in space to deliver high-throughput, high-speed services capable of connecting everywhere and to everyone. The firm designed an advanced, low-Earth-orbit satellite constellation referred to as OneWeb. OneWeb's 5G-ready network will provide connectivity solutions for maritime, aviation, enterprise and government entities, and will cover cell site backhaul. The company powers digital transformation and offers tailored networking solutions for any need, at any level. OneWeb satellites orbit relatively close to the Earth, allowing for better internet access speeds. As they orbit, they interlock with each other electronically to create coverage over the entire planet. Small, low-cost user terminals communicate with the satellite network and provide wireless internet access. The terminals provide connectivity with no change in latency (speed) during satellite handovers in order to ensure continuous quality of voice, gaming and web surfing experience. User terminals consist of a satellite antenna, a receiver and a customer network exchange unit (CNX). The CNX connects the user terminal to the customer's network which in turn connects to end-user devices such as laptops, smartphones, sensors and more. Compared to traditional satellites, OneWeb units have fewer components, are lighter in weight, easier to manufacture and cheaper to launch. They contain on-board propulsion and state-of-the-art positioning GPS sensors that ground-track their placement within meters. The propulsion systems perform maneuvers for steering clear of space debris. When a OneWeb satellite nears the end of its service life, it will de-orbit automatically. Between 2019 and early-2020, OneWeb had launched 40 satellites and was scheduled to launch another 34 in March 2020, bringing the constellation total to 74. In March 2020, the firm filed for Chapter 11 bankruptcy protection. In July 2020, a consortium led by the UK Department for Business Energy and Industrial Strategy.

FINANCIAL DATA: *Note: Data for latest year may not have been available at press time.*

In U.S. $	2020	2019	2018	2017	2016	2015
Revenue	26,520,760	75,773,600	216,496,000	81,254,000		
R&D Expense						
Operating Income						
Operating Margin %						
SGA Expense						
Net Income			-213,184,000	-73,857,000		
Operating Cash Flow						
Capital Expenditure						
EBITDA						
Return on Assets %						
Return on Equity %						
Debt to Equity						

CONTACT INFORMATION:

Phone: Fax:
Toll-Free:
Address: 195 Wood Ln., W., Works Bldg., Fl.3, London, W12 7FQ
United Kingdom

STOCK TICKER/OTHER:

Stock Ticker: Subsidiary   Exchange:
Employees: 80   Fiscal Year Ends:
Parent Company: UK Department for Business Energy and Industrial

SALARIES/BONUSES:

Top Exec. Salary: $ Bonus: $
Second Exec. Salary: $ Bonus: $

OTHER THOUGHTS:

Estimated Female Officers or Directors:
Hot Spot for Advancement for Women/Minorities:

Ooredoo QPSC

NAIC Code: 517210

www.ooredoo.qa

TYPES OF BUSINESS:

Wireless Telecommunications Carriers (except Satellite)
Communications
Mobile Networks
Fixed Networks

BRANDS/DIVISIONS/AFFILIATES:

GROWTH PLANS/SPECIAL FEATURES:

Ooredoo QPSC is an international communications company with a customer base of more than 100 million across the Middle East, North Africa and Southeast Asia. In Qatar, the firm is the leading communications company, delivering services for consumers, businesses, residences and organizations. Services offered include pre-paid and post-paid calling plans, data plans, international calling, internet via fiber cable lines and broadband. Ooredoo's 2G/3G/4G/5G network covers all municipalities of Qatar, and extends to the desert. The company launched its live 5G network on the 3.5GHz spectrum band in 2018, claiming to be the first in the world to do so. Ooredoo's eCommerce platform offers monthly plans, and sells smartphones, tablets, internet devices and related accessories.

CONTACTS: Note: Officers with more than one job title may be intentionally listed here more than once.

Mohammed bin Abdulla Al Thani, CEO
Faisal bin Thani Al Thani, Chmn.

FINANCIAL DATA: Note: Data for latest year may not have been available at press time.

In U.S. $	2020	2019	2018	2017	2016	2015
Revenue	7,865,600,000	8,200,620,000	8,216,400,000	8,902,300,000	8,929,466,368	8,835,398,656
R&D Expense						
Operating Income						
Operating Margin %						
SGA Expense						
Net Income	387,443,000	609,659,000	492,195,000	517,297,000	602,349,952	581,944,448
Operating Cash Flow						
Capital Expenditure						
EBITDA						
Return on Assets %						
Return on Equity %						
Debt to Equity						

CONTACT INFORMATION:

Phone: 974 440002133   Fax: 974 44830011
Toll-Free:
Address: Ooredoo Tower, W. Bay Area, Doha,   Qatar

STOCK TICKER/OTHER:

Stock Ticker: ORDS   Exchange: Qatar
Employees: 15,960   Fiscal Year Ends: 12/31
Parent Company:

SALARIES/BONUSES:

Top Exec. Salary: $ Bonus: $
Second Exec. Salary: $ Bonus: $

OTHER THOUGHTS:

Estimated Female Officers or Directors:
Hot Spot for Advancement for Women/Minorities:

OPTERNA

NAIC Code: 511210B

TYPES OF BUSINESS:

Computer Software: Network Management (IT), System Testing & Storage
Fiber-Optic Infrastructure Products

BRANDS/DIVISIONS/AFFILIATES:

Belden Inc

GROWTH PLANS/SPECIAL FEATURES:

OPTERNA provides enterprise broadband connectivity
solutions through its fiber optic portfolio. Products include
copper products, fiber optics, related equipment cabinets and
accessories, fiber management, distribution hubs and boxes,
splice closures, access and subscriber boxes, panels,
connectors, modules and more. OPTERNA's fiber-to-the-
everywhere (FTTX) solutions span global on- and off-site
premises, including outdoor connectivity. OPTERNA is a
business brand of Belden, Inc., with manufacturing facilities in
Europe, Asia, Africa, the Middle East and the U.S.

CONTACTS: Note: Officers with more than one job title may be intentionally listed here more than once.

Abraham Chandy, Dir.-Oper.
Bret A. Matz, Gen. Mgr.
Javad K. Hassan, Chmn.-NeST Group
David Aldrich, Chmn.-Belden

FINANCIAL DATA: Note: Data for latest year may not have been available at press time.

In U.S. $	2020	2019	2018	2017	2016	2015
Revenue	15,006,000	15,375,000				
R&D Expense						
Operating Income						
Operating Margin %						
SGA Expense						
Net Income						
Operating Cash Flow						
Capital Expenditure						
EBITDA						
Return on Assets %						
Return on Equity %						
Debt to Equity						

CONTACT INFORMATION:

Phone: 315-431-7200   Fax:
Toll-Free:
Address: 6176 E. Molloy Rd., East Syracuse, NY 13057 United States

STOCK TICKER/OTHER:

Stock Ticker: Subsidiary
Employees:
Parent Company: Belden Inc

Exchange:
Fiscal Year Ends: 03/31

SALARIES/BONUSES:

Top Exec. Salary: $ Bonus: $
Second Exec. Salary: $ Bonus: $

OTHER THOUGHTS:

Estimated Female Officers or Directors:
Hot Spot for Advancement for Women/Minorities:

Optical Cable Corporation

www.occfiber.com

NAIC Code: 335921

TYPES OF BUSINESS:

Fiber Optic Cable Manufacturing
Manufacturer
Fiber Optic Cable
Copper Cable
Connectivity Solutions
Communications

BRANDS/DIVISIONS/AFFILIATES:

Applied Optical Systems Inc
Centric Solutions LLC

CONTACTS: *Note: Officers with more than one job title may be intentionally listed here more than once.*

Neil Wilkin, CEO
Tracy Smith, CFO

GROWTH PLANS/SPECIAL FEATURES:

Optical Cable Corporation (OCC) manufactures a range of fiber optic and copper data communications cabling and connectivity solutions mainly for the enterprise market. The company also provides its cabling solutions for various harsh environment and specialty markets (non-carriers), offering integrated suites of high-quality products which operate as a system solution of seamlessly integrate with other providers' offerings. OCC also manufactures and sells products in the wireless carrier markets. Its products are designed for use by enterprise networks, data centers, residences and campuses, as well as for harsh environments such as military, industrial, mining, petrochemical, wireless, carrier and broadcast applications. Products include fiber optic and copper cabling, fiber optic and copper connectors, specialty fiber optic and copper connectors, fiber optic and copper patch cords, pre-terminated fiber optic and copper cable assemblies, racks, cabinets, Datacom enclosures, patch panels, face plates, multi-media boxes, fiber optic reels/accessories and other cable and connectivity management accessories. OCC manufactures its fiber optic cables at its ISO 9001:2015 registered and MIL-STD-790G certified facility in Roanoke, Virginia; its enterprise connectivity products primarily at its ISO 9001:2015 registered facility near Asheville, North Carolina; and its harsh environment and specialty connectivity products at its ISO 9001:2015 registered and MIL-STD-790G certified facility near Dallas, Texas. The company also wholly-owns: Applied Optical Systems, Inc., which markets and sells OCC's harsh environment and specialty connectivity products; and Centric Solutions, LLC, a provider of turnkey cabling and connectivity solutions for the datacenter market.

FINANCIAL DATA: *Note: Data for latest year may not have been available at press time.*

In U.S. $	2020	2019	2018	2017	2016	2015
Revenue	55,277,400	71,324,450	87,828,590	64,092,850	64,616,000	73,568,740
R&D Expense						
Operating Income	-5,533,064	-5,161,701	1,740,374	-1,317,012	-1,216,965	-2,381,798
Operating Margin %		-.07%	.02%	-.02%	-.02%	-.03%
SGA Expense	19,245,500	23,434,360	26,130,960	21,968,760	20,760,740	24,042,550
Net Income	-6,121,224	-5,669,321	1,068,753	-1,738,771	-1,778,822	-4,255,665
Operating Cash Flow	-3,553,137	-283,797	3,206,248	-687,071	3,155,480	1,202,348
Capital Expenditure	168,458	550,397	734,395	583,867	703,401	3,244,793
EBITDA	-4,106,304	-3,433,422	3,478,116	454,345	880,692	-298,656
Return on Assets %		-.14%	.03%	-.04%	-.04%	-.09%
Return on Equity %		-.24%	.04%	-.07%	-.07%	-.15%
Debt to Equity		0.243	0.342	0.512	0.47	0.486

CONTACT INFORMATION:

Phone: 540 265-0690   Fax: 540 265-0724
Toll-Free:
Address: 5290 Concourse Dr., Roanoke, VA 24019 United States

STOCK TICKER/OTHER:

Stock Ticker: OCC   Exchange: NAS
Employees: 317   Fiscal Year Ends: 10/31
Parent Company:

SALARIES/BONUSES:

Top Exec. Salary: $ Bonus: $
Second Exec. Salary: $ Bonus: $

OTHER THOUGHTS:

Estimated Female Officers or Directors:
Hot Spot for Advancement for Women/Minorities:

Orange

www.orange.com

NAIC Code: 517110

TYPES OF BUSINESS:

Telephone Service-Local
Wireless Voice & Data Services
Cable Service
Broadcast Services
Internet & Multimedia Services
Directory Publishing
Corporate & Wholesale Telecommunications

BRANDS/DIVISIONS/AFFILIATES:

Orange Marine
Orange Bank
Orange Money
Orange Fintech

CONTACTS: *Note: Officers with more than one job title may be intentionally listed here more than once.*

Stephane Richard, CEO
Pierre Louette, Deputy CEO
Benoit Scheen, Sr. Exec. VP-Oper., Europe
Elie Girard, Sr.-Strategy & Dev.
Beatrice Mandine, Sr. Exec. VP-Comm. & Brand
Delphine Ernotte Cunci, Deputy CEO-Orange France
Christine Albanel, Sr. Exec. VP-Corp. Social Responsibility & Events
Thierry Bonhomme, Sr. Exec. VP-Orange Bus. Svcs.
Marc Rennard, Sr. Exec. VP-Oper., Africa, Middle East & Asia
Pierre Louette, Deputy CEO-Group Sourcing & Supply Chain

GROWTH PLANS/SPECIAL FEATURES:

Orange is a world-leading telecommunications carrier, serving more than 255 million customers. The firm's activities are divided into: networks, enterprise services, content and financial services. The networks division utilized digital technologies to communication and business purposes. Landline and mobile networks are the hub of the digital revolution. Therefore, this division provides voice, data and video management, coverage for voice, message and internet needs on mobile 3G/4G/4G+/5G networks (whether ready or in development), Internet of Things (IoT) for long-range and light connectivity (Li-Fi) and more. Orange provides 4G mobile service to 70 million customers worldwide. The enterprise service division supports companies active in various sectors via technological and face-to-face collaborative solutions. This business strategy includes various collaborative working methods, information systems and 360-degree customer relations such as email, mobile, social networks and chats. Enterprise solutions serve international carriers, third-party operators, corporate networks, healthcare organizations, broadcasters, telecommunications providers, maritime operations and more. Orange Marine has installed approximately 150,000 miles of submarine fiber optic cables in all of the world's oceans for global connectivity purposes, even at sea. The content division provides television broadcast services, offering fiber-to-the-home (FTTH) connectivity to millions of European households. It also provides high-quality video (UHD) and audio (Dolby Atmos), and is developing a new TV experience with virtual reality. Last, the financial services division offers cloud, data networks and data security for the financial sector. Orange Bank offers mobile banking services, and Orange Money provides mobile payment and money transfer services, serving 54 million customers in 18 countries. Orange Fintech provides reimbursement services between individuals, secure exchanges between banks and payment services providers, money transfer services and more.

FINANCIAL DATA: *Note: Data for latest year may not have been available at press time.*

In U.S. $	2020	2019	2018	2017	2016	2015
Revenue	51,644,510,000	51,604,200,000	50,558,350,000	50,210,140,000	49,992,670,000	49,159,420,000
R&D Expense						
Operating Income	6,964,128,000	7,232,920,000	6,034,356,000	6,741,766,000	6,586,600,000	5,833,985,000
Operating Margin %		.14%	.12%	.13%	.13%	.12%
SGA Expense	10,372,890,000	10,377,770,000	11,086,400,000	10,473,070,000	10,832,270,000	11,035,090,000
Net Income	5,891,409,000	3,672,662,000	2,387,352,000	2,328,707,000	3,585,915,000	3,240,153,000
Operating Cash Flow	15,512,900,000	12,412,030,000	11,614,210,000	12,430,360,000	10,690,550,000	11,639,870,000
Capital Expenditure	10,441,310,000	10,289,810,000	9,336,820,000	9,196,316,000	10,375,330,000	9,494,429,000
EBITDA	17,107,320,000	17,416,430,000	14,484,170,000	13,832,960,000	12,358,270,000	13,709,560,000
Return on Assets %		.03%	.02%	.02%	.03%	.03%
Return on Equity %		.09%	.05%	.05%	.09%	.08%
Debt to Equity		0.165				

CONTACT INFORMATION:

Phone: 33 144442222   Fax: 33 144448034
Toll-Free:
Address: 78 rue Olivier de Serres, Paris, 75015 France

STOCK TICKER/OTHER:

Stock Ticker: ORAN   Exchange: NYS
Employees: 142,150   Fiscal Year Ends: 12/31
Parent Company:

SALARIES/BONUSES:

Top Exec. Salary: $ Bonus: $
Second Exec. Salary: $ Bonus: $

OTHER THOUGHTS:

Estimated Female Officers or Directors: 5
Hot Spot for Advancement for Women/Minorities: Y

Orange Belgium

NAIC Code: 517210

www.orange.be

TYPES OF BUSINESS:
Cell Phone Service
Fixed-Line Services
Mobile Data Services
Fiber Network

BRANDS/DIVISIONS/AFFILIATES:
Orange SA
Orange Communications Luxembourg

CONTACTS: *Note: Officers with more than one job title may be intentionally listed here more than once.*
Xavier Pichon, CEO
Antoine Chouc, CFO
Paul-Marie Dessart, Sec.
Olivier Ysewijn, Chief Strategy Officer
Gabriel Flichy, Chief Network Officer
Stephane Beauduin, Chief Bus. Unit B2B Officer
Sven Bols, Chief Sales & Dist. Officer
Cristina Zanchi, Chief Customer Relationship Officer

GROWTH PLANS/SPECIAL FEATURES:
Orange Belgium, part of the Orange SA group, is a leading provider of mobile phone services, fixed-line and alternative telephone and asymmetric digital subscriber line (ADSL) services for residential and targeted business markets in Belgium and Luxembourg. The company's 2G, 3G, 4G and 4.5G network technologies serve more than 3 million customers. In the residential market, the company offers ADSL (asymmetric digital subscriber line) internet, mobile internet, television channels, pre-paid cards, electronic bill pay and accessories. In the business market, Orange offers integrated mobile and fixed-line solutions for both voice and data transmission. Orange Belgium's HD Voice technology delivers crystal clear calling, with background and other noises muted for enhanced clarity purposes. In the field of mobile data transmission, the firm offers mobile intranet and email access, real-time sales, customer support applications and SIM card-based machine-to-machine data transmission on a secure wireless basis. Via strategic partnerships, the company to provides an extensive Wi-Fi network across the country. Orange retail and ecommerce channels also sell smartphone/mobile phone products. Orange Belgium provides services in Luxembourg through subsidiary Orange Communications Luxembourg. In mid-2021, Orange Belgium announced plans to roll out open and passive fiber-to-the-premise pilot projects in Brussels, starting in Evere and Ixelles and serving approximately 15,000 residents and companies. If successful, Orange Belgium will continue to expand to other municipalities.

FINANCIAL DATA: *Note: Data for latest year may not have been available at press time.*

In U.S. $	2020	2019	2018	2017	2016	2015
Revenue	1,606,475,000	1,638,191,000	1,563,634,000	1,528,706,000	1,517,012,000	1,509,351,000
R&D Expense						
Operating Income	92,256,380	72,055,520	61,572,670	88,178,090	149,642,000	156,140,700
Operating Margin %		.04%	.04%	.06%	.10%	.10%
SGA Expense	75,167,380	70,778,760	80,777,780	81,972,680	71,688,980	70,309,600
Net Income	65,951,520	41,512,320	39,623,450	50,034,210	93,601,550	93,577,120
Operating Cash Flow	420,821,500	414,793,300	319,366,400	325,938,300	365,174,500	417,627,800
Capital Expenditure	217,151,300	220,123,900	219,190,500	230,154,700	204,822,400	328,991,600
EBITDA	454,620,700	414,866,600	340,745,000	359,798,700	387,870,200	392,555,700
Return on Assets %		.02%	.02%	.03%	.05%	.05%
Return on Equity %		.06%	.06%	.08%	.15%	.18%
Debt to Equity		0.827	0.46	0.59	0.731	0.895

CONTACT INFORMATION:
Phone: 32-2745-7111   Fax:
Toll-Free:
Address: Ave. du Bourget 3 Avenue du Bourget 3, Brussels, 1140 Belgium

STOCK TICKER/OTHER:
Stock Ticker: MBSRY   Exchange: GREY
Employees: 1,400   Fiscal Year Ends: 12/31
Parent Company: Orange SA

SALARIES/BONUSES:
Top Exec. Salary: $ Bonus: $
Second Exec. Salary: $ Bonus: $

OTHER THOUGHTS:
Estimated Female Officers or Directors: 2
Hot Spot for Advancement for Women/Minorities:

Orange Polska SA

NAIC Code: 517110

www.orange.pl/start.phtml

TYPES OF BUSINESS:

Local & Long-Distance Telephone Service
Mobile Phone Service
Mobile Internet Services
Equipment Sales
Radio Communications
Fiber-Optic Cable
Internet Portal
e-Commerce Services

BRANDS/DIVISIONS/AFFILIATES:

Orange
Orange Customer Service Sp z o o
Orange Foundation

CONTACTS: Note: Officers with more than one job title may be intentionally listed here more than once.

Maciej Witucki, Pres.
Piotr Muszynski, VP-Oper.
Vincent Lobry, VP-Strategy
Jacek Kunicki, Dir.-Investor Rel.
Maciej Krzysztof Witucki, Chmn.

GROWTH PLANS/SPECIAL FEATURES:

Orange Polska SA is a leading provider of telecommunications services in Poland. The firm's products and services include fixed telephony services, internet access, television and voice over internet protocol (VoIP) as well as mobile telephony services based on LTE (long-term evolution)/UMTS (universal mobile telecommunications service)/CDMA (code-division multiple access) technologies. Orange Polska also provides leased lines, radio-communications and other telecommunications value-added services; sells telecommunications equipment and electronic phone cards; and provides data transmission, multimedia and various types of internet services. Subsidiary Orange Customer Service Sp. z o.o processes mass market and business services such as inquiries, orders and claims; business-to-partner (B2P) services such as data collection for billing, preparation for printing and shipping paper documents, payment settlement, reconciliation entitlements and management of payment channels; and VIP services such as service to customers in VIP category and regulatory intervention. Other offerings by Orange include integrated internet solutions for both institutions and individual clients; telecommunication infrastructure and associated systems, including security and monitoring as well as operating and maintaining networks; telecom services such as television programs and broadband internet access in the province of Podlasie; and organizing training events and recreational activities for business customers. The firm's Orange Foundation is involved in the education of children/youth and health. Orange Polska operates as a subsidiary of Orange SA.

FINANCIAL DATA: Note: Data for latest year may not have been available at press time.

In U.S. $	2020	2019	2018	2017	2016	2015
Revenue	3,153,524,000	3,125,574,000	3,041,995,000			
R&D Expense						
Operating Income	131,807,900	129,889,700	84,126,870			
Operating Margin %		.04%	.03%			
SGA Expense						
Net Income	12,605,330	24,936,630	2,740,289			
Operating Cash Flow	823,456,800	760,704,200	496,540,400			
Capital Expenditure	612,728,600	664,520,100	642,871,700			
EBITDA	911,420,200	877,988,600	802,356,600			
Return on Assets %		.00%	.00%			
Return on Equity %		.01%	.00%			
Debt to Equity		0.763	0.501			

CONTACT INFORMATION:

Phone: 48 225272323   Fax: 48 225272341
Toll-Free:
Address: Al. Jerozolimskie 160, Warszawa, 02-326 Poland

STOCK TICKER/OTHER:

Stock Ticker: PTTWF
Employees: 12,376
Parent Company: Orange SA

Exchange: PINX
Fiscal Year Ends: 12/31

SALARIES/BONUSES:

Top Exec. Salary: $ Bonus: $
Second Exec. Salary: $ Bonus: $

OTHER THOUGHTS:

Estimated Female Officers or Directors: 1
Hot Spot for Advancement for Women/Minorities:

Orbsat Corp

NAIC Code: 517410

orbsat.com

TYPES OF BUSINESS:

Satellite Telecommunications Resellers
Satellite Internet
Communication Services
Asset Tracking
Mobile Satellite Communication

BRANDS/DIVISIONS/AFFILIATES:

Orbital Satcom Corp
Global Telesat Communications Limited
Orbsat Government

GROWTH PLANS/SPECIAL FEATURES:

Orbsat Corp. is a provider of global connectivity services and solutions for commercial, government and individual users, enabling them to communicate, track assets and personnel, or request emergency assistance via satellite from anywhere in the world. The firm's key services include satellite communication solutions, emergency location systems, high-speed satellite internet, global asset and personnel monitoring, customized ground station systems and custom product design. Orbsat provides these products and services to customers in the U.S. and internationally through two subsidiaries: U.S.-based Orbital Satcom Corp. and U.K.-based Global Telesat Communications Limited. The company serves more than 50,000 customers in over 165 countries. In early-2021, Orbsat announced the launch of its new government services business unit, Orbsat Government, dedicated to serving the mobile satellite communication needs of federal government and military customers.

CONTACTS: Note: Officers with more than one job title may be intentionally listed here more than once.

David Phipps, CEO
Theresa Carlise, Treasurer

FINANCIAL DATA: Note: Data for latest year may not have been available at press time.

In U.S. $	2020	2019	2018	2017	2016	2015
Revenue		5,869,558	5,726,572	6,004,955	4,698,638	3,950,601
R&D Expense						
Operating Income						
Operating Margin %						
SGA Expense						
Net Income		-1,379,756	-1,194,706	-3,939,309	-2,589,923	-2,064,211
Operating Cash Flow						
Capital Expenditure						
EBITDA						
Return on Assets %						
Return on Equity %						
Debt to Equity						

CONTACT INFORMATION:

Phone: 305-560-5355   Fax:
Toll-Free:
Address: 18851 NE 29th Ave., Ste. 700, Aventura, FL 33180 United States

STOCK TICKER/OTHER:

Stock Ticker: OSAT
Employees: 10
Parent Company:

Exchange: PINX
Fiscal Year Ends: 12/31

SALARIES/BONUSES:

Top Exec. Salary: $ Bonus: $
Second Exec. Salary: $ Bonus: $

OTHER THOUGHTS:

Estimated Female Officers or Directors:
Hot Spot for Advancement for Women/Minorities:

Pakistan Telecommunication Company Limited www.ptcl.com.pk
NAIC Code: 517110

TYPES OF BUSINESS:
Wired Telecommunications Carriers
Information Technology
Communication Technology
Telecommunications Services
Digital Services
Broadband Services
Cloud Applications
Smart TV Applications

BRANDS/DIVISIONS/AFFILIATES:
Pak Telecom Mobile Ltd
Ufone
U Microfinance Bank Limited
Rozgar Microfinance Bank Limited
DVCOM Data Private Limited
Smart Sky Private Limited

CONTACTS: *Note: Officers with more than one job title may be intentionally listed here more than once.*
Muhammad Sohail Khan Rajput, Chmn.

GROWTH PLANS/SPECIAL FEATURES:

Pakistan Telecommunication Company Limited (PTCL) is Pakistan's largest integrated information and communication technology (ICT) company, and has been in business since 1947. The company offers its digital and telecommunications services to both individual consumers and to businesses. PTCL's services include voice telephone services, video talk, gaming platforms, high-speed broadband internet, power supplies, wireless internet, wireless devices and accessories, cloud applications, as well as smart TV and smart TV applications. For businesses, PTCL offers cloud services, smart cloud Software-as-a-Service, managed services, hosted solutions, businesses connectivity solutions, international business communication solutions, managed WAN, satellite communication, digital radio connectivity, managed security solutions, as well as data platforms, solutions and services. The company operates through its multiple state-of-the art nationwide fiber optic network, digital exchanges, metro fiber and long-distance telephone transmission facilities and international gateways. Subsidiaries of PTCL include: Pak Telecom Mobile Ltd. (doing business as Ufone), a cellular service provider in Pakistan; U Microfinance Bank Limited, which wholly-owns Rozgar Microfinance Bank Limited, offers branch banking and digital commerce services and solutions; DVCOM Data Private Limited, a provider of wireless local loop broadband services; and Smart Sky Private Limited, a provider of direct-to-home television services throughout Pakistan.

FINANCIAL DATA: *Note: Data for latest year may not have been available at press time.*

In U.S. $	2020	2019	2018	2017	2016	2015
Revenue	840,405,800	841,185,200	819,223,300	759,912,500	761,054,400	769,876,800
R&D Expense		7,575,344	1,957,175	2,025,383	2,132,916
Operating Income	76,411,810	75,573,080	69,482,060	29,923,890	41,560,080	27,777,810
Operating Margin %		.09%	.08%	.04%	.05%	.04%
SGA Expense	67,173,930	72,041,990	81,007,640	84,361,020	84,628,900	93,842,360
Net Income	21,251,080	15,435,710	37,077,950	28,196,380	10,537,970	12,132,900
Operating Cash Flow	365,534,900	278,119,500	182,623,000	166,411,500	231,292,100	234,754,300
Capital Expenditure	207,220,100	264,243,900	242,797,900	193,683,200	201,521,200	204,877,000
EBITDA	302,046,200	297,655,900	273,851,400	291,087,400	256,067,300	254,911,800
Return on Assets %		.01%	.02%	.01%	.01%	.01%
Return on Equity %		.03%	.07%	.05%	.02%	.02%
Debt to Equity		0.451	0.301	0.304	0.296	0.217

CONTACT INFORMATION:
Phone: 92 512263732   Fax: 92 512263733
Toll-Free:
Address: Block E, Sector G8/4, Islamabad, 44000 Pakistan

STOCK TICKER/OTHER:
Stock Ticker: PKTLY   Exchange: GREY
Employees: 21,670   Fiscal Year Ends: 06/30
Parent Company:

SALARIES/BONUSES:
Top Exec. Salary: $ Bonus: $
Second Exec. Salary: $ Bonus: $

OTHER THOUGHTS:
Estimated Female Officers or Directors:
Hot Spot for Advancement for Women/Minorities:

Panasonic Corporation

www.panasonic.com/global/home.html

NAIC Code: 334310

TYPES OF BUSINESS:

Audio & Video Equipment, Manufacturing
Lithium Rechargeable Batteries
Home Appliances
Electronic Components
Cellular Phones
Medical Equipment
Photovoltaic Equipment
Telecommunications Equipment

BRANDS/DIVISIONS/AFFILIATES:

Hussmann Corporation

CONTACTS: *Note: Officers with more than one job title may be intentionally listed here more than once.*

Kazuhiro Tsuga, CEO
Shusaku Nagae, Chmn.

GROWTH PLANS/SPECIAL FEATURES:

Panasonic Corporation produces consumer, professional and industrial electronics products, primarily serving the U.S. and Chinese markets. The firm operates through seven business segments: appliances, life solutions, connected solutions, automotive, industrial, China & Northeast Asia and U.S. Company. The appliances segment provides products and services for a wide range of spaces, from homes to offices to stores, with a focus on business-to-consumer (B2C) products such as appliances, beauty and health devices, cooling and heating appliances and more. The life solutions segment produces electric components and building materials for homes, offices and commercial facilities and smart towns, as well as mobility areas such as bicycles and vehicle interior spaces. The connected solutions segment designs and develops customer-oriented business structures using Internet of Things (IoT) technology, which enables Panasonic to offer business-to-business (B2B) solutions for its entire Panasonic group. Furthermore, this division contributes to Panasonic's customers' businesses by providing solutions that connect their products with consumers. The automotive segment produces innovative electronics and devices that provide in-vehicle infotainment, in-vehicle electronics, automotive mirrors and motorized systems such as vehicle batteries. The industrial solutions segment produces B2B solutions such as electronic components, semiconductor failure analysis (FA) and industrial devices, electronic materials and batteries. The China & Northeast Asia segment provides integrated home appliances and residential equipment, as well as electronics systems and solutions for enhancing the supply chain for fresh food, with cold chain at its core. Last, the U.S. Company segment supplies lithium-ion batteries for electric vehicles and electricity storage systems, and, through Hussmann Corporation, provides display merchandisers, refrigerator systems and services to food retailers. Panasonic operates more than 525 subsidiaries and associated companies worldwide. The firm has been in business for more than 100 years. In September 2020, the firm transferred its semiconductor business to Nuvoton Technology Corporation.

FINANCIAL DATA: *Note: Data for latest year may not have been available at press time.*

In U.S. $	2020	2019	2018	2017	2016	2015
Revenue	68,411,700,000	73,089,000,000	72,901,140,000	67,070,110,000	68,988,130,000	70,461,460,000
R&D Expense						
Operating Income	2,634,442,000	3,659,092,000	3,383,459,000	2,451,353,000	3,796,672,000	3,488,013,000
Operating Margin %	.04%	.05%	.05%	.04%	.06%	.05%
SGA Expense	17,027,400,000	17,713,160,000	17,699,850,000	16,831,470,000	16,421,220,000	16,493,390,000
Net Income	2,061,383,000	2,595,134,000	2,155,754,000	1,364,106,000	1,765,008,000	1,639,237,000
Operating Cash Flow	3,929,959,000	1,860,183,000	3,864,923,000	3,519,951,000	3,641,146,000	4,488,534,000
Capital Expenditure	3,153,517,000	3,642,818,000	4,343,685,000	3,121,789,000	2,208,689,000	2,047,273,000
EBITDA	6,375,623,000	6,695,789,000	6,311,500,000	5,200,178,000	4,647,019,000	4,443,663,000
Return on Assets %	.04%	.05%	.04%	.03%	.03%	.03%
Return on Equity %	.12%	.16%	.14%	.09%	.11%	.11%
Debt to Equity	0.579	0.318	0.506	0.602	0.413	0.391

CONTACT INFORMATION:

Phone: 81 669081121   Fax:
Toll-Free:
Address: 1006 Oaza Kadoma, Kadoma City, Osaka, 571-8501 Japan

STOCK TICKER/OTHER:

Stock Ticker: PCRFF   Exchange: PINX
Employees: 271,869   Fiscal Year Ends: 03/31
Parent Company:

SALARIES/BONUSES:

Top Exec. Salary: $ Bonus: $
Second Exec. Salary: $ Bonus: $

OTHER THOUGHTS:

Estimated Female Officers or Directors:
Hot Spot for Advancement for Women/Minorities:

Partner Communications Co Ltd

www.partner.co.il

NAIC Code: 517210

TYPES OF BUSINESS:

Cell Phone Service
Fixed-Line Telephony
Internet Service Provider
Voice over Broadband
Web Video on Demand (VOD)
International Long Distance Telephony

BRANDS/DIVISIONS/AFFILIATES:

S B Israel Telecom Ltd
Partner

CONTACTS: Note: Officers with more than one job title may be intentionally listed here more than once.

Tamir Amar, CFO
Terry Yaskil, VP-Mktg.
Einat Rom, VP-Human Resources
Yaron Eisenstein, VP-IT
Roly Klinger, VP-Legal & Regulatory Affairs
Roly Klinger, VP-Bus. Dev.
Amalia Glaser, VP-Comm. & Corp. Governance Div.
Ori Watermann, VP-Fixed Line Div.
Avi Cohen, VP-Customer Div.
Guy Emodi, VP-Economics, Planning & Corp. Strategy
Guy Emodi, VP-Operator Rel.
Osnat Ronen, Chmn.

GROWTH PLANS/SPECIAL FEATURES:

Partner Communications Co., Ltd. is a leading Israeli telecommunications operator providing consumer and business services under the licensed brand, Partner. The firm's operations are divided into two segments: cellular and fixed-line communications. The cellular segment includes basic cellular telephony services, text messaging, data, airtime, interconnect, roaming, content services and other value-added services. These services are provided via its cellular network, which includes wholesale services to other operators as well as equipment and device sales. The firm provides 4G LTE (fourth generation long-term evolution) coverage. Partner represents an estimated 30% of total Israeli cellular telephone subscribers, with approximately 1.9 million subscribing. The fixed line segment includes internet service provider services, which provides access to the internet, secure business information storage, data center and cloud services; transmission services and primary rate interface; and international long-distance services, outgoing/incoming international telephony hubbing, roaming and signaling, as well as calling card services. S.B. Israel Telecom owns about 30.2% of Partner Communications, and the remainder is free float exchanged.

FINANCIAL DATA: Note: Data for latest year may not have been available at press time.

In U.S. $	2020	2019	2018	2017	2016	2015
Revenue	984,505,300	998,397,700	1,006,116,000	1,008,894,000	1,094,101,000	1,269,144,000
R&D Expense						
Operating Income	27,476,010	23,771,380	36,428,860	87,676,240	45,690,440	18,523,150
Operating Margin %		.03%	.04%	.10%	.05%	.03%
SGA Expense	88,293,680	97,863,980	104,655,800	120,400,500	180,292,000	170,413,000
Net Income	5,248,226	5,865,664	17,596,990	35,193,980	16,053,400	-12,348,770
Operating Cash Flow	242,653,300	258,397,900	192,949,500	300,383,700	291,739,600	284,639,100
Capital Expenditure	176,896,100	194,184,400	154,977,000	116,078,400	60,508,960	110,830,200
EBITDA	250,680,000	247,592,800	202,211,100	261,176,400	234,009,100	228,760,900
Return on Assets %		.00%	.01%	.02%	.01%	-.01%
Return on Equity %		.01%	.04%	.09%	.05%	-.04%
Debt to Equity		1.34	0.856	0.849	1.977	2.497

CONTACT INFORMATION:

Phone: 972 547814888   Fax: 972 547814999
Toll-Free:
Address: 8 Amal St., Afeq Industrial Park, Rosh Ha'ayin, 48103 Israel

STOCK TICKER/OTHER:

Stock Ticker: PTNR
Employees: 2,655
Parent Company:

Exchange: NAS
Fiscal Year Ends: 12/31

SALARIES/BONUSES:

Top Exec. Salary: $ Bonus: $
Second Exec. Salary: $ Bonus: $

OTHER THOUGHTS:

Estimated Female Officers or Directors: 5
Hot Spot for Advancement for Women/Minorities: Y

PCCW Limited

NAIC Code: 517110

www.pccw.com

TYPES OF BUSINESS:

Local & Long-Distance Telephone Services
Telecommunications
Media
Information Technology
Property Development
Property Investment

BRANDS/DIVISIONS/AFFILIATES:

PCCW Media
HKT
Pacific Century Premium Developments
PCCW Solutions
Now TV

CONTACTS: *Note: Officers with more than one job title may be intentionally listed here more than once.*

Bangalore Gangaiah Srinivas, Group Managing Dir.
Hon Hing (Susanna) Hui, CFO
Janice Le, Managing Dir.-TV & News Media
George Fok, Managing Dir.-PCCW Solutions
Tzar (Richard) Kai Li, Chmn.

GROWTH PLANS/SPECIAL FEATURES:

PCCW Limited is a global holding company based in Hong Kong with interests in telecommunications, media, information technology (IT) solutions, property development and investment, among other businesses. Subsidiary PCCW Media is a fully-integrated multimedia and entertainment company that operates a leading payTV service in Hong Kong under the Now TV brand. Now TV offers more than 160 linear channels and an on-demand library of local, Asian and international programming. Premium content can also be accessed by subscribers through the Now Player application. PCCW Medial also provides Chinese language news, financial news and sports programming. HKT is a premier telecommunications service provider in Hong Kong that offers fixed-line, broadband, mobile communication and media entertainment services to consumers and businesses. HKT launched a 5G network in Hong Kong, offering comprehensive coverage across the city. HKT also delivers end-to-end integrated solutions that encompass technologies such as 5G, cloud computing, Internet of Things (IoT) and artificial intelligence (AI) to accelerate digital transformation of enterprises and contribute to Hong Kong's smart city development. Pacific Century Premium Developments covers the firm's property portfolio in Hong Kong and mainland China, and is primarily engaged in developing and managing premium property and infrastructure projects. PCPD also invests in premium-grade buildings in the Asia-Pacific region, including resort development in Hokkaido, Japan and Phang,nga, Thailand, as well as a major office building in Jakarta, Indonesia. PCCW Solutions is an information technology outsourcing and business process outsourcing provider in Hong Kong, mainland China and southeast Asia. This subsidiary offers a wide range of services, including digital solutions, cloud computing, system development, solutions integration, data center hosting, managed services, ecommerce and IoT solutions.

FINANCIAL DATA: *Note: Data for latest year may not have been available at press time.*

In U.S. $	2020	2019	2018	2017	2016	2015
Revenue	4,903,341,000	4,835,679,000	5,006,959,000	4,774,977,000	4,946,902,000	5,066,760,000
R&D Expense						
Operating Income	573,770,400	702,778,600	675,069,600	756,650,200	712,315,700	749,433,000
Operating Margin %		.15%	.13%	.16%	.14%	.15%
SGA Expense	629,446,300	662,052,800	1,671,564,000	1,845,809,000	1,947,881,000	1,873,131,000
Net Income	-131,456,800	87,766,780	115,604,700	289,462,800	264,331,400	295,777,900
Operating Cash Flow	1,636,122,000	1,434,813,000	843,514,800	1,528,895,000	1,282,735,000	1,613,311,000
Capital Expenditure	918,393,700	1,214,300,000	955,768,600	1,215,589,000	1,051,526,000	990,823,800
EBITDA	1,230,153,000	1,473,992,000	1,486,107,000	1,795,417,000	1,574,131,000	1,538,561,000
Return on Assets %		.01%	.01%	.03%	.03%	.03%
Return on Equity %		.04%	.05%	.14%	.18%	.22%
Debt to Equity		3.618	3.052	2.338	3.753	3.455

CONTACT INFORMATION:

Phone: 852 2883 7747   Fax: 852 2962 5634
Toll-Free:
Address: 979 King's Rd., Fl. 39, PCCW Tower, Hong Kong, Hong Kong
Hong Kong

STOCK TICKER/OTHER:

Stock Ticker: PCWLF   Exchange: PINX
Employees: 22,900   Fiscal Year Ends: 12/31
Parent Company: Pacific Century Group Holdings Limited

SALARIES/BONUSES:

Top Exec. Salary: $ Bonus: $
Second Exec. Salary: $ Bonus: $

OTHER THOUGHTS:

Estimated Female Officers or Directors: 2
Hot Spot for Advancement for Women/Minorities: Y

Perusahaan Perseroan PT Telekomunikasi Indonesia Tbk (Telkom)

www.telkom.co.id

NAIC Code: 517110

TYPES OF BUSINESS:

Local Telephone Service
Broadband
Mobile Digital Services
Internet of Things
Voice Services
Data Center
Business Process Outsourcing
Wholesale Telecommunications

BRANDS/DIVISIONS/AFFILIATES:

CONTACTS: Note: Officers with more than one job title may be intentionally listed here more than once.

Ririek Adriansyah, Pres.
Heri Supriadi, Dir.-Finance
Afriwandi, Dir.-Human Capital
Herlan Wijanarko, Dir.-IT & Network
Muhammad Awaluddin, Dir.-Enterprise & Wholesale
Sukardi Silalahi, Dir.-Consumer
Priyantono Rudito, Dir.-Human Capital & Gen. Affairs
Rizkan Chandra, Dir.-Network & Solution
Ririek Adriansyah, Dir.-Compliance & Risk Mgmt.

GROWTH PLANS/SPECIAL FEATURES:

Perusahaan Perseroan PT Telekomunikasi Indonesia Tbk. (Telkom) is a state-owned information and communications technology enterprise, and a telecommunications network in Indonesia. Telkom organizes its business in five segments: mobile, consumer, enterprise, wholesale and international business, and other. The mobile segment offers mobile broadband services, mobile legacy services such as mobile voice and short message services (SMS), and mobile digital services such as financial services, video on demand, music, gaming, Internet of Things (IoT) solutions, big data analytics and digital advertisements. The consumer segment offers fixed voice services, fixed broadband services, internet protocol TV (IPTV), and related consumer digital services. The enterprise segment offers information and communications technology (ICT) and a digital platform that covers enterprise-grade connectivity services, including satellite, information technology (IT) services, data center, cloud, business process outsourcing and related services. The wholesale and international business segment offers wholesale telecommunications carrier services, international business, tower business, and infrastructure and network management services. Last, the other segment comprises digital services offerings such as digital platform, digital content and ecommerce for business-to-business (B2B) to support other Telkom segments. This segment also provides property management across Telkom's property assets throughout Indonesia.

FINANCIAL DATA: Note: Data for latest year may not have been available at press time.

In U.S. $	2020	2019	2018	2017	2016	2015
Revenue	9,574,221,000	9,511,771,000	9,177,140,000	8,999,474,000	8,162,860,000	7,190,120,000
R&D Expense						
Operating Income	3,024,594,000	3,030,418,000	2,698,804,000	3,181,770,000	2,804,407,000	2,345,367,000
Operating Margin %		.32%	.31%	.35%	.34%	.33%
SGA Expense	540,434,400	541,978,000	588,499,500	633,898,200	561,274,300	453,917,100
Net Income	1,477,178,000	1,337,964,000	1,249,132,000	1,552,117,000	1,356,559,000	1,084,167,000
Operating Cash Flow						
Capital Expenditure	2,241,238,000	2,617,970,000	2,444,234,000	2,336,035,000	2,050,521,000	1,965,056,000
EBITDA	5,099,393,000	4,978,774,000	4,283,198,000	4,622,250,000	4,177,245,000	3,673,017,000
Return on Assets %		.09%	.09%	.12%	.11%	.10%
Return on Equity %		.19%	.19%	.25%	.24%	.22%
Debt to Equity		0.324	0.342	0.303	0.313	0.403

CONTACT INFORMATION:

Phone: 6221 808 63539   Fax:
Toll-Free:
Address: Telkom Tower, Fl. 39, Jl. Jendral Gatot Subroto Kav 52 Rt.6/RW.1, Jakarta, 12710 Indonesia

STOCK TICKER/OTHER:

Stock Ticker: TLK
Employees: 25,348
Parent Company:

Exchange: NYS
Fiscal Year Ends: 12/31

SALARIES/BONUSES:

Top Exec. Salary: $ Bonus: $
Second Exec. Salary: $ Bonus: $

OTHER THOUGHTS:

Estimated Female Officers or Directors:
Hot Spot for Advancement for Women/Minorities:

Phazar Antenna Corp

NAIC Code: 334220

TYPES OF BUSINESS:

Antenna Systems & Towers
Wireless Equipment
Contract Manufacturing

BRANDS/DIVISIONS/AFFILIATES:

Antenna Products Corporation
TACSAT-214-SATCOM

CONTACTS: *Note: Officers with more than one job title may be intentionally listed here more than once.*

Robert Fitzgerald, Pres.

GROWTH PLANS/SPECIAL FEATURES:

Phazar Antenna Corp. is the wireless infrastructure antenna division of Antenna Products Corporation (ACP). The firm offers a complete line of distributed antenna system (DAS) and small cell antenna solutions built to meet the needs of wireless service, WiMAX, Wi-Fi and broadband internet system suppliers for the purpose of increasing network data capacity and speed via densification. The DAS antennas for cellular, sensorimotor rhythm (SMR), advanced wireless service (AWS) and personal communication service (PCS) frequencies are installed on utility poles, streetlights, rooftops and lamp posts in urban and remote areas to increase wireless carrier services. These product lines complement APC's existing product lines of cellular, PCS, paging, industrial, scientific, medical, automated meter reading (AMR), omni-directional and sector wireless antennas. The firm's TACSAT-214-SATCOM antenna is custom engineered for special operations soldiers. The antenna is a holster-worn, lightweight mobile system that allows for quick deployment and reliable performance during mission-critical operations. All of Phazar's DAS, oDAS and small cell antennas are designed in-house using state-of-the-art design tools and software. They are available in single, dual, triple, quad and multi-band configurations and in combinations of a plethora of frequencies. Phazar provides fully integrated antenna services, with research and development, engineering, testing, manufacturing, production and tech support housed within its 100,000+ square foot facility located in Texas. Phazar Antenna is utilized by every major U. S. wireless carrier, including Verizon, AT&T, Sprint and T-Mobile.

FINANCIAL DATA: *Note: Data for latest year may not have been available at press time.*

In U.S. $	2020	2019	2018	2017	2016	2015
Revenue	13,837,500	13,500,000	13,125,000	12,500,000	12,000,000	13,000,000
R&D Expense						
Operating Income						
Operating Margin %						
SGA Expense						
Net Income						
Operating Cash Flow						
Capital Expenditure						
EBITDA						
Return on Assets %						
Return on Equity %						
Debt to Equity						

CONTACT INFORMATION:

Phone: 940 325-3301   Fax: 940 325-0716
Toll-Free:
Address: 6300 Columbia Rd., Mineral Wells, TX 76067 United States

SALARIES/BONUSES:

Top Exec. Salary: $ Bonus: $
Second Exec. Salary: $ Bonus: $

STOCK TICKER/OTHER:

Stock Ticker: Subsidiary   Exchange:
Employees: 66   Fiscal Year Ends: 06/30
Parent Company: Antenna Products Corporation

OTHER THOUGHTS:

Estimated Female Officers or Directors: 1
Hot Spot for Advancement for Women/Minorities:

Planet Labs Inc

www.planet.com

NAIC Code: 517410

TYPES OF BUSINESS:

Satellite Telecommunications Services
Satellite Manufacturing
Satellite Imagery
Mapping
Whole-Earth Imaging Datasets

BRANDS/DIVISIONS/AFFILIATES:

Terra Bella
Dove
SkySat
Planet Apps
Planet Explorer
Plant Stories
Planet Basemaps Viewer

CONTACTS: Note: Officers with more than one job title may be intentionally listed here more than once.

Will Marshall, CEO
Martin Van Ryswyk, Sr. VP-Product
Ashley Fieglein Johnson, CFO
Rosanne Saccone, CMO
Laura Malinasky, Chief People Officer
Robbie Schingler, Chief Strategy Officer
Brian Hernacki, Sr. VP-Software

GROWTH PLANS/SPECIAL FEATURES:

Planet Labs, Inc. builds small satellites for Earth observation. The firm has raised significant investor financing. By acquiring Google's satellite business unit, Terra Bella, in exchange for stock in Planet, the company has an excellent base of very high-resolution imaging satellites to complement the medium resolution satellites that had been its main focus. Planet offers customers a diverse selection of 3-meter (nearly 10 feet), 5-meter (more than 16 feet) and 80-centimeter (approximately 2.6 feet) data products under a single roof. Its platform downloads and processes more than 5 terabytes (TB) of data daily, enabling customers to build and run analytics at scale. Users can monitor areas of interest, validate information on the ground and discover trends relevant to one's industry. With over 130 Dove satellites and 21 SkySats satellites in orbit, Planet is able to image anywhere on Earth's landmass every day. Planet Apps enable users to visualize time, analyze change and integrate workflows. Daily imagery can be viewed and downloaded from a browser with Planet Explorer, which encompasses search features, meta-filters and a timeline axis. Planet Stories can be used to observe changes in the environment; and Planet Basemaps Viewer offers access to critical data. Planet Archive dates back to 2009, and provides historical context on preferred areas of interest and deep imagery stacks for analytics and app development. Markets primarily served by the firm include agriculture, government, education, research, energy, infrastructure, finance, forestry, land use, insurance, mapping and maritime. Based in San Francisco, Planet Labs has additional offices in Washington DC and Germany.

Planet Labs offers its employees comprehensive health benefits and company perks.

FINANCIAL DATA: Note: Data for latest year may not have been available at press time.

In U.S. $	2020	2019	2018	2017	2016	2015
Revenue						
R&D Expense						
Operating Income						
Operating Margin %						
SGA Expense						
Net Income						
Operating Cash Flow						
Capital Expenditure						
EBITDA						
Return on Assets %						
Return on Equity %						
Debt to Equity						

CONTACT INFORMATION:

Phone: 415-829-3313   Fax:
Toll-Free:
Address: 645 Harrison St., 4/Fl, San Francisco, CA 94107 United States

STOCK TICKER/OTHER:

Stock Ticker: Private
Employees: 460
Parent Company:

Exchange:
Fiscal Year Ends:

SALARIES/BONUSES:

Top Exec. Salary: $ Bonus: $
Second Exec. Salary: $ Bonus: $

OTHER THOUGHTS:

Estimated Female Officers or Directors:
Hot Spot for Advancement for Women/Minorities:

Plantronics Inc

NAIC Code: 334210

www.poly.com

TYPES OF BUSINESS:

Communications Headsets
Communications Accessories
Specialty Telephone Products
Wireless Headsets

BRANDS/DIVISIONS/AFFILIATES:

Poly
RealPresence

CONTACTS: *Note: Officers with more than one job title may be intentionally listed here more than once.*

Joseph Burton, CEO
Charles Boynton, CFO
Mary Huser, Chief Compliance Officer
Robert Hagerty, Director
Marvin Tseu, Director
Jeff Loebbaka, Executive VP, Divisional
Tom Puorro, Executive VP, Divisional

GROWTH PLANS/SPECIAL FEATURES:

Plantronics, Inc. does business as Poly, and designs, manufactures and markets integrated communication and collaboration solutions. Poly's primary product categories include: enterprise headsets, encompassing corded and cordless communication headsets; consumer headsets, including Bluetooth and corded products for mobile device applications, personal computer and gaming; and voice, video and content sharing solutions, such as open session initiation protocol (SIP) desktop phones, conference room phones and video endpoints (cameras, speakers and microphones). Poly's solutions are designed to work in a wide range of Unified Communications & Collaboration, Unified Communication-as-a-Service and Video-as-a-Service environments. Poly's RealPresence collaboration solutions range from infrastructure to endpoints and allow people to connect and collaborate globally and naturally. The firm also offers comprehensive support services, including support on its solutions and hardware devices, as well as professional, hosted and managed services. Enterprise products are sold through sales representatives, global distributors, channel partners, service providers and resellers. Consumer products are sold through traditional and online consumer electronics retailers, consumer products retailers, office supply distributors, wireless carriers, catalog and mail order companies, and mass merchants. Manufacturing operations are conducted through Plantronics' facility in Tijuana, Mexico, and through contract manufacturers and original design manufacturers in Asia. Plantronics' distribution centers are located in Mexico (serving the U.S., Canada and Latin America regions), Thailand (serving the Asia Pacific region, excluding mainland China), Czech Republic (serving Europe, Africa and Middle East regions), China (serving mainland China), and the U.S. (serving the Americas region).

FINANCIAL DATA: *Note: Data for latest year may not have been available at press time.*

In U.S. $	2020	2019	2018	2017	2016	2015
Revenue	1,696,990,000	1,674,535,000	856,903,000	881,176,000	856,907,000	
R&D Expense	218,277,000	201,886,000	84,193,000	88,318,000	90,408,000	
Operating Income	-261,505,000	-75,626,000	125,532,000	129,222,000	122,967,000	
Operating Margin %						
SGA Expense	595,463,000	567,879,000	229,390,000	223,830,000	221,299,000	
Net Income	-827,182,000	-135,561,000	-869,000	82,599,000	68,392,000	
Operating Cash Flow	78,019,000	116,047,000	121,148,000	137,971,000	146,869,000	
Capital Expenditure	22,880,000	26,797,000	12,468,000	23,176,000	30,661,000	
EBITDA	-573,681,000	125,743,000	146,710,000	150,199,000	143,109,000	
Return on Assets %						
Return on Equity %						
Debt to Equity						

CONTACT INFORMATION:

Phone: 831 426-5858   Fax: 831 426-6098
Toll-Free: 800-544-4660
Address: 345 Encinal St., Santa Cruz, CA 95060 United States

STOCK TICKER/OTHER:

Stock Ticker: POLY
Employees: 8,200
Parent Company:

Exchange: NYS
Fiscal Year Ends: 03/31

SALARIES/BONUSES:

Top Exec. Salary: $ Bonus: $
Second Exec. Salary: $ Bonus: $

OTHER THOUGHTS:

Estimated Female Officers or Directors: 4
Hot Spot for Advancement for Women/Minorities: Y

Sales, profits and employees may be estimates. Financial information, benefits and other data can change quickly and may vary from those stated here.

PLDT Inc

NAIC Code: 517110

www.pldt.com.ph

TYPES OF BUSINESS:

Diversified Telecommunications Services
Telecommunications
Digital Services
Fixed Line
Broadband
Wireless Services

BRANDS/DIVISIONS/AFFILIATES:

Voyager Innovations Holdings Pte Ltd
Multisys Technologies Corporation

CONTACTS: Note: Officers with more than one job title may be intentionally listed here more than once.

Maria Lourdes C. Rausa-Chan, General Counsel
Anabelle L. Chua, Sr. VP-Corp. Finance
Ray C. Espinosa, Head-Regulatory Affairs & Policies
Ernesto R. Alberto, Exec. VP-Enterprise & Intl Carrier Bus.
Claro Carmelo P. Ramirez, Sr. VP
Jun R. Florencio, Sr. VP-Internal Audit & Fraud Risk Mgmt.
Manuel V. Pangilinan, Chmn.
Rene G. Banez, Sr. VP-Supply Chain, Asset Protection & Mgmt.

GROWTH PLANS/SPECIAL FEATURES:

PLDT, Inc. is a telecommunications and digital services provider in the Philippines, serving the fixed line, wireless and broadband markets. The firm operates through three business segments, including wireless, fixed line and other. The wireless segment focuses on driving growth in PLDT's data services while managing its legacy business of voice and short message services (SMS). This division provides mobile telecommunications services such as mobile services, home broadband services, mobile virtual network operations and other services. The fixed line segment provides fixed line telecommunications services, primarily to retail, corporate and small/medium enterprise clients. This division offers data, voice and miscellaneous services, as well as data center, cloud, cybersecurity services and managed information technology. The other segment consists primarily of PLDT's interests in digital platforms and other technologies due to holdings in Voyager Innovations Holdings Pte. Ltd. and Multisys Technologies Corporation.

FINANCIAL DATA: Note: Data for latest year may not have been available at press time.

In U.S. $	2020	2019	2018	2017	2016	2015
Revenue	3,794,156,000	3,546,451,000	3,453,486,000	3,352,325,000	3,464,176,000	3,586,614,000
R&D Expense						
Operating Income	974,866,900	927,220,900	457,762,100	372,468,900	749,276,900	870,435,600
Operating Margin %		.26%	.13%	.11%	.22%	.24%
SGA Expense	958,139,500	997,044,400	1,102,188,000	1,059,804,000	985,054,300	1,029,409,000
Net Income	509,034,500	472,079,000	396,512,000	280,279,200	419,360,300	462,520,400
Operating Cash Flow	1,783,340,000	1,454,576,000	1,281,097,000	1,176,246,000	1,026,621,000	1,461,955,000
Capital Expenditure	1,603,635,000	1,852,828,000	990,818,800	770,406,200	889,154,400	903,932,400
EBITDA	1,949,524,000	1,702,260,000	1,632,394,000	1,562,738,000	1,354,987,000	1,370,540,000
Return on Assets %		.04%	.04%	.03%	.04%	.05%
Return on Equity %		.20%	.17%	.12%	.18%	.18%
Debt to Equity		1.668	1.393	1.483	1.41	1.273

CONTACT INFORMATION:

Phone: 632-816-8556   Fax: 632-840-1864
Toll-Free:
Address: Makati Ave., Ramon Cojuangco Bldg., Makati, 1200 Philippines

STOCK TICKER/OTHER:

Stock Ticker: PHI
Employees: 18,848
Parent Company:

Exchange: NYS
Fiscal Year Ends: 12/31

SALARIES/BONUSES:

Top Exec. Salary: $ Bonus: $
Second Exec. Salary: $ Bonus: $

OTHER THOUGHTS:

Estimated Female Officers or Directors: 10
Hot Spot for Advancement for Women/Minorities: Y

Potevio Corporation

www.cccme.org.cn/shop/cccme3055/index.aspx

NAIC Code: 334220

TYPES OF BUSINESS:

Communications Equipment-Telecom & Mobile
Information Technology
Telecommunications
Equipment
Electronics
Automotive Parts
Terminal Products
Storage

BRANDS/DIVISIONS/AFFILIATES:

Potevio Capitel
Potevio Eastcom
Ningbo Electronics
Beijing Ericsson Potevio
Nanjing Ericsson Panda
Potevio Taili
Potevio Designing & Planning Institute

CONTACTS: Note: Officers with more than one job title may be intentionally listed here more than once.

Liang Sun, Gen. Mgr.-Broadcasting Dept.
Xu Mingwen, VP
Lv Weiping, Chmn.

GROWTH PLANS/SPECIAL FEATURES:

Potevio Corporation is an information technology (IT) products and service provider for the telecommunication industry. Based in China, the company consists of seven subsidiaries: Potevio Capitel, Potevio Eastcom, Ningbo Electronics, Biejing Ericsson Potevio, Nanjing Ericsson Panda, Potevio Taili, and Potevio Designing & Planning Institute for Engineering. Together, these businesses cover both fixed and mobile communications. The firm's product categories consist of communication devices, computer products, electronic apparatus, office supplies, machinery equipment, automotive and motorcycle parts, electrical wire and other electrical parts and components. Products include communication equipment and terminal products include mobile communication network equipment and handsets, optical transmission equipment, communication cables, power connectors, power supplies, microwave communication equipment, telecommunication network operation support systems (OSS), stored program control (SPC) switches, videophones, integrated circuit card payphones, personal handyphone system (PHS) handsets, logistics information systems, ITS series products, office information equipment and much more.

FINANCIAL DATA: Note: Data for latest year may not have been available at press time.

In U.S. $	2020	2019	2018	2017	2016	2015
Revenue	12,618,112,500	12,017,250,000	11,445,000,000	10,900,000,000	10,732,293,749	11,458,648,290
R&D Expense						
Operating Income						
Operating Margin %						
SGA Expense						
Net Income						
Operating Cash Flow						
Capital Expenditure						
EBITDA						
Return on Assets %						
Return on Equity %						
Debt to Equity						

CONTACT INFORMATION:

Phone: 86-10-6268-3863   Fax: 86-10-62683898
Toll-Free:
Address: 6 Beier St., Haidian Distr., Beijing, 100080 China

STOCK TICKER/OTHER:

Stock Ticker: Government-Owned   Exchange:
Employees: 22,100   Fiscal Year Ends: 12/31
Parent Company:

SALARIES/BONUSES:

Top Exec. Salary: $ Bonus: $
Second Exec. Salary: $ Bonus: $

OTHER THOUGHTS:

Estimated Female Officers or Directors: 1
Hot Spot for Advancement for Women/Minorities:

Preformed Line Products Company

www.preformed.com

NAIC Code: 335921

TYPES OF BUSINESS:

Electrical Equipment/Appliances/Tools, Manufacturing
Network Products and Systems
Material & Product Design

BRANDS/DIVISIONS/AFFILIATES:

CONTACTS:
Note: Officers with more than one job title may be intentionally listed here more than once.

Robert Ruhlman, CEO
Michael Weisbarth, Chief Accounting Officer
Dennis Mckenna, COO
Barbara Ruhlman, Director Emeritus
Jon Ruhlman, Director
Caroline Vaccariello, General Counsel
Tim O'Shaughnessy, Vice President, Divisional
John Hofstetter, Vice President, Divisional
David Sunkle, Vice President, Divisional
William Haag, Vice President, Geographical

GROWTH PLANS/SPECIAL FEATURES:

Preformed Line Products Company is an international designer and manufacturer of products and systems employed in the construction and maintenance of overhead and underground networks for the energy, telecommunication, cable operators and information industries. The company has facilities worldwide, including North America, Europe, South Africa, Asia and Asia Pacific. Each of Preformed's domestic and foreign manufacturing facilities are International Standards Organization (ISO) 9001 certified. Products are grouped into three categories: energy, communications and special industries. Energy products are used to support, protect, terminate and secure both power conductor and communication cables and to control cable dynamics such as vibration, etc. Formed wire products are made from stiff wire materials and formed into a helical/spiral shape. Related hardware products include hardware for supporting and protecting transmission conductors, spacers, spacer-dampers, stockbridge dampers, corona suppression devices and various compression fittings for dead-end applications. Communications products are used to protect fixed line communication networks, such as copper cable or fiber optic cable, from moisture, environmental hazards and other potential contaminants. Special industries products include data communication cabinets, hardware assemblies, pole line hardware, resale products, underground connectors, solar hardware systems, guy markers, tree guards, fiber optic cable markers, pedestal markers and urethan products. They are used by energy, renewable energy, communications, cable and special industries such as metal building, tower and antenna industries, agriculture and arborist industries and the marine system industry for various applications.

FINANCIAL DATA:
Note: Data for latest year may not have been available at press time.

In U.S. $	2020	2019	2018	2017	2016	2015
Revenue	466,449,000	444,861,000	420,878,000	378,212,000	336,634,000	354,666,000
R&D Expense	17,625,000	17,187,000	15,107,000	14,327,000	14,025,000	14,879,000
Operating Income	44,416,000	34,993,000	35,368,000	27,093,000	21,533,000	21,102,000
Operating Margin %		.07%	.08%	.07%	.06%	.03%
SGA Expense	91,972,000	88,415,000	81,756,000	77,208,000	73,856,000	67,471,000
Net Income	29,803,000	23,303,000	26,581,000	12,654,000	15,255,000	6,675,000
Operating Cash Flow	41,642,000	27,217,000	22,976,000	33,830,000	25,974,000	20,229,000
Capital Expenditure	24,569,000	29,467,000	9,528,000	11,233,000	24,725,000	10,754,000
EBITDA	56,805,000	47,423,000	46,322,000	39,657,000	33,793,000	23,803,000
Return on Assets %		.06%	.07%	.04%	.05%	.02%
Return on Equity %		.09%	.11%	.05%	.07%	.03%
Debt to Equity		0.231	0.10	0.145	0.192	0.145

CONTACT INFORMATION:

Phone: 440 461-5200   Fax: 440 442-8816
Toll-Free:
Address: 660 Beta Dr., Mayfield Village, OH 44143 United States

STOCK TICKER/OTHER:

Stock Ticker: PLPC   Exchange: NAS
Employees: 2,969   Fiscal Year Ends: 12/31
Parent Company:

SALARIES/BONUSES:

Top Exec. Salary: $ Bonus: $
Second Exec. Salary: $ Bonus: $

OTHER THOUGHTS:

Estimated Female Officers or Directors:
Hot Spot for Advancement for Women/Minorities:

Proxim Wireless Corporation

www.proxim.com

NAIC Code: 334220

TYPES OF BUSINESS:
Wireless Networking Equipment
Home & Office Networking Equipment
Millimeter Wave Products

BRANDS/DIVISIONS/AFFILIATES:
ORiNOCO
Tsunami
Proxim SmartConnect
Proxim ClearConnect
WORP
Proxim FastConnect
SRA Holdings Inc

CONTACTS: Note: Officers with more than one job title may be intentionally listed here more than once.
Fred Huey, CEO
Lee Gopadze, Pres.
David L. Renauld, General Counsel
David L. Renauld, VP-Corp. Affairs
Yoram Rubin, VP-Customer Support & Quality Mgmt.

GROWTH PLANS/SPECIAL FEATURES:

Proxim Wireless Corporation produces and sells advanced Wi-Fi, point-to-point and point-to-multipoint outdoor wireless systems. These systems are primarily built for mission-critical and high-availability communications environments. The company's products are marketed under the ORiNOCO and Tsunami brands, which serve a wide variety of markets, including enterprises, service providers, carriers, governments, municipalities, Wi-Fi operators, hot spot operators and other organizations that need high-performance, secure scalable wireless solutions. Proxim's solutions include smart city, mobility, video surveillance, backhaul, wireless broadband, internet service provider (ISP) and Wi-Fi. Technology-wise, Proxim's proprietary products include: Proxim SmartConnect, an intelligent interface avoidance technology designed to deliver high-performance in high-density environments and under challenging radio frequency interference conditions; Proxim ClearConnect, a suite of interference mitigation technologies ensuring robust and reliable communications in high-density wireless deployments via continuous analysis and automatic link tuning; WORP, a wireless outdoor router protocol that optimizes the performance of multi-stream voice, video and data over wireless networks; and Proxim FastConnect, offering high-speed mobility technology for use on public transportation systems such as buses, trains, metros and ferries. Based in California, USA, the firm has operations all over the world, including Europe, the Middle East, Africa, Asia-Pacific and Latin America. Proxim is majority-held by SRA Holdings, Inc., a Japan-based IT holding company.

Proxim offers its employees medical, dental and vision insurance; short- and long-term disability coverage; flexible spending accounts; and a 401(k) plan.

FINANCIAL DATA: Note: Data for latest year may not have been available at press time.

In U.S. $	2020	2019	2018	2017	2016	2015
Revenue						
R&D Expense						
Operating Income						
Operating Margin %						
SGA Expense						
Net Income						
Operating Cash Flow						
Capital Expenditure						
EBITDA						
Return on Assets %						
Return on Equity %						
Debt to Equity						

CONTACT INFORMATION:
Phone: 408 383-7600   Fax: 408 383-7680
Toll-Free: 800-229-1630
Address: 2114 Ringwood Ave., San Jose, CA 95131 United States

STOCK TICKER/OTHER:
Stock Ticker: PRXM   Exchange: GREY
Employees: 353   Fiscal Year Ends: 12/31
Parent Company: SRA Holdings Inc

SALARIES/BONUSES:
Top Exec. Salary: $ Bonus: $
Second Exec. Salary: $ Bonus: $

OTHER THOUGHTS:
Estimated Female Officers or Directors:
Hot Spot for Advancement for Women/Minorities:

Proximus Group

www.proximus.com/en

NAIC Code: 517110

TYPES OF BUSINESS:

Local & Long-Distance Telephone Services
Cell Phone Services
Internet Services
Television Broadcasting
Network IT Consulting & Sourcing
Media Activities

BRANDS/DIVISIONS/AFFILIATES:

Proximus
Scarlet
Tango
Telindus
BICS
Mobile Vikings

GROWTH PLANS/SPECIAL FEATURES:

Proximus Group is a leading telecommunications company, headquartered in Belgium and operating internationally. The company is 53.51% Belgian state owned. Brands of the firm include: Proximus and Scarlet, providing telephone, internet, television and network-based information and communication technology (ICT) services in Belgium; Tango, a telecom operator in Luxembourg that provides fixed & mobile products; Telindus, an ICT provider in the Netherlands and Luxembourg with a focus on corporate and institutional customers; and BICS (best-in-class solutions), offering international wholesale solutions for voice and mobile data services providers worldwide. In December 2020, Proximus announed it had completed its acquisition of Mobile Vikings, a mobile operator located in Belgium. In 2021 Proximus announced it had acquired full ownership of BICS from MTN and Swisscom, two minority shareholders.

CONTACTS: Note: Officers with more than one job title may be intentionally listed here more than once.

Guillaume Boutin, CEO
Renaud Tilmans, Chief Customer Operations Officer
Didier Bellens, Pres.
Katleen Vandeweyer, Interim CFO
Jim Casteele, Chief Consumer Market Officer
Jan Van Acoleyen, Chief Human Resources Officer
Geert Standaert, CTO
Bruno Chauvat, Exec. VP-Strategy & Content
Bart Van Den Meersche, Exec. VP-Enterprise Bus. Unit
Geert Standaert, Exec. VP-Svc. Delivery Engine & Wholesale
Dominique Leroy, Exec. VP-Consumer Bus. Unit
Stefaan De Clerck, Chmn.

FINANCIAL DATA: Note: Data for latest year may not have been available at press time.

In U.S. $	2020	2019	2018	2017	2016	2015
Revenue	6,650,132,000	6,888,379,000	7,042,322,000	7,011,778,000	7,121,738,000	7,262,242,000
R&D Expense						
Operating Income	978,643,300	662,203,100	923,663,400	950,542,500	1,109,373,000	952,986,000
Operating Margin %		.10%	.13%	.14%	.16%	.13%
SGA Expense	281,008,700	274,899,800	321,327,300	300,557,100	307,887,800	406,851,700
Net Income	689,082,200	455,722,800	620,662,700	637,767,600	638,989,400	588,896,500
Operating Cash Flow	1,850,992,000	2,022,041,000	1,903,528,000	1,796,012,000	1,858,323,000	1,693,383,000
Capital Expenditure	1,330,515,000	1,332,959,000	1,342,733,000	1,208,337,000	1,175,349,000	1,221,777,000
EBITDA	2,387,352,000	2,042,811,000	2,173,541,000	2,150,328,000	2,099,013,000	1,985,388,000
Return on Assets %		.04%	.06%	.06%	.06%	.06%
Return on Equity %		.13%	.17%	.18%	.19%	.17%
Debt to Equity		0.91	0.752	0.65	0.623	0.627

CONTACT INFORMATION:

Phone: 32 22024111   Fax: 32 22036593
Toll-Free:
Address: 27 Blvd. du Roi Albert II, Brussels, 1030 Belgium

STOCK TICKER/OTHER:

Stock Ticker: BGAOF
Employees: 11,423
Parent Company:

Exchange: PINX
Fiscal Year Ends: 12/31

SALARIES/BONUSES:

Top Exec. Salary: $ Bonus: $
Second Exec. Salary: $ Bonus: $

OTHER THOUGHTS:

Estimated Female Officers or Directors: 6
Hot Spot for Advancement for Women/Minorities: Y

Purple Communications Inc

www.purplevrs.com

NAIC Code: 517210

TYPES OF BUSINESS:

Wireless Data Products
Deaf & Speech-Impaired Communications Systems

BRANDS/DIVISIONS/AFFILIATES:

ZP Better Together LLC
POP

CONTACTS: *Note: Officers with more than one job title may be intentionally listed here more than once.*

Sherri Turpin, CEO
Chris Wagner, COO
John Ferron, Pres.
Ray Nunez, VP-Finance
Zarko Roganovic, CTO
Bill Billbrough, CIO
John Goodman, Chief Legal Officer
Francine Cummings, VP-Oper.
Rita Beier Braman, Sr. Dir.-Oper. & Quality, IP-Relay & ClearCaptions
Gordon Ellis, Sr. VP

GROWTH PLANS/SPECIAL FEATURES:

Purple Communications, Inc. is a provider of versatile video relay services (VRS) and professional interpreting for individuals with hearing or speech disabilities. The company offers both major categories of relay services: traditional telecommunications and internet-based services. VRS provides deaf and hard-of-hearing (HOH) individuals and business owners a means to communicate over video desktop and mobile devices (both iOS and Android) with hearing individuals in real-time using American Sign Language (ASL) interpreters. This service is free to deaf and HOH customers. On-site interpreting consists of a team of national-qualified interpreters that can provide services for ASL and English as well as Spanish ASL interpreters. Interpreters provide services for any in-person interpretation needs, including job interviews; special events such as concerts, parties and plays; business meetings; conferences; and employee training. Video remote interpreting (VRI) is an on-demand sign language interpreting service delivered over a live internet video connection. VRI is beneficial for schools, business meetings, medical appointments/hospitals, conferences and more. VRS services are offered 24/7/365 under the Purple brand name. POP is a fully customizable light-emitting diode (LED) light bulb capable of producing millions of colors. When someone calls a Purple customer, Purple sends a signal to the POP to flash, informing the customer that they have an incoming call. POP comprises a management tool built into the mobile app. Purple Communications operates as a subsidiary of ZP Better Together, LLC.

FINANCIAL DATA: *Note: Data for latest year may not have been available at press time.*

In U.S. $	2020	2019	2018	2017	2016	2015
Revenue	160,909,875	153,247,500	145,950,000	139,000,000	137,700,000	135,000,000
R&D Expense						
Operating Income						
Operating Margin %						
SGA Expense						
Net Income						
Operating Cash Flow						
Capital Expenditure						
EBITDA						
Return on Assets %						
Return on Equity %						
Debt to Equity						

CONTACT INFORMATION:

Phone: Fax:
Toll-Free: 800-549-6000
Address: 11900 N. Jollyville Rd. #204209, Austin, TX 78759 United States

STOCK TICKER/OTHER:

Stock Ticker: Private   Exchange:
Employees: 1,520   Fiscal Year Ends: 12/31
Parent Company:

SALARIES/BONUSES:

Top Exec. Salary: $ Bonus: $
Second Exec. Salary: $ Bonus: $

OTHER THOUGHTS:

Estimated Female Officers or Directors: 3
Hot Spot for Advancement for Women/Minorities: Y

Qisda Corporation

NAIC Code: 334419

TYPES OF BUSINESS:

LCD (Liquid Crystal Display) Unit Screens Manufacturing
LCD Flat-Panel Displays
LCD TVs
Projectors
Multifunctional Printers
Mobile Phones
Portable Display Devices

BRANDS/DIVISIONS/AFFILIATES:

CONTACTS: *Note: Officers with more than one job title may be intentionally listed here more than once.*

Peter Chen, CEO
James T. Wong, VP-Mfg. Oper.
Mark Hsiao, Sr. VP-Mfg. Oper.
David Wang, Sr. VP-Admin.
Joe Huang, Sr. VP-Display System Products
Jason Tyan, VP-Medical Devices & Products
April Huang, VP-Precise Optical Products
Chinglung Chen, VP-Mobile Communications Products
K.Y. Lee, Chmn.
Mark Hsiao, Managing Dir.-Qisda (Suzhou)
C.M. Wu, Sr. VP-Supply Chain Mgmt.

GROWTH PLANS/SPECIAL FEATURES:

Qisda Corporation is an original design manufacturer (ODM) and an original equipment manufacturer (OEM) of electronic products for consumer, commercial, medical and industrial applications. Qisda's products include LCD (liquid crystal display) monitors, commercial LCD TVs, all-in-one PCs, projectors, multifunctional printers, mobile phones, car infotainment displays, medical electronics, portable display devices and smart business solutions. The firm has four research and development centers in Taiwan and China, as well as manufacturing locations in China, Mexico and Taiwan. Qisda's in-house manufacturing capabilities include surface-mount technology (SMT), metal stamping, plastic injection and LCD module assembling. Main product categories include displays, imaging devices, smart business solutions, healthcare solutions, opto-mechatronic products, mobile communication devices, industrial solutions and automobile infotainment devices. LCD monitors include wide format models from 15-27 inches, traditional format models from 15-20 inches, monitor-TVs and pen/touch displays. Its LCD TVs include sizes ranging from 15 to more than 45 inches. Qisda's projectors include LCD projectors, home theater projectors and short-throw projectors for home and office settings. Printer offerings include color inkjet printers, color inkjet multifunctional printers, color laser printers (CLPs), color laser multifunctional printers (MFPs), high-speed inkjet and multifunctional printers, image scanners, mobile scanners and medical electronics. Its mobile communications devices include mobile internet devices (MIDs) and tablets, dual mode phones, wireless modules and USB modem modules. Qisda's infotainment products include car electronics, such as navigation systems, TFT-LCD displays and vehicle rear seat entertainment systems; portable display devices, such as mobile digital TVs, e-readers, digital photo frames and GPS units; and general displays for professional, public, industrial and e-signage use. Smart business solutions include light software-hardware integration and innovative Internet of Things (IoT) applications for six major business domains: retail, manufacturing, healthcare, school, enterprise and energy.

FINANCIAL DATA: *Note: Data for latest year may not have been available at press time.*

In U.S. $	2020	2019	2018	2017	2016	2015
Revenue	6,817,870,000	5,341,780,500	5,150,260,000	4,469,530,000	3,988,530,000	4,041,820,000
R&D Expense						
Operating Income						
Operating Margin %						
SGA Expense						
Net Income	226,427,000	125,182,450	131,771,000	190,361,000	125,747,000	68,172,300
Operating Cash Flow						
Capital Expenditure						
EBITDA						
Return on Assets %						
Return on Equity %						
Debt to Equity						

CONTACT INFORMATION:

Phone: 886-3-3595-000   Fax: 886-3-3599-000
Toll-Free:
Address: 157 Shan-ying Rd., Gueishan, Taoyuan, 333 Taiwan

STOCK TICKER/OTHER:

Stock Ticker: 2352   Exchange: TWSE
Employees: 9,985   Fiscal Year Ends: 12/31
Parent Company:

SALARIES/BONUSES:

Top Exec. Salary: $ Bonus: $
Second Exec. Salary: $ Bonus: $

OTHER THOUGHTS:

Estimated Female Officers or Directors: 1
Hot Spot for Advancement for Women/Minorities:

Qualcomm Incorporated

www.qualcomm.com

NAIC Code: 334413

TYPES OF BUSINESS:

Telecommunications Equipment
Digital Wireless Communications Products
Integrated Circuits
Mobile Communications Systems
Wireless Software & Services
E-Mail Software
Code Division Multiple Access

BRANDS/DIVISIONS/AFFILIATES:

CONTACTS: *Note: Officers with more than one job title may be intentionally listed here more than once.*

Steven Mollenkopf, CEO
David Wise, CFO
Jeffrey Henderson, Chairman of the Board
Erin Polek, Chief Accounting Officer
James Thompson, Chief Technology Officer
Michelle Sterling, Executive VP, Divisional
Brian Modoff, Executive VP, Divisional
Donald Rosenberg, Executive VP
Alexander Rogers, Executive VP
Cristiano Amon, President

GROWTH PLANS/SPECIAL FEATURES:

Qualcomm Incorporated provides digital wireless communications products, technologies and services. Its operations are divided into three segments: Qualcomm CDMA Technologies (QCT), Qualcomm Technology Licensing (QTL) and Qualcomm Strategic Initiatives (QSI). QCT designs application-specific integrated circuits based on Code Division Multiple Access (CDMA), Orthogonal Frequency-Division Multiple Access (OFDMA), Time Division Multiple Access (TDMA) and other technologies for use in voice and data communications, networking, application processing, multimedia functions and GPS products. QTL grants licenses and provides rights to use portions of Qualcomm's intellectual property portfolio to third-party manufacturers of wireless products and networking equipment. QSI makes strategic investments in various companies and technologies that Qualcomm believes will open new opportunities for its technologies. Subsidiary RF360 Holdings Singapore Pte. Ltd. (RF360), delivers radio frequency (RF) front-end modules and RF filters into fully integrated systems for mobile devices and fast-growing business segments such as the Internet of Things, drones, robotics, automotive applications and more. Qualcomm Incorporated has pioneered in 3G, 4G and 5G wireless technologies, not just for smartphones and mobile devices, but also for industries and applications including automotive, Internet of Things (IoT), networking, computing and artificial intelligence (AI). The company's non-reporting segments include cyber security solutions, mobile health, small cells and other wireless technology and service initiatives.

U.S. employees of the company receive medical, dental and vision insurance; dependent/health care reimbursement accounts; tuition reimbursement; a 401(k); and an employee stock purchase plan.

FINANCIAL DATA: *Note: Data for latest year may not have been available at press time.*

In U.S. $	2020	2019	2018	2017	2016	2015
Revenue	23,531,000,000	24,273,000,000	22,732,000,000	22,291,000,000	23,554,000,000	25,281,000,000
R&D Expense	5,975,000,000	5,398,000,000	5,625,000,000	5,485,000,000	5,151,000,000	5,490,000,000
Operating Income	6,255,000,000	7,667,000,000	742,000,000	2,614,000,000	6,495,000,000	5,776,000,000
Operating Margin %		.32%	.03%	.12%	.28%	.23%
SGA Expense	2,074,000,000	2,195,000,000	2,986,000,000	2,658,000,000	2,385,000,000	2,344,000,000
Net Income	5,198,000,000	4,386,000,000	-4,864,000,000	2,466,000,000	5,705,000,000	5,271,000,000
Operating Cash Flow	5,814,000,000	7,286,000,000	3,895,000,000	4,693,000,000	7,400,000,000	5,506,000,000
Capital Expenditure	1,407,000,000	887,000,000	784,000,000	690,000,000	539,000,000	994,000,000
EBITDA	7,714,000,000	9,509,000,000	2,842,000,000	4,975,000,000	8,558,000,000	7,805,000,000
Return on Assets %		.13%	-.10%	.04%	.11%	.11%
Return on Equity %		1.50%	-.31%	.08%	.18%	.15%
Debt to Equity		2.737	16.557	0.631	0.315	0.317

CONTACT INFORMATION:

Phone: 858 587-1121　　　　Fax: 858 658-2100
Toll-Free:
Address: 5775 Morehouse Dr., San Diego, CA 92121 United States

STOCK TICKER/OTHER:

Stock Ticker: QCOM　　　　　　　　Exchange: NAS
Employees: 41,000　　　　　　　　Fiscal Year Ends: 09/30
Parent Company:

SALARIES/BONUSES:

Top Exec. Salary: $　　　　Bonus: $
Second Exec. Salary: $　　　Bonus: $

OTHER THOUGHTS:

Estimated Female Officers or Directors: 2
Hot Spot for Advancement for Women/Minorities: Y

Rackspace Technology Inc

www.rackspace.com

NAIC Code: 517110

TYPES OF BUSINESS:

Web Hosting Services
Data Centers
Cloud Computing Services
Server Farms

BRANDS/DIVISIONS/AFFILIATES:

Apollo Global Management LLC
Onica

CONTACTS: *Note: Officers with more than one job title may be intentionally listed here more than once.*

Kevin Jones, CEO
Subroto Mukerji, COO
Amar Maletira, CFO
Amanda Samuels, CMO
Holly Windham, Chief People Officer
Tolga Tarhan, CTO

GROWTH PLANS/SPECIAL FEATURES:

Rackspace Technology, Inc. provides managed cloud services in the business information technology (IT) market worldwide. The firm actively offers four service categories: Cloud, Applications, Data and Security. It delivers advice and integrated managed services across public and private clouds, managed hosting and enterprise applications. The company partners with leading technology platform providers, including VMware, Alibaba Cloud, Amazon Web Services, Google Cloud Platform, Microsoft, OpenStack, Pivotal Cloud Foundry, Oracle and SAP. Rackspace's solutions include application management, business intelligence, database management, digital experience, email hosting, enterprise resource planning (ERP), productivity and collaboration and website hosting. Industries served by the firm include automotive, business services, education, energy, financial services, government, healthcare, manufacturing and retail. Rackspace is owned by private equity firm, Apollo Global Management, LLC. Based in Texas, the company serves approximately 150,000 business customers, including most of the Fortune 100, from data centers on five continents. In November 2020, Rackspace announced it acquired Bright Skies GmbH, a service provider for cloud transformation in Germany with a focus on the modernization of data centers, cloud managed services and artificial intelligence.

FINANCIAL DATA: *Note: Data for latest year may not have been available at press time.*

In U.S. $	2020	2019	2018	2017	2016	2015
Revenue	2,707,100,000	2,438,100,000	2,452,800,000	2,144,700,000		
R&D Expense						
Operating Income	24,700,000	99,500,000	57,800,000	-122,800,000		
Operating Margin %		.04%	.02%	- .06%		
SGA Expense	959,700,000	911,700,000	949,300,000	942,200,000		
Net Income	-245,800,000	-102,300,000	-470,600,000	-59,900,000		
Operating Cash Flow	116,700,000	292,900,000	429,800,000	291,700,000		
Capital Expenditure	116,500,000	198,000,000	294,300,000	189,500,000		
EBITDA	493,300,000	774,100,000	391,600,000	620,600,000		
Return on Assets %		- .02%	- .08%			
Return on Equity %		- .11%	- .52%			
Debt to Equity		4.659	4.651			

CONTACT INFORMATION:

Phone: 210 312-4000   Fax: 210 312-4300
Toll-Free: 800-961-2888
Address: 1 Fanatical Pl., City of Windcrest, San Antonio, TX 78218
United States

STOCK TICKER/OTHER:

Stock Ticker: RXT
Employees: 7,200
Parent Company: Apollo Global Management LLC

Exchange: NAS
Fiscal Year Ends: 12/31

SALARIES/BONUSES:

Top Exec. Salary: $ Bonus: $
Second Exec. Salary: $ Bonus: $

OTHER THOUGHTS:

Estimated Female Officers or Directors: 1
Hot Spot for Advancement for Women/Minorities:

RCN Telecom Services LLC

www.rcn.com

NAIC Code: 517110

TYPES OF BUSINESS:

Local & Long-Distance Telephone Service
High-Speed Internet Access
Cable Television Service

BRANDS/DIVISIONS/AFFILIATES:

TPG Capital

GROWTH PLANS/SPECIAL FEATURES:

RCN Telecom Services, LLC provides advanced high-speed internet, digital TV and phone services to residential and small, medium and enterprise businesses. RCN serves U.S. cities such as Boston, Chicago, Lehigh Valley, New York, Philadelphia and Washington DC. The company's offerings include 100% digital programming, a fiber-optic network and free video on demand. For businesses, RCN's communications products and services include internet, voice, video and network solutions. Bundled packaged deals are also available. RCN Telecom is privately-owned by TPG Capital.

CONTACTS: *Note: Officers with more than one job title may be intentionally listed here more than once.*

Jim Holanda, CEO
Douglas Bradbury, Exec. VP
James Holanda, CEO-Video High-Speed Internet & Premium Voice Svcs
Felipe Alvarez, Pres.-RCN Metro Optical Networks

FINANCIAL DATA: *Note: Data for latest year may not have been available at press time.*

In U.S. $	2020	2019	2018	2017	2016	2015
Revenue	609,375,000	625,000,000	561,500,000	547,468,623	521,398,689	550,000,000
R&D Expense						
Operating Income						
Operating Margin %						
SGA Expense						
Net Income						
Operating Cash Flow						
Capital Expenditure						
EBITDA						
Return on Assets %						
Return on Equity %						
Debt to Equity						

CONTACT INFORMATION:

Phone: 703-434-8200   Fax:
Toll-Free: 800-746-4726
Address: 650 College Rd., Ste 3100, Princeton, NJ 20170 United States

STOCK TICKER/OTHER:

Stock Ticker: Private   Exchange:
Employees: 1,500   Fiscal Year Ends: 12/31
Parent Company: TPG Capital

SALARIES/BONUSES:

Top Exec. Salary: $ Bonus: $
Second Exec. Salary: $ Bonus: $

OTHER THOUGHTS:

Estimated Female Officers or Directors:
Hot Spot for Advancement for Women/Minorities:

Realtime Corporation

www.realtimecorp.com.br

NAIC Code: 511210M

TYPES OF BUSINESS:

Cloud-based Messaging
Web Page Tracking Tools

BRANDS/DIVISIONS/AFFILIATES:

Internet Business Technologies
PowerMarketing
Realtime DMC
iG
HIS
Mobbit
WebSpectator

CONTACTS: Note: Officers with more than one job title may be intentionally listed here more than once.

Andre Tomas Parreira, CEO
Alexandre Botelho, Exec. VP-Sales
David Facter, Dir.-Client Acquisition, U.S.
Gilberto Martins, Head-Brazil Oper.

GROWTH PLANS/SPECIAL FEATURES:

Realtime Corporation is a technology company that offers a variety of cloud-based messaging tools to ensure constant accurate content updates to websites, mobile apps and social channels. Realtime offers its customized services for businesses, individual users and developers. The company's tools allow clients to receive up-to-date site traffic data, including length of visit, page views and number of visitors in real-time. The firm's solutions include PowerMarketing, Realtime DCM, iG, HIS, Mobbit, and WebSpectator. PowerMarketing is a platform for monitoring and interacting in real-time with website visitors (of the company's own website), delivering live and unlimited interaction. Realtime DCM (dynamic cloud manager) is a real-time infrastructure manager for public and private clouds. The iG brand represents the company's online products, including iG email, iG online courses (administrative, management, language, financial and more), iG antivirus security, iG Esoteric psychic services (via telephone, email or online chat), and iG online games (cards, crosswords, roulette and more). HIS is the company's subsidiary and brand of e-Health innovation systems specifically designed for the information systems and technologies sector which caters to healthcare markets, primarily in Brazil. Mobbit boosts Internet of Things (IoT). It develops innovative solutions for live stream management, interaction and dynamic communication, leveraged by mobile devices and the IoT. WebSpectator is a partnership vertical, offering an online advertising solution that combines real-time analytics and ad serving. It measures and monetizes the actual time spent viewing ads or videos. Its technology enables web publishers to earn up to four times the revenue by monetizing TV-type impressions of 20 seconds or more, not simply the number of clicks. Realtime is privately-owned by Internet Business Technologies.

FINANCIAL DATA: Note: Data for latest year may not have been available at press time.

In U.S. $	2020	2019	2018	2017	2016	2015
Revenue						
R&D Expense						
Operating Income						
Operating Margin %						
SGA Expense						
Net Income						
Operating Cash Flow						
Capital Expenditure						
EBITDA						
Return on Assets %						
Return on Equity %						
Debt to Equity						

CONTACT INFORMATION:

Phone: 5.5119752553e+12   Fax:
Toll-Free:
Address: Rua Guararapes, Sao Paulo, SP 2064 Brazil

STOCK TICKER/OTHER:

Stock Ticker: Private   Exchange:
Employees: 100   Fiscal Year Ends:
Parent Company: Internet Business Technologies

SALARIES/BONUSES:

Top Exec. Salary: $ Bonus: $
Second Exec. Salary: $ Bonus: $

OTHER THOUGHTS:

Estimated Female Officers or Directors: 1
Hot Spot for Advancement for Women/Minorities:

Rogers Communications Inc

www.rogers.com

NAIC Code: 517110

TYPES OF BUSINESS:

Cable TV Service
Internet Service Provider
Wireless Phone Service
Telephone Service
Television Broadcasting
Magazine Publishing
Radio Stations
Professional Sports Teams

BRANDS/DIVISIONS/AFFILIATES:

Toronto Blue Jays
Rogers Center
Maple Leaf Sports & Entertainment Ltd
Toronto Maple Leafs
Toronto Raptors
Toronto FC
Toronto Argonauts
Toronto Marlies

CONTACTS: *Note: Officers with more than one job title may be intentionally listed here more than once.*

Alan Horn, CEO, Subsidiary
Deepak Khandelwal, Other Executive Officer
Joseph Natale, CEO
Anthony Staffieri, CFO
Edward Rogers, Chairman of the Board
John Hill, Chief Information Officer
Jorge Fernandes, Chief Information Officer
Graeme McPhail, Chief Legal Officer
Melinda Rogers, Deputy Chairman
Philip Lind, Director
James Reid, Other Executive Officer
Frank Boulben, Other Executive Officer
Dale Hooper, Other Executive Officer
Lisa Durocher, Other Executive Officer
Philip Hartling, President, Divisional
Nitin Kawale, President, Divisional

GROWTH PLANS/SPECIAL FEATURES:

Rogers Communications, Inc. is a Canadian company engaged in providing communications and media. The firm operates in three segments, including wireless, cable and business, and media. The wireless segment offers innovative wireless network technologies and services, providing wireless voice and data communication services to individual consumers, businesses, governments and other telecommunications service providers. The cable and business segment provides high-speed internet, television, voice communication and smart monitoring services through Rogers' fiber and hybrid fiber-coaxial network infrastructure in Ontario, New Brunswick and Newfoundland. The media segment provides services in sports media and entertainment, television and radio broadcasting, multi-platform shopping experiences and digital media. In its sports media and entertainment division, Rogers owns the Toronto Blue Jays Major League Baseball team, and the Rogers Center event venue, which hosts the Blue Jays home games as well as concerts, trade shows and other types of special events. The media segment holds a 37.5% ownership interest in Maple Leaf Sports & Entertainment Ltd, which owns the Toronto Maple Leafs, the Toronto Raptors, Toronto FC, the Toronto Argonauts and the Toronto Marlies, as well as various associated real estate holdings. During 2020, Rogers announced that it began to roll out Canada's first 5G standalone core network, powered by Ericsson, in Montreal, Ottawa, Toronto and Vancouver, and continued to expand its reach across 160 communities throughout the country by year's end.

FINANCIAL DATA: *Note: Data for latest year may not have been available at press time.*

In U.S. $	2020	2019	2018	2017	2016	2015
Revenue	11,530,370,000	12,489,020,000	12,508,080,000	11,718,450,000	11,353,050,000	11,114,430,000
R&D Expense						
Operating Income	2,683,735,000	3,085,591,000	3,125,362,000	2,631,535,000	2,282,708,000	2,237,136,000
Operating Margin %		.25%	.25%	.22%	.20%	.20%
SGA Expense						
Net Income	1,319,082,000	1,692,767,000	1,706,024,000	1,417,682,000	691,855,200	1,144,254,000
Operating Cash Flow	3,580,247,000	3,750,104,000	3,552,904,000	3,262,905,000	3,278,648,000	3,104,648,000
Capital Expenditure	1,962,880,000	2,375,507,000	2,356,450,000	2,067,280,000	1,986,909,000	2,074,737,000
EBITDA	4,731,958,000	5,070,014,000	4,796,586,000	4,379,816,000	3,525,561,000	4,104,731,000
Return on Assets %		.06%	.07%	.06%	.03%	.05%
Return on Equity %		.23%	.28%	.29%	.15%	.25%
Debt to Equity		1.855	1.637	2.00	2.909	2.762

CONTACT INFORMATION:

Phone: 416 935-2303   Fax: 416 935-3548
Toll-Free:
Address: 333 Bloor St. E., Fl. 10, Toronto, ON M4W 1G9 Canada

STOCK TICKER/OTHER:

Stock Ticker: RCI   Exchange: NYS
Employees: 25,300   Fiscal Year Ends: 12/31
Parent Company:

SALARIES/BONUSES:

Top Exec. Salary: $ Bonus: $
Second Exec. Salary: $ Bonus: $

OTHER THOUGHTS:

Estimated Female Officers or Directors: 6
Hot Spot for Advancement for Women/Minorities: Y

Rohde & Schwarz GmbH & Co KG

www.rohde-schwarz.com

NAIC Code: 334515

TYPES OF BUSINESS:

Electronic Test & Measurement Equipment
Electronic Security Products
Test and Measurement Technology
Broadcast Technology
Internet Protocol Network
Secure Network Infrastructure

BRANDS/DIVISIONS/AFFILIATES:

Rohde & Schwarz USA Inc

CONTACTS: Note: Officers with more than one job title may be intentionally listed here more than once.

Christian Leicher, CEO
Peter Riedel, COO

GROWTH PLANS/SPECIAL FEATURES:

Rohde & Schwarz GmbH & Co. KG is a technology firm that develops, produces and sells a wide range of electronic capital goods, with a focus on solutions that contribute to a secure and networked society. The company operates through four divisions: test and measurement technology, broadcast and media technology, aerospace/defense/security, and networks and cybersecurity. The test and measurement technology division serves the mobile radio and wireless sector with test equipment and systems for the development, manufacture and type testing of components and end devices as well as for setting up and monitoring networks. Other markets served by this division include automotive, aerospace, defense, industrial electronics, research and education. The broadcast and media technology division serves network operators, content providers, studios and device manufacturers with solutions for the entire transmission chain of audiovisual content, from camera output to broadcast via terrestrial transmitters, satellites or internet protocol (IP) networks. The aerospace, defense and security division offers communication, reconnaissance and security products for the armed forces, authorities, and organizations with security tasks, and operators of critical infrastructures. Last, the networks and cybersecurity division provides businesses and authorities with secure WAN, LAN and WLAN network infrastructures, and offers products that protect data transmission, end devices and applications. Rohde and Schwarz has branch offices in approximately 60 counties. Subsidiary Rohde & Schwarz USA, Inc. is based in Maryland and serves the U.S. market.

FINANCIAL DATA: Note: Data for latest year may not have been available at press time.

In U.S. $	2020	2019	2018	2017	2016	2015
Revenue	2,901,780,000	2,396,500,000	2,333,340,000	2,167,770,000	2,105,680,000	2,033,770,500
R&D Expense						
Operating Income						
Operating Margin %						
SGA Expense						
Net Income						
Operating Cash Flow						
Capital Expenditure						
EBITDA						
Return on Assets %						
Return on Equity %						
Debt to Equity						

CONTACT INFORMATION:

Phone: 49-89-41-29-0   Fax: 49-89-41-29-12-164
Toll-Free:
Address: Muhldorfstrasse 15, Munich, 81671 Germany

SALARIES/BONUSES:

Top Exec. Salary: $ Bonus: $
Second Exec. Salary: $ Bonus: $

STOCK TICKER/OTHER:

Stock Ticker: Private   Exchange:
Employees: 12,300   Fiscal Year Ends: 06/30
Parent Company:

OTHER THOUGHTS:

Estimated Female Officers or Directors:
Hot Spot for Advancement for Women/Minorities:

Rostelecom PJSC

NAIC Code: 517110

TYPES OF BUSINESS:

Telecommunications Services
Long-Distance & International Phone Service
Pre-Paid Services
Virtual Private Networks

BRANDS/DIVISIONS/AFFILIATES:

Federal Agency for State Property Management

CONTACTS: *Note: Officers with more than one job title may be intentionally listed here more than once.*

Mikhail Oseevskiy, Pres.
Sergey Anokhin, CFO
Inna Pokhodnya, VP-Mktg.
Galina Rysakova, Sr. VP-Human Resources
Kirill Menshov, Sr. VP-IT
Ivan Zima, CTO
Alexander Rogovoy, VP-Legal Affairs
Alexander Rogovoy, VP-Corp. Dev.
Roman Frolov, Chief Accountant
Olga Rumyantseva, Dir.-Corp. Clients Sales Dept.
Anton Khozyainov, Sr. VP
Mikhail Magrilov, VP-Strategy & Operational Efficiency
Vladimir Mironov, VP
Sergey Ivanov, Chmn.

GROWTH PLANS/SPECIAL FEATURES:

Rostelecom PJSC is a telecommunications provider, making use of a digital trunk network to interconnect local public operators in a single national network that supports services throughout Russia. The company offers fixed-line domestic and international long-distance services, as well as internet services, directly to corporate and residential customers. Rostelecom has 13.5 million fixed-line broadband subscribers and 10.8 million pay-TV subscribers, of which over 6.3 million also subscribe to the IPTV service. At the network's core are fiber-optic backbone lines linking Moscow to Novorossiysk, Khabarovsk and St. Petersburg. In addition to fixed line domestic and international long-distance telephony, the firm has expanded its services to include interconnection and voice traffic transit services; data-based services for voice transmission, which use a high quality IP/MPLS-based network; interconnection and IP traffic transit services; virtual private network (VPN) services, which join offices and branches of corporate clients or operators into a private secured telecommunications network; data center services; digital circuits between Europe and Asia; domestic long-distance and international rent of channels; and intelligent network services, such as televoting, freephone (toll free numbers) and mass-calling services. State-controlled Federal Agency for State Property Management (FA SPM) is Rostelecom's majority shareholder.

FINANCIAL DATA: *Note: Data for latest year may not have been available at press time.*

In U.S. $	2020	2019	2018	2017	2016	2015
Revenue	7,439,108,000	4,589,800,000	4,356,080,000	4,153,266,000	4,046,036,000	4,044,798,000
R&D Expense						
Operating Income	950,875,500	433,745,800	443,254,000	480,144,300	517,782,600	507,730,300
Operating Margin %		.09%	.10%	.12%	.13%	.13%
SGA Expense	494,889,500	245,050,700	218,824,900	183,403,700	133,210,200	117,580,800
Net Income	317,090,000	201,005,500	192,531,100	186,314,700	159,844,000	189,674,500
Operating Cash Flow	1,860,698,000	1,352,383,000	1,050,719,000	976,244,400	913,781,200	1,099,769,000
Capital Expenditure	1,849,776,000	1,367,237,000	995,424,000	826,384,600	841,415,500	853,236,200
EBITDA	2,565,068,000	1,415,445,000	1,313,643,000	1,261,899,000	1,218,520,000	1,274,019,000
Return on Assets %		.02%	.02%	.02%	.02%	.03%
Return on Equity %		.06%	.06%	.06%	.05%	.06%
Debt to Equity		0.946	0.774	0.677	0.506	0.515

CONTACT INFORMATION:

Phone: 7 499-999-82-83   Fax: 7 499-999-82-22
Toll-Free:
Address: 30 Goncharnaya St., Bldg. 1, Moscow, 115172 Russia

STOCK TICKER/OTHER:

Stock Ticker: ROSYY   Exchange: PINX
Employees: 15,171   Fiscal Year Ends: 12/31
Parent Company:

SALARIES/BONUSES:

Top Exec. Salary: $ Bonus: $
Second Exec. Salary: $ Bonus: $

OTHER THOUGHTS:

Estimated Female Officers or Directors: 3
Hot Spot for Advancement for Women/Minorities: Y

Samsung Electronics Co Ltd

NAIC Code: 334310

www.samsung.com

TYPES OF BUSINESS:

Consumer Electronics
Semiconductors and Memory Products
Smartphones
Computers & Accessories
Digital Cameras
Fuel-Cell Technology
LCD Displays
Solar Energy Panels

BRANDS/DIVISIONS/AFFILIATES:

Samsung Group

CONTACTS: Note: Officers with more than one job title may be intentionally listed here more than once.

Ki Nam Kim, CEO
Oh-Hyun Kwon, Vice Chmn.

GROWTH PLANS/SPECIAL FEATURES:

Samsung Electronics Co., Ltd., the flagship company of Samsung Group, is a global leader in innovative electronic technologies and products. The company operates through three business areas: consumer electronics, information technology (IT) & mobile communications, and device solutions. The consumer electronics business develops and expands strategic products in regards to consumer electronics, including flat panel televisions and monitors as well as home appliances and health/medical equipment. The IT & mobile communications business sells more than 400 million mobile devices on a global scale every year. This division's telecommunications equipment and solutions power the global expansion of 5G and Internet of Things (IoT), and its digital technology not only captures special moments but enables them to be shared in real-time. The device solutions business designs and manufactures memory technology and products for mobile devices. These solutions include memory semiconductor chips, large-scale integration (LSI) on a single silicon semiconductor microchip for virtual/augmented reality devices, dynamic random access memory (DRAM) and NAND technologies, solid state drive (SSD) components and more. Samsung Electronics also has a foundry business to mass produce 5nm chips using extreme ultraviolet (EUV) lithography. During 2020, Samsung announced it was exiting the liquid crystal display (LCD) business, ending all LCD production by the end of 2020.

FINANCIAL DATA: Note: Data for latest year may not have been available at press time.

In U.S. $	2020	2019	2018	2017	2016	2015
Revenue	213,877,200,000	208,091,400,000	220,167,300,000	216,377,500,000	182,320,200,000	181,224,400,000
R&D Expense	19,067,290,000	17,979,640,000	16,576,870,000	14,771,920,000	12,744,990,000	12,378,590,000
Operating Income	32,508,630,000	25,079,710,000	53,184,740,000	48,450,650,000	26,409,330,000	23,855,860,000
Operating Margin %		.12%	.24%	.22%	.14%	.13%
SGA Expense	23,559,030,000	24,405,650,000	23,696,650,000	29,037,210,000	28,232,130,000	27,314,860,000
Net Income	23,564,500,000	19,422,740,000	39,640,970,000	37,341,220,000	20,245,170,000	16,884,450,000
Operating Cash Flow	58,965,340,000	40,988,540,000	60,541,240,000	56,142,950,000	42,797,340,000	36,182,620,000
Capital Expenditure	36,372,340,000	25,846,650,000	27,616,190,000	39,537,200,000	22,751,460,000	24,730,720,000
EBITDA	60,750,670,000	54,837,100,000	79,765,010,000	71,322,300,000	46,977,950,000	43,052,690,000
Return on Assets %		.05%	.12%	.15%	.09%	.08%
Return on Equity %		.08%	.17%	.21%	.12%	.11%
Debt to Equity		0.012	0.004	0.013	0.007	0.009

CONTACT INFORMATION:

Phone: 82-31-200-1114   Fax: 82-31-200-7538
Toll-Free:
Address: 129 Samsung-ro, Yeongtong-gu, Suwon-si, 443-742 South Korea

STOCK TICKER/OTHER:

Stock Ticker: SSNGY   Exchange: PINX
Employees: 95,798   Fiscal Year Ends: 12/31
Parent Company: Samsung Group

SALARIES/BONUSES:

Top Exec. Salary: $ Bonus: $
Second Exec. Salary: $ Bonus: $

OTHER THOUGHTS:

Estimated Female Officers or Directors:
Hot Spot for Advancement for Women/Minorities:

Sanmina Corporation

www.sanmina.com

NAIC Code: 334418

TYPES OF BUSINESS:

Printed Circuit Assembly (Electronic Assembly) Manufacturing
Assembly & Testing
Logistics Services
Support Services
Product Design & Engineering
Repair & Maintenance Services
Printed Circuit Boards

BRANDS/DIVISIONS/AFFILIATES:

CONTACTS: *Note: Officers with more than one job title may be intentionally listed here more than once.*

Michael Clarke, CEO
David Anderson, CFO
Jure Sola, Chairman of the Board
Brent Billinger, Chief Accounting Officer
Alan Reid, Executive VP, Divisional

GROWTH PLANS/SPECIAL FEATURES:

Sanmina Corporation is a global provider of integrated manufacturing solutions, components, products and repair, along with related logistics and after-market services. With production facilities in 21 countries on six continents, the firm is a world-leading electronics manufacturing services (EMS) provider. Sanmina's end-to-end solutions, combined with its expertise in supply chain management, enable the management of customer products throughout their life cycles. These solutions include: product design and engineering, the manufacturing of components, subassemblies and complete systems, final system assembly and test; direct order fulfillment and logistics services; after-market product service and support; and global supply chain management. Sanmina's integrated manufacturing solutions consists of printed circuit board assembly and test, final system assembly and test, and direct-order fulfillment. Components, products and services by Sanmina include interconnect systems (printed circuit board fabrication, backplane, cable assemblies and plastic injection molding) and mechanical systems (enclosures and precision machining). Services include design, logistics, repair and after-market service and support.

FINANCIAL DATA: *Note: Data for latest year may not have been available at press time.*

In U.S. $	2020	2019	2018	2017	2016	2015
Revenue	6,960,370,000	8,233,859,000	7,110,130,000	6,868,619,000	6,481,181,000	6,374,541,000
R&D Expense	22,564,000	27,552,000	30,754,000	33,716,000	37,746,000	33,083,000
Operating Income	262,212,000	299,870,000	179,197,000	230,955,000	228,486,000	209,431,000
Operating Margin %		.04%	.03%	.03%	.04%	.03%
SGA Expense	240,931,000	260,032,000	250,924,000	251,568,000	244,604,000	239,288,000
Net Income	139,713,000	141,515,000	-95,533,000	138,833,000	187,838,000	377,261,000
Operating Cash Flow	300,555,000	382,965,000	156,424,000	250,961,000	390,116,000	174,896,000
Capital Expenditure	65,982,000	134,674,000	118,881,000	111,833,000	120,400,000	119,097,000
EBITDA	343,879,000	393,331,000	244,093,000	354,165,000	341,438,000	301,771,000
Return on Assets %		.04%	-.02%	.04%	.05%	.11%
Return on Equity %		.09%	-.06%	.09%	.12%	.27%
Debt to Equity		0.211	0.01	0.238	0.27	0.279

CONTACT INFORMATION:

Phone: 408-964-3500   Fax: 408-964-3636
Toll-Free:
Address: 2700 N. First St., San Jose, CA 95134 United States

STOCK TICKER/OTHER:

Stock Ticker: SANM   Exchange: NAS
Employees: 37,000   Fiscal Year Ends: 09/30
Parent Company:

SALARIES/BONUSES:

Top Exec. Salary: $ Bonus: $
Second Exec. Salary: $ Bonus: $

OTHER THOUGHTS:

Estimated Female Officers or Directors:
Hot Spot for Advancement for Women/Minorities:

ScanSource Inc

www.scansource.com

NAIC Code: 423430

TYPES OF BUSINESS:

Data Capture Products, Distribution
Bar Code
Point of Sale
Payments
Security
Unified Communications
Cloud
Telecommunications

BRANDS/DIVISIONS/AFFILIATES:

GROWTH PLANS/SPECIAL FEATURES:

ScanSource, Inc. is a global provider of technology products and solutions. The firm focuses on point-of-sale (POS), payments, barcode, physical security, unified communications and collaboration, cloud and telecom services. ScanSource operates through two business segments: worldwide barcode, networking and security; and worldwide communications and services. Each business segment is led by their own presidents with dedicated sales, merchandising and technical support teams. All ScanSource sales units sell only to resellers. Value-added services include inventory management, financial services, marketing, technical support and customer service.

ScanSource offers its employees comprehensive health benefits, life and disability insurance, retirement and savings options, and a variety of employee assistance programs.

CONTACTS: Note: Officers with more than one job title may be intentionally listed here more than once.

Michael Baur, CEO
Gerald Lyons, CFO

FINANCIAL DATA: Note: Data for latest year may not have been available at press time.

In U.S. $	2020	2019	2018	2017	2016	2015
Revenue	3,047,734,000	3,873,111,000	3,846,260,000	3,568,186,000	3,540,226,000	3,218,626,000
R&D Expense						
Operating Income	62,444,000	105,164,000	104,682,000	93,450,000	98,171,000	104,108,000
Operating Margin %		.03%	.03%	.03%	.03%	.03%
SGA Expense	260,139,000	314,521,000	297,475,000	265,178,000	257,269,000	222,982,000
Net Income	-192,654,000	57,597,000	33,153,000	69,246,000	63,619,000	65,419,000
Operating Cash Flow	226,271,000	-27,127,000	27,871,000	94,876,000	52,211,000	75,522,000
Capital Expenditure	6,387,000	7,215,000	8,159,000	12,432,000	12,081,000	20,762,000
EBITDA	-24,224,000	127,908,000	107,569,000	129,678,000	115,288,000	113,700,000
Return on Assets %		.03%	.02%	.04%	.04%	.05%
Return on Equity %		.06%	.04%	.09%	.08%	.08%
Debt to Equity		0.385	0.287	0.116	0.099	0.007

CONTACT INFORMATION:

Phone: 864 288-2432   Fax: 864 288-5515
Toll-Free: 800-944-2439
Address: 6 Logue Ct., Greenville, SC 29615 United States

STOCK TICKER/OTHER:

Stock Ticker: SCSC   Exchange: NAS
Employees: 2,700   Fiscal Year Ends: 06/30
Parent Company:

SALARIES/BONUSES:

Top Exec. Salary: $ Bonus: $
Second Exec. Salary: $ Bonus: $

OTHER THOUGHTS:

Estimated Female Officers or Directors: 1
Hot Spot for Advancement for Women/Minorities:

SES SA

NAIC Code: 517410

TYPES OF BUSINESS:

Satellite Carrier
Satellite Operations
Broadband Internet Service
Secure Communications
Broadcasting Services
Video on Demand
Direct to Home TV

BRANDS/DIVISIONS/AFFILIATES:

QuetzSat
Ciel
GovSat
YahLive
SES Government Solutions
SES Techcom
HD Plus GmbH
Redu Space Services

CONTACTS: *Note: Officers with more than one job title may be intentionally listed here more than once.*

Steve Collar, CEO
Sandeep Jalan, CFO
Evie Ross, Chief Human Resources Officer
Ruy Pinto, CTO
Gerson Souto, Chief Dev. Officer
Patrick Biewer, Managing Dir.-SES Broadband Svcs.
Wilfried Urner, CEO-SES Platform Svcs.
Frank Esser, Chmn.
Tip Osterthaler, CEO-SES Gov't Solutions

GROWTH PLANS/SPECIAL FEATURES:

SES SA is a leading global satellite communications company that operates more than 50 satellites in geostationary Earth orbit (GEO) and 16 medium Earth orbit (MEO). The firm offers value-added, end-to-end communications solutions, including intelligent software, through two key business units: SES Video and SES Networks. These units connect and enable SES's broadcast, telecom, corporate and government customers to serve their customers on a global scale. The company's satellite operators consist of: wholly-owned QuetzSat, a Mexican satellite operator that provides direct-to-home TV services to areas within Mexico and the U.S.: wholly-owned Ciel, a Canadian satellite service provider that offers digital television and broadband services to homes and businesses throughout North America; 50%-owned GovSat (in partnership with the Luxembourg government), which will procure and launch a dedicated satellite, GovSat-1, for governmental use deploying military frequencies (X-band and military Ka-band) for defense and security purposes; and 35%-owned YahLive, which owns and commercializes 23 Ku-band transponders on the Yahsat 1A satellite to provide direct-to-home TV capacity and services to numerous countries in the Middle East and North/Southwest Africa. SES' service companies include: wholly-owned SES Government Solutions, a provider of secure, reliable and customized satellite communications solutions to the U.S. Government all around the world; wholly-owned SES Techcom, which develops and delivers innovative and tailored end-to-end satellite-enabled solutions and services to governmental, institutional and supranational partners and customers; wholly-owned HD Plus GmbH, which markets HD+, a technical platform for the encrypted transmission and reception of free-to-air channels in high-definition quality via satellite in Germany; and 52%-owned Redu Space Services (a joint venture with QinetiQ Space), which provides a neutral, institutional site that is radio frequency (RF)-protected, with facilities to host, operate and maintain satellite communication infrastructure.

FINANCIAL DATA: *Note: Data for latest year may not have been available at press time.*

In U.S. $	2020	2019	2018	2017	2016	2015
Revenue	2,243,183,000	2,371,347,000	2,362,306,000	2,486,316,000	2,527,612,000	2,461,270,000
R&D Expense						
Operating Income	399,521,100	402,453,300	384,004,500	746,017,000	1,002,224,000	1,093,002,000
Operating Margin %		.17%	.16%	.30%	.40%	.44%
SGA Expense						
Net Income	-105,072,800	361,890,300	357,247,600	728,301,200	1,176,205,000	665,746,200
Operating Cash Flow	1,281,644,000	1,385,617,000	1,455,503,000	1,528,687,000	1,556,666,000	1,772,310,000
Capital Expenditure	256,573,200	373,008,500	400,987,200	587,919,100	757,501,700	694,824,600
EBITDA	1,243,769,000	1,459,901,000	1,511,582,000	1,578,414,000	2,339,336,000	1,849,892,000
Return on Assets %		.02%	.02%	.05%	.08%	.05%
Return on Equity %		.05%	.05%	.09%	.18%	.15%
Debt to Equity		0.61	0.64	0.57	0.62	1.062

CONTACT INFORMATION:

Phone: 352 7107251   Fax:
Toll-Free:
Address: Chateau de Betzdorf, Rue Pierre Werner, Luxembourg, L-6815 Luxembourg

STOCK TICKER/OTHER:

Stock Ticker: SGBAF   Exchange: PINX
Employees: 2,095   Fiscal Year Ends: 12/31
Parent Company:

SALARIES/BONUSES:

Top Exec. Salary: $ Bonus: $
Second Exec. Salary: $ Bonus: $

OTHER THOUGHTS:

Estimated Female Officers or Directors:
Hot Spot for Advancement for Women/Minorities:

Shaw Communications Inc

www.shaw.ca

NAIC Code: 517110

TYPES OF BUSINESS:

Cable TV Service
Internet Service Provider
Satellite Services
Digital Phone Services
Internet Infrastructure Services
Video-On-Demand
Broadcast TV

BRANDS/DIVISIONS/AFFILIATES:

Shaw Fibre+
Shaw Fibre+ Gig
Shaw BlueCurve TV
Shaw Go WiFi
Shaw Mobile
Freedom Mobile

CONTACTS: *Note: Officers with more than one job title may be intentionally listed here more than once.*

Mcaleese Paul, CEO, Divisional
Jay Mehr, Pres.
Vito Culmone, CFO
J. Shaw, Chairman of the Board
Jim Little, Chief Marketing Officer
Zoran Stakic, Chief Technology Officer
Bradley Shaw, Director
Jim Shaw, Director
Janice Davis, Executive VP, Divisional
Trevor English, Executive VP
Peter Johnson, Executive VP
Chris Kucharski, President, Divisional
Ron McKenzie, Senior VP
Ron McKenzie, Senior VP, Divisional

GROWTH PLANS/SPECIAL FEATURES:

Shaw Communications, Inc. is a Canadian telecommunications company focused on seamless connectivity for its global customers. The firm's consumer division provides residential wireline communication services in Canada, connecting them throughout British Columbia, Alberta, Saskatchewan, Manitoba and Northern Ontario. Its Shaw Fibre+ network offers fast and affordable connectivity, and its Fibre+ Gig is available for gigabit download speeds in all of Western Canada. Shaw BlueCurve TV provides access to network programming with the top streaming platforms, whether live or downloaded-to-go. Shaw Go WiFi offers customers free access to hundreds of thousands of hotspots across Canada. Shaw Mobile and Freedom Mobile offer wireless connectivity in British Columbia, Alberta and Ontario. Shaw Direct is one of two licensed satellite video services available in Canada, offering over 350 high-definition video channels and access to over 10,000 on-demand, pay-per-view and subscription movie and television titles. The Shaw business division provides connectivity solutions to business customers of all sizes, leveraging business-grade Fiber+ and fiber-to-the-premise (FTTP) networks. This segment provides businesses with tools and solutions regarding connectivity, managed services, internet, data, WiFi and phone.

FINANCIAL DATA: *Note: Data for latest year may not have been available at press time.*

In U.S. $	2020	2019	2018	2017	2016	2015
Revenue	4,480,073,000	4,424,559,000	4,340,873,000	4,045,074,000	4,046,731,000	4,547,187,000
R&D Expense						
Operating Income	961,140,100	932,140,200	522,827,100	827,740,500	939,597,300	1,186,511,000
Operating Margin %		.21%	.12%	.20%	.23%	.26%
SGA Expense	544,369,900	549,341,300	974,397,200	711,740,800	717,540,800	817,797,600
Net Income	570,055,500	605,684,000	49,714,140	705,112,300	1,010,854,000	709,255,100
Operating Cash Flow	1,590,853,000	1,299,196,000	1,119,397,000	1,244,511,000	1,377,910,000	1,275,996,000
Capital Expenditure	953,683,000	1,075,483,000	1,103,654,000	1,336,482,000	992,625,700	903,140,300
EBITDA	1,962,052,000	1,805,452,000	1,224,625,000	1,619,024,000	1,567,653,000	1,953,766,000
Return on Assets %		.05%	.00%	.06%	.08%	.06%
Return on Equity %		.12%	.01%	.14%	.21%	.17%
Debt to Equity		0.646	0.724	0.699	0.826	0.936

CONTACT INFORMATION:

Phone: 403 750-4500   Fax: 403 750-4501
Toll-Free: 888-472-2222
Address: 630 3rd Ave. SW, Ste. 900, Calgary, AB T2P 4L4 Canada

STOCK TICKER/OTHER:

Stock Ticker: SJR
Employees: 9,500
Parent Company:

Exchange: NYS
Fiscal Year Ends: 08/31

SALARIES/BONUSES:

Top Exec. Salary: $ Bonus: $
Second Exec. Salary: $ Bonus: $

OTHER THOUGHTS:

Estimated Female Officers or Directors: 3
Hot Spot for Advancement for Women/Minorities: Y

Sales, profits and employees may be estimates. Financial information, benefits and other data can change quickly and may vary from those stated here.

Shenandoah Telecommunications Company

www.shentel.com

NAIC Code: 517110

TYPES OF BUSINESS:

Local Exchange Carrier
Broadband Services
Data
Video
Telephone
Fiber Optic Services
Tower Leasing

BRANDS/DIVISIONS/AFFILIATES:

CONTACTS: Note: Officers with more than one job title may be intentionally listed here more than once.

Christopher French, CEO
James Woodward, CFO
David Heimbach, COO
Raymond Ostroski, General Counsel
William Pirtle, Senior VP, Divisional
Edward McKay, Senior VP, Divisional
Thomas Whitaker, Senior VP, Divisional

GROWTH PLANS/SPECIAL FEATURES:

Shenandoah Telecommunications Company (STC) provides a comprehensive range of broadband and wireless communication products and services in the mid-Atlantic region of the U.S. STC's broadband segment provides broadband data, video and voice services to residential and commercial customers of Virginia, West Virginia, Maryland, Pennsylvania and Kentucky, via fiber optic, hybrid fiber and fixed wireless networks. Voice and DSL telephone services are offered to customers in Virginia's Shenandoah County and portions of adjacent counties as a rural local exchange carrier. This division also provides ethernet and wavelength fiber optic services to commercial fiber customers under capacity agreements; and leases dedicated fiber optic strands to customers as part of dark fiber agreements, which are accounted for as leases. STC's tower segment leases space on owned cell towers to the company's broadband segment, and to other wireless carriers. In May 2021, STC and T-Mobile USA, Inc. agreed for T-Mobile to purchase Shentel's wireless business operating assets and related rights utilized to provide wireless telecommunications network and other related services per a previous Sprint/STC agreement for approximately $1.95 billion. The transaction was expected to close by year's end.

STC offers its employees comprehensive health benefits, 401(k), tuition assistance, and a variety of employee training/development and assistance programs.

FINANCIAL DATA: Note: Data for latest year may not have been available at press time.

In U.S. $	2020	2019	2018	2017	2016	2015
Revenue	220,775,000	633,906,000	630,854,000	611,991,000	535,288,000	342,485,000
R&D Expense						
Operating Income	-1,147,000	97,046,000	93,246,000	57,540,000	64,758,000	74,086,000
Operating Margin %		.15%	.15%	.09%	.12%	.22%
SGA Expense	85,016,000	112,540,000	113,222,000	165,937,000	133,325,000	76,367,000
Net Income	126,723,000	54,935,000	46,595,000	66,390,000	-895,000	40,864,000
Operating Cash Flow	302,867,000	259,145,000	265,647,000	222,930,000	161,526,000	119,321,000
Capital Expenditure	120,450,000	155,534,000	136,641,000	146,489,000	173,231,000	69,679,000
EBITDA	47,556,000	260,585,000	263,364,000	228,501,000	170,732,000	146,647,000
Return on Assets %		.03%	.03%	.05%	.00%	.07%
Return on Equity %		.12%	.12%	.21%	.00%	.15%
Debt to Equity		2.217	1.695	2.163	2.694	0.615

CONTACT INFORMATION:

Phone: 540 984-4141   Fax: 540 984-3438
Toll-Free: 800-743-6835
Address: 500 Shentel Way, Edinburg, VA 22824 United States

STOCK TICKER/OTHER:

Stock Ticker: SHEN   Exchange: NAS
Employees: 1,139   Fiscal Year Ends: 12/31
Parent Company:

SALARIES/BONUSES:

Top Exec. Salary: $ Bonus: $
Second Exec. Salary: $ Bonus: $

OTHER THOUGHTS:

Estimated Female Officers or Directors: 3
Hot Spot for Advancement for Women/Minorities: Y

Siemens AG

www.siemens.com

NAIC Code: 334513

TYPES OF BUSINESS:

Industrial Control Manufacturing
Digitalization
Smart Infrastructure
Mobility
Advanced Technologies
Artificial Intelligence
Internet of Things
Robotics

BRANDS/DIVISIONS/AFFILIATES:

Siemens Advanta
Siemens Healthineers AG
Siemens Financial Services
Siemens Real Estate
Next47

CONTACTS: Note: Officers with more than one job title may be intentionally listed here more than once.

Joe Kaeser, CEO
Ralf P. Thomas, CFO
Peter Y. Solmssen, Head-Corp. Legal & Compliance
Joe Kaeser, Head-Controlling
Roland Busch, CEO-Infrastructure & Cities Sector
Hermann Requardt, CEO-Health Care Sector
Michael Suess, CEO-Energy Sector
Siegfried Russwurm, CEO-Industry Sector
Jim Hagemenn Snabe, Chmn.
Barbara Kux, Chief Sustainability Officer

GROWTH PLANS/SPECIAL FEATURES:

Siemens AG is a technology company engaged in electrification, automation and digitalization. Its businesses are grouped into 10 categories. Digital Industries innovates industry-specific automation and digitalization technologies and solutions. Smart infrastructure intelligently connects energy systems, buildings and industries to respond to industry and customer needs, and for efficiency purposes. Mobility offers transport solutions, including rolling stock rail and road automation and electrification, traffic systems and other related systems. Siemens Advanta offers companies digitalization, specifically designed for their future. This category offers related consulting, design, prototyping, platform solutions, data services, and application development in regards to implementation and operation. The portfolio companies business category consists of six umbrella units engaged in the development and production of large drives applications, the manufacture of mechanical driver systems, wind generation, mechanical systems and related components, systems and solutions for electric commercial vehicles, and products and solutions for mail and parcel logistics and baggage/cargo handling. Siemens Healthineers AG provides innovative medical technologies and services across diagnostic and therapeutic imaging, laboratory diagnostics and molecular medicine, as well as digital health and enterprise services. Siemens Financial Services provides business-to-business financial solutions, supporting customer investments with project and structured financing as well as leasing and equipment financing. Global business services innovates, designs, transforms and operates business services for Siemens' units and external customers. These services include digital end-to-end processing as well as professional services. Siemens Real Estate manages the company's global real estate holdings and supports it with forward-looking strategies for tapping into markets worldwide. Last, Next47 is a global venture firm that invests in entrepreneurs engaged in deep technologies such as artificial intelligence (AI), augmented and virtual reality, cybersecurity, autonomous transportation, Internet of Things (IoT), robotics and more.

FINANCIAL DATA: Note: Data for latest year may not have been available at press time.

In U.S. $	2020	2019	2018	2017	2016	2015
Revenue	69,811,110,000	106,110,100,000	101,461,200,000	101,467,300,000	97,307,210,000	92,410,320,000
R&D Expense	5,621,396,000	6,927,476,000	6,790,637,000	6,309,257,000	5,781,449,000	5,477,226,000
Operating Income	5,565,194,000	8,176,131,000	7,223,145,000	8,972,730,000	8,725,931,000	7,000,782,000
Operating Margin %		.08%	.07%	.09%	.09%	.08%
SGA Expense	13,163,420,000	16,304,610,000	15,811,020,000	14,936,220,000	14,256,920,000	13,939,250,000
Net Income	4,923,761,000	6,321,474,000	7,094,859,000	7,386,864,000	6,658,684,000	8,896,980,000
Operating Cash Flow	10,827,390,000	10,331,350,000	10,293,470,000	8,767,472,000	9,298,944,000	8,078,389,000
Capital Expenditure	1,898,641,000	3,188,838,000	3,179,064,000	2,939,596,000	2,608,494,000	2,317,711,000
EBITDA	11,782,820,000	14,833,590,000	15,343,080,000	15,355,290,000	13,631,370,000	12,932,510,000
Return on Assets %		.04%	.04%	.05%	.04%	.06%
Return on Equity %		.11%	.13%	.16%	.16%	.22%
Debt to Equity		0.632	0.596	0.621	0.724	0.774

CONTACT INFORMATION:

Phone: 49 8963633032   Fax: 49 8932825
Toll-Free:
Address: Wittelsbacherplatz 2, Munich, 80333 Germany

STOCK TICKER/OTHER:

Stock Ticker: SIEGY
Employees: 293,000
Parent Company:

Exchange: PINX
Fiscal Year Ends: 09/30

SALARIES/BONUSES:

Top Exec. Salary: $ Bonus: $
Second Exec. Salary: $ Bonus: $

OTHER THOUGHTS:

Estimated Female Officers or Directors: 5
Hot Spot for Advancement for Women/Minorities: Y

Simply Inc

simplyinc.com

NAIC Code: 423690

TYPES OF BUSINESS:

Wireless Handset Distribution
Wireless Handset Design

GROWTH PLANS/SPECIAL FEATURES:

Simply, Inc. is an Apple premier partner authorized to operate retail consumer electronics stores that sell Apple products and provide service by Apple-certified technicians. Simply is the parent of Simply Mac, a chain of more than 45 retail stores across 16 U.S. states. Simply Mac also sells Apple products through its ecommerce site, www.simplymac.com.

BRANDS/DIVISIONS/AFFILIATES:

Simply Mac
www.simplymac.com

CONTACTS: *Note: Officers with more than one job title may be intentionally listed here more than once.*

Reinier Voigt, CEO
Vernon Loforti, CFO
Kevin Taylor, Chairman of the Board

FINANCIAL DATA: *Note: Data for latest year may not have been available at press time.*

In U.S. $	2020	2019	2018	2017	2016	2015
Revenue		30,385,000	11,615,000	13,615,000	39,140,000	47,833,000
R&D Expense						
Operating Income						
Operating Margin %						
SGA Expense						
Net Income		-21,016,000	-27,271,000	-7,540,000	-2,835,000	-1,243,000
Operating Cash Flow						
Capital Expenditure						
EBITDA						
Return on Assets %						
Return on Equity %						
Debt to Equity						

CONTACT INFORMATION:

Phone: 786-254-6709   Fax:
Toll-Free:
Address: 2001 NW 84th Ave., Miami, FL 33122 United States

STOCK TICKER/OTHER:

Stock Ticker: SIMP   Exchange: OTC
Employees: 528   Fiscal Year Ends: 12/31
Parent Company:

SALARIES/BONUSES:

Top Exec. Salary: $ Bonus: $
Second Exec. Salary: $ Bonus: $

OTHER THOUGHTS:

Estimated Female Officers or Directors:
Hot Spot for Advancement for Women/Minorities:

Singapore Technologies Telemedia Pte Ltd www.sttelemedia.com
NAIC Code: 517110

TYPES OF BUSINESS:
Telecommunications Services
Cellular Service
Internet Services
Satellite & Broadcasting Services
Wireless Telecommunications Equipment
Data Centers & Internet Exchange
Network Design & Integration Services
Cloud

BRANDS/DIVISIONS/AFFILIATES:

CONTACTS: Note: Officers with more than one job title may be intentionally listed here more than once.
Stephen Miller, CEO
Johnny Ong, CFO
Chan Jen Keet, VP
Nicholas Tan, Sr. VP-Corp. Planning
Melinda Tan, Media Contact
Richard Lim, Exec. VP-Corp. Svcs.
Kek Soon Eng, Sr. VP-Investee Companies Mgmt.
Alvin Oei, Sr. VP-Intl Bus. Dev.
Melinda Tan, VP-Strategic Rel.
Ek Tor Teo, Chmn.
Steven Terrell Clontz, Sr. Exec. VP-North America & Europe

GROWTH PLANS/SPECIAL FEATURES:
Singapore Technologies Telemedia Pte., Ltd. (ST Telemedia) is an active investor in communications, media, data centers and infrastructure technology businesses worldwide. ST Telemedia's team of industry professionals has deep and broad experience in these sectors worldwide, in both developed and emerging markets. The firm has a long-term view on value creation and works with its portfolio companies and business partners to achieve mutual success. ST Telemedia's investments in communications and media companies are primarily located in the Asia-Pacific region. They enable the company to combine data, mobility, voice and content services with state-of-the-art delivery platforms. ST Telemedia's investments in data centers spans a footprint in key global economic hubs, particularly in China, India, Singapore, Thailand and the U.K. This division's agile and multi-tenant business model enables its global data center assets to be differentiated and diversified. Last, ST Telemedia's infrastructure technology investments are in cutting-edge technology companies that are ready to scale up in areas such as cloud computing, system performance, cybersecurity and advanced analytics. They are at the forefront of technology innovation critical for the digital transformation of governments, enterprises and telecommunications companies. In January 2021, ST Telemedia (60%) announced a joint venture with Hyosung Heavy Industries (40%) to develop and operate data centers, with the first being located in South Korea.

FINANCIAL DATA: Note: Data for latest year may not have been available at press time.

In U.S. $	2020	2019	2018	2017	2016	2015
Revenue	6,055,403,827	5,767,051,264	4,909,244,928	4,669,999,616	4,917,730,816	4,609,133,568
R&D Expense						
Operating Income						
Operating Margin %						
SGA Expense						
Net Income		423,604,672	362,253,824	361,128,768	356,493,568	384,909,632
Operating Cash Flow						
Capital Expenditure						
EBITDA						
Return on Assets %						
Return on Equity %						
Debt to Equity						

CONTACT INFORMATION:
Phone: 65-6723-8777   Fax: 65-6720-7266
Toll-Free:
Address: 1 Temasek Ave., #33-01 Millenia Twr., Singapore, 567710 Singapore

STOCK TICKER/OTHER:
Stock Ticker: Subsidiary   Exchange:
Employees: 23,000   Fiscal Year Ends: 12/31
Parent Company: Temasek Holdings Pvt Limited

SALARIES/BONUSES:
Top Exec. Salary: $ Bonus: $
Second Exec. Salary: $ Bonus: $

OTHER THOUGHTS:
Estimated Female Officers or Directors: 1
Hot Spot for Advancement for Women/Minorities:

Singapore Telecommunications Limited

www.singtel.com

NAIC Code: 517110

TYPES OF BUSINESS:

Telecommunications Services
Local & Long-Distance Services
Cell Phone & Paging Services
Internet Service Provider
IT & Communications Engineering Services
Satellite Services
Virtual Private Networks
Equipment Sales

BRANDS/DIVISIONS/AFFILIATES:

Optus
NCS Pte Ltd
Singtel Digital Media
Singtel Innov8
Amobee
Trustwave

CONTACTS: *Note: Officers with more than one job title may be intentionally listed here more than once.*

Chua Sock Koong, Group CEO
Lim Cheng Cheng, Group CFO
Aileen Tan, Group Human Resources Officer
William Woo, Group CIO
Allen Lew, CEO-Digital Life Group
Bill Chang, CEO-Group Enterprise
Paul OSullivan, CEO-Consumer Group
Mark Chong, Group CTO

GROWTH PLANS/SPECIAL FEATURES:

Singapore Telecommunications Limited (SingTel) is a telecommunication systems/services operator and provider, with operations and investments throughout the world. The firm serves approximately 700 million customers through more than 65 offices located in over 20 countries worldwide. SingTel operates through three business units: consumer, group enterprise and group digital life. The consumer business unit focuses on setting new benchmarks in customer experience in order to provide next-generation communication, infotainment and technology services to consumers and small businesses across Asia Pacific. The group enterprise business unit provides companies and governments with comprehensive and integrated ICT (information and communication technology) solutions that cover mobile, voice and data infrastructure, managed services, cloud computing, IT services and professional consulting. The group digital life business unit drives SingTel's group efforts within the digital space. It focuses on opportunities in digital marketing and data analytics, among other areas. Digital technology solutions encompass customer touch points, payment mechanisms, data analytics infrastructure and more in order to create and capture opportunities that add value to the company's core business strategies. Subsidiaries of SingTel include Optus, offering integrated communications solutions in Australia; NCS Pte. Ltd. offering regional ICT solutions in Asia Pacific and the Middle East; Singtel Digital Media, offering web and mobile services in Singapore; Singtel Innov8, a corporate venture capital fund; Amobee, a global marketing technology company that serves global brands and agencies; and Trustwave, a cybersecurity and managed security services provider. In June 2020, Singtel was awarded the 3.5GHz and the millimeter wave spectrum as part of the 5G license issued by the Infocomm Media Development Authority, paving the way for Singtel's nationwide 5G rollout.

FINANCIAL DATA: *Note: Data for latest year may not have been available at press time.*

In U.S. $	2020	2019	2018	2017	2016	2015
Revenue	12,508,260,000	13,135,400,000	13,256,460,000	12,636,120,000	12,825,010,000	
R&D Expense						
Operating Income	1,467,588,000	1,859,268,000	2,034,314,000	2,083,689,000	2,109,398,000	
Operating Margin %	.12%	.14%	.15%	.16%	.16%	
SGA Expense	2,782,814,000	3,059,334,000	3,431,581,000	3,400,731,000	4,234,373,000	
Net Income	812,545,800	2,339,869,000	4,122,011,000	2,913,173,000	2,926,859,000	
Operating Cash Flow	4,398,682,000	4,058,646,000	4,502,953,000	4,018,646,000	3,514,302,000	
Capital Expenditure	1,804,599,000	1,556,056,000	2,626,370,000	1,904,182,000	1,590,385,000	
EBITDA	3,469,237,000	4,794,822,000	6,676,320,000	5,392,700,000	5,363,589,000	
Return on Assets %	.02%	.06%	.11%	.08%	.09%	
Return on Equity %	.04%	.10%	.19%	.14%	.16%	
Debt to Equity	0.381	0.294	0.29	0.285	0.37	

CONTACT INFORMATION:

Phone: 65-6838-3388   Fax: 65-6732-8428
Toll-Free:
Address: 31 Exeter Rd., 19-00 Comcentre, Singapore, 239732 Singapore

STOCK TICKER/OTHER:

Stock Ticker: SGAPY   Exchange: PINX
Employees: 19,800   Fiscal Year Ends: 03/31
Parent Company:

SALARIES/BONUSES:

Top Exec. Salary: $ Bonus: $
Second Exec. Salary: $ Bonus: $

OTHER THOUGHTS:

Estimated Female Officers or Directors: 5
Hot Spot for Advancement for Women/Minorities: Y

Singtel Optus Pty Limited

www.optus.com.au

NAIC Code: 517110

TYPES OF BUSINESS:

Diversified Telecommunications Services
Mobile Phone Service
Digital Television Service
Local & Long-Distance Phone Service
Business Network Services
Satellite Services
Multimedia Services

BRANDS/DIVISIONS/AFFILIATES:

Singapore Telecommunications Limited

CONTACTS: *Note: Officers with more than one job title may be intentionally listed here more than once.*

Kelly Bayer Rosmarin, CEO
Murray King, CFO
Martin Mercer, Managing Dir.-Strategy & Fixed
David Epstein, VP-Corp. & Regulatory Affairs
Vicki Brady, Managing Dir.-Customer
John Paitaridis, Managing Dir.-Optus Bus.
Gunther Ottendorfer, Managing Dir.-Optus Networks
Austin R. Bryan, VP-Transformation, Consumer Australia
Paul O'Sullivan, Chmn.

GROWTH PLANS/SPECIAL FEATURES:

Singtel Optus Pty. Limited (Optus), a subsidiary of Singapore Telecommunications Limited (Singtel), provides telecommunications services in Australia. Optus' mobile network reaches 98.5% of the Aussie population through its mobile, satellite and broadband networks. The firm's home and mobile network is expanding 5G coverage in select areas, and as the 5G network grows and evolves each day, it will become faster, more responsive and have higher capacity than Optus' 3G and 4G networks. The company's 4G+ coverage reaches all of the country's capital cities as well as more than 700 regional towns. Optus owns and operates its own satellite fleet, which provides satellite-based communications services throughout Australia and Asia. The satellites in orbit are tracked by its ground network of domestic and international Earth stations. Over 1 million Australians utilize Optus for internet services, including digital subscriber line (DSL) connectivity. Optus' regional network invests in and builds the company's regional coverage. In addition, Optus has retail stores throughout Australia, which offer mobile phones, office phones, tablets and other communication devices, as well as related accessories and services. For businesses and enterprises, Optus provides digital transformation services and solutions through its managed cloud strategy, which enables firms to build a simple, secure and cost-effective way for driving business outcomes. The company also provides managed security, security technology, cyber security, digital business solutions, mobility solutions and related consultancy services to businesses, enterprises and all tiers of government entities.

Optus offers employees health insurance, discounted gym memberships, social events, company discounts, flexible compensation options, a public transportation program, career development programs. flexible annual leave and an employee assistance program.

FINANCIAL DATA: *Note: Data for latest year may not have been available at press time.*

In U.S. $	2020	2019	2018	2017	2016	2015
Revenue	4,768,040,000	5,434,520,000	5,478,460,000	5,285,450,000	5,764,390,000	
R&D Expense						
Operating Income						
Operating Margin %						
SGA Expense						
Net Income	1,570,080,000	1,761,130,000	1,898,400,000	1,851,480,000	1,884,220,000	
Operating Cash Flow						
Capital Expenditure						
EBITDA						
Return on Assets %						
Return on Equity %						
Debt to Equity						

CONTACT INFORMATION:

Phone: 61-2-8082-7800   Fax: 61-2-8082-7100
Toll-Free:
Address: 1 Lyonpark Rd., Macquarie Park, NSW 2113 Australia

SALARIES/BONUSES:

Top Exec. Salary: $ Bonus: $
Second Exec. Salary: $ Bonus: $

STOCK TICKER/OTHER:

Stock Ticker: Subsidiary   Exchange:
Employees: 8,400   Fiscal Year Ends: 03/31
Parent Company: Singapore Telecommunications Limited

OTHER THOUGHTS:

Estimated Female Officers or Directors: 1
Hot Spot for Advancement for Women/Minorities:

Sitel Corporation

NAIC Code: 518210

www.sitel.com

TYPES OF BUSINESS:

Communications Consulting-Call Centers
Professional Services
Digital Transformation
Customer Experience
Development Solutions
Data Insights
Digital Experiences

BRANDS/DIVISIONS/AFFILIATES:

EXP+ Empower
EXP+ Engage
EXP+ Explore
EXP+ Evolve

GROWTH PLANS/SPECIAL FEATURES:

Sitel Corporation is an integrated services group. The company partners with clients to effectively harness digital transformation to ensure an innovative, end-to-end solution to managing and enhancing the customer experience. Sitel's solutions consist of four products families: EXP+ Empower, EXP+ Engage, EXP+ Explore and EXP+ Evolve. EXP+ Empower offers learning and development solutions for business employees. EXP+ Engage offers contact center services that are powered by data-driven customer understanding. EXP+ Explore enables users to explore insights from across the business data sources to drive enterprise-wide decision making. EXP+ Evolve offers digital experiences via data-driven and artificial intelligence (AI)-enabled self-service and automation. Industries served by Sitel include retail, travel and hospitality, technology, government, utilities, manufacturing, healthcare, insurance, banking and financial services, communications, media and entertainment.

CONTACTS: *Note: Officers with more than one job title may be intentionally listed here more than once.*

Laurent Uberti, CEO
Olivier Camino, COO
Elisabeth Destailleur, CFO
Martin Wilkinson-Brown, CMO
Jim Flynn, Chief Human Resources Officer
David Slaviero, CTO
David Beckman, Chief Legal Officer
Sean Erickson, Exec. VP-Corp. Dev.
Neal Miller, Chief Tax Officer
Pedro Lozano, Gen. Mgr.-EMEA
Steve Barker, Exec. VP-Global Oper. Support

FINANCIAL DATA: *Note: Data for latest year may not have been available at press time.*

In U.S. $	2020	2019	2018	2017	2016	2015
Revenue	2,100,000,000	1,785,000,000	1,700,000,000	1,615,000,000	1,400,000,000	1,394,000,000
R&D Expense						
Operating Income						
Operating Margin %						
SGA Expense						
Net Income						
Operating Cash Flow						
Capital Expenditure						
EBITDA						
Return on Assets %						
Return on Equity %						
Debt to Equity						

CONTACT INFORMATION:

Phone: 615-301-7100   Fax: 615-301-7150
Toll-Free: 866-957-4835
Address: 3102 W. End Ave., 2 American Ctr., Ste. 900, Nashville, TN 37203 United States

STOCK TICKER/OTHER:

Stock Ticker: Private   Exchange:
Employees: 100,000   Fiscal Year Ends: 12/31
Parent Company:

SALARIES/BONUSES:

Top Exec. Salary: $ Bonus: $
Second Exec. Salary: $ Bonus: $

OTHER THOUGHTS:

Estimated Female Officers or Directors: 1
Hot Spot for Advancement for Women/Minorities:

SK Broadband Co Ltd

www.skbroadband.com/eng/main.do

NAIC Code: 517110

TYPES OF BUSINESS:

Internet Service Provider
Local, Long Distance & International Phone Service
Leased-Line Business Connectivity
VoIP Service
Internet Data Centers

BRANDS/DIVISIONS/AFFILIATES:

SK Telecom Co Ltd

CONTACTS:
Note: Officers with more than one job title may be intentionally listed here more than once.

Jin-Hwan Choi, CEO

GROWTH PLANS/SPECIAL FEATURES:

SK Broadband Co., Ltd. is a Korean provider of telecommunications, high-speed broadband internet, voice, internet data center (IDC) and leased line services. The firm's offerings can be divided into two categories: residential and business services. In addition to basic telephone services, its residential services include fiber-to-the-home (FTTH) internet access, voice over internet protocol (VoIP) service and video-on-demand, cable TV and internet protocol television (IPTV). The company's services for business customers include internet phone, digital fiber-optic, intelligent network, internet leased lines, domestic leased line, virtual private network (VPN), internet data center and content delivery network (CDN), information and communication technology (ICT) and fixed-mobile convergence, data and other services for buildings. A variety of enterprise telephone services are also offered under this category, including general phone services; direct inbound and outbound calling; international calls; and Primary Rate Interface, which automatically dials and receives calls without the need of an operator. IDC services are geared toward content providers and small to medium-sized businesses. It provides direct connections to IXs and ISPs. Additionally, SK Broadband provides managed service solutions to its enterprise customers that provide for 24-hour remote monitoring of data and voice communications infrastructure, LAN/WAN lines and traffic conditions; and carries out preventive examinations and onsite support. SK Broadband is wholly-owned by SK Telecom Co. Ltd.

FINANCIAL DATA:
Note: Data for latest year may not have been available at press time.

In U.S. $	2020	2019	2018	2017	2016	2015
Revenue	3,411,250,000	2,872,370,280	2,730,390,000	2,500,000,000	2,439,430,000	2,323,010,000
R&D Expense						
Operating Income						
Operating Margin %						
SGA Expense						
Net Income	138,446,000	30,078,038	120,312,150	114,583,000	17,842,900	9,212,620
Operating Cash Flow						
Capital Expenditure						
EBITDA						
Return on Assets %						
Return on Equity %						
Debt to Equity						

CONTACT INFORMATION:

Phone: 82-2-626-64534   Fax: 82-2-626-64609
Toll-Free:
Address: SK Namsan Bldg., 24, Toegye-ro, Jung-gu, Seoul, 100-711 South Korea

STOCK TICKER/OTHER:

Stock Ticker: Subsidiary
Employees: 1,583
Parent Company: SK Telecom Co Ltd

Exchange:
Fiscal Year Ends: 12/31

SALARIES/BONUSES:

Top Exec. Salary: $ Bonus: $
Second Exec. Salary: $ Bonus: $

OTHER THOUGHTS:

Estimated Female Officers or Directors:
Hot Spot for Advancement for Women/Minorities:

SK Telecom Co Ltd

www.sktelecom.com

NAIC Code: 517210

TYPES OF BUSINESS:

Wireless Telecommunications Services
Multimedia Broadcasting
Online Shopping
Internet of Things
Telecommunications

BRANDS/DIVISIONS/AFFILIATES:

Eleven Street
SK Hynix Inc
KEB HanaCard Co Ltd
Content Wavve

CONTACTS: *Note: Officers with more than one job title may be intentionally listed here more than once.*

Jung-Ho Park, CEO
Young Sang Ryu, Dir.-Mobile Network Oper.
Dong Seob Jee, Head-Corp. Vision Dept.
Young Tae Kim, Exec. Dir.
Daesik Cho, Chmn.

GROWTH PLANS/SPECIAL FEATURES:

SK Telecom Co., Ltd. is one of Korea's leading wireless telecommunications service provider. The firm continuously engages in the commercial development and implementation of state-of-the-art wireless and fixed-line technologies and services, as well as the development of next-generation businesses such as Internet of Things (IoT) and artificial intelligence (AI) solutions, media, ecommerce, security and other products. SK Telecom commercialized its fifth generation (5G) network, and provides 5G smartphone subscriptions and standalone services. The company's operations are divided into four segments: cellular services, which include wireless voice and data transmission services, sales of wireless devices, IoT solutions and platform services; fixed-line telecommunication services, including fixed-line telephone services, broadband internet services, advanced media platform services (such as internet protocol TV and mobile over-the-top/OTT services) and business communications services; eCommerce services, which include SK Telecom's open marketplace platform, Eleven Street/11st, and related ancillary services; and other businesses; including SK Telecom's portal service, marketing platform business, physical and information security business and certain other miscellaneous businesses. Sister companies include: minority-owned SK Hynix, Inc., which operates SK Telecom's hardware division, manufacturing memory devices and sensors (DRAM, NAND, CIS), modems and system-on-chip (SoC) devices; minority-owned KEB HanaCard Co., Ltd., a credit card services provider offering discounts on some of SK Telecom's wireless network services; and minority-owned Content Wavve, which operates a mobile OTT service.

FINANCIAL DATA: *Note: Data for latest year may not have been available at press time.*

In U.S. $	2020	2019	2018	2017	2016	2015
Revenue	16,821,250,000	16,025,600,000	15,240,070,000	15,823,570,000	15,436,830,000	15,477,400,000
R&D Expense	376,121,100	353,435,200	350,136,800	357,001,900	311,401,600	285,212,400
Operating Income	1,260,267,000	1,054,907,000	1,125,452,000	1,343,582,000	1,430,272,000	1,568,551,000
Operating Margin %		.06%	.07%	.08%	.09%	.10%
SGA Expense	8,778,923,000	8,291,406,000	7,961,691,000	8,120,711,000	7,842,629,000	7,726,875,000
Net Income	1,358,687,000	803,738,200	2,825,017,000	2,348,090,000	1,513,685,000	1,371,559,000
Operating Cash Flow	5,258,150,000	3,600,114,000	3,913,061,000	3,482,465,000	3,832,306,000	3,412,297,000
Capital Expenditure	3,330,693,000	3,176,356,000	2,976,508,000	2,584,514,000	2,823,170,000	2,354,320,000
EBITDA	5,822,032,000	4,964,177,000	6,834,859,000	6,276,920,000	4,926,935,000	4,810,753,000
Return on Assets %		.02%	.08%	.08%	.06%	.05%
Return on Equity %		.04%	.15%	.15%	.11%	.10%
Debt to Equity		0.42	0.382	0.326	0.406	0.43

CONTACT INFORMATION:

Phone: 82-2-6100-2114　　　Fax: 82-2-6110-7830
Toll-Free:
Address: SK T-Tower, 65, Eulji-ro, Jung-gu, Seoul, 100-999 South Korea

STOCK TICKER/OTHER:

Stock Ticker: SKM　　　　　　　　Exchange: NYS
Employees: 41,097　　　　　　　　Fiscal Year Ends: 12/31
Parent Company:

SALARIES/BONUSES:

Top Exec. Salary: $　　　　　Bonus: $
Second Exec. Salary: $　　　　Bonus: $

OTHER THOUGHTS:

Estimated Female Officers or Directors:
Hot Spot for Advancement for Women/Minorities:

Skype Technologies Sarl

www.skype.com

NAIC Code: 511210C

TYPES OF BUSINESS:

Computer Software: Telecom, Communications & VOIP
Voice Communication Services
Video Call Services
Software
Mobile Applications
Group Communication Solutions

BRANDS/DIVISIONS/AFFILIATES:

Microsoft Corporation

CONTACTS: Note: Officers with more than one job title may be intentionally listed here more than once.

Satya Nadella, CEO-Microsoft

GROWTH PLANS/SPECIAL FEATURES:

Skype Technologies Sarl, a subsidiary of Microsoft Corporation, offers software capabilities that enable users to make free voice and video calls over the internet. The firm's proprietary software and mobile applications help people stay connected not only through telephone calls, but also via instant messaging and photo- and file-sharing in real-time. Skype Technologies' additional capabilities include purchasing tickets, surfing the internet for recipes and finding and dropping information into conversations. Skype in the Classroom offers live educational experiences for teachers and their students from over 235 countries, including virtual field trips, talks with guest speakers, collaborative lessons and projects with other classrooms around the world. For businesses and friends who are not online, calling their mobile and landline numbers through Skype-to-Phone is offered at affordable rates. Calls can be made by phone, desktop, tablet, Xbox, Amazon Alexa devices and even connected wearables. Skype numbers are available for purchase in several countries and regions, and can be used across devices. Those with Skype numbers pay a flat fee for unlimited incoming calls.

FINANCIAL DATA: Note: Data for latest year may not have been available at press time.

In U.S. $	2020	2019	2018	2017	2016	2015
Revenue						
R&D Expense						
Operating Income						
Operating Margin %						
SGA Expense						
Net Income						
Operating Cash Flow						
Capital Expenditure						
EBITDA						
Return on Assets %						
Return on Equity %						
Debt to Equity						

CONTACT INFORMATION:

Phone: 352-26-20-15-82   Fax: 352-26-27-05-88
Toll-Free:
Address: 23-29 Rives de Clausen, Luxembourg, L-2165 Luxembourg

STOCK TICKER/OTHER:

Stock Ticker: Subsidiary   Exchange:
Employees: 1,400   Fiscal Year Ends: 12/31
Parent Company: Microsoft Corporation

SALARIES/BONUSES:

Top Exec. Salary: $ Bonus: $
Second Exec. Salary: $ Bonus: $

OTHER THOUGHTS:

Estimated Female Officers or Directors: 1
Hot Spot for Advancement for Women/Minorities: Y

Sales, profits and employees may be estimates. Financial information, benefits and other data can change quickly and may vary from those stated here.

Slack Technologies Inc

slack.com

NAIC Code: 511210C

TYPES OF BUSINESS:

Computer Software, Telecom, Communications & VOIP

BRANDS/DIVISIONS/AFFILIATES:

Slack
Slack Enterprise Grid

CONTACTS: *Note: Officers with more than one job title may be intentionally listed here more than once.*

Stewart Butterfield, CEO
Allen Shim, CFO
Brandon Zell, Chief Accounting Officer
Cal Henderson, Chief Technology Officer
David Schellhase, General Counsel
Tamar Yehoshua, Other Executive Officer
Robert Frati, Senior VP, Divisional

GROWTH PLANS/SPECIAL FEATURES:

Slack Technologies, Inc. is a computer software firm that operates Slack, a platform that enables team communications through a single hub. The platform provides real-time messaging, archiving and searching services primarily for small-to-medium-sized companies or teams. Slack's solutions are divided into two groups: channels and direct messages. Channels provides a way to organize team conversations in open channels and are displayed per subject categories that relate to the project (such as feedback, product, customer service, app, issues, etc.). Direct messages reach colleagues directly and are completely private and secure. Private group features are available for sensitive information, with the ability to invite select team members that no one else can see or join. The direct messages are also categorized by subject for team members to easily see and access. Prices range from free introductory access to $12.50 per month. Free access includes search and browse of 10,000 most recent messages, 10 service integrations, free native apps for iOS/Android/Mac&Windows Desktop and 1:1 voice and video calls, 5GB file storage and two-factor identification. Standard access includes everything in Free, as well as searchable archive with unlimited messages, unlimited service integrations, custom retention policies, guest access, Google Authentication/Apps for Domains sign-on, configurable email ingestion and group voice/video calls, screen sharing, 10GB file storage and custom profiles. Plus access includes everything in Standard, as well as SAML-based single sign-on, compliance exports of all message history, support for external message and archival solutions, 99.99% guaranteed uptime SLA, user provisioning and deprovisioning, real-time active directory sync with OneLogic, Okta and Ping, and 20GB file storage. For enterprise collaboration, Slack offers a communication hub with channels for communication, file-sharing and decision-making purposes, as well as the Slack Enterprise Grid for managing large, complex teams. In December 2020, Slack Technologies agreed to be acquired by salesforce.com inc.

FINANCIAL DATA: *Note: Data for latest year may not have been available at press time.*

In U.S. $	2020	2019	2018	2017	2016	2015
Revenue	630,422,000	400,552,000	220,544,000	105,153,000		
R&D Expense	457,364,000	157,538,000	141,350,000	96,678,000		
Operating Income	-588,278,000	-154,208,000	-143,851,000	-148,503,000		
Operating Margin %	-.93%	-.38%	-.65%	-1.41%		
SGA Expense	664,145,000	345,921,000	196,681,000	141,461,000		
Net Income	-571,058,000	-140,683,000	-140,085,000	-146,864,000		
Operating Cash Flow	-12,389,000	-41,059,000	-35,617,000	-89,806,000		
Capital Expenditure	52,126,000	59,402,000	22,094,000	24,816,000		
EBITDA	-561,151,000	-137,392,000	-129,531,000	-141,716,000		
Return on Assets %	-.43%	-.15%	-.26%			
Return on Equity %	-7.70%					
Debt to Equity	0.277					

CONTACT INFORMATION:

Phone: 415-630-7943   Fax:
Toll-Free:
Address: 500 Howard St., San Francisco, CA 94105 United States

STOCK TICKER/OTHER:

Stock Ticker: WORK   Exchange: NYS
Employees: 2,545   Fiscal Year Ends: 01/31
Parent Company:

SALARIES/BONUSES:

Top Exec. Salary: $ Bonus: $
Second Exec. Salary: $ Bonus: $

OTHER THOUGHTS:

Estimated Female Officers or Directors:
Hot Spot for Advancement for Women/Minorities:

SmarTone Telecommunications Holdings Limited

www.smartoneholdings.com

NAIC Code: 517210

TYPES OF BUSINESS:

Mobile Phone Service
Wireless Data Services
Internet Service
Messaging Services

BRANDS/DIVISIONS/AFFILIATES:

Sun Hung Kai Properties Limited
SmarTone Solutions
Birdie
Sahabat Setia SmarTone
Barkadahan sa SmarTone

CONTACTS: *Note: Officers with more than one job title may be intentionally listed here more than once.*

Josephine Lam, Dir.-Mktg. & Sales
Stephen Chau, CTO
Angus Yiu, Sr. Mgr.-Corp. Planning
Chris Lau, Dir.-Future Svcs.
Patrick Chan, Exec. Dir.
Ping-luen Kwok, Chmn.

GROWTH PLANS/SPECIAL FEATURES:

SmarTone Telecommunications Holdings Limited is a leading telecommunications company with operating subsidiaries in Hong Kong and Macau. The firm provides voice, multimedia and mobile broadband services, as well as fixed fiber broadband services for the consumer and corporate markets. Network development by SmarTone encompass 2G (launched), 3G (launched), 4G (launched) and 5G (launched in 2020). SmarTone has more than 30 stores in Hong Kong. The company provides an omnichannel strategy, offering customers a seamless online-to-offline experience. SmarTone Solutions offers a range of information and communication technology (ICT) space to businesses and public sector organizations in Hong Kong and Macau, helping them to apply conventional and emerging technologies in areas such as digital transformation, customer engagement, cybersecurity and more. The firm's Birdie brand is a digital only mobile operator in Hong Kong. Targeting millennials, Birdie offers products accessible through its mobile app, doing away with contracts and administration fees and emphasizing community engagement via rewards program Birdie Friday and game activities such as Birdie Farm. Sahabat Setia SmarTone and Barkadahan sa SmarTone provide network services and customer care to customers in the Philippines and Indonesia. SmarTone's online store, shop.smartone.com, offers internationally-branded smartphones, smart watches, tablets and accessories, as well as service plans. SmarTone Telecommunications Holdings is a publicly-traded subsidiary of Sun Hung Kai Properties Limited, a real estate developer and investment company based in Hong Kong.

FINANCIAL DATA: *Note: Data for latest year may not have been available at press time.*

In U.S. $	2020	2019	2018	2017	2016	2015
Revenue	901,407,000	1,081,500,000	1,272,484,352	1,110,300,288	2,338,413,824	2,377,043,200
R&D Expense						
Operating Income						
Operating Margin %						
SGA Expense						
Net Income	43,818,100	78,970,800	78,378,904	85,622,456	101,552,952	119,162,640
Operating Cash Flow						
Capital Expenditure						
EBITDA						
Return on Assets %						
Return on Equity %						
Debt to Equity						

CONTACT INFORMATION:

Phone: 852-3128-2828   Fax: 852-2168-3021
Toll-Free:
Address: Fl. 31, Millennium City 2, 378 Kwun Tong Rd., Kowloon, Hong Kong Hong Kong

STOCK TICKER/OTHER:

Stock Ticker: 315   Exchange: Hong Kong
Employees: 1,898   Fiscal Year Ends: 06/30
Parent Company: Sun Hung Kai Properties Limited

SALARIES/BONUSES:

Top Exec. Salary: $ Bonus: $
Second Exec. Salary: $ Bonus: $

OTHER THOUGHTS:

Estimated Female Officers or Directors: 2
Hot Spot for Advancement for Women/Minorities:

SMTC Corporation

NAIC Code: 334418

TYPES OF BUSINESS:

Printed Circuit Assembly (Electronic Assembly) Manufacturing
Electronics Manufacturing Services

BRANDS/DIVISIONS/AFFILIATES:

HIG Capital LLC

CONTACTS: *Note: Officers with more than one job title may be intentionally listed here more than once.*

Edward Smith, CEO
Steven M. Waszak, CFO

GROWTH PLANS/SPECIAL FEATURES:

SMTC Corporation, based in Toronto, provides end-to-end electronics manufacturing services. The company's services include product design, sustained engineering services, printed circuit board assembly, production, enclosure fabrication, cable assembly, precision metal fabrication, systems integration, comprehensive testing services, configuration to order, build to order and direct order fulfillment. SMTC has more than 50 manufacturing and assembly lines at strategically-located facilities in the U.S., Canada and Mexico. The firm's services extend over the entire electronic product life cycle, from new product development and new production introduction through to growth, maturity and end-of-life phases. SMTC offers fully-integrated contract manufacturing services to global original equipment manufacturers (OEMs), technology companies, defense prime contractors, the U.S. Department of Defense and various U.S. government agencies. Focus market sectors include defense, aerospace, industrial, power, clean technology, medical, safety, retail, payment systems, semiconductors, telecommunications, networking, communications, test and measurement. In April 2021, SMTC Corporation was taken private by H.I.G. Capital LLC, a global alternative investment firm.

FINANCIAL DATA: *Note: Data for latest year may not have been available at press time.*

In U.S. $	2020	2019	2018	2017	2016	2015
Revenue	417,212,329	372,511,008	216,131,008	139,231,008	167,868,000	220,616,000
R&D Expense						
Operating Income						
Operating Margin %						
SGA Expense						
Net Income		-5,995,000	-448,000	-7,845,000	-232,000	-4,000
Operating Cash Flow						
Capital Expenditure						
EBITDA						
Return on Assets %						
Return on Equity %						
Debt to Equity						

CONTACT INFORMATION:

Phone: 905 479-1810   Fax:
Toll-Free:
Address: 7050 Woodbine Ave., Markham, ON L3R 4G8 Canada

STOCK TICKER/OTHER:

Stock Ticker: Private   Exchange:
Employees: 2,805   Fiscal Year Ends: 12/31
Parent Company: HIG Capital LLC

SALARIES/BONUSES:

Top Exec. Salary: $ Bonus: $
Second Exec. Salary: $ Bonus: $

OTHER THOUGHTS:

Estimated Female Officers or Directors: 1
Hot Spot for Advancement for Women/Minorities: Y

Socket Mobile Inc

www.socketmobile.com

NAIC Code: 334220

TYPES OF BUSINESS:
Wireless Handheld Computers
Data Collection Devices
Barcode Scanners
RFID Devices
Bluetooth Devices

BRANDS/DIVISIONS/AFFILIATES:
DuraScan
SocketScan
DuraCase
S700
800 Series
D600
S550

CONTACTS: Note: Officers with more than one job title may be intentionally listed here more than once.
Kevin Mills, CEO
Lynn Zhao, CFO
Charlie Bass, Chairman of the Board
Leonard Ott, Chief Technology Officer
Lee Baillif, Vice President, Divisional
James Lopez, Vice President, Divisional

GROWTH PLANS/SPECIAL FEATURES:
Socket Mobile, Inc. is a producer of data collection products for the business market. The company's products are incorporated into mobile applications used in point of sale (POS), enterprise mobility (field workers), asset tracking, manufacturing process and quality control, transportation and logistics (goods tracking and movement), event management (ticketing, entry, access, control and identification), medical and education. Socket Mobile's primary products are cordless data capture devices incorporating barcode scanning and radio frequency identification (RFID)/near field communication (NFC) technologies that connect over Bluetooth. All products work with applications running on smartphones, mobile computers and tablets using operating systems from Apple (iOS), Google (Android) and Microsoft (Windows). Socket Mobile offers an easy-to-use software developer kit to application developers to enable them to provide their users with Socket Mobile's advanced barcode scanning features. The DuraScan linear barcode scanner, laser barcode scanner and universal barcode scanner are designed to be durable and withstand tougher environments. Standard companion cordless barcode scanners include the SocketScan 700 Series, offering 1D linear imaging; and the S700-S760 models offering 2D barcode scanning. Attachable cordless barcode scanners include the SocketScan 800 Series, which are attachable to smartphones, tablets and other mobile devices with a clip of DuraCase, thus creating a one-handed solution. Contactless RFID/NFC reader writers products include the: D600 model, which can read and write many different types of electronic SmartTags or transfer data with NFC; and the SocketScan S550 contactless membership card reader/writer for developers and retail merchants.

Socket Mobile offers its employees health, dental, vision, group life and long-term disability coverage; and 401(k) and stock options.

FINANCIAL DATA: Note: Data for latest year may not have been available at press time.

In U.S. $	2020	2019	2018	2017	2016	2015
Revenue	15,700,040	19,253,100	16,454,430	21,285,800	20,787,590	18,400,180
R&D Expense	3,140,104	3,893,563	3,640,296	3,473,610	2,889,168	2,323,005
Operating Income	76,429	606,370	-585,988	2,417,715	2,563,016	2,128,837
Operating Margin %		.03%	-.04%	.11%	.12%	.12%
SGA Expense	5,118,368	5,600,710	5,402,100	5,498,684	4,982,034	4,482,897
Net Income	-3,278,601	286,586	-571,141	-1,430,731	12,147,090	1,817,672
Operating Cash Flow	804,445	873,534	750,145	2,376,303	879,816	1,352,976
Capital Expenditure	536,481	602,954	423,700	620,575	304,470	391,375
EBITDA	-2,634,971	1,069,300	-153,946	2,731,368	2,842,408	2,326,523
Return on Assets %		.02%	-.03%	-.07%	.80%	.20%
Return on Equity %		.02%	-.04%	-.09%	1.24%	.83%
Debt to Equity		0.054	0.043	0.016	0.02	0.202

CONTACT INFORMATION:
Phone: 510 933-3000 Fax: 510 933-3030
Toll-Free:
Address: 39700 Eureka Dr., Newark, CA 94560 United States

STOCK TICKER/OTHER:
Stock Ticker: SCKT Exchange: NAS
Employees: 48 Fiscal Year Ends: 12/31
Parent Company:

SALARIES/BONUSES:
Top Exec. Salary: $ Bonus: $
Second Exec. Salary: $ Bonus: $

OTHER THOUGHTS:
Estimated Female Officers or Directors:
Hot Spot for Advancement for Women/Minorities:

SoftBank Group Corp

www.softbank.co.jp

NAIC Code: 517110

TYPES OF BUSINESS:

Telecommunications Services
Investment
Managed Funds
Technology
Artificial Intelligence
Robotics
Smartphone Payment
Electricity

BRANDS/DIVISIONS/AFFILIATES:

SoftBank Group Capital Limited
SB Northstar LP
SoftBank Investment Advisers
SoftBank Vision Fund LP
Z Holdings
Arm Limited
Fortress Investment Group LLC
PayPay Corporation

CONTACTS: *Note: Officers with more than one job title may be intentionally listed here more than once.*

Masayoshi Shon, CEO
Marcelo Claure, COO
Ken Miyauchi, COO-SOFTBANK MOBILE Corp.
Ronald D. Fisher, Pres., SOFTBANK Holdings, Inc.
Masayoshi Son, Chmn.

GROWTH PLANS/SPECIAL FEATURES:

SoftBank Group Corp. is a Japanese holding company that operates in the information industry globally. The company has four primary business segments: investment, managed funds, SoftBank and Arm. The investment business is led by SoftBank Group, which conducts investment activities either directly or through subsidiaries. Core companies within this division include Softbank Group, SoftBank Group Capital Limited, SoftBank Group Japan Corporation and SB Northstar LP. The managed funds segment seeks to accelerate the artificial intelligence (AI) platform through investments in tech-enabled growth companies, with current funds including SoftBank Vision Fund I & 2 (SVF1, SVF2) and other small business investment advisor (SBIA)-managed funds. Core companies within this division include SoftBank Investment Advisers, SoftBank Vision Fund LP and SoftBank Vision Fund II-2 LP. The SoftBank segment offers products and services that leverage technology, including AI, Internet of Things (IoT) and robotics, while also expanding into a wide range of other domains domestically and overseas. Core companies within this division include SoftBank and Z Holdings. The Arm segment consists of technologies of processor designer Arm Limited, which are used in the main chips of nearly all smartphones and tablets. In the IoT sector, Arm is a leader in semiconductor technologies and provides high security and energy efficiency for SoftBank Group's own strategies. Other businesses within the SoftBank Group include: Fortress Investment Group LLC, a global investment manager; Fukuoka SoftBank HAWKS Corp., a professional baseball team in Japan; PayPay Corporation, a smartphone payment service using barcodes and QR codes; SoftBank Robotics Group Corp., engaged in the research and development of robot products; and SB Energy Corp., which generates, supplies and sells electricity and energy produced from renewable sources. In December 2020, SoftBank Group agreed to sell a controlling stake in Boston Dynamics to Hyundai Motor Group, with SoftBank retaining an approximate 20% stake.

FINANCIAL DATA: *Note: Data for latest year may not have been available at press time.*

In U.S. $	2020	2019	2018	2017	2016	2015
Revenue	56,488,480,000	87,697,270,000	83,647,050,000	81,292,910,000	83,599,410,000	79,185,170,000
R&D Expense						
Operating Income	-12,571,690,000	19,888,670,000	11,904,220,000	9,204,352,000	8,585,454,000	8,975,031,000
Operating Margin %	-.22%	.23%	.14%	.11%	.10%	.11%
SGA Expense	18,486,730,000	25,450,710,000	23,313,490,000	20,798,140,000	22,353,920,000	21,303,880,000
Net Income	-8,782,078,000	12,888,490,000	9,488,982,000	13,026,480,000	4,330,615,000	6,104,144,000
Operating Cash Flow	10,209,590,000	10,702,640,000	9,942,399,000	13,706,160,000	8,586,723,000	10,550,210,000
Capital Expenditure	11,256,890,000	12,466,130,000	9,725,143,000	8,434,348,000	12,429,650,000	12,766,630,000
EBITDA	21,808,810,000	36,707,900,000	22,710,450,000	24,225,350,000	26,009,310,000	25,262,630,000
Return on Assets %	-.03%	.04%	.04%	.06%	.02%	.04%
Return on Equity %	-.14%	.22%	.24%	.46%	.17%	.28%
Debt to Equity	1.763	1.601	2.667	3.392	3.549	3.439

CONTACT INFORMATION:

Phone: 81-3-6889-2000   Fax:
Toll-Free:
Address: 1-9-1 Higashi Shimbashi, Minato-ku, Tokyo, 105-7303 Japan

STOCK TICKER/OTHER:

Stock Ticker: SFTBF   Exchange: PINX
Employees: 92,069   Fiscal Year Ends: 03/31
Parent Company:

SALARIES/BONUSES:

Top Exec. Salary: $ Bonus: $
Second Exec. Salary: $ Bonus: $

OTHER THOUGHTS:

Estimated Female Officers or Directors:
Hot Spot for Advancement for Women/Minorities:

Sonim Technologies Inc

www.sonimtech.com

NAIC Code: 334220

TYPES OF BUSINESS:

Radio and Television Broadcasting and Wireless Communications
Equipment Manufacturing
Rugged Mobile Devices

BRANDS/DIVISIONS/AFFILIATES:

GROWTH PLANS/SPECIAL FEATURES:

Sonim Technologies, Inc. is a leading U.S. provider of ultra-rugged mobile phones and accessories specifically designed for task workers who are physically engaged in their work environments. The company's phones and accessories are designed to connect workers with voice, data and workflow applications in two end markets: industrial enterprise and public sector. The firm's Android-based devices consolidate and integrate multiple functions into a single ruggedized unit running on commercial wireless networks with improved productivity and safety of task workers. Sonim's products fall into three main categories: ultra-rugged mobile phones based on the Android platform that are capable of attaching to both public and private wireless networks; industrial-grade accessories; and cloud-based software and application services. Customers include construction, energy and utility, hospitality, logistics, manufacturing, public sector and transportation entities that primarily purchase Sonim phones and accessories through their wireless carriers. Sonim sells its products to major wireless carriers such as AT&T, Sprint and Verizon in the U.S. and Bell, Rogers and Telus Mobility in Canada.

CONTACTS:
Note: Officers with more than one job title may be intentionally listed here more than once.

Robert Plaschke, CEO
Peter Liu, Exec. VP-Oper.
Charles Becher, Chief Sales & Mktg. Officer
Joe Hooks, Chief People Officer

FINANCIAL DATA:
Note: Data for latest year may not have been available at press time.

In U.S. $	2020	2019	2018	2017	2016	2015
Revenue	63,992,000	116,251,000	135,665,000	59,031,000		
R&D Expense	16,218,000	26,064,000	23,247,000	13,008,000		
Operating Income	-27,714,000	-21,645,000	5,394,000	-6,770,000		
Operating Margin %		-.19%	.04%	-.11%		
SGA Expense	26,707,000	30,090,000	19,448,000	14,073,000		
Net Income	-29,932,000	-25,834,000	1,277,000	-8,519,000		
Operating Cash Flow	-10,560,000	-33,523,000	3,861,000	-8,906,000		
Capital Expenditure	11,000	1,356,000	2,545,000	1,174,000		
EBITDA	-26,966,000	-19,399,000	5,709,000	-6,249,000		
Return on Assets %		-.42%	-.18%	-.51%		
Return on Equity %		-1.69%				
Debt to Equity		0.014	2.575			

CONTACT INFORMATION:

Phone: 650-378-8100   Fax:
Toll-Free:
Address: 6836 Bee Cave Rd., Bldg. 1, Ste. 279, Austin, TX 78746 United States

STOCK TICKER/OTHER:

Stock Ticker: SONM
Employees: 317
Parent Company:

Exchange: NAS
Fiscal Year Ends: 12/31

SALARIES/BONUSES:

Top Exec. Salary: $ Bonus: $
Second Exec. Salary: $ Bonus: $

OTHER THOUGHTS:

Estimated Female Officers or Directors:
Hot Spot for Advancement for Women/Minorities:

Sony Mobile Communications AB

www.sonymobile.com

NAIC Code: 334220

TYPES OF BUSINESS:

Smartphones
Mobile Phone Accessories
PC Cards
Machine-to-Machine Communications Systems
Communications Products

BRANDS/DIVISIONS/AFFILIATES:

Sony Corporation
Xperia

CONTACTS: *Note: Officers with more than one job title may be intentionally listed here more than once.*

Mitsuya Kishida, CEO
Bob Ishida, Deputy CEO

GROWTH PLANS/SPECIAL FEATURES:

Sony Mobile Communications AB, a wholly-owned subsidiary of Sony Corporation, manufactures audio, video, imaging, game, communications, key device and information technology (IT) products for the consumer and professional markets. Through its Xperia smartphone and smart products portfolio, Sony Mobile Communications delivers technology, premium content and services, along with easy connectivity to Sony's networked entertainment solutions and devices. Sony smart products include wireless listening devices worn on the ear, touchscreen projectors, and an ear-based personal assistant that responds to voice commands. Accessories offered by Sony Mobile Communications include phone covers, stereo headsets, open-ear Bluetooth headsets, cover touch products for smart devices, USB cables, device stands, chargers and charging docks, among other items. Specifically for businesses, Sony Mobile Communications offers Internet of Things (IoT) solutions that support digital transformation, connecting people, things and spaces. These IoT solutions span industry and production, logistics and transportation, and health and wellness. In April 2020, Sony Corporation announced that it will establish an intermediate holding company, Sony Electronics Corporation, that ill incorporate the three businesses that comprise its Electronics Products & Solutions segment (Imaging Products & Solutions, Home Entertainment & Sound, and Mobile Communications).

FINANCIAL DATA: *Note: Data for latest year may not have been available at press time.*

In U.S. $	2020	2019	2018	2017	2016	2015
Revenue	3,358,360,000	4,468,310,000	6,719,170,000	6,764,010,000	9,974,120,000	11,786,700,000
R&D Expense						
Operating Income						
Operating Margin %						
SGA Expense						
Net Income	-256,284,000	-247,096,900	-260,102,000	91,338,500	-546,168,000	-1,818,510,000
Operating Cash Flow						
Capital Expenditure						
EBITDA						
Return on Assets %						
Return on Equity %						
Debt to Equity						

CONTACT INFORMATION:

Phone: 46010-8000000   Fax:
Toll-Free:
Address: Mobilvagen 4, Lund, 221 88 Sweden

SALARIES/BONUSES:

Top Exec. Salary: $ Bonus: $
Second Exec. Salary: $ Bonus: $

STOCK TICKER/OTHER:

Stock Ticker: Subsidiary   Exchange:
Employees: 6,570   Fiscal Year Ends: 03/31
Parent Company: Sony Corporation

OTHER THOUGHTS:

Estimated Female Officers or Directors: 1
Hot Spot for Advancement for Women/Minorities:

Sopra Steria Group SA

NAIC Code: 541512

www.soprasteria.com/en

TYPES OF BUSINESS:
IT Consulting
Business Strategy Consulting
Business Process Outsourcing

BRANDS/DIVISIONS/AFFILIATES:

CONTACTS: Note: Officers with more than one job title may be intentionally listed here more than once.
Vincent Paris, CEO
Christian Levi, Head-Sopra Consulting
Pierre Pasquier, Chmn.

GROWTH PLANS/SPECIAL FEATURES:
Sopra Steria Group SA was founded in 1968, and provides consulting and business process outsourcing services related to information technology (IT), systems integration and overall business strategy and management. The firm divides its business into seven categories: consulting, technology services, systems integration, cybersecurity, software, business process services and infrastructure management. Consulting services offer new and creative approaches, collaborative ways of working and tools to speed a company's digital transformation process. Technology services include artificial intelligence (AI), blockchain, cloud, data, digital interactions, emerging technologies, Internet of Things (IoT) and X-reality. Systems integration addresses the entire application life cycle from systems integration to application management services. Cybersecurity and digital trust solutions address the challenges of threat management, risk assessment and compliance. Software services are specialized for businesses, and are available to clients through banking, finance, human resource and property management application solutions. Business process services (BPS) designs products for outsourcing finance, accounting, human resources and purchasing functions. Infrastructure management (IM) supports information technology infrastructure transformation through technologies integration and services operations around cloud, data centers and end-user environments. The company provides its solutions and services to the aerospace, insurance, social, banking, defense, homeland security, public sector, healthcare, telecommunications, media, entertainment, transport, retail, energy utilities markets among others. Based in Paris, France, Sopra has international offices in 25 countries worldwide. In June 2021, Sopra Steria agreed to acquire Labs, a Norway-based consultancy specializing in digital user experience.

FINANCIAL DATA: Note: Data for latest year may not have been available at press time.

In U.S. $	2020	2019	2018	2017	2016	2015
Revenue	5,235,880,000	4,965,460,000	4,689,550,000	4,551,880,000	4,087,137,824	3,155,268,901
R&D Expense						
Operating Income						
Operating Margin %						
SGA Expense						
Net Income	131,176,000	179,514,000	143,088,000	205,314,000	164,145,000	97,891,600
Operating Cash Flow						
Capital Expenditure						
EBITDA						
Return on Assets %						
Return on Equity %						
Debt to Equity						

CONTACT INFORMATION:
Phone: 33-1-10-67-29-29   Fax: 33-1-40-67-29-30
Toll-Free:
Address: 6 avenue Kleber, Paris, 75016 France

STOCK TICKER/OTHER:
Stock Ticker: SOP
Employees: 46,000
Parent Company:

Exchange: Paris
Fiscal Year Ends: 12/31

SALARIES/BONUSES:
Top Exec. Salary: $ Bonus: $
Second Exec. Salary: $ Bonus: $

OTHER THOUGHTS:
Estimated Female Officers or Directors: 1
Hot Spot for Advancement for Women/Minorities:

Spark New Zealand Limited

www.sparknz.co.nz

NAIC Code: 517110

TYPES OF BUSINESS:

Telecommunications Service
Mobile Phones
Broadband
Landline
Ecommerce
Virtual Store

BRANDS/DIVISIONS/AFFILIATES:

SparkLab.co.nz

CONTACTS: Note: Officers with more than one job title may be intentionally listed here more than once.

Jolie Hodson, CEO
Tessa Tierney, Dir.-Product
Stefan Knight, Dir.-Finance
Matt Bain, Dir.-Mktg.
Heather Polglase, Dir.-Human Resources
Mark Beder, Dir.-Technology
Rod Snodgrass, Head-Telecom Digital Ventures
Chris Quin, Chief Exec.-Telecom Retail
Tim Miles, Chief Exec.-Gne-i
David Yuile, Chief Exec.-AAPT
Justine Smyth, Chmn.

GROWTH PLANS/SPECIAL FEATURES:

Spark New Zealand is a telecommunications and digital services company in New Zealand. Products and services include mobile phones, mobile device accessories, broadband and landline for consumers and businesses. Since 2020, Spark has been launching 5G wireless broadband service to selected locations throughout New Zealand, for consumers and businesses. For businesses, Spark offers an agile strategy that replaces traditional hierarchical control with small, cross-functional and self-managing teams. It also focuses on providing incremental improvements to products and services, looking at the customer's journey from beginning to end. Spark Lab provides online articles (sparklab.co.nz), an events calendar and tools to help businesses in areas such as digital marketing, cyber security, technology and more. Spark offers a virtual and interactive 3D store to better serve customers unable to visit physical stores. As of mid-2021, Spark offered 5G wireless and broadband services to nine locations throughout New Zealand, as well as to four South Island towns.

FINANCIAL DATA: Note: Data for latest year may not have been available at press time.

In U.S. $	2020	2019	2018	2017	2016	2015
Revenue	2,602,489,000	2,551,716,000	2,603,215,000	2,490,788,000	2,426,959,000	2,429,135,000
R&D Expense						
Operating Income	455,508,200	435,924,200	388,052,400	298,836,600	292,308,600	239,359,400
Operating Margin %		.19%	.15%	.12%	.12%	.10%
SGA Expense	472,916,100	456,233,500	509,182,700	520,788,000	483,070,800	499,028,100
Net Income	309,716,500	296,660,600	279,252,600	303,188,600	268,372,700	270,548,600
Operating Cash Flow						
Capital Expenditure	285,055,300	301,012,600	300,287,200	284,330,000	303,188,600	425,044,300
EBITDA	787,710,000	802,942,000	728,958,100	748,542,100	728,232,800	717,352,800
Return on Assets %		.11%	.11%	.13%	.11%	.12%
Return on Equity %		.27%	.24%	.25%	.21%	.21%
Debt to Equity		0.97	0.615	0.419	0.407	0.305

CONTACT INFORMATION:

Phone: 64-9-215-7564	Fax: 64-800-278-320
Toll-Free:
Address: Telecom House, 167 Victoria St., Auckland, 1010 New Zealand

STOCK TICKER/OTHER:

Stock Ticker: NZTCF	Exchange: PINX
Employees: 5,224	Fiscal Year Ends: 06/30
Parent Company:

SALARIES/BONUSES:

Top Exec. Salary: $	Bonus: $
Second Exec. Salary: $	Bonus: $

OTHER THOUGHTS:

Estimated Female Officers or Directors: 2
Hot Spot for Advancement for Women/Minorities:

Speedcast International Limited

www.speedcast.com

NAIC Code: 517110

TYPES OF BUSINESS:

Satellite Network Service Provider.
Communications Technology
Satellite Network

BRANDS/DIVISIONS/AFFILIATES:

Centerbridge Partners LP

CONTACTS: Note: Officers with more than one job title may be intentionally listed here more than once.

Joe Spytek, CEO
Peter Myers, CFO
Chris Hill, CTO

GROWTH PLANS/SPECIAL FEATURES:

Speedcast International Limited is a communications company. The firm's customers are primarily engaged in the maritime, energy, telecommunication, mining, broadcast media, non-government organization (NGO) and government industries. Speedcast's global satellite network and support infrastructure spans across every region in the world. The company's solutions are categorized into: customer experience management, connectivity, professional services, network management and applications and solutions. The customer experience management division works alongside businesses to deliver communication services and support, from implementation to delivery to field support and solution management. The connectivity division unites its diverse connectivity resources into a single, seamless network experience, from both very small aperture terminal (VSAT) two-way satellite ground station and mobile two-way voice and data communication satellite services (MSS). This division has a satellite network of more than 95 satellites and 35+ Speedcast and partner teleports. The professional services division offers problem-solving solutions, enterprise solutions and 24/7/365 support in any time zone and multiple languages. The network management division utilizes a multi-protocol label switching (MPLS) routing technique that directs data from one node to the next based on short path labels rather than long network addresses. It gives a complete view of the customer's network operations, whether it's microwave, fiber, 4G/LTE, terrestrial or satellite services. Last, the applications and solutions division designs solutions to suit its customer's needs, utilizing solutions for Internet of Things (IoT), automation and more. Its solutions are built to satisfy any market, industry, initiative and challenge. In March 2021, Speedcast announced that it successfully completed its restructuring process and emerged from chapter 11 proceedings under the new ownership of Centerbridge Partners LP.

FINANCIAL DATA: Note: Data for latest year may not have been available at press time.

In U.S. $	2020	2019	2018	2017	2016	2015
Revenue	685,300,000	623,000,000	603,832,256	450,877,312	206,055,248	157,050,640
R&D Expense						
Operating Income						
Operating Margin %						
SGA Expense						
Net Income		1,897,396	1,789,901	4,863,276	5,574,120	4,047,364
Operating Cash Flow						
Capital Expenditure						
EBITDA						
Return on Assets %						
Return on Equity %						
Debt to Equity						

CONTACT INFORMATION:

Phone: 832-668-2300   Fax:
Toll-Free:
Address: 4400 S. Sam Houston Pkwy. E., Houston, TX 77048 United States

STOCK TICKER/OTHER:

Stock Ticker: Subsidiary
Employees:
Parent Company: Centerbridge Partners LP

Exchange:
Fiscal Year Ends: 12/31

SALARIES/BONUSES:

Top Exec. Salary: $ Bonus: $
Second Exec. Salary: $ Bonus: $

OTHER THOUGHTS:

Estimated Female Officers or Directors:
Hot Spot for Advancement for Women/Minorities:

Spok Inc
NAIC Code: 517210

www.spok.com

TYPES OF BUSINESS:
Paging Services
Wireless Messaging Services
Instant Text Messaging

BRANDS/DIVISIONS/AFFILIATES:
Spok Holdings Inc
Spok Go

CONTACTS: *Note: Officers with more than one job title may be intentionally listed here more than once.*
Vincent Kelly, CEO
Michael Wallace, CFO
Royce Yudkoff, Chairman of the Board
Timothy Tindle, Chief Information Officer
Calvin Rice, Controller
Bonnie Culp-Fingerhut, Executive VP, Divisional
Sharon Woods-Keisling, Treasurer

GROWTH PLANS/SPECIAL FEATURES:
Spok, Inc., wholly-owned by Spok Holdings, Inc., is a global provider of healthcare communications. The firm delivers clinical information to care teams to improve patient outcomes. Hospitals rely on Spoke Care Connect to enhance workflows for clinicians, support administrative compliance and provide quality experiences for patients. Spok primarily serves customers throughout the U.S., but also in Europe, Canada, Australia, Asia and the Middle East on a limited basis. Spok's products and services include workflow management, secure texting, paging services, contact center optimization and public safety response. The company develops, sells and supports enterprise-wide systems for organizations needing to automate, centralize and standardize their approach to clinical communications. Spok Go is a secure, unified platform that connects clinical teams with people and information needed. The platform provides visibility to clinicians on-the-go, notifies the appropriate care team member on their device of choice, streamlines on-call management, and expedites critical test results. More than 2,200 hospitals use Spok for communication purposes, and over 100 million messages are sent by the firm's customers each month.

Spok offers its employees comprehensive health benefits, retirement and savings plans, training and development opportunities and education assistance.

FINANCIAL DATA: *Note: Data for latest year may not have been available at press time.*

In U.S. $	2020	2019	2018	2017	2016	2015
Revenue	148,180,000	160,289,000	169,474,000	171,175,000	179,561,000	189,628,000
R&D Expense	15,828,000	27,543,000	24,464,000	18,702,000	13,467,000	
Operating Income	3,393,000	-6,291,000	-1,549,000	10,706,000	23,599,000	28,318,000
Operating Margin %		-.04%	-.01%	.06%	.13%	.15%
SGA Expense	85,550,000	64,616,000	68,731,000	97,504,000	94,629,000	107,509,000
Net Income	-44,225,000	-10,765,000	-1,479,000	-15,306,000	13,979,000	84,235,000
Operating Cash Flow	26,163,000	11,693,000	10,315,000	15,556,000	37,461,000	38,012,000
Capital Expenditure	14,707,000	4,837,000	5,915,000	9,214,000	6,254,000	6,374,000
EBITDA	12,449,000	2,958,000	9,220,000	22,330,000	36,562,000	42,288,000
Return on Assets %		-.03%	.00%	-.04%	.04%	.23%
Return on Equity %		-.04%	-.01%	-.05%	.04%	.28%
Debt to Equity		0.046				0.001

CONTACT INFORMATION:
Phone: 800 611-8488   Fax: 508 836-3626
Toll-Free: 800-611-8488
Address: 5911 Kingstown Village Pkwy., Fl. 6, Alexandria, VA 22315
United States

STOCK TICKER/OTHER:
Stock Ticker: SPOK   Exchange: NAS
Employees: 638   Fiscal Year Ends: 12/31
Parent Company: Spok Holdings Inc

SALARIES/BONUSES:
Top Exec. Salary: $ Bonus: $
Second Exec. Salary: $ Bonus: $

OTHER THOUGHTS:
Estimated Female Officers or Directors: 5
Hot Spot for Advancement for Women/Minorities: Y

Sprint Corporation

NAIC Code: 517210

www.sprint.com

TYPES OF BUSINESS:

Mobile Phone and Wireless Services
Internet Service Provider
Wireless Data Services
Long-Range Walkie-Talkie Service
Long-Distance Telephone Service
Network Services

BRANDS/DIVISIONS/AFFILIATES:

Softbank Group Corporation
Sprint
Virgin Mobile
Boost Mobile
Curiosity Internet of Things
T-Mobile

CONTACTS: *Note: Officers with more than one job title may be intentionally listed here more than once.*

Andrew Davies, CFO
Paul Schieber, Chief Accounting Officer
John Saw, Chief Technology Officer
Nestor Cano, COO
Marcelo Claure, Director
Michel Combes, Director
Ronald Fisher, Director
Jorge Gracia, Other Executive Officer
Dow Draper, Other Executive Officer

GROWTH PLANS/SPECIAL FEATURES:

Sprint Corporation is a global communications company offering wireless and wireline communications products and services. The company serves approximately 54.5 million connections and operates wireless and wireline business segments. The wireless segment provides services on a postpaid and prepaid payment basis to retail subscribers, as well as on a wholesale basis, which includes the sale of wireless services that utilize the Sprint network but sold under the wholesaler's brand. The wireline segment provides a wide range of services to other communications companies, as well as targeted business and consumer subscribers. Additionally, this division offers services to Sprint's wireless segment. Its services are provided through an all-digital global wireline network and a Tier 1 internet backbone. Wireline services include domestic and international data communications using various protocols such as multiprotocol label switching technologies, internet protocol, managed network services, voice over internet protocol (VoIP), session-initiated protocol and traditional voice services. Sprint's brands include Sprint, Virgin Mobile and Boost Mobile. Sprint Corporation is engaged in launching a 5G mobile network in the U.S, and hoping to be the first to do so. In addition, Sprint's Curiosity Internet of Things (IoT) platform is a native IoT network and platform for turning collected data from connected devices into actionable intelligence. The platform is 5G ready and designed for the demands of IoT applications and end-uses, including artificial intelligence (AI), robotics and edge computing. Sprint is majority-owned by SoftBank Group Corporation. In April 2020, Sprint and T-Mobile U.S. completed a merger, with the new company to be called T-Mobile.

FINANCIAL DATA: *Note: Data for latest year may not have been available at press time.*

In U.S. $	2020	2019	2018	2017	2016	2015
Revenue		33,600,000,000	32,405,999,616	33,347,000,320	32,180,000,768	34,531,999,744
R&D Expense						
Operating Income						
Operating Margin %						
SGA Expense						
Net Income		-1,943,000,064	7,389,000,192	-1,206,000,000	-1,995,000,064	-3,344,999,936
Operating Cash Flow						
Capital Expenditure						
EBITDA						
Return on Assets %						
Return on Equity %						
Debt to Equity						

CONTACT INFORMATION:

Phone: 800 829-0965   Fax: 913 624-3496
Toll-Free: 800-829-0965
Address: 6200 Sprint Pkwy., Overland Park, KS 66251 United States

STOCK TICKER/OTHER:

Stock Ticker: S   Exchange: NYS
Employees: 28,000   Fiscal Year Ends: 12/31
Parent Company: Softbank Group Corporation

SALARIES/BONUSES:

Top Exec. Salary: $ Bonus: $
Second Exec. Salary: $ Bonus: $

OTHER THOUGHTS:

Estimated Female Officers or Directors: 2
Hot Spot for Advancement for Women/Minorities:

Startec Global Communications Corporation

www.startec.com

NAIC Code: 517110

TYPES OF BUSINESS:

IP Communications Services
Voice Services
Data Services
Internet Access

BRANDS/DIVISIONS/AFFILIATES:

Lingo Communications LLC
CellConnect
MyCountry Number
Direct Dial
10-10-719

CONTACTS: *Note: Officers with more than one job title may be intentionally listed here more than once.*

Chuck Griffin, CEO-Lingo

GROWTH PLANS/SPECIAL FEATURES:

Startec Global Communications Corporation provides telephone, internet and communications services. Startec also works with international long-distance carriers and internet service providers transacting with the world's emerging economies. The company's products include CellConnect long distance, CellConnect Prepaid long distance, Direct Dial long distance, 10-10-719 long distance and MyCountry Number local. CellConnect is an international calling service that allows the user to register up to four phone numbers, including land and cell phone lines, to dial internationally without using PIN numbers. CellConnect Prepaid offers international calls from any cell phone or landline at low rates. Direct Dial provides international long-distance service for home phones and cell phones. Startec's 10-10-719 service, which does not require a calling plan, bills the calls on the company's rates, even if the user is currently under contract with another service provider. MyCountry Number offers one low rate for same-country local calls and unlimited international incoming calls. Startec also offers online account management, online billing for certain services and a referral credit program for users of Direct Dial long distance. The company's services connect worldwide communities including the Pacific Rim, the Middle East, North Africa, Russia, Central Europe and North and South America. It provides services through a network of owned and leased facilities, operating and termination agreements and resale arrangements. Startec technology includes an extensive network of internet protocol (IP) gateways, international gateways, domestic switches and ownership in undersea fiber optic cables. Startec is a subsidiary and brand of Lingo Communications LLC.

FINANCIAL DATA: *Note: Data for latest year may not have been available at press time.*

In U.S. $	2020	2019	2018	2017	2016	2015
Revenue						
R&D Expense						
Operating Income						
Operating Margin %						
SGA Expense						
Net Income						
Operating Cash Flow						
Capital Expenditure						
EBITDA						
Return on Assets %						
Return on Equity %						
Debt to Equity						

CONTACT INFORMATION:

Phone: Fax: 301-610-4301
Toll-Free: 800-827-3374
Address: 400 E. Las Colinas Blvd., Ste. 500, Irving, TX 75039 United States

STOCK TICKER/OTHER:

Stock Ticker: Subsidiary   Exchange:
Employees: Fiscal Year Ends: 12/31
Parent Company: Lingo Communications LLC

SALARIES/BONUSES:

Top Exec. Salary: $ Bonus: $
Second Exec. Salary: $ Bonus: $

OTHER THOUGHTS:

Estimated Female Officers or Directors:
Hot Spot for Advancement for Women/Minorities:

Swisscom AG

NAIC Code: 517110

www.swisscom.ch/en/residential.html

TYPES OF BUSINESS:

Integrated Telecommunications Services
Internet Service Provider
Value-added Services
Mobile Phone Service
Local & Long-Distance Service
IT & Outsourcing Services
5G

BRANDS/DIVISIONS/AFFILIATES:

Swisscom Switzerland
Fastweb
www.bluewin.ch
CT Cinetrade AG

CONTACTS: Note: Officers with more than one job title may be intentionally listed here more than once.

Urs Schaeppi, CEO
Eugen Stermetz, CFO
Klementina Pejic, Human Resources
Christoph Aeschlimann, IT
Jurgen Galler, Head-Strategy & Innovation
Bart Morsellt, Head-Investor Rel.
Mario Rossi, Head-Group Bus. Steering
Michael Rechsteiner, Chmn.
Urs Schaeppi, Head-Switzerland

GROWTH PLANS/SPECIAL FEATURES:

Swisscom AG is one of the leading telecommunications providers in Switzerland. The company operates through three divisions: Swisscom Switzerland, Fastweb and other. Swisscom Switzerland targets residential customers, small- and medium-sized enterprises and wholesalers, and offers 5G service throughout Switzerland. Residential customers receive mobile and fixed-line services, including all telephone, internet and TV services, pay TV, transmissions of sporting events and video on demand from a single source as well as the sale of end devices. This division also provides broadband access lines; operates www.bluewin.ch internet portal; and through CT Cinetrade AG, operates a leading cinema chain in Switzerland. Small- and medium-sized enterprises receive products and services such as fixed-line, mobile telephony, internet, data services and IT infrastructure maintenance. Wholesalers receive services for other telecommunications providers such as regulated access to the last mile as well as commercial voice, data and broadband products. Swisscom Switzerland's IT, network and innovation unit builds, operates and maintains Swisscom's nationwide fixed network and mobile communications infrastructure in Switzerland. Fastweb is one of Italy's largest broadband telecoms companies. The subsidiary is a leader in the development of multimedia and broadband communication services, and offers voice, data, internet and IP TV services, as well as VPN (virtual private network) and mobile services. Fastweb's services are provided directly through its own fiber-optic network or via unbundled fixed access lines and wholesale products of Telecom Italia. The other division comprises the participations, which manages small- and medium-sized enterprises whose activities are mainly related to or help support Swisscom's core business; health, which offers innovating ICT (information and communications technology) solutions for physicians, hospitals and insurers; and connected living, which develops and operates intelligent solutions for energy management.

FINANCIAL DATA: Note: Data for latest year may not have been available at press time.

In U.S. $	2020	2019	2018	2017	2016	2015
Revenue	12,374,860,000	12,768,400,000	13,059,380,000	13,001,410,000	12,980,220,000	13,019,240,000
R&D Expense						
Operating Income	2,127,138,000	2,120,449,000	2,297,710,000	2,369,061,000	2,392,473,000	2,239,738,000
Operating Margin %		.17%	.18%	.18%	.18%	.17%
SGA Expense	415,839,800	527,325,000	564,115,100	594,216,100	928,671,700	969,921,300
Net Income	1,705,724,000	1,864,033,000	1,702,379,000	1,750,318,000	1,788,223,000	1,517,314,000
Operating Cash Flow	4,536,333,000	4,438,226,000	4,147,250,000	4,560,860,000	4,305,559,000	4,311,133,000
Capital Expenditure	2,439,296,000	2,664,497,000	2,680,104,000	2,651,118,000	2,693,482,000	2,705,746,000
EBITDA	4,856,295,000	4,788,290,000	4,686,838,000	4,788,290,000	4,825,080,000	4,541,907,000
Return on Assets %		.07%	.07%	.07%	.08%	.06%
Return on Equity %		.20%	.19%	.22%	.27%	.25%
Debt to Equity		0.884	0.828	0.843	1.047	1.291

CONTACT INFORMATION:

Phone: 4.1058221991e+11   Fax:
Toll-Free:
Address: Alte Tiefenaustrasse 6, Worblaufen, 3048 Switzerland

STOCK TICKER/OTHER:

Stock Ticker: SCMWY
Employees: 19,062
Parent Company:

Exchange: PINX
Fiscal Year Ends: 12/31

SALARIES/BONUSES:

Top Exec. Salary: $ Bonus: $
Second Exec. Salary: $ Bonus: $

OTHER THOUGHTS:

Estimated Female Officers or Directors: 2
Hot Spot for Advancement for Women/Minorities: Y

Sykes Enterprises Incorporated

NAIC Code: 541512

www.sykes.com

TYPES OF BUSINESS:

Computer Integrated Systems Design
Outsourcing Services
Customer Engagement Solutions
Management Services
Consulting
Hosting Services

BRANDS/DIVISIONS/AFFILIATES:

CONTACTS: *Note: Officers with more than one job title may be intentionally listed here more than once.*

Charles Sykes, CEO
John Chapman, CFO
James Macleod, Chairman of the Board
David Pearson, Chief Information Officer
William Rocktoff, Controller
Jenna Nelson, Executive VP, Divisional
James Holder, Executive VP
Lawrence Zingale, Executive VP

GROWTH PLANS/SPECIAL FEATURES:

Sykes Enterprises, Incorporated provides multichannel demand generation customer engagement solutions and services primarily to Global 2000 companies and their end customers. These companies and customers are principally engaged in the financial services, communications, technology, transportation, leisure and healthcare industries. Sykes' differentiated full lifecycle management services platform engages customers at every touchpoint within the customer journey, including digital marketing, digital acquisition, sales expertise, customer service, technical support, and retention, many of which can be optimized by a suite of robotic process automation (RPA) and artificial intelligence (AI) solutions. The firm serves clients in the EMEA (Europe, Middle East and Africa) region, with an emphasis on inbound multichannel demand generation, customer service and technical support. These services are delivered through communication channels such as phone, email, social media, text messaging, chat and digital self-services. In Europe, Sykes also provides fulfillment services such as order processing, payment processing, inventory control, product delivery and product returns handling. Moreover, Sykes provides a suite of solutions such as consulting, implementation, hosting and managed services, all of which generate demand, enhance the customer service experience, promote brand loyalty and brings about high levels of performance and profitability. In June 2021, Sykes Enterprises agreed to be acquired by Sitel Group, a provider of customer experience products and solutions.

FINANCIAL DATA: *Note: Data for latest year may not have been available at press time.*

In U.S. $	2020	2019	2018	2017	2016	2015
Revenue	1,710,261,000	1,614,762,000	1,625,687,000	1,586,008,000	1,460,037,000	1,286,340,000
R&D Expense						
Operating Income	123,337,000	91,511,000	72,603,000	92,301,000	92,562,000	94,645,000
Operating Margin %		.06%	.04%	.06%	.06%	.07%
SGA Expense	421,910,000	412,407,000	407,285,000	376,863,000	351,408,000	297,257,000
Net Income	56,432,000	64,081,000	48,926,000	32,216,000	62,390,000	68,597,000
Operating Cash Flow	175,742,000	101,283,000	109,094,000	134,789,000	130,728,000	120,464,000
Capital Expenditure	52,683,000	38,990,000	55,040,000	68,169,000	78,352,000	49,662,000
EBITDA	148,122,000	159,020,000	135,019,000	166,560,000	163,431,000	151,133,000
Return on Assets %		.05%	.04%	.03%	.06%	.07%
Return on Equity %		.08%	.06%	.04%	.09%	.10%
Debt to Equity		0.274	0.123	0.345	0.369	0.103

CONTACT INFORMATION:

Phone: 813 274-1000   Fax: 813 273-0148
Toll-Free:
Address: 400 N. Ashley Dr., Ste. 2800, Tampa, FL 33602 United States

STOCK TICKER/OTHER:

Stock Ticker: SYKE   Exchange: NAS
Employees: 61,100   Fiscal Year Ends: 12/31
Parent Company:

SALARIES/BONUSES:

Top Exec. Salary: $ Bonus: $
Second Exec. Salary: $ Bonus: $

OTHER THOUGHTS:

Estimated Female Officers or Directors: 3
Hot Spot for Advancement for Women/Minorities: Y

Syniverse Technologies LLC

www.syniverse.com

NAIC Code: 517110

TYPES OF BUSINESS:

Telecommunications & Network Services
Communications Technology Services
Business Management Services
5G Services

BRANDS/DIVISIONS/AFFILIATES:

Carlyle Group (The)

CONTACTS: Note: Officers with more than one job title may be intentionally listed here more than once.

Andrew Davies, CEO
Simeon Irvine, CFO
Sara DeBella, Chief Human Resources Officer
John Wick, CTO
Gary Weisenborn, Sr. VP-Prod. Dev.
David W. Hitchcock, Chief Admin. Officer
Laura Binion, General Counsel
John McRae, Sr. VP-Global Customer Oper.
Ed Lewis, Chief Strategy Officer
Amy Moini, Sr. VP-Global Sales Dev.
Pablo Milikota, Sr. VP-Global Bus. Svcs. & Solutions
David Wasserman, Sr. VP-North America Sales
Michael O'Brien, Sr. VP-Strategic Market Initiatives
James A. Attwood, Chmn.
Mahesh Prasad, Pres., Americas

GROWTH PLANS/SPECIAL FEATURES:

Syniverse Technologies, LLC is a provider of wireless voice and data services for telecommunications companies worldwide, including North America, Asia Pacific, the Caribbean, Latin America, Europe, the Middle East and Africa. The company offers its 1G to 5G services to communications companies and enterprises in approximately 200 countries. These customer companies include mobile operators, cable and internet providers and enterprises as well as machine-to-machine (M2M), voice over internet protocol (VoIP), voice over long-term evolution (VoLTE) and application service providers. Syniverse makes seamless communications between operators, technologies, devices and networks possible for mobile users. Syniverse services can be divided into three primary divisions: messaging solutions, which includes advanced messaging, short message service (SMS) interoperability, multimedia messaging service (MMS) interoperability, mobile video broadcast service, application-to-person (A2P)/enterprise services and value-added messaging services; roaming solutions, which includes roaming hub services, data clearing, financial clearing and settlement, fraud management, roaming interoperability and business intelligence solutions; and network and database solutions, which includes network signaling and transport, interworking gateway, database, data management, number portability and virtual network enablement. Syniverse is owned by The Carlyle Group. In June 2021, Syniverse and AlefEdge announced a collaboration to enable global enterprises and their developers to create their own 5G Edge networks and launch 5G Edge applications and services within mere minutes. The partnership believes 5G Edge API are critical for global enterprises to accelerate and launch their own customized digital transformation strategies.

FINANCIAL DATA: Note: Data for latest year may not have been available at press time.

In U.S. $	2020	2019	2018	2017	2016	2015
Revenue	896,718,154	874,846,980	833,187,600	793,512,000	781,892,000	861,475,000
R&D Expense						
Operating Income						
Operating Margin %						
SGA Expense						
Net Income				-20,799,000	-67,183,000	-50,591,000
Operating Cash Flow						
Capital Expenditure						
EBITDA						
Return on Assets %						
Return on Equity %						
Debt to Equity						

CONTACT INFORMATION:

Phone: 813-637-5000 Fax:
Toll-Free:
Address: 8125 Highwoods Palm Way, Tampa, FL 33647 United States

STOCK TICKER/OTHER:

Stock Ticker: Private
Employees: 2,200
Parent Company: Carlyle Group (The)

Exchange:
Fiscal Year Ends: 12/31

SALARIES/BONUSES:

Top Exec. Salary: $ Bonus: $
Second Exec. Salary: $ Bonus: $

OTHER THOUGHTS:

Estimated Female Officers or Directors: 5
Hot Spot for Advancement for Women/Minorities: Y

TalkTalk Telecom Group Limited

www.talktalkgroup.com

NAIC Code: 517210

TYPES OF BUSINESS:

Wireless Telecommunications Carriers (except Satellite)
Telecommunications
Landline
Broadband
TV
Mobile
Fiber Network

BRANDS/DIVISIONS/AFFILIATES:

Toscafund Asset Management LLP
Penta Capital LLP
Tosa IOM Limited
TalkTalk
TalkTalk Business
FibreNation

GROWTH PLANS/SPECIAL FEATURES:

TalkTalk Telecom Group Limited provides landline, broadband, TV and mobile services to more than 4 million customers. The firm operates in the U.K. and comprises a major broadband network, covering 96% of the population. TalkTalk supplies services to consumers through the TalkTalk brand, to businesses through TalkTalk Business, and by wholesaling to resellers. Subsidiary FibreNation has been rolling out fiber-to-the-premises (FTTP) to consumers and businesses since its 2018 inception. In March 2021, TalkTalk Telecom Group was taken private by Tosca IOM Limited, a newly-formed company by Toscafund Asset Management LLP and Penta Capital LLP.

CONTACTS: Note: Officers with more than one job title may be intentionally listed here more than once.

Tristia Harrison, CEO
Phil Eayres, CFO
Daniel Kasmir, Chief People Officer
Phil Haslam, CTO

FINANCIAL DATA: Note: Data for latest year may not have been available at press time.

In U.S. $	2020	2019	2018	2017	2016	2015
Revenue		2,119,948,544	2,218,671,616	2,199,062,784	2,378,160,384	2,181,601,536
R&D Expense						
Operating Income						
Operating Margin %						
SGA Expense						
Net Income		41,567,620	-102,620,064	71,534,288	2,592,000	87,507,136
Operating Cash Flow						
Capital Expenditure						
EBITDA						
Return on Assets %						
Return on Equity %						
Debt to Equity						

CONTACT INFORMATION:

Phone: 44 020 3417 1000　　Fax:
Toll-Free:
Address: Soapworks, Ordsall Lane, Salford, M5 3TT United Kingdom

STOCK TICKER/OTHER:

Stock Ticker: Private　　　　　　　　Exchange: PINX
Employees: 2,114　　　　　　　　　　Fiscal Year Ends: 03/31
Parent Company: Tosca IOM Limited

SALARIES/BONUSES:

Top Exec. Salary: $　　　　　Bonus: $
Second Exec. Salary: $　　　　Bonus: $

OTHER THOUGHTS:

Estimated Female Officers or Directors:
Hot Spot for Advancement for Women/Minorities:

Tata Communications Limited
NAIC Code: 517110

www.tatacommunications.com

TYPES OF BUSINESS:
Telecommunications Services
Internet Service Provider
VoIP Service
Satellite Communications
Managed Data Network Services
Managed Network Security Services
Outsourced Contact Center Services

BRANDS/DIVISIONS/AFFILIATES:
Tata Group
Oasis Smart SIM Europe SAS

CONTACTS:
Note: Officers with more than one job title may be intentionally listed here more than once.

Amur Swaminathan Lakshminarayanan, CEO
Kabir Ahmed Shakir, CFO
Sumeet Walia, Chief Sales & Mktg. Officer
Aadesh Goyal, Chief Human Resources Officer
Genius Wong, CTO
John Hayduk, Pres., Prod. Mgmt. & Service Dev.
John Freeman, General Counsel
Madhusudhan Mysore, Head-Customer Svcs. & Oper.
Srinivasa Addepalli, Chief Strategy Officer
Natalie Chak, Sr. Mgr.-Corp. Comm.
Michel Guyot, Pres., Global Voice Solutions
Sumeet Walia, Head-Global Enterprise Bus.
Allan Chan, Exec. VP-Global Carrier Solutions
Rangu Saigame, CEO-Growth Ventures
Srinivasan CR, Chief Digital Officer
Sunil Joshi, CEO

GROWTH PLANS/SPECIAL FEATURES:
Tata Communications Limited, a division of Indian conglomerate Tata Group, is a provider of global digital infrastructure services. Tata Communications focuses on helping businesses understand and navigate through the vast potential offered by technologies such as network, mobility, collaboration and security services. It also shapes the future by investing in emerging technologies of Internet of Things (IoT), artificial intelligence (AI), automation and analytics. All of this is delivered seamlessly through the cloud via Tata Communication's wholly-owned advanced subsea fiber optic network. This type of cloud and subsea architecture enables an infinite amount of global connections. Tata Communications is present in more than 200 countries and territories worldwide, serving over 7,000 customers that represent more than 300 of the Fortune 500. Tata connects four out of five mobile subscribers worldwide, and connects businesses to 60% of the world's cloud giants. In December 2020, Tata Communications acquired a majority equity stake of 58.1% in Oasis Smart SIM Europe SAS, a France-based embedded subscriber identity module (SIM) technology provider.

FINANCIAL DATA:
Note: Data for latest year may not have been available at press time.

In U.S. $	2020	2019	2018	2017	2016	2015
Revenue	2,277,820,000	2,322,650,000	2,559,650,000	2,770,260,000	2,733,878,230	2,815,956,640
R&D Expense						
Operating Income						
Operating Margin %						
SGA Expense						
Net Income	-11,275,000	-1,126,370	-50,514,200	-118,095,000	191,309,413	1,346,379
Operating Cash Flow						
Capital Expenditure						
EBITDA						
Return on Assets %						
Return on Equity %						
Debt to Equity						

CONTACT INFORMATION:
Phone: 9122 66592000   Fax:
Toll-Free: 800-266-0660
Address: Tower 4, Fl. 4-8, Equinox Bus. Pk, LBS Marg, Kurla, Mumbai, 400070 India

STOCK TICKER/OTHER:
Stock Ticker: 500483
Employees: 5,654
Parent Company: Tata Group

Exchange: Bombay
Fiscal Year Ends: 03/31

SALARIES/BONUSES:
Top Exec. Salary: $ Bonus: $
Second Exec. Salary: $ Bonus: $

OTHER THOUGHTS:
Estimated Female Officers or Directors: 2
Hot Spot for Advancement for Women/Minorities:

Sales, profits and employees may be estimates. Financial information, benefits and other data can change quickly and may vary from those stated here.

Tata Group

NAIC Code: 331110

www.tata.com

TYPES OF BUSINESS:
Steel Production
Communication & Information Systems
Engineered Products
Energy Utilities
Solar Power
Automobiles
Hotels & Resorts
Pharmaceuticals & Chemicals

BRANDS/DIVISIONS/AFFILIATES:
Tata Sons Private Limited
Tata Consultancy Services
Tata Steel
Tata Motors
Tata Oil Mills Company (TOMCO)
Tata Capital
Tata Communications
Tata Investment Corporation

CONTACTS: *Note: Officers with more than one job title may be intentionally listed here more than once.*
Madhu Kannan, Head-Bus. Dev.
Mukund G. Rajan, Chief Ethics Officer
Nirmalya Kumar, Head-Strategy
Natarajan Chandrasekaran, Chmn.-Tata Sons

GROWTH PLANS/SPECIAL FEATURES:
Tata Group, owned by Tata Sons Private Limited, is an Indian conglomerate that oversees 30 companies across 10 verticals, operating in more than 100 countries worldwide. These verticals include information technology, steel, automotive, consumer and retail, infrastructure, financial services, aerospace and defense, tourism and travel, telecommunications and media, and trading and investments. Information technology is led by Tata Consultancy Services. Tata Steel has an annual crude steel capacity of 36.3 million tons per year. Tata Motors designs, manufactures and markets automobiles across all market segments. Its two iconic brands include Jaguar and Land Rover. Tata Motors has a global network of nearly 100 subsidiaries. The consumer and retail vertical is led by Tata Oil Mills Company (TOMCO), a producer of soaps, detergents, cooling oils, consumer durables, tea, packaged water and more. The infrastructure vertical is engaged in the energy sector, which supplies energy to residences, large cities and industries. Financial services is led by Tata Capital, which offers a range of financial services that cater to individuals and small businesses, including life and non-life insurance products. This division's Tata Asset Management Company offers mutual funds, portfolio management services, alternative investment funds and offshore funds. The aerospace and defense vertical is a global, single-source supplier for fixed wing and rotary wing programs; and provides products and services for the Ministry of Defence, armed forces and Defence Research and Development Organization within India. Tourism and travel encompasses Tata's Taj Mahal hotel, and its airline operations. Telecom and media includes Tata Communications, which owns and operates mobile and internet networks, including fiber, subsea fiber and terrestrial fiber; and Tata Sky, a joint venture direct-to-home entertainment provider. Last, trading and investments offers private trading strategies through Tata International, Tata Industries and Tata Investment Corporation.

FINANCIAL DATA: *Note: Data for latest year may not have been available at press time.*

In U.S. $	2020	2019	2018	2017	2016	2015
Revenue	106,000,000,000	113,000,000,000	109,670,000,000	94,620,050,000	90,672,600,000	
R&D Expense						
Operating Income						
Operating Margin %						
SGA Expense						
Net Income		1,450,911,000	1,381,820,000	3,702,500,000	6,947,020,000	
Operating Cash Flow						
Capital Expenditure						
EBITDA						
Return on Assets %						
Return on Equity %						
Debt to Equity						

CONTACT INFORMATION:
Phone: 91 22-6665-8282   Fax: 91-22-6665-8160
Toll-Free:
Address: 24 Homi Mody St., Mumbai, 400 001 India

STOCK TICKER/OTHER:
Stock Ticker: Private
Employees: 750,000
Parent Company: Tata Sons Private Limited

Exchange:
Fiscal Year Ends: 03/31

SALARIES/BONUSES:
Top Exec. Salary: $ Bonus: $
Second Exec. Salary: $ Bonus: $

OTHER THOUGHTS:
Estimated Female Officers or Directors:
Hot Spot for Advancement for Women/Minorities:

Tata Teleservices Limited

corporate.tatateleservices.com/en-in

NAIC Code: 517110

TYPES OF BUSINESS:

Telecommunications Services
Telecommunications
Mobile
Wireless
Wireline
Digital
Machine-to-Machine
Fiber Optic Network

BRANDS/DIVISIONS/AFFILIATES:

Tata Sons Private Limited
Tata Teleservices (Maharashtra) Limited

GROWTH PLANS/SPECIAL FEATURES:

Tata Teleservices Limited is the telecommunication arm of the Tata Group. The firm is a leading mobile telecom service provider in India, delivering mobile connectivity and services to consumers. Tata Teleservices (Maharashtra) Limited serves the Maharashtra region. The company's integrated solutions include wireline and wireless networks on global system for mobile communications (GSM), code division multiple access (CDMA) for transmitting digital signals simultaneously over the same carrier frequency, and 3G platforms. Non-voice services include eGovernance, machine-to-machine (M2M) and m-Remittance services. For businesses, Tata offers next-generation voice, data and managed solutions to small and large enterprises through its fiber optic network, channel partner network, and sales and service teams.

CONTACTS: Note: Officers with more than one job title may be intentionally listed here more than once.

Amur S. Lakshminarayanan, Chmn.

FINANCIAL DATA: Note: Data for latest year may not have been available at press time.

In U.S. $	2020	2019	2018	2017	2016	2015
Revenue	144,655,000	189,096,000	292,693,000	414,229,000	452,351,000	468,900,000
R&D Expense						
Operating Income						
Operating Margin %						
SGA Expense						
Net Income	-493,567,000	-96,109,100	-1,512,960,000	-363,072,000	-54,048,400	-98,159,400
Operating Cash Flow						
Capital Expenditure						
EBITDA						
Return on Assets %						
Return on Equity %						
Debt to Equity						

CONTACT INFORMATION:

Phone: 91-22-6661 5111   Fax: 91-22-6660-5517
Toll-Free:
Address: D-26, TTC Industria Area, MIDC Sanpada, P.o., Turbhe, Mumbai, 400 703 India

STOCK TICKER/OTHER:

Stock Ticker: 532371
Employees: 368
Parent Company: Tata Sons Private Limited

Exchange: Bombay
Fiscal Year Ends: 03/31

SALARIES/BONUSES:

Top Exec. Salary: $ Bonus: $
Second Exec. Salary: $ Bonus: $

OTHER THOUGHTS:

Estimated Female Officers or Directors:
Hot Spot for Advancement for Women/Minorities:

TCI International Inc

NAIC Code: 334220

TYPES OF BUSINESS:

Transmission, Receiving & Test Equipment
Spectrum Monitoring & Management Systems
Broadcast & Communication Antennas
Communication Intelligence
Direction Finding Systems
System Software

BRANDS/DIVISIONS/AFFILIATES:

SPX Corporation
Blackbird

CONTACTS: *Note: Officers with more than one job title may be intentionally listed here more than once.*

Kevin Davis, VP-Product

GROWTH PLANS/SPECIAL FEATURES:

TCI International, Inc. is a systems engineering and manufacturing company that specializes in spectrum monitoring, signal collection, radio frequency (RF) solutions and radio direction finding solutions, primarily targeting the government, military, civilian and intelligence markets. The company, a subsidiary of SPX Corporation, designs, manufactures, sells and installs high frequency (HF) and medium frequency (MF) broadcast antennas, HF communications antennas and monitoring antennas. The antennas are designed to capture signals from 9 kilohertz (kHz) to 43 gigahertz (GHz). The firm builds and optimizes its antennas for various applications including spectrum monitoring, direction finding (DF), drone detection, signal interception, radio broadcasting and radio communications. TCI also makes computer-controlled radio frequency (RF) distribution systems that interface between multiple-element antenna arrays and communications receivers; specialized receivers for communications, DF/monitoring and COMINT/SIGINT applications; high-speed 32-bit digital signal processors, which deliver signal analysis by simultaneously scanning, detecting, measuring and analyzing RF signals at rates up to 4 GHz per second; and application-specific software to provide real-time control, data processing, digital signal processing, database structures, graphical user interfaces and network management services. TCI's next-generation Blackbird system combines TCI's modular, scalable RF hardware platform and DF/geolocation technology with second-generation Blackbird software, all designed for NextGen automation, smart recording and ease of use. The firm offers installation, training and services in over 105 countries.

FINANCIAL DATA: *Note: Data for latest year may not have been available at press time.*

In U.S. $	2020	2019	2018	2017	2016	2015
Revenue	1,449,350,000	1,414,000,000	1,400,000,000			
R&D Expense						
Operating Income						
Operating Margin %						
SGA Expense						
Net Income						
Operating Cash Flow						
Capital Expenditure						
EBITDA						
Return on Assets %						
Return on Equity %						
Debt to Equity						

CONTACT INFORMATION:

Phone: 510-687-6100   Fax: 510-687-6101
Toll-Free:
Address: 3541 Gateway Blvd., Fremont, CA 94538 United States

STOCK TICKER/OTHER:

Stock Ticker: Subsidiary   Exchange:
Employees: 72   Fiscal Year Ends: 09/30
Parent Company: SPX Corporation

SALARIES/BONUSES:

Top Exec. Salary: $ Bonus: $
Second Exec. Salary: $ Bonus: $

OTHER THOUGHTS:

Estimated Female Officers or Directors:
Hot Spot for Advancement for Women/Minorities:

TCL Technology Group Corporation

www.tcl.com

NAIC Code: 334310

TYPES OF BUSINESS:

Consumer Electronics
Electronic Technology
Electronic Development
Phones
Televisions
Soundbars
Air Conditioners
Headphones

BRANDS/DIVISIONS/AFFILIATES:

GROWTH PLANS/SPECIAL FEATURES:

TCL Technology Group Corporation designs, develops, manufactures and sells electronic products. The firm invests in state-of-the-art facilities where it creates innovative display technologies and develops new production techniques for phones and televisions. TCL introduced its big-screen QLED TV in 2014, pioneering dot color technology; introduced its mini-LED TV in 2019; introduced its Roku TV in 2014; introduced its TV with THX Certified Game Mode setting for big-screen gaming; developed RAY-DANZ technology, which offers an ultra-wide soundstage from a slim 3.1 channel soundbar; and developed a rollable AMOLED smartphone display concept. Other products by TCL include headphones, window and portable air conditioners, air purifiers, and dehumidifiers.

CONTACTS: Note: Officers with more than one job title may be intentionally listed here more than once.

Dongsheng Li, CEO
Bo Liangming, Pres.
Zhao Zhongyao, Sr. VP
Shi Wanwen, Sr. VP
Guo Aiping, Sr. VP
Huang Wei, VP-TCL Group

FINANCIAL DATA: Note: Data for latest year may not have been available at press time.

In U.S. $	2020	2019	2018	2017	2016	2015
Revenue	11,770,800,000	10,743,900,000	16,493,800,000	17,155,400,000	15,365,990,000	15,050,200,000
R&D Expense						
Operating Income						
Operating Margin %						
SGA Expense						
Net Income	776,013,000	523,433,000	591,028,000	544,278,000	237,647,000	380,799,000
Operating Cash Flow						
Capital Expenditure						
EBITDA						
Return on Assets %						
Return on Equity %						
Debt to Equity						

CONTACT INFORMATION:

Phone: 86-755-33311666   Fax:
Toll-Free:
Address: No. 17 Huifeng San Rd., Zhongkai High-Tech Dev. Zone, Huizhou, 516001 China

STOCK TICKER/OTHER:

Stock Ticker: 100
Employees: 48,471
Parent Company:

Exchange: Shenzhen
Fiscal Year Ends: 12/31

SALARIES/BONUSES:

Top Exec. Salary: $ Bonus: $
Second Exec. Salary: $ Bonus: $

OTHER THOUGHTS:

Estimated Female Officers or Directors:
Hot Spot for Advancement for Women/Minorities:

TDC A/S
NAIC Code: 517110

tdc.com

TYPES OF BUSINESS:
Internet Service Provider (ISP)
Telephone Service
Cellular Service
Cable Service
Broadband
Media

BRANDS/DIVISIONS/AFFILIATES:
Macquarie Group Limited
Tele Danmark Commmunications
TDC NET
Nuuday
YouSee
TDC Erhverv
Telmore
Fullrate

GROWTH PLANS/SPECIAL FEATURES:
TDC A/S provides digital telecommunication products and services in the Nordic Region. TDC stands for Tele Danmark Communications, and has been in business since 1882. Subsidiary TDC NET delivers mobile network and landline connectivity for TDC, including fiber and 5G network coverage. Nuuday offers digital services within TV, broadband, network and telephone through brands such as YouSee, TDC Erhverv, Telmore, Fullrate, Hiper, Blockbuster and Relate! TDC A/S operates as a subsidiary of Macquarie Group Limited. In mid-2021, TDC announced plans to establish TDC NET and Nuuday as operationally independent companies and TDC's group functions will be transferred to either TDC NET or Nuuday. TDC A/S will become a holding company of the two entities. The transaction was expected to be complete on December 31, 2021.

CONTACTS: *Note: Officers with more than one job title may be intentionally listed here more than once.*
Henrik Clausen, CEO
Lasse Pilgaard, CFO
Jens Aalose, Chief People Officer
Martin Lippert, Sr. Exec. VP
Eva Berneke, Sr. Exec. VP-TDC Bus.
Ib Konrad Jensen, Chief Press Officer
Miriam Igelso Hvidt, Sr. Exec. VP-Stakeholder Rel.
Niels Breining, CEO-YouSee A
Jens Munch-Hansen, Sr. Exec. VP-TDC Nordic

FINANCIAL DATA: *Note: Data for latest year may not have been available at press time.*

In U.S. $	2020	2019	2018	2017	2016	2015
Revenue	2,643,760,000	2,800,687,000	2,851,955,000	3,330,787,000	3,455,835,000	4,003,845,000
R&D Expense						
Operating Income	250,753,800	237,443,800	438,901,400	517,282,500	592,541,500	749,303,700
Operating Margin %		.07%	.15%	.15%	.17%	.18%
SGA Expense	312,702,800	350,496,700	383,525,200	481,131,900	526,813,100	595,663,600
Net Income	24,812,470	29,413,460	940,573,400	255,190,500	500,028,800	-378,102,600
Operating Cash Flow	894,070,500	857,426,900	880,267,600	1,185,247,000	1,192,642,000	1,284,826,000
Capital Expenditure	778,059,900	825,055,700	599,114,400	737,965,600	731,885,700	739,773,100
EBITDA	1,043,438,000	1,057,077,000	903,272,400	1,276,281,000	1,340,038,000	741,909,200
Return on Assets %		.00%	.10%	.02%	.04%	-.03%
Return on Equity %		.01%	.27%	.06%	.13%	-.12%
Debt to Equity		1.814	1.403	0.686	0.99	1.348

CONTACT INFORMATION:
Phone: 45-66637680   Fax: 45-33157579
Toll-Free:
Address: Teglholmsgade 1, Copenhagen, 0900 Denmark

STOCK TICKER/OTHER:
Stock Ticker: TDCAF   Exchange: PINX
Employees: 7,498   Fiscal Year Ends: 12/31
Parent Company: Macquarie Group Limited

SALARIES/BONUSES:
Top Exec. Salary: $ Bonus: $
Second Exec. Salary: $ Bonus: $

OTHER THOUGHTS:
Estimated Female Officers or Directors: 5
Hot Spot for Advancement for Women/Minorities: Y

TDS Telecommunications LLC

www.tdstelecom.com

NAIC Code: 517110

TYPES OF BUSINESS:

Mobile Phone and Wireless Services
Local Telephone Service
Long-Distance Service
Internet Access

BRANDS/DIVISIONS/AFFILIATES:

Telephone and Data Systems Inc (TDS)
TDS Broadband Service LLC
BendBroadband

CONTACTS: Note: Officers with more than one job title may be intentionally listed here more than once.

Jim Butman, CEO
Vicki L. Villacrez, CFO
Mike Pandow, Sr. VP-Admin.
Mark Barber, VP-Cable Oper.
Vicki L. Villacrez, VP-Finance
Phil LaForge, Pres., TDS Hosted & Managed Svcs.
Kevin Hess, Sr. VP-Gov't & Regulatory Affairs

GROWTH PLANS/SPECIAL FEATURES:

TDS Telecommunications, LLC (TDS Telecom), a wholly-owned subsidiary of Telephone and Data Systems, Inc., is a telecommunications service company that provides voice, internet and entertainment services to rural and suburban communities nationwide. TDS Telecom provides 1.2 million connections to high-speed internet, phone and TV entertainment services to customers in nearly 900 rural, suburban and metropolitan communities. The company deploys up to 1Gig internet access, IPTV services, cable TV options and traditional wireline services. For businesses, TDS Telecom offers advanced communications solutions such as voice over internet protocol (VoIP), high-speed internet, fiber optics, data networking and hosted-managed services. Subsidiary TDS Broadband Service, LLC serves the cable industry within the U.S. states of Arizona, Colorado, Nevada, New Mexico, Utah and Texas. Its cable operations offer businesses metro Ethernet, passive optical network technology, hosted private branch exchange (PBX), carrier backhaul and transport solutions. Subsidiary BendBroadband offers internet, cable TV and telephone services in the state of Oregon.

TDS Telecom offers its employees medical, dental, vision and life insurance; a 401(k) plan; a pension plan; an employee stock purchase plan; flexible spending accounts; education assistance; telephone and Internet discounts; and training and development p

FINANCIAL DATA: Note: Data for latest year may not have been available at press time.

In U.S. $	2020	2019	2018	2017	2016	2015
Revenue	976,000,000	930,000,000	927,000,000	919,000,000	1,151,000,000	1,158,000,000
R&D Expense						
Operating Income						
Operating Margin %						
SGA Expense						
Net Income	100,000,000	92,000,000	89,000,000	138,000,000	42,000,000	46,000,000
Operating Cash Flow						
Capital Expenditure						
EBITDA						
Return on Assets %						
Return on Equity %						
Debt to Equity						

CONTACT INFORMATION:

Phone: 608-664-4000   Fax: 608-664-4035
Toll-Free: 866-571-6662
Address: 525 Junction Rd., Madison, WI 53717 United States

STOCK TICKER/OTHER:

Stock Ticker: Subsidiary   Exchange:
Employees: 2,700   Fiscal Year Ends: 12/31
Parent Company: Telephone and Data Systems Inc (TDS)

SALARIES/BONUSES:

Top Exec. Salary: $ Bonus: $
Second Exec. Salary: $ Bonus: $

OTHER THOUGHTS:

Estimated Female Officers or Directors:
Hot Spot for Advancement for Women/Minorities:

Sales, profits and employees may be estimates. Financial information, benefits and other data can change quickly and may vary from those stated here.

TeamViewer AG

NAIC Code: 511210C

TYPES OF BUSINESS:

Computer Software: Telecom, Communications & VOIP
Screen-Sharing & Conferencing Software

BRANDS/DIVISIONS/AFFILIATES:

TeamViewer
TeamViewer Remote Management
Monitis
TeamViewer Tensor
TeamViewer Pilot
Blizz
TeamViewer Frontline
Ubimax GmbH

CONTACTS: *Note: Officers with more than one job title may be intentionally listed here more than once.*

Oliver Steil, CEO
Karl Markgraf, COO
Stefan Gaiser, CFO
Gautam Goswami, CMO
Rebecca Keating, Sr. VP-Human Resources
Dr. Mike Eissele, CTO
Oliver Steil, Chmn.

GROWTH PLANS/SPECIAL FEATURES:

TeamViewer AG provides cloud-based technologies to enable online remote support and collaboration globally. The TeamViewer remote desktop tool connects to desktop computers, mobile devices and Internet of Things (IoT) devices from anywhere at any time. There are currently (January 2021) over 2.5 billion live TeamViewer identifications that access its remote connection network. TeamViewer Remote Management is the firm's integrated information technology (IT) service management platform with remote monitoring, asset tracking, backup and endpoint protection features. Monitis is a cloud-based, agentless monitoring solution for websites, servers and applications. TeamViewer Tensor offers enterprise remote support, remote access and remote device control software-as-a-service so businesses can deploy and scale in hours, not days. TeamViewer Pilot is an augmented reality solution from which customers can see through their connection partner's smartphone camera to observe any kind of equipment, machinery, infrastructure issue and more. Pilot comes with 3D features for viewing these objects. Blizz is a collaboration companion from TeamViewer that keeps users connected globally via video, voice, instant chat messaging, screen sharing and more on any device, anywhere. TeamViewer can be integrated with business applications such as Microsoft, IBM, salesforce, freshworks and amazonWorkSpaces, among many others. Founded in 2005 in Goppingen, Germany, the company has offices across Europe, the U.S. and Asia Pacific. During 2020, TeamViewer acquired Ubimax GmbH, which offers an integrated augmented reality productivity solution platform to improve work efficiency and simplify the processes of large companies globally. The Ubimax platform was renamed TeamViewer Frontline, an augmented reality frontline workforce solution.

TeamViewer offers employees in-house doctor visits and eye examinations, work development and training programs and other programs and perks.

FINANCIAL DATA: *Note: Data for latest year may not have been available at press time.*

In U.S. $	2020	2019	2018	2017	2016	2015
Revenue	372,939,075	363,843,000	295,327,000	165,904,000		
R&D Expense						
Operating Income						
Operating Margin %						
SGA Expense						
Net Income		13,473,850	-14,183,000	-82,892,200		
Operating Cash Flow						
Capital Expenditure						
EBITDA						
Return on Assets %						
Return on Equity %						
Debt to Equity						

CONTACT INFORMATION:

Phone: 49 7161 60692 50   Fax:
Toll-Free: 800 638 0235
Address: JahnstraÃŸe 30, Goppingen, 73037 Germany

STOCK TICKER/OTHER:

Stock Ticker: TMV   Exchange: Frankfurt
Employees: 841   Fiscal Year Ends: 12/31
Parent Company:

SALARIES/BONUSES:

Top Exec. Salary: $ Bonus: $
Second Exec. Salary: $ Bonus: $

OTHER THOUGHTS:

Estimated Female Officers or Directors:
Hot Spot for Advancement for Women/Minorities:

Tektronix Inc

www.tek.com

NAIC Code: 334515

TYPES OF BUSINESS:

Test & Measurement Equipment
Support Services
Oscilloscopes
Logic analyzers
Video test equipment
Communications test equipment

BRANDS/DIVISIONS/AFFILIATES:

Fortive Corporation
Keithley

CONTACTS: Note: Officers with more than one job title may be intentionally listed here more than once.

Tami Newcombe, Pres.
Fuki Yoneyama, Pres., Japan Region

GROWTH PLANS/SPECIAL FEATURES:

Tektronix, Inc. develops, manufactures and markets test, measurement and monitoring products to a wide variety of customers. The firm's applications and industry solutions include 3D sensing technology, advanced research, automotive, electromagnetic interference (EMI) and electromagnetic compatibility (EMC) testing, education, teaching labs, high-speed serial communications, materials science, engineering, media production and delivery, medical technologies/devices/systems, military, government, power efficiency, wired communications, wireless, radio frequency (RF) testing, semiconductor design and manufacturing. Tektronix's products are categorized into oscillioscopes and probes, analyzers, Keithley (a Tektronix company) products, signal generators, power/measure sources and related supplies, meters, video test equipment, switching and data acquisition systems, semiconductor test systems, components and accessories, software, and refurbished test equipment. The company's calibration and related services are categorized into: calibration services, asset management services, repair services, factory service plans and testing services. Tektronix maintains its headquarters location in Beaverton, Oregon and has offices in 20+ countries. The firm has received more than 700 patents since the year 2000. Tektronix operates as a wholly-owned subsidiary of Fortive Corporation, a diversified industrial growth company encompassing several businesses.

Employee benefits include medical, dental and disability coverage; life insurance; and retirement plans.

FINANCIAL DATA: Note: Data for latest year may not have been available at press time.

In U.S. $	2020	2019	2018	2017	2016	2015
Revenue						
R&D Expense						
Operating Income						
Operating Margin %						
SGA Expense						
Net Income						
Operating Cash Flow						
Capital Expenditure						
EBITDA						
Return on Assets %						
Return on Equity %						
Debt to Equity						

CONTACT INFORMATION:

Phone: 503-627-7111   Fax: 503-627-6108
Toll-Free: 800-833-9200
Address: 14150 SW Karl Braun Dr., Beaverton, OR 97077 United States

STOCK TICKER/OTHER:

Stock Ticker: Subsidiary   Exchange:
Employees: 4,500   Fiscal Year Ends: 12/31
Parent Company: Fortive Corporation

SALARIES/BONUSES:

Top Exec. Salary: $ Bonus: $
Second Exec. Salary: $ Bonus: $

OTHER THOUGHTS:

Estimated Female Officers or Directors:
Hot Spot for Advancement for Women/Minorities:

Tele2 AB

NAIC Code: 517110

TYPES OF BUSINESS:

Fixed & Mobile Telephony
Broadband Services
Data Network Services
Cable TV
Internet of Things

BRANDS/DIVISIONS/AFFILIATES:

GROWTH PLANS/SPECIAL FEATURES:

Tele2 AB is a European alternative telecom developer and provider based in Sweden. The company's networks enable mobile and fixed connectivity, telephone, data network services, television, streaming and global Internet of Things (IoT) solutions for millions of customers, both residential and business. Tele2 offers mobile voice and messaging, mobile handset data, mobile and fixed broadband, business-to-business (B2B) communications services, bundled packages and more to customers in Sweden, Germany, Lithuania, Latvia and Estonia. Tele2's 5G network consists of base stations in Stockholm, Gothenburg and Malmo.

CONTACTS: Note: Officers with more than one job title may be intentionally listed here more than once.

Kjell Johnsen, CEO
Roxanna Zea, Exec. VP-Group Strategy
Lars Torstensson, Dir.-Corp. Comm.
Thomas Ekman, CEO-Tele2 Sweden
Gunther Vogelpoel, CEO-Tele2 Netherlands
Arild Hustad, CEO-Tele2 Norway
Carla Smits-Nusteling, Chmn.
Niklas Sonkin, Exec. VP-Central Europe & Eurasia

FINANCIAL DATA: Note: Data for latest year may not have been available at press time.

In U.S. $	2020	2019	2018	2017	2016	2015
Revenue	3,212,281,000	3,345,955,000	2,867,512,000	3,027,194,000	3,422,530,000	3,248,814,000
R&D Expense						
Operating Income	849,462,900	504,330,800	489,814,200	427,029,900	-157,263,100	273,879,800
Operating Margin %		.15%	.17%	.14%	-.05%	.08%
SGA Expense	792,848,100	841,720,700	767,444,100	801,437,100	1,073,260,000	969,103,800
Net Income	896,158,000	605,342,100	103,188,800	51,412,950	-237,346,400	361,221,300
Operating Cash Flow	1,066,486,000	1,175,360,000	624,213,700	693,409,400	606,914,800	426,908,900
Capital Expenditure	332,672,000	436,707,600	414,206,900	390,133,500	462,595,600	488,120,600
EBITDA	1,531,622,000	1,242,379,000	918,416,700	847,406,400	284,767,200	635,464,100
Return on Assets %		.06%	.01%	.01%	-.05%	.08%
Return on Equity %		.14%	.03%	.02%	-.11%	.15%
Debt to Equity		0.753	0.599	0.622	0.42	0.242

CONTACT INFORMATION:

Phone: 46 856200060   Fax:
Toll-Free:
Address: Skeppsbron 18, Stockholm, SE-103 13 Sweden

STOCK TICKER/OTHER:

Stock Ticker: TLTZF   Exchange: PINX
Employees: 4,295   Fiscal Year Ends: 12/31
Parent Company:

SALARIES/BONUSES:

Top Exec. Salary: $ Bonus: $
Second Exec. Salary: $ Bonus: $

OTHER THOUGHTS:

Estimated Female Officers or Directors: 2
Hot Spot for Advancement for Women/Minorities: Y

Telecom Argentina SA

www.telecom.com.ar

NAIC Code: 517110

TYPES OF BUSINESS:

Local & Long-Distance Telephone Services
Telecommunications
Cable TV
Data Transmission
Internet

BRANDS/DIVISIONS/AFFILIATES:

Nucleo SAE
PEM SAU
Adesol SA
AVC Continente Audiovisual SA
Telecom Argentina USA Inc

GROWTH PLANS/SPECIAL FEATURES:

Telecom Argentina SA is a telecommunications, cable television and data transmission service provider in Argentina. The firm is a leading provider of cable television services across Latin America. Telecom Argentina offers quadruple play services, combining its mobile telephone, cable television, internet and fixed telephone services. The company provides other telephone-related services such as international long-distance and wholesale services, data transmission and information technology (IT) solutions outsourcing, and it installs, operates and develops cable television and data transmission services. Telecom Argentina provides: mobile, cable TV, internet, and fixed and data services in Argentina; mobile, internet and satellite TV services in Paraguay; cable television services in Uruguay; and fixed wholesale services in the U.S. The firm's primary subsidiaries include Nucleo SAE, PEM SAU, Adesol SA, AVC Continente Audiovisual SA, and Telecom Argentina USA, Inc.

CONTACTS:
Note: Officers with more than one job title may be intentionally listed here more than once.

Roberto D. Nobile, CEO
Gonzalo Hita, COO
Gabriel P. Blasi, CFO
Pablo Esses, CIO
Sergio D. Faraudo, Human Capital
Miguel A. Fernandez, CTO
Alejandro D. Quiroga Lopez, Dir.-Legal Affairs
Mariano Cornejo, Dir.-Comm. & Media
Ricardo Luttini, Dir.-Internal Audit
Gonzalo A. Martinez, Dir.-Regulatory Affairs
Guillermo O. Rivaben, Dir.-Mobile Telephony
Maximo D. Lema, Dir.-Wholesale
Paolo Perfetti, Dir.-Network
Carlos Alberto Moltini, Chmn.
Estefano M. Esposizione, Dir.-Procurement

FINANCIAL DATA:
Note: Data for latest year may not have been available at press time.

In U.S. $	2020	2019	2018	2017	2016	2015
Revenue	3,186,875,000	2,504,562,000	1,775,692,000	688,801,100	562,571,300	427,909,200
R&D Expense						
Operating Income	332,587,000	237,919,900	244,492,400	143,263,400	100,373,100	74,283,920
Operating Margin %		.09%	.14%	.21%	.18%	.17%
SGA Expense	878,621,300	667,128,800	471,053,100	217,684,700	178,556,100	136,437,300
Net Income	-60,388,700	-46,451,230	55,940,130	80,623,940	42,002,640	35,958,490
Operating Cash Flow	1,070,671,000	865,761,700	448,302,900	204,275,500	120,090,600	71,980,380
Capital Expenditure	574,406,000	536,767,400	448,873,600	123,609,300	119,815,800	92,078,260
EBITDA	1,068,167,000	861,471,600	453,892,700	210,256,300	144,679,300	109,069,500
Return on Assets %		-.01%	.02%	.14%	.09%	.11%
Return on Equity %		-.02%	.04%	.36%	.22%	.22%
Debt to Equity		0.395	0.263	0.392	0.447	0.084

CONTACT INFORMATION:

Phone: 54 1149684019   Fax:
Toll-Free:
Address: Alicia Moreau de Justo, No. 50, Buenos Aires, C1107AAB Argentina

STOCK TICKER/OTHER:

Stock Ticker: TEO
Employees: 23,254
Parent Company:

Exchange: NYS
Fiscal Year Ends: 12/31

SALARIES/BONUSES:

Top Exec. Salary: $ Bonus: $
Second Exec. Salary: $ Bonus: $

OTHER THOUGHTS:

Estimated Female Officers or Directors: 2
Hot Spot for Advancement for Women/Minorities:

Sales, profits and employees may be estimates. Financial information, benefits and other data can change quickly and may vary from those stated here.

Telecom Egypt SAE
NAIC Code: 517110

ir.te.eg

TYPES OF BUSINESS:
Wired Telecommunications Carriers
Telecommunication Solutions
Voice Over Long-Term Evolution Service

BRANDS/DIVISIONS/AFFILIATES:
Vodafone Egypt

GROWTH PLANS/SPECIAL FEATURES:
Telecom Egypt SAE is a telecommunication solutions provider to consumers and businesses in Egypt. The company's solutions and services encompass mobile, internet and fixed voice, which come in a variety of plans, bundles and packages. Mobile international calling and roaming, broadband, router, call waiting, call filtering, conference calling and a variety of fixed-voice value-added features are provided by Telecom Egypt. Online/mobile payment, bill limit and balance query services are offered by the firm. Telecom Egypt owns a 45% stake in Vodafone Egypt. In mid-2021, Telecom Egypt announced the launch of voice over long-term evolution (LTE) service in Egypt through its 4G network in cooperation with key technology players and handset providers such as Ericsson, Nokia and Huawei.

CONTACTS:
Note: Officers with more than one job title may be intentionally listed here more than once.

Adel Hamed, CEO
Mohamed Shamroukh, CFO
Mohamed Abo-Taleb, CCO
Essam Abdeldayem, VP-Human Resources
Antar Kandil, CIO
Magued Osman, Chmn.

FINANCIAL DATA:
Note: Data for latest year may not have been available at press time.

In U.S. $	2020	2019	2018	2017	2016	2015
Revenue		1,482,490,060	1,411,895,296	1,151,268,736	876,325,056	737,564,800
R&D Expense						
Operating Income						
Operating Margin %						
SGA Expense						
Net Income		226,831,718	216,030,208	195,341,168	165,571,168	181,446,960
Operating Cash Flow						
Capital Expenditure						
EBITDA						
Return on Assets %						
Return on Equity %						
Debt to Equity						

CONTACT INFORMATION:
Phone: 20 231316011   Fax: 20 231316015
Toll-Free:
Address: B7, Smart Village, K28 Cairo-Alexandria Rd., Cairo, 11511 Egypt

STOCK TICKER/OTHER:
Stock Ticker: TEEG   Exchange: GREY
Employees: Fiscal Year Ends: 12/31
Parent Company:

SALARIES/BONUSES:
Top Exec. Salary: $ Bonus: $
Second Exec. Salary: $ Bonus: $

OTHER THOUGHTS:
Estimated Female Officers or Directors:
Hot Spot for Advancement for Women/Minorities:

Telecom Italia SpA

NAIC Code: 517110

www.gruppotim.it/en.html

TYPES OF BUSINESS:

Local Telephone Service
Mobile Communications Services
Internet Access
Data Communications Services
IT Products & Services
Media & TV Broadcasting

BRANDS/DIVISIONS/AFFILIATES:

Vivendi SA
TIM SpA
Gruppo TIM
Telecom Italia Sparkle SpA
Olivetti
INWIT SpA

CONTACTS: *Note: Officers with more than one job title may be intentionally listed here more than once.*

Luigi Gubitosi, CEO
Piergiorgio Peluso, Head-Admin.
Antonino Cusimano, Head-Legal Affairs
Oscar Cicchetti, Head-Strategy
Franco Brescia, Head-Public & Regulatory Affairs
Piergiorgio Peluso, Head-Finance & Control
Simone Battiferri, Head-Bus.
Stefano De Angelis, CEO-Telecom Argentina
Alessandro Talotta, Head-National Wholesale Svcs.
Paolo Vantellini, Head-Bus. Support Office
Salvatore Rossi, Chmn.
Rodrigo Abreu, CEO-TIM Participacoes

GROWTH PLANS/SPECIAL FEATURES:

Telecom Italia SpA, also referred to as TIM SpA and Gruppo TIM, is a leading Italian telecommunications service provider. The company offers both fixed and mobile ultra-broadband services to subscribers in Italy. Its domestic fixed telephone services are offered to retail, wholesale and residential customers. This service included broadband services directly-managed by TIM and excludes satellite, full-infrastructured and fixed wireless service. As for mobile service, the company has roaming agreements with local mobile phone operators in various locations. Telecom Italia Sparkle SpA develops fiber optic networks for wholesale in Europe, the Mediterranean and South America; Olivetti provides office products and services for information technology sectors; and INWIT SpA provides electronic communications infrastructure for housing radio transmission equipment for mobile telephone networks. TIM SpA is authorized to provide services using GSM 900 and GSM 1800 (global system for mobile communication) technology in Italy. In addition, it is 2600 MHz and 1450 MHz licensed. TIM SpA announced that it was working on the country's digital transformation by extending its 5G, fiber optic and long-term evolution (LTE) networks, for its smart home Internet of Things (IoT) product line, for its eGovernment services, for its business virtual services and for cloud computing services. Vivendi SA owns approximately 24% of the company.

FINANCIAL DATA: *Note: Data for latest year may not have been available at press time.*

In U.S. $	2020	2019	2018	2017	2016	2015
Revenue		21,960,220,000	23,140,460,000	24,225,390,000	23,244,310,000	24,091,000,000
R&D Expense						
Operating Income		4,714,838,000	4,568,224,000	5,412,472,000	5,187,665,000	4,819,910,000
Operating Margin %		.21%	.20%	.22%	.22%	.20%
SGA Expense						6,108,885
Net Income		1,119,148,000	-1,723,927,000	1,369,612,000	2,208,973,000	-87,967,940
Operating Cash Flow		7,250,024,000	5,610,400,000	6,596,374,000	6,971,459,000	6,194,409,000
Capital Expenditure		4,458,264,000	5,535,871,000	6,492,522,000	5,691,037,000	6,629,362,000
EBITDA		9,870,736,000	5,822,989,000	9,423,566,000	10,525,610,000	8,057,619,000
Return on Assets %		.01%	- .02%	.02%	.03%	.00%
Return on Equity %		.04%	- .07%	.05%	.09%	.00%
Debt to Equity		1.406	1.21	1.215	1.348	1.642

CONTACT INFORMATION:

Phone: 39-06-36-881   Fax:
Toll-Free:
Address: Via Gaetano Negri, 1, Milan, 20123 Italy

STOCK TICKER/OTHER:

Stock Ticker: TIAJF
Employees: 55,198
Parent Company:

Exchange: PINX
Fiscal Year Ends: 12/31

SALARIES/BONUSES:

Top Exec. Salary: $ Bonus: $
Second Exec. Salary: $ Bonus: $

OTHER THOUGHTS:

Estimated Female Officers or Directors: 1
Hot Spot for Advancement for Women/Minorities:

Telecomunicaciones de Puerto Rico Inc

www.claropr.com

NAIC Code: 517110

TYPES OF BUSINESS:

Local Exchange Carrier
Telecommunications Equipment Rental, Sales & Billing
Wireless Internet Services
Cellular Service
Mobile Network
Cloud
5G

BRANDS/DIVISIONS/AFFILIATES:

America Movil SAB de CV
Claro Puerto Rico
Claro

CONTACTS: Note: Officers with more than one job title may be intentionally listed here more than once.

Enrique Ortiz de Montellano, CEO

GROWTH PLANS/SPECIAL FEATURES:

Telecomunicaciones de Puerto Rico, Inc. (TELPRI), a subsidiary of America Movil SAB de CV and operating through Claro Puerto Rico, is a leading telecommunication services company in Puerto Rico. TELPRI offers wireline and fixed line services to residential and business customers, all marketed under the Claro name. Products and services for residential customers include mobile, internet, TV and fixed telephony, as well as bundled packages. Post- and pre-paid mobile services are offered, as well as services for the deaf community. To business customers, TELPRI provides mobile, internet, data, fixed telephony and cloud services. Data services features IBS trunking, virtual Ethernet link and IP-VPN (virtual private network) services. Finally, to the corporate client, which includes large-scale companies, the firm additionally offers data center services including collocation and virtual servers. In June 2021, TELPRI announced the expansion of its mobile network and 5G coverage, comprising more than 860 antennas throughout Puerto Rico.

FINANCIAL DATA: Note: Data for latest year may not have been available at press time.

In U.S. $	2020	2019	2018	2017	2016	2015
Revenue	926,100,000	882,000,000	840,000,000	800,000,000	1,020,000,000	1,100,000,000
R&D Expense						
Operating Income						
Operating Margin %						
SGA Expense						
Net Income						
Operating Cash Flow						
Capital Expenditure						
EBITDA						
Return on Assets %						
Return on Equity %						
Debt to Equity						

CONTACT INFORMATION:

Phone: 787-792-6052   Fax: 787-282-0958
Toll-Free: 800-781-1314
Address: 1515 FD Roosevelt Ave., Guaynabo, 00968 Puerto Rico

STOCK TICKER/OTHER:

Stock Ticker: Private   Exchange:
Employees: 4,900   Fiscal Year Ends: 12/31
Parent Company: America Movil SAB de CV

SALARIES/BONUSES:

Top Exec. Salary: $ Bonus: $
Second Exec. Salary: $ Bonus: $

OTHER THOUGHTS:

Estimated Female Officers or Directors: 1
Hot Spot for Advancement for Women/Minorities:

Telefonica Brasil SA

www.telefonica.com.br

NAIC Code: 517110

TYPES OF BUSINESS:

Local Telephone Services
Long-Distance Service
Mobile Phone Service
Data Transmission
Pay TV

BRANDS/DIVISIONS/AFFILIATES:

Telefonica SA

GROWTH PLANS/SPECIAL FEATURES:

Telefonica Brasil SA is a leading mobile telecommunications company in Brazil, with a 32.9% market share in the country (based on accesses). The firm's operations consists of local and long distance fixed telephone services, mobile services, data services (including broadband and mobile data), PayTV services via IPTV and DTH satellite technologies, network services, wholesale services, digital services, and the sale of wireless devices and related accessories. Telefonica Brasil is a subsidiary of Telefonica SA, based in Spain.

CONTACTS: *Note: Officers with more than one job title may be intentionally listed here more than once.*

Breno Rodrigo Pacheco de Oliveira, Sec. & Legal Officer
Gilmar Roberto Pereira Camurra, Investor Relations Officer
Cristiane Barretto Sales, Comptroller
Mariano Sebastian de Beer, Gen. Mgr.-Fixed Telephony
Paulo Cesar Pereira Teixeira, Gen. & Exec. Officer
Eduardo Navarro, Chmn.

FINANCIAL DATA: *Note: Data for latest year may not have been available at press time.*

In U.S. $	2020	2019	2018	2017	2016	2015
Revenue	8,374,560,000	8,596,262,000	8,439,859,000	8,390,164,000	8,254,551,000	7,823,138,000
R&D Expense						
Operating Income	1,277,925,000	1,321,585,000	2,111,772,000	1,554,359,000	1,408,361,000	1,257,313,000
Operating Margin %		.15%	.25%	.19%	.17%	.16%
SGA Expense	2,795,609,000	2,791,177,000	2,320,623,000	2,356,284,000	2,324,294,000	2,194,503,000
Net Income	926,369,900	971,127,200	1,733,743,000	894,962,800	793,297,100	664,164,700
Operating Cash Flow	3,755,898,000	3,441,209,000	2,318,859,000	2,454,718,000	2,221,649,000	1,921,899,000
Capital Expenditure	1,609,660,000	1,716,341,000	1,653,972,000	1,624,883,000	1,450,739,000	1,319,086,000
EBITDA	3,720,739,000	3,551,622,000	3,950,278,000	2,845,536,000	2,743,539,000	2,397,451,000
Return on Assets %		.05%	.09%	.05%	.04%	.04%
Return on Equity %		.07%	.13%	.07%	.06%	.06%
Debt to Equity		0.138	0.065	0.078	0.066	0.115

CONTACT INFORMATION:

Phone: 55 1134303687   Fax: 55 1174202240
Toll-Free:
Address: Avenida Engenheiro Luis Carlos Berrini, 1376, 32 d, Sao Paulo, SP 04571-936 Brazil

STOCK TICKER/OTHER:

Stock Ticker: VIV
Employees: 32,759
Parent Company: Telefonica SA

Exchange: NYS
Fiscal Year Ends: 12/31

SALARIES/BONUSES:

Top Exec. Salary: $ Bonus: $
Second Exec. Salary: $ Bonus: $

OTHER THOUGHTS:

Estimated Female Officers or Directors:
Hot Spot for Advancement for Women/Minorities:

Telefonica Chile SA

NAIC Code: 517110

www.telefonicachile.cl

TYPES OF BUSINESS:

Local Telephone Service
Long-Distance Service
Public Telephones
Automated Teller Machines
Managed Network Services
Internet & Broadband Service
Satellite TV Service
IPTV Service

BRANDS/DIVISIONS/AFFILIATES:

Telefonica SA
Telfonica Moviles Chile SA
Telefonica Empresas Chile SA
Telefonica Multimedia
Telefonica Moviles Chile Larga Distancia SA
Telefonica Gestion de Servicios Compartidos
Movistar

CONTACTS: *Note: Officers with more than one job title may be intentionally listed here more than once.*

Roberto Munoz Laporte, CEO
Jose Andres Wallis Garces, Dir.-Corp. Affairs
Victor G. Page, General Counsel
Juan Parra Hidalgo, Controller
Claudio Munoz Zuniga, Chmn.

GROWTH PLANS/SPECIAL FEATURES:

Telefonica Chile SA is the one of the largest telecommunications companies in Chile. A subsidiary of Telefonica SA, the firm offers its products and services under the Movistar brand name. Its services include local telephone service, mobile communications (through Telefonica Moviles Chile SA), broadband service, pay TV services, domestic and international long distance, public telephone service, data transmission and terminal equipment sales and leasing as well as value-added services. The firm provides all of its fixed telephone services through its own digital telecommunications network. The company also maintains public telephones and ATMs. Telefonica Chile offers duo or trio bundled service plans for its pay TV, broadband and voice services. The company operates through a number of majority- and minority-owned subsidiaries. Telefonica Empresas Chile SA provides corporate communications services, such as data and connectivity solutions, IT solutions, telephone and internet protocol (IP) solutions to government agencies, public institutions, businesses and other large national and international organizations. Telefonica Multimedia offers television services, including cable, satellite, broadband and pay TV as well as on-demand video services. Telefonica Moviles Chile Larga Distancia SA is the firm's long-distance carrier, and it provides substantially all of its domestic and international long-distance services with its own equipment and long-distance network. Telefonica Gestion de Servicios Compartidos Chile SA (t-gestiona) provides logistics, treasury, insurance, collection, payment, payroll, personnel and other services to all parts of the company.

FINANCIAL DATA: *Note: Data for latest year may not have been available at press time.*

In U.S. $	2020	2019	2018	2017	2016	2015
Revenue	18,561,080,000	19,017,500,000	1,116,810,000	1,311,960,000	1,142,576,692	1,104,200,207
R&D Expense						
Operating Income						
Operating Margin %						
SGA Expense						
Net Income		4,002,380,000	28,209,600	17,701,100	30,034,049	37,722,888
Operating Cash Flow						
Capital Expenditure						
EBITDA						
Return on Assets %						
Return on Equity %						
Debt to Equity						

CONTACT INFORMATION:

Phone: 562-691-2020   Fax:
Toll-Free:
Address: Ave. Providencia 111, Santiago, 7500775 Chile

STOCK TICKER/OTHER:

Stock Ticker: Subsidiary   Exchange:
Employees: 4,513   Fiscal Year Ends: 12/31
Parent Company: Telefonica SA

SALARIES/BONUSES:

Top Exec. Salary: $ Bonus: $
Second Exec. Salary: $ Bonus: $

OTHER THOUGHTS:

Estimated Female Officers or Directors: 2
Hot Spot for Advancement for Women/Minorities:

Telefonica de Argentina SA

www.movistar.com.ar

NAIC Code: 517110

TYPES OF BUSINESS:

Fixed-Line Telecommunication Services
Internet Service Provider
Data Services
Voice over Internet Protocol (VoIP) Services

BRANDS/DIVISIONS/AFFILIATES:

Telefonica SA
Movistar

CONTACTS: Note: Officers with more than one job title may be intentionally listed here more than once.

Frederico Rava, Pres.

GROWTH PLANS/SPECIAL FEATURES:

Telefonica de Argentina SA is a leading telecommunications service provider in Argentina, operating under the brand name Movistar. The company is owned by companies that are all directly or indirectly owned by Telefonica SA. Telefonica de Argentina's offerings include international long-distance, data transmission, voice over internet protocol (VoIP), mobile, television and internet services. The firm's supplementary service offerings include call waiting and call forwarding through telephones and digital switches. Additionally, the company offers special services, including providing digital links between customers and digital trunk access. Telefonica de Argentina has millions of telephone lines in service. The firm primarily provides services to residential customers, but also caters to professional, commercial and governmental clientele. Besides serving its own customers, Telefonica de Argentina operates a wholesale business that provides network access and the use of its facilities for third-party telecommunications operators, such as cell phone companies. Moreover, the company engages in the sale of telephone booth terminals, batteries, computers, cellular handsets and more.

FINANCIAL DATA: Note: Data for latest year may not have been available at press time.

In U.S. $	2020	2019	2018	2017	2016	2015
Revenue						
R&D Expense						
Operating Income						
Operating Margin %						
SGA Expense						
Net Income						
Operating Cash Flow						
Capital Expenditure						
EBITDA						
Return on Assets %						
Return on Equity %						
Debt to Equity						

CONTACT INFORMATION:

Phone: 54-11-4332-2051   Fax: 54-11-4303-5586
Toll-Free:
Address: Avenida Ingeniero Huergo 723, Buenos Aires, C1107AOH Argentina

STOCK TICKER/OTHER:

Stock Ticker: Subsidiary
Employees: 11,000
Parent Company: Telefonica SA

Exchange:
Fiscal Year Ends: 12/31

SALARIES/BONUSES:

Top Exec. Salary: $ Bonus: $
Second Exec. Salary: $ Bonus: $

OTHER THOUGHTS:

Estimated Female Officers or Directors:
Hot Spot for Advancement for Women/Minorities:

Telefonica del Peru SAA

NAIC Code: 517110

www.telefonica.com.pe/home

TYPES OF BUSINESS:
Local Phone Service
Long-Distance Phone Service
Public Telephones
Cable Television Service
Cellular Service
Internet Service
Calling Cards

BRANDS/DIVISIONS/AFFILIATES:
Telefonica SA
Movistar
Telefonica Moviles Peru SAC
Terra Networks Perus SA
Telefonica Ingenieria de Seguridad
Tgestiona
Wayra Peru Acelerador de Proyectos SAC
Telxius Torres Peru

CONTACTS: *Note: Officers with more than one job title may be intentionally listed here more than once.*
Pedro Cortez Rojas, CEO
Denis Fernandez Armas, Dir.-Network Oper. & Maintenance, Movistar

GROWTH PLANS/SPECIAL FEATURES:
Telefonica del Peru SAA, 98%-owned by the Spanish telecommunications conglomerate Telefonica SA, is one of the largest landline and cellular service providers in Peru. The firm offers both domestic and international long-distance fixed telephone services, public telephone services, data transmission, information technology and internet throughout Peru under the Movistar brand name. Telefonica del Peru operates through several subsidiaries. Telefonica Moviles Peru SAC provides mobile telephone, internet and television services to individual and business customers. Terra Networks Peru SA is a provider of cable internet access. Telefonica Ingenieria de Seguridad offers security engineering services, including installing safety equipment such as alarm systems, fire detection and suppression systems, closed circuit video surveillance cameras and perimeter protection systems. Subsidiary Tgestiona offers outsourced administrative functions to corporate clients, with services in areas such as human resources, property management, collections, logistics management, treasury and accounting. Wayra Peru Aceleradora de Proyectos SAC provides technology innovation and project development services. Telxius Torres Peru is the company's global telecommunications infrastructures subsidiary, with telecommunications towers distributed throughout Peru.

FINANCIAL DATA: *Note: Data for latest year may not have been available at press time.*

In U.S. $	2020	2019	2018	2017	2016	2015
Revenue	1,803,670,000	2,616,568,500	2,491,970,000	2,593,250,000	2,882,688,692	3,008,825,550
R&D Expense						
Operating Income						
Operating Margin %						
SGA Expense						
Net Income	-190,572,000	-127,777,650	-121,693,000	-73,004,700	283,789,472	-153,494,342
Operating Cash Flow						
Capital Expenditure						
EBITDA						
Return on Assets %						
Return on Equity %						
Debt to Equity						

CONTACT INFORMATION:
Phone: 51-1-265-7555   Fax: 51-1-470-7484
Toll-Free:
Address: Avenida Arequipa 1155, Santa Beatriz, Lima 1, Peru

SALARIES/BONUSES:
Top Exec. Salary: $ Bonus: $
Second Exec. Salary: $ Bonus: $

STOCK TICKER/OTHER:
Stock Ticker: Subsidiary   Exchange:
Employees: 4,374   Fiscal Year Ends: 12/31
Parent Company: Telefonica SA

OTHER THOUGHTS:
Estimated Female Officers or Directors:
Hot Spot for Advancement for Women/Minorities:

Telefonica Deutschland Holding AG

www.telefonica.de

NAIC Code: 517210

TYPES OF BUSINESS:

Mobile Telephone Service

BRANDS/DIVISIONS/AFFILIATES:

Telefonica SA
Telefonica Germany GmbH & Co OHG
O2
AY YILDIZ
Blau
Ortel Mobile
AldiTalk
Tchibo mobil

CONTACTS: Note: Officers with more than one job title may be intentionally listed here more than once.

Markus Haas, CEO
Markus Rolle, CFO
Nicole Gerhardt, Chief Human Resources Officer
Mallik Rao, CTO

GROWTH PLANS/SPECIAL FEATURES:

Telefonica Deutschland Holding AG provides telecommunications and connectivity services in Germany. The company offers fixed-line and mobile telephone, internet and data transmission services to residential and business customers. Telefonica Deutschland offers its products and services primarily under the O2 brand, as well as the AY YILDIZ, Blau, Ortel Mobile, AldiTalk and Tchibo mobil brands. Wholly-owned Telefonica Germany GmbH & Co. OHG operates under the holding group's umbrella. In the mobile business, the company provides private and business customers with post- and pre-paid products, as well as mobile data services based on GPRS (general packet radio service), UMTS (universal mobile telecommunications service) and LTE (long term evolution) technology. Fixed services include both DSL telephone and high-speed internet. Telefonica Deutschland began to roll out its 5G network under the O2 brand in late-2020, and plans to continue to expand to across cities each year until its 5G network is nationwide (by 2025).Telefonica Deutschland is part of the Spanish telecommunications group, Telefonica SA, which is headquartered in Madrid.

FINANCIAL DATA: Note: Data for latest year may not have been available at press time.

In U.S. $	2020	2019	2018	2017	2016	2015
Revenue	9,202,425,000	9,039,928,000	8,942,185,000	8,914,085,000	9,165,771,000	9,636,155,000
R&D Expense						
Operating Income	-65,975,960	-151,500,300	-139,282,600	-142,947,900	-496,041,400	-467,940,600
Operating Margin %		- .02%	- .02%	- .02%	- .05%	- .05%
SGA Expense	293,226,500	292,004,700	309,109,600	355,537,100		
Net Income	400,742,800	-259,016,700	-281,008,700	-465,497,000	-215,032,800	-467,940,600
Operating Cash Flow	2,607,272,000	2,461,881,000	2,064,803,000	2,079,464,000	2,271,283,000	2,245,626,000
Capital Expenditure	1,221,777,000	1,180,237,000	1,196,120,000	1,266,983,000	1,263,317,000	2,518,082,000
EBITDA	3,281,693,000	2,803,978,000	2,197,977,000	2,185,759,000	2,536,409,000	2,210,194,000
Return on Assets %		- .01%	- .02%	- .03%	- .01%	- .02%
Return on Equity %		- .03%	- .03%	- .04%	- .02%	- .04%
Debt to Equity		0.64	0.265	0.153	0.183	0.163

CONTACT INFORMATION:

Phone: 49 8924421010   Fax: 49 8924421209
Toll-Free:
Address: Georg-Brauchle-Ring 50, Munich, 80992 Germany

STOCK TICKER/OTHER:

Stock Ticker: TELDF   Exchange: PINX
Employees: 8,271   Fiscal Year Ends: 12/31
Parent Company:

SALARIES/BONUSES:

Top Exec. Salary: $ Bonus: $
Second Exec. Salary: $ Bonus: $

OTHER THOUGHTS:

Estimated Female Officers or Directors:
Hot Spot for Advancement for Women/Minorities:

Telefonica SA

NAIC Code: 517110

TYPES OF BUSINESS:

Fixed Line & Mobile Telecommunications
Internet Access Service
Data Service
Digital Media

BRANDS/DIVISIONS/AFFILIATES:

Telefonica Espana
Telefonica UK
Telefonica Deutschland
Telefonica Brasil
Telefonica HispanoAmerica
Telefonica
Movistar
O2

CONTACTS: *Note: Officers with more than one job title may be intentionally listed here more than once.*

Jose Maria Alvarez-Pallette, CEO
Angel Vila, COO
Laura Abasolo, CFO
Marta Machicot, Chief People Officer
Enrique Blanco, CTO
Ramiro Sanchez de Lerin Garcia-Ovies, General Counsel
Angel Vila Voix, Gen. Mgr.-Corp. Dev.
Angel Vila Voix, Gen. Mgr.-Finance
Guillermo Ansaldo Lutz, Gen. Mgr.-Global Resources
Matthew Key, Chmn.-Telefonica Digital
Eduardo Navarro, Gen. Mgr.-Strategy & Alliances
Eva Castillo, CEO-Telefonica Europe
Jose Maria Alvarez-Pallette, Chmn.
Santiago Fernandez Valbuena, Chmn.-Telefonica Latin America

GROWTH PLANS/SPECIAL FEATURES:

Telefonica SA is a diversified Spanish telecommunications company with operations in 14 countries within Latin American and European markets. The firm maintains strategic partner agreements to offer its services in over 170 countries. Telefonica provides fixed telephony and broadband services, including basic wireline service, long-distance domestic and international service, public telephones, internet service, equipment sales and leasing, cable television, paging and mobile telephony. Business-to-business (B2B) services include cybersecurity, Internet of Things (IoT), big data and cloud. Telefonica's 3337.3 million worldwide customers (as of June 2020) include mobile phone subscribers, fixed telephony customers, internet and data customers, and pay TV subscribers. Telefonica's operations are organized into five geographic regions via primary subsidiaries: Telefonica Espana (Spain), Telefonica U.K., Telefonica Deutschland (Germany), Telefonica Brasil and Telefonica HispanoAmerica (Mexico and South/North America). Approximately 20 million premises had fiber-to-the-home (FTTH) deployment within its Latin American markets. The global resources segment oversees the distributed multinational operations of Telefonica, including network infrastructure, IT, procurement and human resources. Brands of the company include Telefonica, Movistar, Vivo and O2. The firm has been engaged in acquiring and deploying 5G technology throughout select regions. Telefonica has been engaged in During 2020, the firm agreed to merge its U.K. telecommunications business, O2, with that of Liberty Global's U.K. telecommunications business, Virgin Media. The transaction is expected to close mid-2021.

FINANCIAL DATA: *Note: Data for latest year may not have been available at press time.*

In U.S. $	2020	2019	2018	2017	2016	2015
Revenue	52,629,270,000	59,160,880,000	59,491,980,000	63,542,180,000	63,576,390,000	57,691,090,000
R&D Expense						
Operating Income	5,780,227,000	4,448,490,000	8,118,708,000	8,132,148,000	6,593,931,000	3,223,048,000
Operating Margin %		.08%	.14%	.13%	.10%	.06%
SGA Expense	6,559,720,000	11,094,960,000	10,302,020,000	11,169,480,000	12,743,130,000	14,624,670,000
Net Income	1,932,851,000	1,395,269,000	4,069,739,000	3,826,606,000	2,894,390,000	3,353,778,000
Operating Cash Flow						
Capital Expenditure	8,576,874,000	9,357,590,000	10,488,950,000	10,986,220,000	11,224,470,000	11,485,930,000
EBITDA	17,543,500,000	19,664,500,000	21,148,960,000	21,205,160,000	21,222,260,000	16,161,670,000
Return on Assets %		.01%	.03%	.02%	.02%	.02%
Return on Equity %		.05%	.17%	.16%	.12%	.13%
Debt to Equity		2.72	2.399	2.569	2.361	2.465

CONTACT INFORMATION:

Phone: 34 914823734   Fax: 34 914823768
Toll-Free:
Address: Distrito C, Ronda de la Comunicacion, Madrid, 28050 Spain

STOCK TICKER/OTHER:

Stock Ticker: TEF   Exchange: NYS
Employees: 112,797   Fiscal Year Ends: 12/31
Parent Company:

SALARIES/BONUSES:

Top Exec. Salary: $ Bonus: $
Second Exec. Salary: $ Bonus: $

OTHER THOUGHTS:

Estimated Female Officers or Directors: 1
Hot Spot for Advancement for Women/Minorities:

Telefonos de Mexico SAB de CV (Telmex)   www.telmex.com

NAIC Code: 517110

TYPES OF BUSINESS:

Local Telephone Service
Long-Distance Service
Internet Services
Telecom Equipment & Computer Retail
Internet of Things

BRANDS/DIVISIONS/AFFILIATES:

America Movil SAB de CV
Scitum
Infinitum

CONTACTS: *Note: Officers with more than one job title may be intentionally listed here more than once.*

Carlos Slim Domit, Pres.
Sergio Medina Noriega, Dir.-Legal
Arturo Elias Ayub, Dir.-Strategic Alliances & Institutional Rel.
Javier Mondragon Alarcon, Dir.-Regulation & Legal Affairs

GROWTH PLANS/SPECIAL FEATURES:

Telefonos de Mexico SAB de CV, commonly known as Telmex, is a nationwide provider of communications services in Mexico. Telmexes' connectivity solutions provide national and international coverage and robust bandwidths. Its network encompasses approximately 198,835 miles (320,000 kilometers) of fiber optics, which are visible and controllable through the firm's service centers. Collaboration solutions consist of Telmexes' integration of platforms and communication services, which are streamlined for flexible and reliable communication among the entire organization. These services enable customers and clients to incorporate mobility and provide enhanced customer service via video, voice, chat and audio capabilities. Cybersecurity services are provided through subsidiary Scitum, which offers computer security services to businesses so they can protect their information. These solutions help minimize risks, allowing the business to react on time through the security and cyberintelligence tools provided. The services and technologies within the cybersecurity platform are adaptable to the technological, regulatory and business requirements for each organization. Telmex has an of Things (IoT) hub, Infinitum, at KidZania Santa Fe in Mexico City. Infinitum allows children to experience how smart cities and smart homes work via IoT technology. Telmex operates as a subsidiary of America Movil SAB de CV.

FINANCIAL DATA: *Note: Data for latest year may not have been available at press time.*

In U.S. $	2020	2019	2018	2017	2016	2015
Revenue		5,091,560	4,884,980	5,001,470		
R&D Expense						
Operating Income						
Operating Margin %						
SGA Expense						
Net Income						
Operating Cash Flow						
Capital Expenditure						
EBITDA						
Return on Assets %						
Return on Equity %						
Debt to Equity						

CONTACT INFORMATION:

Phone: 52 5552221774   Fax: 52 5555455550
Toll-Free:
Address: Parque Via 190, Colonia Cuauhtemoc, Mexico City, DF 06599 Mexico

STOCK TICKER/OTHER:

Stock Ticker: TMXLF   Exchange: GREY
Employees: 54,317   Fiscal Year Ends: 12/31
Parent Company: America Movil SAB de CV

SALARIES/BONUSES:

Top Exec. Salary: $ Bonus: $
Second Exec. Salary: $ Bonus: $

OTHER THOUGHTS:

Estimated Female Officers or Directors:
Hot Spot for Advancement for Women/Minorities:

Telekom Austria AG

NAIC Code: 517110

TYPES OF BUSINESS:
Wireless & Wireline Phone Services
Internet Services
Mobile Services
Data Services
Cloud
Internet of Things

BRANDS/DIVISIONS/AFFILIATES:
America Movil SAB de CV
A1 Telekom Austria AG
A1
A1 Bulgaria
velcom
Vipnet
Vip mobile
one.Vip

CONTACTS: Note: Officers with more than one job title may be intentionally listed here more than once.
Thomas Arnoldner, CEO
Alejandro Plater, COO
Siegfried Mayrhofer, CFO
Eve Zehetner, Dir.-Human Resources

GROWTH PLANS/SPECIAL FEATURES:
Telekom Austria AG offers digital services and communications solutions in Central and Eastern Europe. The firm serves approximately 25 million customers across seven primary countries, each operating under the A1 brand name, including Austria, Bulgaria, Croatia, Belarus, Slovenia, Serbia and Macedonia. Telekom's fixed line services include voice, internet, data solutions, IT solutions and internet, as well as value-added services and wholesale services. Mobile communications services include switched voice telephone, voicemail, information and entertainment services, mobile commerce, mobile internet access, GPS (global positioning system) services and SMS (short message service) and multimedia messaging services for private and business customers. Subsidiary A1 Digital International GmbH offers cloud services and Internet of Things (IoT) solutions to businesses. Telekom Austria is approximately 28%-owned by the Austrian government, and operates as the European unit of America Movil SAB de CV, which holds a 51% majority stake. In July 2021, Telekom Austria announced that it expanded its international footprint to Turkey, allowing a bandwidth ranging from 2 Mbit to 100 Gbit, with up to 200 Gbit possible in the near future.

FINANCIAL DATA: Note: Data for latest year may not have been available at press time.

In U.S. $	2020	2019	2018	2017	2016	2015
Revenue	5,453,872,000	5,460,526,000	5,419,071,000	5,228,873,000	5,145,467,000	4,919,585,000
R&D Expense						
Operating Income	780,644,600	751,171,700	530,691,000	542,362,700	597,423,300	686,279,400
Operating Margin %		.14%	.10%	.10%	.12%	.14%
SGA Expense	1,218,570,000	1,258,038,000	1,230,362,000	1,215,558,000	1,204,815,000	254,951,900
Net Income	474,563,800	399,475,900	297,255,900	420,857,000	504,387,400	479,668,400
Operating Cash Flow	1,809,524,000	1,781,383,000	1,505,641,000	1,435,356,000	1,460,672,000	1,310,197,000
Capital Expenditure	907,206,000	1,067,677,000	942,550,800	861,868,400	997,535,700	887,817,700
EBITDA	1,903,580,000	1,913,390,000	1,708,599,000	1,718,598,000	1,682,648,000	1,701,655,000
Return on Assets %		.04%	.03%	.04%	.05%	.04%
Return on Equity %		.13%	.09%	.11%	.15%	.16%
Debt to Equity		1.259	1.037	0.863	0.832	1.066

CONTACT INFORMATION:
Phone: 43 506640   Fax: 43 5917182100
Toll-Free:
Address: Lassallestrasse 9, Vienna, AT 1020 Austria

STOCK TICKER/OTHER:
Stock Ticker: TKAGY   Exchange: PINX
Employees: 17,949   Fiscal Year Ends: 12/31
Parent Company: America Movil SAB de CV

SALARIES/BONUSES:
Top Exec. Salary: $ Bonus: $
Second Exec. Salary: $ Bonus: $

OTHER THOUGHTS:
Estimated Female Officers or Directors: 2
Hot Spot for Advancement for Women/Minorities: Y

Telekom Malaysia Berhad

www.tm.com.my

NAIC Code: 517110

TYPES OF BUSINESS:

Wired Telecommunications Carriers
Telecommunications Services
Broadband
Mobile
TV Content
Smart Services

BRANDS/DIVISIONS/AFFILIATES:

Khazanah Nasional Berhad
unifi
TM One
TM Global
Multimedia University
Menara Kuala Lumpur
VADS Berhad
GITN

CONTACTS: *Note: Officers with more than one job title may be intentionally listed here more than once.*

Imri Mokhtar, CEO
Azizi A Haid, COO
Razidan Ghazalli, CFO
Shanti Jusnita Johari, CMO
Sarinah Abu Bakar, Chief Human Resources Officer
M. Umapathy Sivan, CIO

GROWTH PLANS/SPECIAL FEATURES:

Telekom Malaysia Berhad (TM) offers telecommunications services and solutions throughout Malaysia, including broadband, data, telephone, mobile, Wi-Fi, television content and smart services. The company offers its products and services to individual, business, enterprise and government customers as well as to smart cities and living communities. These products, services and solutions are marketed under the unifi, TM One and TM Global brand names. Other entities include: Multimedia University, a private university for computer science and information technology (IT), which comprises three campuses in Melaka, Cyberjaya and Nusajaya; Multimedia College, which offers vocational programs in the fields of multimedia and information technology (IT); Menara Kuala Lumpur, a telecommunications tower; VADS Berhad, an integrated connectivity, information/communications/technology (ICT) and business process outsource (BPO) solutions provider; Yellow Pages, offering an business directory in print and online formats; TM R&D, the innovation engine for TM, and a technology partner for many Malaysian ICT companies; and GITN, which constructs, establishes, maintains and operates integrated telecommunications network infrastructure in Malaysia. TM itself operates as a subsidiary of Khazanah Nasional Berhad, the sovereign wealth fund of the government of Malaysia.

FINANCIAL DATA: *Note: Data for latest year may not have been available at press time.*

In U.S. $	2020	2019	2018	2017	2016	2015
Revenue	2,628,589,000	2,772,599,000	2,865,979,000	2,930,431,000	2,924,563,000	2,842,289,000
R&D Expense				1,624,636	2,061,106	2,594,568
Operating Income	392,725,500	422,259,900	319,059,200	284,384,100	277,934,000	314,015,500
Operating Margin %		.15%	.11%	.10%	.10%	.11%
SGA Expense				106,813,800	107,783,700	95,659,550
Net Income	246,362,800	153,419,000	37,148,400	225,436,400	188,166,800	169,810,900
Operating Cash Flow						
Capital Expenditure	348,472,400	363,433,500	551,915,600	804,728,400	893,186,200	617,652,700
EBITDA	986,954,400	905,868,100	660,911,700	925,363,700	926,648,800	871,605,200
Return on Assets %		.03%	.01%	.04%	.03%	.03%
Return on Equity %		.09%	.02%	.12%	.10%	.09%
Debt to Equity		1.267	1.108	0.896	0.996	0.922

CONTACT INFORMATION:

Phone: 60 322401211   Fax:
Toll-Free:
Address: Fl. 51, North Wing Menara TM, Jalan Pantai Baharu, Kuala Lumpur, 50672 Malaysia

STOCK TICKER/OTHER:

Stock Ticker: MYTEF   Exchange: GREY
Employees: 22,763   Fiscal Year Ends:
Parent Company: Khazanah Nasional Berhad

SALARIES/BONUSES:

Top Exec. Salary: $ Bonus: $
Second Exec. Salary: $ Bonus: $

OTHER THOUGHTS:

Estimated Female Officers or Directors:
Hot Spot for Advancement for Women/Minorities:

Telenet Group NV/SA

www.telenet.be

NAIC Code: 517110

TYPES OF BUSINESS:
Telecommunications Services
Telecommunications
Media Services
Internet
TV
Mobile
Digital Security
Smart Home

BRANDS/DIVISIONS/AFFILIATES:
Liberty Global

GROWTH PLANS/SPECIAL FEATURES:

Telenet Group Holding NV is a Belgium-based provider of media and communication services to public and private sectors. The firm offers internet, TV, mobile, digital security, smart home, streaming and other related services and devices. Telenet has more than 1.6 million broadband internet customers, approximately 3 million mobile customers and 2 million video subscribers. The company's network consists of fiber-optic cable, coaxial cable and wireless infrastructures. Liberty Global owns a 58.28% direct stake in Telenet Group Holding. In mid-2021, Telenet announced that it began testing its 5G network in collaboration with the city of Leuven, which was comprised of 17 cell towers at various locations in Leuven under a temporary license.

CONTACTS: *Note: Officers with more than one job title may be intentionally listed here more than once.*
John Porter, CEO
Erik Van den Enden, CFO
Micha Berger, CTO

FINANCIAL DATA: *Note: Data for latest year may not have been available at press time.*

In U.S. $	2020	2019	2018	2017	2016	2015
Revenue	3,146,320,000	3,156,949,000	3,097,004,000	3,088,760,000	2,967,843,000	2,209,446,000
R&D Expense						
Operating Income	725,857,700	837,528,100	732,407,600	549,321,900	593,089,700	663,530,000
Operating Margin %		.27%	.24%	.18%	.20%	.30%
SGA Expense	708,019,800	665,990,700	653,461,300	593,830,100	603,252,400	343,062,800
Net Income	414,060,200	286,506,700	309,575,100	137,104,100	51,088,600	214,591,700
Operating Cash Flow	1,291,907,000	1,334,791,000	1,314,103,000	1,016,068,000	915,231,900	813,132,900
Capital Expenditure	576,434,400	503,249,900	493,227,700	592,780,500	591,209,300	467,622,900
EBITDA	1,646,222,000	1,582,323,000	1,604,930,000	1,365,876,000	1,136,275,000	1,100,516,000
Return on Assets %		.04%	.05%	.02%	.01%	.05%
Return on Equity %						
Debt to Equity						

CONTACT INFORMATION:
Phone: 32 15333000   Fax: 32 15333999
Toll-Free: 0800 66046
Address: Liersesteenweg 4, Mechelen, 2800 Belgium

STOCK TICKER/OTHER:
Stock Ticker: TLGHY   Exchange: PINX
Employees: 3,431   Fiscal Year Ends: 12/31
Parent Company: Liberty Global

SALARIES/BONUSES:
Top Exec. Salary: $ Bonus: $
Second Exec. Salary: $ Bonus: $

OTHER THOUGHTS:
Estimated Female Officers or Directors:
Hot Spot for Advancement for Women/Minorities:

Telenor ASA

www.telenor.com

NAIC Code: 517210

TYPES OF BUSINESS:

Mobile Telephone Services
Fixed-Line Telephone Services
Cable Services
Satellite Communications
Satellite Television Broadcasting
Internet of Things

BRANDS/DIVISIONS/AFFILIATES:

Telenor Norway
Telenor Sweden
Telenor Denmark
DNA
dtac
Digi
Grameenphone
Telenor Pakistan

CONTACTS: *Note: Officers with more than one job title may be intentionally listed here more than once.*

Sigve Brekke, CEO
Tone Hegland Bachke, CFO
Cecilie Blydt Heuch, Chief People Officer
Ruza Sabanovic, CTO
Morten Karlsen Sorby, Head-Strategy & Regulatory Affairs
Rolv-Erik Spilling, Exec. VP
Hilde M. Tonne, Exec. VP
Berit Svendsen, Exec. VP
Bjorn Magnus Kopperud, Acting Head-Central & Eastern European Oper.
Gunn Waersted, Chmn.
Sigve Brekke, Head-Asia Oper.

GROWTH PLANS/SPECIAL FEATURES:

Telenor ASA, a Norwegian national telecommunications operator and an international provider of mobile services. Telenor's operations are focused in three major areas: mobile, fixed-line and broadcast. With more than 180 million subscribers, mobile services are the firm's chief basis for internationalization and growth, accounting for almost half its external revenue. The company has majority shareholdings in mobile operations in nine markets, including Norway, Denmark, Sweden, Finland, Thailand, Malaysia, Myanmar, Bangladesh and Pakistan. Telenor provides fixed-line telecommunications services to residential and business markets through asymmetric digital subscriber line (ADSL) and fiber-optic lines as well as analogue (PSTN) and digital fixed-line (ISDN) telephony services. In Europe the firm's businesses are Telenor Norway, Telenor Sweden, Telenor Denmark and DNA in Finland. The firm's Asian subsidiaries are dtac in Thailand, Digi in Malaysia, Grameenphone in Bangladesh, Telenor Pakistan and Telenor Malaysia. Telenor's broadcast segment consists of the Canal Digital Group, which provides TV distribution services to approximately 850,000 homes and businesses; transmission and encryption, which provides transmission services for broadcasters through subsidiaries Telenor Satellite Broadcasting and Norkring. The global wholesale business unit is for international wholesale communication, providing services to both internal and external operators. This business unit provides voice, roaming, connectivity and digital services. Telenor Maritime is a mobile operator at sea and a marine communication specialist company. The firm has a global IoT vehicle, Telenor Connexion, which currently connects more than 13 million things, delivering IoT solutions in several markets, including automotive, industrial manufacturing, transportation, logistics, utilities and smart cities. Tapad is a marketing technology company. Tapad develops solutions for unified cross-device marketing with both media execution and data licensing business lines. In November 2020, Telenor agreed to acquire KNL Networks, a Finnish technology company.

FINANCIAL DATA: *Note: Data for latest year may not have been available at press time.*

In U.S. $	2020	2019	2018	2017	2016	2015
Revenue	14,771,980,000	13,671,880,000	13,274,590,000	15,006,050,000	15,808,330,000	15,417,180,000
R&D Expense						
Operating Income	3,067,317,000	3,042,178,000	2,683,016,000	3,197,583,000	3,095,102,000	3,049,756,000
Operating Margin %		.22%	.20%	.21%	.20%	.20%
SGA Expense	904,762,900	936,878,300	1,158,919,000	1,357,385,000	1,642,574,000	1,677,456,000
Net Income	2,085,814,000	934,953,800	1,771,878,000	1,441,342,000	340,639,300	410,643,600
Operating Cash Flow	5,270,767,000	4,116,298,000	4,377,552,000	5,057,387,000	4,784,587,000	4,463,313,000
Capital Expenditure	2,285,362,000	2,644,525,000	2,516,304,000	2,208,502,000	2,853,936,000	2,546,135,000
EBITDA	7,057,440,000	6,032,635,000	5,030,804,000	5,620,067,000	5,100,207,000	4,317,411,000
Return on Assets %		.04%	.07%	.06%	.01%	.02%
Return on Equity %		.18%	.28%	.22%	.05%	.06%
Debt to Equity		3.04	0.897	0.863	1.10	1.024

CONTACT INFORMATION:

Phone: 47 81077000   Fax: 47 67890000
Toll-Free:
Address: Snaroyveien 30, Fornebu, N-1331 Norway

STOCK TICKER/OTHER:

Stock Ticker: TELNF   Exchange: PINX
Employees: 19,000   Fiscal Year Ends: 12/31
Parent Company:

SALARIES/BONUSES:

Top Exec. Salary: $ Bonus: $
Second Exec. Salary: $ Bonus: $

OTHER THOUGHTS:

Estimated Female Officers or Directors: 6
Hot Spot for Advancement for Women/Minorities: Y

Telephone and Data Systems Inc (TDS)

www.tdsinc.com

NAIC Code: 517110

TYPES OF BUSINESS:

Local Telephone Service
Cellular Telephone Services
Internet Access
Printing Services
Long-Distance Telephone Service
Data Networks
Broadband Service

BRANDS/DIVISIONS/AFFILIATES:

United States Cellular Corporation
TDS Telecommunications Corporation
OneNeck
Suttle-Straus Inc

CONTACTS: Note: Officers with more than one job title may be intentionally listed here more than once.

Kenneth Meyers, CEO, Subsidiary
Leroy Carlson, CEO
Douglas Shuma, CFO
Walter Carlson, Chairman of the Board
Kurt Thaus, Chief Information Officer
Jane McCahon, Secretary
Daniel DeWitt, Senior VP, Divisional
Scott Williamson, Senior VP, Divisional
Joseph Hanley, Senior VP, Divisional
Peter Sereda, Senior VP, Divisional

GROWTH PLANS/SPECIAL FEATURES:

Telephone and Data Systems, Inc. (TDS) is a diversified telecommunications service company with wireless telephone and wireline telephone operations. The firm operates primarily through two segments: United States Cellular Corporation (U.S. Cellular) and TDS Telecommunications Corporation (TDS Telecom). U.S. Cellular is one of the U.S.'s largest wireless telecommunications providers, providing services to customers via 6 million connections. This segment focuses on retail consumers, government entities and small-to-mid-size business customers in industries such as construction, retail, agriculture, professional services and real estate. TDS Telecom provides broadband, video and voice services to approximately 1.2 million connections through its wireline and cable divisions. The wireline division has operations located in a mix of rural, small town and suburban markets, with the largest concentrations of customers in the Upper Midwest and the Southeast. Wireline operates several incumbent local exchange carriers and provides telecommunications services as a competitive local exchange carrier in the upper Midwest and the southeast. Wireline provide retail telecommunications services to both residential and commercial customers that reside within its respective service territories. The cable division operates cable systems in markets primarily in Colorado, New Mexico, Oregon, Texas and Utah. In addition, TDS offers hybrid IT solutions, including cloud and hosting solutions, managed services, enterprise application management, advanced IT services, hardware and local connectivity. These solutions are provided via data centers in Arizona, Colorado, Iowa, Minnesota, New Jersey, Oregon and Wisconsin under the OneNeck brand name. In addition, wholly-owned Suttle-Straus, Inc. builds customized print-on-demand marketing portals designed to help large companies manage print collateral and fulfill marketing needs across a network of locations, dealers, franchises, agents or remote sales teams.

TDS offers its employees comprehensive health benefits, life and disability insurance, 401(k) and assistance programs.

FINANCIAL DATA: Note: Data for latest year may not have been available at press time.

In U.S. $	2020	2019	2018	2017	2016	2015
Revenue	5,225,000,000	5,176,000,000	5,109,000,000	5,044,000,000	5,104,000,000	5,176,241,000
R&D Expense						
Operating Income	281,000,000	190,000,000	196,000,000	155,000,000	66,000,000	136,476,000
Operating Margin %		.04%	.04%	.03%	.01%	.03%
SGA Expense	1,681,000,000	1,717,000,000	1,694,000,000	1,686,000,000	1,759,000,000	1,780,463,000
Net Income	226,000,000	121,000,000	135,000,000	153,000,000	43,000,000	219,037,000
Operating Cash Flow	1,532,000,000	1,016,000,000	1,017,000,000	776,000,000	782,000,000	789,694,000
Capital Expenditure	1,368,000,000	957,000,000	776,000,000	685,000,000	636,000,000	800,628,000
EBITDA	1,365,000,000	1,308,000,000	1,276,000,000	892,000,000	1,112,000,000	1,420,682,000
Return on Assets %		.01%	.01%	.02%	.00%	.02%
Return on Equity %		.03%	.03%	.04%	.01%	.05%
Debt to Equity		0.698	0.53	0.571	0.587	0.591

CONTACT INFORMATION:

Phone: 312-630-1900   Fax: 312-630-1908
Toll-Free:
Address: 30 N. LaSalle St., Ste. 4000, Chicago, IL 60602 United States

STOCK TICKER/OTHER:

Stock Ticker: TDS   Exchange: NYS
Employees: 9,400   Fiscal Year Ends: 12/31
Parent Company:

SALARIES/BONUSES:

Top Exec. Salary: $ Bonus: $
Second Exec. Salary: $ Bonus: $

OTHER THOUGHTS:

Estimated Female Officers or Directors: 5
Hot Spot for Advancement for Women/Minorities: Y

Telia Company AB

NAIC Code: 517110

TYPES OF BUSINESS:

Telephone Service
Telecommunications
Mobile
Fixed Voice
Broadband
Television

BRANDS/DIVISIONS/AFFILIATES:

Telia
Call me
Okarte
Ezys
MyCall
Phonero
C More
Halebop

CONTACTS: *Note: Officers with more than one job title may be intentionally listed here more than once.*

Allison Kirkby, CEO
Rainer Deutschmann, COO
Per Christian Morland, CFO
Markus Messerer, CCO
Cecilia Lundin, Chief People Officer
Jan H. Ahrnell, Head-Legal Affairs
Cecilia Edstrom, Sr. VP-Group Comm.
Christian Luga, Head-Finance
Tero Kivisaari, Pres., Mobility Svcs.
Malin Frenning, Pres., Broadband Svcs.
Lars-Johan Jarnheimer, Chmn.
Veysel Aral, Pres., Eurasia

GROWTH PLANS/SPECIAL FEATURES:

Telia Company AB provides telecommunications services, with operations in Denmark, Estonia, Finland, Latvia, Lithuania, Norway and Sweden. The company has about 17 million mobile subscriptions, 1.2 million fixed voice subscriptions, 2.9 million broadband subscriptions and 3.2 million TV subscriptions (as of December 31, 2020). Telia provides mobile voice, data, fixed voice, internet, television and media services, Internet of Things (IoT), cloud, security, information and communication technology services, related devices and more. Brands of the firm include Telia, Call me, Mit Tele, Diil, Telia Cloudy, MLT, Okarte, Amigo, Ezys, MyCall, OneCall, Phonero, Fello, TV4, C More, and Halebop. In June 2021, Telia agreed to sell 49% of its tower business in Norway and Finland to Brookfield and Alecta.

FINANCIAL DATA: *Note: Data for latest year may not have been available at press time.*

In U.S. $	2020	2019	2018	2017	2016	2015
Revenue	10,789,460,000	10,399,330,000	10,108,270,000	9,661,643,000	10,183,150,000	10,472,390,000
R&D Expense	36,049,550	18,387,690	19,839,350	34,597,890	20,928,090	17,782,830
Operating Income	1,302,744,000	1,436,901,000	1,584,607,000	1,486,258,000	1,731,467,000	1,690,216,000
Operating Margin %		.14%	.16%	.15%	.17%	.16%
SGA Expense	2,575,849,000	2,429,352,000	2,213,297,000	2,215,475,000	2,327,252,000	2,432,135,000
Net Income	-2,771,702,000	858,051,900	384,568,900	1,162,295,000	451,466,200	1,034,429,000
Operating Cash Flow	3,486,887,000	3,338,092,000	3,229,459,000	2,851,181,000	3,141,634,000	4,264,130,000
Capital Expenditure	1,658,521,000	1,841,672,000	1,789,655,000	1,984,540,000	2,262,533,000	2,262,049,000
EBITDA	1,236,451,000	3,823,430,000	3,339,422,000	3,789,437,000	4,297,155,000	4,417,885,000
Return on Assets %		.03%	.01%	.04%	.01%	.03%
Return on Equity %		.08%	.03%	.10%	.04%	.08%
Debt to Equity		1.102	0.897	0.882	0.929	0.94

CONTACT INFORMATION:

Phone: 46 850455000   Fax: 46 850455001
Toll-Free:
Address: Stjarntorget 1, Stockholm, 169 94 Sweden

STOCK TICKER/OTHER:

Stock Ticker: TLSNY   Exchange: PINX
Employees: 20,741   Fiscal Year Ends: 12/31
Parent Company:

SALARIES/BONUSES:

Top Exec. Salary: $ Bonus: $
Second Exec. Salary: $ Bonus: $

OTHER THOUGHTS:

Estimated Female Officers or Directors: 7
Hot Spot for Advancement for Women/Minorities: Y

Telia Lietuva AB

www.telia.lt

NAIC Code: 517110

TYPES OF BUSINESS:

Local & Long-Distance Phone Service
Internet Services
Consulting Services
Managed IT Services
VoIP Services
Call Center Services
Network Construction
Next-Generation Services

BRANDS/DIVISIONS/AFFILIATES:

Telia Company AB

CONTACTS: *Note: Officers with more than one job title may be intentionally listed here more than once.*

Dan Stromberg, CEO
Arunas Linge, Dir.-Finance
Nerijus Ivanauskas, Chief Mktg. Officer

GROWTH PLANS/SPECIAL FEATURES:

Telia Lietuva AB provides telecommunications, information technology (IT) and television services from a single source throughout the country of Lithuania. The firm is part of the Telia Company AB, which operates in several countries, from Norway to Turkey. Telia Lietuva's range of products and services include smart TV; mobile telephone, music and entertainment; smart devices and solutions for home and/or office; office equipment maintenance; and IT security. In-late 2020, Telia Lietuva announced that it entered into a strategic partnership with Ericsson to modernize its mobile network and roll out 5G services throughout Lithuania. Therefore, Ericsson would be the sole partner to deliver radio access network technology (RAN) in that country. As a result, Telia Lietuva launched 11 base stations of the 5G technology, operating in Vilnius, Kaunas and Lkaipeda, and two other 5G stations were launched in the Klaipeda Free Economic Zone by the end of 2020. The firm announced plans to provide commercial 5G communication services in Lithuania during 2021.

FINANCIAL DATA: *Note: Data for latest year may not have been available at press time.*

In U.S. $	2020	2019	2018	2017	2016	2015
Revenue	488,943,000	434,842,000	430,631,000	430,388,000	221,862,054	220,258,556
R&D Expense						
Operating Income						
Operating Margin %						
SGA Expense						
Net Income	68,617,100	61,256,400	62,565,400	62,655,500	9,106,964	6,435,225
Operating Cash Flow						
Capital Expenditure						
EBITDA						
Return on Assets %						
Return on Equity %						
Debt to Equity						

CONTACT INFORMATION:

Phone: 370-5-262-15-11   Fax: 370-5-212-66-65
Toll-Free:
Address: Saltoniskiu g. 7, Vilnius, LT-03501 Lithuania

STOCK TICKER/OTHER:

Stock Ticker: TEO1L   Exchange: Vilnius
Employees: 2,001   Fiscal Year Ends: 12/31
Parent Company: Telia Company AB

SALARIES/BONUSES:

Top Exec. Salary: $ Bonus: $
Second Exec. Salary: $ Bonus: $

OTHER THOUGHTS:

Estimated Female Officers or Directors: 4
Hot Spot for Advancement for Women/Minorities: Y

Telkom SA SOC Limited

NAIC Code: 517110

TYPES OF BUSINESS:

Telephony Services
Information Technology
Telecommunications
Broadband Networks
Digital Solutions
Property Management
Data Connectivity
Advertising Solutions

BRANDS/DIVISIONS/AFFILIATES:

Openserve
Telkom Consumer
BCX
Gyro
Telkom Business
Yellow Pages

GROWTH PLANS/SPECIAL FEATURES:

Telkom SA SOC Limited is a leading information and communications technology services provider in South Africa. The company operates through six divisions: Openserve, Telkom Consumer, BCX, Gyro, Telkom Business and Yellow Pages. Openserve builds and operates high-speed broadband networks that link banking systems, hospitals and schools. Telkom Consumer offers fixed and mobile broadband services and voice technology. BCX offers premier end-to-end digital solutions which primarily help businesses to future-proof their operations. Gyro offers three business services: masts and towers, property management and property development. Telkom Business focuses on small and medium enterprises, offering data and voice connectivity, IT services and marketing services. Yellow Pages delivers commercial search solutions and integrated advertising and marketing solutions.

CONTACTS: Note: Officers with more than one job title may be intentionally listed here more than once.

Sipho Maseko, CEO
Dirk Reyneke, CFO
Xoliswa Makasi, Company Sec.
Miriam Altman, Head-Strategy
Praveen Naidoo, Group Exec.-Comm.
Robin Coode, Group Exec.-Acct.
Ouma Rasethaba, Chief Corp. & Regulatory Affairs Exec.
Bashier Sallie, Managing Dir.-Wholesale & Networks
Manelisa Mavuso, Managing Dir.-Consumer Svcs. & Retail
Attila Vitai, Managing Dir.-Telkom Mobile
Vuledzani Nemukula, Group Exec.-Procurement Svcs.

FINANCIAL DATA: Note: Data for latest year may not have been available at press time.

In U.S. $	2020	2019	2018	2017	2016	2015
Revenue	3,128,755,000	3,036,512,000	2,981,559,000	2,978,070,000	2,713,119,000	
R&D Expense						
Operating Income	278,544,400	341,783,900	358,066,300	369,696,500	160,497,400	
Operating Margin %	.08%	.11%	.12%	.12%	.06%	
SGA Expense	287,921,300	256,083,500	392,884,300	303,912,900	361,846,100	
Net Income	43,831,500	203,165,900	221,847,000	276,000,300	163,259,600	
Operating Cash Flow	622,436,300					
Capital Expenditure	560,577,900	551,273,700	565,012,000	616,330,400	431,845,700	
EBITDA	687,565,800	758,582,900	780,825,700	776,391,700	631,885,900	
Return on Assets %	.01%	.05%	.06%	.08%	.05%	
Return on Equity %	.02%	.10%	.11%	.14%	.09%	
Debt to Equity	0.468	0.164	0.265	0.172	0.175	

CONTACT INFORMATION:

Phone: 27 123115322   Fax: 27 813912016
Toll-Free:
Address: 61 Oak Ave., Highveld Techno Park, Centurion, SA 0157 South Africa

STOCK TICKER/OTHER:

Stock Ticker: TLKGY   Exchange: PINX
Employees: 15,099   Fiscal Year Ends: 03/31
Parent Company:

SALARIES/BONUSES:

Top Exec. Salary: $ Bonus: $
Second Exec. Salary: $ Bonus: $

OTHER THOUGHTS:

Estimated Female Officers or Directors: 5
Hot Spot for Advancement for Women/Minorities: Y

Tellabs Inc

NAIC Code: 334210

www.tellabs.com

TYPES OF BUSINESS:
Wireline & Wireless Products & Services
Consulting

BRANDS/DIVISIONS/AFFILIATES:
Marlin Equity Partners LLC

CONTACTS: *Note: Officers with more than one job title may be intentionally listed here more than once.*
Rich Schroder, CEO
Norm Burke, CFO
James M. Sheehan, Chief Admin. Officer
James M. Sheehan, General Counsel
John M. Brots, Exec. VP-Global Oper.
Kenneth G. Craft, Exec. VP-Product Dev.

GROWTH PLANS/SPECIAL FEATURES:
Tellabs, Inc. provides products and services that enable customers to deliver wireline and wireless voice, data and video services to business and residential customers. It operates in two segments: enterprise and broadband. The enterprise segment offers a passive optical local area network (LAN) infrastructure, which is secure, scalable and sustainable. This division serves the business enterprise, federal government, hospitality, higher education, K-12 education, healthcare and transportation industries. The broadband segment offers solutions to service providers that deliver stability and scalability while increasing flexibility. These broadband solutions help telecommunications companies grow HSI (high-speed internet) subscribers, extend service area coverage and offer faster internet service speeds. They also enable Ethernet business services while continuing to support time-division multiplexing (TDM) and automated teller machine (ATM) services. Tellabs offers services such as technical support, professional network services and training. Tellabs is a subsidiary of Marlin Equity Partners, LLC.

FINANCIAL DATA: *Note: Data for latest year may not have been available at press time.*

In U.S. $	2020	2019	2018	2017	2016	2015
Revenue	1,610,256,375	1,533,577,500	1,460,550,000	1,391,000,000	1,372,000,000	1,375,000,000
R&D Expense						
Operating Income						
Operating Margin %						
SGA Expense						
Net Income						
Operating Cash Flow						
Capital Expenditure						
EBITDA						
Return on Assets %						
Return on Equity %						
Debt to Equity						

CONTACT INFORMATION:
Phone: 972-588-7000   Fax:
Toll-Free:
Address: 4240 International Pkwy, St. 105, Carrollton, TX 75007 United States

STOCK TICKER/OTHER:
Stock Ticker: Private
Employees: 9,400
Parent Company: Marlin Equity Partners LLC

Exchange:
Fiscal Year Ends: 12/31

SALARIES/BONUSES:
Top Exec. Salary: $ Bonus: $
Second Exec. Salary: $ Bonus: $

OTHER THOUGHTS:
Estimated Female Officers or Directors: 1
Hot Spot for Advancement for Women/Minorities: Y

Sales, profits and employees may be estimates. Financial information, benefits and other data can change quickly and may vary from those stated here.

Telstra Corporation Limited

www.telstra.com.au

NAIC Code: 517110

TYPES OF BUSINESS:

Wireless & Wireline Telephony Services
Telecommunications
Communications Technology
Mobile
Broadband
Contract Management
5G

BRANDS/DIVISIONS/AFFILIATES:

CONTACTS: *Note: Officers with more than one job title may be intentionally listed here more than once.*

Andrew Penn, CEO
Vicki Brady, CFO
Kate McKenzie, Managing Dir.-Prod. & Innovation
Carmel Mulhern, General Counsel
Will Irving, Managing Dir.-Telstra Bus.
Tony Warren, Managing Dir.-Corp. Affairs
Andrew Keys, Acting Dir.-Investor Rel.
Andrew Penn, Managing Dir.-Finance
Paul Geason, Group Managing Dir.-Enterprise & Govt
Damien Coleman, Sec.
Gordon Ballantyne, Chief Customer Officer
Stuart Lee, Managing Dir.-Telstra Wholesale
Timothy Y. Chen, Pres.

GROWTH PLANS/SPECIAL FEATURES:

Telstra Corporation Limited is a leading telecommunications and technology company based in Australia. Services by the firm include retail mobile, retail fixed and standalone data, and retail fixed standalone voice. Telstra operates through four business segments: consumer and small business, enterprise, networks and IT, and other. Telstra's consumer and small business segment provides telecommunication products, services and solutions across mobiles, fixed and mobile broadband, telephone, Pay TV/IPTV and digital content to both consumer and business customers in Australia. The enterprise segment is responsible for sales and contract management for medium and large businesses and government customers in Australia and globally. This division also provides product management for advanced technology solutions and services, including data and internet protocol (IP) networks and networked appliance systems (NAS) products such as managed networks, unified communications, cloud, industry solutions and integrated services. The networks and IT segment is responsible for planning, design, engineering, architecture and construction of Telstra networks, technology and information technology solutions. Last, the other business segment contains income and expense activities regarding Telstra's product and technology division, its global business services and its new business developments. Telstra's international presence spans more than 20 countries. In Australia, the firm's 5G network covers approximately 50% of the population, offering plans in select areas.

FINANCIAL DATA: *Note: Data for latest year may not have been available at press time.*

In U.S. $	2020	2019	2018	2017	2016	2015
Revenue	17,657,860,000	19,590,630,000	20,173,870,000	20,175,420,000	20,096,310,000	20,183,180,000
R&D Expense						
Operating Income	627,452,300	1,997,920,000	2,489,644,000	3,350,549,000	4,372,776,000	4,790,044,000
Operating Margin %		.10%	.12%	.17%	.22%	.24%
SGA Expense	4,398,371,000	5,650,949,000	5,916,201,000	5,764,960,000	5,408,965,000	5,379,492,000
Net Income	1,410,798,000	1,670,621,000	2,763,427,000	3,017,821,000	4,482,910,000	3,281,521,000
Operating Cash Flow						
Capital Expenditure	2,669,581,000	3,389,328,000	3,825,210,000	4,126,914,000	3,252,824,000	3,957,060,000
EBITDA	7,034,601,000	6,376,901,000	7,913,345,000	8,389,557,000	8,183,250,000	8,455,482,000
Return on Assets %		.05%	.08%	.09%	.14%	.11%
Return on Equity %		.15%	.24%	.26%	.39%	.30%
Debt to Equity		1.033	1.019	1.018	0.923	1.002

CONTACT INFORMATION:

Phone: 61 883081721   Fax: 61 396323215
Toll-Free:
Address: 242 Exhibition St., Level 41, Melbourne, VIC 3000 Australia

STOCK TICKER/OTHER:

Stock Ticker: TLSYY   Exchange: PINX
Employees: 28,959   Fiscal Year Ends: 06/30
Parent Company:

SALARIES/BONUSES:

Top Exec. Salary: $ Bonus: $
Second Exec. Salary: $ Bonus: $

OTHER THOUGHTS:

Estimated Female Officers or Directors: 6
Hot Spot for Advancement for Women/Minorities: Y

Telular Corporation

www.telular.com

NAIC Code: 334220

TYPES OF BUSINESS:

Fixed Wireless Terminals
Wireless Security Products
GPS Products

BRANDS/DIVISIONS/AFFILIATES:

AMETEK Inc
SkyBitz
Telguard

CONTACTS: *Note: Officers with more than one job title may be intentionally listed here more than once.*

Joseph A. Beatty, Pres.
Christopher Bear, VP-Prod. Dev.
George S. Brody, Sr. VP
Henry Popplewell, Sr. VP
Pat Barron, VP
David A. Zapico, Chmn.-AMETEK

GROWTH PLANS/SPECIAL FEATURES:

Telular Corporation designs, develops and distributes products and services that utilize wireless networks to provide data and voice connectivity among people and machines. The company's strategy consists of leveraging domain expertise to identify opportunities for Internet of Things (IoT) solutions to enterprise scale problems. Once identified, Telular utilizes hardware derived from internal designs that connect into the appropriate Telular analytics cloud via a wide range of connectivity options. The firm then rolls the solution out to targeted industries with the goal of delivering a one-year return on investment for customers. Examples for this strategy include trailer tracking, remote oilfield, intermodal asset tracking, local fleet telematics, petroleum logistics, industrial tank monitoring, residential security/home automation, commercial security, fire and personal emergency response systems. Connectivity partners include AT&T, Verizon, Telefonica, Iridium, Inmarsat, Globalstar and Rogers. Ecosystem partners include Sierra Wireless, Salesforce, CISCO Jasper, Windows Azure and Telit. Telular's own brands include: SkyBitz, offering asset tracking and information management services and solutions; and Telguard, offering home security and automation solutions. Telular is a subsidiary of AMETEK, Inc., a global manufacturer of electronic instruments and electromechanical devices.

FINANCIAL DATA: *Note: Data for latest year may not have been available at press time.*

In U.S. $	2020	2019	2018	2017	2016	2015
Revenue	160,875,000	165,000,000	152,500,000	150,000,000	145,000,000	140,000,000
R&D Expense						
Operating Income						
Operating Margin %						
SGA Expense						
Net Income						
Operating Cash Flow						
Capital Expenditure						
EBITDA						
Return on Assets %						
Return on Equity %						
Debt to Equity						

CONTACT INFORMATION:

Phone: 312 379-8397   Fax: 312 379-8310
Toll-Free: 800-835-8527
Address: 200 S. Wacker Dr., Ste. 1800, Chicago, IL 60606 United States

SALARIES/BONUSES:

Top Exec. Salary: $ Bonus: $
Second Exec. Salary: $ Bonus: $

STOCK TICKER/OTHER:

Stock Ticker: Subsidiary   Exchange:
Employees: 155   Fiscal Year Ends: 09/30
Parent Company: AMETEK Inc

OTHER THOUGHTS:

Estimated Female Officers or Directors:
Hot Spot for Advancement for Women/Minorities:

TELUS Corporation

www.telus.com

NAIC Code: 517110

TYPES OF BUSINESS:
Local & Long-Distance Telephone Service
Wireless Phone Service
Internet Service Provider
Paging Services
Mobile Media Services
EMR Technology
Start-up Investments

BRANDS/DIVISIONS/AFFILIATES:
TELUS SmartHome Security
Conservis

CONTACTS: Note: Officers with more than one job title may be intentionally listed here more than once.
Doug French, CFO
Jim Senko, Pres., Divisional
Richard Auchinleck, Chairman of the Board
Andrea Wood, Chief Legal Officer
Darren Entwistle, Director
Eros Spadotto, Executive VP, Divisional
Sandy McIntosh, Executive VP, Divisional
Tony Geheran, Executive VP
Josh Blair, Executive VP
Francois Gratton, Executive VP
Zainul Mawji, President, Divisional
Stephen Lewis, Senior VP

GROWTH PLANS/SPECIAL FEATURES:
TELUS Corporation is a world-leading communications and information technology (IT) company based in Canada. With 15.2 million customer connections, the firm offers wireless, data, internet protocol (IP), voice, television, entertainment, video and security, healthcare and agriculture telecommunications services. TELUS' 4G long-term evolution (LTE) and 5G networks reach 99% of Canadians. Landline services are provided, as well as high-speed internet, television and IPTV services. TELUS SmartHome Security is a complete home monitoring solution. Online security and protection for personal devices and identity is provided by TELUS. Business process and IT solutions include IP networks, hosting, management IT, security and cloud-based services. For the healthcare industry, TELUS offers virtual care for patients and efficiency solutions for healthcare professionals. For the agriculture industry, the company offers agribusiness management platforms. In July 2021, TELUS and Rabobank Group together acquired Conservis, a company that integrates disparate farm technologies into one streamlined interface to manage the business of farming.

FINANCIAL DATA: Note: Data for latest year may not have been available at press time.

In U.S. $	2020	2019	2018	2017	2016	2015
Revenue	12,711,080,000	12,087,990,000	11,678,680,000	10,938,770,000	10,543,540,000	10,299,110,000
R&D Expense						
Operating Income	1,968,680,000	2,429,364,000	2,143,508,000	2,100,423,000	1,776,452,000	1,929,737,000
Operating Margin %		.20%	.18%	.19%	.17%	.19%
SGA Expense	3,066,534,000	2,513,879,000	2,399,536,000	2,150,137,000	2,435,164,000	2,243,765,000
Net Income	1,000,083,000	1,446,682,000	1,325,710,000	1,209,711,000	1,013,340,000	1,145,082,000
Operating Cash Flow	3,789,875,000	3,253,791,000	3,362,333,000	3,270,362,000	2,667,164,000	2,934,792,000
Capital Expenditure	2,338,222,000	3,226,448,000	2,382,136,000	2,552,821,000	2,400,365,000	3,786,561,000
EBITDA	4,518,187,000	4,563,758,000	4,195,874,000	3,954,760,000	3,484,133,000	3,562,847,000
Return on Assets %		.05%	.05%	.05%	.05%	.06%
Return on Equity %		.17%	.17%	.18%	.16%	.18%
Debt to Equity		1.625	1.293	1.491	1.466	1.458

CONTACT INFORMATION:
Phone: 604 697-8044   Fax: 604 432-2984
Toll-Free: 800-667-4871
Address: 510 W. Georgia St., Fl. 7, Vancouver, BC V6B 0M3 Canada

STOCK TICKER/OTHER:
Stock Ticker: TU
Employees: 47,640
Parent Company:

Exchange: NYS
Fiscal Year Ends: 12/31

SALARIES/BONUSES:
Top Exec. Salary: $ Bonus: $
Second Exec. Salary: $ Bonus: $

OTHER THOUGHTS:
Estimated Female Officers or Directors: 1
Hot Spot for Advancement for Women/Minorities:

TESSCO Technologies Incorporated

www.tessco.com

NAIC Code: 423430

TYPES OF BUSINESS:

Wireless Communications Products Distributor
Technology Distribution
Base Station Infrastructure
Network Systems
Installation
Testing

BRANDS/DIVISIONS/AFFILIATES:

CONTACTS: *Note: Officers with more than one job title may be intentionally listed here more than once.*

Aric Spitulnik, Chief Accounting Officer
Robert Barnhill, Director
Murray Wright, President
Douglas Rein, Senior VP, Divisional
Charles Kriete, Senior VP, Divisional
Elizabeth Robinson, Senior VP, Divisional

GROWTH PLANS/SPECIAL FEATURES:

TESSCO Technologies Incorporated is a value-added technology distributor, manufacturer and solutions provider. The company supplies more than 65,000 products from 250 of the industry's top manufacturers in mobile communications, WiFi, Internet of Things (IoT), wireless backhaul, and more. Products are grouped into categories such as base station infrastructure, network systems and installation/test/maintenance. TESSCO's commercial segment consists of two customer markets: public carriers, which are generally responsible for building and maintaining the infrastructure system and provide airtime service to individual subscribers; and value-added resellers and integrators. The strategy of this segment is to increase sales opportunities across its markets and to provide better coverage to customers and better align territories with supplier partners. Sales to the public carrier market accounted for 29% of 2020 revenues, sales to value-added resellers and integrators accounted for 47%, and sales to retailers accounted for 24%. Nearly all (96%) of TESSCO's sales are made to U.S. customers, though the firm sells to customers in nearly 100 countries. In December 2020, TESSCO sold most of its retail inventory, including its mobile device accessory products, to focus on its commercial segment.

TESSCO offers its employees health and retirement benefits, life and disability insurance, product discounts and other assistance plans and programs.

FINANCIAL DATA: *Note: Data for latest year may not have been available at press time.*

In U.S. $	2020	2019	2018	2017	2016	2015
Revenue	540,298,300	606,813,800	580,274,700	533,295,100	530,682,100	549,619,000
R&D Expense						
Operating Income	-15,991,700	8,145,000	7,901,700	3,351,500	9,033,600	14,951,800
Operating Margin %	-.03%	.01%	.01%	.01%	.02%	.03%
SGA Expense	107,814,700	113,213,700	112,326,700	108,416,300	102,932,300	115,936,700
Net Income	-21,568,900	5,545,800	5,195,400	1,445,100	5,340,500	8,634,300
Operating Cash Flow	908,200	8,246,700	-9,247,100	3,051,270	20,141,110	11,079,800
Capital Expenditure	6,845,700	5,164,700	3,539,400	2,563,000	3,513,813	2,950,600
EBITDA	-24,131,300	11,763,900	11,894,300	6,783,800	13,763,600	18,962,000
Return on Assets %	-.10%	.03%	.03%	.01%	.03%	.05%
Return on Equity %	-.22%	.05%	.05%	.01%	.05%	.08%
Debt to Equity	0.137		0.00	0.00	0.015	0.017

CONTACT INFORMATION:

Phone: 410 229-1000   Fax: 410 527-0005
Toll-Free:
Address: 11126 McCormick Rd., Hunt Valley, MD 21031 United States

STOCK TICKER/OTHER:

Stock Ticker: TESS   Exchange: NAS
Employees: 678   Fiscal Year Ends: 03/31
Parent Company:

SALARIES/BONUSES:

Top Exec. Salary: $ Bonus: $
Second Exec. Salary: $ Bonus: $

OTHER THOUGHTS:

Estimated Female Officers or Directors:
Hot Spot for Advancement for Women/Minorities:

Thuraya Telecommunications Company

www.thuraya.com

NAIC Code: 517410

TYPES OF BUSINESS:

Satellite Telecommunications
Mobile Satellite Services
Telecommunications
Mobile Satellite Handsets
Broadband Devices

BRANDS/DIVISIONS/AFFILIATES:

Mubadala Investment Company
Al Yah Satellite Communications Company (Yahsat)

CONTACTS: Note: Officers with more than one job title may be intentionally listed here more than once.

Sulaiman Al Ali, CEO
Khalid Al Kaf, COO
Jassem Nasser, CMO
Adnan Al Muhairi, CTO

GROWTH PLANS/SPECIAL FEATURES:

Thuraya Telecommunications Company is the mobile satellite services subsidiary of Al Yah Satellite Communications Company (Yahsat), a global satellite operator based in the United Arab Emirates. Yahsat itself is wholly-owned by Mubadala Investment Company. Thuraya offers innovative communications solutions to a variety of sectors, including energy, government, broadcast media, maritime, military, aerospace and humanitarian non-government organizations. The company's network enables communications and coverage across two-thirds of the globe by mobile satellite services (MSS), quasi-global very small aperture terminal (VSAT) coverage and through its GSM (global system for mobile) roaming capabilities. Thuraya has established roaming agreements in more than 160 countries, enabling the firm to provide roaming services for postpaid and prepaid customers onto worldwide GSM networks. Thuraya also offers mobile satellite handsets and broadband devices. Product lines are categorized into land voice, land data, marine, aero, machine-to-machine and certified.

FINANCIAL DATA: Note: Data for latest year may not have been available at press time.

In U.S. $	2020	2019	2018	2017	2016	2015
Revenue	180,017,726	184,444,391	175,661,325	167,296,500	159,330,000	141,000,000
R&D Expense						
Operating Income						
Operating Margin %						
SGA Expense						
Net Income						
Operating Cash Flow						
Capital Expenditure						
EBITDA						
Return on Assets %						
Return on Equity %						
Debt to Equity						

CONTACT INFORMATION:

Phone: 971-4-4488888   Fax: 971-4-4488999
Toll-Free:
Address: P.O. Box 283333, Dubai, United Arab Emirates

STOCK TICKER/OTHER:

Stock Ticker: Private   Exchange:
Employees: Fiscal Year Ends:
Parent Company: Mubadala Investment Company

SALARIES/BONUSES:

Top Exec. Salary: $ Bonus: $
Second Exec. Salary: $ Bonus: $

OTHER THOUGHTS:

Estimated Female Officers or Directors:
Hot Spot for Advancement for Women/Minorities:

TIM SA

NAIC Code: 517210

TYPES OF BUSINESS:
Cell Phone Service
Telecommunications Infrastructure
Mobile Telephone
Fixed Telephone
Internet
Broadband

BRANDS/DIVISIONS/AFFILIATES:
Telecom Italia SpA

GROWTH PLANS/SPECIAL FEATURES:
TIM SA (formerly TIM Participacoes SA) provides telecommunications infrastructure and related services throughout Brazil. TIM offers 4G coverage, with services including mobile and fixed telephone, internet and broadband for consumers and enterprises. TIM is a wholly-owned subsidiary of Telecom Italia SpA. In September 2020, TIM Participacoes SA, a former holding company, was merged with and into TIM SA.

CONTACTS: *Note: Officers with more than one job title may be intentionally listed here more than once.*
Pietro Labriola, CEO
Leonardo de Carvalho Capdeville, CTO
Rogerio Tostes, Investor Rel. Officer
Lorenzo Federico Zanotti Lindner, Chief Commercial Officer
Mario Girasole, Chief Regulatory Affairs Officer
Antonino Ruggiero, Chief Wholesale Officer
Daniel Junqueira Pinto Hermeto, Chief Supplies Officer

FINANCIAL DATA: *Note: Data for latest year may not have been available at press time.*

In U.S. $	2020	2019	2018	2017	2016	2015
Revenue	3,353,168,000	3,374,409,000	3,297,537,000	3,152,409,000	3,032,684,000	3,328,126,000
R&D Expense						
Operating Income	538,613,700	867,856,100	461,352,700	368,061,400	260,494,200	387,066,400
Operating Margin %						
SGA Expense	1,045,153,000	1,154,522,000	1,143,601,000	1,051,854,000	1,071,663,000	1,107,456,000
Net Income	355,021,400	703,366,600	494,223,100	239,724,000	145,722,500	402,187,500
Operating Cash Flow	1,684,345,000	1,371,871,000	1,190,242,000	1,049,403,000	969,425,000	830,767,900
Capital Expenditure	755,637,400	748,292,900	744,102,700	805,465,700	874,302,700	925,148,800
EBITDA	1,640,030,000	2,069,294,000	1,214,878,000	1,166,995,000	1,072,860,000	1,386,147,000
Return on Assets %						
Return on Equity %						
Debt to Equity						

CONTACT INFORMATION:
Phone: 55 2141093742   Fax: 55 2141093314
Toll-Free:
Address: Joao Cabral de Melo Neto Ave, 850-South Tower, Fl. 12, Rio de Janeiro, RJ 22775-057 Brazil

STOCK TICKER/OTHER:
Stock Ticker: TIMB   Exchange: NYS
Employees: 9,700   Fiscal Year Ends: 12/31
Parent Company: Telecom Italia SpA

SALARIES/BONUSES:
Top Exec. Salary: $ Bonus: $
Second Exec. Salary: $ Bonus: $

OTHER THOUGHTS:
Estimated Female Officers or Directors:
Hot Spot for Advancement for Women/Minorities:

TKH Group NV

www.tkhgroup.com

NAIC Code: 238210

TYPES OF BUSINESS:

Network Wiring and Electrical Contracting
Telecommunications Infrastructure
Fiber Optic Cable
Security & Closed-Circuit Television Systems

BRANDS/DIVISIONS/AFFILIATES:

CONTACTS:
Note: Officers with more than one job title may be intentionally listed here more than once.

Alexander van der Lof, CEO
Elling de Lange, CFO
Arne Dehn, Managing Dir.-Building Solutions
Alexandervan der Lof, Chmn.

GROWTH PLANS/SPECIAL FEATURES:

TKH Group NV is an internationally-operating group of companies involved in the development of systems and networks for providing information, electro technical engineering, telecommunication and industrial production solutions. The group offers its services under three primary divisions: telecom solutions, building solutions and industrial solutions. The telecom solutions division installs and upgrades fiber-optic cable networks, copper networks and indoor telecom systems, serving customers such as telecom operators, cable operators, service providers, telecom installers and telecom retailers. The building solutions division is focused on three main areas: building technologies, encompassing systems such as intercoms, programmable lighting and motion-activated lighting for public spaces; security systems, including closed-circuit television, control room systems and audio and video analysis technology; and connectivity systems, encompassing specialty cable for energy transmission in both home and industrial settings as well as pre-assembled cable systems engineered to reduce installation time and complexity. The industrial solutions division provides services in two primary areas: connectivity systems, including specialty cable installations for medical, automotive and industrial applications; and manufacturing systems, focused primarily on process-improvement technologies for tire manufacturers and automated handling systems for customers in both food and non-food packaging industries. TKH Group operates on a global scale, with primary activities in Europe, North America and Asia.

FINANCIAL DATA:
Note: Data for latest year may not have been available at press time.

In U.S. $	2020	2019	2018	2017	2016	2015
Revenue		1,610,214,912	1,762,826,368	1,604,609,024	1,484,703,360	1,522,533,248
R&D Expense						
Operating Income						
Operating Margin %						
SGA Expense						
Net Income		123,279,144	117,337,208	94,392,080	94,892,608	95,387,512
Operating Cash Flow						
Capital Expenditure						
EBITDA						
Return on Assets %						
Return on Equity %						
Debt to Equity						

CONTACT INFORMATION:

Phone: 31-53-573-2900   Fax: 31-53-573-2180
Toll-Free:
Address: Spinnerstraat 15, Haaksbergen, 7481 KJ Netherlands

STOCK TICKER/OTHER:

Stock Ticker: TKHGF   Exchange: GREY
Employees: 5,980   Fiscal Year Ends: 12/31
Parent Company:

SALARIES/BONUSES:

Top Exec. Salary: $ Bonus: $
Second Exec. Salary: $ Bonus: $

OTHER THOUGHTS:

Estimated Female Officers or Directors: 1
Hot Spot for Advancement for Women/Minorities:

T-Mobile Polska SA

www.t-mobile.pl

NAIC Code: 517210

TYPES OF BUSINESS:

Mobile Phone Service
Mobile Telephone
Fixed Telephone
LTE Technologies
Wi-Fi
Fiber Optic Network
Devices

BRANDS/DIVISIONS/AFFILIATES:

Deutsche Telekom AG

GROWTH PLANS/SPECIAL FEATURES:

T-Mobile Polska SA is a mobile and fixed telephone service operator in Poland. The company provides mobile services using 2G, 3G and long-term evolution (LTE) technologies, covering nearly 100% of the country's population. T-Mobile Polska also provides voice over LTE and voice over Wi-Fi. As of June 2020, the firm began to provide 5G network services. Fixed-line services are provided through T-Mobile Polska's owned and leased fiber-optic network. The company also offers the entire spectrum of information and communications technology (ICT) services. Related devices such as telephones, tablets, modems and routers, as well as smartwatches are sold through T-Mobile as well. T-Mobile Polska SA is a subsidiary of Deutsche Telkom AG.

CONTACTS: Note: Officers with more than one job title may be intentionally listed here more than once.

Andreas Maierhofer, CEO
Juraj Andras, Dir.-Finance
Dorota Kuprianowcz-Legutko, Dir.-Human Resources
Petri Pehkonen, Dir.-Technology & Innovation
Maciej Rogalski, Dir.-Legal Affairs, Data Protect & Compliance Mgmt
Grzegorz Bors, Dir.-Private Mkt.
Igor Matejov, Dir.-Bus. Mkt.

FINANCIAL DATA: Note: Data for latest year may not have been available at press time.

In U.S. $	2020	2019	2018	2017	2016	2015
Revenue	1,784,640,000	1,664,110,000	1,744,280,000	1,807,580,000	1,663,757,612	1,718,191,477
R&D Expense						
Operating Income						
Operating Margin %						
SGA Expense						
Net Income	106,857,000	104,147,000	-631,373,000	-819,339,000	223,676,481	391,517,316
Operating Cash Flow						
Capital Expenditure						
EBITDA						
Return on Assets %						
Return on Equity %						
Debt to Equity						

CONTACT INFORMATION:

Phone: 4822-413-5881   Fax: 4822-413-6889
Toll-Free:
Address: Al. Jerozolimskie 181, Warsaw, 02-222 Poland

STOCK TICKER/OTHER:

Stock Ticker: Subsidiary   Exchange:
Employees: 4,117   Fiscal Year Ends: 12/31
Parent Company: Deutsche Telekom AG

SALARIES/BONUSES:

Top Exec. Salary: $ Bonus: $
Second Exec. Salary: $ Bonus: $

OTHER THOUGHTS:

Estimated Female Officers or Directors: 2
Hot Spot for Advancement for Women/Minorities:

T-Mobile US Inc

NAIC Code: 517210

www.t-mobile.com

TYPES OF BUSINESS:

Mobile Phone and Wireless Services
Wireless Services
Cellular
Mobile Devices
5G

BRANDS/DIVISIONS/AFFILIATES:

Deutsche Telekom AG
T-Mobile International AG
T-Mobile
Metro by T-Mobile
Sprint Corporation

CONTACTS: *Note: Officers with more than one job title may be intentionally listed here more than once.*

J. Carter, CFO
Timotheus Hottges, Chairman of the Board
Neville Ray, Chief Technology Officer
G. Sievert, COO
John Legere, Director
Peter Ewens, Executive VP, Divisional
Elizabeth McAuliffe, Executive VP, Divisional
David Carey, Executive VP, Divisional
David Miller, Executive VP
Thomas Keys, President, Subsidiary
Peter Osvaldik, Senior VP, Divisional

GROWTH PLANS/SPECIAL FEATURES:

T-Mobile US, Inc. (T-Mobile) is a national provider of wireless voice, messaging and data services, and is one of the largest cellular companies in America. T-Mobile's network is powered by its nationwide 4G long-term evolution (LTE) network, which covers more than 325 million consumers. The firm's 5G network covers 1.6 million square miles, 280 million people and 9,100 cities and towns across the U.S., Puerto Rico and the U.S. Virgin Islands. T-Mobile provides wireless services to 102.1 million postpaid, prepaid and wholesale customers. The company also sells a full range of devices and accessories across its flagship brands, including T-Mobile and Metro by T-Mobile, through its owned and operated retail stores, eCommerce websites, mobile app and customer care channels. Moreover, T-Mobile sells devices to dealers and other third-party distributors for resale through independent third-party retail outlets and a variety of third-party websites. T-Mobile operates as a subsidiary of T-Mobile International AG, which itself is the mobile communications subsidiary of Deutsche Telekom AG. During 2020, T-Mobile completed the acquisition of Sprint Corporation, creating a third giant wireless network operator to compete against AT&T, Inc. and Verizon Communications, Inc.

FINANCIAL DATA: *Note: Data for latest year may not have been available at press time.*

In U.S. $	2020	2019	2018	2017	2016	2015
Revenue	68,397,000,000	44,998,000,000	43,310,000,000	40,604,000,000	37,242,000,000	32,053,000,000
R&D Expense						
Operating Income	7,054,000,000	5,722,000,000	5,309,000,000	4,653,000,000	3,071,000,000	2,278,000,000
Operating Margin %		.13%	.12%	.11%	.08%	.07%
SGA Expense	18,926,000,000	14,139,000,000	13,161,000,000	12,259,000,000	11,378,000,000	10,189,000,000
Net Income	3,064,000,000	3,468,000,000	2,888,000,000	4,536,000,000	1,460,000,000	733,000,000
Operating Cash Flow	8,640,000,000	6,824,000,000	3,899,000,000	7,962,000,000	6,135,000,000	5,414,000,000
Capital Expenditure	12,367,000,000	7,358,000,000	5,668,000,000	11,065,000,000	8,670,000,000	6,659,000,000
EBITDA	20,411,000,000	12,354,000,000	11,760,000,000	10,816,000,000	10,300,000,000	7,162,000,000
Return on Assets %		.04%	.04%	.07%	.02%	.01%
Return on Equity %		.13%	.12%	.22%	.08%	.04%
Debt to Equity		0.793	1.08	0.537	1.197	1.237

CONTACT INFORMATION:

Phone: 425-378-4000   Fax: 425-378-4040
Toll-Free: 800-318-9270
Address: 12920 SE 38th St., Bellevue, WA 98006-1350 United States

STOCK TICKER/OTHER:

Stock Ticker: TMUS
Employees: 50,000
Parent Company: Deutsche Telekom AG

Exchange: NAS
Fiscal Year Ends: 12/31

SALARIES/BONUSES:

Top Exec. Salary: $ Bonus: $
Second Exec. Salary: $ Bonus: $

OTHER THOUGHTS:

Estimated Female Officers or Directors:
Hot Spot for Advancement for Women/Minorities:

TomTom International BV

www.tomtom.com

NAIC Code: 334511

TYPES OF BUSINESS:

Communications Equipment-GPS-Based
Navigation Services
Mapping Technology
PDA & Smartphone Software

BRANDS/DIVISIONS/AFFILIATES:

TomTom

CONTACTS: *Note: Officers with more than one job title may be intentionally listed here more than once.*

Harold Goddijn, CEO
Taco Titulaer, CFO
James Joy, General Counsel
Peter-Frans Pauwels, Mgr.-Online Strategy & e-commerce
Richard Piekaar, Mgr.-Investor Rel.
Taco Titulaer, Treas.
Corinne Vigreux, Managing Dir.-Consumer Bus. Unit
Giles Shrimpton, Managing Dir.-TomTom Automotive
Maarten van Gool, Managing Dir.-Licensing Bus. Unit
Lucien Groenhuijzen, Managing Dir.-Places Bus. Unit
Derk Haank, Chmn.
Kirvan Pierson, Head-Bus. Dev. China

GROWTH PLANS/SPECIAL FEATURES:

TomTom International BV is a manufacturer of portable navigation devices for the automotive, enterprise and consumer markets. TomTom's location-based application components are licensed through its automotive business unit to automotive customers such as vehicle manufacturers and their vendors, for in-vehicle navigation, advanced driver-assistance systems and autonomous driving. These products are offered in a flexible way, but when combined, they create a highly-advanced connected navigation system. Traffic information is provided in real-time, and other live services include electric vehicle information, on-street and off-street parking services, speed camera data, and historical traffic statistics. Enterprise customers include technology companies, geographical information systems (GIS) providers, government bodies and traffic management institutions, which use TomTom's products to create location-enabled applications. This division offers fleet management and logistics solutions. The company's consumer business offers drivers directions, guidance and information for their journeys on the road. The TomTom global positioning system (GPS) helps consumers make smarter decisions to get where they want to be, quickly and safely. TomTom's map data technologies include high-definition maps, advanced driver assistance systems (ADAS) maps and real-time map data. TomTom is headquartered in Amsterdam, with offices in 30 countries and its technologies are trusted by hundreds of millions of people worldwide.

FINANCIAL DATA: *Note: Data for latest year may not have been available at press time.*

In U.S. $	2020	2019	2018	2017	2016	2015
Revenue	645,324,200	856,171,200	839,114,000	1,103,743,000	1,206,296,000	1,229,849,000
R&D Expense	379,823,600	394,371,300	269,833,100	253,954,900	232,715,500	226,570,000
Operating Income	-351,517,500	-282,177,900	3,549,262	-38,068,130	10,866,480	733,066
Operating Margin %		-.33%	.00%	-.03%	.01%	.00%
SGA Expense	175,582,800	198,147,800	175,164,900	336,058,300	336,398,000	312,518,300
Net Income	-314,777,400	773,246,700	54,805,250	-249,226,600	14,645,440	22,141,040
Operating Cash Flow	-24,655,460	114,454,800	279,753,900	211,149,900	176,323,200	145,116,600
Capital Expenditure	7,694,752	29,395,950	102,815,000	146,910,100	143,662,600	131,623,300
EBITDA	-9,104,682	73,162,450	202,848,000	176,964,600	172,036,000	142,925,900
Return on Assets %		.45%	.03%	-.14%	.01%	.01%
Return on Equity %		.88%	.06%	-.23%	.01%	.02%
Debt to Equity		0.034	0.033		0.01	0.046

CONTACT INFORMATION:

Phone: 31-20-757-5000　　　Fax:
Toll-Free:
Address: De Ruyterlade 154, Amsterdam, 1011 AC Netherlands

STOCK TICKER/OTHER:

Stock Ticker: TMOAF　　　　　　Exchange: PINX
Employees: 4,575　　　　　　　　Fiscal Year Ends: 12/31
Parent Company:

SALARIES/BONUSES:

Top Exec. Salary: $　　　　Bonus: $
Second Exec. Salary: $　　　Bonus: $

OTHER THOUGHTS:

Estimated Female Officers or Directors: 3
Hot Spot for Advancement for Women/Minorities: Y

Toshiba Corporation

NAIC Code: 334413

www.toshiba.co.jp

TYPES OF BUSINESS:

Memory Chip Manufacturing
Infrastructure Systems
Digital Products
Electronic Devices
Power Systems
Retail
Identification
Semiconductor

BRANDS/DIVISIONS/AFFILIATES:

CONTACTS: Note: Officers with more than one job title may be intentionally listed here more than once.

Nobuaki Kurumatani, CEO
Norio Sasaki, Vice Chmn.
Hidejiro Shimomitsu, Sr. Exec. VP
Hideo Kitamura, Sr. Exec. VP
Makoto Kubo, Sr. Exec. VP
Satoshi Tsunakawa, Chmn.

GROWTH PLANS/SPECIAL FEATURES:

Toshiba Corporation is a technology firm, offering products and services grouped into three categories: infrastructure systems, digital products and electronic devices and components. Infrastructure systems include power systems, transmission and distribution systems, industrial systems, building systems, information technology (IT) systems, and more. These products and solutions are utilized in fields such as power generation, water and sewage systems, railway systems, and electronic devices. Digital products include: retail solutions, such as point-of-sale, multi-function peripherals, automatic identification systems (including radio frequency/RF), inkjet heads, and barcode printers. Electronic devices and components include semiconductors, storage products, microwave semiconductors and related components. Based in Japan, Toshiba Corporation has factories and laboratories throughout the country, as well as global operations across North and South America, China, Europe, the Middle East, Africa and Asia-Pacific. During 2020, Sharp Corporation exercised its option to acquire the remaining 19.9% of Dynabook shares from Toshiba, which produces laptops and related accessories.

FINANCIAL DATA: Note: Data for latest year may not have been available at press time.

In U.S. $	2020	2019	2018	2017	2016	2015
Revenue	30,959,710,000	33,733,110,000	36,053,410,000	44,484,790,000	51,772,150,000	60,788,310,000
R&D Expense						
Operating Income	1,191,492,000	413,588,100	585,151,600	2,627,583,000	-3,778,927,000	1,556,620,000
Operating Margin %	.04%	.01%	.02%	.06%	-.07%	.03%
SGA Expense	7,191,410,000	7,897,218,000	8,189,437,000	9,192,835,000	11,587,520,000	12,844,900,000
Net Income	-1,046,944,000	9,254,072,000	7,343,036,000	-8,819,405,000	-4,201,301,000	-345,455,900
Operating Cash Flow	-1,298,238,000	1,140,301,000	380,307,500	1,225,311,000	-11,233,600	3,017,928,000
Capital Expenditure	1,234,490,000	1,262,519,000	1,825,761,000	1,650,654,000	2,661,951,000	2,629,246,000
EBITDA	342,350,700	913,209,200	2,098,874,000	3,697,807,000	-3,639,713,000	3,210,854,000
Return on Assets %	-.03%	.23%	.18%	-.20%	-.08%	-.01%
Return on Equity %	-.10%	.90%	6.99%		-.65%	-.03%
Debt to Equity	0.306	0.053	0.499		2.528	0.964

CONTACT INFORMATION:

Phone: 81 334572096   Fax: 81 354449202
Toll-Free:
Address: 1-1, Shibaura 1-chome, Minato-ku, Tokyo, 105-8001 Japan

STOCK TICKER/OTHER:

Stock Ticker: TOSBF   Exchange: PINX
Employees: 128,697   Fiscal Year Ends: 03/31
Parent Company:

SALARIES/BONUSES:

Top Exec. Salary: $ Bonus: $
Second Exec. Salary: $ Bonus: $

OTHER THOUGHTS:

Estimated Female Officers or Directors:
Hot Spot for Advancement for Women/Minorities:

TOT pcl
NAIC Code: 517110

TYPES OF BUSINESS:
Local Telephone Services
International Calling Services
Payphone Installation & Operation
Internet Service Provider

BRANDS/DIVISIONS/AFFILIATES:
Thai Ministry of Finance

GROWTH PLANS/SPECIAL FEATURES:
TOT pcl, 100% owned by the Thai Ministry of Finance, was organized in 2002 as the national telecommunications company of Thailand. TOT offers fixed line, mobile, public and international voice services; internet (including fiber optic), data, international service and internet managed service; multimedia and content services such as eLearning, net-call, eConferencing, mail, smart SMS (short message service), cloud applications, eMarket, iptv (internet protocol television) and Netlog services; and other services such as payment, card, ad billing, contact center and procurement. TOT provides these services for small, medium and large enterprises in the healthcare, finance, energy/utilities, retail, manufacturing, automotive, transportation/distribution, media/entertainment, insurance, technology, education, travel/hospitality and real estate sectors.

CONTACTS: *Note: Officers with more than one job title may be intentionally listed here more than once.*
Montchai Noosong, CEO
Morakot Thienmontree, Sr. Exec. VP-Prod. Dev.
Nutnucha Chaipresert, Sr. Exec. VP-Legal & Beneficial Assurance Mgmt.
Preeya Danchaivijit, Sr. Exec. VP-Finance
Phithakphong Tupinprom, Sr. Exec. VP-Enterprise Effectiveness
Chate Phanchan, Sr. Exec. VP-Mobile Bus.
Rungsun Channarukul, Sr. Exec. VP-Wireless & Universal Svcs. Obligation
Kajhonsak Eiamsopa, Sr. Exec. VP-Metropolitan Sale & Customer Svcs.

FINANCIAL DATA: *Note: Data for latest year may not have been available at press time.*

In U.S. $	2020	2019	2018	2017	2016	2015
Revenue						
R&D Expense						
Operating Income						
Operating Margin %						
SGA Expense						
Net Income						
Operating Cash Flow						
Capital Expenditure						
EBITDA						
Return on Assets %						
Return on Equity %						
Debt to Equity						

CONTACT INFORMATION:
Phone: 66-2240-0701   Fax:
Toll-Free:
Address: 89/2 Moo 3 Chaeng Wattana Rd, Thungsong-Hong, Laks, Bangkok, 10210 Thailand

STOCK TICKER/OTHER:
Stock Ticker: Government-Owned   Exchange:
Employees: Fiscal Year Ends: 12/31
Parent Company: Thai Ministry of Finance

SALARIES/BONUSES:
Top Exec. Salary: $ Bonus: $
Second Exec. Salary: $ Bonus: $

OTHER THOUGHTS:
Estimated Female Officers or Directors: 7
Hot Spot for Advancement for Women/Minorities: Y

Total Access Communication PCL

www.dtac.co.th

NAIC Code: 517210

TYPES OF BUSINESS:

Telecommunications Services
Telecommunications
Wireless
Internet
Wi-Fi
Voice
Smartphones
Tablets

BRANDS/DIVISIONS/AFFILIATES:

Telenor Group
dtac
dtac Reward

GROWTH PLANS/SPECIAL FEATURES:

Total Access Communication PCL, operating under the dtac brand, is a provider of wireless telecommunication service for personal and business use in Thailand. Total Access offers 3G/4G coverage, as well as 4G calling voice over long-term evolution (VoLTE), high-speed internet, Wi-Fi calling, and high definition (HD) voice. The company operates several different services and package options, including postpaid and prepaid. Postpaid services include internet packages such as unlimited internet and add-ons, pay-your-bill debit cards, switch-to-DTAC, international calling and international data roaming. Prepaid services include smart cards for mobile phones (SIMs), unlimited 4G internet service, travel/tourism insurance and add-on packages. Total Access also sells smartphones and tablets, and offers a reward program under the etac Reward name. Smartphone and tablet brands include Huawei, Oppo, dtac, Vivo and more. Total Access Communication operates as a subsidiary of the Telenor Group.

CONTACTS:
Note: Officers with more than one job title may be intentionally listed here more than once.

Sharad Mehrotra, CEO
Rajiv Bawa, Chief Business Officer
Nakul Sehgal, CFO
How Lih Ren, CMO
Nardrerdee Arj-Harnwongse, Chief People Officer
Prathet Tankuranun, CTO
Saranya Sanghiran, Chief Strategy Officer
Darmp Sukontasap, Chief Corp. Affairs Officer
Chaiyod Chirabowornkul, Chief Customer Officer
Boonchai Bencharongkul, Chmn.

FINANCIAL DATA: *Note: Data for latest year may not have been available at press time.*

In U.S. $	2020	2019	2018	2017	2016	2015
Revenue	2,148,911,000	2,308,968,000	2,341,902,000	2,485,288,000	2,612,886,000	2,800,151,000
R&D Expense						
Operating Income	271,918,700	311,075,900	-150,484,900	118,264,000	124,943,800	288,268,100
Operating Margin %		.13%	-.07%	.04%	.05%	.10%
SGA Expense	462,345,200	492,894,600	728,631,400	491,192,300	571,009,900	526,472,700
Net Income	163,868,300	173,968,200	-140,174,900	67,861,600	66,926,460	189,087,900
Operating Cash Flow	832,366,300	564,633,900	585,755,600	876,906,800	854,324,100	794,963,700
Capital Expenditure	667,756,500	579,576,000	814,812,900	640,988,000	562,357,100	780,636,200
EBITDA	961,394,300	957,729,700	657,720,800	972,209,600	872,696,800	884,042,600
Return on Assets %		.03%	-.03%	.02%	.02%	.05%
Return on Equity %		.23%	-.17%	.08%	.08%	.20%
Debt to Equity		2.127	1.716	1.608	1.805	1.212

CONTACT INFORMATION:

Phone: 66 22028000   Fax: 66 22028102
Toll-Free:
Address: 319 Phayathai Rd., Chamchuri Sq. Bldg., Fl. 22-41, Bangkok, 10330 Thailand

STOCK TICKER/OTHER:

Stock Ticker: TACYY
Employees: 5,573
Parent Company: Telenor Group

Exchange: PINX
Fiscal Year Ends: 12/31

SALARIES/BONUSES:

Top Exec. Salary: $ Bonus: $
Second Exec. Salary: $ Bonus: $

OTHER THOUGHTS:

Estimated Female Officers or Directors: 4
Hot Spot for Advancement for Women/Minorities: Y

TPG Telecom Limited

www.tpgtelecom.com.au

NAIC Code: 517110

TYPES OF BUSINESS:

Wired Telecommunications Carriers
Telecommunications Services
Mobile Networks
Fixed Networks
Next-Generation Networks

BRANDS/DIVISIONS/AFFILIATES:

Vodafone
TPG
iiNet
AAPT
Internode
Lebara
felix

CONTACTS: *Note: Officers with more than one job title may be intentionally listed here more than once.*

Inaki Berroeta, CEO
Stephen Banfield, CFO
Rob James, CIO

GROWTH PLANS/SPECIAL FEATURES:

TPG Telecom Limited is an Australian telecommunications company that owns and operates mobile and fixed networks nationwide. TPG Telecom comprises more than 16,777 miles (27,000 km) of metropolitan and inter-capital fiber networks, and its mobile network has over 5,600 sites that cover 23 million Australians. The company's 5G network is rolling out to select areas in Sydney, Melbourne, Brisbane, Adelaide, Canberra, Perth, the Gold Coast, Newcastle, the Central Coast and Geelong, with plans to cover 85% of these cities by the end of 2021. 5G is available in more than 650 Australian suburbs, with approximately 1,600 sites in the planning and design phase. Mobile and internet brands under TPG Telecom include Vodafone, TPG, iiNet, AAPT, Internode, Lebara and felix. In August 2021, TPG Telecom agreed to acquire additional 5G spectrum holdings in the 3.6 GHz band from Dense Air, which will increase TPG's holdings from 60 MHz to 90 MHz in Adelaide and 95 MHz in Brisbane, Perth and Canberra. In Sydney and Melbourne, TPG will acquire 5MHz of 3.6 GHz spectrum, increasing its holdings to 65 MHz after the transaction.

FINANCIAL DATA: *Note: Data for latest year may not have been available at press time.*

In U.S. $	2020	2019	2018	2017	2016	2015
Revenue	3,373,817,000	1,921,447,000	1,935,252,000	1,931,762,000	1,851,954,000	985,464,600
R&D Expense						
Operating Income	176,834,500	418,896,100	463,958,000	463,492,600	391,440,300	259,822,700
Operating Margin %		.22%	.24%	.24%	.21%	.26%
SGA Expense	427,350,100	174,042,400	188,003,000	199,094,000	212,201,400	107,884,600
Net Income	574,712,200	134,797,500	307,831,700	320,939,100	294,414,000	173,809,700
Operating Cash Flow						
Capital Expenditure	530,503,600	556,330,700	741,696,800	446,972,500	217,940,800	119,285,700
EBITDA	864,782,900	445,498,900	653,667,300	691,981,400	659,794,400	376,626,500
Return on Assets %		.03%	.09%	.11%	.14%	.14%
Return on Equity %		.06%	.15%	.20%	.27%	.24%
Debt to Equity		0.489	0.472	0.364	0.761	0.327

CONTACT INFORMATION:

Phone: 61 299644646   Fax: 61 298889148
Toll-Free:
Address: Level 1, 177 Pacific Hwy., Sydney, NSW 2060 Australia

STOCK TICKER/OTHER:

Stock Ticker: TPPTY   Exchange: GREY
Employees: 5,000   Fiscal Year Ends: 07/31
Parent Company:

SALARIES/BONUSES:

Top Exec. Salary: $ Bonus: $
Second Exec. Salary: $ Bonus: $

OTHER THOUGHTS:

Estimated Female Officers or Directors:
Hot Spot for Advancement for Women/Minorities:

Trilogy International Partners Inc
www.trilogy-international.com

NAIC Code: 517210

TYPES OF BUSINESS:
Wireless Telecommunications Carriers (except Satellite)
Wireless Communications
LTE Coverage
Wireless Networks
Fixed Broadband
Wireless Mobile

GROWTH PLANS/SPECIAL FEATURES:
Trilogy International Partners, Inc. is a provider of wireless communications services through its operating subsidiaries in New Zealand and Bolivia, each of which have extensive long-term evolution (LTE) coverage across their wireless networks. 2degrees (73.2%-owned) provides wireless telecommunications and fixed broadband services to 98% of the country's population. NuevaTel (71.5%) is a wireless operator in Bolivia, providing wireless mobile services in urban areas and is deploying fixed wireless in areas that lack residential broadband access. Trilogy International Partners also operates through subsidiary Trilogy International Partners LLC.

BRANDS/DIVISIONS/AFFILIATES:
2degrees
NuevaTel
Trilogy International Partners LLC

CONTACTS: Note: Officers with more than one job title may be intentionally listed here more than once.
Juan Calvo, CEO, Divisional
Stewart Sherriff, CEO, Divisional
Bradley Horwitz, Director
John Stanton, Director
Erik Mickels, Senior VP
Scott Morris, Senior VP

FINANCIAL DATA: Note: Data for latest year may not have been available at press time.

In U.S. $	2020	2019	2018	2017	2016	2015
Revenue	610,299,000	693,927,000	798,175,000	776,810,000	763,416,000	
R&D Expense						
Operating Income	-7,943,000	17,489,000	22,931,000	32,776,000	40,676,000	
Operating Margin %		.03%	.03%	.04%	.05%	
SGA Expense	192,581,000	204,834,000	227,233,000	224,758,000	206,728,000	
Net Income	-47,787,000	2,878,000	-20,205,000	-15,337,000		
Operating Cash Flow	40,876,000	45,671,000	74,602,000	65,013,000	48,967,000	
Capital Expenditure	77,331,000	115,905,000	83,638,000	95,631,000	110,416,000	
EBITDA	96,893,000	139,059,000	130,961,000	144,786,000	141,604,000	
Return on Assets %		.00%	-.03%	-.02%		
Return on Equity %						
Debt to Equity						

CONTACT INFORMATION:
Phone: 425 458-5900   Fax: 425 458-5999
Toll-Free:
Address: 155 108th Avenue NE, Ste. 400, Bellevue, WA 98004 United States

STOCK TICKER/OTHER:
Stock Ticker: TLLYF
Employees: 1,663
Parent Company:

Exchange: GREY
Fiscal Year Ends: 12/31

SALARIES/BONUSES:
Top Exec. Salary: $ Bonus: $
Second Exec. Salary: $ Bonus: $

OTHER THOUGHTS:
Estimated Female Officers or Directors:
Hot Spot for Advancement for Women/Minorities:

Trimble Inc

www.trimble.com

NAIC Code: 334511

TYPES OF BUSINESS:

GPS Technologies
Surveying & Mapping Equipment
Navigation Tools
Autopilot Systems
Data Collection Products
Fleet Management Systems
Outdoor Recreation Information Service
Telecommunications & Automotive Components

BRANDS/DIVISIONS/AFFILIATES:

Applanix
AXIO-NET GmbH
Beena Vision Systems Inc
e-Builder
HHK Datentechnik GmbH
Innovative Software Engineering
MyTopo
Viewpoint

CONTACTS: *Note: Officers with more than one job title may be intentionally listed here more than once.*

Steven Berglund, CEO
Robert Painter, CFO
Ulf Johansson, Chairman of the Board
Julie Shepard, Chief Accounting Officer
Darryl Matthews, Other Corporate Officer
Sachin Sankpal, Senior VP, Divisional
Bryn Fosburgh, Senior VP, Divisional
Michael Bank, Senior VP, Divisional
Ronald Bisio, Senior VP, Divisional
Rosalind Buick, Senior VP, Divisional
Thomas Fansler, Senior VP, Divisional
James Kirkland, Senior VP

GROWTH PLANS/SPECIAL FEATURES:

Trimble, Inc. provides technology solutions used in positioning, modeling, connectivity and data analytics to enable customers to improve productivity, quality, safety and sustainability. These products are sold in more than 150 countries and include more than 2,000 unique patents. Trimble's global operations consist of offices and subsidiaries in nearly 40 countries. The company's subsidiaries include: Applanix, an industry leader in the development and manufacture of integrated Inertial/GPS technology; AXIO-NET GmbH, a provider of reference networked services that deliver highly-accurate, satellite-based positioning and navigation information; Beena Vision Systems, Inc., a manufacturer of vision-based automatic wayside inspection systems for the railroad industry; e-Builder, a provider of integrated, cloud-based construction program management software for facility owners and the companies that act on their behalf; HHK Datentechnik GmbH; a developer and marketer of specialized office management, computer-aided design (CAD) and geographic information system (GIS) software solutions for municipal and cadastral offices, utility suppliers and engineering organizations; Innovative Software Engineering, an engineering and systems integration firm; MyTopo, a provider of navigation-ready mapping services, data and software; Muller-Elektronik GmbH & Co., KG, which develops, produces and sells electronic solutions for agricultural machinery; Stabiplan, which develops and sells design software for MEP engineering in Europe; Trade Service, a provider of standardized product and price information to the mechanical, electrical, plumbing, industrial, automotive and office products industries; and Viewpoint, a global provider of integrated software solutions for the construction industry In February 2020, the firm acquired Kuebix, a privately held transportation management systems provider. In October 2020, Trimble sold its construction logistics business to Command and Alcon, a Thoma Bravo company.

FINANCIAL DATA: *Note: Data for latest year may not have been available at press time.*

In U.S. $	2020	2019	2018	2017	2016	2015
Revenue	3,147,700,000	3,264,300,000	3,108,400,000	2,654,200,000	2,362,200,000	2,290,400,000
R&D Expense	475,900,000	469,700,000	446,100,000	370,200,000	349,600,000	336,700,000
Operating Income	445,600,000	402,700,000	328,900,000	252,900,000	192,600,000	165,800,000
Operating Margin %		.12%	.11%	.10%	.08%	.07%
SGA Expense	767,900,000	834,800,000	829,600,000	706,500,000	633,600,000	629,900,000
Net Income	389,900,000	514,300,000	282,800,000	121,100,000	132,400,000	121,100,000
Operating Cash Flow	672,000,000	585,000,000	486,700,000	411,900,000	407,100,000	354,900,000
Capital Expenditure	56,800,000	69,000,000	67,600,000	43,700,000	26,300,000	44,000,000
EBITDA	670,100,000	634,400,000	566,400,000	467,500,000	390,400,000	376,500,000
Return on Assets %		.08%	.06%	.03%	.04%	.03%
Return on Equity %		.18%	.11%	.05%	.06%	.05%
Debt to Equity		0.557	0.64	0.332	0.212	0.275

CONTACT INFORMATION:

Phone: 408 481-8000   Fax: 408 481-2218
Toll-Free: 800-874-6253
Address: 935 Stewart Dr., Sunnyvale, CA 94085 United States

STOCK TICKER/OTHER:

Stock Ticker: TRMB   Exchange: NAS
Employees: 11,402   Fiscal Year Ends: 12/31
Parent Company:

SALARIES/BONUSES:

Top Exec. Salary: $ Bonus: $
Second Exec. Salary: $ Bonus: $

OTHER THOUGHTS:

Estimated Female Officers or Directors: 5
Hot Spot for Advancement for Women/Minorities: Y

TruConnect Communications Inc

www.truconnect.com

NAIC Code: 517110

TYPES OF BUSINESS:

Local Exchange Carrier
Wireless Telecommunications Services
Internet
Broadband Services
Telephone Services
Telephone Devices

BRANDS/DIVISIONS/AFFILIATES:

GROWTH PLANS/SPECIAL FEATURES:

TruConnect Communications, Inc. is a U.S. wireless telecommunications service provider. The company offers Lifeline and pay-as-you-go affordable plans. Lifeline is a state and federal government program that provides wireless internet and mobile broadband service to low-income consumers. This program is only available to consumers who can provide documentation for eligibility based on either income or participation in public assistance programs such as Supplemental Nutrition Assistance Program (SNAP) and Medicaid. Only one Lifeline service is allowed per household. TruConnect currently offers Lifeline service to residents in select states. Phones for sale by TruConnect range from $50 to $200, and consumers can also bring their own devices for service plans. Phones can be picked up at TruConnect corporate stores, branded partner locations and through authorized dealers.

CONTACTS: Note: Officers with more than one job title may be intentionally listed here more than once.

Nathan Jonson, Co-CEO
Matthew Johnson, Co-CEO
Brian Kushner, Pres.
Lucy Sung, COO
Samuel Braff, Chief Product Officer
Aleksandr Gudkov, CTO
Danielle Perry, CIO
John Debus, Treas.
Shahin Sazej, Sr. VP-Systems
Nathan Johnson, Chmn.

FINANCIAL DATA: Note: Data for latest year may not have been available at press time.

In U.S. $	2020	2019	2018	2017	2016	2015
Revenue	148,050,000	141,000,000	138,000,000	132,300,000	126,000,000	122,000,000
R&D Expense						
Operating Income						
Operating Margin %						
SGA Expense						
Net Income						
Operating Cash Flow						
Capital Expenditure						
EBITDA						
Return on Assets %						
Return on Equity %						
Debt to Equity						

CONTACT INFORMATION:

Phone: 323-776-9880   Fax:
Toll-Free:
Address: 1149 S. Hill St., H-400, Los Angeles, CA 90015 United States

STOCK TICKER/OTHER:

Stock Ticker: Private   Exchange:
Employees: 326   Fiscal Year Ends: 12/31
Parent Company: TSC Acquisition Corporation

SALARIES/BONUSES:

Top Exec. Salary: $ Bonus: $
Second Exec. Salary: $ Bonus: $

OTHER THOUGHTS:

Estimated Female Officers or Directors:
Hot Spot for Advancement for Women/Minorities:

True Corporation Public Company Limited true.listedcompany.com

NAIC Code: 517110

TYPES OF BUSINESS:

Wired Telecommunications Carriers

BRANDS/DIVISIONS/AFFILIATES:

TrueMove
TrueVisions
TrueOnline
TrueMoney
TrueMusic
TrueYou
TrueID
Charoen Pokphand Group

CONTACTS: *Note: Officers with more than one job title may be intentionally listed here more than once.*

Dhanin Chearavanont, Chmn.

GROWTH PLANS/SPECIAL FEATURES:

True Corporation Public Company Limited is a telecommunication conglomerate in Thailand. The company's products for individuals and businesses are marketed under the True brand name in various ways. TrueMove is a mobile operator that provides 2G, 3G, 4G and 4.5G service, covering 98% of the Thai population. TrueVisions is a nationwide pay TV and HD TV operator, with millions as premium and standard customers and other customers who utilize True's free-to-air content. TrueOnline offers broadband internet and WiFi through a fiber network, serving more than 13 million homes nationwide. TrueMoney is a payment services provider that offers pre-paid cards for a variety of purposes. TrueMusic is an online entertainment provider, offering television programming, news, sports information and music. TrueYou is an eCommerce website and mobile app through which users can purchase food, gifts, travel discounts and more. The company's digital platform offers solutions that utilize cutting-edge technologies, including Internet of Things (IoT), artificial intelligence (AI) and TrueID. The TrueID application combines a variety of digital content such as movies, TV, music, sports and lifestyles in a single platform. True Corporation operates as a subsidiary of Charoen Pokphand Group, which holds an approximate 50% stake in the company.

FINANCIAL DATA: *Note: Data for latest year may not have been available at press time.*

In U.S. $	2020	2019	2018	2017	2016	2015
Revenue	4,434,715,000	4,522,348,000	5,192,206,000	4,533,481,000	4,001,771,000	3,811,226,000
R&D Expense						
Operating Income	341,596,400	170,085,200	654,748,500	188,948,700	-15,774,020	147,841,600
Operating Margin %						
SGA Expense	864,023,700	905,855,100	1,143,390,000	1,068,654,000	950,111,000	757,095,700
Net Income	33,639,160	180,861,600	225,713,600	74,521,140	-90,301,860	141,549,200
Operating Cash Flow	1,415,611,000	462,804,300	1,216,993,000	160,217,600	259,774,400	106,945,100
Capital Expenditure	2,401,497,000	1,489,186,000	2,239,794,000	1,526,695,000	1,507,586,000	1,689,588,000
EBITDA	2,001,289,000	1,430,370,000	1,763,635,000	1,470,035,000	976,509,600	882,170,400
Return on Assets %						
Return on Equity %						
Debt to Equity						

CONTACT INFORMATION:

Phone: 66 26431111   Fax: 66 28599134
Toll-Free:
Address: 18 True Tower, Ratchapisek Rd., Bangkok, 10310 Thailand

SALARIES/BONUSES:

Top Exec. Salary: $ Bonus: $
Second Exec. Salary: $ Bonus: $

STOCK TICKER/OTHER:

Stock Ticker: TCPDF   Exchange: PINX
Employees: Fiscal Year Ends: 12/31
Parent Company: Charoen Pokphand Group

OTHER THOUGHTS:

Estimated Female Officers or Directors:
Hot Spot for Advancement for Women/Minorities:

TTEC Holdings Inc

www.ttec.com

NAIC Code: 541800

TYPES OF BUSINESS:

Customer Support Services
Customer Experience
Digital Consulting
Customer Acquisition

BRANDS/DIVISIONS/AFFILIATES:

TTEC Digital
TTEC Engage

CONTACTS: *Note: Officers with more than one job title may be intentionally listed here more than once.*

Kenneth Tuchman, CEO
Regina Paolillo, CFO
Margaret McLean, Chief Risk Officer
Martin DeGhetto, Executive VP, Divisional
Steven Pollema, Executive VP, Divisional
Judi Hand, Executive VP

GROWTH PLANS/SPECIAL FEATURES:

TTEC Holdings, Inc. is a global customer experience company that designs, builds and operates omnichannel customer experiences on behalf of its customers' brands. The firm helps these global companies increase revenue and reduce costs by delivering personalized customer experiences across every interaction channel and phase of the customer lifecycle. TTEC provides end-to-end customer engagement services, technologies, insights and innovations. The company is organized into two centers of excellence: TTEC Digital and TTEC Engage. TTEC Digital provides digital consultancy for designing and building human centric, tech-enabled, insight-driven customer experience solutions. TTEC Engage is the company's global hub of operational excellence providing clients with turnkey customer acquisition, care, revenue growth and digital trust and safety services. Together, TTEC Digital and TTEC Engage offers Humanify, which drives measurable results for clients through delivery of personalized omnichannel interactions that are seamless and relevant. TTEC Holdings delivers these services in 24 countries from 85 customer engagement centers on six continents. The firm primarily serves the following industries: automotive, communications, healthcare, financial services, government, logistics, media, entertainment, retail, technology, travel and transportation. In March 2021, TTEC Holdings agreed to acquire Avtex, a full-service customer experience technology and solutions leader.

FINANCIAL DATA: *Note: Data for latest year may not have been available at press time.*

In U.S. $	2020	2019	2018	2017	2016	2015
Revenue	1,949,248,000	1,643,704,000	1,509,171,000	1,477,365,000	1,275,258,000	1,286,755,000
R&D Expense						
Operating Income	213,765,000	129,191,000	99,637,000	120,476,000	89,194,000	100,094,000
Operating Margin %		.08%	.07%	.08%	.07%	.08%
SGA Expense	203,902,000	202,540,000	182,428,000	182,314,000	175,797,000	194,606,000
Net Income	118,648,000	77,164,000	35,817,000	7,256,000	33,678,000	61,666,000
Operating Cash Flow	271,920,000	237,989,000	168,345,000	113,152,000	107,897,000	133,750,000
Capital Expenditure	59,772,000	60,776,000	43,450,000	51,958,000	50,832,000	66,595,000
EBITDA	266,619,000	198,610,000	154,091,000	167,128,000	126,916,000	157,235,000
Return on Assets %		.06%	.03%	.01%	.04%	.07%
Return on Equity %		.20%	.10%	.02%	.09%	.14%
Debt to Equity		0.997	0.817	0.967	0.612	0.231

CONTACT INFORMATION:

Phone: 303 397-8100   Fax: 303 397-8668
Toll-Free: 800-835-3832
Address: 9197 S. Peoria St., Englewood, CO 80112 United States

STOCK TICKER/OTHER:

Stock Ticker: TTEC   Exchange: NAS
Employees: 49,500   Fiscal Year Ends: 12/31
Parent Company:

SALARIES/BONUSES:

Top Exec. Salary: $ Bonus: $
Second Exec. Salary: $ Bonus: $

OTHER THOUGHTS:

Estimated Female Officers or Directors: 4
Hot Spot for Advancement for Women/Minorities: Y

Turkcell Iletisim Hizmetleri AS

www.turkcell.com.tr/en/aboutus

NAIC Code: 517210

TYPES OF BUSINESS:

Cell Phone Service
Value-Added Services
Mobile Media Content
Mobile Internet

BRANDS/DIVISIONS/AFFILIATES:

Turkcell Holding AS
Cukurova Telecom Holdings Limited
Telia Sonera Finland Oyj
Cukurova Finance International Limited
Alfa Telecom Turkey Limited

CONTACTS: *Note: Officers with more than one job title may be intentionally listed here more than once.*

Kaan TerzioÄŸlu, CEO
Osman Yilmaz, Exec. VP-Finance
Omer Barbaros Yis, Exec. VP-Marketing
Serkan Ozturk, Mngr.-IT & Communication
Tayfun Cataltepe, Exec. VP-Corp. Strategy & Regulations
Selen Kocabas, Assistant Gen. Mgr.-Corp. Mktg. & Sales Group
Burak Sevilengul, Assistant Gen. Mgr.-Retail Mktg.
Hulusi Acar, Assistant Gen. Mgr.-Retail Sales
Ekrem Yener, Assistant Gen. Mgr.-Intl Expansion
Ilter Terzioglu, Assistant Gen. Mgr.-Strategic Projects
Bulent Aksu, Chmn.
Lale Saral Develioglu, Assistant Gen. Mgr.-Intl Affairs

GROWTH PLANS/SPECIAL FEATURES:

Turkcell Iletisim Hizmetleri AS is a telecommunications service provider based in Turkey, with more than 35.5 million total subscribers, including mobile, fixed and internet protocol television (IPTV) subscribers in Turkey alone. Other areas served by Turkcell include Ukraine, Belarus, Cyprus and Germany. The firm offers wireless and value-added mobile communications services and prepaid and postpaid high-quality wireless telephone voice services. It also provides mobile voice and data services over its global system of mobile communication (GSM) network, which covers the Turkish population living in settlements of 1,000 people or more, the majority of the country's tourist areas and principal inter-city highways. Currently, Turkcell operates under a 25-year GSM license, which expires in 2023; a 20-year 3G license, which expires in 2019; and a 13-year 4.5/LTE license which is good through April 2029. Turkcell Holding AS holds a 51%-stake in the company, which itself is 52.91%-owned by Cukurova Telecom Holdings Limited and 47.09%-owned by Telia Sonera Finland Oyj. Cukurova is 51%-owned by Cukurova Finance International Limited and 49%-owned by Alfa Telecom Turkey Limited. In July 2021, Turkcell announced its subsidiary Turkcell Enerji Ã‡ozumleri ve Elektrik SatiÄŸ Ticaret A.S (Turkcell Enerji) had signed a share transfer agreement to acquire the shares of Boyut Grup ENerji Elektrik Uretim ve Insaat Sanayi ve Ticaret A.S. (Boyut Grup Enerji).

FINANCIAL DATA: *Note: Data for latest year may not have been available at press time.*

In U.S. $	2020	2019	2018	2017	2016	2015
Revenue	3,383,487,000	2,922,345,000	2,475,380,000	2,049,835,000	1,660,783,000	1,484,522,000
R&D Expense						
Operating Income	772,534,900	664,834,900	563,423,300	426,375,300	305,467,700	287,477,400
Operating Margin %		.21%	.22%	.17%	.17%	.18%
SGA Expense	244,419,800	268,357,900	264,275,300	301,102,800	279,142,100	293,795,200
Net Income	492,587,000	377,423,900	234,961,100	230,085,800	173,464,300	240,377,400
Operating Cash Flow	1,522,117,000	1,049,392,000	677,756,000	360,541,100	70,583,380	221,038,400
Capital Expenditure	904,669,600	681,172,800	631,314,400	477,817,400	422,844,800	534,425,800
EBITDA	1,326,834,000	1,069,665,000	903,066,800	681,939,500	540,452,000	526,781,900
Return on Assets %		.07%	.05%	.06%	.05%	.08%
Return on Equity %		.19%	.13%	.13%	.10%	.13%
Debt to Equity		0.702	0.824	0.551	0.433	0.243

CONTACT INFORMATION:

Phone: 90 2123131244   Fax: 90 2165044058
Toll-Free:
Address: Aydinevler Mahallesi Inonu Caddesi No. 20, B Block, Maltepe, Istanbul, Turkey

STOCK TICKER/OTHER:

Stock Ticker: TKC
Employees: 24,675
Parent Company:

Exchange: NYS
Fiscal Year Ends: 12/31

SALARIES/BONUSES:

Top Exec. Salary: $ Bonus: $
Second Exec. Salary: $ Bonus: $

OTHER THOUGHTS:

Estimated Female Officers or Directors: 4
Hot Spot for Advancement for Women/Minorities: Y

Uniden Corporation

www.uniden.co.jp/english

NAIC Code: 334220

TYPES OF BUSINESS:

Communications Equipment-Wireless Devices
Wireless Communications Devices
Electronics
Manufacture
Marine Electronics
Two-Way Radios
Digital Tuners
HD TV

BRANDS/DIVISIONS/AFFILIATES:

Uniden America Corporation
Uniden Australia Proprietary Limited
Uniden Vietnam Limited
Uniden China

GROWTH PLANS/SPECIAL FEATURES:

Uniden Holdings Corporation, based in Japan, provides wireless communications devices through its global companies. The group manufactures and markets wireless communication equipment and consumer products such as CB radios, marine electronics, two-way radios, scanners, high-definition televisions, digital tuners for homes and cars and more. Group companies include Uniden America Corporation, Uniden Australia Proprietary Limited, Uniden Vietnam Limited and Uniden China.

CONTACTS: Note: Officers with more than one job title may be intentionally listed here more than once.

Takeyuki Nishikawa, Pres.
Tatsuhiro Muto, CFO

FINANCIAL DATA: Note: Data for latest year may not have been available at press time.

In U.S. $	2020	2019	2018	2017	2016	2015
Revenue	185,786,000	144,087,300	137,226,000	117,642,000	117,114,954	151,310,523
R&D Expense						
Operating Income						
Operating Margin %						
SGA Expense						
Net Income	-4,284,380	16,834,440	16,032,800	13,282,000	-42,439,908	3,688,051
Operating Cash Flow						
Capital Expenditure						
EBITDA						
Return on Assets %						
Return on Equity %						
Debt to Equity						

CONTACT INFORMATION:

Phone: 81-3-5543-2800   Fax: 81-3-5543-2921
Toll-Free:
Address: 2-12-7 Hatchobori, Chuo-ku, Tokyo, 104-8512 Japan

STOCK TICKER/OTHER:

Stock Ticker: 6815   Exchange: Tokyo
Employees: 789   Fiscal Year Ends: 03/31
Parent Company:

SALARIES/BONUSES:

Top Exec. Salary: $ Bonus: $
Second Exec. Salary: $ Bonus: $

OTHER THOUGHTS:

Estimated Female Officers or Directors:
Hot Spot for Advancement for Women/Minorities:

United Online Inc

NAIC Code: 517110

TYPES OF BUSINESS:

Internet Service Provider

BRANDS/DIVISIONS/AFFILIATES:

B Riley Financial Inc
NetZero
Juno

CONTACTS: *Note: Officers with more than one job title may be intentionally listed here more than once.*

Edward Zinser, CFO
Howard Phanstiel, Director
Mark Harrington, Executive VP
Shahir Fakiri, General Manager, Divisional
Bryant Riley, Chmn.-B. Riley Financial

GROWTH PLANS/SPECIAL FEATURES:

United Online, Inc., a subsidiary of B. Riley Financial, Inc., provides consumer products and internet and media services over the internet. These products feature value-priced internet access through the NetZero and Juno brands. The brands offer a variety of plans, and customers can choose the option that best meets their connection needs. NetZero offers mobile and home wireless broadband services. NetZero mobile broadband provides high-speed, affordable internet access to on-the-go consumers. There are four value-priced NetZero mobile broadband plans to choose from. Customers are not required to sign a contract, cannot incur overage charges and can upgrade their data plan at any time. New customers can try the service free for up to one year with the purchase of a NetZero hotspot or NetZero stick. NetZero home wireless broadband is a secure, wireless internet access service designed for home or office use. NetZero and Juno each offer a variety of plans, including a full range of dial-up and digital subscriber line (DSL) internet access services. Customers who purchase the accelerated dial-up service (either NetZero HiSpeed or Juno Turbo) can surf the web at up to 5 times the speed of standard dial-up. The Toll-free service allows customers who live in hard-to-serve areas to connect to the internet using a toll-free 800 access number. DSL service is available in select cities and includes Norton Antivirus online and MegaMail with built-in spam and email virus protection. Additionally, United Online provides advertising solutions to marketers with brand and direct response objectives through a full suite of display, search, email and text-link opportunities across its internet properties.

FINANCIAL DATA: *Note: Data for latest year may not have been available at press time.*

In U.S. $	2020	2019	2018	2017	2016	2015
Revenue	189,150,000	194,000,000	193,000,000	191,000,000	184,400,000	151,118,000
R&D Expense						
Operating Income						
Operating Margin %						
SGA Expense						
Net Income						
Operating Cash Flow						
Capital Expenditure						
EBITDA						
Return on Assets %						
Return on Equity %						
Debt to Equity						

CONTACT INFORMATION:

Phone: 818 287-3000   Fax: 818 287-3001
Toll-Free:
Address: 21301 Burbank Blvd., Woodland Hills, CA 91367 United States

STOCK TICKER/OTHER:

Stock Ticker: Subsidiary   Exchange:
Employees: 625   Fiscal Year Ends: 12/31
Parent Company: B Riley Financial Inc

SALARIES/BONUSES:

Top Exec. Salary: $ Bonus: $
Second Exec. Salary: $ Bonus: $

OTHER THOUGHTS:

Estimated Female Officers or Directors:
Hot Spot for Advancement for Women/Minorities:

United States Cellular Corporation

www.uscellular.com

NAIC Code: 517210

TYPES OF BUSINESS:

Mobile Phone and Wireless Services
Wireless Services
Telecommunications
Voice
Data Services

BRANDS/DIVISIONS/AFFILIATES:

Telephone and Data Systems Inc

CONTACTS: *Note: Officers with more than one job title may be intentionally listed here more than once.*

Kenneth Meyers, CEO
Steven Campbell, CFO
Leroy Carlson, Chairman of the Board
Douglas Chambers, Chief Accounting Officer
Michael Irizarry, Chief Technology Officer
Paul-Henri Denuit, Director Emeritus
James Barr, Director Emeritus
Jay Ellison, Executive VP
Deirdre Drake, Executive VP

GROWTH PLANS/SPECIAL FEATURES:

United States Cellular Corporation (U.S. Cellular) is a leading U.S. wireless telecommunications firm. U.S. Cellular provides wireless voice and data services to 5 million customers nationwide, including 4.4 million postpaid, 0.5 million prepaid and 0.1 million reseller and other connections. The company maintains interests in consolidated and investment wireless licenses that cover portions of 21 states. U.S. Cellular offers a range of wireless devices such as handsets, modems, mobile hotspots, home phone and tablets for use by its customers. The firm has also installed service repair programs at certain facilities, which assist customers with over-the-counter exchanges, Smartphone advance exchanges, loaner phones, device recycling and device returns. U.S. Cellular sells wireless devices to agents and other third-party distributors for resale. The wireless services segment provides a variety of packaged voice and data pricing plans. The company offers post-pay plans and prepaid plans. Moreover, U.S. Cellular services include connected home, a self-installed home security and automation system for home monitoring purposes. U.S. Cellular also offers data-services and app-like experiences to non-smartphone devices via a technology known as binary runtime environment for wireless (BREW). These enhanced data services include downloading news, weather, sports information, games, ring tones and other services. In addition, U.S. Cellular has recently engaged in VoLTE (voice over long-term evolution) trials, with plans to upgrade equipment in select markets to allow the trial processes to continue following the services official launch. Telephone and Data Systems, Inc. owns approximately 82% of the company.

U.S. Cellular offers its employees medical, dental and vision coverage; life insurance and AD&D; short- and long-term disability; a 401(k) and Roth IRA; a pension plan; and tuition reimbursement.

FINANCIAL DATA: *Note: Data for latest year may not have been available at press time.*

In U.S. $	2020	2019	2018	2017	2016	2015
Revenue	4,037,000,000	4,022,000,000	3,967,000,000	3,890,000,000	3,939,000,000	3,996,853,000
R&D Expense						
Operating Income	193,000,000	130,000,000	150,000,000	60,000,000		68,816,000
Operating Margin %		.03%	.04%	.02%		.02%
SGA Expense	1,368,000,000	1,406,000,000	1,388,000,000	1,412,000,000	1,480,000,000	1,493,730,000
Net Income	229,000,000	127,000,000	150,000,000	12,000,000	48,000,000	241,347,000
Operating Cash Flow	1,237,000,000	724,000,000	709,000,000	469,000,000	501,000,000	555,114,000
Capital Expenditure	1,190,000,000	916,000,000	520,000,000	654,000,000	496,000,000	866,400,000
EBITDA	1,045,000,000	997,000,000	971,000,000	456,000,000	813,000,000	1,096,278,000
Return on Assets %		.02%	.02%	.00%	.01%	.04%
Return on Equity %		.03%	.04%	.00%	.01%	.07%
Debt to Equity		0.564	0.396	0.441	0.445	0.457

CONTACT INFORMATION:

Phone: 773 399-8900   Fax: 773 399-8936
Toll-Free: 888-944-9400
Address: 8410 W. Bryn Mawr Ave., Chicago, IL 60631 United States

STOCK TICKER/OTHER:

Stock Ticker: USM   Exchange: NYS
Employees: 5,500   Fiscal Year Ends: 12/31
Parent Company: Telephone and Data Systems Inc

SALARIES/BONUSES:

Top Exec. Salary: $ Bonus: $
Second Exec. Salary: $ Bonus: $

OTHER THOUGHTS:

Estimated Female Officers or Directors: 6
Hot Spot for Advancement for Women/Minorities: Y

Veon Ltd

NAIC Code: 517210

TYPES OF BUSINESS:

Cell Phone Service
Wireless Internet Service
IPTV
Fixed-Line Telephony
Digital

BRANDS/DIVISIONS/AFFILIATES:

Veon
Beeline
Kyivstar
banglalink
Jazz
Djezzy

GROWTH PLANS/SPECIAL FEATURES:

Veon Ltd. is a global provider of connectivity and internet services, serving more than 213 million customers. The company's services include fixed-line telecommunication, broadband, voice, wireless internet, data and digital, which are offered to customers in 9 countries, including Russia, Pakistan, Ukraine, Bangladesh, Uzbekistan, Kazakhstan, Kyrgyzstan, Georgia and Armenia. The firm provides services under the Veon, Beeline, Kyivstar, banglalink, Jazz, ShopUp and Toffee brands. In July 2021, Veon announced it would exercise its put option to sell its stake in Djezzy.

CONTACTS: *Note: Officers with more than one job title may be intentionally listed here more than once.*

Sergi Herrero, Co-CEO
Kaan Terzioglu, Co-CEO
Serkan Okandan, CFO
Jeffrey D. McGhie, General Counsel
Dmitry G. Kromsky, Head-CIS Bus. Unit
Anton Kudryashov, Head-Russia Bus. Unit
Ahmed Abou Doma, Head-Africa & Asia Bus. Unit
Romano Righetti, Group Chief Regulatory Officer
Gennady Gazin, Chmn.
Maximo Ibarra, Head-Italy

FINANCIAL DATA: *Note: Data for latest year may not have been available at press time.*

In U.S. $	2020	2019	2018	2017	2016	2015
Revenue	7,980,000,000	8,863,000,000	9,086,000,000	9,474,000,000	8,885,000,000	9,625,000,000
R&D Expense						
Operating Income	1,597,000,000	2,235,000,000	1,501,000,000	1,655,000,000	1,354,000,000	808,000,000
Operating Margin %		.25%	.17%	.17%	.15%	.08%
SGA Expense	2,522,000,000	2,741,000,000	3,418,000,000	3,470,000,000	3,366,000,000	4,563,000,000
Net Income	-349,000,000	621,000,000	582,000,000	-483,000,000	2,328,000,000	-655,000,000
Operating Cash Flow	2,443,000,000	2,949,000,000	2,515,000,000	2,475,000,000	1,875,000,000	2,033,000,000
Capital Expenditure	1,778,000,000	1,683,000,000	1,948,000,000	2,037,000,000	1,651,000,000	2,207,000,000
EBITDA	3,413,000,000	4,227,000,000	3,260,000,000	2,902,000,000	3,113,000,000	2,301,000,000
Return on Assets %		.04%	.03%	-.02%	.08%	-.02%
Return on Equity %		.25%	.15%	-.09%	.48%	-.15%
Debt to Equity		6.329	1.789	2.381	1.354	2.15

CONTACT INFORMATION:

Phone: 31 207977200   Fax: 31 207977201
Toll-Free:
Address: Claude Debussylaan 88, Amsterdam, 1082 MD Netherlands

STOCK TICKER/OTHER:

Stock Ticker: VEON   Exchange: NAS
Employees: 46,132   Fiscal Year Ends: 12/31
Parent Company:

SALARIES/BONUSES:

Top Exec. Salary: $ Bonus: $
Second Exec. Salary: $ Bonus: $

OTHER THOUGHTS:

Estimated Female Officers or Directors: 1
Hot Spot for Advancement for Women/Minorities:

Verio Inc

www.verio.com

NAIC Code: 517210

TYPES OF BUSINESS:

Internet Service Provider
Domain Name Registration
Web Site Hosting
Virtual Private Networks
Ecommerce Services

BRANDS/DIVISIONS/AFFILIATES:

Nippon Telegraph and Telephone Corporation (NTT)
NTT Communications

CONTACTS: *Note: Officers with more than one job title may be intentionally listed here more than once.*

Hideyuki Yamasawa, CEO
Fred Martin, Sr. VP-Oper.
Tomoyuki Sakae, VP-Corp. Svcs.
William Gunther, VP-Systems Dev. & Architecture
Fred Martin, Sr. VP-Customer Service
Fred White, VP-Product Mgmt.
Wataru Imajuku, VP-Global Service Dev. & Japanese Sales

GROWTH PLANS/SPECIAL FEATURES:

Verio, Inc. offers shared website hosting solutions, domain name registration, virtual private server (VPS) hosting and other online services to individuals and small-to-medium-sized businesses. The company's hosting plans include free site-building software, as well as access to more than 200 other tools and services. Domain name registrations have hundreds of new domains available, as well as pre-registration services for soon-to-be-released domain extensions. Domain name Trademark capabilities are also available. Verio offers secure customer data and payments with SSL Certificates to enhance customer confidence from the business' website, to help boost Google rankings and utilizing encryption at lower costs. Email services through Microsoft offers businesses the latest in business-class email management and collaboration, including email, calendar, contact and task management from anywhere, any time. Verio's marketing services provide solutions for generating more traffic to the business' website, including design services, marketing services, Google Workspace, search engine optimization, search engine marketing, email marketing and more. Marketing strategies include website, advertising and website traffic management and analytics. Verio operates as a wholly-owned subsidiary of NTT Communications, which itself is a subsidiary of Nippon Telegraph and Telephone Corporation.

FINANCIAL DATA: *Note: Data for latest year may not have been available at press time.*

In U.S. $	2020	2019	2018	2017	2016	2015
Revenue						
R&D Expense						
Operating Income						
Operating Margin %						
SGA Expense						
Net Income						
Operating Cash Flow						
Capital Expenditure						
EBITDA						
Return on Assets %						
Return on Equity %						
Debt to Equity						

CONTACT INFORMATION:

Phone: 855-765-0425   Fax:
Toll-Free:
Address: 10 Corporate Dr., Ste. 300, Burlington, MA 01803 United States

STOCK TICKER/OTHER:

Stock Ticker: Subsidiary   Exchange:
Employees: 1,960   Fiscal Year Ends: 03/31
Parent Company: Nippon Telegraph and Telephone Corporation (NTT)

SALARIES/BONUSES:

Top Exec. Salary: $ Bonus: $
Second Exec. Salary: $ Bonus: $

OTHER THOUGHTS:

Estimated Female Officers or Directors:
Hot Spot for Advancement for Women/Minorities:

VeriSign Inc

NAIC Code: 511210E

TYPES OF BUSINESS:

Computer Software: Network Security, Managed Access, Digital ID,
Cybersecurity & Anti-Virus
Domain Name Registration

BRANDS/DIVISIONS/AFFILIATES:

Registry Services
Security Services

GROWTH PLANS/SPECIAL FEATURES:

VeriSign, Inc. is a global provider of domain name registry services and internet security, enabling internet navigation for many of the world's most recognized domain names and providing protection for websites and enterprises around the world (Registry Services). VeriSign's Registry Services ensure the security, stability, and resiliency of key internet infrastructure and services, including the .com and .net domains, two of the internet's root servers and operation of the root-zone maintainer functions for the core of the internet's Domain Name System. The company manages and protects the DNS infrastructure for more than 163.7 million .com and .net domain names, and processes more than 219 billion query transactions daily.

Employees of VeriSign receive a flexible benefits package that includes health, dental, vision, disability and life insurance; flexible spending accounts; a 401(k); an employee assistance program; a group legal plan; domestic partner coverage; tuition ass

CONTACTS: *Note: Officers with more than one job title may be intentionally listed here more than once.*

James Bidzos, CEO
George Kilguss, CFO
Todd Strubbe, Executive VP
Thomas Indelicarto, Executive VP

FINANCIAL DATA: *Note: Data for latest year may not have been available at press time.*

In U.S. $	2020	2019	2018	2017	2016	2015
Revenue	1,265,052,000	1,231,661,000	1,214,969,000	1,165,095,000	1,142,167,000	1,059,366,000
R&D Expense	74,671,000	60,805,000	57,884,000	52,342,000	59,100,000	63,718,000
Operating Income	824,201,000	806,127,000	767,392,000	707,722,000	686,572,000	605,946,000
Operating Margin %		.65%	.63%	.61%	.60%	.57%
SGA Expense	186,003,000	184,262,000	197,559,000	211,705,000	198,253,000	196,914,000
Net Income	814,888,000	612,299,000	582,489,000	457,248,000	440,645,000	375,236,000
Operating Cash Flow	730,183,000	753,892,000	697,767,000	702,761,000	667,949,000	651,482,000
Capital Expenditure	43,395,000	40,316,000	37,007,000	49,499,000	169,574,000	40,656,000
EBITDA	883,659,000	895,717,000	892,728,000	785,226,000	754,904,000	656,772,000
Return on Assets %		.32%	.24%	.17%	.19%	.17%
Return on Equity %						
Debt to Equity						

CONTACT INFORMATION:

Phone: 703 948-3200   Fax:
Toll-Free: 800-922-4917
Address: 12061 Bluemont Way, Reston, VA 20190 United States

STOCK TICKER/OTHER:

Stock Ticker: VRSN   Exchange: NAS
Employees: 872   Fiscal Year Ends: 12/31
Parent Company:

SALARIES/BONUSES:

Top Exec. Salary: $ Bonus: $
Second Exec. Salary: $ Bonus: $

OTHER THOUGHTS:

Estimated Female Officers or Directors:
Hot Spot for Advancement for Women/Minorities:

Verizon Communications Inc

www.verizon.com

NAIC Code: 517110

TYPES OF BUSINESS:

Mobile Phone and Wireless Services
Telecommunications Services
Cable TV Subscriptions
Long-Distance Services
High-Speed Internet Access
Video-on-Demand Services
e-Commerce & Online Services

BRANDS/DIVISIONS/AFFILIATES:

Verizon Wireless
BlueJeans Network Inc

CONTACTS: *Note: Officers with more than one job title may be intentionally listed here more than once.*

Kumara Gowrappan, CEO, Divisional
Hans Vestberg, CEO
Matthew Ellis, CFO
Anthony Skiadas, Chief Accounting Officer
Marc Reed, Chief Administrative Officer
Kyle Malady, Chief Technology Officer
Craig Silliman, Executive VP, Divisional
Rima Qureshi, Executive VP
Ronan Dunne, Executive VP
Tami Erwin, Executive VP

GROWTH PLANS/SPECIAL FEATURES:

Verizon Communications, Inc. is a world-leading provider of communications services. The company operates through its subsidiaries, with products and services categorized into two primary segments: wireless and wireline. The wireless segment consists of wireless voice and data services and equipment sales, which are provided to consumer, business and government customers throughout the U.S. This division does business as Verizon Wireless and represents approximately 70% of Verizon's aggregate revenues. Wireless' network technology platform is currently 4G LTE (long-term evolution), but the segment is engaged in 5G wireless technology development and its ecosystems for fixed and mobile 5G wireless services are intact. This division offers various post-paid account service plans, including unlimited plans, shared data plans, single connection plans and other plans tailored to the customer's need. Pre-paid connection plans are available and feature domestic unlimited voice and unlimited domestic/international text. Access to the internet is available on all smartphones and nearly all basic phones; and network access needed to deliver various Internet of Things (IoT) products and services is also provided. The wireline segment consists of video and data services, corporate networking solutions, security and managed network services, and local and long-distance voice services. Wireline products and services are provided to consumers in the U.S., as well as to carriers, businesses and government customers both in the U.S. and worldwide. These products are built around a fiber-based network (as well as a copper-based one, to a lesser degree), supporting data, video and advanced business services in areas where high-speed connections is needed. During 2020, Verizon acquired video conferencing service BlueJeans Network, Inc.; agreed to acquire Tracfone Wireless, Inc. from America Movil, which provides pre-paid and mobile services in the U.S.; and agreed to acquire Bluegrass Cellular, a rural wireless operator serving central Kentucky.

Verizon offers comprehensive employee benefits.

FINANCIAL DATA: *Note: Data for latest year may not have been available at press time.*

In U.S. $	2020	2019	2018	2017	2016	2015
Revenue	128,292,000,000	131,868,000,000	130,863,000,000	126,034,000,000	125,980,000,000	131,620,000,000
R&D Expense						
Operating Income	28,798,000,000	30,470,000,000	26,869,000,000	29,188,000,000	27,059,000,000	33,060,000,000
Operating Margin %		.23%	.21%	.23%	.21%	.25%
SGA Expense	31,573,000,000	29,990,000,000	31,083,000,000	28,336,000,000	31,569,000,000	29,986,000,000
Net Income	17,801,000,000	19,265,000,000	15,528,000,000	30,101,000,000	13,127,000,000	17,879,000,000
Operating Cash Flow	41,768,000,000	35,746,000,000	34,339,000,000	25,305,000,000	22,715,000,000	38,930,000,000
Capital Expenditure	20,318,000,000	18,837,000,000	18,087,000,000	17,830,000,000	17,593,000,000	27,717,000,000
EBITDA	44,934,000,000	44,145,000,000	41,859,000,000	42,281,000,000	41,290,000,000	49,177,000,000
Return on Assets %		.07%	.06%	.12%	.05%	.07%
Return on Equity %		.34%	.32%	.92%	.67%	1.24%
Debt to Equity		1.94	1.992	2.637	4.681	6.313

CONTACT INFORMATION:

Phone: 212 395-1000   Fax:
Toll-Free: 800-837-4966
Address: 1095 Avenue of the Americas, New York, NY 10036 United States

STOCK TICKER/OTHER:

Stock Ticker: VZ
Employees: 132,200
Parent Company:

Exchange: NYS
Fiscal Year Ends: 12/31

SALARIES/BONUSES:

Top Exec. Salary: $ Bonus: $
Second Exec. Salary: $ Bonus: $

OTHER THOUGHTS:

Estimated Female Officers or Directors: 5
Hot Spot for Advancement for Women/Minorities: Y

ViaSat Inc

NAIC Code: 334220

www.viasat.com

TYPES OF BUSINESS:

Telecommunications Equipment-Digital Satellite
Networking & Wireless Signal Processing
Satellite Broadband Internet Service Provider

BRANDS/DIVISIONS/AFFILIATES:

CONTACTS: *Note: Officers with more than one job title may be intentionally listed here more than once.*

Mark Dankberg, CEO
Shawn Duffy, Chief Accounting Officer
Keven Lippert, Chief Administrative Officer
Mark Miller, Chief Technology Officer
Girish Chandran, Chief Technology Officer
Robert Blair, General Counsel
Melinda Del Toro, Other Executive Officer
Ken Peterman, President, Divisional
Kevin Harkenrider, President, Divisional
David Ryan, President, Divisional
Richard Baldridge, President
Bruce Dirks, Senior VP, Divisional
Doug Abts, Vice President, Divisional
Marc Agnew, Vice President, Divisional

GROWTH PLANS/SPECIAL FEATURES:

ViaSat, Inc. provides advanced satellite and wireless communications and secure networking systems, products and services. The company operates in three segments: government systems, commercial networks and satellite services. The government systems segment encompasses products serving defense customers, including its tactical data link product line; tactical networking and information assurance, enabling the government and military to secure information up to top secret levels; and government satellite communication systems. Current defense products include multifunctional information distribution system (MIDS) terminals for military fighter jets and their successor, MIDS joint tactical radio system (MIDS-JTRS) terminals, 'disposable' weapon data links and portable small tactical terminals. The commercial networks develop and produce a variety of advanced end-to-end satellite and other wireless communication systems and ground networking equipment and products that address five key markets: consumer, enterprise, in-flight, maritime and ground mobile applications. Satellite communication systems for this segment include fixed satellite networks, mobile broadband satellite communication systems, antenna systems and satellite networking development. The satellite services segment, like the commercial networks segment, offers wholesale and retail broadband services, as well as managed broadband wireless networking services, and mobile satellite broadband services to airborne- and marine-based customers. Launched satellites by the firm include: ViaSat-1, in 2011; and ViaSat-2, in 2017; with three ViaSat-3 class satellites under construction. In addition, ViaSat has a joint venture with Eutelsat which operates two businesses: one operates Eutelsat's KA-SAT satellite and wholesale broadband business, and the other purchases KA-SAT capacity and markets retail broadband internet services throughout Europe and the Mediterranean.

ViaSat offers employee benefits such as health, 401(k) and tuition reimbursement, depending on the location.

FINANCIAL DATA: *Note: Data for latest year may not have been available at press time.*

In U.S. $	2020	2019	2018	2017	2016	2015
Revenue	2,309,238,000	2,068,258,000	1,594,625,000	1,559,337,000	1,417,431,000	
R&D Expense	130,434,000	123,044,000	168,347,000	129,647,000	77,184,000	
Operating Income	38,421,000	-60,620,000	-92,187,000	36,459,000	41,119,000	
Operating Margin %	.02%	-.03%	-.06%	.02%	.03%	
SGA Expense	523,085,000	458,458,000	385,420,000	333,468,000	298,345,000	
Net Income	-212,000	-67,623,000	-67,305,000	23,767,000	21,741,000	
Operating Cash Flow	436,936,000	327,551,000	358,633,000	411,298,000	296,937,000	
Capital Expenditure	761,078,000	686,820,000	584,487,000	585,658,000	450,625,000	
EBITDA	382,247,000	258,142,000	154,208,000	283,389,000	285,421,000	
Return on Assets %	.00%	-.02%	-.02%	.01%	.01%	
Return on Equity %	.00%	-.04%	-.04%	.02%	.02%	
Debt to Equity	1.04	0.73	0.533	0.489	0.845	

CONTACT INFORMATION:

Phone: 760 476-2200   Fax: 760 929-3941
Toll-Free:
Address: 6155 El Camino Real, Carlsbad, CA 92009 United States

SALARIES/BONUSES:

Top Exec. Salary: $ Bonus: $
Second Exec. Salary: $ Bonus: $

STOCK TICKER/OTHER:

Stock Ticker: VSAT   Exchange: NAS
Employees: 5,800   Fiscal Year Ends: 03/31
Parent Company:

OTHER THOUGHTS:

Estimated Female Officers or Directors:
Hot Spot for Advancement for Women/Minorities:

Viavi Solutions Inc

www.viavisolutions.com

NAIC Code: 334220

TYPES OF BUSINESS:

Communications and Commercial Optical Products
Network Systems
Security Products
Systems Enablement and Consulting

BRANDS/DIVISIONS/AFFILIATES:

Optically Variable Pigment
Optically Variable Magnetic Pigment

CONTACTS: Note: Officers with more than one job title may be intentionally listed here more than once.

Oleg Khaykin, CEO
Amar Maletira, CFO
Paul McNab, Chief Marketing Officer
Richard Belluzzo, Director
Kevin Siebert, General Counsel
Luke Scrivanich, General Manager, Divisional
Ralph Rondinone, Senior VP, Divisional
Gary Staley, Senior VP, Divisional

GROWTH PLANS/SPECIAL FEATURES:

Viavi Solutions, Inc. is a global provider of network test, monitoring and assurance solutions to communications service providers, enterprises and their ecosystems. The company's solutions deliver end-to-end visibility across physical, virtual and hybrid networks, which enables Viavi customers to optimize connectivity, quality of experience and profitability. The firm also produces thin film coatings, which provide light management solutions to various markets. Viavi operates through three business segments: network enablement, service enablement and optical security and performance products. Together, the network enablement and service enablement segments enable networks to provide agile, flexible, programmable and cost-effective transmission capacity and speed to their customers. These segments provide products and solutions for the deployment of next-generation network technologies, including optical fiber-to-the-home and to everywhere. The optical security and performance products segment produces and provides Viavi's anti-counterfeiting products and solutions, including its Optically Variable Pigment (OVP) and Optically Variable Magnetic Pigment (OVMP) technologies. These technologies protect the integrity of banknotes and other high-value documents by delivering optical effects which are very easy for consumers to recognize but difficult for counterfeiters to reproduce. This division also provides optical technologies for government, healthcare, consumer electronics and industrial markets. In early-2021, Viavi relocated its headquarters from California to Arizona, and announced that its optical security and performance products segment plans to establish a new manufacturing facility in Chandler, Arizona. The company's San Jose, California office continues to operate as a center of excellence and sales office.

Viavi offers its employees medical, dental and vision benefits, wellness initiatives, retirement benefits, stock compensation and an employee stock purchase plan.

FINANCIAL DATA: Note: Data for latest year may not have been available at press time.

In U.S. $	2020	2019	2018	2017	2016	2015
Revenue	1,136,300,000	1,130,300,000	880,400,000	811,400,000	906,300,000	1,709,100,000
R&D Expense	193,600,000	187,000,000	133,300,000	136,300,000	166,400,000	313,200,000
Operating Income	121,600,000	82,800,000	13,400,000	35,200,000	17,600,000	-17,800,000
Operating Margin %		.07%	.02%	.04%	.02%	- .01%
SGA Expense	315,000,000	343,500,000	324,500,000	300,500,000	351,100,000	463,500,000
Net Income	28,700,000	5,400,000	-46,000,000	166,900,000	-99,200,000	-88,100,000
Operating Cash Flow	135,600,000	138,800,000	66,000,000	80,000,000	52,900,000	82,300,000
Capital Expenditure	31,900,000	45,000,000	42,500,000	38,600,000	35,500,000	101,500,000
EBITDA	235,500,000	185,800,000	98,100,000	287,500,000	60,400,000	91,100,000
Return on Assets %		.00%	- .02%	.09%	- .05%	- .04%
Return on Equity %		.01%	- .06%	.23%	- .11%	- .08%
Debt to Equity		0.833	0.811	1.22	0.895	0.536

CONTACT INFORMATION:

Phone: 408-404-3600   Fax: 408-404-4500
Toll-Free:
Address: 7047 E. Greenway Pkwy., Ste. 250, Scottsdale, AZ 85254 United States

STOCK TICKER/OTHER:

Stock Ticker: VIAV
Employees: 3,600
Parent Company:

Exchange: NAS
Fiscal Year Ends: 06/27

SALARIES/BONUSES:

Top Exec. Salary: $ Bonus: $
Second Exec. Salary: $ Bonus: $

OTHER THOUGHTS:

Estimated Female Officers or Directors:
Hot Spot for Advancement for Women/Minorities:

Sales, profits and employees may be estimates. Financial information, benefits and other data can change quickly and may vary from those stated here.

Virgin Media Business Ltd

www.virginmediabusiness.co.uk

NAIC Code: 517110

TYPES OF BUSINESS:

Fixed-line Telecommunications
High-Speed Internet Services
Telephony Services
Voice Services
Business Telecommunications
Data Services

BRANDS/DIVISIONS/AFFILIATES:

Virgin Media Limited

CONTACTS: *Note: Officers with more than one job title may be intentionally listed here more than once.*

Peter Kelly, Managing Dir.
Mike Smith, Managing Dir.-Business
Luke Milner, Dir.-Finance
Michelle King, Dir.-Dev. & Strategy
Alison Bawn, Dir.-People
Phil Stewart, Dir.-Customer Service
Brendan Lynch, Dir.-Bus. & Partner Markets
Lee Hull, Dir.-Public Sector

GROWTH PLANS/SPECIAL FEATURES:

Virgin Media Business Ltd., a division of Virgin Media Limited, is a leading telecommunications provider for small- and medium-sized businesses as well as for enterprises and public sector entities within the U.K., Scotland and northern Ireland. The firm offers a national product portfolio of broadband, internet, mobile, voice over internet protocol (VoIP) solutions, site connectivity, virtual private networks (VPNs) and phone lines. Virgin Media works with approximately 600 wholesale partners to service businesses and public sector organizations in the U.K. The company's wholly-owned network hosts 84% of Ethernet services entirely on their own, connects hundreds of data centers and points of presence, and carries over 35% of the U.K.'s broadband traffic. Virgin Media Business' office locations include: Reading, Berkshire, Hammersmith, Bristol, Peterborough, Nottingham, Staverton, Swansea, Bradford, Stockton on Tees, Liverpool, Manchester, Knowsley and Gateshead, England; Edinburgh, Scotland; and Belfast, Ireland.

FINANCIAL DATA: *Note: Data for latest year may not have been available at press time.*

In U.S. $	2020	2019	2018	2017	2016	2015
Revenue	1,084,820,000	1,110,900,000	1,058,000,000	1,030,000,000	1,020,432,000	960,000,000
R&D Expense						
Operating Income						
Operating Margin %						
SGA Expense						
Net Income						
Operating Cash Flow						
Capital Expenditure						
EBITDA						
Return on Assets %						
Return on Equity %						
Debt to Equity						

CONTACT INFORMATION:

Phone: 44-173-323-0666   Fax:
Toll-Free:
Address: Southgate House, Bakewell Rd., Orton Southgate,
Peterborough, PE2 6YS United Kingdom

STOCK TICKER/OTHER:

Stock Ticker: Subsidiary   Exchange:
Employees: Fiscal Year Ends: 12/31
Parent Company: Virgin Media Limited

SALARIES/BONUSES:

Top Exec. Salary: $ Bonus: $
Second Exec. Salary: $ Bonus: $

OTHER THOUGHTS:

Estimated Female Officers or Directors:
Hot Spot for Advancement for Women/Minorities: Y

Virgin Media Limited

www.virginmedia.com

NAIC Code: 517210

TYPES OF BUSINESS:

Wireless Service
Cable TV
Internet Service Provider
Fixed Line & Mobile Telephony
Digital
Broadband

BRANDS/DIVISIONS/AFFILIATES:

Liberty Global plc
Telefonica SA
VMED O2 UK Limited (Virgin Media O2)

GROWTH PLANS/SPECIAL FEATURES:

Virgin Media Limited, a subsidiary of VMED O2 UK Limited, is a leading entertainment and communications company serving the U.K. The company provides broadband, TV, phone and mobile services to consumers and businesses, of which the services can be bundled. Virgin Media offers TiVo and digital set-top boxes; subscription video on-demand services; and pay-per-view services. It operates a digital cable platform that includes access to hundreds of linear television channels. Virgin Media is a subsidiary of telecommunications and television giant, Liberty Global plc. Parent company VMED O2 UK, doing business as Virgin Media O2, is a 50:50 joint venture between Liberty Global plc and Telefonica S.A. that combines Virgin Media with Telefonica's O2 mobile operator to create a leading U.K. mobile platform, bringing together 5G technology with gigabit broadband.

CONTACTS: *Note: Officers with more than one job title may be intentionally listed here more than once.*

Lutz Schuler, CEO
Patricia Cobian, CFO
Adrian Di Meo, CIO
Philipp Wohland, Chief People Officer
Jeanie York, CTO
Richard Williams, Dir.-Investor Relations
Kay Schwabedal, Chief Digital Officer

FINANCIAL DATA: *Note: Data for latest year may not have been available at press time.*

In U.S. $	2020	2019	2018	2017	2016	2015
Revenue	6,963,080,000	6,778,630,000	7,030,768,500	6,695,970,000	5,912,270,000	6,846,130,000
R&D Expense						
Operating Income						
Operating Margin %						
SGA Expense						
Net Income	53,358,500	-442,404,000	-46,953,900	-117,239,000	-351,334,000	-210,347,000
Operating Cash Flow						
Capital Expenditure						
EBITDA						
Return on Assets %						
Return on Equity %						
Debt to Equity						

CONTACT INFORMATION:

Phone: 44-800-052-0626   Fax:
Toll-Free:
Address: 160 Great Portland St., London, W1W 5QA United Kingdom

STOCK TICKER/OTHER:

Stock Ticker: Subsidiary   Exchange:
Employees: 11,800   Fiscal Year Ends: 12/31
Parent Company: Liberty Global plc

SALARIES/BONUSES:

Top Exec. Salary: $ Bonus: $
Second Exec. Salary: $ Bonus: $

OTHER THOUGHTS:

Estimated Female Officers or Directors:
Hot Spot for Advancement for Women/Minorities:

Vocus Group Limited

NAIC Code: 517110

www.vocusgroup.com.au

TYPES OF BUSINESS:

Wired Telecommunications Carriers

BRANDS/DIVISIONS/AFFILIATES:

Dodo
iPrimus
Slingshot
Flip
Orcon
Australia Singapore Cable

CONTACTS: *Note: Officers with more than one job title may be intentionally listed here more than once.*

Kevin Russell, Managing Dir.
Ellie Sweeney, COO
Nitesh Naidoo, CFO
Amber Kristof, Dir.-People & Culture
Robert Mansfield, Chmn.

GROWTH PLANS/SPECIAL FEATURES:

Vocus Group Limited provides retail, wholesale and corporate telecommunications services across Australia and New Zealand through various brands. The company's range of products and services span connectivity, cloud, data center, voice and security. Vocus owns and operates the group's telecom network, which comprises approximately 18,640 miles (30,000 km) of fiber optic cable. Vocus' internet services include business internet, business nbn (national broadband network) satellite service, enterprise internet, IP transit carrier grade internet and add-on products such as distributed denial-of-service (DDoS) protection. Internet services also include connectivity solutions. The firm's Commander brand focuses solely on business communications, offering communications and technology solutions to Australian businesses. Dodo is a leading Australian brand that serves individuals and families with affordable and easy-to-use telecommunications and insurance products nation-wide. Dodo also provides power and gas in selected Australian states. iPrimus offers broadband, home phone and mobile phone products and services to the Australian market. Slingshot offers broadband services in New Zealand. Flip is a no-frills, budget-friendly internet provider in New Zealand. Orcon offers broadband services to New Zealand residential customers. Beyond Australia and New Zealand, Vocus built, owns and operates the Australia Singapore Cable, a 2,858 miles (4,600 km) fiber network that delivers connectivity via direct-current interconnects in Perth, Jakarta and Singapore, enabling low-latency connections to Asian hubs such as Hong Kong.

FINANCIAL DATA: *Note: Data for latest year may not have been available at press time.*

In U.S. $	2020	2019	2018	2017	2016	2015
Revenue	1,221,160,000	1,457,934,400	1,401,860,000	1,420,960,000	600,344,000	109,167,000
R&D Expense						
Operating Income						
Operating Margin %						
SGA Expense						
Net Income	-122,355,000	47,337,045	45,082,900	-1,143,340,000	46,319,300	14,502,100
Operating Cash Flow						
Capital Expenditure						
EBITDA						
Return on Assets %						
Return on Equity %						
Debt to Equity						

CONTACT INFORMATION:

Phone: 61-3-9923-3000   Fax: 61-3-9674-6599
Toll-Free:
Address: 452 Flinders St., Fl. 10, Melbourne, VIC 3000 Australia

SALARIES/BONUSES:

Top Exec. Salary: $ Bonus: $
Second Exec. Salary: $ Bonus: $

STOCK TICKER/OTHER:

Stock Ticker: VOC   Exchange: ASX
Employees: 2,032   Fiscal Year Ends: 06/30
Parent Company:

OTHER THOUGHTS:

Estimated Female Officers or Directors:
Hot Spot for Advancement for Women/Minorities:

Vodafone Group plc

www.vodafone.com

NAIC Code: 517210

TYPES OF BUSINESS:

Cell Phone Service
Mobile Communications
Fixed Communications
Unified Communications
Cloud Hosting
Internet of Things
Carrier Services

BRANDS/DIVISIONS/AFFILIATES:

TPG Telecom

CONTACTS: Note: Officers with more than one job title may be intentionally listed here more than once.

Nick Read, CEO
Margherita Della Valle, CFO
Ahmed Essam, Chief Commercial Operations Officer
Leanne Wood, Chief Human Resources Officer
Johan Wibergh, Group Technology Officer
Rosemary Martin, General Counsel
Warren Finegold, Dir.-Strategy & Bus. Dev.
Matthew Kirk, Dir.-External Affairs
Morten Lundal, Chief Commercial Officer
Philipp Humm, CEO-Northern & Central Europe
Paulo Bertoluzzo, CEO-Southern Europe
Nick Jeffery, Dir-Group Enterprises
Gerard Kleisterlee, Chmn.
Nick Read, CEO-Asia-Pacific, Africa & Middle East Region

GROWTH PLANS/SPECIAL FEATURES:

Vodafone Group plc is a group of world-leading telecommunications companies, with a global network throughout Europe, Asia Pacific, Africa and the Americas. The firm's solutions include mobile communications, fixed communications, unified communications, cloud and hosting, Internet of Things (IoT) and carrier services. Mobile solutions include voice and data, and managed messaging. Fixed communications solutions include open/interconnected software-defined networks, IP-VPN service, international Ethernet service, LAN/WLAN service, satellite services, internet access and network gateway protection. Unified communications solutions include conferencing/collaboration services, contact center service, customer interaction service, call recording for compliance purposes, fixed voice service and global SIP trunking. Cloud and hosting solutions include agile, intelligent, global cloud products for any business. These solutions include colocation, managed hosting services, professional services, private cloud, cloud platforms, productivity solutions and public cloud services. IoT solutions help unlock new revenue streams, improve efficiency and increase customer engagement and loyalty via solutions relating to narrowband-IoT, digital buildings, IoT managed tablets, fleet telematics, usage-based motor insurance, vehicle manufacturers, integrated terminals, asset tracking, monitoring/control, smart grid and smart meters, connected retail display cabinets and satellite IoT. These products and services primarily serve large and multinational businesses, small and medium businesses, international public sectors and industries such as automotive, banking/finance, health, manufacturing, retail, smart cities, transportation/logistics and utilities. In July 2020, the $15 billion merger of TPG Telecom and Vodafone Hutchison Australia was completed, with the new company named TPG Telecom.

FINANCIAL DATA: Note: Data for latest year may not have been available at press time.

In U.S. $	2020	2019	2018	2017	2016	2015
Revenue	54,948,200,000	53,350,110,000	56,899,380,000	58,194,460,000	63,477,510,000	
R&D Expense						
Operating Income	10,933,680,000	4,956,749,000	5,324,504,000	4,493,696,000	2,762,317,000	
Operating Margin %	.20%	.09%	.09%	.08%	.04%	
SGA Expense	11,758,380,000	11,363,750,000	11,796,260,000	12,741,910,000	13,447,510,000	
Net Income	-1,124,035,000	-9,798,651,000	2,979,914,000	-7,693,530,000	-6,234,190,000	
Operating Cash Flow	21,233,260,000	15,858,660,000	16,616,170,000	17,377,330,000	16,237,710,000	
Capital Expenditure	9,291,614,000	9,958,704,000	9,973,365,000	10,826,170,000	18,364,840,000	
EBITDA	21,717,080,000	11,098,620,000	18,910,660,000	19,043,840,000	16,267,150,000	
Return on Assets %	-.01%	-.06%	.02%	-.04%	-.03%	
Return on Equity %	-.01%	-.12%	.03%	-.08%	-.06%	
Debt to Equity	1.024	0.782	0.487	0.478	0.445	

CONTACT INFORMATION:

Phone: 44 163533251   Fax: 44 1635238080
Toll-Free:
Address: Vodafone House, The Connection, Newbury, Berkshire RG14 2FN United Kingdom

STOCK TICKER/OTHER:

Stock Ticker: VOD   Exchange: NAS
Employees: 105,000   Fiscal Year Ends: 03/31
Parent Company:

SALARIES/BONUSES:

Top Exec. Salary: $ Bonus: $
Second Exec. Salary: $ Bonus: $

OTHER THOUGHTS:

Estimated Female Officers or Directors: 2
Hot Spot for Advancement for Women/Minorities: Y

Vonage Holdings Corp

www.vonage.com

NAIC Code: 517110

TYPES OF BUSINESS:
VOIP Telecommunications

BRANDS/DIVISIONS/AFFILIATES:

CONTACTS: *Note: Officers with more than one job title may be intentionally listed here more than once.*
David Pearson, CFO
Jeffrey Citron, Chairman of the Board
David Levi, Chief Accounting Officer
Randy Rutherford, Chief Legal Officer
Rishi Dave, Chief Marketing Officer
Vinod Lala, Chief Strategy Officer
Sagi Dudai, Chief Technology Officer
Alan Masarek, Director
Omar Javaid, Other Executive Officer
Susan Quackenbush, Other Executive Officer

GROWTH PLANS/SPECIAL FEATURES:

Vonage Holdings Corp. offers a cloud communications platform that enables businesses of all sizes to collaborate and to engage their customers efficiently, across any device. These business/enterprise customers can choose among two delivery models: purchase a Vonage software-as-a-service (SaaS) model for a complete and configured unified communications solution; or purchase a Vonage application program interface (API) platform with a platform-as-a-service (PaaS) model, which comprises the firm's cloud communication in programmable modules, delivered via APIs. All of Vonage's cloud communications solutions are designed to allow businesses to be more productive by integrating communications with all their existing business productivity tools. The company's programmable solutions enable customers to engage via embedded voice, chat or messaging to create seamless and contextual communications that makes doing business easier. For consumer customers, Vonage enables users to access and utilize its services through a single identity, either a number or user name, regardless of how they are connected to the internet. This technology enables Vonage to offer individual customers attractively-priced voice and messaging services and other features worldwide, across a variety of devices. The company's consumer market primarily consists of those under-served within the North American region.

FINANCIAL DATA: *Note: Data for latest year may not have been available at press time.*

In U.S. $	2020	2019	2018	2017	2016	2015
Revenue		1,189,346,000	1,048,782,016	1,002,286,016	955,620,992	895,072,000
R&D Expense						
Operating Income						
Operating Margin %						
SGA Expense						
Net Income		-19,482,000	35,728,000	-33,933,000	17,907,000	22,655,000
Operating Cash Flow						
Capital Expenditure						
EBITDA						
Return on Assets %						
Return on Equity %						
Debt to Equity						

CONTACT INFORMATION:
Phone: 732 528-2600   Fax: 732 287-9119
Toll-Free: 800-980-1455
Address: 23 Main St., Holmdel, NJ 07733 United States

STOCK TICKER/OTHER:
Stock Ticker: VG   Exchange: NYS
Employees: 2,264   Fiscal Year Ends: 12/31
Parent Company:

SALARIES/BONUSES:
Top Exec. Salary: $ Bonus: $
Second Exec. Salary: $ Bonus: $

OTHER THOUGHTS:
Estimated Female Officers or Directors: 1
Hot Spot for Advancement for Women/Minorities:

VTech Holdings Limited

www.vtech.com

NAIC Code: 334210

TYPES OF BUSINESS:
Cordless Telephone Sets
Electronic Learning Products
Contract Manufacturing Services
Data Networking Products
Cordless Phones
Telecommunications

BRANDS/DIVISIONS/AFFILIATES:
Vtech
Leap Frog

CONTACTS: *Note: Officers with more than one job title may be intentionally listed here more than once.*
Allan Chi Yun Wong, CEO
King Fai Pang, Pres.
Andy Leung Hon Kwong, CEO-Contract Mfg. Svcs.
William To, Pres., Vtech Electronics North America
Gordon Chow, Pres., Vtech Technologies Canada
Nicholas Delany, Pres., Vtech Communications, Inc.
Allan Chi Yun Wong, Chmn.

GROWTH PLANS/SPECIAL FEATURES:
VTech Holdings Limited is a global electronic learning products company, as well as a manufacturer of cordless phones. Based in Hong Kong, the firm has manufacturing facilities in China and Malaysia, and various operations across 14 countries and regions worldwide. VTech's products and services are categorized into three business divisions: electronic learning products, telecommunication products and contract manufacturing services. Electronic learning products include learning-based toys for children aged from infancy through toddler/preschool, as well as kid-based smart watches, tablets, laptops, desktops and phones. These products are offered in more than 30 languages. Telecommunications products include cordless phones and handsets for residential and commercial use. Other offerings within this division include a variety of wireless monitoring systems, audio/video baby monitors and conference phone systems. Last, contract manufacturing services include professional audio equipment, hearables, medical/health products and industrial products. VTech's products are marketed under the VTech and Leap Frog brands. In April 2021, VTech Holdings acquired a production facility in Tecate, Mexico from QSC, LLC for manufacturing wood enclosure loudspeakers.

FINANCIAL DATA: *Note: Data for latest year may not have been available at press time.*

In U.S. $	2020	2019	2018	2017	2016	2015
Revenue	2,165,500,000	2,161,900,000	2,130,100,000	2,079,300,000	1,856,500,000	
R&D Expense	81,700,000	77,200,000	77,600,000	77,200,000	56,300,000	
Operating Income	219,700,000	193,200,000	231,300,000	200,000,000	202,300,000	
Operating Margin %	.10%	.09%	.11%	.10%	.11%	
SGA Expense	368,100,000	371,900,000	397,300,000	412,200,000	324,700,000	
Net Income	190,700,000	171,300,000	206,300,000	179,000,000	181,400,000	
Operating Cash Flow	237,000,000	249,300,000	175,700,000	185,300,000	216,700,000	
Capital Expenditure	34,600,000	37,300,000	37,600,000	35,700,000	41,600,000	
EBITDA	276,900,000	231,200,000	267,400,000	234,800,000	237,400,000	
Return on Assets %	.17%	.16%	.19%	.18%	.20%	
Return on Equity %	.32%	.27%	.34%	.32%	.34%	
Debt to Equity	0.245			0.002		

CONTACT INFORMATION:
Phone: 852 26801000   Fax: 852 26801300
Toll-Free:
Address: 57 Ting Kok Rd., Tai Ping Ctr., Block 1, 23/Fl, Hong Kong, Hong Kong Hong Kong

STOCK TICKER/OTHER:
Stock Ticker: VTKLF
Employees: 26,000
Parent Company:

Exchange: PINX
Fiscal Year Ends: 03/31

SALARIES/BONUSES:
Top Exec. Salary: $ Bonus: $
Second Exec. Salary: $ Bonus: $

OTHER THOUGHTS:
Estimated Female Officers or Directors:
Hot Spot for Advancement for Women/Minorities:

Westell Technologies Inc

NAIC Code: 334210

www.westell.com

TYPES OF BUSINESS:

Telecommunications Equipment-High-Speed Data Transmission
Distributed Antenna Systems
Digital Repeaters
Passive System Components
Remote Units
Integrated Cabinets
Power Distribution
Fiber Network Connectivity

BRANDS/DIVISIONS/AFFILIATES:

CONTACTS: *Note: Officers with more than one job title may be intentionally listed here more than once.*

Thomas Minichiello, CFO
Kirk Brannock, Chairman of the Board
Alfred John, President
Jesse Swartwood, Senior VP, Divisional

GROWTH PLANS/SPECIAL FEATURES:

Westell Technologies, Inc. is a provider of in-building wireless, intelligent site management, cell site optimization and outside plant solutions, with a focus on innovation and differentiation of telecommunication networks, where end-users connect. The firm operates in three segments: in-building wireless (IBW), intelligent site management (ISM) and communications network solutions (CNS). The IBW segment offers solutions that enable cellular and public safety coverage in stadiums, arenas, malls, buildings and other indoor areas not served well or at all by existing outdoor cellular networks. For cellular service, solutions include distributed antenna system (DAS) conditioners and digital repeaters. For the public safety market, solutions include Class A repeaters, Class B repeaters and batter backup units. IBW also offers ancillary products that consist of passive system components and antennas for both the cellular service and public safety markets. The ISM segment offers a suite of remote units, which provide machine-to-machine (M2M) communications that enable operators to remotely monitor, manage and control physical site infrastructure and support systems. Remote units can be and often are combined with Westell's Optima management software system. ISM also offers support services such as maintenance agreements, and deployment services such as installation. The CNS segment offers a wide range of hardened network infrastructure offerings suitable for indoor and outdoor use. They include integrated cabinets, power distribution products, copper and fiber network connectivity products and Tier-1 network interface units. Westell's customers primarily consist of communication service providers, systems integrators, neutral host operators and distributors.

Westell offers its employees comprehensive medical benefits, a 401(k) plan and paid time off.

FINANCIAL DATA: *Note: Data for latest year may not have been available at press time.*

In U.S. $	2020	2019	2018	2017	2016	2015
Revenue		43,570,000	58,577,000	62,965,000	88,203,000	84,127,000
R&D Expense						
Operating Income						
Operating Margin %						
SGA Expense						
Net Income		-11,382,000	31,000	-15,941,000	-16,212,000	-58,007,000
Operating Cash Flow						
Capital Expenditure						
EBITDA						
Return on Assets %						
Return on Equity %						
Debt to Equity						

CONTACT INFORMATION:

Phone: 630 898-2500   Fax: 630 375-4931
Toll-Free:
Address: 750 N. Commons Dr., Aurora, IL 60504 United States

STOCK TICKER/OTHER:

Stock Ticker: WSTL   Exchange: NAS
Employees: 102   Fiscal Year Ends: 03/31
Parent Company:

SALARIES/BONUSES:

Top Exec. Salary: $ Bonus: $
Second Exec. Salary: $ Bonus: $

OTHER THOUGHTS:

Estimated Female Officers or Directors: 2
Hot Spot for Advancement for Women/Minorities:

WIND Hellas Telecommunications SA

www.wind.com.gr

NAIC Code: 517210

TYPES OF BUSINESS:

Mobile Telephone Service
Business Services
Internet Services

BRANDS/DIVISIONS/AFFILIATES:

Crystal Almond Holdings Limited
Crystal Almond SARL

CONTACTS: Note: Officers with more than one job title may be intentionally listed here more than once.

Nasos Zarkalis, CEO
Harris Kyriakopoulos, CFO
Michalis Anagnostakos, Gen. Mngr.- Mktg.
Nikos Babalis, Gen. Mngr.-Informatics & Transformation
Antonis Tzortzakakis, Chief Commercial Officer
Yiannis Gavrielides, Exec. Dir.-Online Mktg. Comm. & Consumer Prepaid
George Tsaprounis, Exec. Dir.-Corp. Affairs
Nikos Babalis, Chief Network Officer
Nikos Panopoulos, Exec. Dir.-Supply Chain & Facilities Mgmt.

GROWTH PLANS/SPECIAL FEATURES:

WIND Hellas Telecommunications SA is one of the largest telecommunications operators in Greece. WIND's principal business is the provision of mobile telecommunications services, including voice, broadband, internet and related value-added services, to pre-paid and contract customers. The company also offers businesses with network services with a variety of options, such as a voice mailbox, online payment solutions, teleconference services, caller ID, call waiting, call barring, call forwarding and mobile email. WIND offers 2G, 3G, 4G and 5G network coverage, including 4G LTE services in select Grecian cities. Internet and fixed programs are available. WIND also sells devices such as cell phones, tablets, mobile broadband, wearables, smart home and related accessories, as well as fixed devices, routers, modems, power connectors and extenders. WIND operates as a subsidiary of Crystal Almond SARL, itself a subsidiary of Crystal Almond Holdings Limited. WIND announced in December 2020 that its 5G Network would begin operating in Athens and Thessaloniki. As part of a 5G pilot program, the firm has installed and operates a 5G pilot network in Kalamata, to evaluate operational elements of the technology.

FINANCIAL DATA: Note: Data for latest year may not have been available at press time.

In U.S. $	2020	2019	2018	2017	2016	2015
Revenue	642,369,420	611,780,400	582,648,000	591,745,000	501,495,000	900,000,000
R&D Expense						
Operating Income						
Operating Margin %						
SGA Expense						
Net Income						
Operating Cash Flow						
Capital Expenditure						
EBITDA						
Return on Assets %						
Return on Equity %						
Debt to Equity						

CONTACT INFORMATION:

Phone: 30-210-615-8000   Fax: 30-210-510-0001
Toll-Free:
Address: 66 Kifissias Ave., Athens, 15125 Greece

STOCK TICKER/OTHER:

Stock Ticker: Private   Exchange:
Employees: 1,520   Fiscal Year Ends: 12/31
Parent Company: Crystal Almond Holdings Limited

SALARIES/BONUSES:

Top Exec. Salary: $ Bonus: $
Second Exec. Salary: $ Bonus: $

OTHER THOUGHTS:

Estimated Female Officers or Directors: 1
Hot Spot for Advancement for Women/Minorities:

Windstream Holdings Inc   investor.windstream.com/home/default.aspx

NAIC Code: 517110

TYPES OF BUSINESS:

Telephone Service--Local Exchange Carrier & Diversified
Network Communications
Technology Solutions
Broadband
Internet
Cloud
Digital Transformation
Fiber Optic

BRANDS/DIVISIONS/AFFILIATES:

CONTACTS: *Note: Officers with more than one job title may be intentionally listed here more than once.*

Anthony Thomas, CEO
Robert Gunderman, CFO
Michael Flannery, CMO
Alan Wells, Director
Kristi Moody, General Counsel
Jeffery Small, President, Divisional
Layne Levine, President, Divisional

GROWTH PLANS/SPECIAL FEATURES:

Windstream Holdings, Inc. is a provider of advanced network communications and technology solutions for residences and businesses throughout the U.S. The firm also offers broadband, entertainment and security solutions to consumers and small businesses primarily in rural areas within 18 states. For residential consumers, Windstream's products and services keep the home environment connected via high-speed internet, digital TV and phone. For small and mid-sized businesses, products and solutions include internet, voice, unified communications, cloud and security. For enterprises, the firm offers multi-location networking, an office suite platform, SD-WAN, cloud, security and unified communications solutions and services. Windstream also offers digital transformation services for wholesale customers, including content and media providers, cloud and data center operators, international carriers, resale partners, cable operators, wireless and traditional network service providers and more. Wholesale solutions include scalable fiber optic connectivity, 5G fixed wireless service, wavelengths and Ethernet. Industries served by Windstream span healthcare, retail, K-12 education, higher education, hospitality, banking, government, content and media. Windstream owns and operates a nationwide network with over 170,000 fiber route miles, as well as a proprietary cloud core architecture. During 2020, Windstream announced that the U.S. Bankruptcy Court confirmed its plan of reorganization. Windstream completed the process and emerged from Chapter 11 bankruptcy protection as a private company.

FINANCIAL DATA: *Note: Data for latest year may not have been available at press time.*

In U.S. $	2020	2019	2018	2017	2016	2015
Revenue	4,987,515,000	5,115,400,000	5,713,099,776	5,852,899,840	5,386,999,808	5,765,300,224
R&D Expense						
Operating Income						
Operating Margin %						
SGA Expense						
Net Income		-3,517,000,000	-723,000,000	-2,116,600,064	-383,500,000	27,400,000
Operating Cash Flow						
Capital Expenditure						
EBITDA						
Return on Assets %						
Return on Equity %						
Debt to Equity						

CONTACT INFORMATION:

Phone: 501 748-7000   Fax:
Toll-Free: 866-445-5880
Address: 4001 N. Rodney Parkham Rd., Little Rock, AR 72212 United States

STOCK TICKER/OTHER:

Stock Ticker: Private   Exchange:
Employees: 11,080   Fiscal Year Ends: 12/31
Parent Company:

SALARIES/BONUSES:

Top Exec. Salary: $ Bonus: $
Second Exec. Salary: $ Bonus: $

OTHER THOUGHTS:

Estimated Female Officers or Directors: 3
Hot Spot for Advancement for Women/Minorities: Y

XIUS

NAIC Code: 511210C

TYPES OF BUSINESS:

Computer Software, Telecom, Communications & VOIP
Payment Processing Solutions

BRANDS/DIVISIONS/AFFILIATES:

Megasoft Limited
XIUS AMPLIO
XIUS Infinet
XIUS Inergy
XIUS PowerRoam
XIUS Payment Manager
XIUS Wireless Wallet
X-Connect

CONTACTS: Note: Officers with more than one job title may be intentionally listed here more than once.

G.V. Kumar, CEO
Shridhar Thathachary, CFO
Sridhar Lanka, VP-Eng.
Kevin Bresnahan, Exec. VP-Oper.
Derek Bowman, Dir.-Bus. Dev.
Umakanta Mansingh, Head-Quality
Sundaresan Nandyal, Head-Global Sales

GROWTH PLANS/SPECIAL FEATURES:

XIUS, a subsidiary of Indian company Megasoft Limited, is a mobile technology specialist focused on real-time transaction processing in mobile infrastructure, mobile payments and over-the-top (OTT) solutions. The company's mobile infrastructure solutions division provides mobile virtual network operator (VNO) services, a mobile services platform, 4G LTE services, Internet of Things (IoT) connectivity and control, solutions its XIUS AMPLIO mobile infrastructure solutions platform, real-time billing through its XIUS INfinet product, real-time mobile services through its XIUS INergy application, and steering of roaming services through its XIUS PowerRoam solution. The mobile commerce division provides domestic and international recharge services through XIUS Payment Manager, mobile payment technology via its XIUS Wireless Wallet application, mobile banking as well as mobile kiosks that offer mobile operator services via its Active Poster product; an end-to-end platform for payment banks to set up technology infrastructure and launch services, and a secure authentication online/mobile platform called eCognito. The mobile-enabled solutions division consists of business intelligence and geo-referencing, which allows the mining of data and creation of custom views, reports and dashboards, along with the capability of viewing key information data on a map; and retail consumer engagement, providing consumer mobile interaction and engagement data to brands and retailers. IoT solutions include X-Connect, X-Fleet, X-Care device management, X-Asset Tracking/Management, and X-Manufacturing. XIUS is headquartered in Massachusetts, with a global delivery center in Hyderabad, India, and operations in the U.S., Mexico, Malaysia and India.

FINANCIAL DATA: Note: Data for latest year may not have been available at press time.

In U.S. $	2020	2019	2018	2017	2016	2015
Revenue	507,385,000	480,600,000	480,612,000	385,400,000	354,955,000	
R&D Expense						
Operating Income						
Operating Margin %						
SGA Expense						
Net Income	-3,782,000	33,419,000	86,900,000	26,000,000	21,856,000	
Operating Cash Flow						
Capital Expenditure						
EBITDA						
Return on Assets %						
Return on Equity %						
Debt to Equity						

CONTACT INFORMATION:

Phone: 781-904-5000   Fax: 781-904-5601
Toll-Free:
Address: 15 Tyngsboro Rd., Unit 8C, North Chelmsford, MA 01863
United States

STOCK TICKER/OTHER:

Stock Ticker: Subsidiary   Exchange:
Employees: Fiscal Year Ends: 03/31
Parent Company: Megasoft Limited

SALARIES/BONUSES:

Top Exec. Salary: $ Bonus: $
Second Exec. Salary: $ Bonus: $

OTHER THOUGHTS:

Estimated Female Officers or Directors:
Hot Spot for Advancement for Women/Minorities:

Zoom Video Communications Inc

zoom.us

NAIC Code: 511210C

TYPES OF BUSINESS:

Computer Software, Telecom, Communications & VOIP

BRANDS/DIVISIONS/AFFILIATES:

Zoom
Zoom Room

CONTACTS: *Note: Officers with more than one job title may be intentionally listed here more than once.*

Eric Yuan, CEO
Kelly Steckelberg, CFO
Janine Pelosi, Chief Marketing Officer
Aparna Bawa, General Counsel

GROWTH PLANS/SPECIAL FEATURES:

Zoom Video Communications, Inc. designs and develops cloud-based video and web conferencing software. Zoom's software unifies cloud video conferencing, online meetings, group messaging and conference room solutions into one simple-to-use platform. The company's solutions work across multiple room systems. Zoom's software conferencing application program interface (API) runs within a business' conference room or workspace. Cloud video conferencing features include HD video and voice, full-screen with gallery views, dual stream/dual screen, feature-rich mobile apps, and various ways to join the conferences (Zoom Room, view-only, voice only and more). Zoom products are secure, with secure socket layer encryption, AES 256-bits encryption, HTTPS access, role-based access control features and administration control features. The firm also offers a hybrid cloud service with 24/7 online monitoring and instant global service backup. Partner integrations provide content sharing, scheduling/starting meetings, unified log-in, marketing/process automation and room collaboration. Pricing plans range from free to $100 per month, among other options. Zoom is headquartered in San Jose, California, with additional U.S. offices in California, Colorado and Kansas, as well as international offices in Sydney, London, Paris and Amsterdam. The Coronavirus pandemic spurred phenomenal growth in Zoom meetings. The firm reported usage of up to 300 million meeting participants per day in the first quarter of 2020, compared to 10 million per day in December 2019. For all of 2020, the firm reported over 3.3 trillion annual meeting minutes.

FINANCIAL DATA: *Note: Data for latest year may not have been available at press time.*

In U.S. $	2020	2019	2018	2017	2016	2015
Revenue	622,658,000	330,517,000	151,478,000	60,817,000		
R&D Expense	67,079,000	33,014,000	15,733,000	9,218,000		
Operating Income	12,696,000	6,167,000	-4,833,000			
Operating Margin %	.02%	.02%	- .03%			
SGA Expense	427,487,000	230,335,000	109,798,000	39,127,000		
Net Income	25,305,000	7,584,000	-3,822,000	-14,000		
Operating Cash Flow	151,892,000	51,332,000	19,426,000	9,361,000		
Capital Expenditure	38,225,000	30,450,000	9,738,000	4,824,000		
EBITDA	29,145,000	13,175,000	-2,047,000	1,219,000		
Return on Assets %	.03%	.03%	- .04%			
Return on Equity %	.04%	.11%				
Debt to Equity	0.078					

CONTACT INFORMATION:

Phone: 650-397-6096   Fax:
Toll-Free: 888-799-9666
Address: 55 Almaden Blvd., Fl. 6, San Jose, CA 95113 United States

STOCK TICKER/OTHER:

Stock Ticker: ZM   Exchange: NAS
Employees: 4,422   Fiscal Year Ends: 01/31
Parent Company:

SALARIES/BONUSES:

Top Exec. Salary: $ Bonus: $
Second Exec. Salary: $ Bonus: $

OTHER THOUGHTS:

Estimated Female Officers or Directors:
Hot Spot for Advancement for Women/Minorities:

ZTE Corporation

www.zte.com.cn

NAIC Code: 334210

TYPES OF BUSINESS:

Telecommunications Equipment Manufacturing
Optical Networking Equipment
Intelligent & Next-Generation Network Systems
Mobile Phones

BRANDS/DIVISIONS/AFFILIATES:

CONTACTS: Note: Officers with more than one job title may be intentionally listed here more than once.

Ziyang Xu, CEO
Junshi Xie, COO
Ying LI, CFO
Zixue Li, Chmn.

GROWTH PLANS/SPECIAL FEATURES:

ZTE Corporation is one of China's largest telecommunications equipment providers, specializing in customized network solutions for telecom carriers in more than 160 countries. The company develops and manufactures telecommunications equipment for voice, data, multimedia and wireless broadband applications. ZTE's business is organized into seven primary product divisions: device, including smartphones, gateways and mobile hotspot solutions; wireless, including base stations, controllers and network management solutions; bearer, including data communication and optical transmission solutions; cloud computing, cloud platform, cloud storage and distributed databases; cloud infrastructure, including cloud hardware and telecom cloud platform; cloud core network, including 5G common core, packet core, IMS& CS, UDC and orchestration and management; video, including video conferencing system, public safety, cloud desktop, advanced metering infrastructure and cloud contact center; fixed access, including optical and copper access equipment and solutions, and customer-premises equipment (CPE) such as telephones, routers, switches, gateways and more; and energy products, including telecom energy, government & enterprise energy and ZEGO IDC. ZTE's products and solutions include consulting services, customer support, integration services, tools, learning services, managed services and UniCare service transformation services. The firm has global sales outlets throughout North America, Latin America, Africa, Europe, the Commonwealth of Independent States, China and Asia-Pacific.

FINANCIAL DATA: Note: Data for latest year may not have been available at press time.

In U.S. $	2020	2019	2018	2017	2016	2015
Revenue	15,899,620,000	14,220,480,000	13,401,840,000	17,053,810,000	15,865,530,000	15,701,470,000
R&D Expense	2,319,028,000	1,966,540,000	1,709,152,000	2,031,477,000	2,000,103,000	1,912,101,000
Operating Income	875,867,200	1,458,167,000	932,144,000	1,216,585,000	400,613,000	537,057,000
Operating Margin %		.10%	.07%	.07%	.03%	.03%
SGA Expense	1,555,999,000	1,592,488,000	1,636,818,000	2,036,280,000	2,051,078,000	1,932,044,000
Net Income	667,599,500	806,788,700	-1,094,498,000	715,935,900	-369,460,700	502,748,200
Operating Cash Flow	1,603,688,000	1,167,043,000	-1,444,259,000	1,131,533,000	824,393,300	1,160,478,000
Capital Expenditure	1,014,254,000	1,026,630,000	765,099,800	937,829,000	627,276,000	386,965,400
EBITDA	1,650,465,000	1,953,812,000	-556,227,700	1,642,410,000	441,761,900	1,198,083,000
Return on Assets %		.04%	-.05%	.03%	-.02%	.03%
Return on Equity %		.20%	-.26%	.16%	-.08%	.12%
Debt to Equity		0.371	0.103	0.095	0.19	0.203

CONTACT INFORMATION:

Phone: 86 75526770000   Fax: 86 75526770286
Toll-Free:
Address: Hi-tech Rd. S., No. 55, Shenzhen, Guangdong 518057 China

STOCK TICKER/OTHER:

Stock Ticker: ZTCOF
Employees: 73,709
Parent Company:

Exchange: PINX
Fiscal Year Ends: 12/31

SALARIES/BONUSES:

Top Exec. Salary: $ Bonus: $
Second Exec. Salary: $ Bonus: $

OTHER THOUGHTS:

Estimated Female Officers or Directors:
Hot Spot for Advancement for Women/Minorities:

ADDITIONAL INDEXES

Contents:

INDEX OF FIRMS NOTED AS HOT SPOTS FOR ADVANCEMENT FOR WOMEN & MINORITIES

Advanced Info Service plc
Advanced Micro Devices Inc (AMD)
Akamai Technologies Inc
Alaska Communications Systems Group Inc
Altice USA Inc
Anixter International Inc
Asia Satellite Telecommunications Holdings Ltd
AT&T Inc
Axiata Group Berhad
Bangkok Cable Co Ltd
BCE Inc (Bell Canada Enterprises)
Belden Inc
Bell Aliant Inc
Bell MTS Inc
Bezeq-The Israel Telecommunication Corp Ltd
Bharti Airtel Limited
BlackBerry Limited
Bouygues SA
Broadcom Inc
BT Global Services plc
BT Group plc
Celestica Inc
Cellcom Israel Ltd
Ceske Radiokomunikace as
China Mobile Limited
China Telecom Corporation Limited
Chunghwa Telecom Co Ltd
Cincinnati Bell Inc
Cisco Systems Inc
Colt Technology Services Group Limited
Comcast Corporation
Corning Incorporated
COSMOTE Mobile Telephones SA
Cox Communications Inc
Cricket Wireless LLC
Deutsche Telekom AG
Digi.com Bhd
DirecTV LLC (DIRECTV)
EarthLink LLC
Elisa Corporation
Empresa Nacional de Telecommunications SA (Entel)
Equinix Inc
Extreme Networks Inc
F5 Networks Inc
Flex Ltd
Frontier Communications Corporation
Garmin Ltd
Gilat Satellite Networks Ltd
GoDaddy Inc
Hellenic Telecommunications Organization SA
HP Inc
Huawei Technologies Co Ltd

Hutchison Telecommunications Hong Kong Holdings Limited
Iliad SA
Ingram Micro Mobility
Inmarsat Global Limited
Intel Corporation
Internap Corporation
International Business Machines Corporation (IBM)
Jabil Inc
Juniper Networks Inc
Koninklijke Philips NV (Royal Philips)
Kratos Defense & Security Solutions Inc
L3Harris Technologies Inc
Liberty Global plc
LM Ericsson Telephone Company (Ericsson)
Lumen Technologies Inc
M1 Limited
Maxis Berhad
McAfee Corp
Microsoft Corporation
Millicom International Cellular SA
MiTAC Holdings Corp
Momentum Telecom
NETGEAR Inc
Neustar Inc
Newfold Digital Inc
Nokia Corporation
Orange
Partner Communications Co Ltd
PCCW Limited
Plantronics Inc
PLDT Inc
Proximus Group
Purple Communications Inc
Qualcomm Incorporated
Rogers Communications Inc
Rostelecom PJSC
Shaw Communications Inc
Shenandoah Telecommunications Company
Siemens AG
Singapore Telecommunications Limited
Skype Technologies Sarl
SMTC Corporation
Spok Inc
Swisscom AG
Sykes Enterprises Incorporated
Syniverse Technologies LLC
TDC A/S
Tele2 AB
Telekom Austria AG
Telenor ASA
Telephone and Data Systems Inc (TDS)
Telia Company AB
Telia Lietuva AB
Telkom SA SOC Limited
Tellabs Inc
Telstra Corporation Limited
TomTom International BV

TOT pcl
Total Access Communication PCL
Trimble Inc
TTEC Holdings Inc
Turkcell Iletisim Hizmetleri AS
United States Cellular Corporation
Verizon Communications Inc
Virgin Media Business Ltd
Vodafone Group plc
Windstream Holdings Inc

INDEX OF SUBSIDIARIES, BRAND NAMES AND AFFILIATIONS

Brand or subsidiary, followed by the name of the related corporation

10-10-719; **Startec Global Communications Corporation**
2degrees; **Trilogy International Partners Inc**
3; **Hutchison Telecommunications Hong Kong Holdings Limited**
800 Series; **Socket Mobile Inc**
A1; **Telekom Austria AG**
A1; **America Movil SAB de CV**
A1 Bulgaria; **Telekom Austria AG**
A1 Telekom Austria AG; **Telekom Austria AG**
a4; **Altice USA Inc**
AAPT; **TPG Telecom Limited**
ACS Long Distance LLC; **Alaska Communications Systems Group Inc**
ACS of Alaska LLC; **Alaska Communications Systems Group Inc**
ACS of Anchorage LLC; **Alaska Communications Systems Group Inc**
ACS of Fairbanks LLC; **Alaska Communications Systems Group Inc**
ACS of the Northland LLC; **Alaska Communications Systems Group Inc**
ACS Wireless Inc; **Alaska Communications Systems Group Inc**
ACX; **Juniper Networks Inc**
Adaptive Network; **Ciena Corporation**
Adaptive Service Intelligence; **NetScout Systems Inc**
Adesol SA; **Telecom Argentina SA**
Advent International; **Laird Connectivity**
AGC Networks Ltd; **Black Box Corporation**
AISWare; **AsiaInfo Technologies Limited**
Al Yah Satellite Communications Company (Yahsat); **Thuraya Telecommunications Company**
Alaska Communications Internet LLC; **Alaska Communications Systems Group Inc**
AldiTalk; **Telefonica Deutschland Holding AG**
Alfa Telecom Turkey Limited; **Turkcell Iletisim Hizmetleri AS**
All3Media; **Liberty Global plc**
Altice; **Altice Europe NV**
Altice; **Altice Portugal SA**
Altice Empresas; **Altice Portugal SA**
Altice Group; **Altice Portugal SA**
Altice Mobile; **Altice USA Inc**
Altice NV; **Altice Portugal SA**
AMD; **Advanced Micro Devices Inc (AMD)**
America Movil SAB de CV; **Embratel Participacoes SA**
America Movil SAB de CV; **Telecomunicaciones de Puerto Rico Inc**
America Movil SAB de CV; **Telefonos de Mexico SAB de CV (Telmex)**

America Movil SAB de CV; **Telekom Austria AG**
AMETEK Inc; **Telular Corporation**
Amobee; **Singapore Telecommunications Limited**
Antenna Products Corporation; **Phazar Antenna Corp**
Apollo Global Management Inc; **Intrado Corporation**
Apollo Global Management LLC; **Rackspace Technology Inc**
Apollo OPT; **ECI Telecom Ltd**
AppDynamics Inc; **Cisco Systems Inc**
Applanix; **Trimble Inc**
Applied Optical Systems Inc; **Optical Cable Corporation**
AQCOLOR; **BenQ Corporation**
Arcoa; **Far EasTone Telecommunications Co Ltd**
ARISE analytics Inc; **KDDI Corporation**
Arm Limited; **SoftBank Group Corp**
AS Watson Group (HK) Limited; **CK Hutchison Holdings Limited**
Asavie; **Akamai Technologies Inc**
Asia Satellite Telecommunications Company Limited; **Asia Satellite Telecommunications Holdings Ltd**
AsiaSat 5; **Asia Satellite Telecommunications Holdings Ltd**
AsiaSat 6; **Asia Satellite Telecommunications Holdings Ltd**
AsiaSat 7; **Asia Satellite Telecommunications Holdings Ltd**
AsiaSat 8; **Asia Satellite Telecommunications Holdings Ltd**
AsiaSat 9; **Asia Satellite Telecommunications Holdings Ltd**
Aspect Via; **Aspect Software Inc**
Aspirasi; **Axiata Group Berhad**
AT&T; **AT&T Inc**
AT&T Inc; **AT&T Mexico SAU**
AT&T Inc; **AT&T Mobility LLC**
AT&T Inc; **Cricket Wireless LLC**
AT&T Inc; **DirecTV LLC (DIRECTV)**
AT&T PREPAID; **AT&T Inc**
AT&T Wireless; **AT&T Mobility LLC**
Athlon; **Advanced Micro Devices Inc (AMD)**
ATI; **Advanced Micro Devices Inc (AMD)**
ATLAS P25; **EF Johnson Technologies Inc**
au Data MAX Plan; **KDDI Corporation**
au Data MAX Plan Netflix Pack; **KDDI Corporation**
au Flat Plan 7 Plus; **KDDI Corporation**
Australia Singapore Cable; **Vocus Group Limited**
Avaya Inc; **Avaya Holdings Corp**
AVC Continente Audiovisual SA; **Telecom Argentina SA**
AWG-WIFI; **Boingo Wireless Inc**
Axiata Digital Labs; **Axiata Group Berhad**
AXIO-NET GmbH; **Trimble Inc**
Axway AMPLIFY; **Axway Inc**
AY YILDIZ; **Telefonica Deutschland Holding AG**
Azteca America; **HC2 Holdings Inc**
B Communications; **Bezeq-The Israel Telecommunication Corp Ltd**
B Riley Financial Inc; **United Online Inc**
Bangkok Cable Ventures Co Ltd; **Bangkok Cable Co Ltd**

INDEX OF SUBSIDIARIES, BRAND NAMES AND AFFILIATIONS, CONT.

INDEX OF SUBSIDIARIES, BRAND NAMES AND AFFILIATIONS, CONT.

INDEX OF SUBSIDIARIES, BRAND NAMES AND AFFILIATIONS, CONT.

INDEX OF SUBSIDIARIES, BRAND NAMES AND AFFILIATIONS, CONT.

INDEX OF SUBSIDIARIES, BRAND NAMES AND AFFILIATIONS, CONT.

INDEX OF SUBSIDIARIES, BRAND NAMES AND AFFILIATIONS, CONT.

INDEX OF SUBSIDIARIES, BRAND NAMES AND AFFILIATIONS, CONT.

INDEX OF SUBSIDIARIES, BRAND NAMES AND AFFILIATIONS, CONT.

INDEX OF SUBSIDIARIES, BRAND NAMES AND AFFILIATIONS, CONT.

INDEX OF SUBSIDIARIES, BRAND NAMES AND AFFILIATIONS, CONT.

A Short Telecommunications Industry Glossary

3G Cellular: Short for third-generation, this term refers to high speed enhancements to mobile telephone service. 3G enables wireless e-mail, Internet browsing and data transfer. 3G will be largely replaced by advanced 4G and 5G technologies.

3GPP: Third Generation Partnership Project. It is an organization set up to create and monitor advanced 3G wireless standards.

4G Cellular: An advancement in speed and capabilities over 3G wireless networks. 4G not only features high data transfer speeds, it also has an enhanced ability to support interactive multimedia, internet access, mobile video and other vital tasks. It will eventually be surpassed by 5G and higher networks, with 5G beginning to rollout on a major basis in the 2020s.

5G Cellular: A wireless technology that is expected to produce blinding download speeds of one gigabyte per second (Gbps), and perhaps as high as 10 Gbps. The first specifications for 5G were agreed to by the global wireless industry from 2017 to 2019. Significant rollout was expected to begin in the early 2020s. While certain 5G features can be used to boost speeds of earlier 4G networks, a true rollout requires major investment in new cellular infrastructure and systems.

802.11: See "Wi-Fi."

802.11n (MIMO): Multiple Input Multiple Output. MIMO is a standard in the series of 802.11 Wi-Fi specifications for wireless networks. It can provide very high speed network access. 802.11n also boasts better operating distances than many networks. MIMO uses spectrum more efficiently without any loss of reliability. The technology is based on several different antennas all tuned to the same channel, each transmitting a different signal. Advancements include MU-MIMO (Multi-User MIMO) and OFDMA (Orthogonal Frequency-Division Multiple Access), each of which improves network throughput.

802.15: See "Ultrawideband (UWB)." For 802.15.1, see "Bluetooth."

802.15.1: See "Bluetooth."

802.16: See "WiMAX."

Access Network: The network that connects a user's telephone equipment to the telephone exchange.

Active Server Page (ASP): A web page that includes one or more embedded programs, usually written in Java or Visual Basic code. See "Java."

Active X: A set of technologies developed by Microsoft Corporation for sharing information across different applications.

ADN: See "Advanced Digital Network (ADN)."

ADSL: See "Asymmetrical Digital Subscriber Line (ADSL)."

Advanced Digital Network (ADN): See "Integrated Digital Network (IDN)."

Analog: A form of transmitting information characterized by continuously variable quantities. Digital transmission, in contrast, is characterized by discrete bits of information in numerical steps. An analog signal responds to changes in light, sound, heat and pressure.

Analog IC (Integrated Circuit): A semiconductor that processes a continuous wave of electrical signals based on real-world analog quantities such as speed, pressure, temperature, light, sound and voltage.

Analytics: Generally refers to the deep examination of massive amounts of data, often on a continual or real-time basis. The goal is to discover deeper insights, make recommendations or generate predictions. Advanced analytics includes such techniques as big data, predictive analytics, text analytics, data mining, forecasting, optimization and simulation.

ANSI: American National Standards Institute. Founded in 1918, ANSI is a private, non-profit organization that administers and coordinates the U.S. voluntary standardization and conformity assessment system. Its mission is to enhance both the global competitiveness of U.S. business and the quality of U.S. life by promoting and facilitating voluntary consensus standards and conformity assessment systems, and safeguarding their integrity. See www.ansi.org.

APAC: Asia Pacific Advisory Committee. A multi-country committee representing the Asia and Pacific region.

Applets: Small, object-based applications written in Java that net browsers can download from the Internet on an as-needed basis. These may be software, accessories (such as spell checkers or calculators), information-packed databases or other items. See "Object Technology."

Application Service Provider (ASP): A web site that enables utilization of software and databases that reside permanently on a service company's remote web server, rather than having to be downloaded to the user's computer. Advantages include the ability for multiple remote users to access the same tools over the Internet and the fact that the ASP provider is responsible for developing and maintaining the software. (ASP is also an acronym for "active server page," which is not related.) For the latest developments in ASP, see "Software as a Service (SaaS)."

Applied Research: The application of compounds, processes, materials or other items discovered during basic research to practical uses. The goal is to move discoveries along to the final development phase.

ARPANet: Advanced Research Projects Agency Network. The forefather of the Internet, ARPANet was developed during the latter part of the 1960s by the United States Department of Defense.

ARPU: See "Average Revenue Per User (ARPU)."

Artificial Intelligence (AI): The use of computer technology to perform functions somewhat like those normally associated with human intelligence, such as reasoning, learning and self-improvement.

ASCII: American Standard Code for Information Exchange. There are 128 standard ASCII codes that represent all Latin letters, numbers and punctuation. Each ASCII code is represented by a seven-digit binary number, such as 0000000 or 0000111. This code is accepted as a standard throughout the world.

ASEAN: Association of Southeast Asian Nations. A regional economic development association

established in 1967 by five original member countries: Indonesia, Malaysia, Philippines, Singapore, and Thailand. Brunei joined on 8 January 1984, Vietnam on 28 July 1995, Laos and Myanmar on 23 July 1997, and Cambodia on 30 April 1999.

ASP: See "Application Service Provider (ASP)."

Asymmetrical Digital Subscriber Line (ADSL): High-speed technology that enables the transfer of data over existing copper phone lines, allowing more bandwidth downstream than upstream.

Asynchronous Communications: A stream of data routed through a network as generated instead of in organized message blocks. Most personal computers use this format to send data.

Asynchronous Transfer Mode (ATM): A digital switching and transmission technology based on high speed. ATM allows voice, video and data signals to be sent over a single telephone line at speeds from 25 million to 1 billion bits per second (bps). This digital ATM speed is much faster than traditional analog phone lines, which allow no more than 2 million bps. See "Broadband."

ATCA: Advanced Telecommunications Computing Architecture. It is a set of standards widely used in telecommunications equipment due to the rapid growth of VOIP. ATCA technology increases performance and reliability by optimizing the architecture specifically for communications servers by eliminating proprietary communications port specifications.

Average Revenue Per User (ARPU): A measure of the average monthly billing revenue of a wireless company on a per user basis.

Backbone: Traditionally the part of a communications network that carries the heaviest traffic: the high-speed line or series of connections that forms a large pathway within a network or within a region. The combined networks of AT&T, MCI and other large telecommunications companies make up the backbone of the Internet.

Bandwidth: The data transmission capacity of a network, measured in the amount of data (in bits and bauds) it can transport in one second. A full page of text is about 15,000 to 20,000 bits. Full-motion, full-screen video requires about 10 million bits per second, depending on compression.

Basic Cable: Primary level or levels of cable service offered for subscription. Basic cable offerings may include retransmitted broadcast signals as well as local and access programming. In addition, regional and national cable network programming may be provided.

Basic Research: Attempts to discover compounds, materials, processes or other items that may be largely or entirely new and/or unique. Basic research may start with a theoretical concept that has yet to be proven. The goal is to create discoveries that can be moved along to applied research. Basic research is sometimes referred to as "blue sky" research.

Baud: Refers to how many times the carrier signal in a modem switches value per second or how many bits a modem can send and receive in a second.

Beam: The coverage and geographic service area offered by a satellite transponder. A global beam effectively covers one-third of the earth's surface. A spot beam provides a very specific high-powered downlink pattern that is limited to a particular geographical area to which it may be steered or pointed.

Binhex: A means of changing non-ASCII (or non-text) files into text/ASCII files so that they can be used, for example, as e-mail.

Bit: A single digit number, either a one or a zero, which is the smallest unit of computerized data.

Bits Per Second (Bps): An indicator of the speed of data movement.

Blog (Web Log): A web site consisting of a personal journal, news coverage, special-interest content or other data that is posted on the Internet, frequently updated and intended for public viewing by anyone who might be interested in the author's thoughts. Short for "web log," blog content is frequently distributed via RSS (Real Simple Syndication). Blog content has evolved to include video files (VLOGs) and audio files (Podcasting) as well as text. Also, see "Real Simple Syndication (RSS)," "Video Blog (VLOG)," "Moblog": "Podcasting," and "User Genercated Content (UGC)."

Bluetooth: An industry standard for a technology that enables wireless, short-distance infrared connections between devices such as cell phone headsets, Palm Pilots or PDAs, laptops, printers and Internet appliances.

BPL: See "Broadband Over Power Lines (BPL)."

BPO: See "Business Process Outsourcing (BPO)."

Bps: See "Bits Per Second (Bps)."

Brand: A marketing strategy that places a focus on the brand name of a product, service or firm in order to increase the brand's market share, increase sales, establish credibility, improve satisfaction, raise the profile of the firm and increase profits. Also, see "Brand."

Branding: A marketing strategy that places a focus on the brand name of a product, service or firm in order to increase the brand's market share, increase sales, establish credibility, improve satisfaction, raise the profile of the firm and increase profits. Also, see "Brand."

Broadband: The high-speed transmission range for telecommunications and computer data. Broadband generally refers to any transmission at 2 million bps (bits per second) or higher (much higher than analog speed). A broadband network can carry voice, video and data all at the same time. Internet users enjoying broadband access typically connect to the Internet via DSL line, cable modem or T1 line. Several wireless methods offer broadband as well.

Broadband Over Power Lines (BPL): Refers to the use of standard electric power lines to provide fast Internet service. Internet data is converted into radio frequency signals, which are not affected by electricity. Subscribers utilize special modems.

Browser: A program that allows a user to read Internet text or graphics and to navigate from one page to another. The most popular browsers are Microsoft Internet Explorer and Netscape Navigator. Firefox is an open source browser introduced in 2005 that is rapidly gaining popularity.

B-to-B, or B2B: See "Business-to-Business."

B-to-C, or B2C: See "Business-to-Consumer."

Business Process Outsourcing (BPO): The process of hiring another company to handle business activities. BPO is one of the fastest-growing segments in the offshoring sector. Services include human resources management, billing and purchasing and call centers, as well as many types of customer service or marketing activities, depending on the industry involved. Also, see "Knowledge Process Outsourcing (KPO)" and Business Transformation Outsourcing (BTO)."

Business Transformation Outsourcing (BTO): A segment within outsourcing in which the client company revamps its business processes with the goal of transforming its business by following a collaborative approach with its outsourced services provider.

Business-to-Business: An organization focused on selling products, services or data to commercial customers rather than individual consumers. Also known as B2B.

Business-to-Consumer: An organization focused on selling products, services or data to individual consumers rather than commercial customers. Also known as B2C.

BYOD: Bring Your Own Device. The trend of employees bringing their own, favorite laptops, tablets and cellphones into the office, as opposed to using equipment issued by the company. Similar phrases include BYOP (Bring Your Own Phone) and BYOT (Bring Your Own Technology).

Byte: A set of eight bits that represent a single character.

Cable Modem: An interface between a cable television system and a computer or router. Most cable modems are external devices that connect to the PC through a standard 10Base-T Ethernet card and twisted-pair wiring. External Universal Serial Bus (USB) modems and internal PCI modem cards are also available.

CAFTA-DR: See "Central American-Dominican Republic Free Trade Agreement (CAFTA-DR)."

Call Automation: Part of the telephone equipment revolution, including voice mail, automated sending and receiving of faxes and the ability for customers to place orders and gather information using a touch-tone telephone to access sophisticated databases. See "Voice Mail."

Call Center: A department within a company or a third-party organization that manages inbound and outbound telephone calls. This organization usually processes orders, provides technical support and/or provides marketing support. Call centers are frequently provided on an outsourced basis by service firms in lower-cost nations.

Capex: Capital expenditures.

Captive Offshoring: Used to describe a company-owned offshore operation. For example, Microsoft owns and operates significant captive offshore research and development centers in China and elsewhere that are offshore from Microsoft's U.S. home base. Also see "Offshoring."

CAR: See "Committed Access Rate (CAR)."

Carrier: In communications, the basic radio, television or telephony center of transmit signal. The carrier in an analog signal is modulated by varying volume or shifting frequency up or down in relation to the incoming signal. Satellite carriers operating in the analog mode are usually frequency-modulated.

CDMA: See "Code Division Multiple Access (CDMA)."

CDMA 1xRTT: See "Code Division Multiple Access (CDMA)."

CDMA2000: The commercial name for a high-speed version of 3G CDMA, based on and compatible with current 2G CDMA networks. See "EV-DO (CDMA 2000 1xEV-DO)."

CDMAOne: See "Code Division Multiple Access (CDMA)."

Cellular Mobile Telephone Service: Refers to the method in which advanced mobile telephone systems hand off calls to the nearest "cells" as the users travel. Cells represent the range of fixed antenna. In the best systems, cells overlap so that there is less possibility of service interruptions.

CEM: Contract electronic manufacturing. See "Contract Manufacturing."

Central American-Dominican Republic Free Trade Agreement (CAFTA-DR): A trade agreement signed into law in 2005 that aimed to open up the Central American and Dominican Republic markets to American goods. Member nations include Guatemala, Nicaragua, Costa Rica, El Salvador, Honduras and the Dominican Republic. Before the law was signed, products from those countries could enter the U.S. almost tariff-free, while American goods heading into those countries faced stiff tariffs. The goal of this agreement was to create U.S. jobs while at the same time offering the non-U.S. member citizens a chance for a better quality of life through access to U.S.-made goods.

CGI: See "Common Gateway Interface (CGI)."

CGI-BIN: The frequently used name of a directory on a web server where CGI programs exist.

Channel Definition Format (CDF): Used in Internet-based broadcasting. With this format, a channel serves as a web site that also sends an information file about that specific site. Users subscribe to a channel by downloading the file.

Churn Rate: The percentage of customers of subscribers who terminate contracts in a given time period.

CLEC: See "Competitive Local Exchange Carrier (CLEC)."

Client/Server: In networking, a way of running a large computer setup. The server is the host computer that acts as the central holding ground for files, databases and application software. The clients are all of the PCs connected to the network that share data with the server. This represents a vast change from past networks, which were connected to expensive, complicated "mainframe" computers.

Cloud: Refers to the use of outsourced servers to store and access data, as opposed to computers owned or managed by one organization. Firms that offer cloud services for a fee run clusters of servers networked together, often based on open standards. Such cloud networks can consist of hundreds or even thousands of computers. Cloud services enable a client company to immediately increase computing capability without any investment in physical infrastructure. (The word "cloud" is also broadly used to describe any data or application that runs via the Internet.) The concept of cloud is also increasingly linked with software as a service.

Cloud Computing: See "Cloud".

CMOS: Complementary Metal Oxide Semiconductor. The technology used in making modern silicon-based microchips.

Coaxial Cable: A type of cable widely used to transmit telephone and broadcast traffic. The distinguishing feature is an inner strand of wires surrounded by an insulator that is in turn surrounded by another conductor, which serves as the ground. Cable TV wiring is typically coaxial.

Code Division Multiple Access (CDMA): A cellular telephone multiple-access scheme whereby stations use spread-spectrum modulations and orthogonal codes to avoid interfering with one another. IS-95 (also known as CDMAOne) is the 2G CDMA standard. CDMA2000 is the 3G standard. CDMA in the 1xEV-DO standard offers data transfer speeds up to 2.4 Mbps. CDMA 1xRTT is a slower standard offering speeds of 144 kbps.

Codec: Hardware or software that converts analog to digital and digital to analog (in both audio and video formats). Codecs can be found in digital telephones, set-top boxes, computers and videoconferencing equipment. The term is also used to refer to the compression of digital information into a smaller format.

Co-Location: Refers to the hosting of computer servers at locations operated by service organizations. Co-location is offered by firms that operate specially designed co-location centers with high levels of security, extremely high-speed telecommunication lines for Internet connectivity and reliable backup electrical power systems in case of power failure, as well as a temperature-controlled environment for optimum operation of computer systems.

Committed Access Rate (CAR): A premium level of access from the Internet carrier to the customer.

Common Gateway Interface (CGI): A set of guidelines that determines the manner in which a web server receives and sends information to and from software on the same machine.

Communications Satellite Corporation (COMSAT): Serves as the U.S. Signatory to INTELSAT and INMARSAT.

Competitive Local Exchange Carrier (CLEC): A newer company providing local telephone service that competes against larger, traditional firms known as ILECs (incumbent local exchange carriers).

Compression: A technology in which a communications signal is squeezed so that it uses less bandwidth (or capacity) than it normally would. This saves storage space and shortens transfer time. The original data is decompressed when read back into memory.

COMSAT: See "Communications Satellite Corporation (COMSAT)."

Contract Manufacturing: A business arrangement whereby a company manufactures products that will be sold under the brand names of its client companies. For example, a large number of consumer electronics, such as laptop computers, are manufactured by contract manufacturers for leading brand-name computer companies such as Dell and Apple. Many other types of products, such as shoes and apparel, are made under contract manufacturing. Also see "Original Equipment Manufacturer (OEM)" and "Original Design Manufacturer (ODM)."

Cookie: A piece of information sent to a web browser from a web server that the browser software saves and then sends back to the server upon request. Cookies are used by web site operators to track the actions of users returning to the site.

CRM: See "Customer Relationship Management (CRM)."

Customer Relationship Management (CRM): Refers to the automation, via sophisticated software, of business processes involving existing and prospective customers. CRM may cover aspects such as sales (contact management and contact history), marketing (campaign management and telemarketing) and customer service (call center history and field service history). Well known providers of CRM software include Salesforce, which delivers via a Software as a Service model (see "Software as a Service (Saas)"), Microsoft and Oracle.

Cyberspace: Refers to the entire realm of information available through computer networks and the Internet.

D-AMPS: See "Time Division Multiple Access (TDMA)."

Dark Fiber: A reference to fiber optic bandwidth that is not being utilized.

Data Over Cable Service Interface Specification (DOCSIS): A set of standards for transferring data over cable television. DOCSIS 3.0 will enable very high-speed Internet access that may eventually reach 160 Mbps.

Datanets: Private networks of land-based telephone lines, satellites or wireless networks that allow corporate users to send data at high speeds to remote locations while bypassing the speed and cost constraints of traditional telephone lines.

Decompression: See "Compression."

Dedicated Internet Access (DIA): A high speed Internet service with dedicated access from the carrier to the customer.

Demographics: The breakdown of the population into statistical categories such as age, income, education and sex.

Development: The phase of research and development (R&D) in which researchers attempt to create new products from the results of discoveries and applications created during basic and applied research.

DIA: "Dedicated Internet Access (DIA)."

Digital: The transmission of a signal by reducing all of its information to ones and zeros and then regrouping them at the reception end. Digital transmission vastly improves the carrying capacity of the spectrum while reducing noise and distortion of the transmission.

Digital Local Telephone Switch: A computer that interprets signals (dialed numbers) from a telephone caller and routes calls to their proper destinations. A digital switch also provides a variety of calling features not available in older analog switches, such as call waiting.

Digital Rights Management (DRM): Restrictions placed on the use of digital content by copyright holders and hardware manufacturers. DRM for Apple, Inc.'s iTunes, for example, allows downloaded music to be played only on Apple's iPod player and iPhones, per agreement with music production companies Universal Music Group, SonyBMG, Warner Music and EMI.

Digital Signal Processor: A chip that converts analog signals such as sound and light into digital signals.

Digital Subscriber Line (DSL): A broadband (high-speed) Internet connection provided via telecommunications systems. These lines are a cost-effective means of providing homes and small businesses with relatively fast Internet access. Common variations include ADSL and SDSL. DSL competes with cable modem access and wireless access.

Digital Transformation (DX): The implementation of digital technologies into as many areas of a business as reasonably possible Goals may include: to fundamentally change how the enterprise operates: how data is gathered and tracked: how innovation is launched: and how value is delivered to customers. The hoped-for result is to create new operating efficiences and develop new revenue or profit opportunities, while better positioning the enterprise for the future. Also abbreviated as DX or DT.

Direct Broadcast Satellite (DBS): A high-powered satellite authorized to broadcast television programming directly to homes. Home subscribers use a dish and a converter to receive and translate the TV signal. An example is the DirecTV service. DBS operates in the 11.70- to 12.40-GHz range.

Disaster Recovery: A set of rules and procedures that allow a computer site to be put back in operation after a disaster has occurred. Moving backups off-site constitutes the minimum basic precaution for disaster recovery. The remote copy is used to recover data if the local storage is inaccessible after a disaster.

Discrete Semiconductor: A chip with one diode or transistor.

Disk Mirroring: A data redundancy technique in which data is recorded identically on multiple separate disk drives at the same time. When the primary disk is off-line, the alternate takes over, providing continuous access to data. Disk mirroring is sometimes referred to as RAID.

Distributor: An individual or business involved in marketing, warehousing and/or shipping of products manufactured by others to a specific group of end users. Distributors do not sell to the general public. In order to develop a competitive advantage, distributors often focus on serving one industry or one set of niche clients. For example, within the medical industry, there are major distributors that focus on providing pharmaceuticals, surgical supplies or dental supplies to clinics and hospitals.

Domain: A name that has server records associated with it. See "Domain Name."

Domain (Top-Level): Either an ISO country code or a common domain name such as .com, .org or .net.

Domain Name: A unique web site name registered to a company, organization or individual (e.g., plunkettresearch.com).

DS-1: A digital transmission format that transmits and receives information at a rate of 1,544,000 bits per second.

DSL: See "Digital Subscriber Line (DSL)."

Duplicate Host: A single host name that maps to duplicate IP addresses.

DX: See "Digital Transformation (DX)."

Dynamic HTML: Web content that changes with each individual viewing. For example, the same site could appear differently depending on geographic location of the reader, time of day, previous pages viewed or the user's profile.

EDI: See "Electronic Data Interchange (EDI)."

Electronic Data Interchange (EDI): An accepted standard format for the exchange of data between various companies' networks. EDI allows for the transfer of e-mail as well as orders, invoices and other files from one company to another.

E-Mail (eMail): The use of software that allows the posting of messages (text, audio or video) over a network. E-mail can be used on a LAN, a WAN or the Internet, as well as via online services or wireless devices that are Internet enabled. It can be used to send a message to a single recipient or may be broadcast to a large group of people at once.

EMEA: The region comprised of Europe, the Middle East and Africa.

EMS: Electronics Manufacturing Services. See "Contract Manufacturing."

Enhanced 911 (E911): A Federal Communication Commission rule that all wireless carriers must be able to identify a 911 caller by telephone number and location to within 100 meters.

Enhanced Data Rate for Global Evolution (EDGE): Technology that uses enhanced TDMA to achieve 3G transmission speeds and is compatible with GSM and TDMA networks.

Enterprise Resource Planning (ERP): An integrated information system that helps manage all aspects of a business, including accounting, ordering and human resources, typically across all locations of a major corporation or organization. ERP is considered to be a critical tool for management of large organizations. Suppliers of ERP tools include SAP and Oracle.

ERP: See "Enterprise Resource Planning (ERP)."

Ethernet: The standard format on which local area network equipment works. Abiding by Ethernet standards allows equipment from various manufacturers to work together.

eTOM: A business process flow standard created by the TeleManagement Forum.

EU: See "European Union (EU)."

EU Competence: The jurisdiction in which the European Union (EU) can take legal action.

European Community (EC): See "European Union (EU)."

European Union (EU): A consolidation of European countries (member states) functioning as one body to facilitate trade. Previously known as the European Community (EC). The EU has a unified currency, the Euro. See europa.eu.int.

EV-DO (CDMA 2000 1xEV-DO): A 3G (third generation) cellular telephone service standard that is an improved version of 1xRTT. The EV-DO (Evolution-Data Optimized) standard introduced in 2004 allows data download speeds of as much as 2.4 Mbps. A version introduced in 2006 allows up to 14.7 Mbps data download speeds. EV-DO is also known as CDMA 2000 1xEV-DO. EV-DO's capabilities are used by the entertainment industry to enable video via cell phone.

Extensible Markup Language (XML): A programming language that enables designers to add extra functionality to documents that could not otherwise be utilized with standard HTML coding. XML was developed by the World Wide Web Consortium. It can communicate to various software programs the actual meanings contained in HTML documents. For example, it can enable the gathering and use of information from a large number of databases at once and place that information into one web site window. XML is an important protocol to web services. See "Web Services."

Extranet: A computer network that is accessible in part to authorized outside persons, as opposed to an intranet, which uses a firewall to limit accessibility.

FASB: See "Financial Accounting Standards Board (FASB)."

FCC: See "Federal Communications Commission (FCC)."

FDDI: See "Fiber Distributed Data Interface (FDDI)."

Federal Communications Commission (FCC): The U.S. Government agency that regulates broadcast television and radio, as well as satellite transmission, telephony and all uses of radio spectrum.

Femtocell: A device used to boost performance of cell phones on a local basis, such as in a consumer's home or office. It utilizes nearby licensed wireless spectrum. The femtocell, in the form of a small box, routes wireless phone calls from a cell phone handset to the central office of a cellular service provider via a consumer's high speed Internet line.

Fiber Distributed Data Interface (FDDI): A token ring passing scheme that operates at 100 Mbps over fiber-optic lines with a built-in geographic limitation of 100 kilometers. This type of connection is faster than both Ethernet and T-3 connections. See "Token Ring."

Fiber Optics (Fibre Optics): A type of telephone and data transmission cable that can handle vast amounts of voice, data and video at once by carrying them along on beams of light via glass or plastic threads embedded in a cable. Fiber optics are rapidly replacing older copper wire technologies. Fiber optics offer much higher speeds and the ability to handle extremely large quantities of voice or data transmissions at once.

Fiber to the Home (FTTH): Refers to the extension of a fiber-optic system through the last mile so that it touches the home or office where it will be used. This can provide high speed Internet access at speeds of 15 to 100 Mbps, much faster than typical T1 or DSL line. FTTH is now commonly installed in new communities where telecom infrastructure is being built for the first time. Another phrase used to describe such installations is FTTP, or Fiber to the Premises.

Fiber to the Node (FTTN): Refers to the extension of a fiber-optic system through the last mile so that it touches a central neighborhood junction close to the home or office where it will be used. The remaining distance is covered by existing copper phone line that uses DSL (digital subscriber line) technology to speed data transfer.

File Transfer Protocol (FTP): A widely used method of transferring data and files between two Internet sites.

Financial Accounting Standards Board (FASB): An independent organization that establishes the Generally Accepted Accounting Principles (GAAP).

Firewall: Hardware or software that keeps unauthorized users from accessing a server or network. Firewalls are designed to prevent data theft and unauthorized web site manipulation by "hackers."

Firmware: A software program or string of code programmed on a hardware device. Firmware is usually stored in the read only memory (ROM) of the device, and essentially provides the control program for that device.

Fixed Wireless: Refers to the use of Wi-Fi, WiMAX or other wireless receivers that remain fixed in a stationary place, to provide Internet service.

FOMA: Freedom of Mobile Multimedia Access. See "Wideband CDMA."

Fourth-Party Logistics (4PL): A service that integrates a company's third-party logistics providers into a single entity for ease of use. Often formed by a telecommunications company, a 4PL is also called a lead logistics provider. A 4PL service provider provides a top layer of business processes, generally technology-driven, to the client's supply chain. Also see "Third-Party Logistics (3PL)."

Frame Relay: An accepted standard for sending large amounts of data over phone lines and private datanets. The term refers to the way data is broken down into standard-size "frames" prior to transmission.

Free Space Optics (FSO): A cost-effective alternative to fiber-optic broadband access, FSO uses lasers, or light pulses, to send packetized data in the terahertz spectrum range. Air, rather than fiber, is the transport medium.

Frequency: The number of times that an alternating current goes through its complete cycle in one second. One cycle per second is referred to as one hertz: 1,000 cycles per second, one kilohertz: 1 million cycles per second, one megahertz: and 1 billion cycles per second, one gigahertz.

Frequency Band: A term for designating a range of frequencies in the electromagnetic spectrum.

FTP: See "File Transfer Protocol (FTP)."

FTTC: Fiber to the curb. See "Fiber to the Home (FTTH)."

FTTP: Fiber to the premises. See "Fiber to the Home (FTTH)."

Fuzzy Logic: Recognizes that some statements are not just "true" or "false," but also "more or less certain" or "very unlikely." Fuzzy logic is used in artificial intelligence. See "Artificial Intelligence (AI)."

GAAP: See "Generally Accepted Accounting Principles (GAAP)."

Gateway: A device connecting two or more networks that may use different protocols and media. Gateways translate between the different networks and can connect locally or over wide area networks.

GDP: See "Gross Domestic Product (GDP)."

General Packet Radio Service (GPRS): A system for mobile communications, GPRS providers faster data transmission than GSM networks. See "Global System for Mobile Communications (GSM)."

Generally Accepted Accounting Principles (GAAP): A set of accounting standards administered by the Financial Accounting Standards Board (FASB) and enforced by the U.S. Security and Exchange Commission (SEC). GAAP is primarily used in the U.S.

Geostationary: A geosynchronous satellite angle with zero inclination, making a satellite appear to hover over one spot on the earth's equator.

Gigabyte: 1,024 megabytes.

Gigahertz (GHz): One billion cycles per second. See "Frequency."

Global Positioning System (GPS): A satellite system, originally designed by the U.S. Department of Defense for navigation purposes. Today, GPS is in wide use for consumer and business purposes, such as navigation for drivers, boaters and hikers. It utilizes satellites orbiting the earth at 10,900 miles to enable users to pinpoint precise locations using small, electronic wireless receivers.

Global System for Mobile Communications (GSM): The standard cellular format used throughout Europe, making one type of cellular phone usable in every nation on the continent and in the U.K. In the U.S., Cingular and T-Mobile also run GSM networks. The original GSM, introduced in 1991, has transfer speeds of only 9.6 kbps. GSM EDGE offers 2.75G data transfer speeds of up to 473.6 kbps. GSM GPRS offers slower 2.5G theoretical speeds of 144 kbps.

Globalization: The increased mobility of goods, services, labor, technology and capital throughout the

world. Although globalization is not a new development, its pace has increased with the advent of new technologies.

GPRS: A system for mobile communications, GPRS providers faster data transmission than GSM networks. See "Global System for Mobile Communications (GSM)."

GPS: See "Global Positioning System (GPS)."

Graphic Interchange Format (GIF): A widely used format for image files.

Gross Domestic Product (GDP): The total value of a nation's output, income and expenditures produced with a nation's physical borders.

Gross National Product (GNP): A country's total output of goods and services from all forms of economic activity measured at market prices for one calendar year. It differs from Gross Domestic Product (GDP) in that GNP includes income from investments made in foreign nations.

GSM: See "Global System for Mobile Communications (GSM)."

GSM EDGE: See "Global System for Mobile Communications (GSM)."

GSM GPRS: See "Global System for Mobile Communications (GSM)."

Handheld Devices Markup Language (HDML): A text-based markup language designed for display on a smaller screen (e.g., a cellular phone, PDA or pager). Enables the mobile user to send, receive and redirect e-mail as well as access the Internet (HDML-enabled web sites only).

HDML: See "Handheld Devices Markup Language (HDML)."

HDSL: See "High-Data-Rate Digital Subscriber Line (HDSL)."

HDSPA: See "High Speed Packet Access (HSPA)."

Headend: A facility that originates and distributes cable service in a given geographic area. Depending on the size of the area it serves, a cable system may be comprised of more than one headend.

Hertz: A measure of frequency equal to one cycle per second. Most radio signals operate in ranges of megahertz or gigahertz.

HFC: Hybrid Fiber Coaxial. A type of cable system.

High Speed Packet Access (HSPA): A 3G wireless standard introduced in 2007 that encompasses two protocols: High Speed Downlink Packet Access (HSDPA) and High Speed Uplink Packet Access (HSUPA). Downlink speeds can reach up to 14.4 Mbps while uplink speeds of up to 5.76 Mbps. (These are theoretical speeds.) HSPA+ is an advanced technology with the following theoretical download speeds: Release 8, 42 Mbps: Release 9, 84 Mbps: Release 10, 168 Mbps.

High-Data-Rate Digital Subscriber Line (HDSL): High-data-rate DSL, delivering up to T1 or E1 speeds.

Homes Passed: Households that have the ability to receive cable service and may opt to subscribe.

HSDPA: See "High Speed Packet Access (HSPA)."

HSPA: See "High Speed Packet Access (HSPA)."

HTML: See "Hypertext Markup Language (HTML)."

HTML5: A specification for Internet development that represents the fifth major revision of the Hypertext Markup Language, or HTML. HTML5 is designed to better handle the types of Internet content that are rapidly growing in popularity, such as online video, audio and interactive documents and pages. For example, HTML5 enables the designer to embed images, audio and video directly into a web-based document.

HTTP: See "Hypertext Transfer Protocol (HTTP)."

Hypertext Markup Language (HTML): A language for coding text for viewing on the World Wide Web. HTML is unique because it enables the use of hyperlinks from one site to another, creating a web.

Hypertext Transfer Protocol (HTTP): The protocol used most frequently on the World Wide Web to move hypertext files between clients and servers on the Internet.

ICANN: The Internet Corporation for Assigned Names and Numbers. ICANN acts as the central coordinator for the Internet's technical operations.

ICT: See "Information and Communication Technologies (ICT)."

iDEN: A packet switched cellular mobile telephone standard. It is a proprietary standard of Nextel. The maximum data speed is 19.2 kbps. This standard is considered 2.5G. It was introduced in 2001.

IDN: See "Integrated Digital Network (IDN)."

IEEE: See "Institute of Electrical and Electronic Engineers (IEEE)."

IFRS: See "International Financials Reporting Standards (IFRS)."

ILEC: See "Incumbent Local Exchange Carrier (ILEC)."

IM: See "Instant Messaging (IM)."

IMT-Advanced: See "Long-Term Evolution (LTE)."

Incumbent Local Exchange Carrier (ILEC): A traditional telephone company that was providing local service prior to the establishment of the Telecommunications Act of 1996, when upstart companies (CLECs, or competitive local exchange carriers) were enabled to compete against the ILECS and were granted access to their system wiring.

Industry Code: A descriptive code assigned to any company in order to group it with firms that operate in similar businesses. Common industry codes include the NAICS (North American Industrial Classification System) and the SIC (Standard Industrial Classification), both of which are standards widely used in America, as well as the International Standard Industrial Classification of all Economic Activities (ISIC), the Standard International Trade Classification established by the United Nations (SITC) and the General Industrial Classification of Economic Activities within the European Communities (NACE).

Information and Communication Technologies (ICT): A term used to describe the relationship between the myriad types of goods, services and networks that make up the global information and communications system. Sectors involved in ICT include landlines, data networks, the Internet, wireless communications, (including cellular and remote wireless sensors) and satellites.

Information Technology (IT): The systems, including hardware and software, that move and store voice, video and data via computers and telecommunications.

Infrastructure: 1) The equipment that comprises a system. 2) Public-use assets such as roads, bridges, water systems, sewers and other assets necessary for public accommodation and utilities. 3) The underlying base of a system or network. 4) Transportation and shipping support systems such as ports, airports and railways.

Infrastructure (Telecommunications): The entity made up of all the cable and equipment installed in the worldwide telecommunications market. Most of today's telecommunications infrastructure is connected by copper and fiber-optic cable, which represents a huge capital investment that telephone companies would like to continue to utilize in as many ways as possible.

Initial Public Offering (IPO): A company's first effort to sell its stock to investors (the public). Investors in an up-trending market eagerly seek stocks offered in many IPOs because the stocks of newly public companies that seem to have great promise may appreciate very rapidly in price, reaping great profits for those who were able to get the stock at the first offering. In the United States, IPOs are regulated by the SEC (U.S. Securities Exchange Commission) and by the state-level regulatory agencies of the states in which the IPO shares are offered.

INMARSAT: The International Maritime Satellite Organization. INMARSAT operates a network of satellites used in transmissions for all types of international mobile services, including maritime, aeronautical and land mobile.

Instant Messaging (IM): A type of e-mail that is viewed and then deleted. IM is used between opt-in networks of people for leisure or business purposes.

Institute of Electrical and Electronic Engineers (IEEE): An organization that sets global technical standards and acts as an authority in technical areas including computer engineering, biomedical technology, telecommunications, electric power, aerospace and consumer electronics, among others. www.ieee.org.

Integrated Circuit (IC): Another name for a semiconductor, an IC is a piece of silicon on which thousands (or millions) of transistors have been combined.

Integrated Digital Network (IDN): A network that uses both digital transmission and digital switching.

Integrated Services Digital Networks (ISDN): Internet connection services offered at higher speeds than standard "dial-up" service. While ISDN was considered to be an advanced service at one time, it has been eclipsed by much faster DSL, cable modem and T1 line service.

Intellectual Property (IP): The exclusive ownership of original concepts, ideas, designs, engineering plans or other assets that are protected by law. Examples include items covered by trademarks, copyrights and patents. Items such as software, engineering plans, fashion designs and architectural designs, as well as games, books, songs and other entertainment items are among the many things that may be considered to be intellectual property. (Also, see "Patent.")

INTELSAT: The International Telecommunications Satellite Organization. INTELSAT operates a network of 20 satellites, primarily for international transmissions, and provides domestic services to some 40 countries.

Interactive TV (ITV): Allows two-way data flow between a viewer and the cable TV system. A user can exchange information with the cable system—for example, by ordering a product related to a show he/she is watching or by voting in an interactive survey.

Interexchange Carrier (IXC or IEC): Any company providing long-distance phone service between LECs and LATAs. See "Local Exchange Carrier (LEC)" and "Local Access and Transport Area (LATA)."

Interface: Refers to (1) a common boundary between two or more items of equipment or between a terminal and a communication channel, (2) the electronic device that interconnects two or more devices or items of equipment having similar or dissimilar characteristics or (3) the electronic device placed between a terminal and a communication channel to protect the network from the hazard of excess voltage levels.

International Financials Reporting Standards (IFRS): A set of accounting standards established by the International Accounting Standards Board (IASB) for the preparation of public financial statements. IFRS has been adopted by much of the world, including the European Union, Russia and Singapore.

International Telecommunications Union (ITU): The international body responsible for telephone and computer communications standards describing interface techniques and practices. These standards include those that define how a nation's telephone and data systems connect to the worldwide communications network.

Internet: A global computer network that provides an easily accessible way for hundreds of millions of users to send and receive data electronically when appropriately connected via computers or wireless devices. Access is generally through HTML-enabled sites on the World Wide Web. Also known as the Net.

Internet Appliance: A non-PC device that connects users to the Internet for specific or general purposes. A good example is an electronic game machine with a screen and Internet capabilities.

Internet of Things (IoT): A concept whereby individual objects, such as kitchen appliances, automobiles, manufacturing equipment, environmental sensors or air conditioners, are connected to the Internet. The objects must be able to identify themselves to other devices or to databases. The ultimate goals may include the collection and processing of data, the control of instruments and machinery, and eventually, a new level of synergies, artificial intelligence and operating efficiencies among the objects. The Internet of Things is often referred to as IoT. Related technologies and topics include RFID, remote wireless sensors, telecommunications and nanotechnology.

Internet Protocol (IP): A set of tools and/or systems used to communicate across the World Wide Web.

Internet Protocol Television (IPTV): Television delivered by Internet-based means such as fiber to the home (FTTH) or a very high speed DSL. Microsoft is a leading provider of advanced IPTV software. SBC and BT are two leading telecom firms that are using Microsoft's new software to offer television services over high speed Internet lines.

Internet Protocol Version 6 (IPv6): The next-generation of IP standard. IPv6 is intended to first work with, and eventually replace, IPv4. Version 6 will enable a vastly larger number of devices to each utilize one internet address (an IP address) at one time. Specifically, it will allow for 340 trillion, trillion, trillion addresses.

Internet Service Provider (ISP): A company that sells access to the Internet to individual subscribers. Leading examples are MSN and AOL.

Internet Telephony: See "Voice Over Internet Protocol (VOIP)."

Intranet: A network protected by a firewall for sharing data and e-mail within an organization or company. Usually, intranets are used by organizations for internal communication.

IoT: See "Internet of Things (IoT)."

IP: See "Intellectual Property (IP)."

IP Number/IP Address: A number or address with four parts that are separated by dots. Each machine on the Internet has its own IP (Internet protocol) number, which serves as an identifier.

IP VOD: See "VOD-Over-IP."

IPL: International Private Line.

IPv6: See "Internet Protocol Version 6 (IPv6)."

IS-95: See "Code Division Multiple Access (CDMA)."

ISDN: See "Integrated Services Digital Networks (ISDN)."

ISO 9000, 9001, 9002, 9003: Standards set by the International Organization for Standardization. ISO 9000, 9001, 9002 and 9003 are the highest quality certifications awarded to organizations that meet exacting standards in their operating practices and procedures.

IT: See "Information Technology (IT)."

IT-Enabled Services (ITES): The portion of the Information Technology industry focused on providing business services, such as call centers, insurance claims processing and medical records transcription, by utilizing the power of IT, especially the Internet. Most ITES functions are considered to be back-office procedures. Also, see "Business Process Outsourcing (BPO)."

ITES: See "IT-Enabled Services (ITES)."

ITU: See "International Telecommunications Union (ITU)."

ITV: See "Interactive TV (ITV)."

Java: A programming language developed by Sun Microsystems that allows web pages to display interactive graphics. Any type of computer or operating systems can read Java.

Joint Photographic Experts Group (JPEG): A widely used format for digital image files.

Ka-Band: The frequency range from 18 to 31 GHz. The spectrum allocated for satellite communications is 30 GHz for the up-link and 20 GHz for the downlink.

Kbps: One thousand bits per second.

Kilobyte: One thousand (or 1,024) bytes.

Kilohertz (kHz): A measure of frequency equal to 1,000 Hertz.

Knowledge Process Outsourcing (KPO): The use of outsourced and/or offshore workers to perform business tasks that require judgment and analysis. Examples include such professional tasks as patent research, legal research, architecture, design, engineering, market research, scientific research, accounting and tax return preparation. Also, see "Business Process Outsourcing (BPO)."

LAC: An acronym for Latin America and the Caribbean.

Landline: Refers to standard telephone and data communications systems that use in-ground and telephone pole cables, as opposed to wireless cellular and satellite services.

LATA: See "Local Access and Transport Area (LATA)."

LDCs: See "Least Developed Countries (LDCs)."

Leased Line: A phone line that is rented for use in continuous, long-term data connections.

Least Developed Countries (LDCs): Nations determined by the U.N. Economic and Social Council to be the poorest and weakest members of the international community. There are currently 50 LDCs, of which 34 are in Africa, 15 are in Asia Pacific and the remaining one (Haiti) is in Latin America. The top 10 on the LDC list, in descending order from top to 10th, are Afghanistan, Angola, Bangladesh, Benin, Bhutan, Burkina Faso, Burundi, Cambodia, Cape Verde and the Central African Republic. Sixteen of the LDCs are also Landlocked Least Developed Countries (LLDCs) which present them with additional difficulties often due to the high cost of transporting trade goods. Eleven of the LDCs are Small Island Developing States (SIDS), which are often at risk of extreme weather phenomenon (hurricanes, typhoons, Tsunami): have fragile ecosystems: are often dependent on foreign energy sources: can have high disease rates for HIV/AIDS and malaria: and can have poor market access and trade terms.

LEC: See "Local Exchange Carrier (LEC)."

Li-Fi: Optical wireless systems that operate somewhat like Wi-Fi, but they utilize light to transfer data.

LINUX: An open, free operating system that is shared readily with millions of users worldwide. These users continuously improve and add to the software's code. It can be used to operate computer networks and Internet appliances as well as servers and PCs.

LMDS: Local Multipoint Distribution Service. A fixed, wireless, point-to-multipoint technology designed to distribute television signals.

Local Access and Transport Area (LATA): An operational service area established after the breakup of AT&T to distinguish local telephone service from long-distance service. The U.S. is divided into over 160 LATAs.

Local Area Network (LAN): A computer network that is generally within one office or one building. A LAN can be very inexpensive and efficient to set up when small numbers of computers are involved. It may require a network administrator and a serious investment if hundreds of computers are hooked up to the LAN. A LAN enables all computers within the office to share files and printers, to access common databases and to send e-mail to others on the network.

Local Exchange Carrier (LEC): Any local telephone company, i.e., a carrier, that provides ordinary phone service under regulation within a service area. Also see "Incumbent Local Exchange Carrier (ILEC)" and "Competitive Local Exchange Carrier (CLEC)."

Long Term Evolution (LTE): An advanced wireless technology expected to deliver wireless Internet access speeds equal to ultrafast DSL speeds. The technology may be useful not only for cell phones, but also for connecting items like digital cameras to the Internet. LTE implementations are planned by such operators as Verizon Wireless, AT&T and Vodafone. It will compete with WiMAX. Practical LTE data transfer speeds may reach 100 to 1,000 Mbps.

LTE: See "Long-Term Evolution (LTE)."

M2M: See "Machine-to-Machine (M2M)."

Machine Learning: The ability of a computer or computerized device to learn based on the results of previous actions or the analysis of a stream of related data. It is a vital branch of Artificial Intelligence that uses advanced software in order to identify patterns and make decisions or predictions.

Machine-to-Machine (M2M): Refers to communications from one device to another (or to a collection of devices). It is typically through wireless means such as Wi-Fi or cellular. Wireless sensor networks (WSNs) will be a major growth factor in M2M communications, in everything from factory automation to agriculture and transportation. In

logistics and retailing, M2M can refer to the advanced use of RFID tags. See "Radio Frequency Identification (RFID)." The Internet of Things is based on the principle of M2M communications. Also, see "Internet of Things (IoT)."

MAN: See "Metropolitan Area Network (MAN)."

Managed Service Provider (MSP): An outsourcer that deploys, manages and maintains the back-end software and hardware infrastructure for Internet businesses.

Market Segmentation: The division of a consumer market into specific groups of buyers based on demographic factors.

Mbps (Megabits per second): One million bits transmitted per second.

M-Commerce: Mobile e-commerce over wireless devices.

Media Oriented Systems Transport (MOST): A standard adopted in 2004 by the Consumer Electronics Association for the integration of or interface with consumer electronics (such as iPods) into entertainment systems in automobiles.

Megabytes: One million bytes, or 1,024 kilobytes.

Megahertz (MHz): A measure of frequency equal to 1 million Hertz.

Mesh Network: A network that uses multiple Wi-Fi repeaters or "nodes" to deploy a wireless Internet access network. Typically, a mesh network is operated by the users themselves. Each user installs a node at his or her locale, and plugs the node into his/her local Internet access, whether DSL, cable or satellite. Other users within the mesh can access all other nodes as needed, or as they travel about. A mesh network can provide access to an apartment complex, an office building, a campus or an entire city. Meraki is a leading node brand in this sector.

Metropolitan Area Network (MAN): A data and communications network that operates over metropolitan areas and recently has been expanded to nationwide and even worldwide connectivity of high-speed data networks. A MAN can carry video and data.

Microprocessor: A computer on a digital semiconductor chip. It performs math and logic operations and executes instructions from memory. (Also known as a central processing unit or CPU.)

Microwave: Line-of sight, point-to-point transmission of signals at high frequency. Microwaves are used in data, voice and all other types of information transmission. The growth of fiber-optic networks has tended to curtail the growth and use of microwave relays.

Miles of Plant: The number of cable plant miles laid or strung by a cable system: the cable miles in place.

MIME: See "Multipurpose Internet Mail Extensions (MIME)."

MIMO: See "802.11n (MIMO)."

MMS: See "Multimedia Messaging System (MMS)."

Mobile Virtual Network Operator (MVNO): A seller of cellular service that doesn't own its own cellular network. Instead, it buys all access and network services from a major provider such as Sprint Nextel, and then resells that service under its own brand.

Moblog: Mobile blog. This is a blog created by cell phone or other mobile device. It often consists largely of photos taken by a cell phone's built-in camera. Also, see "Blog (Web Log)."

Modem: A device that allows a computer to be connected to a phone line, which in turn enables the computer to receive and exchange data with other machines via the Internet.

Modulator: A device that modulates a carrier. Modulators are found in broadcasting transmitters and satellite transponders. The devices are also used by cable TV companies to place a baseband video television signal onto a desired VHF or UHF channel. Home video tape recorders also have built-in modulators that enable the recorded video information to be played back using a television receiver tuned to VHF channel 3 or 4.

MOST: See "Media Oriented Systems Transport (MOST)."

MP3: A subsystem of MPEG used to compress sound into digital files. It is the most commonly used format for downloading music and audio books. MP3 compresses music significantly while retaining CD-like quality. MP3 players are personal, portable devices used for listening to music and audio book files. See "MPEG."

MPEG, MPEG-1, MPEG-2, MPEG-3, MPEG-4: Moving Picture Experts Group. It is a digital standard for the compression of motion or still video for transmission or storage. MPEGs are used in digital cameras and for Internet-based viewing.

MPLS: See "Multi-Protocol Label Switching (MPLS)."

MSO: See "Multi-System Operator (MSO)."

MSO: See "Multi-System Operator (MSO)."

Multicasting: Sending data, audio or video simultaneously to a number of clients. Also known as broadcasting.

Multimedia Messaging System (MMS): See "Text Messaging."

Multiple System Operator (MSO): An individual or company owning two or more cable systems.

Multipoint Distribution System (MDS): A common carrier licensed by the FCC to operate a broadcast-like omni-directional microwave transmission facility within a given city. MDS carriers often pick up satellite pay-TV programming and distribute it, via their local MDS transmitter, to specially installed antennas and receivers.

Multi-Protocol Label Switching (MPLS): A technology that enables network operators to route Internet traffic around network failures and bottlenecks.

Multipurpose Internet Mail Extensions (MIME): A widely used method for attaching non-text files to e-mails.

Multi-System Operator (MSO): Refers to companies that operate cable TV (and/or direct-broadcast satellite TV) systems in multiple cities or regions.

MU-MIMO: Mulit-User, Mutiple-Inut, Multiple-Output. See "802.11n (MIMO)."

MVNO: See "Mobile Virtual Network Operator (MVNO)."

NAFTA: See "North American Free Trade Agreement (NAFTA)."

NAICS: North American Industrial Classification System. See "Industry Code."

Nanosecond (NS): A billionth of a second. A common unit of measure of computer operating speed.

National Telecommunications and Information Administration (NTIA): A unit of the Department of Commerce that addresses U.S. government telecommunications policy, standards setting and radio spectrum allocation. www.ntia.doc.gov.

Network: In computing, a network is created when two or more computers are connected. Computers may be connected by wireless methods, using such technologies as 802.11b, or by a system of cables, switches and routers.

Network Numbers: The first portion of an IP address, which identifies the network to which hosts in the rest of the address are connected.

Node: Any single computer connected to a network or a junction of communications paths in a network.

North American Free Trade Agreement (NAFTA): A trade agreement signed in December 1992 by U.S. President George H. W. Bush, Canadian Prime Minister Brian Mulroney and Mexican President Carlos Salinas de Gortari. The agreement eliminates tariffs on most goods originating in and traveling between the three member countries. It was approved by the legislatures of the three countries and had entered into force by January 1994. When it was created, NAFTA formed one of the largest free-trade areas of its kind in the world.

NS: See "Nanosecond (NS)."

NTIA: See "National Telecommunications and Information Administration (NTIA)."

Object Technology: By merging data and software into "objects," a programming system becomes object-oriented. For example, an object called "weekly inventory sold" would have the data and programming needed to construct a flow chart. Some new programming systems–including Java–contain this feature. Object technology is also featured in many Microsoft products. See "Java."

OC3, up to OC768: Very high-speed data lines that run at speeds from 155 to 39,813.12 Mbps.

ODM: See "Original Design Manufacturer (ODM)."

OECD: See "Organisation for Economic Co-operation and Development (OECD)."

OEM: See "Original Equipment Manufacturer (OEM)."

OFDM: See "Orthogonal Frequency Division Multiplexing (OFDM)."

OFDMA: Orthogonal Frequency-Division Multiple Access. See "802.11n (MIMO)."

Offshoring: The rapidly growing tendency among U.S., Japanese and Western European firms to send knowledge-based and manufacturing work overseas. The intent is to take advantage of lower wages and operating costs in such nations as China, India, Hungary and Russia. The choice of a nation for offshore work may be influenced by such factors as language and education of the local workforce, transportation systems or natural resources. For example, China and India are graduating high numbers of skilled engineers and scientists from their universities. Also, some nations are noted for large numbers of workers skilled in the English language, such as the Philippines and India. Also see "Captive Offshoring" and "Outsourcing."

Onshoring: The opposite of "offshoring." Providing or maintaining manufacturing or services within or nearby a company's domestic location. Sometimes referred to as reshoring.

Open Source (Open Standards): A software program for which the source code is openly available for modification and enhancement as various users and developers see fit. Open software is typically developed as a public collaboration and grows in usefulness over time. See "LINUX."

Optical Fiber (Fibre): See "Fiber Optics (Fibre Optics)."

Organisation for Economic Co-operation and Development (OECD): A group of more than 30 nations that are strongly committed to the market economy and democracy. Some of the OECD members include Japan, the U.S., Spain, Germany, Australia, Korea, the U.K., Canada and Mexico. Although not members, Estonia, Israel and Russia are invited to member talks: and Brazil, China, India, Indonesia and South Africa have enhanced engagement policies with the OECD. The Organisation provides statistics, as well as social and economic data: and researches social changes, including patterns in evolving fiscal policy, agriculture, technology, trade, the environment and other areas. It publishes over 250 titles annually: publishes a corporate magazine, the OECD Observer: has radio and TV studios: and has centers in Tokyo, Washington, D.C., Berlin and Mexico City that distributed the Organisation's work and organizes events.

Original Design Manufacturer (ODM): A contract manufacturer that offers complete, end-to-end design, engineering and manufacturing services. ODMs design and build products, such as consumer electronics, that client companies can then brand and sell as their own. For example, a large percentage of laptop computers, cell phones and PDAs are made by ODMs. Also see "Original Equipment Manufacturer (OEM)" and "Contract Manufacturing."

Original Equipment Manufacturer (OEM): 1) A company that manufactures a component (or a completed product) for sale to a customer that will integrate the component into a final product. The OEM's customer will put its own brand name on the end product and distribute or resell it to end users. 2) A firm that buys a component and then incorporates it into a final product, or buys a completed product and then resells it under the firm's own brand name. This usage is most often found in the computer industry, where OEM is sometimes used as a verb. Also see "Original Design Manufacturer (ODM)" and "Contract Manufacturing."

Orthogonal Frequency Division Multiplexing (OFDM): An alternative to CDMA cell phone technology backed by Flarion Technologies, Inc. OFDM is a frequency-division multiplexing system that uses closely spaced, eight-sided subcarriers to transmit data.

Outsourcing: The hiring of an outside company to perform a task otherwise performed internally by the company, generally with the goal of lowering costs and/or streamlining work flow. Outsourcing contracts are generally several years in length. Companies that hire outsourced services providers often prefer to focus on their core strengths while sending more routine tasks outside for others to perform. Typical outsourced services include the running of human resources departments, telephone call centers and computer departments. When outsourcing is performed overseas, it may be referred to as offshoring. Also see "Offshoring."

P2P: See "Peer-to-Peer (P2P)."

Packet Switching: A higher-speed way to move data through a network, in which files are broken down into smaller "packets" that are reassembled electronically after transmission.

PAS: See "Personal Access System (PAS)."

Passive Optical Network (PON): A telecommunications network that brings high speed fiber optic cable all the way (or most of the way) to the end user. Also, see "Fiber to the Home (FTTH)."

Patent: An intellectual property right granted by a national government to an inventor to exclude others from making, using, offering for sale, or selling the invention throughout that nation or importing the invention into the nation for a limited time in exchange for public disclosure of the invention when the patent is granted. In addition to national patenting agencies, such as the United States Patent and Trademark Office, and regional organizations such as the European Patent Office, there is a cooperative international patent organization, the World Intellectual Property Organization, or WIPO, established by the United Nations.

Pay Cable: A network or service available for an added monthly fee. Also called premium cable. Some services, called mini-pay, are marketed at an average monthly rate below that of full-priced premium.

Pay Cable Unit: Each premium service to which a household subscribes.

Pay-Per-View (PPV): A service that enables television subscribers, including cable and satellite viewers, to order and view events or movies on an individual basis. PPV programming may include sporting events.

PBX: A central telephone system within a large business office used to route incoming and outgoing calls to various employees and onto long-distance networks. PBX functions are typically enhanced by the application of computer functions, such as voice mail and call forwarding.

PC: See "Personal Computer (PC)."

PCS: See "Personal Communication Service (PCS)."

Peer-to-Peer (P2P): Refers to a connection between computers that creates equal status between the computers. P2P can be used in an office or home to create a simple computer network. However, P2P more commonly refers to networks of computers that share information online. For example, peer-to-peer music sharing networks enable one member to search the hard drives of other members to locate music files and then download those files. These systems can be used for legal purposes. Nonetheless, they became notorious as systems that enable members to collect music and videos for free, circumventing copyright and other legal restrictions. At one time Napster was widely known as a P2P music system that enabled users to circumvent copyright.

Personal Access System (PAS): A type of mobile phone service that is very popular in China. Unlike traditional cellular mobile phone service, a PAS customer typically cannot roam beyond their home service area. However, monthly charges tend to be much lower.

Personal Communication Service (PCS): A type of cellular mobile telephone service.

Personal Computer (PC): An affordable, efficient computer meant to be used by one person. The device may be a desktop computer or a laptop. Frequently, the PC is connected to a local area network (LAN), or uses wireless methods such as Wi-Fi to access the Internet. PCs are used both in the home and in the office. There is no firm agreement on whether tablets should be regarded as PCs.

Personal Handyphone System (PHS): A type of mobile phone service that is very popular in Japan. Unlike traditional cellular mobile phone service, a PHS customer typically cannot roam beyond their home service area. However, monthly charges tend to be much lower.

PHS: See "Personal Handyphone System (PHS)."

Podcasting: The creation of audio files as webcasts. Podcasts can be anything from unique radio-like programming to sales pitches to audio press releases. Audio RSS (Real Simple Syndication) enables the broadcast of these audio files to appropriate parties. Also see "Real Simple Syndication (RSS)," "Video Blog (VLOG)" and "Blog (Web Log)."

Point-to-Point Protocol (PPP): A protocol that enables a computer to use the combination of a standard telephone line and a modem to make TCP/IP connections.

PON: See "Passive Optical Networking (PON)."

POP: An acronym for both "Point of Presence" and "Post Office Protocol." Point of presence refers to a location that a network can be connected to (generally used to count the potential subscriber base of a cellular phone system). Post office protocol refers to the way in which e-mail software obtains mail from a mail server.

Port: An interface (or connector) between the computer and the outside world. The number of ports on a communications controller or front-end processor determines the number of communications channels that can be connected to it. The number of ports on a computer determines the number of peripheral devices that can be attached to it.

Portal: A comprehensive web site for general or specific purposes.

Positioning: The design and implementation of a merchandising mix, price structure and style of selling to create an image of the retailer, relative to its competitors, in the customer's mind.

Powerline: A method of networking computers, peripherals and appliances together via the electrical wiring that is built in to a home or office. Powerline competes with 802.11b and other wireless networking methods.

Predictive Analytics: See "Analytics."

Product Lifecycle (Product Life Cycle): The prediction of the life of a product or brand. Stages are described as Introduction, Growth, Maturity and finally Sales Decline. These stages track a product from its initial introduction to the market through to the end of its usefulness as a commercially viable product. The goal of Product Lifecycle Management is to maximize production efficiency, consumer acceptance and profits. Consequently, critical processes around the product need to be adjusted during its lifecycle, including pricing, advertising, promotion, distribution and packaging.

Product Lifecycle Management (PLM): See "Product Lifecycle (Product Life Cycle)."

Proportionate Subscribers: The number of subscribers, usually to a mobile telecommunications system, relative to the interest owned in the system by an investor or investors. For example, a firm with a 100% ownership interest in a wireless business with 100,000 subscribers would have 100,000 proportionate subscribers, but a firm with a 25% interest in a system with 100,000 subscribers would be attributed 25,000 proportionate subscribers for that system.

Protocol: A set of rules for communicating between computers. The use of standard protocols allows products from different vendors to communicate on a common network.

PSTN: See "Public Switched Telephone Network (PSTN)."

Public Switched Telephone Network (PSTN): A term that refers to the traditional telephone system.

QoS: See "Quality of Service (QoS)."

Quality of Service (QoS): The improvement of the flow of broadband information on the Internet and other networks by raising the data flow level of certain routes and restricting it on others. QoS levels are supported on robust, high-bandwidth technologies such as 4G.

R&D: Research and development. Also see "Applied Research" and "Basic Research."

Radio Frequency Identification (RFID): A technology that applies a special microchip-enabled tag to an individual item or piece of merchandise or inventory. RFID technology enables wireless, computerized tracking of that inventory item as it moves through the supply chain from factory to transport to warehouse to retail store or end user. Also known as radio tags.

RBOC: See "Regional Bell Operating Company (RBOC)."

Real Simple Syndication (RSS): Uses XML programming language to let web logs and other data be broadcast to appropriate web sites and users. Formerly referred to as RDF Site Summary or Rich Site Summary, RSS also enables the publisher to create a description of the content and its location in the form of an RSS document. Also useful for distributing audio files. See "Podcasting."

Regional Bell Operating Company (RBOC): Former Bell system telephone companies (or their successors), created as a result of the breakup of AT&T by a Federal Court decree on December 31, 1983 (e.g., Bell Atlantic, now part of Verizon).

Request for Bids (RFB): A request for pricing and supporting details, sent by a firm that requires products or services, outlining all the firm's requirements. Proposing companies are asked to place a bid based on the requested goods or services.

Request for Quotation (RFQ): A proposal that asks companies to submit pricing for goods or a described level of services. See "Request for Bids (RFB)."

Reshoring: See "Onshoring."

RF: Radio Frequency.

RFID: See "Radio Frequency Identification (RFID)."

RoHS Compliant: A directive that restricts the total amount of certain dangerous substances that may be incorporated in electronic equipment, including consumer electronics. Any RoHS compliant component is tested for the presence of Lead, Cadmium, Mercury, Hexavalent chromium, Polybrominated biphenyls and Polybrominated diphenyl ethers. For Cadmium and Hexavalent chromium, there must be less than 0.01% of the substance by weight at raw homogeneous materials level. For Lead, PBB, and PBDE, there must be no more than 0.1% of the material, when calculated by weight at raw homogeneous materials. Any RoHS compliant component must have 100 ppm or less of mercury and the mercury must not have been intentionally added to the component. Certain items of military and medical equipment are exempt from RoHS compliance.

Router: An electronic device that enables networks to communicate with each other. For example, the local area network (LAN) in an office connects to a router to give the LAN access to an Internet connection such as a T1 or DSL. Routers can be bundled with several added features, such as firewalls.

RSS: See "Real Simple Syndication (RSS)."

SaaS: See "Software as a Service (SaaS)."

Satellite Broadcasting: The use of Earth-orbiting satellites to transmit, over a wide area, TV, radio, telephony, video and other data in digitized format.

Scalable: Refers to a network that can grow and adapt as customer needs increase and change. Scalable networks can easily manage increasing numbers of workstations, servers, user workloads and added functionality.

SDSL: See "Digital Subscriber Line (DSL)."

Semiconductor: A generic term for a device that controls electrical signals. It specifically refers to a material (such as silicon, germanium or gallium arsenide) that can be altered either to conduct electrical current or to block its passage. Carbon nanotubes may eventually be used as semiconductors. Semiconductors are partly responsible for the miniaturization of modern electronic devices, as they are vital components in computer memory and processor chips. The manufacture of semiconductors is carried out by small firms, and by industry giants such as Intel and Advanced Micro Devices.

Serial Line Internet Protocol (SLIP): The connection of a traditional telephone line, or serial line, and modem to connect a computer to an Internet site.

Server: A computer that performs and manages specific duties for a central network such as a LAN.

It may include storage devices and other peripherals. Competition within the server manufacturing industry is intense among leaders Dell, IBM, HP and others.

Server-Based SVOD Programming: Programming that is delivered directly to the customer's TV from where it is stored on the content provider's servers. In contrast, non-server-based SVOD (satellite TV) needs a storage device at the customer's location (such as a PVR or DVR) to store and play VOD content for the viewer's TV. Server-based SVOD surpasses non-server-based SVOD in its ability to simultaneously send or receive more than one video stream to or from the customer.

Service Level Agreement (SLA): A detail in a contract between a service provider and the client. The agreement specifies the level of service that is expected during the service contract term. For example, computer or Internet service contracts generally stipulate a maximum amount of time that a system may be unusable.

Set-Top Box: Sits on top of a TV set and provides enhancement to cable TV or other television reception. Typically a cable modem, this box may enable interactive enhancements to television viewing. For example, a cable modem is a set-top box that enables Internet access via TV cable. See "Cable Modem."

Short Messaging System (SMS): See "Text Messaging."

SIC: Standard Industrial Classification. See "Industry Code."

Simple Mail Transfer Protocol (SMTP): The primary form of protocol used in the transference of e-mail.

Simple Network Management Protocol (SNMP): A set of communication standards for use between computers connected to TCP/IP networks.

SIP (SIPphone): SIP stands for Session Initiated Protocol. An SIP telephone, or SIPphone, is a telephone that can make calls at no cost to any other SIPphone, anywhere in the world, via the Internet. Both telephones must be equipped with a SIPphone adapter or an Internet-connected softphone.

Six Sigma: A quality enhancement strategy designed to reduce the number of products coming from a manufacturing plant that do not conform to specifications. Six Sigma states that no more than 3.4 defects per million parts is the goal of high-quality output. Motorola invented the system in the 1980s in order to enhance its competitive position against Japanese electronics manufacturers.

SLIP: See "Serial Line Internet Protocol (SLIP)."

Smartphones: Mobile devices that have the capability to perform complex tasks and run user-generated programs. Newer devices include high-speed Internet access by connecting to wireless data services. Examples include Apple's iPhone, Research in Motion's BlackBerry and various devices with Google's Android operating system.

SMDS: See "Switched Multimegabit Data Service (SMDS)."

SMS: See "Short Messaging System (SMS)."

SMTP: See "Simple Mail Transfer Protocol (SMTP)."

Social Media (Social Networks): Sites on the Internet that feature user generated content (UGC). Such media include wikis, blogs and specialty web sites such as MySpace.com, Facebook, YouTube, Yelp and Friendster.com. Social media are seen as powerful online tools because all or most of the content is user-generated.

Software as a Service (SaaS): Refers to the practice of providing users with software applications that are hosted on remote servers and accessed via the Internet. Excellent examples include the CRM (Customer Relationship Management) software provided in SaaS format by Salesforce. An earlier technology that operated in a similar, but less sophisticated, manner was called ASP or Application Service Provider.

SONET: See "Synchronous Optical Network Technology (SONET)."

Spam: A term used to refer to generally unwanted, solicitous, bulk-sent e-mail. In recent years, significant amounts of government legislation have been passed in an attempt to limit the use of spam. Also, many types of software filters have been introduced in an effort to block spam on the receiving end. In addition to use for general advertising purposes, spam may be used in an effort to spread computer viruses or to commit financial or commercial fraud.

Streaming Media: One-way audio and/or video that is compressed and transmitted over a data network. The media is viewed or heard almost as soon as data is fed to the receiver: there is usually a buffer period of a few seconds.

Subscriber: A term used interchangeably with household in describing cable, Internet access or telephone customers.

Subscription Video On Demand (SVOD): Allows subscribers unlimited access to selected VOD television programming for a fixed monthly fee.

Subsidiary, Wholly-Owned: A company that is wholly controlled by another company through stock ownership.

Supply Chain: The complete set of suppliers of goods and services required for a company to operate its business. For example, a manufacturer's supply chain may include providers of raw materials, components, custom-made parts and packaging materials.

SVOD: See "Subscription Video On Demand (SVOD)."

Switch: A network device that directs packets of data between multiple ports, often filtering the data so that it travels more quickly.

Switched Multimegabit Data Service (SMDS): A method of extremely high-speed transference of data.

Synchronous Optical Network Technology (SONET): A mode of high-speed transmission meant to take full advantage of the wide bandwidth in fiber-optic cables.

System (Cable): A facility that provides cable television service in a given geographic area, consisting of one or more headends.

T1: A standard for broadband digital transmission over phone lines. Generally, it can transmit at least 24 voice channels at once over copper wires, at a high speed of 1.5 Mbps. Higher speed versions include T3 and OC3 lines.

T3: Transmission over phone lines that supports data rates of 45 Mbps. T3 lines consist of 672 channels, and such lines are generally used by Internet service providers. They are also referred to as DS3 lines.

Tablet: A mobile computing device that offers similar functionality as a smartphone, except with a larger viewing area and a more complex processor. However, some tablets do not have the ability to make phone calls. Examples include the Apple iPad and Samsung Galaxy tablet. Tablets are designed to interact with the user primarily through a touchscreen rather than a keyboard. While tablets offer many PC-like functions, there is no firm agreement as to whether they should be counted as part of the PC market.

TCP/IP: Transmission Control Protocol/Internet Protocol. The combination of a network and transport protocol developed by ARPANet for internetworking IP-based networks.

TDMA: See "Time Division Multiple Access (TDMA)."

Telecommunications: Systems and networks of hardware and software used to carry voice, video and/or data within buildings and between locations around the world. This includes telephone wires, satellite signals, wireless networks, fiber networks, Internet networks and related devices.

Telepresence: The use of highly sophisticated digital video cameras, microphones and high speed Internet connections to create a video conference for remote participants that is nearly life-like. Conference participants may consult with each other from specially-equipped rooms that can be almost anywhere in the world. With the most advanced equipment, such as that produced by Cisco, the images on screens can be near life-size and the results can be of almost face-to-face quality.

Telnet: A terminal emulation program for TCP/IP networks like the Internet, which runs on a computer and connects to a particular network. Directions entered on a computer that is connected using Telnet will be read and followed just as if they had been entered on the server itself. Through Telnet, users are able to control a server and communicate with other servers on the same network at the same time. Telnet is commonly used to control web servers remotely.

Text Messaging: The transmission of very short, text messages in a format similar to e-mail. Generally, text messaging is used as an additional service on cell phones. The format has typically been SMS (Short Messaging System), but a newer standard is evolving: MMS (Multimedia Messaging System). MMS can transmit pictures, sound and video as well as text.

Third-Party Logistics (3PL): A specialist firm in logistics, which may provide a variety of transportation, warehousing and logistics-related services to buyers or sellers. These tasks were previously performed in-house by the customer. When 3PL services are provided within the client's own facilities, it can also be referred to as insourcing. Also see "Fourth-Party Logistics (4PL)."

TIME: Telecommunications, Information Technology, Media and Electronics.

Time Division Multiple Access (TDMA): A 2G digital service for relatively large users of international public-switched telephony, data, facsimile and telex. TDMA also refers to a method of multiplexing digital signals that combines a number of signals passing through a common point by transmitting them sequentially, with each signal sent in bursts at different times. TDMA is sometimes referred to as IS-136 or D-AMPS.

Token Ring: A local area network architecture in which a token, or continuously repeating frame, is passed sequentially from station to station. Only the station possessing the token can communicate on the network.

Transactional VOD: Allows VOD customers to pay a single price for a single VOD program or a set of programs rather than paying a set fee for a set amount of VOD programming (as in SVOD services).

Transistor: A device used for amplification or switching of electrical current.

TV over IP: See "Internet Protocol Television (IPTV)."

U-Commerce (U Commerce): Ubiquitous Commerce, Universal Commerce or Ultimate

Commerce (ubiquitous meaning ever-present), depending on whom you ask. It describes the concept that buyers and sellers have the potential to interact anywhere, anytime thanks to the use of wireless devices, such as cell phones, by buyers to connect with sellers via the Internet where orders can be placed online and payments can be made via credit card or PayPal. The Association for Information Systems states that the qualities of U-Commerce include ubiquity, uniqueness, universality and unison.

Ultra 3G Cellular: See "4G Cellular."

Ultrawideband (UWB): A means of low-power, limited-range wireless data transmission that takes advantage of bandwidth set aside by the FCC in 2002. UWB encodes signals in a dramatically different way, sending digital pulses in a relatively secure manner that will not interfere with other wireless systems that may be operating nearby. It has the potential to deliver very large amounts of data to a distance of about 230 feet, even through doors and other obstacles, and requires very little power. Speeds are scalable from approximately 100 Mbps to 2Gbps. UWB works on the 802.15.3 IEEE specification.

UMA: See "Unlicensed Mobile Access (UMA)."

UMTS: Universal Mobile Telecommunications System. See "Wideband CDMA."

Unified Communications: The use of advanced technology to replace traditional telecommunications infrastructure such as PBX, fax and even the desktop telephone. Special software operating on a local or remote server enables each office worker to have access, via the desktop PC, to communications tools that include VOIP phone service, email, voice mail, fax, instant messaging (IM), collaborative calendars and schedules, contact information such as address books, audio conferencing and video conferencing.

Uniform Resource Locator (URL): The address that allows an Internet browser to locate a homepage or web site.

Universal Mobile Telecommunications System (UMTS): An overarching standard based on W-CDMA technology. See "Wideband CDMA."

UNIX: A multi-user, multitasking operating system that runs on a wide variety of computer systems, from PCs to mainframes.

Unlicensed Mobile Access (UMA): A standard technology developed for GSM cellular phone networks. UMA is designed to enable access to the Internet and to VOIP telephony for dual mode cellular phone handsets that are capable of switching from cellular to Wi-Fi and back.

URL: See "Uniform Resource Locator (URL)."

User Generated Content (UGC): Data contributed by users of interactive web sites. Such sites can include wikis, blogs, entertainment sites, shopping sites or social networks such as Facebook. UGC data can also include such things as product reviews, photos, videos, comments on forums, and how-to advice. Also see "Social Media (Social Networks)."

UWB: See "Ultrawideband (UWB)."

Value Added Tax (VAT): A tax that imposes a levy on businesses at every stage of manufacturing based on the value it adds to a product. Each business in the supply chain pays its own VAT and is subsequently repaid by the next link down the chain: hence, a VAT is ultimately paid by the consumer, being the last link in the supply chain, making it comparable to a sales tax. Generally, VAT only applies to goods bought for consumption within a given country: export goods are exempt from VAT, and purchasers from other countries taking goods back home may apply for a VAT refund.

V-Chip: A system built into TV sets that helps parents screen out programs with questionable parental guideline ratings. Consumers can purchase a special set-top box that performs the same function.

VDSL: Very high-data-rate digital subscriber line, operating at data rates from 55 to 100 Mbps.

Vendor: Any firm, such as a manufacturer or distributor, from which a retailer obtains merchandise.

Very Small Aperture Terminal (VSAT): A small Earth station terminal, generally 0.6 to 2.4 meters in size, that is often portable and primarily designed to handle data transmission and private-line voice and video communications.

Video Blog (VLOG): The creation of video files as webcasts. VLOGs can be viewed on personal computers and wireless devices that are Internet-enabled. They can include anything from unique TV-like programming to sales pitches to music videos, news coverage or audio press releases. Online video is one of the fastest-growing segments in Internet usage. Leading e-commerce companies such as Microsoft, through its MSN service, Google and Yahoo!, as well as mainstream media firms such as Reuters, are making significant investments in online video services. Real Simple Syndication (RSS) enables the broadcasting of these files to appropriate parties. Also see "Real Simple Syndication (RSS)," "Podcasting" and "Blog (Web Log)."

Video On Demand (VOD): A system that allows customers to request programs or movies over cable or the Internet. Generally, the customer can select from an extensive list of titles. In some cases, a set-top device can be used to digitally record a broadcast for replay at a future date.

Virtual Private Network (VPN): Cordons off part of a public network to create a private LAN.

VLOG: See "Video Blog (VLOG)."

VOD: See "Video On Demand (VOD)."

VOD-Over-IP: VOD (video on demand) television viewing that is distributed via the Internet.

Voice Mail: A sophisticated electronic telephone answering service that utilizes a computer. Voice mail enables users to receive faxes and phone messages and to access those messages from remote sites.

Voice Over Internet Protocol (VOIP): The ability to make telephone calls and send faxes over IP-based data networks, i.e., real-time voice between computers via the Internet. Leading providers of VOIP service include independent firms Skype and Vonage. However, all major telecom companies, such as SBC are planning or offering VOIP service. VOIP can offer greatly reduced telephone bills to users, since toll charges, certain taxes and other fees can be bypassed. Long-distance calls can pass to anywhere in the world using VOIP. Over the mid-term, many telephone handsets, including cellular phones, will have the ability to detect wireless networks offering VOIP connections and will switch seamlessly between landline and VOIP or cellular and VOIP as needed.

VOIP: See "Voice Over Internet Protocol (VOIP)."

VPN: See "Virtual Private Network (VPN)."

WAN: See "Wide Area Network (WAN)."

WAP: See "Wireless Access Protocol (WAP)."

W-CDMA (WCDMA): See "Wideband CDMA."

Web 2.0: Generally refers to the evolving system of advanced services available via the Internet. These services include collaborative sites that enable multiple users to create content such as wikis, sites such as photo-sharing services that share data among large or small groups and sites that enable consumers to form groups of people with similar interests. Common features of Web 2.0 are tagging, social networks and folksonomies.

Web of Things: See "Internet of Things (IoT)."

Web Services: Self-contained modular applications that can be described, published, located and invoked over the World Wide Web or another network. Web services architecture evolved from object-oriented design and is geared toward e-business solutions. Microsoft Corporation is focusing on web services with its .NET initiative. Also see "Extensible Markup Language (XML)."

Webmaster: Any individual who runs a web site. Webmasters generally perform maintenance and upkeep.

Website Meta-Language (WML): A free HTML generation toolkit for the Unix operating system.

WFH: Work from home.

Wide Area Network (WAN): A regional or global network that provides links between all local area networks within a company. For example, Ford Motor Company might use a WAN to enable its factory in Detroit to talk to its sales offices in New York and Chicago, its plants in England and its buying offices in Taiwan. Also see "Local Area Network (LAN)."

Wideband CDMA: A high-speed version of CDMA based on Qualcomm technology. Significantly modified by Japanese and European manufacturers, it is used as a 3G technology outside the U.S. with

Japan's Freedom of Multimedia Access (FOMA) and Europe's Universal Mobile Telecommunications System (UMTS). It is also known as "IMT-2000 Direct Spread."

WiFi: See "Wi-Fi."

Wi-Fi: Wireless Fidelity. Refers to 802.11 wireless network specifications. The 802.XX standards are set by the IEEE (Institute of Electrical and Electronics Engineers). Wi-Fi enables very high speed local networks in homes, businesses, factories, industrial and transportation infrastructure, public spaces and vehicles. Wi-Fi networks enable computing devices of all types to connect to each other and to the internet, including smartphones, laptops, desktops and tablet computers. In addition, Wi-Fi enables machine-to-machine (M2M) communication between devices, providing a backbone for the Internet of Things. These networks can be made reasonably secure when strong passwords are required and additional cybersecurity measures are in place. (Also, see 'Internet of Things".)

WiMAX: An advanced wireless standard with significant speed and distance capabilities, WiMAX is officially known as the 802.16 standard. Using microwave technologies, it has the theoretical potential to broadcast at distances up to 30 miles and speeds of up to 70 Mbps. The 802.XX standards are set by the IEEE (Institute of Electrical and Electronics Engineers).

Wireless: Transmission of voice, video or data by a cellular telephone or other wireless device, as opposed to landline, fiber or cable. It includes Bluetooth, Cellular, Wi-Fi, WiMAX and other local or long-distance wireless methods.

Wireless Access Protocol (WAP): A technology that enables the delivery of internet pages in a smaller format readable by screens on smartphones.

Wireless LAN (WLAN): A wireless local area network. WLANs frequently operate on 802.11-enabled equipment (Wi-Fi).

Wireline (in telecommunications): See "Landline."

WLAN: See "Wireless LAN (WLAN)."

WML: See "Website Meta-Language (WML)."

Workstation: A high-powered desktop computer, usually used by engineers.

World Trade Organization (WTO): One of the only globally active international organizations dealing with the trade rules between nations. Its goal is to assist the free flow of trade goods, ensuring a smooth, predictable supply of goods to help raise the quality of life of member citizens. Members form consensus decisions that are then ratified by their respective parliaments. The WTO's conflict resolution process generally emphasizes interpreting existing commitments and agreements, and discovers how to ensure trade policies to conform to those agreements, with the ultimate aim of avoiding military or political conflict.

World Wide Web: A system (the internet) that provides enhanced access to various sites on the Internet through the use of hyperlinks. Clicking on a link displayed in one document takes you to a related document. The World Wide Web is governed by the World Wide Web Consortium, located at www.w3.org. Also known as the web.

WoT: Web of Things. See "Internet of Things."

WPA: Wireless Protected Access. A basic security standard for wireless networking, including Wi-Fi.

WTO: See "World Trade Organization (WTO)."